GREAT AGES
AND IDEAS
OF THE
JEWISH PEOPLE

GROWTH IN JEWISH HISTORY

═══BIBLICAL AGE═══

ISRAELITE RELIGION

PRIESTLY   PROPHETIC

HEBREW BIBLE

(Hebrew)

═══HELLENISTIC AGE═══

DIASPORA JUDAISM   PALESTINIAN JUDAISM

HELLENISTIC LITERATURE   SADDUCEES, ESSENES, PHARISEES

Septuagint   Written and Oral Law

Philo   Hillel

(Hebrew, Aramaic, Greek)

═══TALMUDIC (RABBINIC) AGE═══

BABYLONIAN JUDAISM   PALESTINIAN JUDAISM

BABYLONIAN TALMUD   PALESTINIAN TALMUD

Abba Arika, Rabina II   Johanan ben Zakkai, Judah Ha-Nasi

Mishna   Midrash

(Hebrew, Aramaic, Greek)

═══JUDEO—ISLAMIC AGE═══

RABBINIC JUDAISM

NORMATIVE—PHILOSOPHIC—MYSTICAL (KABBALA)

ARABIC AND HEBREW LITERATURE—RESPONSA

Saadia   Maimonides

(Hebrew, Arabic, Aramaic)

═══EUROPEAN AGE═══

RABBINIC JUDAISM

TALMUD AND SHULHAN ARUKH

NORMATIVE JUDAISM   HASKALAH   HASIDISM (KABBALA)

Vilna Gaon   Moses Mendelssohn   Israel Baalshem Tob

(Hebrew, Aramaic, Yiddish, and European tongues)

═══MODERN AGE═══

TRADITIONAL AND RABBINIC JUDAISM

LIBERAL-REFORM—CONSERVATIVE—ORTHODOX

AMERICAN JEWRY—ISRAEL—DIASPORA JEWRY

(Hebrew, Yiddish, and all major tongues)

GREAT AGES
AND IDEAS
OF THE
JEWISH PEOPLE

BY

SALO W. BARON, GERSON D. COHEN

ABRAHAM S. HALKIN

YEHEZKEL KAUFMANN

RALPH MARCUS, CECIL ROTH

Edited, with an Introduction, by
LEO W. SCHWARZ

RANDOM HOUSE, NEW YORK

A Publication of Hadassah

Manufactured in the United States of America
by H. Wolff, New York

Second Printing

"The ideals of the spirit consciously held by any portion of mankind lend freedom to thought, grace to feeling: and by sailing up this one stream we may reach the fountain-head whence all spiritual forces emanate and about which, as a fixed pole, all currents eddy."

LEOPOLD ZUNZ

FOREWORD

This book is an exploration of the long history of the Jewish people and an interpretation of the major ideas and values that have grown out of that unique historical experience. It is a human story that combines an inventory of the past with an assessment of the present. If the focus is on a single people, the panorama that comes into view, though different from that of other cultures, is part and parcel of the heritage of mankind.

The idea of asking experts to apply historical knowledge to contemporary issues originated in the leadership of Hadassah, the Women's Zionist Organization of America.

From its inception in 1952, the plan of the book was under discussion by a group of scholars and laymen who comprised the National Education Advisory Committee of Hadassah. The editor was commissioned in the winter of 1953 to form a collegium of scholars for the preparation of the material in accordance with the general principle stated in the first paragraph. The chapters were written as follows: Chapters 1-4 by Yehezkel Kaufmann of the Hebrew University of Jerusalem; Chapters 5-6 by Ralph Marcus of the University of Chicago; Chapters 7-8 by Gerson D. Cohen of Columbia University; Chapters 9-10 by Abraham S. Halkin of the City College of New York; Chapters 11-12 by Cecil Roth of the University of Oxford; and Chapters 13-18 by Salo W. Baron of Columbia University. Although the whole text has been integrated by the editor to form a consecutive narrative, the final responsibility for the substance of each section belongs to the individual writer.

For assistance in formulating the plan of the book the editor is deeply indebted to Professor Shalom Spiegel of the Jewish Theological

Seminary and Professor Harry A. Wolfson of Harvard University. He is grateful to Dr. Moshe Greenberg of the University of Pennsylvania for undertaking, at short notice, to translate Professor Kaufmann's Hebrew manuscript. Special thanks are due to Dr. Leo Roberts of Cambridge, Massachusetts, for generous counsel and help. Appreciation is also due to Dr. Ira Eisenstein of Chicago, Illinois, Dr. Judah Goldin of New York, and to the other members of the National Education Advisory Committee of Hadassah for their continual interest and advice. Finally, the gratitude of all concerned with the project is extended to Mrs. Samuel Rosensohn and Mrs. Benjamin Gottesman, who were President and Chairman of Education of Hadassah during the time of the book's preparation. Without their vision and zeal, the book would not have been initiated or completed.

L.W.S.

New York, June, 1956

CONTENTS

FOREWORD   vii

INTRODUCTION: *Historians to the Reader*   xiii

THE BIBLICAL AGE
by Yehezkel Kaufmann

1 THE GENESIS OF ISRAEL   3

The Ancient Near Eastern Legacy, The Nature of the Pagan Religion, The Religious Idea of Israel, Moses and Monotheism, The Covenant at Sinai, Religious Revolution in the Desert

2 ISRAEL IN CANAAN   30

Conquest and Settlement, Early Popular Religion, The Kingdom of God, Monarchy and Prophecy, The Battle Against Baal Worship

3 THE AGE OF CLASSICAL PROPHECY   57

Historical and Ideological Background, The Primacy of Morality, The View of History, Vision of the End of Days: Isaiah, The Josianic Reform, The Fall of Judah: Jeremiah

4 THE EMERGENCE OF JUDAISM   76

The Crisis of Faith, A New Self-Awareness: the Second Isaiah, The Restoration: Ezra and the Torah Book, New Ideas and Ideals, Judaism and Hellenism

THE HELLENISTIC AGE
by Ralph Marcus

5 THE CHALLENGE OF GRECO-ROMAN CULTURE   95

Resemblance to the Modern World, Response in Palestine, Hellenistic Influence on Diaspora Judaism

6 THE ACHIEVEMENT OF HELLENISTIC JUDAISM 122

Loyalties and Tradition, The Spell of Judaism, Gentile-Jewish Relations, A Portrait of Philo, Zion as Fact and Idea, The Legacy to Western Civilization

THE TALMUDIC AGE
by Gerson D. Cohen

7 TALMUDIC SOCIETY 143

Talmudic Society: Time and Place, Emergence of the Talmudic Community, Commonwealth within an Empire, The Institutional Pillars

8 THE RABBINIC HERITAGE 173

Torah: Scripture and Tradition, The New Hero Type, Theological Idiom, The Election of Israel, The Holy Land, The Legacy of Talmudic Civilization

THE JUDEO-ISLAMIC AGE
by Abraham S. Halkin

9 THE GREAT FUSION 215

A New Historic Pattern, Intellectual Transformation, The Bible: Agent of Enlightenment, A Flowering of Hebrew Literature

10 REVOLT AND REVIVAL IN JUDEO-ISLAMIC CULTURE 234

Cultural Tensions, The Karaites, The Nature of Rationalism, Maimonides and His Critics, The Mysticism of the Kabbala, The Legacy

THE EUROPEAN AGE
by Cecil Roth

11 A MILLENNIUM IN EUROPE 267

The European Experience, Contemporary Significance, The Vital Institutions, Intellectual Standards, The Influence of Judaism

12 THE SUCCESS OF THE MEDIEVAL JEWISH IDEAL 287

The Home, The Synagogue, The Jewish Quarter, The Visitor, Heritage to Posterity

THE MODERN AGE
by Salo W. Baron

13 THE DYNAMICS OF EMANCIPATION 315

Emancipation in Western Democracies, Springtime of Nations, The Price of Liberty, The Climax of Emancipation

14 THE IMPACT OF NATIONALISM 338

Character of Modern Nationalism, Antisemitism, Old and New, Ambiguities of Racialism, Varieties of Jewish Nationalism

15 THE ENDURING HERITAGE 360

A Classic Minority, Varieties of Religious Adjustment, New Cultural Molds, Rebirth of Literature and the Arts

16 THE CHALLENGE OF MATERIAL CIVILIZATION 391

Changing Population Trends, Migration: Fact and Fiction, Economic Change and Social Attitudes, Impact on Various Isms

17 THE EMERGENCE OF ISRAEL 420

Religious Motivations, The Humanitarian Element, Cultural Aspirations, Political Drives, The Palestine Mandate, The State of Israel

18 THE AMERICAN EXPERIENCE 455

Welfare Pioneering, Religious Currents, Cultural and Educational Experiments, A Creative Culture in the Making, Patterns of Survival

SUGGESTIONS FOR FURTHER READING 485

INDEX 499

INTRODUCTION: HISTORIANS
TO THE READER

It may be well to begin by stating briefly the assumptions that are implicit in our attempt to distill an almost four-thousand-year cultural experience and draw lessons and meaning from it. Conscious of the complexities of our present civilization as well as its fascinations, we are concerned with transmitting the best of our heritage. We have learned from our day-to-day existence that the growing mastery of nature does not inevitably improve the quality of man or his social relations and institutions. Automobile, freezer, and telephone have enhanced family comforts; medical and hygienic services have extended our lives. But the increase of physical comfort has at the same time increased intellectual and spiritual discomfort, or as it has been nicely put, nuclear fission has created moral confusion.

Whether we are living in an Aspirin Age or a Golden Age is perhaps a matter of opinion. The historian looks with suspicion on figures of speech. In any case, it is a fact that we are living in an age that has at its disposal unprecedented stores of knowledge. Yet it is difficult for even the best-educated person to master more than a small fraction of these accumulated stores. In this respect the historian is in a more advantageous position, because his profession requires him to collect, order, and record the data of human experience. But behind words are men and behind men are ideas and ideals. Hence the historian seeks also to discover how human society came to be what it is, to interpret the facts and make their significance clear.

That is the function which the historian will try to perform in this book. He will bring you into his workshop—his mind and his library. He will present to you—humbly, for he knows his limitations—the fruit of a lifetime of labor and reflection. He will communicate his conviction that history is something alive, that it is around us and within us. Indeed, he will go further and claim that understanding of both present and past is not only useful but imperative.

THE USE OF HISTORY

Can we say that the past is intimately involved in our present fate?

One common answer to this question is that "history is bunk." This is a view too common in the United States to be overlooked by anyone seriously interested in discovering the role of history in human affairs. It is representative of the mechanical mind of the twentieth century. A scornful attitude to history—that is, to human experience and aspiration—is the mark of a mind which, despite a mastery of wires and springs, would turn the clock back.

Somewhat more sophisticated but not far removed from this view is that in which newspaper headlines figure as the sheet anchor of history. Of course, it is true that what is the future at breakfast has become the past at dinner. But to live within a time span of twenty-four hours is to live within the narrowest of strait jackets. It not only has great drawbacks, it has great dangers. For in foreshortening the long continuity of human growth, we become victims rather than makers of history. Whenever a civilization has hardened or been retarded, you may be sure that the people and especially their rulers have been dominated by this mollusk conception of history.

Newspaper headlines, like human beings, have an ancestry. Every event, every fact, and for that matter every illusion grows out of the seedbed of time, as imaginative intellects have always and everywhere recognized. Since Darwin the knowledge of evolution in nature and man—the continuous process of growth and development—has become the leaven of every cultivated mind. Every scientific invention of the twentieth century rests upon a discovery in the nineteenth century and earlier. The whole of psychological research documents Wordsworth's dictum that the child is father of the man. In other words, every facet of our daily existence is historical. To obscure this fact, or to be ignorant of it, is to deny life, or at the very least to cramp it unnecessarily. When one who holds great power casts all past experience to the winds, the result is incalculable suffering for mankind and destruction of much that is good in our heritage. Knowledge of the past may not prevent the repetition of error or erase human fallibility. But ignorance of the past is a certain road to the reenactment of the tragedy and folly which glut the pages of man's past record.

Thus knowledge of history is in actuality liberation from the strait jackets of time and ignorance. The use of history—placing experience in the service of man and his world—is a method of improving human relations as well as a way of increasing understanding and enjoyment of life. History has made man but has also been made by him. That is our conviction. We deny the doctrine of historical inevitability. Nothing is "inevitable" until after it happens.

The turn of events in the middle of the twentieth century requires a reexamination of the interaction between the individual and society. Our fundamental convictions and allegiances, both as Americans and as Jews, are being hammered out on the anvil of changing political and cultural ideas. There are new ingredients in this social ferment, but the pattern of crisis and reconstruction is as old as the human race. Those who want to participate in capturing the future— and we may assume that anyone who takes the trouble to read this book is to be counted among them—must consciously or unconsciously conclude that they are not only the creatures but also the creators of history.

A TOOL OF THE MIND

The central question that we as historians ask ourselves is: To what extent has past experience made us what we are, and what is there in that experience that can serve our needs in the future?

As historians we have no pat answer to this supremely important question. Looking over the sweep of Jewish history, however, we do note that earlier generations have lived through similar situations and have evolved methods and ideas for surviving the greatest catastrophes. On Sinai and in the surrounding desert, Moses formulated a conception of society that fused his people into a nation with specific goals. Seeing the Judean state completely destroyed in 586 B.C.E. and his people driven to a foreign country, the prophet Jeremiah proclaimed a supranational doctrine that halted a threatened extinction. When the Romans destroyed both the Herodian state and the center of sacrificial worship in Jerusalem in the first century, the statesmanship of Johanan ben Zakkai and his school led to a complete reconstruction of the theory and practice of Judaism in the Greco-Roman world. As the political map and cultural topography of the world changed in succeeding centuries because of the conquests of Islam and the domination of the Christian nation-state, other outstanding Jewish leaders continued to develop social techniques and to reconstruct intellectual concepts. This whole rich heritage is again being put to the test of the modern age of science and industrialism. For the past century or more Jews have wrestled with the problem of survival and adjustment. Some of the attempted solutions have failed; a few have led to positive results. But the quest for solutions continues. The reader is surely involved in this quest, and so are the historians.

Without getting into a technical discussion of historical method, let us try to state the aim of our approach to history. We hope to get at the substance of history the way an anatomist charts the human body, and we hope to reveal its meaning as the poet catches the essence of thought and the beat of the heart. This dual task is primarily intellectual: to select out of accumulated knowledge and experience the data that are relevant to the quest for survival, adaptation, and expression. If this task is accomplished with imagination and sympathy, then the achievement—in this instance, the book in your hands—should be an intellectual aid to every self-conscious and intelligent Jew in America.

Now the point of the last paragraph is not really novel. Influential historians from Thucydides to Toynbee have been moved by similar intentions. They were convinced that the past had shaped the present in which they were deeply involved, that the narration and re-creation of their own span of experience would serve as manuals for future statesmen. Indeed, all the influential histories were written in periods of crisis and catastrophe, of upheaval and change. Hence the recurrence (but not repetition) of historical experience. Croce summed up the matter in a famous epigram: "All history is contemporary history." His remark has been the subject of much debate, yet this much of what is implied in it appears to be valid: the past is not a fossil; it is omnipresent and, above all, living. For the central concern of the historian is life—its tragedies and triumphs, its humor and vanity, its mysteries and follies and truths.

Illustrations abound in the long experience of the Jewish people. It will serve our purpose to linger for a few moments over the historians who have recorded this millennial drama. For history, too, has a history.

The first Jewish historian, and perhaps the first historian of any consequence, created the work which comprises the first two parts of the Hebrew Bible. This anonymous writer was (it is believed) a refugee, broken-hearted at the destruction of the Judean state and appalled by the decimation of his people and their exile to a foreign land. He selected out of numerous chronicles, registers, codes, and poetic and prophetic anthologies such material as suited his purpose and molded a comprehensive portrait of the Jewish people from their beginnings to the Babylonian Dispersion. He summoned up remembrance of things past, drew events together in a grand unity, and transfused into the chaotic present the exhilarating ideas and hopeful promises of the Prophets.

The crisis that inspired a subsequent historical work was the Roman ravaging of Jerusalem and destruction of the Second Temple in 70 C.E. The patriotic version of that epic struggle by Justus of Tiberias has disappeared, but his contemporary, a cosmopolitan "collaborator" of the Romans, Josephus, produced two historical works which have survived. Josephus' *Ancient History of the Jews* is a full-dress portrait. It evidences a mastery of historical records of the ancient world, both Jewish and Greco-Roman; the writing is stamped with an awe of Judaism and the belief that Judaism is superior to pagan religions of the classical world. Yet both the *History* and *The Jewish War* are polemic and apologetic accounts. On the one hand Josephus attempted to refute the Hellenic critics of the Jews, and on the other hand he undertook to defend himself against his "would-be detractors." In a way these imposing works became prototypes of a genre of historical writing which unconsciously confuses a bruised ego with national catastrophe.

In the first part of the nineteenth century European Jews were caught in the vortex of civil and political emancipation that stemmed from the French Revolution. Scholars used the new scientific ideas and tools to investigate their threatened heritage. Out of the ferment in Germany arose a brilliant circle of scholar-writers—Leopold Zunz, Heinrich Graetz, and others. Probing anew the sources of Jewish culture, Graetz finally embodied his research and thought in a great eleven-volume work. The popularity of the six-volume English condensation of his *History of the Jews* is a tribute to the majestic sweep of Graetz's knowledge and to his felicity of style. However, when we examine this work a century after its original publication, certain defects stand out sharply. Despite his optimism for the future, which gives the reader a sense of the unfinished business of Judaism, Graetz was impaled on the dilemma posed by the intellectual currents of his age. He frequently sounds like a German schoolmaster, unshakable in his principles and cocksure of his interpretations. Actually, he had little understanding of some of the richest strains in the manifold culture of Judaism. He rubbed out the historic treasures of Eastern European Jewries as though they were a pupil's unsatisfactory writing on a blackboard. Finding the expression of mysticism in the Kabbala and Hasidism repugnant to his own intellectual presuppositions, he minimized their role and misconstrued the social and emotional tensions which produced them. He identifies Judaism with a contemporary version of rationalism and converted Judaism into a mission. "Out of Zion," he declared, "went forth rationalistic teaching." Graetz died in 1891, without feeling the new tremors that were already rumbling beneath the surface of European society.

They were felt and understood by the eminent historian Simon M. Dubnow, who emerged from Polish Jewry and was one of the martyrs of 1941. Persecution and migration were to him not merely evils of the past, but a living personal and national experience. He understood both the decadent and renascent trends in Jewish life as reactions to a new historical complex, fashioned by the dominant forces of nationalism and antisemitism. Although he appreciated the positive side of Zionism, Dubnow pinned his faith on the survival value of the corporate Jewish minorities in the new European states after World War I. Adopting the philosophy of modern nationalism, he saw the fulfillment of Jewish history in what is known as Diaspora Nationalism. He wanted to stem the corrosive forces of his time, and his great *World History of the Jewish People* (unfortunately only some of his shorter works have so far been translated into English) is a monument of permanent value. But events have moved too fast and history has brutally demolished the cornerstone on which Dubnow built. At the time of his death a new catastrophe was writing an epitaph on the tombstones of Slavic and German Jewries. World War II radically altered the map of the world and among the casualties were the ancient landmarks of European Jewry.

These changes, and the forces underlying them, call for a hard look at new features; our mid-twentieth-century crisis presses for a rebuilding of the community and a reploughing of the intellectual soil. And this brings us to the psychological orientation of the present work. As in earlier periods of upheaval, so now there is an inescapable need to mobilize all the resources that history has placed at our command. Past experience, employed intelligently and imaginatively, is part of the design and material that can form the bridge into the future. The role of historians is to provide their audience with a tool. The tool we shall attempt to fashion in this work is a distillation of those Judaic ideas and values which have stood the test of time.

THE SHAPE OF IDEAS

To achieve the goal set forth in the last sentence would be formidable enough even if a series of volumes were at our disposal. What makes it in some modest measure possible in one volume are certain limitations which we have imposed upon ourselves. For one thing, we will not duplicate the dozen or more Jewish histories now on the library shelves. We have selected the great ages of our historical drama and made them the framework of the story. Each of these ages stretches over many centuries, touches several continents, embraces a complex of cultures, leaves its peculiar imprint upon human experience. Out of innumerable events, movements, personalities, institutions, and records, we have selected only a few of the most characteristic and significant for purposes of illustration. For these are the frame on which the web of ideas and values are woven. Tracing this web is the main theme of our work. We have tried to extract and interpret the fundamental ideas in all their variations and combinations so that they evolve into forms that will serve our own needs.

This task is more easily stated than achieved, especially within the confines of less than six hundred pages. Obviously, we cannot render an account of the whole Jewish intellectual tradition. We have had to pause, reflect, reassess—in other words, to choose, as if a conflagration were in the offing, what is most precious in our heritage. This approach, though it has the disadvantage of incompleteness, has the advantage of immediate relevance. And it has resulted in what we consider a living context for the substance of the book. For each of the great ages portrayed here is considered from the vantage ground of its fundamental tensions: the conflicts of Judaism with prevailing or contending religions and cultures, the methods by which these tensions were resolved, and the impact these struggles have had upon the historic personality of the Jewish people throughout the ages.

To avoid the stereotypes of conventional history—but at the same time to hew closely to historical fact—the book does not conform to a fixed design, with each epoch portrayed and each idea analyzed in accordance with a blueprint. On the contrary, a true understanding of history requires a large degree of flexibility in the interpretation of human achievement. Consequently, each of the epochs of Judaism in its procession through the centuries—the Biblical, the Hellenistic, the Rabbinic, the Islamic, the European, and the modern—has been described and interpreted by a historian who has devoted his prime energies over many years to that cultural zone. While each encounter of Judaism with other cultures has certain similarities to contemporary struggles within Western civilization, each in turn has basic and definable differences. That is why each writer has undertaken to portray his particular area with its particular presuppositions, but with an eye on present-day reality as well. It is these two factors which account for the variation of exposition and of techniques of presentation in the different sections of the volume. It would be strange not to find great diversity in a half-dozen historians of varied backgrounds and temperaments, engaged in re-creating so vast a sweep of life and time.

Efforts to do this have in the past been made almost entirely by specialists whose work is embalmed in studies too technical to be intelligible to even the serious layman. The task is by no means clear-cut. Living ideas are so intimately tied up with events and people that they can be analyzed and formulated only with infinite delicacy.

The pitfalls in the way of accomplishing our goal are innumerable. It is important for the reader as well as the historian to be aware of them. Perhaps the best way of illustrating these difficulties, and at the same time bringing the story of the book into perspective, is to sketch some of the unique features of the Jewish historical experience.

THE UNIQUE FEATURES OF JEWISH HISTORY

No history is simple, and Jewish history in particular is so varied and so complex that it has baffled even the ablest historians. At least two modern writers of universal history, Spengler and Toynbee, could not fit this history into their theories and brushed aside quite unhistorically what they regarded as a "deviation." This poses for the scholar and the reader alike a real and fascinating problem; and even if we cannot resolve it we will make an honest attempt to understand it. Of course, we do not pretend that, even with the instruments of science and the new insights of social science, we can fully explain the cause and character of so unique a cultural evolution as the Jewish experience. Would any social scientist claim, for example, that the impulses of masses of men and women under conditions of emotional strain have been completely recorded even by the most advanced mechanical and cybernetic devices? Surely not. However, if we cannot always discern the root causes of historical currents, we can describe their visible impacts.

One source of puzzlement is the time depth of Jewish history. Americans of the middle twentieth century are accustomed to centennial and, more rarely, tercentennial celebrations. Modern Europeans revere national institutions that originated with the industrial and political revolutions of the eighteenth century and, in exceptional instances, with the breakup of feudal medieval society. But Jews living in the United States annually celebrate or commemorate, as in the Passover and Hanukka festivals, events that occurred thousands of years ago. The Hebrew calendar year in which this book is published is 5717.

Even if you discard the legendary calendar date, this book itself encompasses at least 3,500 years, and according to the estimates of some Biblical scholars, as much as 4,000 years. If you were to make an age chart of the member states of the United Nations, you would find that most of them are by comparison mere striplings. They came into existence in modern times or even, like the republic of Israel, during the middle decades of the twentieth century. As for the ages of the *peoples* living within these member states (and, for that matter, those living in nonmember states), only the Chinese and the Hindus can claim equal or greater longevity. Indeed, Dubnow attempted to prove that the Jewish people and their culture are "coextensive with the whole of history." While this claim does not hold up under factual scrutiny, it is safe to say that the Jews have an endurance record in the arena of history. The time depth of Jewish history invites one to think not only in terms of decades and generations, but of centuries and millennia.

A second unique feature of Jewish history is the geographical span. Unlike the histories of the Chinese and the Hindus, which in the main were confined to single areas, Jewish history touches and is intermingled with that of almost every part of the earth. The main body of Jews lived in Palestine only during the first third of their history. Even during that period they were almost totally displaced during the Babylonian Exile, and between the restoration under Cyrus and the destruction of the state by Titus, a larger part of their population was in lands outside of Palestine. Political misfortune altered but did not stunt their growth. Jewish communities, from Hellenistic times to the present, by voluntary migration or actual expulsion, spread out in circle after circle, generally with the northward and westward movement of economic and cultural centers. They were found in every major country and state on the five continents, and everywhere they developed their historical heritage in some form. So this global dispersion imposes upon the student the huge but exhilarating obligation of becoming acquainted with world geography throughout the ages.

Because our main interest in this book is something more than chronology and geography, we have chosen only such dates and places as are directly related to the origin, growth, and migration of ideas of enduring value. However, when the historical spotlight is turned on cultural evolution, we face complex and tantalizing problems. Ideas, like men, are gregarious, migratory, unpredictable, and like the mind of man, their life is partly conscious and partly unconscious.

Let us take an illustration. King David and Flavius Josephus could each look out from the heights of Judea, but the life and world their eyes saw and their minds grasped existed in each instance in a vastly different context. As soon as we attempt a historical portrait for each context or framework, we must distinguish not only biological and social changes but also different psychological and mental structures. To be sure, geneticists have established the basic similarity of all members of the species; but they have no doubt about the reality of the differences created by nature and nurtured in individual and social organisms. If you could examine the unpublished diaries of Ben-Gurion and compare his life with that of David as portrayed in the Bible and of Josephus as recounted in his *Autobiography,* you would find it easy to discover each one's place in time and space. But as soon as you tackled the minds and emotions of these men and their relations to the cultural milieu of which they were also products, you would find yourself in the midst of all sorts of puzzling problems. For example, how did these men and their contemporaries solve the problem of living at once within the world and outside of it? To what extent did Hellenism enter into the heart of Judaism in the case of Josephus and his older contemporaries Philo of Alexandria and Hillel of Jerusalem? At what points do these world views blend and conflict?

For those of us who share in the general culture and at the same time are devoted to Jewish culture, this is a living problem. But the solution was not—and is not—easy. Indeed, the chapters on Hellenistic and Talmudic Judaism in this book contain somewhat different conclusions, based upon the same data, arrived at by two students of this problem. Let us assume that you wish to lift your historical sights even higher and compare what you have found out about

David, Josephus, and Ben-Gurion and their periods with their counterparts in the contemporary world: you would find yourself perplexed and fascinated by data so infinitely diverse that any understanding or synthesis of them would seem impossible. Yet it is possible. Historical knowledge and historical thinking have made it so.

Perhaps these observations can be made more real by looking at the same example from another angle of vision. Running like a thread of many colors through our millennial history is a unique—and rarely treated—political experience. King David lived in a world of absolutist empires and states. Josephus lived in the Roman multinational state where cosmopolitanism and multiple citizenship were the order of the day. Ben-Gurion has lived through an age of nation-states when the doctrine of self-determination and international welfare and law were the axes of international society. In the eighteen hundred years separating Josephus and Ben-Gurion—the time period in which Toynbee considers the Jewish people a "fossil" in Western Christian society—Jews lived in many nations, empires, and states. Most historians either regard them as part of another political entity or simply relegate them to a footnote. Even Graetz and Dubnow did not satisfactorily solve this problem of historical treatment. Graetz, failing to find a unifying political principle, weaves his story back and forth from general to Jewish frameworks. Dubnow, on the other hand, did find a unifying principle, but considered it "the national spirit undergoing continuous evolution during thousands of years." As this quotation suggests, Dubnow developed an organic conception of Jewish history, but he too neglected or preferred to minimize certain political data. The fact is that in these eighteen hundred years the Jews, while deprived of political "sovereignty," did possess self-government. In some instances, as in the Persian and Islamic empires or in Poland before its partitions, the high degree of self-government was almost equal to sovereignty. Moreover, even the European ghettos had community self-determination. Or, to put it in another way, we may say that in response to the dynamics of history, the Jews substituted community power for state power, and thus they constitute a significant example for the philosophers and proponents of a twentieth-century world federation of peoples.

Perhaps the most distinctive and yet the most elusive material of all are cultural elements that distinguish Jewish history. In this sphere the range of experience has been so broad and so deep that no single set of formulas or gauges applies. There is the important element of language, for example. Anyone wishing to follow the history of the United States can do so with books and documents in the English language, but the man has not yet been born who could master all the languages and literatures in which the cultures of the Jewish people are expressed. The Hebrew language, written and spoken continuously for thirty-five hundred years or more, is a major conduit through which culture flowed. Witness the Bible, the Mishna, the Shulhan Arukh, the poetry of Bialik and Tchernichovski, and the Hebrew press of Israel today. Aramaic too has a long history, with parts of the Book of Daniel and the Talmud, and the Zohar to its credit. Philo of Alexandria wrote in Greek, which in his time had become the vehicle of daily Jewish speech and literary expression. In the Middle Ages, Arabic took its place side by side with Hebrew, and in both tongues we possess secular and religious masterpieces by Saadia Gaon, Judah Halevi, and Moses Maimonides. When the modern Romance languages began to take form in Europe, Jews learned them. The earliest French is embedded in the Hebrew commentaries of the French master Rashi and his contemporaries, and Castilian Spanish is still found among the surviving descendants of Jews expelled from Spain in 1492. In modern times the culture of Jews has been expressed in almost every tongue: Heine wrote in German, Dubnow in Hebrew and Russian, Edmond Fleg in French —any anthology of modern Jewish literature will suggest other tongues. An engrossing cultural phenomenon is the development of the Yiddish language many centuries ago and its flowering in the last century.

But the variety does not stop with language. The dispersal of Jewish communities throughout the world invariably brought both plain people and intellectuals into relation with most of the historic peoples and their cultures. There was a continual absorption-rejection process which operated unconsciously on a kind of sociological principle of assimilation or survival. It is impossible, of course, to separate, weigh, and label the elements of a cultural compound as the scientist isolates and identifies chemical elements. Yet a scholar blessed with a keen-edged intellect and a strong imagination can dissect a cultural fusion as a great critic can evaluate a novel or a musicologist a symphony.

A glance at the mainstream of the Jewish cultural tradition shows all the intellectual currents that have gone into the making of Western civilization. Archeology has brought to light the similarities between the life and thought of Biblical culture and the Semitic, Egyptian, and Hellenic cultures of antiquity. The digs and finds of this new species of detective-adventures are as dramatic—witness the Dead Sea discoveries of the nineteen forties and nineteen fifties—as a Broadway or Hollywood whodunit; but in this book we are concerned only with the meaning of the new facts for our major theme.

Among other things, a revision of the tenets of Biblical Higher Criticism has become necessary. The accepted Hebrew text of the Bible is daily being vindicated by irrefutable contemporary evidence. Moreover, one of the extraordinary illusions of the Higher Critics has also been shattered. On the basis of certain similarities between ancient Judaism and surrounding cultures, they had concluded that the Mosaic code, the belief in monotheism, and other key ideas were simply taken over by the Jews, and consequently they questioned and frequently denied the uniqueness of Judaism. Well, they—and we —know better now. The facts tell another story—an eloquent one. "Though the Old Testament contains a synthesis of the best that had been contributed by the ancient East," writes Professor William F. Albright, the preeminent archeologist and Biblical scholar, "it was transmuted by Hebrew religious insight into a work which rises mountain-high above even the highest hills of Egypt and Mesopotamia, and which is permeated through and through with the elusive fragrance of Palestine."

Succeeding chapters in this book will show how Judaism—engaged in a long struggle with pagan religions and philosophies of early and late antiquity, and fighting off idolatry, immoralism, and polytheism —left its impress on Western culture, especially through its derivatives, Christianity and Islam. Today, particularly in the United States, expounders of Judaism are grappling with current scientific and democratic thought in the hope of adapting the basic Jewish tradition and ethics to twentieth-century culture. Sink your shafts deep, then, into the cultures of the Jewish people and you will be sure to come up with astonishing results. And you will find that, far from being engaged in an academic pursuit, you are being brought to the heart of one of the profoundest issues facing us all.

HISTORIAN, READER, AND HISTORY

To overcome many of the obstacles mentioned in the foregoing pages, the writers of this book have pooled their specialized knowledge. They have been enabled to deal quite successfully with what may be called the factual element in history: population and vital statistics of the inhabitants of well-developed and sensibly governed areas; modes of earning a living and accumulating wealth in modern communities; blood groups and net reproduction rates in given states; social and political proclivities that are reflected in developed social institutions; the data of manuscript and printed literature, and so on. Where life lends itself to scientific analysis, the evidence of investigation by generations of scholars has led to some valid generalization.

Yet the writers are bound to fall short of writing history with the "scientific accuracy" that certain nineteenth-century scholars thought was possible. For the domain of history is life—a hot, throbbing organism whose subtlety and suppleness continue to elude the most sensitive and flexible scientific tools. If we could read the many tons of documents and books on the catastrophe of the Six Million, the depth, character, and significance of so great a tragedy would still pass our understanding. Or to take another contemporary example, if we could master all the available evidence on the new republic of Israel, we should still find it impossible to tabulate "scientifically" all the complex forces and all the emotions and ideas that gave it birth. We should have to press into service the great unconscious and creative aid of the mind—poetic intuition.

It is time to add a final word about the overarching theme of this book. For we are concerned with something more than the story of Jewish history, however fascinating and important that story may be. Our concern is primarily with the way in which the ideas and values developed in the course of that history anchored themselves in the mind and spirit of the people and how they have been transmitted to the present generation.

We do not hesitate to say that four thousand years of experience have evolved a cluster of ideas and values that are uniquely Jewish and that remain significant for modern men and women. They have been creative forces, building human character to an extraordinary degree and raising standards of social conduct. No other culture has produced a greater faith in the goodness of human nature and in the efficacy of human institutions. The fusion of the idea of nationality with the ideal of universality—a fusion which has not yet been satisfactorily solved in political democracy or international law—is another of the dominant strivings of Judaism. These, and other ideas which will be elucidated throughout this book, are challenging for all of us; and they are decisive for anyone bred in democratic culture and interested in the fate of the human race.

It is necessary to add that the writers have not attempted to mold the ideas and values described in the following pages into a substantive theory of Judaism. We have left this great question open to the reader. Nevertheless, we have not hesitated to take a stand and commit ourselves on many burning historical and contemporary issues in order to help clarify and enrich the reader's understanding.

It is our hope that anyone who follows our account through to the end will find in addition to essential information a pool of ideas which can be drawn upon for intellectual stimulation and the formulation of communal policy. And perhaps the reader will find something more: that as a participant in the latest chapter of this story he has the power to help create the next chapter.

THE
BIBLICAL
AGE

YEHEZKEL KAUFMANN

Yehezkel Kaufmann, a Biblical scholar of the first rank, was born in 1890 in the Ukraine and studied in Odessa. Broadening his studies in the fields of political economy, history of religion, and philosophy, he received his doctorate from the University of Berne in Switzerland and taught in Berlin. He published studies in German and Hebrew and then settled in Palestine in 1929. He has been Professor of Bible at the Hebrew University in Jerusalem since 1949. Among his numerous publications in Hebrew are In Exile and Alien Lands, *a philosophy of Jewish history, and the monumental eight-volume* History of the Religion of Israel *(1937-56). The following chapters, written expressly for this volume, comprise the first extensive presentation of his writing in the English language. Professor Kaufmann wrote these chapters in Hebrew and they were rendered into English by Dr. Moshe Greenberg of the University of Pennsylvania.*

1

THE GENESIS OF ISRAEL

About thirty-five hundred years ago, in the lands now called the Near East, a small band of nomads wandered with their flocks into Palestine. After many adventures their descendants conquered the land and made it the seedbed of a new religion. In the course of time their new world view and their sacred writings became a basic element in the thought of western man. The long road they traveled to greatness begins in the ancient past, amid the civilizations that once flourished along the rivers Tigris and Euphrates.

THE ANCIENT NEAR EASTERN LEGACY

The cuneiform records of western Asia begin to speak of a peculiar group of migrants who wander from land to land, making their living as laborers, slaves, and mercenary soldiers. They appear in Babylonia, Assyria, western Mesopotamia, Asia Minor, Canaan, and Egypt; the cuneiform sources call them "Habiru."

Precisely what the term Habiru means is still an unsettled question. One view regards it as denoting a social category of nomadic raiders. Others take it to be an ethnic term, equivalent to the Biblical "Hebrew"—a gentilic denoting descent from Eber (the great-great-grandson of Noah), and applicable to the peoples of Arabia, Aram, Ammon, Moab, Edom, and Israel. The latter view seems likely to be correct. Toward the end of the third millennium, then, the "sons of Eber" began their migration which went on for centuries and carried them throughout the civilized lands of the ancient Near East.

Our sources indicate that this was not, for the most part, a mass movement, but one of individuals, of small bands and families. These migrants were not seeking a national territory; it was enough for them to have found a means of subsistence. And yet there do appear to have been ethnic units among the Habiru who retained their individuality and who were looking for a land they could call their own. The patriarchal ancestors of Israel—Abraham "the Hebrew" and his offspring—were evidently of this sort. When they entered Canaan in the second half of the second millennium B.C.E., it was not as soldiers, slaves, or hirelings, but as distinct, independent tribes. A sense of kinship united them, and their common purpose was to find land upon which they could settle.

Among the extra-Biblical documents that mention the Habiru there is, however, no reference to these tribes. The Tell-el-Amarna letters, sent from Canaan to the Egyptian Pharoah in the fifteenth and fourteenth centuries B.C.E., have often been cited as bearing witness to the Israelite occupation of Canaan. These letters do indeed report that Habiru bands are disrupting Egyptian control of Canaan, and that the natives are falling away to them. But the Biblical evidence argues against identifying these Habiru with the Israelites. They can hardly be related to the Patriarchs, for the latter are represented in the Bible, not as mercenaries or raiders, but as herdsmen and farmers, seeking to live at peace with their Canaanite neighbors. The conquering tribes of Joshua's time are even more unlike the el-Amarna Habiru. For the Israelite invaders were an organized tribal alliance, fighting on their own under a single leader against all the kings of Canaan. They have little in common with the Habiru raiders and mercenaries of the el-Amarna letters, who hire themselves out to the rival kings and play a large role in their anti-Egyptian intrigues. In short, the extra-Biblical material on the Habiru cannot be brought into connection with the Israelite occupation of Canaan without obscuring and distorting the plain meaning of the Biblical narratives.

Nonetheless, the information regarding the Habiru migrations is of value for understanding the background of Israelite origins. To begin with, we see that the wandering of the Israelite tribes into Canaan was part of the spread of the Habiru groups throughout the ancient Near East. The Biblical story which has the family of Abraham wander north, then southwest—from Ur of the Chaldees to Harran, thence to Canaan—is thus placed in its proper historical setting. This itinerary is important because it confutes the notion that the Israelite tribes were desert barbarians with a low culture and religion at the time of the Exodus and Conquest.

As a matter of fact the tribes did not originate in the desert at all. They came from Babylonia and lived for a while in Upper Mesopotamia, whence they came to Canaan and eventually to Egypt; their stay in the desert after the Exodus was a relatively short affair. During many generations they lived in lands of high culture. They were not only influenced by the culture of the peoples among whom they lived, they intermarried with them, and thus became ethnically mingled with them. The Patriarchs marry Aramean women; Judah and Simon take Canaanite wives; Tamar, the ancestress of the most important Judahite clans, Perez and Zerah, is a Canaanite; and the mother of Ephraim and Manasseh is Asenath, the Egyptian wife of Joseph. The Israelite tribes were an ethnic conglomerate and their early culture was likewise composed of many elements.

The most ancient of these elements go back to proto-ethnic times, to the period when the tribes had not yet branched off from the common Semitic stock. The tribal structure of Israelite society dates from this early period. In retaining this structure Israel was distinct from the Canaanites, who by the el-Amarna period had become organized into many city-states. The Israelites, on the other hand, kept their tribal organization after they settled in Canaan, and even after they established a kingdom. Also stemming from proto-ethnic times is, doubtless, the form of divination in which oracles are delivered by a prophet-seer of the Arabic *kahin* type. It is characteristic of the *kahin* that he is not connected with sanctuary or cult. He is a visionary, a poet, possessing a familiar spirit who reveals hidden things to him. He interprets portents, goes out to war, and, at times, even becomes the leader of a tribe. Such, too, is the nature of the ancient Israelite seer. It is possible that Israel's divination by lot is likewise a practice which goes back to earliest times.

Babylonian civilization contributed another important element to the culture of early Israel. Israelite traditions regarding the Creation, the Antediluvians, the Flood, and the Tower of Babel have striking parallels in Babylonian literature which show that the tribes were influenced by Mesopotamian culture during their stay in that area. The social and legal background of the patriarchal narratives likewise reveals cultural contacts with Mesopotamian legal traditions. Elements of Israel's hymnal and wisdom literature, along with certain cultic practices, also stem from the period of the tribes' stay in the land between Ur and Harran.

Once the Hebrew tribes reached Canaan their language underwent a change, and the original dialect was transformed into "the language of Canaan." Literary materials that have been unearthed at Ugarit* indicate that Biblical idiom has roots in the literary language of Canaan. This connection is doubtless ancient, from before the descent of the tribes into Egypt. And so, together with the language, the literature of Canaan was also adopted by the tribes. In that early period several religious and cultural features of the Canaanites were taken over: such divine epithets as 'elyon (most high), 'adon, and ba'al (both mean "lord") are Canaanite. The 'ephod as a cultic garment and an instrument of divination also seems to derive from Canaanite usage. From Canaan come the names of the sacrifices, shelem, 'asham, kalil, and others; with them came, surely, something of sacrificial techniques. Some of the "dionysiacal" elements of the cult, such as the wine festival, wine libation, and frenzied cultic prophesying—which was widespread in Canaan and Asia Minor—were derived from Canaan. From Canaan came the hymnal style of Hebrew, and other literary features. The legend of the wise and righteous Daniel, who is mentioned together with Noah and Job in Ezekiel 14 and 28, is Canaanite.

There is a distinctive Egyptian element in Israelite culture. This is visible, in the first place, in the Egyptian coloring of the Joseph narrative and the account of the Egyptian sojourn of the tribes. It is seen in the Egyptian names of the priestly tribe—Moses, Phinehas, Hur, Pashhur, and others. The Aaronites may well have adopted certain Egyptian cultic practices. Egyptian wisdom in large measure, and hymnal literature to a lesser degree, had an influence on early Israel. The magical wonder—for example, the staff which becomes a serpent—is ultimately of Egyptian derivation, although in Israel it was transformed into a divine wondrous sign destined to become one of the typical and enduring expressions of the Israelite idea.

In the culture and religion of the Israelite tribes during the period of their crystallization into a nation one can thus see clearly the impact of the peoples among whom they lived for centuries. At that

* Ugarit was an ancient city on the coast of Syria destroyed about 1300 B.C.E. and rediscovered by a French archeological expedition in 1929. Excavation there is still going on. Among the most important finds to date are large portions of the long-lost Canaanite religious and mythological literature. The Ugaritic language is a dialect closely akin to Biblical Hebrew, with a good number of identical phrases and idioms. Ugaritic literature also provides much material illuminating hitherto unintelligible allusions in our Bible.

time—the second half of the second millennium B.C.E.—there had already long been in existence a highly developed polytheism, which conceived of exalted gods, creators of the world and of human civilization and maintainers of right and justice. There were intricately developed cultic forms, magnificent temples, and an advanced level of art that had produced a complex religious symbolism. A rich mythological literature was in existence, as well as a varied hymnal, which included both individual and national psalms. At work within these religions was an aspiration to express deity in universalistic terms, and a tendency toward monism is also evident—a tendency to regard the many gods as manifestations of one supreme divinity. There were legal, ethical and wisdom literatures informed with high and noble sentiments. The Israelite tribes lived for many generations in this highly civilized environment; their cultural level at the time when they became a nation reflected that of their surroundings.

The foregoing implies that the religion of the Israelite tribes at the Exodus and during the Desert Wandering was not animism, demonism, or totemism. Their religious level was that of the prevailing sophisticated polytheism. In the view of Wellhausen,* a view which to a considerable degree still dominates the field of Biblical study, the idea of a universal god made its first appearance in Israel in the eighth century, not before Amos, and then only as the result of the Assyrian menace, thanks to which Israel was drawn out of its narrow nationalistic confines. Until then Israel is assumed to have confined the domain of its God to the boundaries of Palestine. But this notion is naïvely unhistorical; for the idea of a universal god, the creator and sustainer of all, was prevalent in the polytheistic world well before Israel became a nation, and owes nothing to the Assyrian menace. The initial level of Israelite religion—and this cannot be emphasized too often—was set by the cultural level of the surroundings in which Israel first found itself: creation legends, cultic practices, priesthood, prophecy, psalms, wisdom, law, and ethics were all a heritage of the ancient Near East.

And yet there did appear in Israel an entirely new religious idea, an original creation and one that had no roots in polytheistic civiliza-

---

* Julius Wellhausen (1844-1918) was a German Biblical scholar and Orientalist. In his *Prolegomena to the History of Israel* (1882, English translation 1885) he presented what became the classic critical view of the cultural history of Israel. It is only in the past few decades that Biblical scholarship has begun to free itself from the spell of Wellhausen's brilliant work. The advances of archeology have done much to undermine Wellhausen's conclusions (he worked primarily with the internal evidence of the Bible); his method, however, remains exemplary.

tion. Essentially nonpagan, this notion in seeking expression gave rise to a new sphere of culture. The elements derived from without served it as building materials, but only after they had been fundamentally transformed. The appearance of the idea among the tribes of Israel, marking as it did the rise and early history of Israel, was an event of lasting historical moment.

THE NATURE OF THE PAGAN RELIGION

Before we can appreciate the significance of Israelite religion we must free ourselves of the idea, prevalent throughout Biblical and post-Biblical Jewish literature and in Christian and Islamic thought as well, that paganism—the religion of all the nations of antiquity— was the "worship of wood and stone," the worship of material objects and "dumb idols." We must, in short, cease to mistake paganism for fetishism.

The discovery that wood and stone were not gods is in itself completely trivial; it was surely not by virtue of this discovery that Israelite religion made its great impression on the world. It need hardly be said that this discovery does not give rise to a belief in one god. But the main point is that the conception of paganism as fetishism is false. To be sure, there was a certain element of fetishism in the popular religion of the pagans, and it was this that several of the Greek philosophers ridiculed (Heraklites, Xenophanes, and others). The fetishistic aspect of paganism is, however, quite peripheral, and by no means expresses its essence. Pagan religion was not the worship of wood and stone.

The basis of pagan religion is the deification of natural phenomena. To the pagan, all the manifestations of nature are divine powers, aspects of a mysterious supernatural vitality. The heaven, the earth, the sea, the sun, moon, and stars, the wind, the mountains and rivers—are all divine beings. The creative imagination of man molded the mysterious vitality that reveals itself in the phenomena of nature into the image of living persons. It gave them plastic form and thus created a universe of spirits, of gods and goddesses individual in body and character, who lived out their personal lives everywhere in the universe. The deification of nature gave rise to the worship of natural gods, personal gods whose lives were bound up in the processes of nature. Observing natural events, such as lightning or thunder, dawn or dusk, the pagan created stories about the life of the gods. Such stories about what happened to the gods constitute mythology. Myths tell of the birth of gods and goddesses, their growth, marriage, generations, wars, death and resurrection.

Every pagan religion has its theogony, an account of the birth of the gods. The gods evolved; they were born or created out of some primeval substance which precedes them in time and transcends them in power. This is the great symbol of the essence of paganism: the gods are not ultimately sovereign; they emerge out of a pre-existent realm and are subject to a transcendent order. The deification of nature entails the imposition of natural or supernatural compulsion upon the gods. They are subject to "biological" conditions: they must eat and drink, they grow old, become sick, and die. Sexual impulses rule them. Some gods are "by nature" good, others evil; they are at war with each other, and the forces of evil are a real threat to the good gods so that they must always fight for their lives. Sinful impulses also hold sway over the gods: they commit sin and are subject to its consequences. They are subject to the decrees of fate—the Greek *moira,* the Latin *fatum.* Paganism thus does not accord ultimate freedom to its gods.

Corresponding to the mythological conception of deity is the magical character of the pagan cultus. Magic is an art whose purpose is to move occult powers to act in a desired manner. It utilizes means which are automatically efficient, irrespective of the will of the gods. There are words and incantations, colors, substances, gestures, and the like which are in themselves charged with magical power; whoever possesses the secret knowledge of these means is thereby enabled to work magic. By magic alone one can make rain and stop it, make ill and heal, bring victory or defeat. The power of magic transcends the gods: they themselves employ it, for they too are in need of this almighty instrument which is independent of them and their will. The gods are great magicians, and there are even skilled specialists in this art among them.

The pagan cultus is fundamentally magical. Cultic activity is conceived as having an inherent, automatic effectiveness, which is independent of the gods. The cult is not merely the command of the gods to man, not entirely a law which derives from their will; it is ultimately above the gods. They are in need of it; their lives depend on it. It is conceived as the "navel of the universe," a mysterious source of the vital power of the gods and the universe. On a primitive level the conception is crude: man builds a house for the god, appoints it with furniture, serves the god meals in it, and generally attends there to all his needs. On a higher level, cultic activity is regarded as charged with a mysterious, magical power.

But on all levels pagan religion sees the cult as activating the transcendent source of power upon which both the gods and the world depend. To be sure, the pagan also believes that his service can incline the favor of the gods toward him, can move them to prosper him. Thus the worshiper does implore the graciousness of the gods, often to a considerable extent. But the very entreaty is at bottom grounded on a magical conception of the cultic act: man gives something to the god, he heightens the god's power and fulfills his want; therefore, he looks to the god for grace and reward.

The heart of the pagan idea, then, is the conception of a primordial, supradivine realm which is the womb of all being, contains the roots and patterns of all nature, and out of which the gods themselves have emerged. The multitude of natural phenomena and with it the multitude of the gods stem from the infinite fertility of the primordial sphere. Multiplicity is fundamental to paganism; it serves to symbolize its basic idea: the subjection of all, deity included, to a transcendent, primeval realm.

Needless to say, this fundamental conception was never explicitly formulated by paganism, never abstracted and expressed as a philosophic postulate. It was rather an intuitive perception, inarticulate but all-pervasive as a primary category of thought, as the very structure of the pagan world view. Paganism everywhere believed the deity to be subject to a superior realm and obedient to its sovereign laws; this is as true of the primitive as of the most advanced stages of pagan religion. Though the idea was never formulated explicitly, all of pagan creativity serves as its symbol and manifestation.

THE RELIGIOUS IDEA OF ISRAEL

One people, however, and it alone, conceived a different world view: the people of Israel.

The Israelite religious idea is that the will of God is transcendent and sovereign over all. Israelite religion does not subject the Deity to a primeval realm and an imposed pattern. Its primary category, differing fundamentally from that of paganism, is the absolute freedom of the Godhead. It liberates the Godhead from mythological and magical subjection: Israelite religion has no theogony; its God did not emerge from a preexistent substance, nor is He subject to or dependent upon anything outside or above Himself. He was not born, and has no lineage. He is ageless, and has no sexual qualities: Israelite religion has no male and female deities, no engendering of or by

Deity. Its God does not die and is not resurrected. He is prior to all and rules all: He fashions light and creates darkness, He is God of good and God of evil. He was not born from the universe, nor the universe from Him. All that is was created by His will, by His word; "He spoke—and it was."

Israel's God is equally free from subjection to magic. Israelite religion knows of no objects, acts, or formulas charged with inherent, automatic power, independent of the will of God, which therefore may be utilized by God for His own need. This is to say that it has no magic in the pagan sense.

To be sure, the Israelite man of God works wonders; but in the Biblical period wonders are not performed by established techniques possessing mysterious powers; they are done without any special equipment, by the grace of God alone. The Biblical wonder is a wondrous *sign:* not a sign of the power of the man of God or his techniques, but of God's power and the sovereignty of His will. The classic type of Biblical wonderworking is found in the story of Exodus 4, where the God who appears to Moses in the Burning Bush sends him to work wonders before the eyes of the people so that they may believe in him. The techniques are: to cast his staff on the ground, to place his hand in his bosom, and to pour water from the Nile onto the ground. These are all quite ordinary acts involving the plainest objects; no incantation accompanies them to activate occult forces. The wonder is performed solely through the grace of God. Because of this, a science of wonderworking, analogous to the art and science of pagan magic, never developed in Israel. The Israelite wonderworker was not a specialist, a professional wizard who had mastered the traditional esoteric lore of his art, as were, say, the Egyptian magicians. The God of the Bush does not reveal magical secrets to Moses; He merely commands him to do certain things; the wonder follows as an act of divine grace, and the human agent is viewed as no more than the bearer—for the moment —of this grace. Inasmuch as the wonder is not the result of special skill, it cannot be performed at man's bidding; it is a single, unique event which occurs only at God's pleasure and only as a sign of His sovereign rule.

The cult of Israelite religion differs from that of paganism no less radically. The Israelite cult is not conceived of as charged with mysterious, transcendental power upon which the life and strength of the deity are dependent. It is not the "navel of the universe" through which power flows to the deity to heighten his vitality. Israel's God is not in need of the cultus. Whereas the pagan cult implies the divine subjection to a supernal realm above the gods,

Israel's represents man's subjection to the will of God and the recognition of His supremacy.

Having liberated deity from mythological-magical subjection, Israelite religion did away with the pagan conception of the power of fate over all—divine and human beings alike obeying dark, blind fate, irrational and amoral yet all-powerful. In its stead Israelite religion postulated the universal rule of a purposeful intelligence, a God who acts with a moral purpose, whose fundamental attribute is goodness. Along with divine freedom, Israelite religion affirmed human freedom. The omnipotent Creator has set norms for the physical realm—natural law—but for man He has set religious and moral norms—the divine commandments. In contrast to the rigid realm of nature, however, man, created in God's image, possesses the gift of moral freedom; he may do either good or evil at will. This freedom of choice implies the possibility of rebellion against God. And indeed, man did rebel: he forgot his Creator, and gave the homage due to God to no-gods, violated the laws of God and did much evil on earth; it is this sin of man which is the source of evil in the world. This brought down on man a host of afflictions, the divine punishment for his sinful rebellion. The tension between the rebellious will of man and the word of God is what makes human history. The drama of man's defiance of the divine command is being played out upon the world's stage. The battle will end at the End of Days.

In this way Israelite religion replaced the mythological wars of the gods with the historical struggle of man against the word of God. And so while there is no strife between good and evil gods, no autonomous powers of evil that menace the dominion of the Lord, there is another sort of cosmic battle, another kind of divine drama. This drama unfolds in the dimension of human history and morality, in the life of man who opposes God's will. There is no divine power that is arrayed against God; His antagonist is man, in whom He Himself implanted the freedom to rebel as the necessary concomitant of endowing him with free will and making him a moral creature.

The religion of Israel effected a revolution in the world view of man. An abyss separates it from paganism. The motto of the new faith was "the Lord is One," but it is a mistake to think that a merely arithmetic difference sets off Israel's religion from paganism. The pagan idea does not approach Israelite monotheism as it diminishes the number of its gods. The Israelite conception of God's unity entails His sovereign transcendence over all. It rejects the pagan idea of a realm beyond deity, the source of mythology and magic.

The affirmation that the will of God is supreme and absolutely free is a new, nonpagan category of thought.

Nowhere in the Bible is the Israelite idea stated explicitly, nor, for that matter, is it ever so stated in later Jewish literature. It appears rather as a primal intuition informing all of Israelite creativity. The ancient creativity of Israel was not scientific or philosophic; it expressed itself in song and story, seer and lawgiver, psalm and prayer, and a lofty faith. The new religious conception pervades every aspect of Israel's creativity: legend, cult, ethics, wisdom, priesthood, prophecy, and kingship. It speaks in the history of the nation, and as if from a hidden center dominates all.

Still, it is surprising that the Bible fails even to hint at the contrast between its world view and that of paganism. After all, the Bible is the archantagonist of idolatry; from beginning to end it is at war with heathendom. But because it misconceives of pagan religion as the worship of wood and stone, it never really comes to grips with the essence of polytheism, the belief in mythological gods. In the entire Bible there is not one word of polemic directed explicitly at any mythological notion. That is why the Bible fails to express the real contrast between Israelite religion and mythological polytheism. Over against all forms of paganism Israel's religion has no theogony; but the contrast is nowhere stated. Israel knows of no sexuality in its Deity; it knows of no primordial realm or magical forces independent of the Deity; yet none of these things is said in so many words, least of all formulated in abstract concepts.

Hence it is a mistake to suppose that Israel's monotheism grew out of the polemic against idolatry—more particularly, out of the great prophetic denunciations of idol worship, especially those of the Second Isaiah, as is sometimes asserted. It is a mistake because the Israelite idea never found expression in those polemics and denunciations. Nevertheless, the idea pervades all levels of Biblical literature: ancient folk tales, early, popular prophecy, laws of the cult, and wisdom writings alike. There is no mythological or magical stratum in Biblical literature; "discoveries" of such strata are the fruit of a superficial interpretation of Biblical phenomena in the light of pagan institutions. Fossil remains of ancient myths stemming from before the rise of the Israelite religion are to be found in the Bible, but living myths—whether Israelite or foreign—are absent. Most remarkable of all is the Bible's seeming ignorance of the fact that the *pagans* believe in mythological gods. It repeatedly asserts the naïve notion that they worship gods of wood and stone, but fails to disparage a single pagan myth. This can have but one meaning: all of Biblical literature was created in a monotheistic environment, at a time after the profound religious revolution that marked the beginning of Israel's life as a nation took place. It was this revolution that brought about the rise of a civilization that was monotheistic to the core.

Israelite religion did not, of course, spring full-blown into existence. Like every cultural phenomenon, it underwent an evolution in time. It arose in the wilderness, took on new forms in Canaan, and reached a climax in the middle of the eighth century with the rise of classical prophecy. After the destruction of the Temple, it evolved forms enabling it to exist apart from its land. It developed a new doctrine of retribution. A stage was reached when it declared war upon the religion of the heathen and aspired to become a universal religion. But this development was organic, like that of a living organism, all of whose stages are latent in the seed but appear only gradually, one by one. In the life of Israel the seed of a new religious idea was sown in antiquity; throughout the ages this idea continued to realize and embody in new forms the latent possibilities it harbored.

Why was Israel thus unique among all the peoples in its religious world view? The believer answers: Israel was chosen; the empirical historian can only say: here is revealed the creative genius of the nation. Neither answer is completely satisfying, for no creation of the spirit can be completely explained; there is an ultimate mystery which always eludes us. We may be able to describe the historical circumstances of its appearance; that is the most we can hope for.

MOSES AND MONOTHEISM

Biblical tradition has it that the first men were monotheists, that Adam, Cain, Abel, and the succeeding generations were worshipers of the one God; idolatry is not mentioned in Genesis 1-11. Idolatry arose with the dispersal of mankind and the confusion of tongues, that is, the origin of idolatry is coeval with the origin of the nations. Knowledge of the one God is kept alive in this period only by a select few: Abraham, Isaac, and Jacob know Him, as do Melchizedek, King of Shalem, Job, and his friends—who are evidently thought of as belonging to patriarchal times. It is only in the time of Moses that monotheism becomes the faith of an entire nation, of Israel.

No creditable evidence is forthcoming to support the existence of monotheism among primitive men. The historicity of the Biblical tradition concerning the monotheism of the Patriarchs is difficult to determine. History knows only of national cultures and national religions, and historical monotheism existed in antiquity as the national religion of Israel. We know of no other monotheistic nations, nor of monotheistic individuals outside of Israel, in the ancient world. We may say, therefore, that the empirical history of monotheism does not antedate the rise of Israel.

According to the Biblical account, the appearance of monotheism in Israel is bound up with the events of the Exodus and the man Moses. In the time of Rameses II (ca. 1301-1235 B.C.E.), famed for his extensive building operations, a group of Hebrew tribes which had migrated to Egypt were impressed into forced labor. They were compelled to build, or participate in the building of, the cities Pithom and Rameses. These tribes were a distinct group, knit together by kinship and a common tradition; they called themselves Bne Yisrael, "Sons of Israel," Israelites. They had come to Egypt not as slaves or laborers but as herdsmen and farmers, free men. To be impressed into service was an insult and a crime, for it violated the customary protection that sojourners had a right to expect in a foreign land. Feeling ran high and apparently led to a movement of rebellion. As a result the tribes were treated with even greater severity, which in turn intensified the ferment of rebellion. Were they destined to be reduced to permanent slavery? Reminiscences of their ancestors' wanderings in Canaan welled up in their hearts: their ancestors had aspired to settle some day in that land and take possession of it. Now the longing to be free and possess the land aroused and unified them. Individuals could escape into the desert, but for the masses, with their wives and children, there was no possibility of flight. Groaning under their burdens, they could only plan and hope for an opportunity to escape.

During those dark days there arose among them a man of genius and leader of men, mighty in will and spirit, whose splendor is not dulled by the thirty centuries that separate us from him: the man Moses. He fulfilled the longing of his tribesmen for freedom, but his achievement was not merely political. It was his prophetic genius that transformed the liberation of the tribes into the birth of a nation, an event which proved to be one of the crucial junctures of human history. He entered the scene, apparently toward the end of Rameses' reign, and carried through the emancipation during the first years of Rameses' successor, Merneptah (1235-27). At first his people's distress drives Moses into the wilderness, and there he hears the voice of God. He returns to his people transformed: he is now a prophet and a messenger of God. His reappearance in this new role astounds his kinsmen; never before has anyone come as a messenger, an apostle of Deity. For Moses is, so far as we know, the first apostolic prophet not only in Israel but in world history. His message, stirring and disturbing, is met with belief and disbelief; but henceforth he is to lead the people with an iron hand, whether they will or no.

We have an account of the experience in the wilderness that made Moses a prophet and a messenger. The account—in Exodus 3:1-4:17 —is a prophetic legend, told simply and yet with great art. Its level is that of the folk, and yet it contains profound symbolism. Legendary as it is, there can be no doubt that it reveals a historic moment; it is the record of the fateful turning point in the life of a colossus of the spirit.

According to this account the hidden name of God, YHWH,* was first revealed in the theophany at the Burning Bush. The name is interpreted as "I am that which I am," a cryptic phrase meaning, perhaps, the Eternal Being, the Everlasting. This is the first revelation of God in the history of the Israelite people. Here for the first time God calls Israel "my people" (Exodus 3:7, 10) and commissions a prophet to carry them His message. In the vision of the Bush, God sets Israel apart as the sphere of His revelation in history: henceforth He will send Israel prophets throughout the generations, henceforth Israel will be God's people. Moses is the first messenger-prophet, but in time to come the messenger-prophet will be a permanent feature of the life of ancient Israel. The concept will pass over into Christianity, where Jesus appears as a messenger, and his disciples are called apostles. Centuries later another prophet will arise in the wilderness, Muhammad, who calls himself "messenger of God." The story of the Bush marks the first appearance of the prophet who is jealous for his God and who fights heathendom. Before this there is no battle for the sake of the "jealous God"; Moses is His first champion. He is sent to Pharaoh, the head of heathendom's empire, to make him know God, to convey to him the command of God, to fight his arrogance and lay him low in the name of YHWH. With the coming of Moses the contrast between Israel and its God and the pagan world suddenly manifests itself in its full proportions.

In the story of the Bush there thus appear at once and for the first time those features which provide the historical framework for Israelite monotheism throughout all the ages: the name YHWH, the people of Israel, the election of Israel, apostolic prophecy, and the battle with heathendom. We may safely assert, therefore, that the story marks the beginning of an epoch.

The symbolism of the story gives concrete expression to the new re-

* These are the Hebrew consonants of the Ineffable Name of God. Long before the Christian era Jews had substituted for it *'adonay* (my Lord) or *'elohim* (God). In the course of time the tradition of its correct pronunciation was lost; a widely accepted modern conjecture is *Yahweh*. The form Jehovah is an erroneous—though by now traditional—hybrid of the consonants JHVH (Latin for YHWH) and the vowels of *'adonay*, with which vowels the Name is usually supplied in the Hebrew Bible to indicate that this is how it is to be read.

ligious idea that was revealed to Moses in the desert of Sinai: the will of God governs all. God appears in a flame burning in a dry thorn bush; the bush burns but is not consumed—something transcending nature is at work. Here is the symbol of a Deity who rules nature, by whose will a dry bush survives the fire. God gives Moses three wondrous signs: his staff becomes a serpent, his hand becomes leprous, and water turns to blood. There is a similarity between these wonders and the magic performed by the Egyptian wizards, so that many scholars have been misled into taking the Burning Bush and similar stories for typical magic stories. But this is a fatal error. We have already pointed out that the pagan magician utilizes means which are thought of as possessing inherent, automatic power independent of the gods; that he is an expert who has acquired the esoteric knowledge needed to manipulate the forces of the occult. Hence his power is not dependent upon the will of the gods; on the contrary, he is capable of coercing the gods, if need be, to do his will. This is never the case in the Bible, especially in our story. God does not disclose to Moses magical secrets such as wonderworking names, incantations, or other secret lore. The acts he is told to perform—casting his staff, placing his hand in his bosom, pouring water—are all thoroughly commonplace. The wonder happens not by virtue of these acts but by the will of God who commanded them; it is a sign, not of Moses' power but of the supreme rule of God. The Author of these signs is all-powerful: He "hath made man's mouth . . . maketh a man dumb, or deaf, or seeing, or blind." The story of the Bush introduces the account of the prodigies that took place in Egypt (the ten plagues), in which God shows Himself the lord of all nature, of water, land, living creatures, wind, fire, hail, light and darkness, and so forth; in which the heathen learns that "there is none like unto YHWH our God," and "that the earth is YHWH's." The wonder legend of the Bush serves, then, as an expression of the idea of a God supreme above all; this is the new idea that flashed upon Moses in his desert vision.

There is equally profound meaning in representing the God of the Bush as a hidden God, whose name has hitherto been unknown. Moses himself is as ignorant of the name of the God that appears to him as are the people to whom he brings His message. To be sure, He is identified as the "God of the Fathers," but it is assumed that the people have forgotten their ancestral God and no longer worship Him. Traditional scholars have been puzzled by this circumstance, and have given it forced interpretations. But the idea is rich with meaning: if the God who reveals himself to Moses has hitherto been unknown, it is because He is outside the sphere of the mythological-magical religion of the pagans. The world of men has not known *Him*, has not built *Him* temples, represented *Him* in images, recounted *His* mythical adventures. This being unknown means that He is other than all the pagan gods of nature.

Moreover, although there is no people who worship this hidden God, He alone sustains the entire heathen world in His mercy. Neither does Israel recognize Him—yet He calls them "my people" and comes to save them from their bondage in the abundance of His kindness. The God who is unknown because He is unknowable thus discloses Himself to Moses as the God of goodness and mercy, God of the world and God of Israel.

Moses appeared before the tribes of Israel as a prophet-messenger with news of redemption from the bondage of Egypt. He also brought them word of the self-disclosure of the supreme, hidden God, together with the tidings of Israel's election. When they left Egypt they were to worship God at Mount Horeb; they were to become the people of God. There was nothing in what Moses said that was beyond the understanding of his fellow tribesmen. It is true that implicit in the Israelite idea of a God above nature is a tremendous abstraction, which was formulated philosophically only after centuries and under the impact of Greek thought. But in its intuitive form the notion of a supreme, omnipotent God, who performs wonders, who is good and abundant in mercy, and who reveals His word to man in prophetic visions, is fully within the reach of the popular mind. It was a novel and marvelous message indeed, but precisely because of this it could move men of simple faith, and stir their souls to the very depths —all the more so as preached by one uniquely endowed for leadership. The work of Muhammad furnishes a striking historical parallel here. He too appeared as a prophetic messenger of God, bringing to men of the desert the new message of the oneness of Allah. He too declared war upon the faith of his people in natural gods. Allah is one and above nature! This gospel fired the Arabs, gave birth to a tremendous religious movement among them, revolutionized their lives, and raised up zealots and mighty warriors for their God.

The new religious idea, never and nowhere contemplated in paganism, was first embodied in national forms. It was universal in essence, but its historical manifestation was bound up with the life of a people in the making, the tribes of Israel. The vision of the Bush laid the foundation of the national monotheism of ancient Israel. Only after a millennium did the new idea begin to exert an influence beyond the confines of Israel and become what it had always been potentially, a force in universal history.

There is no doubt that it was precisely the religious aspect of

Moses' message, new and potentially universal as it was, that gave deeper meaning to its national aspect. In this also Muhammad's activity may serve as an illuminating example. Although his new message to the Arab tribes was essentially religious, it consolidated them into a political and military unit, and brought them out of the desert to conquer lands and peoples at sword's point. The new idea had a similar effect upon the Israelite tribes: it uplifted them, welded them into a people, and infused divine significance into their history. In whatever befell them they now discerned the hand of God; every event was transformed into part of a divine drama. To be sure, all this was still far in the future, yet we may suppose that Moses at least was aware of the mighty power latent in his religious message. And something of the light he radiated must have been reflected in the faces of the people.

THE COVENANT AT SINAI

The first years of Merneptah's reign were filled with crises. Canaan rebelled and had to be subdued; soon afterward war with the Lybians broke out. It is also likely that after Rameses' death the spate of building operations fell off, so that the slave levies were not so closely supervised as before. The time seemed ripe for the liberation of the tribes. We may assume that there is a historical kernel to the stories of the ten plagues. Natural calamities probably struck Egypt and the tribes saw in them the finger of God. Inspired by Moses, their faith was strengthened and they took courage. In the month of Abib (Spring-Fruit) in about 1230 B.C.E., Moses gave the signal and the tribes went forth "with an high hand," suddenly and "in haste." Their immediate goal was to escape into the wilderness.

The tribes had lived in "the land of Rameses" (Goshen), in the district of the city Rameses (Zoan, Tanis), in northern Egypt. On the night of the Exodus they journeyed from Rameses to Succoth. It appears that the events that immediately followed took place in the northern rather than the southern part of the wilderness of Sinai. The tribes had first of all to get out of the reach of Egyptian forces. They must therefore have gone eastward, into the desert of the Sinai isthmus between Egypt and Edom-Midian. Here are found wells and pasturage, and even some patches of arable land. This would seem to be the site of the forty-year wandering. Here, and not in the southern triangle where Christian tradition places the site of Mount Sinai, are we to look for the mountain of God. According to Exodus 14:2, the fleeing tribes were compelled to change their course and turn northward, toward the Mediterranean Sea. They encamped facing Baal Zephon, on the shore of the Mediterranean. Here too wells are still found, and nearby is a body of water called Lake Sirbonis, divided from the sea by a narrow strip of land. The lake is quite deep, and occasionally its waters are covered by a deceptive layer of sand that cannot support the weight of a man. The narrow land passage is at times submerged under water. At this treacherous spot whole armies have perished. It would seem that this is the Red Sea (*Yam Suf*) of the Exodus story. The Egyptians apparently sent out a force to compel the fugitives to return, and the two companies met in the area of Lake Sirbonis. The fugitives managed to escape under cover of night. As for the pursuers, some were overwhelmed by a sudden rise in the tide, while others may have stumbled upon the quicksand covering the lake and sunk to the bottom. Such would appear to be the core of the story about the crossing of the Red Sea. The Israelites saw the hand of God in their escape. A triumphal inscription of Merneptah mentions the encounter as a victory of his army against Israelite nomads in Canaan (the area of Lake Sirbonis was considered within the boundaries of Canaan), but it must be kept in mind that such inscriptions were in the nature of military communiqués and are as veracious.

At any rate, the liberation was a success. The fugitives escaped to the desert while the pursuing Egyptians were miraculously struck down. A wave of enthusiasm swept the tribes in their first encampment as free men. For the first time they celebrated their independence under the desert sky. They baked *matzoth*—bread of haste—and glorified the hidden God, their Redeemer. For the first time the wilderness rang with a song to YHWH: "Sing ye unto YHWH for He is highly exalted: the horse and his rider hath He thrown into the sea"; "YHWH is a man of war, YHWH is His name . . . fearful in praises, doing wonders." This was the first festival of the new religion, the first embodiment of a new popular cult. It was not a mythological festival, celebrating an event in the life of a god, but a historical one, celebrating the deed of God who redeems man. It was based on the work of a prophet-messenger, and it was characteristic of the new faith.

The appearance of Moses marks the beginning of that uniquely Israelite phenomenon, apostolic prophecy. Prophets are, of course, found in many places, but the pagan prophet delivers oracles and foretells the future only for those who inquire of him. And he is usually paid for his services. The messenger-prophet, on the other hand, comes before men on his own impulse, unasked and unsought, in the name of God. At times he is persecuted; he feels his mission an intolerable burden, and he fulfills it only under the duress of the divine imperative. The work of the pagan prophet and diviner is not informed by any idea, it is rather a kind of vocation. Not so Israel's apostolic prophecy: it is bound up with a religious and ethical doctrine which it urges, and it creates a civilization on the basis of that doctrine. For many generations Israelite prophecy was the ardent champion of monotheism and its moral imperatives against the idolatrous leanings of the people. Indeed, prophecy was the very fountainhead of Israelite religion. It was in a prophetic vision that this faith first appeared, and prophets ever conceived its noblest ideals. Nowhere else can so intimate a relation be found between prophecy and the creation of a culture.

The Pentateuchal narratives about Moses bear the stamp of prophetic teaching. Moses stands at the head of the tribes as their leader. His authority over them stems from his being the messenger of God. He is concerned with their security, with their food and water supply, but his activity is centered about the inculcation of his new message. All that he does provides a vehicle for this task. He performs a series of miracles in the wilderness, but only to confirm his mission. Moses does not act as a priest. It is in the role of a prophet that he performs cultic acts.

The goal of the tribes was the land of Canaan, the land of their fathers' sojournings. But Moses led them first into the wilderness to induct them into the Covenant and make them a people. His aim was at once political and religious. And so he led them to the mountain of God, the place where YHWH had first revealed Himself to him.

The narrative represents the Covenant at Sinai as the crucial event in the life of the Israelite tribes. It is described as a majestic and unparalleled theophany: a divine revelation to an entire people in public view. The Sinai saga bears features similar to the story of the Bush. The God who appeared to Moses in the stillness of the desert as a flame in the Bush manifests Himself here in thunder, lightning, and fire to the eyes of all. This manifestation is likewise a wondrous sign whose purpose is to instill forever in the hearts of the onlookers a firm belief in God and Moses. The primary motif of this revelation is the speech of God, His word and command to the people. The fire, the cloud, and the thunder are only a background for the speech, for the "Giving of the Torah."

The making of the Covenant, following the theophany, bears the prophetic stamp as well. Its ritual is cultic, but its content prophetic: the "Book of the Covenant" (Exodus 24:4,7) is the written words of God. The ritual is described in detail in Exodus 24. Moses builds an altar at the foot of the mountain and sets up twelve pillars, one for each of the tribes. Israelite youths offer up on it whole and peace offerings. Moses sprinkles half the sacrificial blood on the altar, then recites the Book of the Covenant to the people and sprinkles the other half upon them, saying, "Behold the blood of the Covenant which the Lord hath made with you concerning all these things!" There follows a sacral meal in the presence of God. Moses, Aaron, and the elders go up the mountain to YHWH; they bow down to Him from afar; they partake of the sacral meal before Him. As an extraordinary favor they are permitted to behold the God of Israel—"and beneath His feet there was the like of a paved work of sapphire"—and yet remain alive.

This story bears every mark of antiquity and folkloristic naïveté. Stone pillars are not yet prohibited, and serve here as "witnesses" to the Covenant. A meal is prepared in the presence of the God. The theophany itself is depicted in highly anthropomorphic terms. We seem to be on the threshold of paganism, and yet precisely at this point we can see most clearly how the new faith refashioned the ancient materials. No image, no pillar, stands for the Deity in the ritual. The prophet acts as God's deputy, bringing His word to the people. There is, to be sure, a sacral meal, but only in the presence of God, "from afar." The pagan conceives of his gods as actually eating and drinking at divine and human feasts. Here the mythological meal is transformed into an act of divine favor. The Deity appears not in order to partake, but in order to confirm His presence at the making of the Covenant. Even in this ancient story the climax of the ritual is prophetic. It is a theophany, the immediate perception that the Covenant is divine and that the words are the words of God.

The laws connected with the theophany at Sinai are the Ten Commandments (Exodus 20:2-17) and the larger and smaller Books of the Covenant (Exodus 20:22-23:33; 34:6-26). These laws contain specifically Israelite as well as general Near Eastern elements. To the former we may account the religious, cultic, and ethical laws that are related to Israel's monotheism; to the latter, the civil and criminal laws as well as the bulk of the ethical. The general elements are, of course, the older and have their parallels in the legal and wisdom literature of the ancient Near East. They are a legacy from the civilizations with which Israel was in contact before becoming a nation. These common traditions were current among the people at this time orally and in writing, and Moses drew upon them. What is new is the Israelite element that sprang from the religious-national movement Moses inspired. The laws of the Pentateuch combined both elements, and in the amalgamation the older were themselves recast.

The Ten Commandments have a unique place among the Penta-teuchal laws. They alone were given by God in an august theophany without the mediation of a prophet. They were inscribed on the stone Tablets of Testimony and placed in the Ark. An examination of their content tells much about the nature of the Covenant and the Torah which was its basis.

The first four Commandments (Exodus 20:2-11) are religious, specifically Israelite. The first obligates Israel to be faithful to the God who brought it out of Egypt, and not to deify any other being. The second prohibits the worship of idols and images—supposedly the religion of the nations. Monotheism is here expressed in the epithet "jealous God," which is given to YHWH. The third commandment enjoins Israel to preserve the sanctity of the hidden Name which was disclosed to it. The fourth prescribes the hallowing of the Sabbath. Here a cosmogonic motive is given—"For on six days the Lord created heaven and earth and rested on the seventh"—which emphasizes the fact that YHWH alone created the world. In Deuteronomy 5, however, an ethical-historical motive appears: the Sabbath commemorates the liberation from Egyptian bondage.

The last six Commandments have a universal character. They prescribe honoring of parents and respect for the sanctity of life, marriage, property, and justice. The last prohibits envious scheming. These imperatives do not derive originally from Israelite monotheism, nor were they first enunciated by Moses. The legal and wisdom literature of pre-Biblical antiquity gave them prominent expression. Even the Biblical view insists that man had to obey the moral law from the time of Adam onward. Having violated it, antediluvian humanity was doomed to the Flood, and the cities of Sodom and Gomorrah were destroyed. The heathen, too, who are not condemned for their idolatry, are nonetheless punished for moral corruption—in spite of their not having received the Torah. Thus the Bible itself implies that the universal moral rules of the Sinaitic Covenant were already well known and in force among men—whether in theory or in practice—long before Israel stood at Sinai.

While the laws of universal morality were not new in their content, the source of their authority was newly formulated at Sinai. When the hidden God revealed Himself to Israel, by framing moral rules as expressions of His will He put their authority on a new basis. The moral law was indeed binding upon the pagans as well, but inasmuch as they knew not God they were ignorant of its true source. Now God revealed His name to Israel and declared morality to be His will, the foundation of His Torah. This restatement lent new authority to morality, for now the moral imperative was absolute, supreme, everlasting, inasmuch as it was divine.

It is true that paganism also sought to strengthen morality by religious sanctions. But the essential nature of its gods was not moral but mythological: lusts control them, evil motivates them, they sin, murder, steal, fornicate. Hence pagan justice and morality cannot derive from the sacred will of the gods to absolute good. The source of justice and morality in the pagan conception is not a sovereign moral will but *wisdom*—human or divine. Legislators and moralists are, in the first place, wise rulers and sages who innovated good laws and mores in their wisdom. There are wise gods also, who know good laws, and at times they reveal something of their knowledge to men. In the Israelite conception justice and morality belong to the realm of prophecy, not wisdom. The legislator is a prophet, not a sage. The prophet brings man the divine imperative from a God over whom no evil impulses hold sway, whose will is essentially moral and good. The God of Sinai, who has no mythological attributes, does have moral attributes and these are revealed to the prophet: "A God merciful and gracious, long suffering and abundant in mercy and truth; keeping mercy unto the thousandth generation . . ." (Exodus 34:6ff.).

The ethics of the Covenant were not given to the individual but to the entire nation; similarly its rewards and punishments are communal and not individual. It is, however, a mistake to suppose that this reflects a primitive level of ethical consciousness, one that has not yet attained to the awareness of the individual and his responsibilities— as embodied in the supposedly more advanced wisdom literature of the Bible and the ancient Near East. For the event at Sinai took place quite late in human history—even according to the Biblical chronology (twenty-six generations after the Creation). The confederation of Israelite tribes moved, as has been stressed above, in a world of high and ancient civilization; individual morality and individual retribution were ideas that had long been in existence. Nor can Israel be said to have been a primitive, "natural" ethnic community; it was rather a child of prophecy. It became a nation through a Covenant which was based on a divine law. This Covenant imposed a new moral responsibility on the tribes in addition to and beyond that of the individual. Having been elected *en masse,* and having heard together the divine moral commands, the people as a whole become answerable for their moral state. An intensification of moral demands is the outcome of the prophetic and communal nature of the Sinaitic Covenant. Morality ceases to be a private affair. In time the classical prophets were to draw the ultimate conclusions from this restatement of the moral law.

RELIGIOUS REVOLUTION IN THE DESERT

The message of Moses, the Exodus, and the Covenant at Sinai brought about a religious revolution among the tribes of Israel: polytheism perished forever from their midst. Of this we have monumental proof in the fact that the Bible no longer knows what polytheism really is and throughout, from its earliest to its latest parts, represents pagan religion purely as fetishism, as the worship of wood and stone or the host of heaven. Nothing is said of the genuine pagan belief in mythological gods. This can only mean that even the earliest parts of the Bible were created after the death of the gods in Israel, in a monotheistic environment from which mythological polytheism had been uprooted. Of the early Israelite pantheon there remained only a few names, and they became epithets of the one God: *'adon, shadday, 'elyon, el ro'i,* and perhaps also *beth'el.* In addition, the popular religion still harbored shades of the rejected deities in the form of satyrs, to whom the people sacrificed "in the field" (Leviticus 17:5, 7). One of these—the only one who is mentioned by name—is Azazel (Leviticus 16:8-10, 26), a denizen of the desert, the symbol of an ancient and forgotten "impurity." Of prime significance is the fact that the ancient gods did not become baleful spirits, demons who fight God and harm men. The Bible knows of no harmful or evil gods. Evil too comes from YHWH, and evil spirits are His messengers (angels), a fact which by itself testifies to the profundity of the monotheistic revolution: good and evil now spring from the same divine realm.

The new faith begins at once to create a new conceptual universe. In place of the pagan realm of divine mythology it sets up the realm of human history. The people of YHWH, having come into being through the Covenant, constitute a national-historical sphere of divine revelation paralleling the natural sphere of pagan divine activity. The basis of the Covenant is the divine word. In theory and in practice the tribal confederation is the kingdom of God. The leader of the confederation is neither a king nor a priest, but a prophet, a spokesman of God. The work of Moses and the events that befall the tribes under his leadership are the materials out of which historical legends are spun. The saga of Israel emerges as the history of the kingdom of God, with its triumphs and failures.

Replacing the mythological accounts of the life of the gods by the historical chronicle of man makes it necessary to reformulate the history of mankind from its very beginnings. In the Pentateuch this history appears in three strata: universal history down to the confusion of tongues, the patriarchal period, and the history of the people of

Israel from its origin to its entry into Canaan. The materials of the first stratum are the oldest. They are paralleled in the literatures of Near Eastern antiquity, and so must be considered as part of the pre-Israelite legacy. The materials of the second stratum are later, but are also to be accounted as pre-Israelite in the main. The third is the Israelite stratum. It is a product of the religious movement inspired by Moses, its stories are the first fruits of historic monotheism. Later, perhaps, the patriarchal narratives received their monotheistic stamp, while the reworking of the universal history probably came last. While we are unable to follow the details of this process, it seems likely that it began with the stories of the Mosaic age.

The Israelite idea strove to find expression in new cultic forms as well. The initial level of the new cultus was prophetic and popular. Its first embodiments were in song, dance, festival, and sacrifice. Exodus 15 indicates that the first cultic activity after the escape was a prophetic-popular ceremony involving song and dance. Led by Moses, the people celebrate their miraculous rescue in a paean to God, after which Miriam, the prophetess, leads the women in dance to the sound of timbrels and singing. The Covenant ceremony, including its cultic aspects, is, as we have seen, prophetically inspired.

The Passover festival, the first established by the new religion, certainly goes back to pre-Israelite times. It is rooted in the belief that demonic danger threatens the firstborn of man and beast on the night of the full moon of the month Abib. Each year on this night a sacrifice was offered and some of its blood placed on the lintel and doorposts; everyone remained indoors for fear of the terror without. Israelite religion re-created this ancient festival, turning it into a historical celebration. The notion of annual demonic danger gave way to the one-time danger of the plague that struck the Egyptian firstborn on the night of the Exodus. The danger came from God Himself. Thereafter the ceremony served merely as a historical reminiscence of Israel's redemption on that night. The ritual is popular, not priestly: it is a home service performed by members of the household; priest and altar are unnecessary. This was the character of the festival until the Josianic reform.

Alongside of the popular forms there arose a priestly cult grounded on the ideas of the new faith. The literary product of the ancient Israelite priesthood is the priestly stratum of the Torah (most of which is found from Exodus 25 to Numbers 36). Its laws and prescriptions give us an excellent idea of the part the priesthood played in the formation of Israelite monotheism.

The portable desert sanctuary of Israel, the Tent of Meeting, is a priestly creation. While the gorgeous Tabernacle, adorned with silver and gold and constructed out of boards and curtains, is, of course, legendary, the stories about the Tent have a historical core. The first sacred object of the new faith, the stone Tablets of the Covenant, were placed in the Ark, which in turn was set in the Tent of Meeting. The Tent's primary significance was as an oracle, the place where Moses received and transmitted to the people the words of God. The Aaronite priesthood converted this oracular Tent into a sanctuary, a place of sacrifice and ceremonial.

The heart of the priestly Tent was the Ark and the Cherubim. Now a sacred ark holding the idol image of the god is a common feature of pagan religion, and cherubim with outspread wings were an Egyptian figure whose function was to protect the god from demonic harm. Carrying the ark in ritual processions was viewed as carrying the god himself. Out of these ancient elements the Israelite priesthood fashioned a new monotheistic symbol. The Ark holds not the image of God, but the Tablets, the embodiment of His word; the Cherubim watch not over the Deity but over the sign of His Covenant with Israel (the Cherubim themselves represent the divine chariot, the symbol of God's omnipresent rule). Finally, what was carried about in the Ark was not the Deity or His image but the witness to His Covenant.

It may be assumed that a regular, daily order of service was performed in the desert Tent, similar to the daily service found in ancient Egypt, Mesopotamia, and elsewhere. Its elements were in all likelihood a daily sacrifice, an "eternal light," shewbread, and incense.

The meaning of the cult, however, underwent a fundamental change. We have already seen that the pagan cult was mythological and magical. It was related to events in the life of the gods; it was thought to be charged with magic, supradivine power, independent of the gods and necessary to their existence; it was an esoteric science of the mysteries of being, of the forces which were the vital principle both of the gods and the world. Israel's cult has no mythical elements: its festivals commemorate events in history, in the life of God's creatures. No Israelite ritual is thought of as affecting the life or vitality of God. No ceremony is intended to protect God or man from the destructive power of demonic impurity. One of the most remarkable features of the priestly code is its new conception of impurity. In the pagan world impurity is viewed as a supernatural, baleful force. In the priestly code impurity has no power at all. Purification rites are not designed as a protection against any harm that stems from it. Demonic powers are here no longer an independent realm. Stripped of any power, they survive only residually as the condition of impurity, which is to be carefully separated from the holy. It is the holy alone, the realm of the one God, that possesses power and is, therefore, potentially dangerous. All power has been concentrated in YHWH, the God of good and evil. How and when this change took place in the concept of impurity we do not know. But it is one of the great contributions of the priesthood to the monotheistic revolution.

For the priestly code, as for the Bible generally, the value of the cult is not in its inherent efficacy, but in its being a divine command —not the product of magical science, but the will of God, a commandment or *mitzvah* given to man by His prophet. In this we see a union of priesthood and prophecy, with the authority of the one derived from the revelation of the other. The purpose of the cult is to bring man close to God, to sanctify him by implanting in him awe in the presence of the divine. It is thus not man's protection and maintenance of the Deity, but the Deity's gracious gift to man.

The creative enthusiasm stirred up by the new faith and its prophet filled the life of the tribes with enchantment. The desert environment played its part as well. This wild land breathed a fresh, pristine atmosphere untouched by pagan civilization. Here the old forms could be sloughed off and new ones begin to take shape.

But the tribes were not beduin. They had found in the desert a refuge from tyrannic oppression, yet the austerity of life there was difficult to endure. The old hope of settling in Canaan was reawakened. This national hope took on new significance from the religious revolution. What they now desired was not only a territory for settlement, but also a land to consecrate to the supreme God, a land in which He would dwell and be worshiped, which he would reign over as King. Thus the wish to settle became a prophetic ideal, the natural complement to the redemption from Egypt.

Some time after the Covenant at Sinai the tribes tried to invade Canaan from their provisional base at Kadesh. The attempt miscarried, with the result that a revolt against the authority of Moses broke out. The tribal alliance was for the moment threatened with disintegration, but Moses' towering personality carried the day. The despair reflected in the revolt indicated that the time was not yet ripe. It was necessary to fortify the spirit of this people, to educate and toughen the youth, to implant faith in them, to make them good soldiers in the Lord's battles. And so they stayed in the vicinity of Kadesh for about a generation. Then they made a detour to Trans-Jordan to search out a new base and prepare for the conquest of the land. They defeated the Amorite kings of Trans-Jordan—Sihon and Og—

and took possession of their land. But they still aspired to cross over into Canaan, the land promised them by God. And so they pitched camp at the Jordan, facing Jericho, in the plains of Moab, at Abel-Shittim.

It was here, according to the Biblical account, that Israel first fell into the sin of idolatry, the worship of Baal Peor, a Canaanite-Moabite god. This story of Israel's first idolatry is highly instructive. Note that the sin arises from contact with a pagan nation. There are no Israelite gods whose worship is revived. Even the Golden Calf that Israel made while still at Mount Sinai, although it constituted an idolatrous deviation, had not been made in the name of a strange god —"Tomorrow shall be a feast unto YHWH!" Aaron cried before its altar (Exodus 32:5). The first regression into pagan worship thus occurs on the boundary of Moab. But special circumstances are involved. The people "began to commit harlotry with the daughters of Moab" (Numbers 25:1), and it is the Moabite women who seduce them into worshiping their gods. The sin is therefore not so much due to a weakness of faith as to a weakness of the flesh. According to Numbers 31:16, the availability of the women was a clever device of Balaam to inveigle Israel into idol worship. Already in this story, then, idolatry is viewed as foreign to Israel, something into which the people are drawn only under the stress of special circumstances.

After this Moses dies, and the leadership of the people falls to Joshua, his faithful servant and disciple. Joshua has been endowed by Moses with something of his spirit, and is charged to conquer Canaan and give it as a possession to the children of Israel.

2

ISRAEL IN CANAAN

For thirty years after the death of Merneptah in 1227, internal disorders racked Egypt. Nor did the accession of Rameses III (1195-64) restore peace to the land. On the contrary, it marked the beginning of a period of warfare in which the very existence of Egypt was threatened. Lybians again attacked from the west, while from the north a new wave of Sea Peoples—the Philistines and related tribes—engulfed the western coasts of the Mediterranean. They overwhelmed the empire of the Hittites and swept through Canaan, leaving a ruin in their wake. Now they were preparing to overrun Egypt.

In the eighth year of his reign Rameses marched out to meet them and succeeded in blocking their advance, but he was unable to drive them out of Canaan. Some settled on the coast, where they founded the Philistine pentapolis (the five cities Gaza, Ashkelon, Gath, Ashdod, and Ekron) which was to distress Israel for centuries. Rameses managed to defeat the Lybians three years later, and for the next twenty years Egypt enjoyed peace. But the political situation in Canaan had by now altered fundamentally; the land was in fact no longer part of the Egyptian empire. Rameses still maintained a garrison at Beth Shean, but its authority was entirely nominal. The repeated crises had exhausted Egypt and undermined its will to empire.

After the death of Rameses, Canaan ceased being part of the Egyptian domain.

CONQUEST AND SETTLEMENT

The Israelite tribes entered Canaan during the period of disorders in Egypt after Merneptah's death. They appear to have crossed the Jordan at the beginning of the reign of Rameses III, a short while before the coming of the Sea Peoples. The account of Joshua's wars (Joshua 1-12) does not mention the Philistines, which suggests that the phase of the Conquest in which Joshua participated took place before the Philistines consolidated their five cities. The Biblical narrative describes the invading Israelites as an organized confederation of twelve tribes. Their Conquest is depicted as having been accomplished in a few decisive battles under the generalship of Joshua. The Egyptians are not even mentioned, a circumstance which points to the disintegration of Egypt's authority that had occurred in the troubled years after Merneptah's death.

If the tribes did enter the land at the beginning of Rameses' reign, they had managed to gain control of the hill country and had even begun to threaten the lowlands before Egypt's resurgence. The disunited Canaanite cities were unable to withstand the onslaught of tribes fighting together under a man who was thought to be a prophet and man of God. They were paralyzed by a "God-sent fear." The vanquished were put to the ban. Great numbers must have fled —probably northward—in the face of the victorious invaders. By the time peace had been restored to Egypt the Israelites had taken firm possession of the hill country, and the Philistines of the coastal plain. The Egyptians reconciled themselves to the situation, retaining their border posts and some measure of control over the coastal road. But before long their rule in the land of Canaan came to an end.

The tribes were unable to dispossess the Canaanites entirely. They could not conquer the coast, nor the northern part of the land: Tyre, Sidon, and the area of Lebanon. But they succeeded in getting hold of a continuous territory within which only pockets of Canaanites remained—the largest of these being one in the valley of Jezreel, which was finally conquered during Deborah's judgeship. The tribes thus occupied an ethnically homogeneous area, for the few remaining Canaanite enclaves—such as Gezer or Jebus (Jerusalem)— had no effect on the ethnic or cultural makeup of the people. Neither in population nor in culture did a Canaanite-Israelite amalgam come into being. Israelite religion never became syncretistic, never worshiped a Canaanite-Israelite god "YHWH-Baal." To be sure, modern histories of ancient Israel do tell of such things, but they are scholarly inventions founded on a mistaken interpretation of the Biblical evidence.

The Israelites in Canaan were a people distinct ethnically and culturally. Their vitality was the wellspring of an original national culture, and every aspect of their life became an embodiment of the monotheistic idea. Canaan provided the geographic setting in which a monotheistic civilization could flourish.

It is true that the Bible charges pre-Exilic Israel with the sin of idolatry, that it regards idolatry as the one fatal sin that brought on Israel's collapse and exile. Nor can this oft-repeated charge be denied. The existence of idolatry in pre-Exilic Israel is a hard fact. But the nature of this idolatry must be properly assessed.

Biblical literature testifies throughout that the idolatry prevalent in Israel was fetishistic: the worship of wood and stone. Biblical writers reproach Israel only for serving images; they know of no other idolatry. This incessant reproach is sufficient in itself to demonstrate that genuine mythological-magical polytheism was nonexistent in Israel. Its idolatry was—as is charged by the Bible—the product of foreign influences. It was something external and peripheral, the superstitious worship of imported figurines—male "Baalim" and female "Ashtaroth" (so the anonymous, merely sexually differentiated foreign images are called). The vulgar imagined that some benefit could be derived from these objects. But they worshiped them privately, in "back alleys." Thus Rachel steals the teraphim, Laban's "gods"— doubtless thinking that they could avail her—but she does not hesitate to put them under her camel saddle and sit on them (Gen. 31: 19, 30 ff.). David's wife also has teraphim, but when necessary she places them in his bed to deceive his pursuers (I Sam. 19:13 ff.). There were certainly more serious manifestations of idolatry in Israel, but it was always fetishistic. Zealots would not acquiesce even in this pagan vestige. It was pagan-inspired, and the like of it was practiced among the heathen. Even to give divine honor to idols is a grave profanation of YHWH's name, an unforgivable sin for the people of God. When the Bible attributes Israel's calamities to persistent national idolatry, it is only this vestigial idolatry that can be intended.

Such idolatry played no productive role in Israelite culture. It was a dead and withered branch. On the other hand, the living, authentic polytheism of the pagans served always as the fountainhead of a rich, variegated creativity. It was a world view which found expression in all forms of culture: in song, dance, cult, prophecy, the arts, and so forth. But this fecundity derived from a vigorous faith in living gods, while Israel's fetishistic idolatry had no creative force. And this situation is faithfully reflected in the Bible, where idolatry exists only as a sin, a monstrosity—not as a source of creativity. The cultural growth of the nation is rooted solely in the religion of YHWH.

EARLY POPULAR RELIGION

Our knowledge of the premonarchic age (Joshua, Judges, I Samuel 1-12) is based upon contemporaneous materials. They may be taken, therefore, as a faithful mirror of the condition of the people in that age. The material contains occasional references to idol worship, but with few exceptions these references occur only in the historiosophic framework of the narratives, that is, in the interpretative comment of the editors and compilers, comment designed to connect the stories and explain the causal interrelation of events. This historiosophy is extremely simple: every national calamity is caused by national sin; the historically decisive national sin of Israel is idolatry; *ergo,* every calamity implies the presence of idolatry.

In the body of the narratives, on the other hand, idolatry rarely plays any role whatsoever. In Joshua 1-12 idolatry is not mentioned, nor is it mentioned in the stories about Ehud, Deborah, Jephthah, Samson, and the concubine at Gibeah. Judges 17-18 tells of Micah's image, but this image belongs to the cult of YHWH, and does not involve the worship of Baal or any other foreign god. No allusion to idolatry is found in the stories concerning the house of Eli and the destruction of the Shiloh sanctuary; Eli's house perished through the sin of his sons, who despised the holy things and the sanctuary, not through any sin of idol worship. Nor does idolatry appear in the narratives of Saul's rise to kingship. It is mentioned in the stories concerning Gideon and Abimelech, though only peripherally; it is for the murder of his brothers that Abimelech dies, not because of idolatry.

When we examine the individual stories we find that, popular as they are, they could only have sprung from monotheistic soil.

The Song of Deborah (Judges 5), whose antiquity is conceded on all hands, is a fine specimen. A deep-seated, though popular—one might even say primitive—monotheism pervades the entire song. YHWH seems to be a national God; He is a God of war. Israel's enemies are His; the tribes march off "to help YHWH." He shines forth from Seir, from "the plain of Edom." Yet He is the only God, at whose appearance the earth quakes, the heavens rain, the mountains melt; the stars are His host, they too fight the Canaanites. YHWH thus is sovereign over all. Here, as throughout the Bible, the enemies of YHWH are the hostile nations, never their gods; God has only human enemies, no divinity fights against Him—neither god nor demon. The Song of Deborah is thus composed exclusively of monotheistic elements.

The stories concerning the Conquest in Joshua 2-12 exemplify one basic idea: Israel's victories over the Canaanite kings despite their chariotry and walled cities could never have been achieved without divine help, without the wonders of the one almighty God. He divided the Jordan before them, broke down the walls of Jericho, melted the heart of the Canaanites, subjugated the coalitions of southern and northern kings, rained hailstones down upon the fleeing enemy in the descent of Beth Horon, and halted the sun in midcourse for Joshua until the end of the fighting. According to the Biblical writer himself, the story of the sun's stoppage is derived from an ancient collection of songs called "The Book of Yashar" which indicates how ancient is the notion that YHWH controls all the phenomena of nature.

The narratives of Judges and Samuel provide intimate glimpses of the daily life of a simple folk. The atmosphere is filled with a pristine faith in the nearness of God. The pagan feels a similar sense of nearness, but it is because he has deified the forces of nature which surround him. In Israel, although nature is not divine, the Deity is still close at hand, for He graciously reveals Himself to His people.

God and His angels appear both in night visions and in the light of day as well. Gideon sees an angel in the form of a wayfarer, sitting under a terebinth near his father's winepress. The angel speaks to Gideon and commissions him to rescue Israel from the oppression of the Midianites. Gideon presents an offering to him; the angel touches it with the end of his staff and it goes up in flame, after which the angel himself disappears. Samson's mother, the wife of Manoah, first meets an angel in the field; later the angel reappears to Manoah and his wife together. They take him for a man of God, although his appearance is indeed supernaturally awesome, "like that of an angel of God." He announces to them the birth of Samson, and then goes up to heaven in a tongue of fire. God reveals himself to the dozing Samuel in the Shiloh sanctuary in the flickering light of the dying lamp. Literally to see God is a terrible thing, portending death, but occasionally it is granted as a special boon (Judges 6:22-4; 13: 22ff.). In a broader sense every manifestation of God is an act of His special grace. He shows His gracious concern for His chosen ones by raising up prophets for them, and providing them with mighty nazirites such as Samson, who performs amazing feats of strength and courage, impelled by the spirit of YHWH. "Men of God," privy to God's secrets, wander through the land; their countenance is "like the countenance of an angel of God, very terrible."

Grounded in the feeling of God's nearness was the faith that He answers those who inquire of Him, reveals to them the secrets of the future, and guides them aright in all their concerns. In Israel as elsewhere people sought divine guidance at every turn, through oracles like the priestly *ephod* or through a prophet (a "seer"). Oracles determined whether or not there would be war, who should be king, who was the unknown criminal. Men sought oracles in commonplace matters as well. For example, Kish, Saul's father, lost some she asses; after a futile search, Saul and his servant come to the "seer" Samuel to inquire about the lost animals, ready to pay a quarter silver shekel for the information. Samuel disclosed to them that the asses had been found.

Sanctuaries and high places to YHWH were everywhere. There were public high places serving a given locality, and central national sanctuaries such as those at Shechem, Shiloh, Mizpah, and Beth-el; there were also private sanctuaries, such as that of Micah the Ephraimite, who had a "house of God," with an image, an *ephod,* and *teraphim* —all in the name of YHWH—and a Levite priest to serve in it. There were open field altars, permanent and temporary ones. The sacred paraphernalia of the desert Tent were deposited at Shiloh—according to Joshua 18:1, the Tent of Meeting was pitched there. But what was suitable for the desert was totally unfit for Palestine, with its severe rainstorms. And so we find the Ark housed in a temple at Shiloh in the time of Eli—although it appears to have been for a while at Beth-el and elsewhere. As the tribes occupied the country the necessarily centralized cult of the Wandering came to an end. Altars, high places, and sanctuaries were erected wherever the people settled. Only on the festivals or for some extraordinary event was it the custom to go to a large temple to worship in festive throngs, to sacrifice and fulfill vows.

Temple and high place were focal points of public and private life. The Danites are happy to have abducted Micah's priest along with his cultic equipment for their own temple in the city of Dan. The temple serves as the public treasury. In it the celebration of the wine harvest takes place. The temple city is the locale of great fêtes and dances. At the temple the private prayer of the individual is offered up to God; there the pilgrim family partakes of the sacred feast, with its patriarchal head distributing "portions" to his wives and children.

One might occasionally be favored there with a special blessing by the priest. At the high place public sacrifice is held, after which the specially invited guests retire to a private chamber where the "man of God" pronounces a blessing over the meat and the cook distributes the courses.

At the temple covenants and agreements are sealed: Joshua makes a covenant with the people at the temple of YHWH in Shechem, and sets up there a stone pillar as "witness." Jephthah recites the terms of his agreement with the elders of Gilead "before YHWH at Mizpah." At Mizpah too, Saul is chosen king, and there Samuel deposits the "Law of the Monarchy" before YHWH.

In the time of Samuel "prophesying" bands roam the land. These are not authentic prophets who speak the word of God, but ecstatic "prophesyers." Such "prophesying" was the raving of frenzied enthusiasts, and is found in many places and many ages. It was prevalent in Canaan as well. Often it takes the form of communal ecstasy, in which an entire group of people is infected with frenzy. The movement that was current in Israel during Samuel's time was of this sort. Its manifestations were popularly regarded as produced by the Divine Spirit, and therefore akin to prophecy. "Prophesying" was connected with cult and temple. There was a certain orgiastic element in the popular cult, involving singing and dancing to the accompaniment of musical instruments. The ecstatics gathered at the high places, and used to descend "prophesying" and playing their instruments, arousing others as they went. Cultic "prophesying" however, was an eccentric feature of Israelite religion. Ordinarily the temples and high places were not scenes of orgiastic frenzy. They were the centers of the normal, conventional religious life of the people.

All of the variegated aspects of life that can be seen in the picturesque Biblical stories are intimately bound up with the religion of YHWH, and with that religion alone. To YHWH belong the temples and high places, the altars, sacrifices and vows. It is true that according to Judges 6 there was an altar to Baal to be found at Ophrah, Gideon's home town; and Judges 9:4 speaks of a temple to *Baal berith* (Baal of the covenant). But it is not clear that the reference is to the Canaanite Baal, for at that time it was customary to use *baal* (lord) as an epithet for YHWH also—such loyal monotheists as David and Saul use it in this way. But because *baal* was popular as a divine epithet among the Canaanites as well, it seems to have been opposed by Israelite zealots.

In any event, Baal appears only in these stories and nowhere else. Gideon finds no other Baal altars to demolish outside of Ophrah, nor is any other judge represented in the original narratives (as opposed to the editorial framework) as eradicating idolatrous cults. Only YHWH is God. There is no mention of any mythological ceremony, no altars to Ashtoret, no allusion to a syncretistic naturalization of YHWH into the Canaanite pantheon—for example, by being made kin to Baal. YHWH is a national God who fights Israel's battles, but this does not exclude Him from the daily life of the common man. Hannah, taunted by her rival, pours out her soul to YHWH in His temple, because she has no other God beside Him.

Having settled in Canaan, Israel became an agricultural nation, and naturally enough, its religion adapted itself to this change. Agricultural festivals developed, along with religious practices connected with insuring fertility of the soil. There is no evidence, however, that Canaanite fertility rituals had any direct influence on the course of this development. Rather, it was a natural internal evolution. No similarity between YHWH's role as fructifier of earth and the mythological roles of Baal and Astarte-Ashera in pagan fertility rituals is discernible. Fertility of the earth and the womb are assured by nothing more than YHWH's blessings, His gracious gifts to man.

Particularly salient is the monotheistic character of prophecy—the most significant expression of Israelite religion. Just as all cultic institutions belong to YHWH, so too do all forms of spiritual manifestation. The narratives are filled with theophanies and inspired men: God's spirit activates judges and nazirites, Hannah dedicates her son to temple service, Samson's mother devotes her son to nazirite-hood and the battles of YHWH. "From among your sons I raised up prophets, and from among your youth nazirites," says Amos in God's name when speaking of these times. If a vestige of paganism lingered in the realm of the cult, no such vestige is visible in the prophetic realm. Paganism raises up no Israelite prophet or any other form of inspired person. The Canaanite Baal never reveals himself to anyone. Baal has no angels, nor is anything said to be done by his command. The only divine source of inspiration for the Israelite is YHWH. Conflict between the new faith and the remnants or influences of paganism occurred only in the realm of the cult; in the realm of the spirit they did not occur. Just as the Bible knows of no wars between gods, so it knows of no conflict between Israelite prophets claiming to be inspired by rival gods. Israel's prophecy is wholly monotheistic.

In one story a sort of conflict between YHWH and a pagan god is recorded. It is a story characteristic of the times, and indeed, of later ages as well. I Samuel 5-6 tells of the great disgrace YHWH brought upon the Philistine god Dagon. Interestingly enough, this humiliation also occurs in a cultic setting: The Philistines capture the

Ark, bring it to Ashdod, and place it before Dagon in his temple. The next morning Dagon is found prostrate before the Ark. He is restored to his place, but on the next day is fallen again, this time with his head and both hands severed and cast upon the threshold. After this blow and the plagues that break out in their cities the Philistines are compelled to return their trophy to its rightful place, to Israel. This is the whole story. The god Dagon is a mere idol. There is not a word that hints at an encounter between YHWH and a living god Dagon. Moreover, from the whole tenor of the story it is clear that the narrator imagines the Philistines themselves as believing only in the dumb idol Dagon—this is their "god!"

THE KINGDOM OF GOD

That this period is one of original, monotheistic creativity becomes especially evident when its characteristic political institution is considered, namely, the institution of the Judges. For here there can be no question of a Canaanite-Israelite cross-influence. This peculiarly Israelite development cannot be explained, as we shall see, except by assuming that the tribes had already become consolidated as a monotheistic nation in the wilderness.

The Canaanite political unit was the city-state ruled over by a king. At the period of the Conquest there were dozens of such units throughout the country. Militarily they were far superior to the Israelite tribes, who at best could muster only a rustic army of swordsmen against trained armies bolstered by professional mercenaries and equipped with iron chariotry.

Yet the victorious tribes adopted neither the Canaanite political structure nor its military art. The Israelite socio-political unit after the Conquest, as before, was the tribe. Nowhere in Palestine did a Canaanite-Israelite city-state arise to continue the pre-Conquest pattern. The Canaanite cities of the valley of Jezreel (and Hazor) had kings before the battle with Deborah and Barak; afterward the kings disappeared; no Israelite-Canaanite successors inherited their thrones. When kingship finally came to Israel with Saul it was an entirely new invention, having no Canaanite roots whatsoever. (Abimelech's kingdom bears no relation to the Canaanite model. To begin with, it appears rather late, and having appeared is quite ephemeral. Further, it seems to have had a tribal basis, with aspirations toward becoming pan-Israelite [Judges 9:22, 55]. Finally, the current scholarly notion that Shechem was at this time a Canaanite city is at best doubtful.) As for the military, Israel's army after the Conquest remained rustic, composed of popular levies of sword bearers. It was not until Solomon's reign that Israel finally developed horse and chariot warfare. This goes far to show how distinct Israel's culture was in Canaan, and how free from foreign admixture.

The institution of the Judges that Israel developed in Canaan is a typical and peculiarly Israelite expression of its early monotheism. During the period of the Judges the tribal organization is still in full force. The tribe itself is the autonomous territorial unit. At its head stand the elders, the clan heads, who dispense justice and make all decisions affecting the general welfare of their tribe. There is no supratribal government. Only in extraordinary cases do tribes act in concert—and even then it is by the joint decision of the tribal elders. This popular civil government by elders has rightly been called primitive democracy, since the elders represent the tribe and, when necessary, the entire people. Its origin goes back to pre-Israelite times, long before the monotheistic revolution.

Superimposed upon the authority of the elders, however, is the authority of inspired men, the Judges. This institution is not only peculiarly Israelite, its function even in Israel is confined to the early period and then forever disappears. It never developed fixed forms, and never created a political body. But it was a well-established, functioning idea. In times of national crises, when Israel's enemies had the upper hand, an inspired man would arise, sent by God to save the people.

Under normal circumstances the primitive democracy of the elders sufficed for the government of the tribes. But in periods of stress it was inadequate, and then the hidden kingdom represented by inspired men, God-sent saviors, revealed itself. Among these Judges were full-fledged prophets such as Deborah and Samuel; a visionary such as Gideon; an inspired, though rude, nazirite, whose birth was announced by an angel—Samson; and an ecstatic such as Saul (who still belongs to this era). But the "spirit of YHWH" seizes such men as Jephthah, Othniel, and Ehud as well, and makes them saviors of the nation. In distress the people cry out to YHWH, expecting Him to send help; and He answers in a vision, or sends an angel, or activates His spirit and raises up an inspired man or prophet. The authority of the judge was not viewed as secular, or merely political, but as deriving from the kingship of God. "I shall not rule over you," says Gideon to the people who have asked him to become king, "nor shall my sons rule over you; YHWH shall rule over you" (Judges 8:23). That this is no mere phrase is evident from Samuel's opposition to the people's request for a human king. When he finally accedes to the popular demand it is only because God has told him, "Listen to whatever the people say to thee, for they have not rejected thee, but Me, that I should not be king over them" (I Samuel 8:7). This is the early Israelite theocracy—a prophetic theocracy, with inspired men at its head, as contrasted with the later priestly theocracy of Second Temple times.

The rule of inspired men continued for several generations. By its very nature it was discontinuous and sporadic. Since inspiration was a gift of God, and each instance of it a fresh act of grace, there could be no hereditary succession to judgeship, no genealogical qualifications, nor even the transmission of authority to a disciple. Each judge was commissioned individually by God; his authority and mission come from God, not from his predecessor. The Judges are not even caliphs in the Muslim sense—continuous successors to the religious authority of Muhammad. Nor is the institution of Judges founded, in the first instance, on the notion that human kingship is a sin, the usurpation of a divine privilege, such as we find at the root of the Muslim theocracy. The institution of the Judges is based upon faith in the election of Israel by the one God. The life of Israel is the historical sphere of divine revelation; YHWH, who is the supreme King, makes manifest His kingship in Israel's history by sending it apostles to save it from oppression. The appearance of inspired saviors is the concrete proof of Israel's election and of God's kingship. The tribes did not establish a monarchy, not because they opposed it in principle, but because their supreme confidence in the kingship of God was constantly being substantiated by the rise of His apostle-Judges.

When we inquire as to the origin of this institution we can find but one answer: a historical experience that implanted in the people the firm faith that YHWH would always send it apostle-saviors in time of need. Thus the line of Judges properly begins, not with Othniel and Ehud, but with Moses and Joshua. For the first apostle-savior was Moses, and his emancipation of the enslaved tribes served as a model for all the Judges. Moses redeemed Israel from Egypt, Joshua conquered the land for them—such marvelous successes by God's apostles was more than enough to instill in the hearts of the people the confidence that God would forever save them through His messengers. This mood is expressed in the words of the ancient song, "So Israel dwells secure, alone the Fountain of Jacob, upon a land of grain and wine. . . . Happy art thou O Israel, Who is like thee a people triumphant through YHWH . . ." (Deuteronomy 33:28ff.). It is the feeling that made possible the succession of charismatic

Judges. The phenomenon of the Judges thus serves as a monumental testimony to the narratives concerning Moses and Joshua.

The Kingdom of God was a noble ideal and a sublime vision; it succeeded in emancipating Israel and conquering Canaan. But it failed in the long struggle with the neighboring peoples—Moab, Philistia, and the rest—who warred incessantly with Israel and aimed to conquer it. It also failed to insure domestic tranquillity and justice. The Book of Judges depicts the period in dark colors. The compiler is an open advocate of the monarchy—he lived, perhaps, at the time of David or Solomon—and views the preceding period as one of decline and failure. He ascribes the failure to the sin of the people, who permitted themselves to be seduced by their neighbors to the worship of the Baals and the Ashtorets. As a result they were punished by God with continuous defeats, from which they were finally rescued only by the monarchy.

And yet the stories themselves preserve a different evaluation of the time. It was the time when God was King over Israel. There was sin, to be sure, but, more important, there were YHWH's apostle-saviors, through whom YHWH manifested His rule. Gideon refuses to accept the people's offer of kingdom—YHWH's rule must go on. Samuel looks back to the time before Saul as the age when "YHWH was your King" (I Samuel 12:12). This evaluation surely reflects the feeling of those days, when the people believed that they "dwelt secure" in the shelter of the Most High, that no man could take from them what God had given them through His apostles. And if an enemy should rise up, a savior would soon appear to rescue the people "triumphant through YHWH." These are testimonies to a simple but profound faith in the one God who had established His kingdom in Israel—if YHWH was with them, what had they to fear? The institution of the Judges thus reflects the marvelous religious idealism that prevailed in Israel after the revolution of Moses' time.

It was a period of rich literary creativity, in poetry and prose, in writing and orally.

We may assume that the "Book of the Wars of YHWH"—Numbers 21:14—was completed at this time. From the single fragment that remains we can conjecture that it contained epic songs about the Exodus and the events that occurred in the wilderness. At about this time, too, the "Book of Yashar" seems to have been begun. Several fragments of this work are embedded in our Bible, so that we are able to speak with some assurance of its content. It was a book of poetry on themes beginning with the wars of Conquest and extending to the period of the monarchy. One fragment is found in Joshua 10:12-13, which describes Joshua's command to the sun and moon to stand still. The Song of Deborah may also have belonged to this collection.

We may ascribe to this period the oral and written composition of the main narratives and legends of the Torah, the Book of Joshua, Judges, and I Samuel 1-12. The material covers the history of man from the Creation of the rise of Israel, and the history of Israel to the end of the "Kingdom of God" (in the time of Samuel). The three strata which comprise the bulk of this literature have been described and discussed above (pages 25-26).

This literature is a great monotheistic history of the world. The ancient mythological elements that are embedded in it have been so transformed as to amount to a new creation. Only here and there can one find a reminiscence of the world that was. In this saga there are no gods beyond the One, and this One has no "biography," or history. The narrative opens with the creation of the world and man; it knows of no previous events in the life of God. Genesis is the first philosophy of history, a history conceived of dramatically as the arena of a struggle between two protagonists: rebellious man and the will of God. We have already discussed how the drama of the struggle of powers in the world is transferred in the Bible from the mythological to the historical realm. The idea is that the freedom God gave man in order to make him a moral being has been turned to evil use by man. This sin brings down on man the punishment of divine justice, in the form of troubles and afflictions. The tension between the will of man and that of God is the motive force of all history.

The opening scene of the history tells of the rebellion of Adam and Eve against the divine command. It goes on to unfold the tale of the corrupt generation of the Flood and its annihilation, and ends with the uprising and dispersal of the builders of the Tower of Babel. The fundamental principle of Biblical historiosophy serves to explain Israel's career, but in Genesis the vista is universal. In the first scene—from Creation to the Confusion of Tongues—mankind is monotheistic: it rebels and is punished, but does not worship idols. With the rise of nations, however, the rebellion is climaxed by the appearance of idolatry. While indeed there is no explicit account of this fateful turn, the fact is that the Bible knows of no monotheistic nation before the emergence of Israel. It seems to assume that national man forgot God and made himself gods of wood and stone. Thereafter monotheism remained the legacy of a select few, the Patriarchs, Melchizedek and others. The coming of Moses ushers in the third period: the dispensation of monotheism to a national group, to Israel, which is chosen out of all the idolatrous nations by the grace of God and is redeemed through His apostle Moses.

It seems certain that this monotheistic view of human history is rooted in the historic sense of the Israelite nation, in its consciousness of itself as unique, elected—a feeling that it had from the time of the religious revolution in the days of Moses. There is no reason to defer the development of Israel's historic sense to the days of the monarchy. For, in contrast to that of other nations, Israelite historiography was national, not dynastic. Genesis relates the histories of the Patriarchs and of nations; kings are mentioned only incidentally. The goal of the story is the emergence of the people of Israel. And so the career of mankind is unfolded: the antediluvians and the annihilation of their line, the evolution of the nations from the sons of Noah, and the further emergence of new peoples through the generations until the last and youngest of all emerges—Israel. With Israel's birth the period of the formation of nations comes to an end. And it is this infant people that became the people of God. Such a broad historic canvas is necessary only because it is a nation that is endeavoring to find its place in world history—a nation, not a dynasty or a kingdom. The nation was elected long before a human king reigned over it; after the Patriarchs came a period of prophetic-apostolic rulers, not a kingdom.

The religious-national historic sense that was awakened in Israel during this period aroused the desire to give form not only to the saga of the past, but also to the actual facts of Israel's history from its birth as a nation. Israel's career was recorded not only in song and legend, but in prose narratives as well. The heroes of these accounts were the men whom the spirit of God raised up to be leaders and saviors. During this period the Book of Joshua and the stories about the Judges down to Samuel were composed. The whole of the Book of Joshua bears an antique stamp, for the latest event recorded in it is the displacement of the Danites to the north, which occurred before the war with Sisera. Joshua 13:1-6 promises explicitly that Israel will yet dispossess all those Canaanites that Joshua failed to dislodge: the people of Tyre, Sidon, and the Lebanon as far as Hamath, and also the Philistines. The history of the peoples who remained within the unconquered part of Israel's promised land is thus beyond the vista of this writer. There is, moreover, no allusion to the monarchy throughout the book. It was surely composed in the period of the Judges, although, to be sure, in its present form it shows signs of later editing.

Hymnal literature was also composed at this time. From the well-developed hymnals of Mesopotamia, Egypt, and Canaan, Israel may have adapted psalms of praise and thanksgiving, laments, and the like. The Book of Psalms preserves several specimens of the psalmody of this period.

One such is the majestic Psalm 29, in which remote echoes of mythological hymns are still audible. The psalm is, at bottom, a paean to the "Voice of YHWH," i.e., to YHWH as the God of storm and thunder. The divine "Voice" peals over the sea, shakes the land, sets the desert quaking, terrorizes all creatures. At the sound of it the "sons of gods" bow down to YHWH. Canaanite expressions and motifs found in Ugaritic literature are in evidence: "sons of gods," the thunder god, Lebanon and Sirion, the Wilderness of Kadesh, and the deity's ascending his throne. Yet in Israel these elements were embodied in a monotheistic psalm.

We may also date Psalms 68, 80, and 83 to our period. In 68:5, God is called "rider on the clouds," an epithet drawn from Ugaritic terminology. The psalm is a song of victory and includes a description of a triumphal procession. Psalms 80 and 83 are national laments and petitions for divine help. While the background of 80 is national, it is primarily a prayer on behalf of the Joseph tribes ("Ephraim, Benjamin and Manassah"). The enemy's oppression in both psalms recalls the stress of the period of the Judges. Note that Psalm 83:10ff. mentions Deborah's battle with Sisera and Gideon's with Midian. Since these psalms make no mention of the monarchy it is safe to assume that they precede it.

Wisdom literature is similarly part of the ancient Near Eastern legacy that Israel shared with its neighbors. In pre-Solomonic times sages and parable-makers were already found in Israel: Ethan, Heman, Calcol, and Darda (I Kings 5:11) appear to have been Edomites who introduced the wisdom of the "Easterners" to Israel. The book of Judges contains several examples of popular wisdom and phrase-making. Thus Samson is credited with a clever riddle and a sharp epigrammatic retort, "From the eater came forth edibles, and from the fierce, sweets," "Had you not ploughed with my heifer, you had not found out my riddle." Gideon parries the attack of the Ephraimites, who are angry at his failure to call them to fight Midian, with the gracious "Are not the gleanings of Ephraim better than the harvest of Ebiezer [Gideon's clan]?" A symbolic riddle appears also in the dream of the Midianite soldier in Judges 7:13f. Jotham, son of Gideon, tells a fable which is a fine satire on kingship—stemming, it would appear, from Canaan.

Our period, then, was a highly creative one, and its creations for the most part bear the impress of the monotheistic idea. As for the "idolatry" of the time, it was but a superficial phenomenon with no deep or lasting effect.

MONARCHY AND PROPHECY

The "Kingdom of God" lasted for about two hundred years—about 1230-1024 B.C.E.—from the Exodus to the founding of the monarchy. It was, as we have said, a product of Israel's religious idealism and it enjoyed great success for a while. There was, however, a fatal flaw in this "kingdom": it failed to set up a stable and continuous government. It always depended on the enthusiasm of the moment, on the spiritual excitement of a crisis, on the popular expectation of an inspired savior.

Of Israel's enemies the two most dangerous were Ammon-Moab to the east and the Philistines to the west. The one never forgot that Israel had taken part of their land, the "land of Sihon," and were ever stirring up war; while the other had established themselves in the low coastlands, and with the passage of time became the decisive military power of Palestine. In the decades before the rise of the Israelite monarchy they succeeded in subjugating the entire land. The unstable prophetic "kingdom" was unable to endure this tremendous stress. The need for a new political order was felt on all sides; the demand for a king began to be heard in Israel.

The Israelite monarchy was a prophetic creation. Samuel was the last representative of the old order of prophet-judges. The people turn to him with the plea to give them a king "that our king may defend our right, and lead us, and fight our wars." Samuel opposes the request, sensing in it a lack of faith in the saving might of God. In the end, however, he yields to the people and anoints a king for them. This was the last great political act of ancient prophecy: the creation of Israel's national monarchy. The monarchy did not arise as an extension of previous city or tribal monarchies. Nor did it grow out of a series of petty internecine wars, or from the rise to dominance of one tribe over the rest. It was from the beginning a national institution, embracing all the tribes, and it was the product of a prophetic election, of a divine oracle (I Samuel 9-10). Both circumstances mark the monarchy as the direct successor of the "Kingdom of God" which preceded it, and which aspired always to be national in its scope.

The historic nexus between the monarchy and prophecy is conspicuous in the character of the Israelite kings. Saul, the first king, is an ecstatic. After he is anointed king, he leaves Samuel, meets with a "prophesying" band, is himself seized by the "spirit," and so is transformed into "another man." He goes out to his first battle against the Ammonites after the "spirit of God" rushes upon him, which brings the Judges to mind. At Naioth in Ramah he "prophesies" before Samuel and lies naked and prostrate all day and night.

In fact, the first three kings of Israel are all inspired men. Saul "prophesies," David is a divinely inspired poet, Solomon has divine wisdom. Of David, too, it is said that with his anointment by Samuel, the "spirit of YHWH" seized him (I Samuel 16:13). Of his poetry David says, "The spirit of YHWH spoke through me, and His word was on my tongue" (II Samuel 23:2). Solomon is possessed of "divine wisdom" to do justice (I Kings 3:28), and has prophetic dreams besides. The kingdom of the "spirit" thus goes on even after the prophetic "Kingdom of God" has passed away.

From the century of the first three inspired kings (ca. 1024-931) we have a wealth of vivid narratives, comprising some fifty-eight chapters, from I Samuel 9 to I Kings 11, written by a prose artist of genius. A whole gallery of personalities passes before us, depicted in brilliant colors. The broad canvas unfolds in scenes of courage, glory, struggle for power, lust, crimes, and love. Each episode is candidly realistic, no attempt is made to draw a curtain over anything. There can be no doubt that the real character of the Israelite monarchy is portrayed in these stories.

Politically speaking, there was, of course, no innovation in the institution of monarchy. Throughout the Near East it was the long-standing, recognized form of government. In fact monarchy was viewed as a primary form of the state, with kings conceived of as the successors to gods or demigods who reigned in primeval times. The derivative nature of Israelite monarchy is frankly expressed in the Bible itself, where it is said to make Israel "like all the nations" (I Samuel 8:5, 20; compare Deuteronomy 17:14). From the socio-political viewpoint Israel's king was essentially identical with his Near Eastern brothers, he was an absolute autocrat.

There appears to be a certain democratic element in Israel's monarchy expressed in the notion that it is based on a covenant between the people and the king, made before God. But the content of the covenant is nonetheless autocratic: the people are made subject to the sovereign rule of the king. This provision is set forth in detail in the "Law of the Monarchy" drawn up by Samuel (I Samuel 8:11ff.). In accordance with it the people are the king's slaves, and their property and children his; all weapons are the king's, he levies tithes from the fields and the herds, and has a free hand in raising corvées. The symbols of Israel's monarchy are one with those of neighboring kingdoms: the anointing with oil, the crown and the throne, as in Egypt and Canaan. The king appoints priests, and has the special right of offering sacrifices in the temple. In all these matters Israelite monarchy is similar to those of the rest of the Near East.

And yet Israel's monarchy did not escape the impress of Israelite religion.

In the pagan world the king was the center, not only of political and economic life, but of religious life as well. He was often regarded as a divine being, or at least as possessed of superhuman powers. The king is the highest embodiment of the people and its gods. He is the life source of his people; the blessings of earth, flocks, and children stem from him. The belief in the divinity of kings is found among both primitive and highly civilized nations; it existed in Egypt, Mesopotamia, Asia Minor, and Canaan. The living or dead king could be deified. The king had a central role in the cult, as he often played the part of god and priest in the dramatic rituals of the festivals. The god was the king himself, dying and arising to new life. Thus the mysterious cycle of death and revival was bound up with the king.

Some scholars are of the opinion that in Israel too the king was deified; that here too he played a central role in ritual dramas, suffering, dying and coming to life again; that he was responsible for the nation's fertility and peace. For example, that is how they understand the royal epithet "The breath of our nostrils, the anointed of YHWH" in Lamentations 4:20. To be sure, the prophets opposed these conceptions and rituals, but they could make little headway against the popular, syncretistic religion in which the king played a divine role.

This opinion is unquestionably wrong. It is disproved by the abundant evidence of the stories concerning the first three kings, Saul, David, and Solomon. It is true enough that the king had the right to offer sacrifice in the temple, and that in this sense he was a priest. But the king is neither a god nor the son of a god, and his role in the cult is not central. The cult laws of the Torah give him no place at all. And in the stories telling of the cultic acts of the kings there is no mention of dramatic or mystery rites. Kings appear always with the people or leading the people. When the ark is being transferred to Jerusalem, David dances before YHWH with "the whole house of Israel"; Solomon prays to God before the people, kneels, spreads his hands heavenward, sacrifices—and "all Israel with him." There is no merit to the argument that the prophetic redaction of the Biblical books obliterated the guilty evidence of Israel's deification of its kings, and the cultic role that royalty played. In the prophets' repeated enumerations of Israel's sins we never hear once of the sin of deifying kings—living or dead—or of their role as god-priests. Surely, if such pagan notions and practices had existed in the popular religion the prophets would not have hesitated to denounce them.

The Israelite character of the monarchy is evident in all the narratives concerning it. Israel's monarchy was unrelated to the Canaanite model. The latter was aristocratic and ruled city-states, while the former was popular and national. Nor did David inherit any privileges from the early Jebusite kings of Jerusalem. When he took the city it had no king. Israel's monarchy was not connected with the priesthood, but with prophecy, as we have seen. Prophecy set the tasks: to fight the enemies of the nation and to judge righteously. The kings are thus the successors to the Judges, with all their military and civil functions, and like them have no specific cultic role. The king's contact with divinity stems not from his nature or descent— Saul is a farmer, David a shepherd—but from the divine spirit which rests on him. The king is the "anointed of YHWH," not His son. Anointing causes the divine spirit to rest on Saul and David, making them inspired men. This idea testifies to the prophetic roots of the monarchy. Throughout its history the monarchy is in some measure dependent upon prophecy. Several political upheavals were instigated by the prophets. The faith in the eternity of the Davidic dynasty was grounded on the prophecy of Nathan (II Samuel 7). The idea that the king was dependent on the prophet is exemplified in the remarkable phenomenon of prophetic opposition to kings who violated moral or religious laws: Nathan against David, Ahijah against Solomon and later against Jeroboam, Elijah against Ahab, Micaiah against Ahab, Elisha against Jehoram and Ahab's house, Amos against Jeroboam II, Jeremiah against Jehoiakim, and many more. No parallel phenomenon exists in the history of monarchies. It is additional evidence that the Israelite model was a product of monotheism.

The many narratives concerning the first three kings agree on a most important point: no idolatry existed in Israel during their rule. There are sins and punishments—defeats in battle, famine, plagues, and so forth—but no national idolatry and no national calamity which is explained as a punishment for idolatry. What is most remarkable is the way idolatry suddenly and entirely disappears from the history starting with the reign of Saul: between I Samuel 8 and I Kings 10 we never hear that Israel worshiped other gods. Saul is a great zealot: he extirpates the "wizards and familiar spirits," persecutes the Gibeonites in his "jealousy on behalf of Israel"—but we hear nothing of his eradicating pagan cults. David is regarded as utterly loyal to YHWH, loving Him and beloved by Him. The *teraphim* that his wife Michal, the daughter of Saul, keeps in his house are not considered idolatrous by the writer, who appears to view them as harmless furniture. The idolatry of the period of the Judges seems to have withered away of itself, without a struggle. This serves to show how superficial and peripheral that idolatry was, how shallow its roots in the life of the people. Only at the end of Solomon's reign does idolatry reappear, but not as a national sin. Solomon builds high places to the gods of his foreign wives. The sin is therefore private to the old king, whose wives have turned his heart.

The period of early monarchy is, like that of the Judges, a time of monotheistic creativeness in literature and life. During this time the Book of Judges—with its adjunct, I Samuel 1-12—was composed. The background of the book is an unqualified admiration for the monarchy, in contrast to which the preceding age appears as one of sin, rebellion, and failure. With the founding of the kingdom foreign domination came to an end, and the internal anarchy in politics and morality also disappeared. The monarchy is the supreme token of YHWH's grace toward Israel. Both the stories and their historiosophic framework are monotheistic in their outlook. During this period the superb stories of I Samuel were also composed—the narratives concerning the life of Saul and David and their descendants. A brilliant novelistic art, thoroughly imbued with monotheism that could only have sprung from a monotheistic environment, reveals itself here. Most of the stories are historical novels, but there are also a few authentic historical records among them. The whole is fixed in a prophetic framework: events are the embodiment and fulfillment of the word of God through His prophets, all history is thus the realization of a divine plan.

The Book of Ruth is also a product of these times. It is not, as the prevailing view maintains, a tendentious work of the Second Temple era, but a simple, exquisite idyl with no ulterior purpose. It bears the marks of a local Bethlehemite story of early times. The story tells of the Moabite Ruth, a simple, devoted girl, all love and loyalty. Ruth cleaves to her Israelite mother-in-law Naomi, and returns with her to Palestine. Through good fortune she comes to marry into an eminent Israelite family, from whom David later was born. This is a story of devoted love. Reflected in it is the ancient form of "conversion"—complete ethnic, social, and religious assimilation—which existed in pre-Exilic Israel before the innovation of religious proselytism. The viewpoint is, of course, monotheistic: YHWH rules all lands. But religion is conceived in national-territorial terms: each people has its god; Ruth thus comes under the wing of Israel's god when she comes to Palestine with Naomi. The writer extols Ruth's two qualities, high morality and religion. The former is exemplified in her love and loyalty, and as a reward it is given to her to become part of Israel and cleave to its God.

The period also saw the crystallization of the bulk of the Torah literature, those various scrolls which were to be collected and sealed as the Torah book in the time of Ezra. In Josiah's time the stratum involving the centralization of the cult was added to Deuteronomy, and other prophetic passages are also later accretions. But the body of the Torah is ancient, not later than the early monarchy. Its laws reflect the institutions of premonarchic times. They give the king no role, either judicial or military. They do not mention the privileges of the royal officialdom, the widespread bureaucracy which was a product of the monarchy. The "Law of the Monarchy" is ascribed to Samuel, not to Moses, thus indicating its lateness. It is viewed as a law stemming not from God but from a covenant between the king and the people made in His presence. The prophetic element of the Torah gives more room to the monarchy. The promise of royal offspring is one of the blessings given to the Patriarchs (Genesis 17:6, 16; 35:11). In the predictions the Davidic empire is reflected: Edom's subjection to Israel (Genesis 25:22ff.); Israel's domination of its neighbors (Genesis 27:28ff.). Balaam foresees the glory of David's kingdom and his great triumphs: "A star shall come forth out of Jacob, a sceptre shall rise out of Israel, which will shatter the corners of Moab. . . ." (Numbers 24:17ff.). Only the initial period of the monarchy is mirrored here, however; the Torah makes no allusions to the promise of an everlasting dynasty which was made to David and which played so great a part in later history.

The fact that the Torah contains no laws for the king or his officialdom shows that it was not the actual law of the land. Its literary form, mingling profane laws, ceremonial regulations, and moral exhortations indiscriminately, also argues against its having been the state constitution. The Torah was rather a moral and religious guide, set in a narrative framework but containing also some legal elements. It was an ideal. In actuality common law, judicial decisions, and royal laws were in force, these were the law of the land alongside of the divine law and, in many cases, differing from it. Precisely because the Torah literature had this idealistic character, it was cultivated in various circles and underwent several formulations and crystallizations before its components were collected and fixed in the course of time.

Biblical and post-Biblical tradition make David and Solomon literary figures. David is the psalmist, Solomon the poet and sage; the one is said to have authored the Book of Psalms; the other, the Song of Songs, Proverbs, and Ecclesiastes. There is doubtless a historical germ in this tradition. David played the harp before Saul; the Book of Samuel, moreover, ascribes several poetical creations to him (the lament over Saul and Jonathan, over Abner, a psalm of thanksgiving, and his poetic "last words"). The psalm in II Samuel 22 (Psalms 18) gives the impression of being a personal thanksgiving of David. In all likelihood, several of the royal psalms are from David's pen, or at least from his age, as for example 60:8-11 (108:8-14), 2, 89, 132, and perhaps also 20, 21, and 110. It is a plausible assumption that David and his court poets cultivated hymnal literature.

According to I Kings 5:9-14, Solomon was a poet and parable-maker, apparently of the Aesopic type, with trees, animals, insects, and fish the subject matter. His wisdom is comparable to that of Egypt and the "Easterners," plentiful examples of which have been preserved for us. It deals with moral and utilitarian matters, phrased sententiously or in fables. I Kings 10:1 makes Solomon out to be a witty solver of riddles as well. Nothing has been preserved of such Aesopic fables and riddles, although some samples of the epigrammatic wisdom of Solomon and his time may well be included in the Book of Proverbs.

Other considerations also support the historicity of these traditions. Tradition's psalmist, David, is known from the narratives to have been a man of deep religious sentiment. Tradition's sage, on the other hand, is portrayed as a worldly and materialistic king, loving pomp and women. His wisdom has its parallels among the nations, and, indeed, many foreigners are said to have come to hear it. Such cosmopolitanism is, in fact, quite typical of ancient Near Eastern wisdom, and Israel's is no exception to the rule. Although international wisdom took on monotheistic dress in Israel, its content remained universalistic, non-Israelite, throughout the Biblical period. The morality of Biblical wisdom has no specifically Israelite element. There is no mention, for example, of giving rest to the worker on the Sabbath, or of observing the tithe for the poor. Nor does it ever deal with any of the historical questions that concerned the prophets. The people of Israel is never referred to in the wisdom literature. Nor does it reflect in any way the polemic against idolatry, despite the fact that wisdom concepts were involved, as for example that of idolatry as foolishness. Israelite wisdom thus retained its general character, its ancient pre-Israelite stamp. It was a legacy of ancient culture that flourished in Israel, especially in the time of the royal sage.

In the age of David and Solomon new symbols based on the monarchic idea were created, which became permanent features of Israelite religion. The belief in Israel's ultimate redemption was eventually to be bound up with David and his dynasty: the last redeemer, the Messiah, will be a descendant of David. Not even Christianity, which became the faith of many nations, could do away with this symbol. Its Messiah is, to be sure, the "Son of God" but he is the "son of David" as well. David himself aspired to create permanent symbols of God's graciousness toward Israel. He regarded his kingship as an everlasting work of God. This notion was no mere flourish, but a deep religious conviction. After God gave Israel the land of Canaan for a permanent possession, he graciously gave it the monarchy—also a permanent gift. David was chosen to save Israel from all its enemies and establish a mighty kingdom; his reign is no less a divine act of grace, an everlasting one. And thus it is David who conceives the idea of building a royal capital. He captures Jebus (Jerusalem), a city bordering on the territory of Judah and the Joseph tribes but belonging to neither, and builds it up as "the city of David." This becomes the "Chosen City," at once a symbol of Israel's kingdom and the dynasty of David. To this new city he transfers the Ark. The city of David thus becomes the home of the ancient witness to the Sinaitic Covenant, with the added implication that the Davidic dynasty has inherited and now embodies the blessing of that Covenant, and is as everlasting. David further plans to build a magnificent temple, a royal chapel in Jerusalem for the God of Israel. This temple will be the cultic center of the entire kingdom. There were, of course, temples before David, but never one that was a symbol of the monarchy. Saul built altars, but not a temple. David envisions a Chosen Temple in the Chosen City in which the Ark will be housed.

Now the Ark was a portable *sacrum,* housed in the Tent; neither was ever connected with a particular holy place. But David conceives the idea of establishing the Ark in a fixed, chosen place. He was not concerned to do away with the other sanctuaries and centralize all worship in Jerusalem—as was the later intent of the Josianic reform —but he did create the idea of a chosen city and temple which ripened in time into the particular doctrine of centralization found in Deuteronomy—the basis of that reform. It was David's genius that made the chosen dynasty, city, and temple into permanent symbols of the religion of Israel. The aspiration of the Davidic house to symbols of permanence is expressed with greatest clarity in Nathan's vision and David's prayer in II Samuel 7. With David, the history of Jerusalem as the eternal Holy City begins.

David was unable to carry through his plan of building a temple because of the many wars that sapped his energy. But built it was by Solomon, the great royal builder. No more than David did Solomon intend to abolish the local sanctuaries, and like him he nonetheless envisioned his Temple as the "Chosen House," the unique habitation of Deity. He enshrined the Ark in the Temple, whereupon it forever ceased to be a portable *sacrum*. Its sanctity, with that of the Temple, became inseparable from the sanctity of the site. Thus the Temple, too, became an eternal symbol of Israelite religion that no physical destruction could eradicate.

THE BATTLE AGAINST BAAL WORSHIP

The Books of Kings fix the beginning of Israel's decline and fall after the close of Solomon's reign. As a matter of fact, the decline had already set in during his last days. The aged king was prevailed upon by his foreign wives to serve other gods. Because of this sin the kingdom was divided after his death in the days of his son Rehoboam. Jeroboam, son of Nebat, the king of the northern ten tribes, sought to dissuade his people from worshiping at the Jerusalem Temple. To this end he set up two golden calves, one in Dan and one in Beth-el. The Biblical historian regards this worship as idolatrous. In addition he henceforth reckons a new national sin to Israel's account—the sin of the high places. Deuteronomy forbids the worship of God at the high places after the building of the central sanctuary. To the ancient historian, this meant that to worship at the high places after Solomon's time was illegal. But in fact this worship went on until the time of Josiah, and even the righteous kings of Judah failed to abolish it. Hence even the worship of Judah was illegal, let alone that of Israel, where the sin of the high places was aggravated by that of the calves. Nor was Israel innocent of the worship of foreign gods. Such sins, continuing for generations, finally brought about the fall of both kingdoms. This historiosophic viewpoint is set forth in detail in II Kings 17.

However, an objective assessment of the narratives reveals that until the end of Omri's reign (875 B.C.E.) no real pagan worship existed in northern Israel. Jeroboam's calves were not consecrated to a foreign god; they were made in honor of the God of Israel, presumably representing His bearers, much like the Cherubim of the Ark. The historian execrates them as idolatrous. It may be that in the course of time some sort of fetishistic homage came to be paid to them by the vulgar. But the fact that neither Elijah nor Elisha combats the calves is enough to show that they were not considered idolatrous in the north. Neither was there a national pagan cult in Judah. The sin of the aged Solomon was private; he built pagan altars for his foreign wives, but he did not involve the people in this worship. In both kingdoms, then, worship was carried on at high places, and some paganizing deviations occurred, but the historian knows of no national and public cult of any foreign god. Baal worship is absent during this period.

The first instance of public Baal worship occurs during the reign of of Ahab (875-854). It is the worship of the Sidonian Baal. This cult was imported into Israel by Ahab's Sidonian wife, the brazen Jezebel; it had no popular roots. At Jezebel's instigation Ahab builds an altar and sanctuary to Baal at Samaria. The queen brings in her train four hundred "prophets of Baal," and priests of Baal and Asherah are her pensioners. Thus the cult of Baal is celebrated publicly and with royal pomp under the auspices of the palace. This is the first time we hear of such a cult in Israelite Palestine. It is possible that the splendor of this cult had an effect on certain Israelite circles; yet the account of its extirpation by Jehu mentions only one temple to Baal in the north. In any event, this was a new phenomenon in Israel. The public worship of a pagan god agitated many spirits, and a bloody struggle began.

The fight against Baal was initiated by the prophets. For the first time in Israel's history zealots appear, who fight paganism and die for the "sanctification of the Name." The zealots attack the Baal cult, and Jezebel retaliates with a murderous persecution of the prophets of YHWH. There are a great throng of anonymous prophets who die for their zeal. Above them all towers the majestic figure of Elijah, the solitary prophet, "hairy, with a leather girdle about his loins," who lives on mountain tops, and is transported by the "spirit." Elijah succeeds in arousing the fervor of the people, and puts to death the Baal "prophets." Jezebel threatens his life, and he must flee to the desert. At Mount Horeb the word of God comes to him in an august and sublime theophany. He is told to anoint a new king over Israel—that is, to destroy Ahab's house—and to anoint Elisha as his successor. Elisha will carry out the annihilation of Ahab's line.

The struggle that broke out between the court and the prophets had a moral as well as a religious aspect. For Jezebel taught Ahab not only how to acquiesce in the worship of Baal, but also how "to govern the kingdom of Israel." Ahab coveted the vineyard of Naboth the Jezreelite, but Naboth refused either to sell him the vineyard or to take another in its place. Thus thwarted, Ahab fell into a sudden rage, but Jezebel showed him how to achieve his desire. She staged a public trial of Naboth, hired perjurers to testify against him that he "cursed God and the king," and had him executed. Ahab went to take over the vineyard. On his way Elijah suddenly appeared and thundered at him, "Hast thou slain and also taken possession!" Then Elijah uttered what the Baal worship had never called forth from him: a prophecy of the utter extermination of Ahab's house: "At the place where the dogs licked Naboth's blood there will dogs lick your blood also" (I Kings 21:19). An equally ignominious death is in store for Jezebel, nor will the rest of the line be spared. Ahab is stunned, he rends his clothes, puts on sackcloth, and goes about "softly."

The Baal cult appeared in Judah at the same period. It was imported by Athaliah, the daughter of Jezebel. We hear that it continued there during the reigns of Jehoram, Ahaziah, and Athaliah—a total of seventeen years (850-836). The cult was violently abolished in Israel and in Judah at about the same time.

The revolution came in 842, during the reign of Joram, the son of Ahab. Elisha entered into a conspiracy with Jehu, one of Joram's generals, and anointed him king. Jehu killed Joram and Jezebel and the entire house of Ahab. Then he cunningly entrapped all the votaries of Baal in the Baal temple at Samaria and put them to death. The pillars of Baal were torn down, his image burned, and the temple turned into an outhouse. With this the Baal cult was forever destroyed (II Kings 10:27). It is never again mentioned by the Biblical historian of Kings in connection with the Northern Kingdom.

About six years later a similar revolution took place in Judah. Here it was the priest Jehoiada who initiated it. He conspired with the officers of the army, and with their support crowned Jehoash, the son of Ahaziah; Athaliah was put to death. The Baal temple was torn down, his idols and altars were broken, and Mattan, the Baal priest, was slain before the altars. For the next hundred years no pagan worship appeared in Judah. In the time of Ahaz there was a new wave of paganizing but apparently not as overt as that of Jezebel. Hezekiah, son of Ahaz (719-691), purged the land of pagan worship and for the first time moved to abolish the high places—in accord with the demand of Deuteronomy. But there was a new influx of paganism during the reign of his son Manasseh, who reigned a long time (691-638) and seems to have been a devotee of pagan cults during most of his reign. There is no doubt that Assyrian influence was involved. Manasseh was the Jezebel of Judah. He turned the Jerusalem temple itself into a pagan Pantheon, and for the loyalists this was a time of grief and terror. Amon, Manasseh's son, followed in his father's steps (638); his ministers conspired against him and assassinated him. He was succeeded by his son Josiah (638-609), who carried out a radical reformation. He purged the pagan cults, leaving hardly a remnant. He also completed the abolition of the high places and brought their priests to Jerusalem. Josiah's purge extended even to the northern cities of Beth-el and the cities of Samaria. The kings who reigned after him—Jehoiakim and Zedekiah—were not paganizers.

Our survey has indicated that the manifestations of paganism in Israel during the period of the First Temple were in essence what they were during the time of the Judges: sporadic, superficial phenomena, lacking popular roots in either the north or the south. Despite the pagan deviations—most of which are attributable to the influence of the foreign women of royal households—the monotheistic creativeness of Israel continued. The period saw the composition of a good part of Biblical literature: the Books of Samuel, the sources of the Books of Kings, the story of Jonah, the bulk of Psalms, the Book of Job, and the bulk of Proverbs. But above all, it was the age of classical prophecy.

3

THE AGE OF CLASSICAL PROPHECY

With the last rays of the Northern Kingdom's setting sun in the period of Jeroboam, the son of Joash, classical prophecy emerged. It manifested itself at approximately the same time in the Northern and Southern Kingdoms, its first representatives being the Judean Amos and the northern Hosea. Its last spokesman was Malachi. These new prophets span a period of three hundred years (750-430 B.C.E.), during which the most fateful events in the life of the monarchy took place. They prophesy the fall of the Northern and Southern Kingdoms, they console and encourage the Babylonian exiles, and rouse the remnant to undertake the Restoration. They subject the people to ceaseless denunciation, and suffer and die for so doing. But the nation hallowed their words and set them alongside of its ancient sacred legacy, the Torah of Moses.

HISTORICAL AND IDEOLOGICAL BACKGROUND

The immediate occasion of the rise of the new prophecy was the political and social ruin caused by the wars with Israel's northern neighbor, Aram, which continued for more than a century. They raged intensely during the reign of Ahab, and did not end until the time of Jeroboam II (784-744). While the nation as a whole was impoverished, a few—apparently of the royal officialdom—grew wealthy as a result of the national calamity. Many of the people were compelled to sell their houses and lands, with the result that a sharp social cleavage arose: on the one hand a mass of propertyless indigents, on the other a small circle of the rich. A series of disasters struck the nation—drought, famine, plagues, death, and captivity (Amos 4:6-11), but the greatest disaster of all was the social disintegration due to the cleavage between the poor masses and the wealthy, dissolute upper class. The decay affected both Judah and Israel.

High-minded men were appalled at this development. Was this the people whom YHWH had brought out of Egypt, to whom He had given the land and a law of justice and right? It seemed as if the land were about to be inherited by the rich, who would squander its substance in drunken revelry. It was this dissolution that brought the prophetic denunciations to white heat. The decay continued through the reign of Jeroboam II, even after the victory over Aram, and may even have become worse. For the victory was taken as a sign of divine favor and was celebrated in a fever of sacrifices, songs, and temple revels. The tumult distracted attention from the social crisis, and the people failed to perceive that such living and such festivals were a violation of the Covenant and a desecration of the name of God. Within prophetic circles moral indignation grew, and was given voice by the new prophets.

Historical circumstances do not, of course, fully explain the entire phenomenon. Classical prophecy formulated new religious and moral ideas which flowed forth from the rock of Israelite religion and became a mighty stream. But it was the moral indignation aroused by the social decay of the times that struck the rock and released the latent flood.

Following the pattern of all Israelite prophecy, the classical prophets are apostles. They do not merely respond to inquiries made of them but act on their own as messengers of God. The line of apostolic prophets went on unbroken in Israel, from Moses to Malachi.

At the same time classical prophecy—like the popular prophecy which preceded it—has an element of divination in it. The literary prophets, too, are possessed of supernatural divinatory powers which are employed to predict not only events of general or national concern, but also the future of individuals—at times in minute detail. Thus, for example, Amos prophesies to Amaziah, the Beth-el priest, what is to befall him (Amos 7:17), and Jeremiah does the same for Hananiah (Jeremiah 28:16f.) and Pashhur (20:4ff.).

Nonetheless, classical prophecy cannot be considered as properly belonging in the category of oracle-giving. We know of no literary prophet who divined or prophesied for pay, although to be sure, great prophets of earlier times—such as Samuel and Ahijah of Shiloh—did so. The essence of apostolic prophecy was independence, freedom from all material values. The known literary prophets are purely apostles. Prophecy is thus restored in this period to the level prevailing in the days of Moses and Joshua. It was not for hire.

What distinguishes Israelite prophecy from that of all other peoples is its ideological role. From the time of Moses until the time of Amos, prophecy was the standard-bearer of the popular religion, and was itself popular in character. Amos begins an epoch in which Israelite religion reaches a new climax. The new prophecy conceives of ideas which the religion of the previous age never attained. As a result there develops a certain rift between prophecy and popular religion, because the new ideas are not immediately adopted by the people but remain for some generations the property of a small circle. This ideological gap produces great tension; the prophets' diatribes seem exaggerated and the king and people occasionally resort to persecution.

And yet the innovations derive from the heart of Israelite religion. Classical prophecy does not so much repudiate the popular religion, from which it receives its fundamental notions, as rise beyond it to new heights.

The monotheistic idea of one God—creator, sustainer, and just judge—is rooted in the popular religion. The idea was not an invention of the literary prophets, as some current opinion would have it, but was part of the ancient inherited faith. The prophets flourish in the environment of Israel's fundamental idea, which is of Deity as the supreme, sovereign will, unlimited by nature or compulsion of fate. Their prophecy knows of no popular or priestly mythology, no magical ritual, nor does it combat any such phenomena. It is not aware of the real meaning of paganism, nor does it polemicize against it. For it developed in a monotheistic nation which for centuries had been nonpagan.

The one universal, sovereign God made Himself known only to Israel. The other nations worship gods of wood and stone. Israel alone has been gifted with a steady line of prophets. Israel is holy; its land is holy and God dwells in its sanctuaries. The pagans' lands are "impure ground." Classical prophecy shares the view that God does not hold the idolatry of the nations against them; they are judged only for moral sins. The prophets prophesy concerning the nations, but they were sent only to Israel and only in Israel can they as a rule fulfill their task. They too regard Israel as a community pledged to observe a specific religion and morality by the Covenant which God made with it in antiquity. The duty to be loyal to God and refrain from idol worship is incumbent on Israel alone, and derives from this Covenant.

Yet although classical prophecy was rooted in the popular religion, it brought Israelite religion to a new climax.

THE PRIMACY OF MORALITY

It is the literary prophets who conceived the idea of the primacy of morality, the doctrine that morality is superior to the cult, that what God requires of man is morality, not ritual. The cult appears to be repudiated. Such utterances as those with which Amos astonished the festive throngs at YHWH's temple in north Israel were never heard before:

> *I hate, I despise your feasts,*
> *And I will take no delight in your solemn assemblies.*
> *Yea, though ye offer me burnt-offerings and your meal-offerings,*
> *I will not accept them;*
> *Neither will I regard the peace-offerings of your fat beasts.*
> *Take thou away from Me the noise of thy songs;*
> *And let Me not hear the melody of thy psalteries.*
> *But let justice well up as waters,*
> *And righteousness as a mighty stream.*
>
> (Amos 5:21-24)

And at approximately the same time Isaiah was saying the same thing to the people coming to sacrifice and pray to God in the Jerusalem temple:

> *To what purpose is the multitude of your sacrifices unto Me?*
> *Saith the Lord;*
> *I am full of the burnt-offerings of rams,*
> *And the fat of fed beasts;*
> *And I delight not in the blood*
> *Of bullocks, or of lambs, or of he-goats. . . .*
> *Your new moons and your appointed seasons*
> *My soul hateth;*
> *They are a burden unto Me;*
> *I am weary to bear them. . . .*

Wash you, make you clean,
Put away the evil of your doings
From before Mine eyes,
Cease to do evil;
Learn to do well;
Seek justice, relieve the oppressed,
Judge the fatherless, plead for the widow.

(Isaiah 1:11-17)

Variations on this theme are found in Hosea, Micah, Jeremiah, the Second Isaiah, and Zachariah 1-8; reflections of it also occur in the writings of those prophets who do not state it explicitly. It is a revolutionary religious idea.

What is here rejected is not the cultic act of the wicked individual, who is unacceptable to the Deity because of his sins. That the good deed of the righteous man is more pleasing to God than the sacrifices of the wicked is expressed in the wisdom literature of Egypt as well as in Biblical wisdom. What the literary prophets condemn is the cult of the entire people: its festivals, sacrifices, temples, songs, and so forth. Now this cult of Israel is the whole of the YHWH cult; there is no other nation in the world that serves Him. Hence the prophetic repudiation of Israel's cult implies that the cult in its entirety is of no value to God. Such an idea could not have been conceived on heathen soil, for as we have seen, the pagan cult is thought to affect the gods. The life of the gods depends on the cult, and the priest is charged with the mysteries of the life, death, and resurrection of the gods. Festivals celebrate events in their lives, sacrifices renew their vitality and power. The doctrine of the primacy of morality, then, implies a revolution in religious concepts; it deprives the cult of any inherent, absolute value.

The roots of this revolutionary concept are found in the early religion. The Torah has already stripped the cult of any magical, transcendent value and transformed it into a divine command, an expression of divine grace, and not a divine need. It becomes a token of, and a means for maintaining, intimacy with God, an expression of reverence and homage to the name of God, a memorial to His grace and Covenant. But the primacy of morality is not explicitly stated in the early Biblical literature. The Torah is a conglomerate of moral, secular, and ritual laws indiscriminately juxtaposed. Nowhere is it said that the moral takes priority over the ritual. Nor is the idea voiced anywhere in the historical books. Samuel says to Saul: "Hath YHWH as great delight in burnt-offerings and sacrifices, as in hearkening to the voice of YHWH? Behold, to obey is better than sacrifice . . ." (I Samuel 15:22f.). That is, obedience to God (in this case, the execution of the ban against the Amalekites) is of a higher order than sacrifice; but nothing is said here with regard to the superiority of morality to the cult. Amos was the first to utter this idea, and thereafter it dominates classical prophetic literature. Although the seed of the idea was present in the Israelite conception of the cult as a command and an expression of divine grace, it was not until the emergence of the great prophets that it was given full and final utterance.

The Israelite conception as expressed by the prophets considers both cult and morality as aspects of the divine command and Covenant. For it is certain that prophecy did not unconditionally repudiate the cult or utterly deny its value. But Israelite religion raised morality to the level of an absolute religious value, because it regarded morality as essentially divine. Moral attributes are of the essence of God Himself; He who requires righteousness, justice, and compassion of man is Himself righteous, just, and compassionate. The moral man thus shares, so to speak, in divinity. Paganism aspired to apotheosis, seeking by means of mysterious cultic rites to deify man. Israelite religion had no room for such a notion. Man cannot become God in life or afterward. But man can and must become Godlike in his moral attributes. Such is the moral "apotheosis" that Judaism requires. Its fullest expression is in the Rabbinic exhortation: "Be like Him: as He is gracious and merciful so be thou gracious and merciful . . ." (Shabbat 133b).

THE VIEW OF HISTORY

Classical prophecy also views history in a new light. It makes morality a decisive factor in national history. That God justly recompenses man, individually and corporately, according to his moral condition is, of course, fundamental to Israelite thought. The moral law is obligatory on all mankind; it is the basis of Divine Providence and can be seen at work even in the fate of the pagans (the generation of the Flood, Sodom and Gomorrah). Israel is peculiar in being judged not only on the basis of its morality, but for its religious state as well. Idolatry is a sin for Israel, but not for the nations. In addition, Israel was given a special moral law at Sinai, for which it is held especially responsible and whose observance is crucial for its well-being: the moral-legal code of the Torah.

And yet the view throughout early Biblical literature is that only one sin is historically decisive, the sin of idolatry. Other religious and moral sins are punishable, but national collapse and exile result only from a breach of the Covenant which involves the worship of other gods. This is the prevailing view throughout the Books of Kings and is epitomized in II Kings 17:7-23: Israel's fateful sin was to worship other gods, to follow the customs of the nations, to serve the calves, sacrifice at high places, worship the host of heaven, use magic and divination, and so forth. In the narratives of the historical books we find, to be sure, accounts of moral sins and their dire consequences. There is David's crime with Bath-Sheba, for which Nathan calls down terrible punishment; the death of the child and, later, Absalom's rebellion are viewed as effects of this sin. Ahab's house is condemned to extinction for the murder of Naboth. Yet these individual moral sins are not viewed as constituting a fateful, continuous sin, a historical sin which implicates the whole nation, a debit which grows from generation to generation. There is only one such national sin: idolatry. That the moral corruption of the nation brought about its fall is never alluded to in the Books of Kings. We never hear of such corruption—or that there were prophets who denounced Israel for it.

The same historical view prevails in the Torah. The Torah is a religious-moral law which Israel is duty-bound to observe in its entirety. Yet it is for one sin only that the punishments of destruction and exile are explicitly threatened. It is the sin of worshiping other gods (Leviticus 26:30, Deuteronomy 4:25-28 and 6:12-15, and elsewhere).

The revolutionary idea of classical prophecy is that Israel's history is determined by two factors, the moral as well as the religious, and that both are equally decisive. The prophets reproach the nation for two evils, one moral, the other religious. For both they announce impending doom; both are viewed as causes of Israel's downfall. There is a national religious sin—idolatry—and a national moral sin—social corruption, perversion of justice, robbery of the poor. Amos, the first literary prophet, concerns himself almost exclusively with the latter. He takes up the cause of the poor against the exploitation and extortions of the rich, who "sell the righteous for silver, and the needy for a pair of shoes" (Amos 2:6). "And they lay themselves down besides every altar upon clothes taken in pledge, and in the house of their God they drink the wine of them that have been fined" (2:8); "who store up violence and robbery in their palaces" (3:10); who spend their time "thrumming on the psaltery" and "drinking wine in bowls," stretched out in revelry (6:5ff.); who have denuded the land of justice and right, "making the ephah small and the shekel great, and falsifying the balances of deceit" (8:5).

This is a new type of denunciation. It is, of course, an old idea that God dooms people for grave moral sins such as murder, robbery, and Sodomic immorality. But the prophets address their rebuke to the commonplace, "venial" sins: bribe-taking, biased justice, false scales, extortion from the poor and defenseless, raising prices, and the like. For such sins they prophesy destruction and exile. The moral demand here reaches its climax. God made Himself known to Israel, made with it a moral-religious Covenant, intended it to be a holy nation dedicated to do His will. But a people perverting justice, practicing violence, drunken and debauched, is no people of God! For the prophets, justice and righteousness are not a private affair. The entire nation is responsible for the moral state that prevails in it. Hence it will be judged as a whole both for idol worship and for moral sin on the day of reckoning.

VISION OF THE END OF DAYS: ISAIAH

Classical prophecy gave a new content to Israelite eschatology.

The bitter wars with Aram deeply disturbed sensitive men in Israel, and gave rise to an anxious searching of soul. Why had God inflicted this terrible enemy on Israel? In the time of Ahab and Jezebel, God's wrath was ascribed to the worship of Baal and the wickedness of Ahab's house. For this Elijah predicts a harsh retribution. The sword of Hazael, king of Aram, will be unsheathed against Israel; only the "seven thousand" who "did not bow down to Baal" will remain. The disastrous Aramean wars are thus designed to purge Israel, allowing only a remnant to survive. This is the first expression of the prophetic doctrine of the "remnant of Israel." Elisha anointed Hazael king and prophesied to him that he was to make a great slaughter in Israel. It was doubtless expected that the extermination of Ahab's house by Jehu would assuage the wrath of God. And yet during Jehu's reign, Israel's peril increased, while in the days of Jehoahaz, his son, Aram made Israel "like the dust in threshing." The people looked to God for rescue and dreamed of "the Day of YHWH," in which judgment and vengeance would be wreaked on the enemy while Israel triumphed. The dream seemed near fulfillment during the time of the victorious Jeroboam, the son of Joash (784-744 B.C.E.), who restored Israel's boundaries "from the entrance of Hamath to the Sea of the Arabah."

In the midst of this atmosphere of hopeful expectation classical prophecy appeared with its message of reproach and even greater chastisement. But these prophets were not merely prophets of doom, they were primarily rebukers: their great demand is for repentance. The affliction would not cease until Israel repented of its sin, and the repentance must be twofold: religious and moral. The people must root out idol worship from its midst and along with it the moral evil. No amount of offerings, sacrifices, and hymns could reconcile God to this people in their present state. YHWH has inflicted a series of disasters upon Israel to turn them to repentence, says Amos, but they have not turned; and so they will suffer yet the more (Amos 4:6-12). Vainly do they await "the Day of YHWH," for the day, when it comes, will be "darkness and not light" (Amos 5:18ff.). It will be a day of reckoning for Israel no less than for the nations—an idea that came to prevail in the writings of all the classical prophets. Chastisements will follow hard upon one another, and only if Israel repents will a "remnant" be permitted to survive (Amos 5:15). This twofold message announcing doom and calling to repentance is echoed by all the successors of Amos.

In their moral pathos, the fury of their censure, and the fervor of their call for repentance the prophets of Israel are a unique phenomenon in world history. They attain their greatest heights, however, in their vision of salvation. While on the one hand they include Israel among those to be judged by God on the day of reckoning, on the other they embrace all the nations in their vision of His saving. Isaiah, who was the first to conceive this vision, gave voice thereby to the tremendous optimism of Israelite religion.

The decline of Aram took place in the days of Isaiah. A mightier power, Assyria, now entered upon the stage of history. The reign of Tiglath-Pileser III (745-727 B.C.E.) saw the emergence of Assyria as a world empire. By incessant wars Tiglath-Pileser subjugated peoples and countries and reduced them to vassalage. In the year 734 he conquered the northern districts of Israel and deported their inhabitants. The truncated north became subject to Assyria, and Judah followed suit. In 732, Tiglath-Pileser captured Damascus and put an end to the Aramean kingdom. Ten years later Sargon captured Samaria and exiled Israel from its land. A heavy cloud hung over the future of Judah, and during Hezekiah's reign (719-691 B.C.E.) it seemed as if the end had come. Sennacherib (705-681 B.C.E.) set out to capture Jerusalem; in 701 he attacked Judah and reduced all its fortified cities except Jerusalem. The royal city was besieged, and Hezekiah yielded to the point of paying tribute, but refused to open the gates to the Assyrian. Isaiah encouraged the king with the prophecy that Sennacherib would never capture the city. And, in fact, he did not, for a plague apparently broke out in the Assyrian army, and he was compelled to hurry home.

In spite of his message of cheer to besieged Jerusalem, the bulk of Isaiah's prophecy is reproach and warning of punishment. He predicts that cities will be destroyed, homes abandoned, the earth desolated so that not even a tenth of its population would remain. Assyria is for him the "rod of YHWH's wrath," the instrument that He has fashioned to punish Israel and the nations for their sin (Isaiah 10:5ff.). But Isaiah does not regard Assyria as just another passing episode. There is a divine plan discernible in the turbulent events of the time. The affliction is intended to chasten Israel, but this is not its ultimate meaning. Isaiah envisions the disturbances of his day as the prelude to a cosmic revolution, to the remaking of all mankind.

It is characteristic of Isaiah that he not only demands a return to God, but prophesies its coming about—symbolically he names his son Shear Yashub, "a remnant shall return." The return thus becomes a promise, an eschatological certainty, part of the divine plan for the End of Days. It will not be transient, but genuine and whole-hearted, a permanent, perfect return to God. Isaiah envisions an eschatological return—an end of sin, when the terrible empire of heathendom will have played out its role. At present God has surrendered the world to this empire, and has given free rein to tyranny and rapine. Now Assyria lords it over the world with un-bridled fury, "for to destroy is in his heart, and to cut off not a few nations" (Isaiah 10:7). It knows not the God who raised it up to be His "rod of wrath," and is ignorant of its role as His mere tool. But Assyria will be broken on the mountains of Israel, when it comes up against Jerusalem to conquer it. This defeat will not touch Assyria alone, for then a new epoch will open in world history. "This is the design that is planned for the whole earth, and this is the Hand that is stretched out over all the nations" (Isaiah 14:26).

The fall of Assyria will not only mark the end of heathendom's empire, heathendom itself shall then cease to be. Isaiah is the first prophet to envision an end to the dominion of heathenism. God's coming to save Jerusalem and crush the armies of Assyria will be a new theophany of world-wide scope. "On that day they shall cast away every man his idols of silver, and his idols of gold" (Isaiah 31:7). "In that day shall man regard his Maker, and his eyes shall look to the Holy One of Israel" (17:7). An end will then come to Israel's subjection and exile: "It shall be in that day, that a great horn shall be blown; and they shall come that were lost in the land of Assyria, and they that were dispersed in the land of Egypt, and

they shall worship the Lord in the holy mountain in Jerusalem"
(27:13). The glory of the Davidic dynasty shall be restored. The
new kingdom shall be righteous and peaceful; its king will be "a
branch from the stock of Jesse"

> *And the spirit of the Lord shall rest upon him,*
> *The spirit of wisdom and understanding,*
> *The spirit of counsel and might,*
> *The spirit of knowledge and of the fear of the Lord . . .*
> *And the wolf shall dwell with the lamb,*
> *And the leopard shall lie down with the kid;*
> *And the calf and the young lion shall feed together;**
> *And a little child shall lead them . . .*
> *For the earth shall be full of the knowledge of the Lord,*
> *As the waters cover the sea.*
>
> (Isaiah 11:1ff.)

But the new Israel will not stand isolated; it shall be "an ensign
of the peoples" whom "nations shall seek." Thus even the nations
erstwhile heathen, shall now be inspired by the spiritual kingdom
at the holy mountain.

Isaiah's vision of heathendom's end is connected with his vision
of universal peace. The great seer is the originator of that idea, too.
In an early prophecy concerning the "day of YHWH" he envisions
a time when God will visit doom

> *Upon all that is proud and lofty,*
> *And upon all that is lifted up, so that it shall be brought low; . . .*
> *And upon every lofty tower*
> *And upon every fortified wall;*
> *Upon all the Tarshish-ships*
> *And upon all boats of delight.*
>
> (Isaiah 2:12ff.)

God will demolish the fortifications and armaments of man, and
destroy the treasures amassed in violence and war. On that day
the Lord alone shall be exalted; men shall cast away their images
of silver and gold, and idolatry shall utterly pass away. In this same
prophecy Isaiah envisions the reign of universal peace; with the
end of heathendom shall come an end to war.

It shall come to pass in the end of days,
That the mountain of the Lord's house shall be established at the top of
  mountains,
And shall be exalted above the hills;
And all nations shall look to it.

* The translation of this line is based upon the superior reading of the text of
Isaiah *a* among the Dead Sea Scrolls.

And many peoples shall go and say:
"Come ye, and let us go up to the mountain of the Lord,
To the house of the God of Jacob;
And He will teach us of His ways
And we will walk in His paths."
For out of Zion shall go forth instruction
And the word of the Lord from Jerusalem.
He shall judge between the nations,
And decide for many peoples;
So that they shall beat their swords into plowshares,
And their spears into pruning-hooks;
Nation shall not lift up sword against nation,
Neither shall they learn war any more.

(Isaiah 2:2-4)

In this vision idolatry is viewed as the product of human arrogance, the fruit of man's aspiration to dominate the world, to be "like God." Here too idolatry is regarded as fetishism—the worship of silver and gold images—but it is pagan man's trust in the supremacy of his own wisdom that is the ultimate cause of his "making" himself "gods." The deification of his handiwork is at bottom a deification of himself as man-god. This idolatry is symbolized in man's desire to fortify himself with towers and walls, to conquer every height, to amass silver, gold, and all luxuries. Isaiah regards idolatry as the source of moral evil as well as a rebellion against God. For the pagan lust for power and wealth sets man against man in an endless struggle for domination. The Assyrian monarch is idolatry incarnate: he trusts in his power and wisdom, is filled with pride, lusts after the wealth of nations, seeks to subjugate peoples and to destroy them (Isaiah 10:5-14). He vaunts himself as being above the gods, and boasts of having attained "the height of the mountains, to the uttermost parts of Lebanon" (37:24). The end of idolatry is therefore the end of moral evil, of violence and warfare as well. When all the nations acknowledge the God of Israel, and come flocking to the mountain of His house, the age of eternal peace shall have arrived.

Thus the prophet sees in the end of one epoch the beginning of another. The storm which is about to break over the earth will sweep away wickedness. God will arraign Israel, too, and only after his judgment will Israel become truly the people of God. But then Israel will assume a new and nobler role: it will become the bearer of God's message to all the peoples.

In this vision the universalism of Israelite religion reached a new level. The early religion of Israel, as embodied in the literature of the Torah and the Former Prophets, is universalistic. It regards the God of Israel as the creator of the world, the sole sustainer of all that is. While He made Himself known only to Israel, He rules all the nations, although they are ignorant of Him and worship wood and stone in His stead. Moreover, the Bible, as we have seen, depicts primeval man as monotheistic until the generation of the Confusion of Tongues. From the start mankind was monotheistic, as from the start the nations were polytheistic, and remained so even after Israel, late-come, was singled out to be the people of God. Thus the world latterly became divided into two distinct realms: Israel and the nations. Israel received the religion of the one God as an eternal heritage in the Covenant of Sinai and the Torah of Moses. Idolatry is the heritage of the nations. "Take ye good heed unto yourselves," warns Moses, ". . . lest thou lift up thine eyes unto heaven, and when thou seest the sun and the moon and the stars, all the host of heaven, thou be drawn away and worship them, and serve them, which the Lord thy God hath allotted unto all the peoples under the whole heaven" (Deuteronomy 4:19). This division of mankind is considered permanent; that it will ever come to an end is beyond the scope of the Torah and Former Prophets. It is true that here and there the pious wish is voiced that the nations also shall acknowledge the power of Israel's God, but there is no confident expectation of a time when idolatry will be cut off, no idea of a divine plan to have the nations ultimately share in the faith that God gave to Israel.

The universalism of the early religion is thus historical, or legendary, while that of classical prophecy is eschatological. The early religion saw monotheism as the common heritage of all men only in the distant past. From their inception the nations sank into idolatry, and idolatry will remain their portion forever. The new message of classical prophecy was that monotheism was again to become the faith of all mankind. At the End of Days, God shall make Himself known to all nations as He did to Israel. History moves toward the end of paganism, toward the triumph of the divine moral law, the kingdom of justice and peace. Idolatry is a passing phase. Sprung from rebellion, it will be consumed in the crucible of affliction. This view lent new meaning to the idea of Israel's election: Israel has been chosen to be the instrument of universal redemption; God will reveal Himself to all mankind through His miraculous rescue of Israel. When the heathen empire storms Jerusalem it will be shattered by the hand of God. In this wondrous event the glory of Israel's God will be manifest to all nations. They will then abandon their idols and return to Him.

All humanity is here made an object of divine grace alongside of Israel. The national limits of the old religion have been transcended. Zion, formerly a national and cultic symbol, becomes the site of universal redemption at the End of Days. The "remnant" of Israel will be redeemed in Zion, but Zion is destined to become the fountainhead of grace for all nations as well. Such is Israel's new mission: to become "a light unto the nations," in the language of the Second Isaiah (Isaiah 49:6).

This vision opens a new epoch in Israelite as well as world history. With it Israelite religion takes the first step toward becoming a factor in universal history. Heretofore it confined itself to the people and the land of Israel; it was involved in the destiny of one nation and its symbols were national and territorial. It was not designed for the nations at large. There was a constant battle with Israelite deviations into idolatry, but no thought of declaring war upon the idolatry of the nations. Indeed, it was firmly believed that God Himself had "allotted" idolatry to those who practiced it. Here for the first time the idea that Israel's religion could be a universal religion flashes forth, and with it the idea of combating the idolatry of the nations. In this crucial moment Israelite religion discovered its role in universal history. It is true that Judaism's war upon paganism was not properly joined until later; neither Isaiah nor his successors demanded a missionary propagation of the faith, nor were they sent to the nations to preach monotheism. The prophets regard the end of idolatry as an eschatological event, a divine work of redemption at the End of Days. Nevertheless, the vision of idolatry's end must be considered as the preliminary skirmish in the war of Judaism and Christianity with paganism. It is the beginning of paganism's fall.

Isaiah was a visionary and a dreamer. He pictured the end as the collapse of Assyria's armies on the mountains of Israel, and envisaged the coming of universal peace within the frame of the events of his time. But his dream did not come true. When Assyria did eventually fall, it was only to be succeeded by another heathen empire. Yet the value of Isaiah's vision is not dependent upon its historical framework. The significance of his insight transcends his specific historical situation. It is the eternal insight that man can be redeemed only by conquering "idolatry," as Isaiah conceived it: man's self-deification; man's trust in his own handiwork (e.g., in his technological "know-how"), in high towers and Tarshish ships; his avarice, his violent impulses, his lust to dominate. Redemption will come only when he recognizes his moral obligation as divine and absolute. There is no saving political or economic doctrine. Man's redemption can be realized only when his moral condition is perfected, only when "Jerusalem" triumphs over "Babylon." Isaiah bequeathed to us the legacy of redemptive idealism, and so his vision has eternal validity.

THE JOSIANIC REFORM

Sennacherib failed to capture Jerusalem; Judah could breathe easy again. But the respite was momentary, for Assyria's might was not a whit lessened. During the reign of Esarhaddon, we see Hezekiah's son, Manasseh, entirely subjected to Assyrian control. Manasseh's servility led him, it would seem, into becoming an ardent and zealous pagan. He purchased peace at the price of political and religious thralldom. In the view of the loyalists of God such thralldom was a dreadful calamity and a portent of divine wrath. But Manasseh crushed all opposition and in the process "filled Jerusalem with innocent blood from one end to the other." The pious—those "who moaned and groaned"—looked on with horror as he turned the very house of YHWH into a pagan temple. Could there be any hope for such a people? The subjection to Assyria, extending as it did even to the realm of religion, gave rise to a mood of remorse and soul-searching, a longing for reconciliation with God.

Out of this mood was born the Josianic reform. In 622 B.C.E., Josiah purged the Jerusalem Temple and the entire land of Manasseh's pagan cults and of the pagan vestiges that lingered from earlier days. The immediate cause of the reform was the discovery of "the book of the Torah" in the Temple. This book was, according to the current scholarly consensus, the Book of Deuteronomy, in which the requirement of centralized worship and the prohibition of worship at the high places are found. Josiah fulfills this demand also; he puts an end to the cult of the high places and transfers its priests to Jerusalem. Furthermore, he assembles the people at the Temple, reads to them the newly found book, and makes a covenant obligating them to obey all that is written therein. This act has great significance: Josiah is the only king who made a covenant on the basis of "the book of the Torah"; in so doing he gave this book the force of a state law. Heretofore the Torah literature was a religious, cultic, juristic-moralistic ideal, corresponding in part to actual practice, but never possessing constitutional validity. Its influence was much like that of the wisdom literature—didactic and edifying. Josiah made the book discovered in the Temple the law of the land. In this we can see the aspiration of the time to crystallize the fluid tradition of Torah literature into a fixed, canonical book. The penitant mood of that and the succeeding generations awakened the desire to found the life of the nation on the solid rock of "the book of the Torah" which had been transmitted from hoary antiquity. By this alone could they cleave to God and do His will. The book which was found in the days of Josiah—Deuteronomy—was the first crystallization of the Torah; it was given constitutional force by Josiah. Later, in the time of Ezra and Nehemiah, the process was completed with the canonization of the whole Torah. Josiah's act thus prepared the way for the Judaism of Second Temple times which based its life on the Torah book.

The Josianic reform was doubtless accompanied by high hopes for divine salvation and the end of heathen domination. When Assyria collapsed before the combined attack of Babylonians, Medians, and barbarian tribes—Nineveh fell in 612 B.C.E.—the prophet Nahum celebrated the event as heralding the redemption of all mankind. But these hopes were disappointed, for a new heathen empire arose in Assyria's place. Josiah, the righteous king, was slain in 609 in an encounter with Pharaoh Necho as the latter marched to fight the Babylonian king. In the ensuing struggle to succeed Assyria, Babylonia emerged victorious. In 605, Nebuchadnezzar defeated Pharaoh Necho and established himself firmly in the seat of empire. The prophet Habakkuk looks on horrified at the rise of the "bitter and impetuous nation" that marches through the earth "to possess dwelling-places that are not his." He cries "violence" to God, and can console himself only with the thought that soon the end shall come also to this new ravager.

THE FALL OF JUDAH: JEREMIAH

The kingdom of Judah shifted restively in the grip of the Babylonian overlord. To submit or to fight was the question that agitated and divided the leaders of the nation. These last melancholy years of the kingdom saw the advent of Jeremiah, one of the most uncompromising of the prophets of denunciation and doom. In his youth he championed the Josianic reform, but the reform did not fulfill his expectations. Weighing the life of the people in the balance of the prophetic ideal, he found it wanting. The reform did not penetrate below the surface, did not revolutionize life. The people had bound themselves by the covenant to fulfill the precepts of the book of the Torah "with their whole heart and soul," yet they violated the covenant, did not repent whole-heartedly. Traces of pagan practices still subsisted. There were women—apparently survivors of Manasseh's generation—who made "cakes to the Queen of Heaven" (Jeremiah 7:17ff.; 44:16-19, 25). Especially appalling was the moral corruption that went on undiminished. There were wicked men whose houses were "filled with deceit," who ignored the rights of orphan and poor. Stealing, murder, adultery, false swearing—this is Jeremiah's summary of the moral decay (7:9). "For every brother acteth subtly, and every neighbor goeth about with slanders. . . . And truth they speak not; they have taught their tongue to speak lies . . ." (9:3ff.). For all these sins Jeremiah prophesied doom and destruction, death and exile. Furthermore, inasmuch as the people had not repented sincerely God would visit on them the sins of Manasseh's generation as well (15:4)—the generation who set up their abominations in the temple and burned their children at the altars of Topheth (7:30-34; 19; 32:34f.).

The people were affronted by this reproach and this warning of doom, feeling it was unmerited. Nor did they believe that Jerusalem and the Temple would be surrendered by God to the hand of an enemy. The people trusted in the Temple of YHWH, in the sacred cult performed there, and in the Name of YHWH that dwelled in His House. It was unthinkable that He should give His only sanctuary on earth over to the heathen. But Jeremiah lashes out furiously against this confidence, and he draws the ultimate inference from the doctrine of the primacy of morality. No cultic act, no sacrifice, prayer, or fast can atone for moral corruption; worship done by villains is a profanation of the Name. The people have turned the House of God into a den of robbers; God must, therefore, destroy His Temple. "This house shall be like Shiloh, and this city desolate, without an inhabitant" (Jeremiah 26:9). Outraged by this prophecy —uttered in the very court of the Temple—the priests and the people sought to kill Jeremiah, and he was rescued from them by Ahikam, the son of Shaphan.

But the trend of events confirmed his dire warnings. The rise of the Babylonian Empire appeared to Jeremiah as a token of God's persisting wrath. When Nebuchadnezzar became king, Jeremiah prophesied that God would set him over all the nations. The nation that would not submit to his yoke would perish by sword, famine, and plague (27: 5ff., 13). In the days of Jehoiakim (608-598), Jeremiah prophesies that the king of Babylon shall come "and destroy this land." Jehoiakim seeks to kill Jeremiah and his secretary, Baruch, but they manage to escape. Meanwhile, a movement of revolt gathers headway: preparations are made for war; popular prophets announce the near collapse of Babylonia. Jehoiakim revolts, and Nebuchadnezzar counters in 598 by besieging Jerusalem. The Judean king dies during the siege and his son Jehoiachin ascends the throne in 597. Jehoiachin submits, and opens the city. Nebuchadnezzar plunders the Temple, carries off the Temple and palace vessels, and deports the king along with several thousands of the upper class. Undaunted, the popular prophets now prophesy the speedy return of the Temple vessels and the exiles, and the imminent fall of Babylonia.

Jeremiah denies these prophecies; on the contrary, even the remaining vessels will soon be carried off to Babylon (27:16-28:17). He writes a letter to the exiles warning them that their stay will be a long one, and they had best give up hope for a speedy return (29). Throughout the whole reign of Zedekiah (597-586) he demands submission to Babylonia, but the King and officers ignore him.

In 588, the ninth year of his reign, Zedekiah revolts, and the desperate struggle of the tiny nation against the world empire begins. There is no doubt that the rebels drew their strength from a deep religious faith. In this their resistance was similar to that of the zealots who fought Rome at the end of the Second Temple. There was frightful suffering, but until the last moment the people hoped for divine succor. For nearly three years the siege went on, famine ultimately bringing the city to its knees. In 586 Jerusalem fell, Zedekiah was taken captive, the Temple was burned, and Judah went into exile.

Even during the siege Jeremiah continued preaching submission. His speeches enraged the government; he was imprisoned and an attempt was made to sink him in a pit of mire. We can understand Jeremiah only from the viewpoint of his prophetic idealism, which differed radically from the popular idealism that sustained the revolt. For Jeremiah the basic fact was that the people had not repented whole-heartedly, hence it must still undergo a period of chastisement. Nebuchadnezzer did not rise to power on his own, but was merely performing the task assigned to him by God. He was "the servant of YHWH" (Jeremiah 27:6), the instrument of divine chastisement. Jeremiah allots seventy years to the Babylonian domination, seventy years which are to be at the same time the period of Israel's penitence (25:11ff.; 29:10-13). Submission to the Babylonian yoke is therefore submission to the will of God, and recognition of the fact that the hour of salvation has not yet come. The people do not yet merit God's help because they have not returned to Him whole-heartedly. To accept the yoke of Babylon is an expression of contrition. On the other hand, the revolt and the expectation of divine succor are tantamount to a rejection of the prophetic demand to right the moral and religious wrongs of the nation. Jeremiah prophesied that the expectation was vain and the revolt doomed to failure. Its consequence could only be complete destruction and exile.

But Jeremiah was not merely a prophet of doom, he also brought a message of consolation. He is the first to set a time limit to the sway of the heathen empire, a limit of seventy years. His example was followed by all succeeding reckoners of the End and millenarians.

At the end of seventy years Jeremiah forsees a great war of all nations against each other (25:15-19). In this war heathendom will perish. Judah and Israel shall then return to their land, "unto the goodness of the Lord, to the corn, and to the wine, and to the oil, and to the young of the flock and of the herd" (31:11ff.); all distress and grief shall pass away. Zion shall be acknowledged the holy city, and in it shall reign a scion of David (33:20-26). Then God shall make a new covenant with Israel.

I will put My law in their inward parts,
And in their heart will I write it . . .
And they shall teach no more every man his neighbor and every man
his brother,
Saying: "Know the Lord";
For they shall all know Me,
From the least of them
Unto the greatest of them,
Saith the Lord . . . (Jeremiah 31:33ff.)

And I will make an everlasting covenant with them,
That I will not turn away from doing them good;
And I will put My fear in their hearts, that they shall never depart
from me.
(Jeremiah 32:40)

Jeremiah is among the great universalistic prophets; he too prophesies the end of idolatry at the End of Days. The End will come when the nations realize that manufactured gods are no-gods (16:19-20). God will also show mercy to Israel's wicked neighbors and restore them to their lands. If they learn to swear by His name, "then shall they be built up in the midst of My people" (12:14-17). We also find Jeremiah polemicizing against idolatry in the style of the Second Isaiah, and it seems that his Aramaic letter to the exiles—"Thus shall ye say unto them: 'The gods that have not made the heavens and the earth, these shall perish from the earth, and from under the heavens' " (10:11)—is intended to inform the nations of his prophecy concerning idolatry's end. It is Jeremiah, then, who first carries the battle against idolatry into its own territory.

4

THE EMERGENCE OF JUDAISM

The Fall of Judah brought to a close an era full of splendor, creativeness, and courage. One might say that the history of Israel as a nation came to an end, and the history of Judaism began. To be sure, the people of Israel lived on and were as productive after the Fall as before, but the conditions of their existence were radically altered. Israel ceased being a "normal" nation.

The Fall shattered the national and territorial bases of Israel's culture and religion. It was not only the people that went into exile, but their religion as well; the Exile was no less an "Exile of the *Shekinah*" (the Divine Presence). Israel and its faith were now confronted by a great test. Although Israelite religion was universal in essence, it had evolved in national forms. The land of Israel was its territorial sphere, the life of Israel was the sphere of its historic expression; its holy land was Palestine, its festivals, temples, priests, and prophets were exclusively Israelite. Until the Fall it existed as a national religion, like the religions of Egypt, Canaan, Moab, and the other nations of antiquity. It was an organic part of the national culture, like the language, poetry, literature, and social forms. The Fall put an end to this state of affairs. Israel was uprooted from its land and scattered among the nations; the national culture in which the religion had been historically rooted collapsed. The crucial question was, could Israelite religion survive the collapse of its national foundations? Could it subsist on foreign soil, or would it go the way of other national religions?

THE CRISIS OF FAITH

By the end of the Babylonian Exile it had become clear that the people and the religion had stood the test. Israelite religion began revealing its universal significance. In the first place it demonstrated its capacity for keeping Israel an identifiable national-religious unit even in foreign lands. Although its national and territorial basis had been destroyed, its inner strength remained undiminished. The Diaspora gradually assimilated the foreign, pagan culture, but did not accept pagan religion. After half a century of exile the exiles were still determined to return to their land. This is an unparalleled phenomenon. It testifies to the distinctiveness of Israelite religion, to its vitality, which proved to be independent of time and place and unabated by pagan civilization.

How is this strength to be explained? An answer suggests itself when we survey the later history of the spread of Judaism, Christianity, and Islam over a period of fifteen hundred years. During this time the nations among whom the Jews live undergo a great religious transformation: they give up their pagan religions and adopt monotheism. The process moves in one direction only—from paganism to monotheism. There is no instance of an opposite movement. This historical circumstance implies a law of evolution, and it appears to be an irreversible law. It is that monotheism represents a higher religious stage than paganism. Monotheism won over its foe where and whenever the battle was joined. In Israel after the Fall this law is seen in operation: the passage from paganism to monotheism occurred at the time of the Exodus, and Israel never retraced its steps to return to its former religious stage. For centuries there were idolatrous deviations, there was the "sin" of idolatry, but idolatry could never again become the national religion of Israel. The religious revolution of the age of Moses established forever a gap between the religious level of Israel and its neighbors. The test of the Exile proved that not even national dissolution could eliminate this gap and restore Israel to the religious community of the nations. The exiles were influenced by the surrounding culture of the pagans; they participated in their political and economic life; but they could not descend to the level of pagan religion. Despite the high degree of cultural assimilation the religious contrast set up an impassable barrier between the exiles and their environment.

We are therefore entitled to say that it was the monotheistic character of the Israelite nation that prevented its being absorbed into its surroundings. The deportees of pagan nations adopted the local alien cults out of a faith in their validity, with the result that the new gods eventually displaced the old national gods. Once the religious barrier was removed, assimilation soon became total. But no degree of cultural assimilation was sufficient to inspire in the Jews a belief in the pagan gods. As a result they remained religiously and hence nationally distinct.

Thus the factor which operates decisively in the later history of Jewry is already at work in this period: the Jews are unable to adopt the religion of their environment by belief, when they do adopt it, it is by force. Such conversion is faithless and takes place because of material considerations. This is the iron law of the Exile. It is strikingly expressed in the words of the elders to Ezekiel: "Let us become like the nations, like the families of the earth, to serve wood and stone" (Ezekiel 20:32). Jews can accept paganism only as the worship of no-gods, as the service of "wood and stone." The elders are not voicing a sober demand, but rather their desperation at the terrible spiritual burdens of the exiled community. Individuals may have found relief in a cynical "service of wood and stone," but the people as a whole could not adopt this unfaith.

The religious factor separating Israel from the nations operated as an objective historical necessity. But the people, of course, did not feel their separateness as something imposed upon them, for they kept faith with their God with all their heart and soul. It is true that the Fall came as a dreadful blow to the exiles and for a while overwhelmed them with despair. If God cast them away and gave them over into the hand of their enemies, was there room for further hope? No calamity, however, could shake their awareness of their religious superiority to the pagan world. Stripped of every national possession, they still clung to their knowledge of God and His Torah. This unique heritage went with them into exile. So the die was cast: Israel could not and would not surrender the gift God had made it; it remained true to Him despite the Fall.

And so begins the remarkable history of post-Exilic Judaism. Not only did the Jewish people refuse to adopt pagan religion, but at the very moment of national failure the last vestiges of paganism were forever obliterated from their midst. The Fall is the great watershed of Israel's religious life. From earliest times the sin of "idolatry" had existed in Israel, and the zealots of every age had combated it.

After the Fall, however, "the evil genius of idolatry died." During the period of the Second Temple, and forever after, idolatry ceases to exist.

This is not to be interpreted as the transformation of a polytheistic people into monotheists. Israel had long ago become a monotheistic people. But on the popular level monotheism had not been carried through consistently in the cultic sphere. Vestiges of an ancient fetishistic idolatry, reinforced by foreign influences, continued to exist among the people down to the Fall of Judah. It was the catastrophe of the Fall that aroused in the people a spirit of remorse. The pious viewed the sin of idolatry as the crucial national sin. The prophets had predicted doom for the worship of gods of wood and stone. God-fearing kings such as Asa, Jehoshaphat, Hezekiah, and Josiah had destroyed idolatrous cults, but had been unable to root out idolatry entirely. The Fall worked a revolution. The nation accepted the verdict that God's wrath had poured down upon them for the sin of idolatry, and they drew the ultimate conclusion from their monotheistic faith: all traces of idol-worship must be extirpated. It was thus in the realm of the cult that the final victory of monotheism in Israel took place. Henceforth Israel was a nation jealous for its Jealous God.

A NEW SELF-AWARENESS: THE SECOND ISAIAH

It is in this period that Israel's battle against the paganism of the nations was fully joined. Isaiah was the first to conceive of the end of idolatry; Habakkuk and Jeremiah polemicize briefly against Gentile idolatry; but it remained for the Second Isaiah, who flourished at the close of the Exile, to open a full-scale attack on the religion of the nations. His taunts and satires are aimed at idolatry *per se,* the idolatry of all men, not of Israel alone. A front is formed against the religion of the nations which will be extended to whatever land the Jewish Diaspora inhabits. The Second Isaiah is the spokesman for the entire nation. The foreign environment has the effect of heightening Israel's consciousness of its election. It not only remains true to its God, but aspires to broadcast the knowledge of Him throughout the world. Israel becomes, in the words of the Second Isaiah, "the Servant of YHWH." There is a quarrel between Israel and the nations; loyal to its God, Israel is derided and abused by the nations among whom it is dispersed. But Israel fights back, and in the end will be vindicated by a glorious redemption in which the glory of its God will be revealed to all mankind. Israel's religion shall emerge triumphant over paganism, so that the redemption will be national for Israel but spiritual for the rest of mankind. Jerusalem shall become the holy city of all men, and the servant of YHWH shall be exalted and glorified before the eyes of all.

It is a remarkable fact of Israelite history that during the political nadir of the Babylonian Exile the first proselytes to Judaism make their appearance. The Second Isaiah mentions them as "those who joined themselves to YHWH" (Isaiah 56:3-7). They are aliens who have adopted Israelite religion out of religious conviction, an entirely new phenomenon. Formerly one became "converted" to Israelite religion by living in the land of Israel, assimilating Israel's culture, severing all connections with one's homeland and adopting the worship of the national God. The religious assimilation of such "converts" was merely one aspect of their total assimilation into the environment of Israelite Palestine. Now, however, "those who joined themselves to YHWH" attached themselves to a community in exile; the act involved their religious beliefs only.

This was a novelty, and it was to be a long time before the institution of proselytism fully matured. For the present, the novitiates were uncertain of their status. Were they full-fledged members of the Israelite community? The prophet encourages them and promises them that they will share in the ingathering of Israel's dispersed, that God will bring them to His holy mountain and make them rejoice in His Temple.

The appearance of such persons marks the beginning of Israel's impact on the heathen world. The thin trickle of adherents was to become by the beginning of the common era a mighty stream of proselytes and "fearers of God." It was among them that Christianity was eventually to strike roots. Heathendom's wall had been breached.

The Jewish Diaspora was a religious-national body the like of which the pagan world had never seen. It remained loyal to its God yet did not worship him cultically. It was a cultless religious community. For at this time cult and sacrifice were inseparable; sacrifice was the heart of the cult, and without it there could be no normal cult. Yet the Diaspora did not set up altars or build temples and offer sacrifices. It regarded foreign lands as "impure soil," and the singers of Zion's Temple shrank even from singing "the songs of YHWH" in a foreign land (Psalms 137:4). We know of only one temple built by a Diaspora community, the Elephantine temple, erected by an out-of-the-way garrison of Jewish mercenaries in southern Egypt. For the Diaspora as a whole there was only one holy site—Jerusalem—and only one legitimate temple—the one lying in ruins in Zion. Hence no sacrifice could be offered to God; amidst the impurity of pagan lands there could be no cult in any conventional sense.

Under these circumstances a new cult began to be fashioned in the Exile, a cult without sacrifice. This cult comprised fasts in memory of the national calamities attending the Fall (Zechariah 7:3,5; 8:19), confession, and prayer (Isaiah 58). Three times a day Jews knelt and prayed in the direction of Jerusalem (Daniel 6:11). Worship in the synagogue came into being. This worship had no sacrifice, and was independent of a fixed holy city or temple; it was a new creation of Judaism. The Sabbath came to have an important place in the life of the Babylonian Exile. This sublime moral-religious institution had no parallel in paganism. By its nature the Sabbath had no firm roots in the temple cult, so that its observance was possible in the Exile. In all likelihood other festivals were also observed as far as it was possible to do so without sacrifice and temple.

THE RESTORATION: EZRA AND THE TORAH BOOK

The new form of worship was superior to the cult of sacrifices, yet the people continued to hope for the renewal of the sacred ritual in the Jerusalem Temple as of old. In the Diaspora they felt themselves estranged from God and His sanctuary, and they were unable to make the offerings prescribed in the Torah. Their national and eschatological ideals were bound up with Jerusalem and the dynasty of David. Longing for Zion is the theme of the prophet of the age, the Second Isaiah, and the fruit of these longings was the Restoration that took place in the days of Cyrus. This too is one of the marvels of Jewish history after the Fall.

In 539 B.C.E. the Neo-Babylonian empire fell; Cyrus the Persian captured Babylon and founded the Persian world empire. The following year he issued an edict permitting the Jews to return to Jerusalem to rebuild their Temple, and a considerable number of the Babylonian community of exiles seized the opportunity to return. They settled in the tiny Persian province of Judah that consisted almost entirely of Jerusalem and its environs. They were headed by Zerubbabel, the son of Shaltiel—of the Davidic line—and by Joshua, the son of Jehozadak the priest. But "the enemies of Judah and

Benjamin" interfered with the rebuilding of the Temple and managed to delay it for many years. It was not until 516 that the work was completed and the full cult could be reinstituted.

Now the people again inhabited their national land and possessed anew a national body, a sphere in which a national culture could flourish. But the political hopes of the nation were not fulfilled. The Davidic dynasty was not restored, and the greater part of the nation remained in the Diaspora. The walls of Jerusalem remained breached until the year 445, when they were repaired by Nehemiah. Nevertheless, the return and the rebuilding of the Temple did fill a religio-national need. They were an expression of the spirit of repentance. With a great effort the people restored the legitimate cult in the holy land and the chosen city, and so demonstrated their loyalty to God and their yearning to be reconciled with Him. In return they prayed He would show them mercy and renew their days as of old. This was the messianic background of the Restoration.

About a century after the return under Zerubbabel, in the time of Ezra and Nehemiah, an event of enormous significance took place: the Torah was fixed and canonized. In this undertaking, too, the motive was the consciousness of sin. The idea was that true repentance could be shown only if Israel made God's Torah the basis of its life. Now the Torah was a national heritage of Israel from earliest times, but in previous ages it had existed as a type of literature, composed in varied styles and variously formulated by the circles of priests and scholars who cultivated it. It was not a unified book with a fixed and stabilized text. Because of this fluidity it was hard to use as a clear guide in life.

The new aspiration to live by the Torah made it necessary to collect the ancient scrolls, to combine and consolidate them into an organized, integral whole that the people might know the will of God. There arose a desire to establish a canon of sacred writings, authorized by the consent of the people and the sages. The crystallization of a sacred canon was begun in the time of Ezra and Nehemiah with the formation of the Torah book. Josiah had already made the Book of Deuteronomy, discovered in his reign, the law of the land, and had made a covenant with the nation concerning its observance. The undertaking in the time of Ezra and Nehemiah occurred under altered circumstances, and on a much broader basis. Ezra, the priest-scribe, came from Babylonia in 457 and he brought with him a Torah book representing the priestly tradition of the Babylonian exiles. Arrived in Jerusalem, he doubtless encountered differing traditions. The resolve to make the Torah the basis of national life required the organization of these traditions into one book, and Ezra and the collegium of Jerusalem priests and sages took this task upon themselves. Supporting them were "the officers and elders," the autonomous administrators of the province of Judah. Thus the undertaking became a national concern. Later Nehemiah added his authority. The work went on for some thirteen years, during which Ezra also established a class of "interpreters," teachers of the Torah recruited for the most part from among the Levites. It seems that the redaction had been completed even before the coming of Nehemiah, and that the report of the work of the distinguished priest-scribe had already been circulated among the people.

On New Year's Day in 444 the completed Torah was publicly read before the assembled throng in Jerusalem. Ezra stands on a wooden platform, opens the book, and all the people rise. Before reading, Ezra makes a benediction, to which they respond with "Amen" and bow down to the ground. Then they listen with fear and trembling to the words of the Book. The reading takes some six hours, and as it proceeds the "interpreters" explain the difficult passages. The people are moved to tears, for they hear words of God that they knew not before. This public recitation of the Torah is regarded as a special, self-contained ceremony; it is not carried out in the Temple precinct and is not connected with any other cultic act. In this solemn act the Torah was given anew to Israel. Now, however, it was no longer the special possession of the priests, "the holders of the Torah," but was the property of the entire people, who participated in its study. Thus Israelite religion created a noble symbol: the word of God embodied in a book accepted as authoritative by the whole nation, a guide to sanctifying life to the service of God.

To this first stratum of sacred writings there were later added two others, the Prophets and the Hagiographa.

With the formation of a canonical Book of the Torah, oral tradition takes on a new role: it is assigned the task of interpreting the written Torah and of enlarging its domain by a creative exegesis (midrash), to cover every phase of life. The Torah becomes the object of searching study; the science of Torah is developed, and its proponents are the scribes and sages, the new teachers of the people replacing the priest. There is a growing awareness that only through the science of Torah is its fulfillment possible; only through midrash is it possible to discover in the Torah the answers to the ever changing problems of life. After the public reading on New Year's Day a Great Assembly is called to make a new covenant with the people concerning the observance of the Torah. At the same time the assembly draws up a "sure agreement" listing a series of self-imposed injunctions belonging to the category of Oral Law. The people pledge themselves to observe the Torah in accordance with the interpretation of the learned scholars of their age. Both the written and the oral Torah thus began to work on the life of the people simultaneously. This is what is related in Nehemiah 8-10; it is a turning point in the history of Israel.

NEW IDEAS AND IDEALS

It is a widespread notion among historians of Israel that post-Exilic Judaism is epigonous, that its creative impulse waned, that it became petrified. Judaism is alleged to have placed greater value on the observance of externals than on its ethico-religious content. Prophecy ceased, to be replaced by the casuistic study of the letter of the law. The universalism of the prophets—so it is said—gave way to a narrow, nationalistic exclusivism. This evaluation, however, is incorrect. Israelite religion continued fertile and creative throughout the period of the Second Temple, and in spite of appearances the direction of this creativeness was universalistic. Indeed, the Judaism of this age attained heights of universalism beyond anything achieved in the pre-Exilic period.

During the period of the Second Temple monotheism held absolute sway over the entire people; idolatry disappeared. When Antiochus Epiphanes issues a decree enjoining the people to sacrifice to foreign gods they are horrified and rise in armed rebellion. Many undergo torture and death for the "sanctification of the Name." Furthermore we find Jews actively combating paganism everywhere. The prophets only spoke of the end of idolatry; the Judaism of Second Temple times worked to bring it about. Jewish propaganda among the Gentiles increased from generation to generation, reaching vast proportions by the end of our period. Hellenistic Judaism was especially active in this direction. The universalistic essence of Judaism is strikingly exemplified by this popular campaign against idolatry.

Jewish worship during this period became further refined and more catholic. Although the synagogue service was viewed as a parallel to the sacrificial cult of the temple and a substitute for it, in reality it was a new, original creation. The core of the service was not sacrifice, but the soliloquy of the heart and the utterance of the lips. Public reading of the word of God from the Torah and the Prophets was likewise an important element. During this period the ancient hymns were gathered into one collection, the Book of Psalms, which came to be used in the cult. Prayer was gradually formulated and developed into an independent liturgy. Before this, prayer had been for the most part extemporized, according to the need of the moment; in the Torah it is not considered a fixed obligation. Now the form of prayer is fixed together with its times and seasons, and assuming an obligatory character, it takes on the nature of a full-fledged cult. Prayer as a form of the service of God is an innovation of Second Temple times. The new service was independent of any holy site; it could be performed everywhere, within or without the boundaries of Palestine. It thus contributed to the aspiration of Israelite religion to become a universal faith.

The crystallization of the Torah into a canonized book also did much to bring out the universal essence of Israel's religion. The Sacred Scripture becomes the bearer and symbol of the religion, the vehicle by which man is put in touch with the holy. It is the embodiment of the divine word, and makes that word accessible to all men. Historically this was a national literature, properly belonging to one people only, but Israelite religion achieved in it self-contained expression. It could now be possessed anew by any people—it could even be separated from Israel, and history shows that such a separation actually took place. The Samaritans—an ethnic conglomerate of Israelite and foreign elements—adopted Israel's Torah and began tracing their ancestry to the Joseph tribe, claiming to have exclusive possession of the "correct" traditions of Israel. Through Christianity many nations adopted Israel's Bible and began regarding themselves as "true Israel," even to the point of persecuting the Jews for not being as "truly" Israel. The crystallization of the word of God in the Book of the Torah, the repository of divine wisdom, was the necessary prelude to this process.

Toward the end of the fifth or the beginning of the fourth century B.C.E., classical prophecy came to an end. The last of the line of classical prophets is Malachi. And yet prophetic activity did not altogether cease. Prophetic legends continued to be produced—some of which are preserved in the narratives of the Book of Daniel (Daniel 1-6). In the Hasmonean period (142-76 B.C.E.) a literature of prophetic visions again arises, but now in a new form. There are no longer apostle-prophets who come before the people in the name of God. Anonymous (or pseudonymous) prophets—among whom there were doubtless genuine visionaries—were the authors of this new literature. They refrained from writing under their own names, and preferred to ascribe their works to ancient worthies. Of this apocalyptic literature only the Book of Daniel was accepted into the Biblical canon. The rest of it—the Ethiopic and Slavonic Enoch, Jubilees, the Testament of the Twelve Patriarchs, Baruch, Fourth Ezra, and others—remained extracanonical. This literature develops into the Aggada of the Talmud and Midrash; it is also the soil from which early Christian literature sprang.

The apocalyptic literature testifies to the profound changes that Israelite religion underwent in the second half of the Second Temple period. Angelology takes on a new dress. The angels of the Bible are divine agents whose personalities are eclipsed by their function; they are for the most part anonymous and featureless. In the apocalypses, however, angels take on distinct personalities, are assigned fixed roles, and are given names. The first names appear in the Book of Daniel (Gabriel, Michael); many more are mentioned in the extracanonical literature. Satan takes on a new role. While the Bible depicts him always as a member of the divine entourage, the apocalypses promote him to the head of evil spirits. He and his hosts constitute a veritable "kingdom," in opposition to God and His angels. His domain is the underworld, the realm of sin and evil.

At the same time eschatological notions undergo a transformation. Biblical eschatology concerns itself with events that are to take place in this world: the collapse of the heathen empires, the judgment of the nations and the wicked, Israel's redemption, the ingathering of the exiles, the restoration of the Davidic monarchy, the reign of justice, eternal peace. These images remain, but apocalyptic literature sets them a new pattern of transcendental other-worldly visions. At the End of Days there will be not only an earthly war between Israel and the heathen world, but a heavenly battle between the angels of God and the forces of Satan. Judgment Day will also see the doom of the evil spirits that make men stumble.

During our period there develops the image of the messianic redeemer. In Biblical literature the redeemer is God; in the extracanonical literature, as well as in Rabbinic Aggada, he is the messianic King. The image of the Messiah is twofold; he is at once earthly and heavenly. He is the son of David and is expected to restore Israel's monarchy; at the same time he is the "Son of Man," a supernatural being who will judge the sinful angels, conquer Satan, and establish the kingdom of God. The idea of a heavenly redeemer is already hinted at in the Bible: Malachi 3:1 speaks of an angel who shall prepare the way before the God of Judgment on Doomsday, and at the end of the chapter we hear that Elijah—the heavenly man—will come before the great Day of YHWH to bring peace to the earth. According to Daniel 12:1, Michael, the patron angel of Israel, is to fill the role of redeemer. These ideas are crystallized in the extracanonical literature; they dominate early Christian writings.

Against this background a radical change in the concept of the relationship of the soul to God takes place. The Biblical view is that such a relationship exists only during man's life on earth. Death, the realm of "impurity," severs man forever from contact with the holy, and hence from God. "The dead do not praise Yah nor all those who go down into Silence" (Psalms 115:7)—this is the prevailing conception in Biblical literature. It is a melancholy view, in strange contrast to the fundamental optimism of Israelite religion. Grounded in it is Job's wretchedness when he contemplates the injustices of Divine Providence. Ecclesiastes' denial of ultimate values is its child. For Biblical man the problem was not merely one of human destiny; it challenged the sovereignty of God as well. Death seemed to put a limit to divine justice, it appeared to remove man from the realm of divine retribution to beyond God's reach. The thought drove him to despondency.

During Second Temple times new horizons open. The new eschatology includes the belief in retribution for the soul after death, in a Last Judgment for both living and dead, in Paradise and Hell, in resurrection and the Age to Come. The notion of resurrection had already made its appearance in the Bible (e.g., Daniel 12:2, "And many of them that sleep in the dust of the earth shall wake. . . ."); the other images prevail throughout the post-Biblical literature. They became fundamental beliefs of Judaism. Man thus remained within reach of God and His judgment even after death. This brought about a reassessment of man's nature and the meaning of his deeds: man became immortal; his deeds took on eternal significance.

Some scholars are of the opinion that this change took place under the influence of foreign—particularly Persian—ideas. This is questionable; even if true, however, it was the indirect influence of the ideological climate, not the outcome of direct borrowing from the original sources. The Hellenistic period abounded in syncretistic tendencies which were transcultural, and something of these tendencies may have infiltrated Israelite religion, perhaps through Greek mediation. But whatever was adopted from abroad was so transformed as to amount to a new creation, just as was the case with the ancient Near Eastern materials that Israel refashioned at its beginning.

Thus the apocalyptic kingdom of Satan is not a primordial, independent realm, as is the realm of Ahriman, the Persian god of evil. There is no genuine dualism in the Israelite concept. The Satanic kingdom is nothing more than the dominion of sin, of rebellion against God, which was ever regarded in Israelite religion as the fountainhead of evil. In the same way the new angelology is not an expression of dualism, but serves rather to underscore the majesty and exaltedness of the Deity.

The rise of the new doctrine of retribution is another case in point. It did not arise out of the problem of the fate of the individual, the problem that exercises the wisdom writers (Job, Ecclesiastes); it is not at bottom a response to the individual's plea for just deserts. Significantly, it is not at all a product of wisdom, but of later prophetic literature: it is dealt with in the Book of Daniel and the extracanonical apocalypses. The problem is the destiny of the people of Israel and its religion. The new doctrine included, of course, a solution to the problem of the individual, but the doctrine arose out of the national issue. The burning question in apocalyptic literature concerns, first of all, the national-religious adversity. Why is Israel downtrodden? How long will heathendom reign? Goaded on by this enigma, Israelite religion evolved its new doctrine of retribution.

The ancient national blessings promised in the Torah and the Prophets were still looked for. The later writers, too, dream of the ingathering of the dispersed, of a rebuilt Jerusalem and a restored monarchy, of earthly prosperity. But it would seem that these rewards were no longer fully satisfying. Israel's battle with the pagans was not for material values. Jewry was fighting for the sake of God. And the new doctrine opened the way to the Divine Presence. Death itself became rich with promise: it became a way to God. The thought that death removed man from God, even if a man died a martyr, was too cruel to bear. It was a dreadful flaw in divine justice. Now the flaw was repaired. The new doctrine was first enunciated in the visions of the Book of Daniel which arose out of the agony of the Syrian-Greek persecution in the days of Antiochus IV. The national and religious redemption embraces the living and the dead; it carries with it the promise of eternal life in the Divine Presence. In this way the ancient yearnings for intimacy with God, so movingly expressed by the Psalmist—"My soul thirsteth for Thee, My flesh pineth away for Thee"—were finally fulfilled. The Biblical idea that man was created in the image of God, and that God had made him "but a little less than the angels," attained its full meaning.

In the new doctrine of retribution the basic idea of Israelite monotheism reached its ultimate expression. Although Israelite religion had done away with the multiplicity of divine powers by making the one God omnipotent, a shadow of the former plurality still lingered on in the concept of "impurity." The realm of impurity was set apart from the holy, it was something un-Godly. Death also was removed from God. Although Israelite religion had no room for a god of death, the nether world of the shades—by virtue of belonging to the realm of impurity—existed, as it were, beyond the domain of God. We have already seen that in the ancient religion the nether world was outside the scope of divine justice—here the righteous man is not rewarded nor the wicked punished. It was, then, virtually an autonomous sphere, and the domain of God was correspondingly contracted. The new doctrine of retribution changed all this. While not abolishing the notions of impurity connected with death, it nonetheless transferred death to the realm of God. The soul of the deceased "ascends" heavenward and his body too is kept by God and his angels until the Judgment. The souls of the righteous are with God. Thus a remarkable metamorphosis occurs: the nether world, the sphere of the impurity of death, is embraced by divine justice. The last trace of an independent realm is erased; the idea of unity reaches its limit.

And so we may confidently say that even if alien ideological influences were at work here, Judaism was not conscious of their foreignness. What it absorbed became bone of its bone—although it is true that there was some opposition for a time (e. g., on the part of the Sadducees). The new doctrine remedied what was a serious defect in ancient Israelite religion when compared with the religion of Egypt or Persia or with the Hellenistic mysteries. It is doubtful that paganism could have been bested without this doctrine. The most sensational tidings of both Christianity and Islam were, after all, the doctrines of the Resurrection and the Last Judgment.

The universalistic tendency of Israelite religion during this age is evident not only in its quarrel with paganism and its propaganda, but also in its condemnation of the Gentiles for their paganism. The view of Biblical writers is that idolatry, though fatal to Israel, is not reckoned against the nations; they are judged only for moral sins. That idolatry is a sin also for the nations is perhaps hinted at in Jeremiah 50:38 and Daniel 5:23. In the post-Biblical literature of Judaism it becomes a dominant theme: idolatry is a sin for all peoples, and is the source of moral evil as well. Consequently Judaism's verdict concerning the nations becomes the more severe. But this severity does not spring from a spirit of narrow exclusiveness. On the contrary, it is the outcome of the view that Israel's monotheism is a universal faith, designed for the nations as well as for Israel. To cling to idolatry is therefore a sin for all men, and all men will be punished for it. This condemnation of pagan man was taken over from Judaism by Christianity and Islam.

A product of this aspiration to universality was the institution of proselytism. Biblical religion knows of new adherents, but their "conversion" is a gradual process, not a single, deliberate act. The early "convert" was the foreigner who decided to settle in Israelite Palestine, who gradually assimilated Israel's culture and religion, and ended by worshiping Israel's God. The new proselytism which was purely religious originated in the Exile. Its first representatives were those "who joined themselves to YHWH," mentioned by the Second Isaiah. But it was more than a century before the institution of proselytism, with its ritual that immediately conferred full membership in the household of Israel, was finally developed. And so we find the Judaizing Samaritans—alien adherents to Judaism—rejected in the time of Zerubbabel (Ezra 4:1-3). Similarly, at the time of Ezra the foreign, though non-idolatrous, wives of Jews were forcibly separated from their husbands. It is quite plain that the ceremony which could at once have equalized foreigner and Jew, and allowed them to marry, had not yet come into being. Exactly when it was instituted we cannot say; that it had evolved by Hasmonean times is evident from the forcible conversion of the Edomites by John Hyrcanus.

Proselytism is a uniquely Jewish innovation; it has no parallel in the ancient world. In it the universal essence of Isralite religion is given final expression, and the national symbols of Israelite religion became supranational. Through it Judaism was enabled to become a world religion. Christianity and Islam adopted proselytism, and by it were enabled to win many nations. That Judaism itself did not enjoy similar success, despite its innovation of proselytism, cannot be attributed—as is usually done by Christian historians—to any alleged Jewish exclusivism. Israel's political and material failure stood in the way of its advancement. The nations could not bring themselves to accept the religion of a people whom they had defeated and enslaved. But they could and did accept Israelite monotheism after it had become separated from the people of Israel, and had been brought to them by prophets whom Israel would not acknowledge. This happened twice in history: in Christianity and in Islam. Because of this circumstance the universal religion of Judaism remained the national faith of the people of Israel.

JUDAISM AND HELLENISM

During the very period in which the edifice of Judaism was being consolidated, the culture of Greece—the glory of polytheistic civilization—was reaching its climax. Both of these cultures have points in common, and yet they are utterly distinct. They were destined to conflict with each other and to influence each other, but they forever remained two worlds. Judaism embodied the idea of divine revelation, of prophecy and the holy spirit. Its faith was in a God who gave man Torah and *mitzvot* to show him the path of life and virtue. It aspired to mold life in accordance with the inspired utterances of its ancient prophets. Greek culture was distinguished by its idea of scientific reason. It aspired to perfect a system of thought, a world view based on rational awareness. It had faith in the redeeming power of the intellect. It created science and philosophy and believed that reason could show man the path of life and virtue.

In the time of Alexander the Great of Macedonia, Greek enlightenment began to be diffused among many nations. It was spread by Greeks and Macedonians who lived in the areas under Hellenistic rule. The upper classes were its primary devotees. In the course of time Hellenism conquered Rome also, and with this conquest attained universal dominion. At the same time Judaism was the heritage of a scattered, exiled, and subject people. The Hasmonean kingdom was a mere episode; Rome put an end to it and vanquished Jewry.

And yet the lesson of history is that the men of that age accepted the Jewish gospel of a redeeming God and rejected the Greek gospel of redeeming reason. The struggle between monotheism and paganism ended with the utter collapse of paganism, and the debris buried Hellenistic enlightenment as well. This is certainly not without significance. It indicates that there was something in Judaism that overbore the great appeal of Hellenism. The heart of man was captivated by the message of the one supreme God, sovereign and unfettered by blind fate, a God whose sacred moral will governs all, and is the source of man's moral obligation. The spirit of man was elevated by the message of his moral freedom and the injunction, "So choose thou life!" The soul of man responded to the tidings of a gracious and merciful God. The moral pathos of prophecy triumphed over the moral philosophy of reason. Men were dismayed and yet heartened by the demand for repentance that Christianity and Islam adopted from Judaism and announced to many peoples. Repentance was the way to the redemption of man. The war upon paganism was at the same time a war upon the idolatrous deification of reason, the faith that rational knowledge could save man. Moral goodness shall redeem, not the power of the intellect! And since man can choose goodness, the keys to redemption are in his hands. The nations knelt before these tidings.

Has the warning against the idolatrous worship of reason become irrelevant today? The events of our time show clearly that the prophetic demand for a turn of heart is still relevant. If the prophetic pathos no longer moves us, if the light of Isaiah's vision has indeed failed, we must ask in trepidation, is there yet hope for man?

THE
HELLENISTIC
AGE

RALPH MARCUS

Born in San Francisco, California, in 1900, Ralph Marcus was educated in the public schools of New York City and pursued graduate studies in classical and Semitic philology at Harvard University and at Columbia University, where he received his doctorate in 1927. He has taught Semitic languages at Columbia and the Jewish Institute of Religion in New York City. Since 1943 he has served as Professor of Hellenistic Culture in the Oriental and Greek departments and in the Theological Faculty at the University of Chicago. He has been an Exchange Professor at the University of Frankfort and will lecture in 1957 at the University of Utrecht as a Fulbright Exchange Professor. He is the author of almost two hundred monographs and studies in the fields of Biblical, Hellenistic, and ancient Near Eastern literature, history, and religion and is a contributor to the Encyclopedia Britannica and the Merriam-Webster Dictionary. Among his notable works are translations of Josephus and Philo in the Loeb Classical Library.

5

THE CHALLENGE
OF GRECO-ROMAN CULTURE

The medieval poet and philosopher Judah Halevi has his protagonist declare in the second book of the *Kuzari* that "Israel among the nations is like the heart among the members of the body, stronger and healthier than all of them." To the Hebrews, as to other ancient peoples, the heart was the seat of mental and emotional as well as physical activity; so perhaps it is not too fanciful to suggest, translating Halevi's statement into modern anthropological terms, that just as man is distinguished from all the other animals by his greater ability to adapt himself to changes in his natural environment, so the Jews are distinguished from all other peoples by their greater ability to adapt themselves to changes in their cultural environment. The Jews have always shown remarkable skill in nicely combining flexibility and inflexibility. How they managed to maintain the core of their ethnic-religious culture after long centuries of intimate contact with the Babylonian, Egyptian, Hittite, Canaanite, Assyrian, Persian, Greek, and Roman cultures has remained an enigma to historians and a mystery to theologians. For though we may agree with Toynbee that of two neighboring peoples one will become great by accepting the challenge presented by a drastically changed environment, while the other will stagnate through failure to meet the challenge, we still do not know by what device of evolution or providence the one people, and not the other, stands up to the challenge.

Such reflections suggest themselves as we set out on this survey of Judaism over a period of some six centuries, roughly from 300 B.C.E. to 300 C.E., a period during which the Jews were in close contact with the two great peoples of the West, the Greeks and the still not fully christianized Romans—the former prominent for intellectual and artistic achievement, and the latter for political power. Not only were the Jews perilously tested in battle with the armies of Ptolemaic Egypt and Seleucid Syria and the Roman legions; they were constantly exposed to the cultures of these peoples, both in Palestine and in many communities of the Diaspora. Yet the body of Judaism remained intact, even if changes occurred in its structure.

Before we go any further, let us take a look at this period in the larger perspective of world history and in the light of our present-day philosophy of history. We may distinguish three chief eras of close and continuous contact between Mediterranean Europe and the Near East, eras that had a fateful bearing on the cultural history of a much larger part of mankind. These are the Bronze Age, roughly from 3000 to 1200 B.C.E.; the Hellenistic-Roman period; and the twentieth century. In the period here surveyed, Europe, as represented by the Greeks and Romans, was in more intimate contact with the Orient, represented by Jews, Egyptians, Phoenicians, Syrians, Asianics—in a word, the peoples of Asia Minor—and Iranians, than it had been for the previous thousand years, or was to be for another fifteen hundred years, except perhaps briefly during the Crusades. In this long perspective, we may regard the impact of Hellenism upon the Jews and the Jews' reaction to it as part of the rhythmic ebb and flow between the cultures of the East and the West. At the same time we find that the Jews, though classed by the Greeks and Romans with the peoples of the Orient, were in many ways as different from their Eastern neighbors as from the Europeans, and in some ways, particularly in their civic conscience, they were closer to Greece than to the Orient. To guard against an oversimplified conception of "Eastern" and "Western" cultures, it should be borne in mind that one of the great "Oriental" nations, the Iranians or Persians, were descendants of the invaders of Asia, who were cousins of the invaders of Italy and Greece; that is, the Iranians were members of the Indo-European family.

RESEMBLANCE TO THE MODERN WORLD

The first dramatic meeting of East and West, that between the Persian armies of Xerxes and the citizen militias of Greece in the fifth century B.C.E., is memorialized in the *History* of Herodotus and the *Persae* of Aeschylus. We have no such memorials to Alexander the Great's reversal of this movement when he invaded Asia in 334 B.C.E. Yet later historical sources enabled us to follow Alexander's triumphs for the next ten years till his death in 323 B.C.E., by which time he had established the military and political power of the West over an immense area extending from the eastern border of Iran to the western border of Egypt. The conquests of Alexander, political as well as military, brought about a momentous change in the cultural pattern of the Mediterranean and Near Eastern area. It introduced the period of Hellenistic culture, which is commonly dated from about 300 to 100 B.C.E. To the cultural historian, however, appreciative of the primacy of religion and of the fact that the Near East remained largely Hellenistic in culture even under Roman rule, the period may be regarded as lasting till 325 C.E., when Christianity became the state religion of the Roman Empire.

Let us now consider the characteristics of this Hellenistic culture, which left a deep impression on Diaspora Jewry and at last touched Palestinian Jewry at various less vital but still significant points. "Hellenistic," of course, must not be confused with "Hellenic"; the latter term denotes Greek culture in the period before Alexander, the so-called classical period, while the former refers to the fusion of Greek and Oriental culture in the period after Alexander, when most of the urban populations of the Levant were as much at home in the Greek lingua franca, the *koiné*, as modern Levantines are in French. Once a neglected subject, Hellenistic culture has come to be regarded by most scholars as being in many ways more interesting than that of the classical period, not least because of its remarkable resemblances to our own.

One significant similarity is that Alexander and some of the rulers who followed him, encouraged by the philosophers at their courts, were inspired by the idea of a world civilization. "Ecumenical," which appears so often in the writings of modern Protestant theologians, is derived from the Greek word *oikoumenē,* which means "inhabited land" and assumed in Hellenistic thought the connotation of something like "one world" or "the brotherhood of man," although, of course, without the full Biblical flavor of the latter phrase. Alexander himself deliberately sought to fuse the best elements of Greek and Persian culture; among other things, he encouraged intermarriage between his Macedonian officers and the women of the Persian aristocracy. His successors established scores of Greek city-states throughout Egypt, Palestine, Phoenicia, Syria, Asia Minor, Mesopotamia, Iran, and adjacent regions. These new foundations or refoundations of older Oriental cities became centers of Greek political institutions, science, and art in western Asia and North Africa.

At the same time that Greek culture was spreading throughout the *oikoumenē* or inhabited world by means of the *polis*, or city-state, with its council, assembly, magistrates, civic cult, gymnasium, temple, and public buildings, the *polis* itself as an autonomous political entity, resembling a modern state, was giving way to the *oikoumenē* in the political thinking of most educated men, whether Greeks or Orientals. In fact, two polar movements were greatly intensified in this age, one of them toward individualism and the other toward world citizenship, or cosmopolitanism. The latter term was a creation of Stoic philosophy, itself a product of the Hellenistic period. Along with the idea of world community there flourished, first in Greek philosophy and later in Roman law, the idea of a "law of nations." Maintaining itself through all the ideological battles of medieval and early modern times, this idea may be regarded as the secular counterpart of the Judeo-Christian notion of world brotherhood.

Its manifestations still abstract, there was a growing consciousness of the individual's place in society and of the relation of one society to another. More colorful were certain other ideas characteristic of the Hellenistic period. For example, there was a mounting curiosity about the beliefs and customs of foreign peoples, especially those of the Orient, with whom Westerners were becoming better acquainted through exploration and trade. And there seems to have been a large appetite for the multiplying accounts of ideal societies, usually located in faroff places. Such utopian literature satisfied the nostalgic desire to escape the painful present by evoking a golden past or anticipating a golden future. It played the same role among the pagans as did the prophetic and apocalyptic books among the Jews. This romantic political bent found some satisfaction in the growth of the idea of a divine ruler, whether in the person of a Hellenistic king or a Roman emperor, who in the language of many public inscriptions and in the orations of Greek philosophers was proclaimed "a savior and benefactor of the human race."

The complexity of social and economic relations in the Hellenistic-Roman period also reminds us startlingly of our own age. The ideas of socialism and communism assumed concrete form in proletarian strikes and slave revolts. The contrasts between rich and poor provoked the savage criticism of pagan satirists and aroused the benevolent concern of the Stoic philosophers, whose reactions were not very different from those of the authors of Ezra-Nehemiah and Ben Sira. Concern for the less privileged classes, especially women and slaves, was becoming marked. Not only did the average woman in a Hellenistic city emerge from the strict seclusion which classical Greek authors have made familiar, but many Hellenistic women achieved important civic office, to say nothing of unusually influential queens, of whom Cleopatra is only the most picturesque example. Perhaps the position of the Hasmonean queen Salome Alexandra was a reflection of the newly emancipated status of women in the Hellenistic age.

As the position of women improves, romantic love appears in literature. It is a mistake to suppose that the ancients were unfamiliar with the idea. As only one example, there is Apollonius Rhodius' poem about the Argonauts, in which he describes how the young Medea fell in love with Jason at first sight, and how her knees trembled and how she blushed and almost swooned and in general behaved like the heroine of an early Victorian novel. Actually the first European novels appeared in the Hellenistic period; what we call the Greek Romances are stories full of romantic lovers separated by cruel parents, or kidnaped heroines and dauntless rescuers, and of other vicissitudes that are amusingly reminiscent of nineteenth-century backstairs paper novels and twentieth-century movie serials like *The Perils of Pauline*. If there is a difference, it is that the Greek romances are improved by philosophical and religious sentiments. In both Hellenistic and Latin poetry the "slavery of love" is celebrated in much the same fashion as it was fifteen hundred years later by the troubadors and minnesingers and writers of chivalrous epics.

Slaves begin to be regarded with more humane feelings and are given greater legal protection. Foreign groups in Rome, Alexandria, Antioch, and other large cities organize themselves in societies whose object is to make them feel more at home and to assure them of various material and spiritual benefits. The period witnesses the rise of "benevolent societies," or fraternities, of guilds and clubs, that give the individual more status and more comfort. They are comparable to the more formal organization of Jewish communities in the Diaspora.

Greek intellectual activity takes the form of greater specialization in natural science and technology. Owing in part to fuller acquaintance with Babylonian texts translated from cuneiform into Greek, the sciences, especially astronomy and mathematics, undergo a development that was not surpassed until the sixteenth century. If there was no lack of mechanical skill in the Hellenistic age, there was a lack of the social and economic incentive that would have placed it in the service of industry. Slaves were cheap, and besides, the interest was in theoretical rather than applied science. Plutarch tells us that Archimedes was characteristically reluctant to invent military and naval machines for the ruler of Syracuse. The term "liberal arts" is a reflection of the Greek distinction between studies suitable to gentlemen and those which they called "mechanical."

The spirit of Hellenistic culture is further illustrated in literature and art. Both are full of vivid contrasts, such contrasts as one expects to find in a complex and sophisticated urban society. On the one hand we have the ideal of heroic life, on the other the ideal of quietism. In the midst of constant warfares, stress is laid on peace and family virtues and comforts. Over against individualism we find the preaching of retirement and resignation, often ending in pessimism. Poetry and painting frequently picture a quiet country life in opposition to the tumult of the city. Together with an interest in types and in allegorical abstract symbolism, we have genre studies and individualistic realism. In literature the tendency to ornament and baroque is matched by the use of naturalism and purism.

Religion and ethics play a dominant role in the philosophies of the schools, replacing to some extent both the state religion and mythology in the thinking of educated people. There was no lack of keen critics of idolatry and mechanical sacrifices. The Epicurean philosophy taught that although the gods exist they do not intervene in human affairs, and that it is man's duty as well as to his advantage to free himself of the superstitious fear of death and future punishment. No wonder the Rabbis used the word *apikoros,* a corruption of *Epikouros,* to designate an unbeliever. Stoicism, probably the most popular philosophy among all classes, amounting almost to a religion, sought to rationalize the Olympian gods by means of allegorical explanations of the myths found in Homer, Hesiod, and others. Divine names were given fanciful etymologies, so that the gods appear as abstractions or personifications of natural forces or moral qualities. For example, the accusative case of the name *Zeus* is *Zēna,* and the *Zēna* is facilely brought into relation with the common Greek verb *zēn* "to live," and in this way Zeus becomes a symbol of the vital power of nature. Moreover, the widespread tendency to identify Greek gods and goddesses with their counterparts among the deities of the Egyptians, Syrians, Iranians, and other peoples naturally gave rise to a conception, however vaguely defined, of a universal divine power, whether male or female, or in the form of a divine triad, that foreshadows the trinitarian monotheism of Christianity.

In perspective, none of the aspects of Hellenistic-Roman culture appears to be as significant as religion, for it was at this time that the chief religions of the West and of western Asia (except for Islam) were born or about to to born: Rabbinic Judaism, Christianity, Mandaism, Manicheanism, Gnosticism, the Oriental-Greek mystery cults, and the quasi-religions of Orphism, Hermeticism, and Neo-Pythagoreanism.

In the pagan religion of the Hellenistic-Roman period we have the same revealing contrasts as in other fields. Side by side with manifestations of popular religion such as divination, astrology—the favorite of several emperors—and magic (in which Hebrew divine names played a prominent part), we find a sublimation of religious feeling in ascetic and mystical movements, such as Orphism with its demand for purification of body and soul, and the mystery-cults with their initiations, revelations, and preaching of salvation in a life after death. One of the greatest modern authorities on Greek religion, Professor Martin P. Nilsson of Lund University in Sweden, epitomizes the subject of Hellenistic-Roman religion, to which he has devoted more than fifty years of study, by singling out as the three chief pillars of the new pagan religion the monotheistic tendency, the belief in power, and the contempt for materialism.

When Alexander the Great took the place of the last Achemenian king of Persia as ruler of western Asia, including Palestine, the inhabitants of Judea had been aware of the achievements of the Greeks and Macedonians during most of the preceding two centuries of Persian rule. Judean taxes had contributed to the expenses of the wars between Persia and Greece; Judea probably furnished supplies to the navy of its neighbor, Phoenicia, which was an important part of the Persian fleet; she had been importing Greek products and Greek wares, and was familiar with Greek, especially Athenian, coinage. Thus the Jews were not confronted by complete strangers in the persons of the Greco-Macedonian armies that rapidly conquered Palestine and occupied its chief cities.

Let us briefly examine the condition in which the Jewish community of Palestine found itself on the eve of Alexander's conquest of the Persian Empire. Judea was a small territory, most of which served as a kind of appendage to the disproportionately large capital city of Jerusalem. The religious leaders of the small and not too prosperous province of Yehud, as the Persians called it, whether statesmen like Zerubbabel and Nehemiah, prophets like Malachi,

Zechariah, and Second Isaiah, or priests like Ezra, had succeeded in molding a surprisingly homogeneous state. The chief traits of their culture were the acceptance of the Mosaic Torah as a kind of civic-religious constitution; the strongly centralized cult administered by the Zadokite priesthood of Jerusalem; universal education for the male children of most citizens; the beginnings of what we may call adult education through the synagogues in communities outside Jerusalem; devotion to the glorious memories of Davidic kingship; and a hope for the ultimate triumph of the God of Israel over the false gods of the Gentiles.

This cultural homogeneity was remarkable not for a complete absence of tensions and differences of opinion—which would be an unnatural state of affairs for any free people—but for the fact that it was maintained in spite of these tensions and differences. There was tension between universalists and nationalists or isolationists, the former to be identified perhaps with the descendants of the Judeans who had escaped deportation to Babylonia, the latter with the returned exiles. There was tension between the higher priests, who were conservative, and the lower priests, including the Levites and lay scholars, who were not only more liberal in their interpretation of Scripture but were also interested in democratizing the cult and improving the condition of the lower classes. There was tension between those who favored alliances through marriage or political interest with the Samaritans and other neighboring peoples, and those who feared any such contact. There was tension, reflected in the prophecies of the Second Isaiah, between the more sober, institutional-minded religious leaders and the more mystical or romantic types, who were impressed by the dramatic myth of Zoroastrianism and therefore inclined toward dualism, who believed in angels and demons, and speculated about a day of judgment and a future life of rewards and punishments for the good and the wicked.

But in spite of these tensions there was enough momentum in the great traditions canonized in the five books of Moses, the histories of the Kingdom, the messages of the Prophets, and other writings to enable the Jews of the post-Exilic period not only to withstand the forces of disintegration during Persian rule but also to resist the even more powerful pressures of the Greco-Roman, Christian, and Moslem cultures throughout the centuries to come.

RESPONSE IN PALESTINE

The stories told by Josephus and the Rabbis about Alexander the Great being welcomed to Jerusalem by the high priest and a solemn procession of Jewish dignitaries are probably historical fiction; yet there can be no doubt that the Macedonian king's victorious campaign in Palestine, Egypt and Syria had an immediate impact upon Judea. For one thing, Alexander left Macedonian garrisons in Samaria and other cities not too far away; for another, the Macedonian kings who followed Alexander as rulers of Palestine—the Antigonids of Greece, the Ptolemies of Egypt, and the Seleucids of Syria—built a network of Hellenistic cities on the very borders of Judea. During the early Hellenistic period there were some thirty such centers of more or less Hellenistic culture along the coasts of Philistia and Phoenicia, in Trans-Jordan, and immediately north and south of Judea. Since most of these Hellenistic or Hellenistic-Oriental *poleis* were within a radius of about fifty miles from Jerusalem, and some were important seaports, others administrative centers of the Ptolemies and Seleucids, it is clear that many Jews had abundant opportunity to become acquainted with the political forms, as well as the religion and the art, of the Greeks.

Hellenistic influences made themselves felt both indirectly and directly soon after the Ptolemies began their hundred-year rule of Palestine in 300 B.C.E. We know from recent archeological discoveries that the Hellenistic cities on the borders of Judea were rich in Greek architecture and art, and we can even specify in some detail just what Greek styles were most popular. Bearing the heads and insignia of Green-Oriental gods carved in relief, silver and bronze coins of the Greek and Hellenistic-Oriental cities circulated freely in Palestine, so that the Jews were acquainted with Greek myths and cults.

Even provincial cities in Palestine were at times centers of Hellenistic culture, as is shown by the number of famous pagan poets and philosophers who came from the region: for example, Menippus, Meleager, and Philodemus of Gadara, which was a few miles from the Jordan and the Lake of Galilee; Boethus of Sidon in Phoenicia; and Antiochus of Ascalon in Philistia.

Nor is it an accident that some of the Greek myths most popular at this time had their setting in or near Palestine. The rock from which Perseus rescued Andromeda was near Jaffa, and Herakles was sometimes identified with the Semitic god Melkarth of Tyre in Phoenicia. Moreover, a Greek writer named Claudius Iolaus wrote about the ancient friendship of Judeans and Spartans—a friendship that is alluded to in the First Book of Maccabees, which says that Areus, the king of Sparta, wrote to the Jewish high priest Onias III, reminding him that "the Spartiates and the Jews are brothers and are of the stock of Abraham."

More direct, of course, was the effect of Ptolemaic rule in Palestine during the third century B.C.E. Although we have no detailed knowledge of this period, except for a few brief intervals, we do have a fair general idea of the course of events, thanks not only to Josephus and certain pagan writers on Hellenistic history, but especially to the Zenon papyri discovered in Egypt about thirty years ago. This valuable collection of contemporary documents contains many letters written from and about Palestine by a certain Zenon, the business agent of Apollonius, finance minister under the Egyptian King Ptolemy II Philadelphus, who ruled during the first half of the third century B.C.E.

From these various sources it appears that while the Ptolemaic rulers maintained strict control over the political and economic life of Palestine, the Jews were allowed a large measure of cultural and religious freedom. But though the Jewish community was represented, at least in form, by the high priests of the Oniad family (descendants of the line of Zadok going back to the time of Solomon), the actual conduct of internal affairs—especially the collection of taxes for the Ptolemaic treasury—and of political relations with the Egyptian rulers was in the hands of the Tobiad family. This family were descendants of "Tobiah the Ammonite," a nominal Jew according to the Book of Nehemiah, who was hostile to the religious reforms of Nehemiah and Ezra.

In the Hellenistic period a descendant and namesake of Tobiah served as a local military commander of the Ptolemaic government and made his headquarters in a fortified castle in Trans-Jordan (modern Araq el-Emir), which from the appearance of the extant ruins was a mixture of Persian and Greek styles. This Tobiah was on rather free and easy terms with King Ptolemy II Philadelphus, if we may judge from two of his letters included among the Zenon papyri. Although he was related to the high priests of Jerusalem, he did not hesitate to use pagan religious expressions in his Greek letters.

A later Tobiad, named Joseph, was a nephew of the high priest Onias II and served as tax collector in Palestine for King Ptolemy III Euergetes. He seems to have been a rival of the high priest for chief authority in the Jewish community, although we are not clear about how authority was divided between them. It is clear, however, from the detailed, though sometimes embellished, account given by Josephus of the struggle for power between various Tobiads and Oniads (both families being divided in political loyalties), that there was a considerable amount of Hellenization among the ruling classes of Jews, whether they lived in Jerusalem or in such marginal regions as Trans-Jordan. Throughout this whole period many of the relatives and friends of the Oniad high priests (and later some of the usurping high priests themselves) behaved like the Roman Catholic clerics in high office during the Renaissance: outwardly observant of the Mosaic Law but rather pagan in feeling and thought.

With the conquest of Palestine by the Seleucid king Antiochus III the Great about 200 B.C.E., there was no important immediate change in the civic status of the Jews, except that Antiochus, more liberal than the Ptolemies, granted the Jewish community a sort of charter of liberties which recognized their right to be governed by their own "constitution" (*politeia*), namely, the Mosaic Law. Unfortunately, the relations between the Seleucid rulers and their Jewish subjects soon deteriorated for a variety of reasons. Antiochus' son, Seleucus IV, attempted to seize the deposits of money in the treasury of the Temple in Jerusalem and Antiochus IV Epiphanes interfered with the religious observances of pious Jews and tried to introduce pagan customs into Jerusalem and the towns of Judea. But these things were more than a manifestation of anti-Jewish feeling. They were in large measure the result of the struggle for political and economic power between two factions of the Jewish ruling classes, both of them largely Hellenized and contemptuous of the religious as well as national traditions of their fellow Jews.

Probably the most powerful single motive for the invasion of Judea by the Syro-Macedonian armies of the Seleucids was the solicitation of the Hellenized Jewish aristocrats, both priestly and lay, who thought it would be to their advantage to have Jerusalem made into a Hellenistic *polis*, perhaps with the new name of Antioch. Their attitude is described in archaic Biblical Hebrew by the author of I Maccabees as follows: "In those days there went out from Israel lawless ones and they persuaded many, saying, Let us go and make a covenant with the Gentiles around us because from the time that we were separated from them many evils have come upon us." More precise is the account given in II Maccabees, originally written in Greek, that Jason, brother of the high priest Onias III, bribed the Seleucid king to make him high priest in place of his brother and to let him build a gymnasium and an *ephebeum* (a Hellenistic youth center) in Jerusalem. "And when the king assented," this author continues, "Jason on coming into power, at once proceeded to transform his coreligionists into a Greek mold." Besides building a gymnasium in the very shadow of the Temple, Jason encouraged the priests to neglect their duties in order to take part in athletic games, dressed as Greeks, and he even sent envoys to represent Jerusalem at the pagan festival in honor of Herakles at Tyre, giving them three hundred silver drachmas to contribute to the cost of the pagan sacrifices! It would be hard to imagine a severer blow to the morale of pious Jews. The acts of the Hellenizers must have seemed even more offensive than the subsequent attempt of Antiochus Epiphanes to forbid the practice of Judaism.

This desperate illness of the Jewish nation found its desperate cure in the armed revolt led by the Hasmonean Mattathias and his sons against the Jewish "loyalists" and their Seleucid masters. Supported by the great masses of Jews, the Hasmoneans not only won religious freedom, but established an independent state, even adding new territory and forcibly Judaizing the neighboring lands of Idumea and Galilee. Their imperialist activities later incurred the strong disapproval of some of the unworldly Hasidim or "pious ones," from whom the Essenes sprang.

Yet the same foreign influences that provoked the Jews to revolt under Mattathias were at work, even if much less strongly and consistently, during most of the hundred-year rule of the Hasmoneans, especially in the second half of the period. The necessity of maintaining diplomatic relations with Rome and other states involved the training of Jewish envoys and officials versed in Greek and Hellenistic usages.

On the other hand, these envoys to the West may sometimes have been the bearers of Jewish culture to the Gentiles, or by helping to better the morale of Diaspora Jews, may have helped to make converts to Judaism. A Roman writer of historical anecdotes named Valerius Maximus tells us that in the year 139 B.C.E. the praetor of Rome "forced the Jews to go back to their homes because they tried to corrupt Roman morals through their cult of Jupiter Sabazius" (probably an error for YHWH Sabaoth, "the Lord of Hosts"). Since this happened about a year after the Hasmonean ruler Simon sent Numenius, son of Antiochus, and Antipater, son of Jason, as envoys to the Roman Senate, one suspects that the presence of the Jewish dignitaries in Rome stimulated the Jewish community there to further zeal in calling attention to the virtues of Judaism.

It is not surprising to find presumably pious Jews like these envoys bearing Greek names and having fathers with Greek names. This was a common occurrence throughout the Hellenistic-Roman period. Nor were Greek names by any means confined to important officials dealing with foreign governments. The Mishnaic treatise *Pirke Abot,* which gives the chain of scholarly tradition from Moses to the time of Rabbi Judah the Patriarch, shows that several of the great Pharisaic authorities also bore Greek names: for example, Antigonus of Socho, Dositheus, a pupil of Shammai, and Tryphon or Terpon (Tarphon).

The later Hasmoneans diverged more and more from the policies and practices of the earlier Maccabees and their Hasidic supporters. John Hyrcanus, son of Simon and grandson of Mattathias, broke with the Pharisees and became an adherent of the Sadducees, the successors of the priestly Hellenizers who had been attacked by his grandfather. Jewish rulers became increasingly involved in foreign wars and international politics, grew dependent on foreign mercenaries, and showed a marked tendency to imitate the style of Hellenistic kings, as in coinage and titulary.

Various events intensified the process of Hellenization and, in a lesser degree, Romanization. There were the intervention of Rome in Palestine under Pompey the Great in 63 B.C.E., the quarrels between the rival Hasmonean claimants to the throne, and the eventual recognition of the Idumean Herod as king of Judea in 40 B.C.E.—although the essence of Judaism was not greatly affected. The process naturally continued throughout the long reign of Herod and the half-century of rule by Roman procurators down to the outbreak of the Jewish revolt against Rome in 66 C.E. In some ways this growing Hellenization is even more apparent, curiously enough, in the very period (the first three centuries of the common era) when the Rabbis of Palestine were consolidating the foundations of Talmudic Judaism.

Let us illustrate some of these various forms of Hellenistic-Roman influence. First of all there is the impressive fact that the Hebrew and Aramaic languages of the early Talmudic period contained well over two thousand words of Greek and Latin origin. These foreign words were by no means confined to the speech of officials and learned Jews, but formed part of the everyday speech of the people, and supplied important terms in such fields as government, economy, law, and technology as well as art, science, and even theology. Any number of instances of the invasion of Greek and Latin into Jewish life could be cited, some of them amusing. For example, when the Rabbis decreed after the war of Quietus in 117 C.E. that no man should teach his son Greek, the very word they used to refer to this war was not the common Hebrew word *milhamah* but the Greek word *polemos.* Again, when a Palestinian rabbi in a popular sermon referred to "the chair of Moses," one of the usual architectural features of a synagogue, he called the chair by its Greek name *kathedra*.

At this point we may comment on what is perhaps the most remarkable example of the way the current of Hellenistic art flowed all about the citadel of Jewish religious life in Palestine without noticeably affecting it. No institution or religious form is more nearly central to Rabbinic and therefore to medieval and modern Judaism than the synagogue, that miniature and local counterpart of the Temple in Jerusalem (a *miqdash me'at,* "small sanctuary," some of the Rabbis called it), so admirably able to take the place of the Temple when the Romans destroyed it. Almost all the synagogues, of which about forty dating from the Roman period have been excavated in Palestine, were built in the form of the Hellenistic-Roman basilica, a rectangular public building divided by two rows of columns into three aisles. The outer pillars, the decorations of the capitals, the architectural moldings, and the occasional mosaics are all provincial adaptations of Hellenistic style. Nor is this all. A crucial synagogue inscription of dedication, found in Jerusalem itself and dating from the first century of the common era, is written neither in Hebrew nor in Aramaic but in Greek. It reads in part: "Theodotus, son of Vettenus, a priest . . . built this synagogue for the reading of the Law and the teaching of the commandments."

Certainly it was difficult for Jews, even when they avoided visiting the Hellenistic cities near them, to escape the almost obtrusive presence of Greco-Roman architecture and plastic art. Especially was this so after the time of Herod the Great, whose reconstruction of the Temple in Jerusalem, together with his other numerous building activities there, was matched by his beautification of such cities as Caesarea and Samaria, as well as his capital. Indeed, one can still see in Jerusalem such Hellenistic-Oriental monuments as the tombs of the Judges, the tomb of Absalom, the tomb of Jehoshaphat, and the like. There are too the multiplying discoveries of Hellenistic tomb paintings at Marisa, Beth Shearim, Beit Jibrin, Sheikh Ibreiq, and elsewhere in Palestine. All this material has recently been described by Professor Erwin Goodenough of Yale in the first four volumes of his imposing series *Jewish Symbols in the Graeco-Roman Period.*

How significant was all this varied and attractive array of Hellenistic art, technology, science, and thought in the inner life of the Jews of Palestine? In trying to answer this question we shall treat separately the three great social-religious parties or schools of thought or, to use the somewhat misleading traditional term, "sects" into which Palestinian Jewry was divided in the Hellenistic-Roman period. These "sects" (the word is a translation of Josephus' Greek term *haireseis,* meaning something like "schools of thought," or perhaps "denominations") were the Sadducees, the Pharisees, and the Essenes.

As we have seen, the Sadducees were the priestly and lay aristocrats. It was in their interest to be socially and religiously conservative, since their revenues and authority were based on the priestly privileges specified in the Laws of Moses, the "constitution" of the Jewish state. They could hardly be expected to favor changes in the Law proposed by the liberal and democratic Pharisees in the interest of the nonpriestly population. Devotion to the older prophetic ideals played no part in the Sadducees' conservatism, so there was nothing to prevent them from taking the lead in the bold attempt to Hellenize Judea in the days of Antiochus Epiphanes. Although this attempt was thwarted by the heroic resistance of the Maccabees, several of the later Hasmonean rulers, more favorably inclined to the Sadducean minority than to the Pharisaic majority in the Sanhedrin, or Senate, exhibit the influence of Hellenistic political practice and policy. Nevertheless, the Sadducees were only temporarily in the ascendant during the late Hellenistic and early Roman periods, and with the fall of the Jewish state in 70 C.E. they disappeared from the scene. Nor did their temporary political ascendancy succeed in vitally affecting the social and political thinking of the Jews.

The Pharisees, whose name means Separatists, perhaps earned the title not only because they separated themselves from the later worldly-minded Hasmoneans, but also because they vigorously opposed Hellenistic customs, even if they did not entirely escape such foreign influence. It is to the Pharisees that we owe the preservation of Prophetic Judaism with its stress upon the primacy of social justice and its messianic belief in the ultimate conversion of all mankind to a belief in the fatherhood of God and the brotherhood of man. To our generation this ideal is a commonplace, though one which is more honored in the breach than in the observance. But at the time of which we speak this messianic hope was a bold and original program, all the bolder and original for not being merely the evangelistic theme of a few inspired and undisciplined prophets or the utopian speculation of a few superior Greek thinkers. Rather it was the consistent political and religious plan of an entire community, whose way of life or *halakha* embodied the plan to a remarkable degree, especially in view of foreign rule and internal dissension. This way of life is well documented for us in the considerable body of literature known as Talmudic in the broad sense.

With regard to Hellenistic-Roman influence on Pharisaic Judaism, it is necessary to observe from the outset that while there is plenty of evidence that the Rabbis were well acquainted with Greco-Roman religious, legal and social institutions and attitudes, it does not follow from the existence of such knowledge among their leaders that the Jews belonging to the Pharisaic majority were influenced by Hellenistic-Roman culture. No doubt there are striking similarities between the legal formulas used in contracts of sale, marriage, divorce, and so on by the Jews and by the Greeks in Egypt. This has been established since the discovery of hundreds of legal papyri from Ptolemaic and Roman Egypt. But the resemblances may well be due, as the late Professor Louis Ginzberg suggested, to the common origin of these formulas in the cuneiform law of ancient Mesopotamia. As for the influence of Roman law on Jewish Palestine, though this question was raised several centuries ago, the matter is still undecided. One of the foremost students of this particular branch of comparative law, Professor Boaz Cohen, has judiciously remarked that since a critical comparison between Roman and Jewish law has only recently been begun, "It would be premature to make any statement on the question whether the Jews and the Romans had profited to any great extent from each other's legal experience."

Pagan legal and economic influences apart, can we say that Greco-Roman culture penetrated to the heart of Pharisaic Judaism and affected the thought of the great Rabbinic authorities? Did it affect the norms of interpretation they set up, norms that served as the framework of the great Talmudic commentary on Biblical law? Professor David Daube of Oxford has suggested that Hillel's pioneer formulation of methods of interpretation was derived from Hellenistic rhetoric, but his arguments are inconclusive. It is not enough to show, as he does, that there is a similarity between Hillel's distinction of written from oral law and that made by the Greeks, or between Hillel's attempt and that of the Greeks to reconcile authority and reason. It would not be difficult to find the same methods used by jurists in India and China in an early period, and one would therefore be inclined to suppose that such methods of interpretation naturally arise in any society where certain general principles of law and authoritative codes of law are found.

Granted that some of the social and economic institutions and legal forms of the Palestinian Jewish community were influenced by those of their Hellenistic and Roman rulers and neighbors, we are not obliged to conclude that these foreign influences affected the essential character of Pharisaic Judaism. At best, the effect of such influences was a greater emphasis than ever upon those beliefs and practices, inherited from Prophetic Judaism and adapted to their own times, that made the Pharisees and their supporters feel spiritually superior to the intellectual Greeks and the politically powerful Romans. This is not to say that Pharisaic Judaism was better off for not being greatly influenced by the philosophy and science of the Greeks or the laws and military techniques of the Romans. But it cannot be maintained with complete impartiality that Christianity, which did absorb these Greco-Roman influences, has given the world a higher religion or ethic than did the Pharisees, who preserved the most universal ideals of Prophetic Judaism by "building a fence around the Torah." And if we, their descendants, have considerably lowered that fence in order to be able to enjoy the cultural achievements of the Gentiles, we can still be grateful to the builders of the fence for making us aware that we are equal contributors with the Greeks and the Romans in creating European civilization.

The third great "sect" or social-religious party among the Palestinian Jews of our period was that of the Essenes, whose name goes back to the Aramaic word *hasēn,* which like the corresponding Hebrew term *hasidim* means "pious ones" or "saints." Philo and Josephus have long familiarized us with the remarkable communal organization of the Essenes, who lived apart from the mass of Jews. Characteristic of the sect were their archaic religious practices, which demanded great strictness in ritual purity; their doctrine of good and evil spirits, which bordered on non-Jewish dualism; their interest in faith healing and in apocalyptic visions; and their almost Calvinistic doctrine of election and theological determinism.

In distinction from the Pharisees and Sadducees, many of whose beliefs are described in early Rabbinic sources, and also in the Gospels, the Essenes cannot be clearly identified with any group mentioned in Rabbinic literature. So there has been uncertainty about their exact relation to the other "sects," and it has not been possible to decide whether their beliefs and practices were merely a development of certain older Israelite tendencies (the so-called nomadic tradition exemplified by the ancient Rechabites) or whether they were derived from foreign cultures, Iranian or Greek or both. During the early part of this century, however, a number of scholars came to believe that the Essenes were responsible for the apocalyptic books among the Apocrypha and Pseudepigrapha (the early Jewish books which were not accepted into the Biblical canon), such as Enoch, Jubilees, the Testaments of the Twelve Patriarchs, and the like, which contain ideas that resemble those ascribed to the Essenes by Philo and Josephus.

This reasonable conjecture has become almost a certainty through the sensational discovery in 1947 by a Palestinian Arab shepherd of the Dead Sea Scrolls. These are Hebrew scrolls that were sealed in clay jars and hidden in a cave on the western shore of the Dead Sea in a part of the wilderness of Judea called Wadi Qumran. Since this discovery French and British archeologists working in Jordan have explored a large number of caves in the same region and uncovered hundreds of fragments of Biblical and Apocryphal writings. Various tests have shown, at least to the satisfaction of the vast majority of the experts in this field, that the Qumran scrolls were written some time between the Maccabean revolt and the destruction of Jerusalem, that is, between 170 B.C.E. and 70 C.E.

One of these scrolls contains the regulations of a sort of monastic community, called *yahad,* striking in its similarity to the communal organization of the Essenes as described by Philo and Josephus. Other Qumran scrolls contain doctrines that resemble those found in the apocalyptic books, mentioned above, that had been thought by some scholars to be of Essene origin. There is little doubt that these Qumran covenanters were identical with or closely related to the Essenes. And since we now appear to have some of the ancient writings of the Essenes in their original language, we can more accurately appraise their place in the history of Judaism and their relation to contemporary groups.

The Essenes, I venture to suggest on the basis of the new evidence, were a Pharisaic subgroup among whom apocalyptic speculation, ethical and cosmic dualism, pessimism, and contempt for private property figured with special prominence. They observed most of the written and oral laws prescribed in the Pharisaic Halakha, but in a manner that was mystical, esoteric, and archaic. Moreover, their preoccupation with the power of evil in this world and their separateness from the general community were apparently regarded by the Pharisaic authorities as verging on sectarianism and on Gnosticism, with its belief that the world of matter was created not by God but by an evil principle opposed to God. Since the Essenes revered Moses as the lawgiver chosen to reveal God's will, they could not wholly accept Gnostic dualism. Yet they came so perilously close to it that it would not be unfair to characterize the Essenes as Gnosticizing Pharisees. So far as we can see at present, this Gnosticizing tendency was the result of contact with pagan Gnostics, who combined certain tenets of Platonic, Pythagorean, and Iranian theology into a kind of philosophic religion or theosophy.

In one form or another this Gnostic strain has reappeared from time to time in Jewish history. Examples are the publication of the Zohar in thirteenth-century Spain; the mystical circle of Cordovero, Isaac Luria, and others in sixteenth-century Safed; and the rise of Hasidism in eighteenth-century Galicia. This sometimes subterranean, sometimes triumphantly emergent, Gnostic-Kabbalistic-Hasidic Judaism is perhaps the most remarkable example of Hellenistic influence on the Hebrew-speaking Jews of Palestine as opposed to the Greek-speaking Jews of the Diaspora.

HELLENISTIC INFLUENCE ON DIASPORA JUDAISM

The Greek word *diaspora* occurs several times in the Greek Bible as a rendering of several different Hebrew words all meaning "dispersion" and referring to the Jewish communities scattered throughout Babylonia, Egypt, and the Mediterranean littoral after the destruction of Jerusalem in 586 B.C.E.

The western Diaspora in the Hellenistic-Roman period alone concerns us here. Although the story is full of gaps, we have a fairly detailed knowledge of certain significant incidents in the histories of such communities as Antioch, Alexandria, and Rome, the three chief cities of the Greco-Roman world. We also have a pretty good idea of the distribution of the Jews during this period as a whole. There are inscriptions from European and Asiatic cities, papyri from Egypt, and copies of official decrees concerning the civic rights of Jewish communities, all providing us with instructive glimpses into certain aspects of the life of Jews in these regions.* There is a sufficient amount of Hellenistic Jewish literature to enable us to form a judgment about the religion and general thinking of Greek-speaking Jews. The reports of early Christian missionaries also throw some light on the religious attitudes of Jews in the Diaspora. And the considerable number of references to Jews in pagan Greek and Latin writings

---

* A considerable settlement of Jews in the West before the time of Alexander the Great was the military colony established by the Persian rulers of Egypt on the island of Yeb (later called Elephantine), near the first cataract of the Nile, early in the fifth century B.C.E. Of this group of Aramaic-speaking Jews we have some knowledge, owing to a number of papyri in that language which were found by the German excavators of Yeb some fifty years ago. It is possible that after the Macedonians conquered Egypt from the Persians some of these Jewish colonists migrated to other cities in Egypt to become the nuclei of Greek-speaking communities. But it appears that most of the Jewish communities in the Hellenistic Diaspora were founded by emigrants from Judea after the conquests of Alexander the Great.

provide some insight into Gentile attitudes toward the Jews living in their midst. Finally, we have a substantial part of the writings of those two exceptionally Hellenized Jews, the philosopher Philo of Alexandria and the historian Josephus of Jerusalem. Their works are not only invaluable contemporary sources for the history of the Jews in the first century of the common era, but they contain as well revealing portraits of their authors. Both writers are loyal to Judaism, but in different ways, and the very differences in training, character, and temperament of the two help us to understand the impact of Hellenism on Jewish intellectuals.

Both Josephus and Philo assert with conscious pride that their coreligionists were invited to settle in centers such as Alexandria and Antioch by kings no less illustrious than Alexander the Great and Seleucus I. Unfortunately both authors were writing with an apologetic slant, so that most historians hesitate to take their statements at face value. Still, we may assume that Jews were in Egypt, Phoenicia, and Syria and in some of the Greek islands and coastal cities of Asia Minor early in the Hellenistic period. For one thing, the historian Hecataeus of Abdera, who lived shortly after 300 B.C.E., is quoted by Josephus as saying that after Alexander's death many thousands of Jews migrated to Egypt and Phoenicia because of the disturbances in Syria. In the same work Josephus reports that Aristotle's disciple Clearchus wrote a book on sleep that contained an anecdote about a remarkable Jew whom Aristotle had met in Asia Minor. This Jew, said Aristotle, "was Greek not only in language but also in soul," a Jew who was thoroughly Hellenized, in other words. Even if such a meeting never took place, it is clear that Clearchus was writing in the early Hellenistic period and that Greek readers expected to find Hellenized Jews in Asia Minor at this time.

Although we have no accurate notion of the chronologies of Greek-speaking Jewish settlements in Hellenistic cities, we know that by the first century C.E. there were a great many Jewish communities "spread out over all the continents and islands," as Philo says, even if we have to dismiss his further statement that these Diaspora Jews "seemed not much less numerous than the indigenous inhabitants." The fact is that the Jewish population of the Roman Empire in Philo's time was something like ten per cent, or about six out of sixty millions. Undeniably impressive, though, is the list of more than two hundred Jewish communities in the Hellenistic-Roman Diaspora that emerges from scattered sources in papyri, inscriptions, the Talmud, Philo, Josephus, early Christian literature, and pagan historians. These communities extended from Spain to southern Russia in Europe, through North Africa and western Asia. We have little knowledge of them, in some cases only a personal name or two. But with regard to the large settlements in Antioch, Alexandria, and Rome we have enough information about the civic rights and over-all organization of the Jews to gauge the attitudes of the Hellenistic and Roman rulers toward them (mostly favorable) and those of the Gentile populations (mostly unfavorable).

Philo and Josephus were indulging in rhetoric when they insisted that the Jews had long enjoyed full citizenship (*politeia*) in Hellenistic cities. Both undoubtedly had the same reason for exaggeration: they were writing at a time when antisemites (an inaccurate but now accepted word for anti-Jewish agitators) were attempting to persuade the Roman authorities to revoke the privileges of the Jews in those cities. A few individual Jews may have been singled out for the honor of citizenship because of some special service or through the favor of a Gentile magistrate, but the great majority cannot have been citizens, for this would have involved full participation in civic life, including, of course, pagan festivals and sacrifices abhorrent to observant Jews.

Instead of citizenship the Jewish residents of Alexandria, Antioch, Ephesus, and other Hellenistic cities had the status of *isopoliteia* or "quasi-citizenship." Accordingly, organized in a separate corporation or *politeuma* within the *polis,* they enjoyed religious and cultural autonomy, and exemption from those civic obligations that conflicted with the Jewish religion. This meant that in Egypt, Syria, and Asia Minor the Jews, if not on a par with the Greeks and Macedonians, who alone were full citizens, enjoyed about the same advantages. In this they were unlike the native Oriental population, and their favored position naturally contributed to the rise of popular resentment against them. Violence broke out from time to time, especially in the period of Roman rule, but of this we shall speak later.

Although we have no official decrees from the early centuries of the period that attest the granting of special civic rights to the Jews by the kings and city authorities, we do have such documents from the Roman era. The Roman Senate and later the emperors merely continued the earlier practice of recognizing the special status of Jewish residents in Hellenistic cities.

Here, for example, from Josephus, is part of a decree issued by Dolabella, appointed governor of the province of Asia by Julius Caesar, to the officials of the city of Ephesus.

> Alexander, son of Theodorus, the envoy of Hyrcanus, the son of Alexander [Jannaeus], the high priest and ethnarch of the Jews, has explained to me that his coreligionists cannot undertake military service because they may not bear arms or march on days of the Sabbath,

nor can they obtain the native foods to which they are accustomed. I, therefore, like the governors before me, grant them exemption from military service and allow them to follow their native customs and to come together for sacred and holy rites in accordance with their law, and to make offerings for their sacrifices [in Jerusalem].

Among the papyri recovered from the soil of Egypt is a long letter from the Roman emperor Claudius to the Alexandrians. In this document, written a few years after the pogrom against the Jews in Alexandria, Claudius, who was by no means partial to the Jews (it was in his reign that many of them were expelled from Rome), takes occasion to warn both the Jews and the Gentiles of that city not to prolong their quarrel. At the same time he announces his intention of preserving the privileges which the Jews had enjoyed since the time of the Emperor Augustus. This portion of the letter reads as follows:

Therefore I now again call upon the Alexandrians to be mild and humane toward the Jews, who have for many years lived in the same city, and not to profane any of the rites observed by them in the worship of their God but to allow them to observe their own customs as in the time of the divine Augustus, which customs, after hearing both sides, I also have sanctioned. On the other hand, I expressly forbid the Jews to agitate for more rights than they formerly had or in future to send two embassies as if they lived in two cities, which has never been done before, or to force their way into the games of the gymnasiarch or the kosmetes, while enjoying their own privileges and sharing an abundance of generous advantages in a foreign city, or to bring in and admit Jews who sail from Syria or [Upper] Egypt. Otherwise I will prosecute them in all ways as fomenting a common plague of the whole world.

Nothing could make plainer the impatience of the Roman emperor in the face of what he considered an attempt by the Jews to exceed the rights which earlier emperors had granted them, and equally plain is his resolve not to permit the antisemites in Alexandria to deprive them of those rights. The same or similar rights had been granted them by the Ptolemaic kings of Egypt, as is clear not only from express claims made by Jewish writers but from a number of Greek inscriptions found in different parts of Egypt. These record the dedications of synagogues in honor of various reigning Ptolemaic kings and queens, the donors being "the Jews of such and such a place." We also have a good many inscriptions from various cities in Asia Minor, where the local Jewish communities are described in the same loose terms, but it is evident from various literary sources that each community had its local governing body which supervised the internal affairs of the *politeuma* and saw to it that the officials of the city respected the special rights granted to the Jews by various Hellenistic rulers and their Roman successors.

The Greek historian Strabo, a contemporary of Augustus, briefly describes the civic status of the Jews in the city-state of Cyrene in North Africa (modern Libya). As preserved by Josephus, the passage reads:

> There were four classes in the state of Cyrene. The first consisted of citizens, the second of farmers, the third of resident aliens, and the fourth of Jews. This people has already made its way into every city, and it is not easy to find any place in the habitable world which has not received this nation and in which it has not made its power felt.

Further on, Strabo tells us that in the great city of Alexandria the Jews were ruled by an ethnarch of their own,

> who governs the people and adjudicates suits and supervises contracts and ordinances, just as if he were the head of a sovereign state.

Later the Emperor Augustus replaced the ethnarch with a *gerousia,* or senate, whose ordinances were carried out by magistrates.

During the Ptolemaic era the Jewish communities of Egypt were not only protected in the observance of their religion but were probably well treated on the whole. There were exceptions, as when Ptolemy VII Physcon was at war with his brother Ptolemy VI Philometor and found the majority of Egyptian Jews siding with his rival; or when Cleopatra was at war with her unfilial son Ptolemy Lathyrus, and relied for military leadership on two Jewish generals named Hananiah and Hilkiah. It may be that throughout this period the Egyptian natives as well as certain ambitious Greeks were hostile to the Jews, but we have no record of any overt antisemitism among the populace until the Romans made Egypt a province of the Empire.

In Rome itself, where the government was consistently opposed to granting much freedom to any social or religious organization for fear of subversive political activity, the Jews were not organized into one large corporation or *politeuma,* as they were almost everywhere else in the Diaspora. Instead they were organized in separate congregations called *synagogai* (the synagogue building itself being called *proseucha,* a Greek loan-word in Latin, meaning "house of prayer"). Quite possibly, on special occasions the heads of the various congregations consulted together or joined in presenting petitions to the Roman Senate or imperial chancellery. They certainly did so at the time when the Alexandrian Jews sent an embassy to the Emperor Gaius Caligula to complain of the pogrom abetted by the Roman governor of Egypt and to plead with Gaius not to drive the Jews to despair by demanding that they worship him as a god.

At first the Jews were settled mostly in suburban Rome, across the Tiber (near present-day Vatican City). Most of them, Philo tells us, were Roman freedmen, "for having been brought to Italy as captives, they were freed by their owners and not forced to violate any of their ancestral customs." Later on, Jews settled in other parts of Rome. In the early empire there were thirteen congregations, known to us chiefly from the Greek inscriptions found on tombstones. Three of these congregations were named after famous Romans, one after King Herod, three after districts in Rome, and six (in the fashion of modern *schuls*) after the founders' places of origin. The synagogue officials had charge also, it seems, of the civic affairs of the local community. To some extent the structure of the community resembled that of the pagan social-religious societies, which in turn imitated the organization of a Hellenistic-Roman city-state. It has been suggested that the local senate (*gerousia*) or council of each congregation may also have been modeled on the Sanhedrin in Jerusalem, but we are still ignorant of most of the details of communal organization.

As a result of special circumstances—for example, the coming to power of a minister who happened to dislike Jews—there were several expulsions of Jews from Rome during the early empire. It is probable that the expulsion under Tiberius (who also banished the Egyptian worshipers of Isis for a time) may have been because of the antisemitism of Tiberius' favorite minister Sejanus. Philo tells us that after Sejanus' death the emperor, realizing that the Jews had been slandered by Sejanus, ordered the Roman officials in all places to permit the Jews to observe their own customs without interference.

That the Jews in Rome were treated considerately during the late republic and early empire seems to be indicated by their numbers and influence, by the gibes of Roman satirists, and by occasional unprejudiced references in the works of pagan historians. For example, Suetonius writes that no group in Rome mourned the death of Julius Caesar more conspicuously than the Jews. We know of the great dictator's official acts of kindness to the Jews of Palestine, Egypt, and Asia Minor. Presumably he was as well disposed toward the Jews of Rome. Again, the Emperor Augustus, according to Philo, allowed the Jews in Rome to receive monthly doles of money or grain like the rest of the population, and if the distribution fell on the Sabbath, he ordered the Roman officials to reserve the Jews' share until the next day.

Of course, there were emperors, like the mad Gaius and the tyrannical Domitian, who pursued antisemitic policies, but such policies were exceptions to the general rule of imperial tolerance during most of our period. And even Gaius, who threatened to set up his statue as an object of worship in the Temple of Jerusalem and the synagogues of the Diaspora, stayed his hand for a time out of friendship for Agrippa.

Nor did the Jews lack friends at court. Poppaea, the wife of Nero, interceded for some Jewish captives at the request of Josephus himself, who was introduced to her by the Jewish actor Aliturus. Startlingly enough, an Alexandrian antisemitic agitator on trial for treason before Claudius went so far as to accuse the emperor of being the illegitimate or cast-off son of the Jewess Salome. A cousin of the Emperor Domitian, Flavius Clemens, was convicted of "atheism," a charge successfully brought against Romans who, according to Dio Cassius, "had been drifting into a Jewish way of life." Finally, the anonymous writer of a papyrus found in Oxyrhynchus in Egypt asserts that the Emperor Trajan (the same Trajan whose legions killed many Jews during the war of Quietus in 117 c.e.) greeted a Jewish delegation in Rome most cordially, having already been won over to their side by the Empress Plotina. And in this same papyrus the antisemitic leader Hermaiscus, on trial for treason or lèse-majesté, dares to say to the emperor, "It hurts me to see your cabinet [or privy council] filled with Jews." The charge was, of course, a wild exaggeration, yet it shows that the antisemites from Alexandria were aware that Roman Jews had some influence at court.

We have all too little knowledge of the economic and social condition of the many Jewish settlements scattered throughout the lands bordering the Mediterranean. Just as the biochemist is forced to collect and treat a ton or so of animal entrails in order to extract a few grams of a precious medical substance, so the historian must comb through a small library of pagan, Jewish, and Christian works, besides many papyri and inscriptions, in order to extract a few significant facts about the social and economic history of the various communities in the Diaspora. Professor V. Tcherikover of the Hebrew University has studied all the literary material and papyri from Egypt, and has given us a convenient summary of his findings.

It appears that the Jews in Ptolemaic and Roman Egypt were engaged in a variety of occupations, of which banking and money-lending (so monotonously singled out by critics of the Jews) were probably the least frequent. Most of the Jews in Egypt seem to have been farmers, farm laborers and tenants, cattle breeders, craftsmen, soldiers, tax collectors, and the like; that is to say, they were humble and not too prosperous workers. It was natural for them to turn to agriculture and craftsmanship, the occupations most common in their Palestinian homeland. To be sure, there were some merchants, especially in Alexandria, as we know from Philo (they are rarely mentioned in the papyri), but their number was comparatively small. It was small because the Ptolemaic kings, as Professor Tcherikover points out, distrusted businessmen as representing a threat to the royal monopolies in various essential products. Later, in Egypt under Roman rule, most trade was in the hands of the guilds of Roman merchants (*collegia mercatorum*), and since these guilds were closely associated with pagan cults, it would have been impossible or at least very difficult for Jews to gain admission to them.

The originally numerous Jewish slaves in Egypt were in the course of time ransomed by their coreligionists, but rich Jews, to whom there are incidental allusions, were probably conspicuous by their rarity. There was the Alabarch (financial officer) Alexander, who once loaned 200,000 drachmas to Herod Agrippa. But the charge so frequently made by medieval and modern antisemites, that Jews are generally rich and usurious, is one that is hardly ever made in antiquity. It is worth mentioning here that in the Roman period the Jews of Egypt were required to pay a head tax higher than that of the Greek residents and just as high as that of the native Egyptians— a necessity that the Jews resented not so much for economic reasons as out of injured pride. After the destruction of the Temple of Jerusalem in 70 c.e. every Egyptian Jew from the age of three to sixty was obliged by Rome to pay a special "Jewish tax," which replaced the voluntary yearly half-shekel contribution to the Temple treasury.

Little as we know about the economic and social status of Egyptian Jewry, even less do we know about that of the Jews in Rome. Here too, as in Egypt, the originally numerous Jewish slaves seem speedily to have been ransomed by their coreligionists or else freed by their Gentile masters, who found them unsuitable for domestic service because of their peculiar religious customs. From a good many inscriptions we learn that some Jews were craftsmen, as in Egypt, which is not surprising. What is surprising are the references in literary sources to Jewish actors, such as Aliturus. Whether they were observant Jews or merely of Jewish origin, we do not know. It has been suggested, but on insufficient evidence, that a good many Jews were profitably employed in the importation and transport of grain, which was an important part of Rome's economic activity even before the decadent days of bread and circuses.

Since there were at least thirteen separate congregations in Rome, each of some size and stability, and since the various Jewish cemeteries have yielded valuable tombstones and sarcophagi, it is tempting to suppose that Roman Jewry as a whole was not too impoverished during the early empire. Yet we find in the Jewish inscriptions references to "friends of the poor," as well as to officials in charge of distributing alms to the needy. Such references, taken together with the sneer about "Jewish beggars" found in the satires of Juvenal, support the conjecture that Roman Jewry was not disproportionately or conspicuously prosperous.

As for the many Jewish settlements scattered throughout Syria and Asia Minor and adjacent countries, we are again limited to a few isolated facts gleaned mostly from inscriptions or incidental allusions in pagan or Christian literature. We find mention of benefactions made by presumably wealthy Jewish individuals to their local communities. In the busy and sometimes thriving coastal city of Smyrna a certain Eirenopoios, whose name is obviously the Greek translation of Solomon, gave seven pieces of gold for the balustrade of a synagogue. In another city, Phocaea, a Jew named Tation built a synagogue and a colonnade "at his own expense." In still another city of Asia Minor, Ephesus, a Jew was one of the "chief physicians," presumably one of the ten such officials appointed by the city.

One could go on at some length selecting from the inscriptions and literary sources picturesque bits that give a momentary glimpse of one small area of the social and economic life of Diaspora Jewry. Unfortunately we cannot yet sketch that life as a whole, and perhaps shall never be able to do so. All that we can say with any certainty is that a considerable number of Jewish communities in the Greco-Roman world were secure and prosperous enough to maintain a cultural life of their own for several centuries; that they made a deep impression on the Gentile and early Christian historians of the time; and that they attracted the sympathetic interest, and sometimes (as in the case of the communities in Alexandria, Rome, and Antioch) the slightly envious admiration, of their coreligionists in Palestine.

6

THE ACHIEVEMENT
OF HELLENISTIC JUDAISM

The experience of the Jews in the Hellenistic Age, as sketched in the last chapter, foreshadows an intellectual development that was anything but simple, yet in the perspective of some twenty centuries the general outlines emerge clearly enough. Accordingly, we turn to our main topic, which is the religious or cultural life of the Jews in the Hellenistic-Roman Diaspora. We say religious or cultural because the two were practically synonymous in ancient Judaism.

From the long shelf of Hellenistic Jewish writings at our disposal it would be easy to cull a large number of passages showing that the great majority of Jews, though they lived in the midst of a Gentile culture that was in some ways superior to their own, remained loyal in thought and practice to the teaching of the Torah, the Prophets, and the other Scriptures. All these writings, diverse as they are in form and content, sound the same note, which is that of a proud Jewish consciousness. It is sounded in the historical romance of III Maccabees; in the poetic drama on the Exodus by Ezekiel Tragicus; in the legendary narratives of Eupolemus and Artapanus; in the vigorous glorification of the Torah and polemic against idolatry known as *The Wisdom of Solomon;* in the gnomic morality of the anonymous Jewish poet writing under the name of Phocylides; in the histories of Biblical antiquity and of the war against Rome; in the great apologetic treatise *Against Apion* by Josephus; and in the philosophical-allegorical treatises of Philo.

This body of Hellenistic Jewish literature, most of which remained unknown to the Jews of Palestine, was preserved through the succeeding centuries by Christian scribes and theologians as a sort of arsenal in their intellectual warfare with pagans. For their Jewish predecessors made out a forceful case for the thesis that the Greek philosophers had originally learned their wisdom from Moses and his followers, and powerfully defended the thesis that Jewish monotheism was superior to pagan polytheism and idolatry.

But are these literary demonstrations of Jewish loyalty—mostly written in Alexandria—representative of Diaspora Judaism as a *whole?* Any generalization from them is bound to be inconclusive, just as the evidence derived from the numerous synagogue and sepulchral inscriptions is inconclusive. For the synagogues and sepulchres were communal Jewish property and stood in protected sites, whereas no monuments, or very few, were left by Jews who became pagans or, later on, Christians.

LOYALTIES AND TRADITION

The fact is, we have no wholly reliable method for determining what proportion of Diaspora Jews remained loyal to their religion and "race" and what proportion apostatized. Various kinds of indirect evidence, however, enable us to state with confidence that the great majority of Diaspora Jews, no matter how Hellenized they were in externals such as language, housing, institutional forms and the like, remained believing and observant Jews and continued to regard Jerusalem as their holy city and Palestine as their holy land, even after the destruction of the Temple.

There are four kinds of such indirect evidence: (1) the statements of pagan writers, most of them unfriendly to the Jews, precisely because this "unsocial" people refused to participate fully in pagan culture; (2) Christian writings, extending from St. Paul to the Church Fathers who were active in different parts of the Greco-Roman world and who everywhere attacked the Jews for refusing to give up their Torah and accept Jesus as their Messiah; (3) incidental references in Palestinian apocryphal and Rabbinic literature to the active participation of Diaspora Jewry in the Temple cult, the synagogue liturgy and the study of the Law—significantly, there is no mention in this literature of disloyalty to tradition on the part of Diaspora Jews; and

(4) statements made by Hellenistic Jewish writers indicating that Jewish customs were regularly observed in the local communities, together with spontaneous expressions of loyalty to Judaism found in sepulchral inscriptions, and similar sources. We shall confine ourselves to a few illustrations drawn from the last category.

Josephus tells us that throughout the Diaspora, as well as in Palestine, the local Jewish communities kept careful records of priestly genealogies, which indicates the general concern for such laws as those connected with priestly marriage and divorce, revenues, participation in the synagogue service and other forms of observance. And Philo, in his description of the pogrom in Alexandria under Gaius, reports that the Jews of the city were celebrating the festival of Sukkoth at the time, and were living in booths. Philo states that during the pogrom some Jewish women refused to eat pork when seized by the mob, and others did so only under threat of violence. In another treatise Philo reminds his antisemitic opponents that the Emperor Augustus did not expel the Jews from Rome and deprive them of Roman citizenship merely because they clung to their Jewish way of life.

Other communities besides the Alexandrian provide examples of Jewish loyalty, as the numerous inscriptions in Rome testify. And there is an inscription from Stobi, a remote provincial town in Macedonia, probably dating from the second century c.e., which was designed to honor a certain Tiberius Polycharmus Achyrius, the "father" of the congregation and builder of its synagogue, and which tells us in his own words that he "lived his whole life in accordance with Judaism."

These are stray bits of evidence, but we are justified in taking them at their face value, and in their light it is reasonably certain that Philo and Josephus were overstating the case only a little when they proudly asserted, in almost the same language, that the Jews "are taught the laws from their earliest youth and carry them as though engraved in their souls."

If most of the Jews in the Diaspora were faithful to traditional Judaism, not all Jews believed in or practiced the same kind of Judaism. Thus we find Philo criticizing two kinds of Jews, both more or less within the fold. On the one hand he finds fault with those Jews who consider only the literal text of Scripture and neglect the allegorical or philosophical meaning, and on the other hand, with those who pay little or no attention to the literal meaning, and are interested only in the allegory.

Roughly speaking, one may say that among the Jews of ancient

Alexandria, and probably elsewhere, there were three "denominations" corresponding to the liberal, conservative and orthodox groups that are found among the Jews of the United States and England today. But this correspondence must not be taken too literally. For the fact is that if ancient "liberal" Jews, for example, resemble modern liberal Jews in their receptivity to Gentile culture, it would be a serious error to suppose that any Jew, no matter how liberal and how tolerant of certain aspects of Greek thought, could have remained a member of the Jewish community in the Hellenistic-Roman period if, like most modern liberal Jews, he had failed to observe the Sabbath rest or the dietary laws, or had absented himself from the synagogue service; or if, like most liberal Jews and many conservative Jews of today, he had doubted the divine inspiration of Scripture. In fact, most Greek-speaking Jews seem to have believed, as Philo did, that even the Greek translation of the Hebrew Bible was divinely inspired.

Yet as traditional in observance and in theology as even the most liberal Jews of the Hellenistic-Roman Diaspora seem to have been, we must not suppose that they and their more conservative coreligionists were immune to the religious and social beliefs and practices of their Gentile neighbors. Both in the literature of Hellenistic Judaism and in the archeological remains, we have abundant proof that Jewish communities and Jewish individuals were affected by Greco-Roman culture in a number of ways.

One major proof is that imposing monument of Hellenistic Jewish literature known as the Septuagint, the Greek translation of the Hebrew Bible carried out by a group of Alexandrian Jewish scholars, with the assistance of colleagues sent from Palestine, during the third and second centuries B.C.E. No work was ever more fateful, for without it the earliest Christian missionaries would have been in no position to convert large numbers of Greek-speaking Gentiles and so make it possible for Christianity to become a world religion in the course of three centuries. Now there can be no question of the essential Jewishness of the Septuagint both in purpose and content. It was designed to meet the educational and liturgical needs of the Diaspora Jews, of whom the vast majority were ignorant of Hebrew. But the Septuagint also exhibits marked Hellenistic influences. There occur in it, for example, Greek mythological terms like "Titan"; Hebrew names are often Hellenized; Greek metrical forms are used in poetic passages, as in the Book of Proverbs; on occasion attempts are made to smooth out awkward Hebraisms; the translation of some passages, as in parts of Isaiah, reveal an astonishing acquaintance with technical Greek terminology. Thus there is no doubting the presence of Hellenistic elements in the Greek Bible, though it may be said of them, paradoxical as it sounds, that they are merely forms of Jewishness in a Hellenistic environment.

Our second example of Hellenistic influence is more surprising. We find that the Jews of Egypt, although they had their own judicial organization, were influenced by the principles of Hellenistic common law, as Professor V. Tcherikover, the eminent papyrologist, has discovered. Yet even here it is not necessary to suppose that the legal authorities of the Egyptian Jewish community used Hellenistic laws when these were in flagrant contradiction to Biblical laws. In all probability this Hellenistic influence was restricted to cases in which traditional Jewish law could not conveniently or prudently be enforced.

But what shall we say about the disconcerting practice occasionally found among the Roman Jews of burying their dead in coffins decorated with pagan motifs—cherubs, for instance—or inscribing on tombstones such pagan formulas as *dis manibus,* "to the spirits of the lower world," or *oudeis athanatos,* "no one is immortal." Obviously these Jews were not converts to paganism or they would never have buried their dead in Jewish cemeteries; nor would they have employed, as they sometimes did, Jewish symbols, like the menorah, along with pagan ones. If, then, they employed pagan symbolism and formulas, it was either because of such practical necessities as having to buy ready-made coffins at short notice, or because they were ignorant of the religious significance of pagan symbols.

Such Hellenization, whether it occurred in art or law or organization, is of an external kind. It has a sort of counterpart in the rhetorical Hellenization to be found in the writings of that devout Jew and severe critic of pagan religion, Philo of Alexandria.

No Jew of the Diaspora tried more consistently and conscientiously to demolish the pretensions of Greek religious philosophy than Philo. He never wearied of pointing out the impiety and absurdity of Greek polytheism and idolatry. And yet Philo does not hesitate, when it suits his rhetorical purpose, to write as though he were a great admirer of Greek mythology. For example, in his treatise *Embassy to Gaius,* a polemic against that mad emperor, Philo complains that Gaius has paraded as Dionysus and Herakles, though he possessed none of the virtues of these gods.

This use of Greek myths to drive home an argument is not confined to Philo but occurs in Josephus and others. It illustrates the willingness of certain Jews to bring even Greco-Roman religion and culture into play to support a Jewish moral and hence an anti-Gentile conviction.

Much the same kind of Hellenization characterizes those Hellenistic Jewish writers who employ Greek literary forms to impress their Gentile neighbors or to convince them that Judaism is superior to pagan culture. We may cite such examples as the drama on the Exodus, in which Ezekiel Tragicus transformed the simple prose style of the Septuagint narrative into the lively meter of Attic drama; the prophecies of an unknown Jewish poet, written in the Homeric meter of the pagan Sibylline Oracles; and the eulogy of Judaism in the form of a philosophical symposium that concludes the so-called *Letter of Aristeas*. Many writings of this sort have no doubt been lost, but those extant bring home to us how thoroughly acquainted Diaspora Jews were with the chief poetic, historical and philosophical compositions of the Greeks. Further, these writings show that, while liberally educated Jews admired the intellectual and artistic achievements of the Gentiles, they had no doubt of the superiority of Jewish culture. Of course, the great majority of Diaspora Jews were far better acquainted with their own than with Greco-Roman literature.

But we should not overlook the fact that there were some Jews who preferred to dissociate themselves entirely from their coreligionists and sought to identify themselves with the Gentile majority. How many Jews apostatized to paganism we do not know, but there is reason to believe, if we may rely on negative evidence, that it was relatively small. The motives behind such apostasy were long ago analyzed by Philo, who was not only a learned theologian but a perceptive social psychologist. Following the helpful interpretation of Philo by Professor Harry A. Wolfson of Harvard University, we find that the apostates to paganism were chiefly of three sorts: (1) those who forsook Judaism out of the weakness of the flesh, that is, out of a desire to enjoy some of the luxuries forbidden to Jews; (2) the social climbers, those whom Wolfson describes as progressing "from a front row in the synagogue to a place at the tail-end of the mystery-processions of the heathen"; and (3) the intellectually uprooted or freethinking Jews, who found Jewish culture much less attractive than Greco-Roman culture with its wealth of poetry, philosophy, art and science.

Far more serious were the inroads made by the young Christian Church upon the traditional loyalties of Diaspora Jews. Even the oldest Christian community, that established by the immediate followers of Jesus in Jerusalem, was made up not only of Palestinian Aramaic-speaking Jews but also of Greek-speaking Jews from Cyrene, Alexandria, Cilicia in Asia Minor, and other parts of the Diaspora. After the stoning of Stephen, his associates went to Phoenicia, Cyprus, and Antioch, "preaching the word to none but unto the Jews only." In Antioch itself, where the disciples of Jesus were first called "Christians," some of the leading missionaries, like Lucius of Cyrene, were Jews from the Diaspora.

Although Paul, himself a Diaspora Jew, is known as the great "Apostle to the Gentiles," it is clear from the Book of Acts and his Epistles that he and his colleagues addressed themselves primarily to "God-fearing" Gentiles, that is, semiproselytes to Judaism, who were thus in some measure prepared to understand the preaching of the Gospel. They quoted the Septuagint to the Greek-speaking Jews to convince them that the life and works of Jesus were truly the fulfillment of Biblical prophecy.

Perhaps historians of Christianity have not sufficiently appreciated the fact that Paul's peculiar theological dialectic, with its frequent elliptical references to Scriptural narratives and ideas and its rabbinical method of interpretation, would have been practically unintelligible to the Gentile members of his audience had there been no learned Jews around to supply the missing links in Paul's involved and hurrying argument.

Again, many of the early Christian missionaries were of Jewish origin. Among the better known are Timothy, whose mother was Jewish, Aquila and Priscilla of Pontos, and Apollos of Alexandria.

We have no means of knowing just how many Diaspora Jews became converts to Christianity during the first three centuries; yet it is safe to say that large as the number may have been absolutely, it was small by the side of the number of Jews who remained loyal to the tradition of their fathers. Otherwise there would be no explanation for the fact that both Christian and pagan writers of this period are constantly critical of the Jews for their stubborn adherence to their own way of life.

THE SPELL OF JUDAISM

Whatever losses the Jewries of the Diaspora may have suffered through conversions to paganism or Christianity, they themselves made a considerable number of converts from among the Gentiles. For the most part these were not full converts, circumcised and baptized and assuming all the responsibilities of the faith in practice as well as belief; they were rather "God-fearers" or semiproselytes, persons who accepted monotheism, believed the Scriptures to be divinely inspired, observed the Sabbaths and festivals so far as was practicable, and abstained from the more flagrant practices of paganism.

Like other Oriental religions, Judaism probably attracted converts by its antiquity, exotic rites, and foreign vocabulary, and the prestige that resulted from the widespread notion among Greeks and Romans that wisdom had originally come from the East. Hence the popularity in the Hellenistic-Roman period of the cults of the Egyptian Isis, the Syrian "Goddess," the Iranian Mithra, and the Anatolian Cybele.

But apart from all this, Judaism, with its worship of an invisible God too great to be comprehended, had a special appeal for the more philosophical and spiritual Gentiles. Something of the sort is suggested in a statement quoted by St. Augustine from Varro, the Roman historian of religion, to the effect that the ancient Romans had worshiped without images for a hundred and eighty years, "and if this condition had continued, the gods would be worshiped more purely"; and Augustine adds that Varro cited the Jews to prove his point.

Another reason for the appeal of Judaism to some Gentiles was its austere morality, in contrast to the dissolute way of living common among the upper classes in large cities like Rome, Alexandria and Antioch. True, this particular appeal is not clearly documented in the ancient sources; yet it is so consistently stressed in Jewish apologetic works of the period that we can hardly escape the conclusion, supported by such eminent students of the subject as the Protestant scholar Emil Schuerer, that Jewish morality played an important part in winning Gentile converts to Judaism.

The question whether these conversions were owing chiefly to the efforts of Jewish missionaries or to the spontaneous actions of Gentiles attracted by what they observed of Jewish life is one that cannot be answered with certainty. Still, there are reasons for thinking that most conversions came about through Jewish efforts. So at least two ancient sources testify. One is the statement attributed to Jesus, "Woe to you scribes and Pharisees, for you compass sea and land to make one proselyte." The other, in Horace, is in a humorous vein.

> *If you don't grant this,*
> *A great band of poets—for we are many—*
> *Will come to my aid and like the Jews*
> *We'll just force you to join our crowd.*

Both statements are exaggerations but not pure inventions.

Nor is there any certainty concerning what proportion of converts remained at the semiproselyte stage, without becoming full-fledged Jews; what proportion took the further step; or what proportion fell away altogether and returned to paganism or, after the middle of the first century c.e., went over to the newly founded Christian Church.

That some converts fell back into paganism is frankly admitted by Josephus. "Of the many Greeks who have come to accept our laws, some have remained loyal, while others, not having the persistence to stay, have again apostatized." It is also quite clear that from the middle of the first century on, a large number of the Gentile "God-fearers" became converted to Christianity, but whether their number exceeded that of the semiproselytes who remained loyal to Judaism is wholly a matter of conjecture.

Apparently the Jews were content to have Gentiles become semi-proselytes without always insisting on their going on to accept all the obligations of Judaism as full-fledged converts. At any rate, Philo announces that "all those who have seen fit to worship the Creator and Father of the universe, if not from the beginning, at least later, and have embraced the idea of one [divine] ruler instead of many, must be considered our dearest friends and closest kin." And the fact is that these semiconverted "God-fearers" gave not only moral but material support to Judaism. They contributed to the Temple treasury, as is shown by a passage in Josephus: "No one need wonder that there was so much wealth in our Temple, for all the Jews throughout the habitable world and those who worship God [the *sebomenoi* or semiproselytes], even those from Asia and Europe, have been contributing to it for a long time."

That some "God-fearers" did become full converts is indicated in several passages in ancient pagan writings. One of these passages occurs in a satire of the Roman poet Juvenal, who despised not only Jews but Orientals in general, and even "Greeklings." He is speaking of the full conversion to Judasim of Romans whose fathers were "God-fearers":

> Some have a father who reveres the Sabbath day,
> And worship nothing but the clouds and a heavenly spirit.
> They see no difference between the flesh of man and swine,
> Of which their fathers would not eat, and presently
> Are circumcised. Taught now to scorn Rome's laws,
> They learn, observe and honor Jewish law alone,
> Which Moses handed down to them in secret scrolls,
> So as not to show the way to one of different faith
> And lead none but the circumcised to a fountain sought.
> This is the father's fault, who every seventh day
> Rested and gave no thought to other things in life.

And a Greek historian in Rome, Dio Cassius, writing about 200 C.E., remarks that he does not know the origin of the name "Jew" or when it was first applied to the nation, but "it extends to other men, even men of different race who zealously follow their laws."

GENTILE-JEWISH RELATIONS

On the darker side of Gentile-Jewish relations, the Hellenistic period was one of marked cultural and political change, accompanied by widespread feelings of insecurity. As usually happens in such circumstances, foreign groups were regarded with profound distrust. It is small wonder, therefore, that we hear less about Gentile converts to Judaism in the Greco-Roman world than about critics and opponents of the Jews. Antisemitism took two forms.

One form was religious and cultural and arose from the feeling, common among upper-class Greeks and Romans, that the Jews had no right to consider themselves the cultural equals of the Gentiles; that they were arrogant in refusing to worship the pagan gods; that they were given to absurd superstitions; and that they were haters of the rest of mankind, a disturbing element in the Hellenistic-Roman world.

The other form of antisemitism was political and arose from the feeling of the native populations of Hellenistic cities in Egypt, Syria and Asia Minor, chiefly in the period of Roman rule, that the Jews who resided among them had undeservedly been given special rights and privileges, whether by Hellenistic kings or Roman emperors. The political form of antisemitism was particularly strong in Roman Egypt and Roman Syria, for in the one case the Egyptians already detested the Jews on cultural grounds, while in the other the Syrians were looked down upon by the Jews.

In both areas, and to a lesser extent in Asia Minor, the Jews often served as outlets for the resentment which the dissatisfied populations felt against their rulers, but did not usually dare to express directly. In this respect antisemitism in the Hellenistic-Roman period was not essentially different from antisemitism in the Middle Ages or in modern times.

But ancient antisemitism was notably different from that of later periods in at least two respects. For one thing, there was extremely little or no hostility to Jews for economic reasons; at least no pagan writer ever mentions the subject. For another, there is nothing in antiquity comparable to the relentless antisemitism of the Christian Church, until recent times constantly stirred up by theologians and influential members of the clergy.

Yet there is some resemblance between the religious-cultural antisemitism of educated Greeks and Romans and the antisemitism of the Christian theologians. The Greeks and Romans could not bear to see a small, separate, and politically weak people cast doubts upon their most sacred beliefs, claiming that the Hebrew Scripture alone contained divinely inspired truth, while what was true in Greek philosophy came from Moses and the Prophets. To the Christians it was equally offensive to have the Jews claiming that Christian theologians had perverted Scripture in order to prove that Jesus of Nazareth was the Jewish Messiah, as well as the savior of the Gentiles.

A PORTRAIT OF PHILO

The lives and works of few individuals among Diaspora Jews are known to us. Fortunately, one of these is Philo of Alexandria, whose extant writings fill a good many volumes, and whose genius extended the frontiers of Hellenistic Judaism. Owing to his position in the community, his learning and character, and his influence on European thought, he is eminently worthy of special attention.

We have few facts about his life. Born about twenty years before the beginning of the common era, he lived till the middle of the first century C.E., and was thus a younger contemporary of the great Palestinian teacher Hillel, who incidentally may have come to Jerusalem from Alexandria rather than Babylonia, as has long been thought. That Philo's family was illustrious and wealthy we know from Josephus as well as other sources. Philo headed the small delegation of Alexandrian Jews who went to Rome in 40 C.E. to seek the protection of the emperor against the depredations of anti-Jewish mobs in Alexandria. Philo's younger brother Alexander held the important office of Alabarch in the Roman government in Egypt. One of his nephews, Marcus Lysimachus, married the daughter of King Agrippa I of Judea. Another nephew, Tiberius Julius Alexander, an apostate from Judaism, had a brilliant civil and military career in the imperial service. Tiberius served successively as procurator of Judea, as prefect or governor of Egypt, and as chief of staff to Titus in the war against the Jews. As procurator he executed a number of Jewish Zealots or anti-Roman extremists; as prefect of Egypt he put down a Jewish rebellion with such violence that thousands of the rebels were killed. And finally, in his military capacity, he was largely responsible for the success of the Romans in taking Jerusalem by siege and for the leveling of its chief buildings, the Temple among them.

As a devoted Jew, Philo must have been appalled at his apostate nephew's career, or as much of it as he lived to see. For death probably spared him the anguish of the war against the Jews of

Palestine in which Tiberius played so prominent a part. Whatever Philo's feelings toward his nephew, they do not show through the impersonal rhetoric of his remarks about the contrast between the morality of Mosaic Law and that of pagan rulers. It may be, though, that it was with Tiberius in mind that Philo warned his fellow Jews against marrying Gentile women.

Further details about Philo's family life are lacking except for an ancient story about his wife, who being asked why she did not wear gold ornaments like other women of her class, replied, "The virtue of her husband is sufficient ornament for the wife." In view of Philo's repeated denunciations of the frivolity and immorality of women, this story is especially piquant. Either his wife was a woman of great magnanimity or else she was outside the orbit of her husband's misogyny.

Thanks to his material advantages and native endowment Philo acquired a thorough education in Greek literature and philosophy, together with an apparently thorough grounding in Jewish tradition. Although he uses the Greek translation of the Hebrew Bible as possessing authority in its own right, there is reason to believe that he knew enough Hebrew to be able to compare the text of the Greek version with that of the original. But he wrote in Greek and there is no doubt that he thought of himself as an heir of Greek culture almost as much as of Judaism. It is amazing that one so devoted to Jewish custom and so immersed in public affairs found time to acquire his profound knowledge of the works of Homer, Plato, Aristotle, the Attic tragic writers and lyric poets, the philosophers and rhetoricians of the Hellenistic age, the authors of the New Comedy, and other authors besides. Philo also had a considerable knowledge of the theater, the plastic and graphic arts, and architecture, to say nothing of technology and science. He even found time to attend pagan games and athletic contests, if one may judge from his frequent allusions to such spectacles.

Sincere and consistent in his admiration of the Greek genius, he was critical and reserved in his attitude toward the Roman government, though less so toward the comparatively liberal reign of Augustus. He was at no pains to conceal his contempt and distrust of the unfriendly Egyptians, whether natives or Greco-Egyptians of the Alexandrian upper class. In one passage he speaks of the Egyptians as "an evil seed, whose souls represent a mixture of the venom of asps and the bad temper of their native crocodiles."

How much of his time was occupied in political activity on behalf of his fellow Jews there is no way of telling, but there is reason to suppose that he regarded public service as a necessary and justifiable sacrifice. "There was a time," he writes, "when I had leisure for philosophy . . . but envy suddenly fell upon me and incessantly pulled me down with violence until it plunged me into the great sea of political cares . . . but if there unexpectedly comes to me a brief spell of fair weather and calm in the midst of political turmoil, I rise to the surface and almost float on the air."

Philo's preference for scholarly pursuits was no handicap to him as a leader in Jewish communal affairs. The combination of scholarship and statesmanship, if it is uncommon in our own country, is by no means rare in both ancient and modern Europe and Asia. In Philo's writings, even the most abstract, there are many shrewd observations about politics; so we may safely assume that he was a not inept adviser on public affairs. Speaking of his trying experience with the Emperor Gaius, he says, "As I think myself to be somewhat more prudent because of my age and training, I was rather fearful where the others were joyful . . . but while I was depressed, I kept my uneasiness concealed because it was not safe to show my feelings." He had no occasion to choose between prudence and heroism, or between the interests of his own community and those of the Jews of the empire as a whole. So he writes, "For what religion or righteousness is there in showing that we are Alexandrians when we are menaced by the danger that hangs over the universal political community of Jews?" In the end he trusted less in his own understanding than in the help of God. "Our hope in God the savior will remain indestructible in our souls, for He has often saved our nation from hopeless straits."

Far more important, however, than Philo the statesman is Philo the religious philosopher. Professor Wolfson has stated that "Philo is the direct or indirect source of this [religious] type of philosophy, which continues uninterruptedly in its main assertions for well-nigh seventeen centuries, when at last it is openly challenged by Spinoza." Again, there is the opinion of a distinguished French scholar, Emile Bréhier, that Philo's expression of the love of God is a new thing in Greek literature.

Among Philo's great achievements is his fusion of Greek allegory and Palestinian midrash into a consistent body of doctrine, which in its sustained symbolism and architectonic structure reminds one of that great medieval synthesis, Dante's *Divine Comedy*. Further, he demonstrated to educated Jews and Greeks alike that the Mosaic Law, as the revealed will of God, necessarily contains the scientific, philosophical, and moral truths that pagan philosophers had discovered by natural reason, as well as deeper truths that remained unrevealed to them. Again, Philo skillfully adapted the mystical idealism of his admired teacher Plato to prove the essential rightness of the Biblical account of creation and its teachings about the human soul. He sought to expose the errors of the materialistic Stoics at the same time that he made use of their philosophical terminology, together with that of other schools of thought. He transformed the doctrine found earlier in both Palestinian and Alexandrian Judaism that Torah is another name for wisdom, both divine and human, by showing that this wisdom (*hokmah*) is the same as *sophia,* or Greek science in its best sense. He subtly explained how the human reason is related to the cosmic reason or Logos, and how this in turn is related to God's creative wisdom. The account of all this, and more, is to be found in Professor Wolfson's monumental study of Philo.

As for Philo's relation to contemporary Rabbinic thought, there is room for an honest difference of opinion, for it is not easy to compare Philo's thoroughly Hellenized theology with the popular and unphilosophical Aggada of the Palestinian teachers. But the similarities appear to be more significant than the differences. Philo and the Pharisaic authorities were close in their essential views about man's duty to God and to his fellow man; certainly they were closer to one another than to the pagan philosophers of their day.

ZION AS FACT AND IDEA

In the preceding chapter we dealt with the relations of the Jews in the Greco-Roman Diaspora to their Gentile neighbors. We now turn to another, equally important, aspect of Diaspora Judaism, namely, the relation of the Jewish communities scattered throughout the Greco-Roman world to the Jewish community of Palestine, the traditionally holy land, and to that of Jerusalem, the traditionally holy city. On this subject, unlike some of the others we have touched upon, the materials are abundant. It is no problem to determine how the Jews of Alexandria, Rome, Antioch and other cities felt about Palestine and Jerusalem, for we have evidence from all quarters—Jewish, pagan and Christian—to show that the vast majority of Jews throughout the *oikoumene* looked upon Palestine as their spiritual homeland.

First of all, loyalty to the Temple cult took concrete form in the annual contribution of a half-shekel from individuals in all parts of the Diaspora. A graphic instance of the concern felt by the Jews for the safe delivery of these funds is found in Cicero's oration of 59 B.C.E. in defense of Lucius Valerius Flaccus, who had been accused of maladministration while acting as governor of the Province of Asia. The charges included his embezzlement of moneys collected by the Jews of Asia for the Temple in Jerusalem. In the course of his speech Cicero grudgingly testifies to the loyalty of Roman Jews toward the Temple in the following words.

> Next comes the malicious accusation about the gold of the Jews. No doubt that is the reason why this case is being tried not far from the Aurelian Terrace. Because of this charge, Laelius, you chose this place and that crowd over there. You know how large that group [of Jews] is, how unified they are, and how much strength they show in political meetings.

Like a clever lawyer, Cicero was trying to stir up resentment against the Jews in order to win sympathy for his client, but the fact remains that Flaccus' attempt to impound the money sent to Jerusalem from Asia aroused intense and vocal indignation among the Jews of Rome.

Half-shekel contributions and other voluntary offerings were not the only manifestations of loyalty to the Temple in Jerusalem. Many Diaspora Jews went further in their reverence for the holy city and ritual tradition by making pilgrimages to Jerusalem for the three great pilgrim festivals, Tabernacles, Passover, and Pentecost, especially on the Passover. Here we have not only the express testimony of Philo and Josephus, but the evidence of early Rabbinic legislation designed to provide for the reception of large numbers of pilgrims from the Diaspora and to safeguard them against exploitation by the landlords and shopkeepers of Jerusalem.

Not only did the pious Jews of the Diaspora who could afford it visit Jerusalem for festivals, but many of them also came to die and be buried in the soil of the holy land. Recent excavations of burial sites of the third and fourth centuries C.E. at Beth Shearim in Lower Galilee have uncovered a good many inscriptions in Greek showing that the large necropolis there was "the central burying-ground of the Jews of the Diaspora," probably because it contained the tomb of Rabbi Judah ha-Nasi.

In recent years several scholars have compiled anthologies of Jewish writings throughout the centuries illustrating devotion to the Zionist ideal. A compilation of passages on the same theme drawn solely from the Jewish literature of the Hellenistic-Roman period would itself make up a small volume. One such passage is from the Sibylline Oracles, and celebrates the preeminence of Jerusalem:

> *No longer let thy heart be vexed in thy breast, O thou blessed*
> *Offspring of God, abundant in wealth, sole desirable blossom,*

> *Excellent light and nobly sought goal, desirable* chaste-tree,
> *Pleasant Judea, thou beautiful city, inspired of song.*

The second, from Philo, that eloquent spokesman of the thoroughly Hellenized Jews, is significant because it seems to be the most ancient example of a conscious and unapologetic "double loyalty"—loyalty to one's Diaspora community combined with loyalty to the spiritual homeland.

> For so populous are the Jews that no one country can hold them, and for that reason they settle in the most populous and most prosperous cities in Europe and Asia, both in the islands and on the mainland, and while they believe the sacred city [of Jerusalem], where the holy temple of the Most High God is established, to be their mother-city, yet they consider the various cities which they have inhabited from the time of their fathers and grandfathers and great-grandfathers and ancestors still farther back, where they were born and reared, to be their fatherlands.

THE LEGACY TO WESTERN CIVILIZATION

As we saw at the beginning of this section, the Hellenistic-Roman period was in some respects curiously like our own. This is not to say that history repeats itself, certainly not in an integral fashion. This or that configuration may repeat itself, but the recurrence of any large number of them together is not likely. So it would be simple innocence to suppose that present-day Jewry, whether in the Diaspora or in the state of Israel, might predict its future on the strength of what is known about the history of Palestinian and Diaspora Judaism in the Hellenistic-Roman period. Our history is an inseparable part of world history, and the modern world is very different from the world of Philo, Josephus, Hillel, and Rabbi Judah ha-Nasi.

Yet it is possible to single out achievements and events in ancient Jewish history and say of them that they are the forerunners of movements and influences in the later history of Judaism in particular and of Western culture in general that still have meaning and relevance for our own time.

Let us try to enumerate some of the consequences in Judeo-Christian culture of the long association of the Jews in Palestine and the Diaspora with the Greeks and Romans. The consequences mentioned here represent only a part of the legacy of Hellenistic Judaism, but they all bring home to us the fact that Jewish creativeness did not end with the Prophets of the Bible, nor disappear in the powerful flood of Gentile culture that swept over the Jewish communities of Palestine and the Diaspora.

The heroic revolt of the small band of villages led by Mattathias and Judas Maccabeus, as related in the Books of the Maccabees, has become the classic prototype of religious-nationalist resistance to tyranny in the West. The whole tradition of Christian martyrology stems directly from the apocryphal literature on the Jews of Palestine who submitted to torture rather than give up their ancestral beliefs and practices.

The pattern of religious conversion to Christianity—its forms of baptism and catechism, and the like—largely follows that established by Jewish missionaries in their efforts to win proselytes or semi-proselytes among the Gentiles of the Greco-Roman world.

The forms of divine service, the reading and interpretation of Scripture, the recitation of stated prayers and psalms, and other elements of the liturgy used in both the western and eastern branches of the Christian Church are chiefly modeled on the liturgy of the synagogue as it took shape during the Hellenistic-Roman period.

The religious thought of Christianity in antiquity and later of Islam in the Middle Ages is heavily indebted to the philosophical allegory of Philo of Alexandria. For it was Philo who first and most successfully integrated the principles of Judaism with the teachings of the Greek philosophers, especially Plato, and so may be regarded as the founder of Christian and Muslim philosophy, as Professor Wolfson has brilliantly demonstrated. Philo's theory of the Logos as the manifestation of the transcendent God in the physical universe and in the human mind was the most important immediate source of the doctrines of the Christian Trinity.

The translation of the Hebrew Bible into Greek by the Jewish scholars of Alexandria, and its circulation among the Jews of the Diaspora and the "God-fearing" Gentiles who were attracted to the synagogue, made it possible for the missionaries sent out by the small Aramaic-speaking Christian community of Jerusalem to preach the Gospel to Jews and Gentiles in the Diaspora. Had there been no Bible in Greek and no Greek-speaking Jewish congregations throughout the Greco-Roman world, Christianity would no doubt have remained a minor Jewish heresy. Again, the pattern of early Christian monasticism was laid down by the Essenes of Palestine, who, organized in separate communities, lived under strict ascetic discipline, practiced agriculture and simple crafts, and avoided the luxuries of urban society. From these same Essenes, and from circles closely related to them, came the body of Jewish Gnostic doctrine and the mystical-allegorical literature that eventually took the form of the Zohar and other Kabbalistic writings that profoundly influenced, not only later Judaism in Spain, Italy, Palestine, and Eastern Europe, but also Christian thought during the Renaissance and the seventeenth century.

The massive and durable structure of normative or Talmudic Judaism was erected during the Hellenistic-Roman period on the foundations of Biblical prophetic teaching. While this was wholly the work of Pharisaic teachers, who were hostile to Greco-Roman culture, it was nevertheless the case that as a result of their contact with Greek science and art, and with Roman political forms, they became all the more conscious of the specific tasks to which they felt they had to educate the Jewish masses during this period of subjection to two culturally dominant peoples.

It was also in the Hellenistic-Roman period that the pattern of professional and literary antisemitism was first worked out by men like Apion of Alexandria, Apollonius Molon, and others of that stamp. At the same time the first systematic refutations of antisemitic propaganda were produced by men like Philo and Josephus. Josephus' work *Against Apion* remains a classic exposition of Jewish contributions to culture, which it would be difficult to match for effective eloquence in the entire history of this melancholy genre.

These are a few of the achievements of a great age in the history of the Western world and in the history of Judaism. Various historians may summarize its achievements in various ways, each according to his own philosophy of history. For me there are two aphorisms that best distill the wisdom of Judaism in the Hellenistic-Roman period. One is Philo's saying, "Kinship is not measured by blood alone but by likeness of conduct and pursuit of the same end." The other is the statement of the Palestinian Rabbis that "all the righteous of the nations of the world have a share in the world to come."

THE
TALMUDIC
AGE

GERSON D. COHEN

Gerson David Cohen was born in New York City in 1924 and was educated in the Rabbi Isaac Elchanan Yeshiba, the College of the City of New York, the Jewish Theological Seminary, and Columbia University. Between 1947 and 1950 he was Cyrus Adler Scholar and Harry Halpern Fellow in Talmud at the Jewish Theological Seminary and is now Librarian and Instructor in Jewish Literature and Institutions there. Since 1950 he has been Gustav Gottheil Lecturer in Semitic Languages at Columbia. He has contributed studies and articles both in English and in Hebrew to journals, including a noteworthy paper on "Hannah and Her Seven Sons in Hebrew Literature" in the Mordecai M. Kaplan Jubilee Volume. With the late Professor Alexander Marx he edited The Seder Olam *and he is currently preparing for publication* Abraham Ibn Daud's History of Tradition. *In addition to research, teaching, and writing, he has lectured widely in learned institutions and public forums.*

7

TALMUDIC SOCIETY

The earliest document of Jewish history, the Hebrew Bible, contains a record of the birth of the people of Israel and of its slow growth into a small but cohesive ethnic-religious group. The sources of the next stage of this history portray the period of the Jews' schooling in Western civilization and the emergence of a new Jewish culture. It is in this Talmudic stage of its development that the Jewish people undergoes a metamorphosis so thorough and so pervasive as to cast its character in a mold that remains practically unchanged to modern times. This mold, called Talmudic or Rabbinic Judaism, became the abiding legacy of Talmudic civilization to future generations of Jews and Judaically oriented Gentiles.

In its Talmudic stage, Judaism became a universalist religion which welcomed into its fold—and what is more astonishing, into the community of Jews—all who would accept its discipline. Greeks, Romans, and Arabs were preached to and converted. For the first time in recorded history a closed society opened its doors to all with an invitation to *equal* membership. The effects of this metamorphosis in Judaism were to become cataclysmic for Western—as well as for Oriental—civilization. The change from the religion-of-one-people to the people-of-one-religion enabled Jews and Judaism to transcend the limitations of land, language, and even conflicting economic-political interests.

Talmudic civilization was to become the basis of Jewish—and to a large extent Christian and Muslim—communal life in the Middle Ages. To understand the medieval world even superficially requires some appreciation of Rabbinic polity and religion. More important, the painful readjustment which the modern world—and within it the Jews of Europe and the United States—has had to undergo in the past two centuries is in many respects but a revolt against, or at least a reorientation to, the laws of life originally formulated by the Rabbis and their disciples. Ultimately, to understand the modern spirit historically is to comprehend the Rabbinic-Talmudic tradition from which it emerged.

Like the Bible, the Talmud has had special historic and religious significance for the Jews. It is the repository of the civilization which produced their morality and religious vocabulary and their heroes and hero types. To Christians, the Talmud represents the age of Jesus, Paul, and the Church Fathers. It is the soil from which the New Testament and Christianity sprang to revolutionize the history of the world. Hence the period has been the subject of intense, if not always dispassionate, study by Christian and Jewish scholars. The major events and developments are fairly clear. Yet because the period is of such crucial importance, even the most fundamental facts about it have given rise to diametrically opposite interpretations. The phenomenon is not peculiar to the study of the Talmud. The Reformation, the American Civil War, and the Russian Revolution have often generated considerable heat in discussions of what should long ago have passed into the realm of simple fact. Still, it is true that no book has a longer history as a subject of emotional controversy than the Talmud. Above all, it is important to recognize that although in recent times the controversy may have become less intense—though inflammatory anti-Talmudic diatribes continue to appear occasionally to this day—its tone and content remain the same.

To the historian it is self-evident that the Talmud ought not be arraigned like a prisoner in the dock. It is of little importance whether a statement or congeries of statements within the corpus of Jewish literature is more ethical than a Gentile one, or less so. The Talmud, we believe, is in no more need of defense or exposure than the Bible, Homer, or Plato. Rabbinic society and religion, being the products of human activity, beliefs, and aspirations, had their nadir as well as their peak. Our task will be merely to understand the phenomena and to describe them as best we know how.

Now to the Talmudically oriented Jew the Talmud is not primarily a record of the past, but a regimen for the present and the future. "Our merciful Father," the daily Jewish liturgy reads, "inspire us to understand and to discern, to perceive, learn, and teach, to *observe, do and fulfill* lovingly all the instructions of Thy Torah." Each person must strive as best he can to apply the Talmud to his life.

The Talmud is often but an outline, and the details must be filled in anew as fresh problems arise in every generation. Accordingly, it has never ceased to grow in size and scope. As each generation encounters problems not mentioned (or even imagined) in Rabbinic literature, it inquires of its rabbis what the law should be. These authorities then attempt to elicit from the Talmud and its principles the key to their own decisions. The Responsa (or *Teshubot*), as these official replies are called, at once take their place in the chain of Rabbinic tradition and precedent.

Actually, the Responsa are but an extension of a practice that began in the Talmudic age. As life grows more complex, so do the questions and, quite naturally, the answers to them. However, if the yoke of the Law is to be kept intact, life must be related to it. The modern Talmudist must, therefore, search the records of academic discussion as far removed from his time as twenty centuries to gain some insight into problems posed by modern conditions. Are "eye-banks" permissible, since they enhance human life? Or do they violate the sacred Jewish principle forbidding the mutilation of the dead? May a Jew consent to a medical autopsy? What is the status of a woman whose husband is missing and whom official agencies list as legally dead, but who is never known for certain to have died? May his wife remarry, according to Jewish law? These are some of the problems the twentieth-century Talmudist has been called upon to answer. No shade of Judaism, from ultra-Orthodox to Reform, has yet discarded the practice of at least consulting this Rabbinic record for illumination of the present. The Talmud is very much alive to Jews wherever they live within the tradition.

TALMUDIC SOCIETY: TIME AND PLACE

The age and culture designated as Talmudic extends in time from the conquests of Alexander the Great in Asia about 330 B.C.E. until 500 C.E., shortly before the rise of Islam, a period of about eight centuries. Obviously no single label can do it justice. For aside from the fact that the culture of any people is never of a piece over so long a time span, these eight centuries were cataclysmic in their overall effects on the history of the Mediterranean peoples. To treat these centuries as a unit requires by-passing some of the most outstanding events in all history. Within this span of centuries, empires were conquered and dismembered; dynasties rose and fell; the character of almost all peoples was challenged by new habits of thought and radically different patterns of life.

Almost throughout this vast extent of time, the Jews of Palestine, not to speak of those outside the country, were subjects of foreign rulers—Greek, Roman, and Christian—who imposed their own forms of government on Jewish society. As early as the third century B.C.E. the Jews first experienced the taste of an agressive Hellenistic culture that would soon push its way into every part of Jewish life. The Maccabean revolt and the ultimate victory of the insurgent party won for the people a short spell of independence (140-63 B.C.E.) which has left an indelible mark on all aspects of Jewish literature and thought.

The Jewish state, despite its brief life span, saw the emergence of contending religious ideals and sects which have been immortalized by the Talmud, Josephus, and the New Testament, and which have aroused renewed interest since the recent discovery of the Dead Sea Scrolls. The state lasted less than a century, yet its rulers engaged in a program of territorial expansion which was followed by the forced conversion of whole cities to the faith of Israel. Despite the bitter animosities, and even bloody conflicts, between sizable segments of the people and their priest-kings, the era of Hasmonean rule was later fondly remembered as an age "when the hands of Israel were superior to those of the Gentiles."

In 63 B.C.E., Pompey put an end to the independent Jewish state and pruned its territorial holdings, and six years later a Roman governor reorganized the administration of the country along economically and militarily manageable lines. To the renewed experience of foreign domination the Jews reacted with new social and religious responses, many of which became fixed as part of the enduring legacy of Rabbinism. The desperate revolt of the years 66-73 C.E. and the destruction of the Temple by Titus were the final fruits of a century of seething debate and activity, religious as well as political. A second desperate effort at regaining independence in 133, crushed as brutally as the first, broke the backbone of the country. Nevertheless, Jewish society continued to develop in Palestine for three centuries more, hoping against hope for the promised return and restoration. To appreciate the soil on which Talmudic civilization flourished, a knowledge of the saga of the Second

Commonwealth is essential, and some account of it has been given in preceding chapters.

The temporal extent of Talmudic culture is further complicated by the geographic dispersal of the Jews throughout the civilized world. At the center of Jewish life throughout the Talmudic age was the Jewish community in Palestine. However, in Rome and in Alexandria, the two "mother cities" of Mediterranean culture, large Jewish communities lived and experienced a history of their own. Different societies required special adjustments and new formulation, as the culture of Alexandrian Jewry well demonstrates. Almost simultaneously, a vast Jewish community in Babylonia (Iraq) flowered quite beyond the reach of Hellenistic-Roman-Christian control. In time, the Babylonian community rivaled in wealth and influence that of the Palestinian center, finally surpassing it and exerting its own Mesopotamian influence on the Law of the homeland.

In each of these centers the Jews spoke different languages: Hebrew and Aramaic in Palestine, Greek in Egypt, Latin in Rome, and Babylonian Aramaic in Mesopotamia. Furthermore, the religious sources make no effort to conceal differences in religious practice between the Jews of Palestine and Babylonia. Life in Babylonia meant adjustment to a Parthian culture, to a different social, economic, and religious environment from that found in Palestine. However, from the Jewish point of view, adherence to the Law meant conforming to the religious standards codified in Palestinian schools and Palestinian law books, and on occasion these were irrelevant to Babylonian Jewish needs. Accordingly, changes were introduced in Babylonia of which the Palestinian Jews either did not approve or did not know. In the course of time not inconsiderable theological differences emerged between some of the major Jewish centers of settlement, which, in turn, reflected themselves in different ritual usages.

Is it possible, then, to speak of a "Talmudic civilization," a single Jewish culture pattern that includes the major motifs of life of all the Jewish communities throughout eight centuries? Our answer is yes, and is perhaps best explained by an analogy. Just as it is possible to speak of an American pattern, and to include in that category the environment and culture of such contrasting types as the Bostonian aristocrat, the sharecropper of Georgia, and the factory worker of Detroit as representing, through all their real differences, a distinct civilization quite different from the culture of England, so it is possible to formulate real and pertinent characterizations of the Talmudic period as a whole. It will be noted that there are immense gulfs—economic, political, social, cultural and religious—dividing the Americans that we have mentioned; and the same holds true of the Jews of the Talmudic age. It would be pointless to deny or minimize the differences between Jews in different centuries and communities, or even the differences between social and ideological groups of Jews within one community. If anything, a study of these contrasts would portray all the more vividly the vital character of the ideological currents in the ancient world. The contrast, let us say, of the Rabbi of the first century with the Galilean peasant of his day only helps us better to understand the great events of that crucial century in Palestine: the victory of Pharisaism over sectarianism, the messianic aspirations of the people, with their organized revolts and spontaneous uprisings, the rise of Christianity, and the downfall of the Jewish commonwealth. By such an analysis the Rabbinism of the first century would come into full relief as a dynamic religious movement, one which propagated not only a ritual but a complete orientation to life, and which included a political outlook, a social program, and an economic viewpoint.

Given the impossibility of pursuing such a study within the limits of this book, there still remains much that can properly be said of the Talmudic period. We shall therefore try to delineate those features of the Talmudic culture pattern which make it distinguishable from other stages in Jewish religious and cultural development both before and after.

EMERGENCE OF THE TALMUDIC COMMUNITY

What makes it possible to study Talmudic culture as a unit is the basic homogeneity of social organization and religious orientation throughout the far-flung Jewish settlements in the Rabbinic age. Of the instruments by which the values of Judaism were inculcated in the dispersed masses of native Jews and converts, the organized community—with its media for supervision, discipline, instruction, and self-defense—was doubtless one of the most effective and certainly the most enduring. That the Talmudic community structure served as the model for all subsequent Jewish communal life derived, apart from the conservative bent of all Jewish tradition, from the functions it performed not only for Jews but for the Gentile world as well. And these functions changed little throughout the many centuries before the emancipation of the Jews and their absorption into modern national states.

"Jewish community" implies the existence of an alien or Gentile community from which the Jews were distinguished by birth, often by distinct residential areas, but principally by institutions making for a separate social and cultural life. The cohesiveness of the Jewish community ever since Talmudic times stems in large measure from ethnic origin, from the status of birth. However, the Jews superimposed on their natural differences a rationale which was peculiarly religious and which was motivated by the challenge of, and conflict with, the alien world. The Jews were no longer a people concentrated in one country composed of local communities of Jerusalemites, Jezreelites, Samarians, or the like. Talmudic Jewry consisted of a people dispersed from Persia and Mesopotamia in the east, to Rome and perhaps even Spain in the west. All the Jews of Palestine, even if at any time during the Talmudic stage they constituted the majority of the Jewish people, comprised but one community of Jews among many. The Jewish communities of Alexandria, Antioch, Rhodes, and Rome were equally members of the same people in the eyes of the Jews as well as of the Gentiles. Moreover, even within Palestine one had to distinguish between the Jewish communities, on the one hand, and the Samaritan and Gentile (Canaanite, Greek, Roman), on the other.

The Jewish community drew its strength from the desire of Jews to preserve their identity and cultural autonomy in a world where they were always outnumbered and in cultures where they refused to feel at home. Quite apart from the Jews' own feelings, their Gentile neighbors all over the world regarded them as an alien group whose fatherland was Palestine. These universal sentiments about the Jews of the Diaspora did not center upon them alone, but were in keeping with the ethnic classification of all persons in the ancient world. When in Rome, a person may have been expected to do as the Romans did, but that could in no way earn for him the status of a Roman. An Athenian and his descendants remained Athenians no matter how long they or their forebears had dwelt in Rome, if they had not been formally admitted to Roman citizenship. The refusal of the Jews to admit the Samaritans into partnership with them would have been understood perfectly by their Athenian contemporaries, who never contemplated admitting the thousands of metics living in Athens to membership in the city democracy. Ethnic difference was accepted as a natural fact of life. That the ethnic differences of Jews had special overtones is one of the leit-motifs of all Jewish history.

To the overwhelming majority of Jews the ethnic classification of persons and groups was a most welcome practice, and they saw no reason to seek its change. It provided them with a natural barrier which intensified the physical and spiritual separation from the Gentiles, which was what they desired to begin with. As the children of Israel, the people God had chosen, they stood bound by the Covenant entered into at Mount Sinai, and were harnessed by the yoke of the Torah to a unique way of life which transcended time and country. Wherever they happened to live, they felt enjoined by the Biblical command: "Thou shalt not make marriages with them; thy daughter thou shalt not give unto his son, nor his daughter shalt thou take unto thy son. . . . For thou art a holy people unto the Lord thy God: the Lord thy God hath chosen thee to be his own treasure, out of all peoples that are on the face of the earth." Holiness to the Jews signified separation and removal, a form of *imitatio dei*. God had said: "Ye shall be holy; for I the Lord your God am holy." To the Jew this meant: "As I am separated [from the world], so you shall keep yourselves separated [from the rest of the world]." To be a kingdom of priests and a holy nation, they said, meant to keep themselves "removed from the peoples of the world and their abominations." Community—living close together in a group—would make this separation easier and more secure.

However paramount the ethnic-religious function of community may have been, it helped produce something far more religiously revolutionary and enduring than itself. Community in the religious sense was a prime instrument in the achievement of religious universalism. After the exile of Jehoiachin and the aristocracy of Jerusalem to Babylon, the people of Judea were known to have read their exiled brethren out of the religious body of Israel: "They are far from the Lord! Unto us [alone, who remained in Judea] is this land given for a possession." Ezekiel's retort to this high-handed but quite traditional mode of thinking marks a new era in religious life. "Thus saith the Lord God: Although I have removed them far off among the nations, and although I have scattered them among the countries, yet have I been to them as a little sanctuary in the countries, where they are come." Approximately eight centuries later a Palestinian rabbi penetratingly remarked that the "little sanctuary" referred to the synagogues and houses of study of Babylonia. Strictly speaking he may have been anachronistic, but his exegesis was doubtless in keeping with the fruit of Ezekiel's school of thought. God's sanctuary-in-miniature would go wherever the Jews went, without priests or sacrifice, but with the mere recitation of prayer and of Scripture. The first Jewish community arose in alien Babylon; its precedent endures in every synagogue, church, and mosque on the face of the earth. Never again could monotheism be restricted to one locality, for the creator of heaven and earth would hence-forth be worshiped everywhere.

The ethnic ties of the dispersed people were incalculably strength-ened by a monotheistic form of worship which at once set them apart from the rest of the pagan world. However, what is most astonishing to the later observer is the relative homogeneity of the Jewish communities dispersed over the breadth of Asia, Africa, and Europe. No matter where one turned, and despite all the variations in local custom, the underlying core of faith, tradition, and *practice* was the same. How was this basic uniformity achieved in the absence of a centralizing agency with disciplinary powers, and in the absence of modern media of communication?

The answer lies in the sanctification of a book, in the acceptance by Jews everywhere of the Pentateuch as the divinely revealed Law. How and when this adoption of the finally redacted Torah was achieved has been discussed in the section on the Biblical age. As soon as the Torah became the holy code of the people, every facet of life described or enjoined by the Book was raised to religious significance. The language of the Book, the laws, the history of the people—all became part of the religion, links in the covenant between God and Israel. The Sabbath and festivals, the regulations of family life and levitical purity, the dietary laws of Leviticus and Deuteronomy, the laws of usury and slavery, and a host of other regulations of daily routine immediately became the law of the Jews everywhere. The same Torah had declared Palestine the one holy land, and the Temple in Jerusalem the one place where sacrifices could lawfully be offered. Three times a year every Jewish male was obliged to make the pilgrimage to the Temple. Since the Law in effect enjoined the people to gravitate to the country of their fathers, the adoption of the Torah as the law of life made the acceptance of Palestinian *interpretation* of the Torah a foregone conclusion. As it was in Palestine, so must it be elsewhere. After all, Scripture had formulated the ritual with specific reference to the Land of Promise; the community abroad must strive to be an extension, a replica, of the actual sanctuary and its community.

The Palestinian community never hesitated to assert its hegemony over the Jews of the Diaspora. The victories of the Jews of Palestine, like the festival of Hanukka, were proclaimed as the victory of Jewry at large, and the celebrations were mandatory upon all. Regular communications were sent from Palestine to the "exiles" regulating the Jewish calendar and soliciting help for the Temple or for other special needs. Some six hundred fifty years after the canonization of the Torah, the Mishna was promulgated by the court of Rabbi Judah the Patriarch as the official code of Jewish law. The Torah of Moses was to be applied to life in accordance with the norms prescribed in the Mishna, itself the product of centuries of Palestinian interpretation and application of the Torah. The homogeneity of Jewish usage and Jewish community organization was now assured, for the structure of the community in Palestine automatically became the model for the Jews of Syria and Rome, Babylonia, and Alexandria. The Jews of Europe, North Africa, and Asia lived throughout the Middle Ages in communities which often varied in detail but whose underlying structure conformed to Talmudic precept and precedent.

The major change from Biblical to post-Biblical society in the internal administration of Jewish life lay in the new type of civil and religious leadership governing communal and national affairs. The Davidic dynasty, momentarily revived by Zerubbabel's short-lived administration, was replaced by the high-priesthood, which in Maccabean times openly donned the royal purple and the pretensions that went with it. The removal of the Hasmonean house and the relegation of the high-priesthood to purely cultic jurisdiction coincided with the loss of Jewish independence and the incorporation of Palestine into the Roman imperial framework. During the six centuries of the Second Commonwealth, the powers of the high-priesthood form an arc, mounting steadily until the first half of the first century B.C.E., and then swinging downward until its elimination in the year 70 C.E.

External power politics were not solely responsible for the change in the fortunes of the priestly class. The internal metamorphosis of Jewish religious life brought to the fore a new class of religious teachers who vigorously propagated their doctrine of a life according to Torah and ultimately succeeded in gaining control over all aspects of autonomous Jewish life. The net effect of the instruction and subsequent rule of these scribes, and later on the Rabbis, was to shift the authority of religious codification and instruction from the priesthood to the scholar, and the responsibility for ritual performance from the Temple and the priest to the synagogue and the individual.

The rise of the rabbinic class in the Jewish community is traceable to the disappearance of that unique class of religious preachers of Biblical society, namely, the prophetic school. In Biblical times, the function of the prophets was to communicate divine revelation, that is, the word of the Lord on all problems on which God might choose to disclose his will: the building of a temple, the choice of a king, the sacrificial cult, social justice, and even foreign policy. The Torah itself, though of priestly orientation, had been revealed to a prophet rather than to a king or a priest. However, with the arrival of Ezra and the adoption of the Torah as the law book of the nation of Judea, prophecy was deprived of its major reasons for existence.

What need was there of prophets if the revelation was now available in one book, in other words, if all prophecy had already been anticipated. So long as there had been no single Torah, but a number of codes circulating in different areas of the land, the prophets were indispensable for information concerning God's wish. However, Ezra produced and made binding a book which was all-inclusive. "Ye shall not add unto the word which I command you, neither shall you diminish from it, that ye may keep the commandments of the Lord your God which I commanded you." A continuing revelation through the mouths of prophets would make the written word, the Torah, superfluous. The adherent of the written Torah sensed intuitively that prophetic revelation jeopardized his hallowed text, for at any moment it might be undermined completely.

Prophets, or foretellers of the future, did not pass out of Jewish society at once. Down to the destruction of the Temple men continued to appear claiming direct knowledge of the future, and even the Pharisees acknowledged that prophecy was still a possibility. But on one point the teachers of the Torah would not budge. A prophet could not proclaim the Law, for that had already been committed to writing. Prophets might well have the key to the outcome of future events, but requiring fulfillment were the demands of the present, and they were set down in a book. The new claimant to religious knowledge was the interpreter of the Book, the scribe or sage, who indicated how the revelation of Moses applied to each person here and now.

The young Christian Church, with its new scripture, was to be faced in the second century with a similar problem. That this church, too, had to stamp out prophecy, the claim of individuals to communication from Heaven, demonstrated the incompatibility of a continuing revelation with a scripture. Ultimately Christianity followed the example of Judaism and placed all religious authority in the hands of its bishops, the recognized interpreters of its new gospel.

The promulgation of the Torah as the code of the nation and its individuals made the Law an open book, free for all to study and to fulfill. Inevitably, one of the special functions of the priesthood in Biblical times—knowledge of the Torah and instruction in its application—became public domain. The priest, in the view of the scribes, retained only the prerogative expressly delegated to him by the Torah, ministration of Temple ritual.

To be sure, the priests did not easily submit to a new doctrine which would deprive their class of much of its power. The recognition of the high priest and his staff by the Persian and Hellenistic rulers gave the priesthood a secure hold on the reins of Jewish government. However, the priestly group had to contend throughout Temple days with a vigorous and growing class that denied its absolute right to power. The concrete issue around which their disputes revolved was which class, priestly or learned laity, was the legitimate ruler of autonomous civil as well as religious Jewish life.

COMMONWEALTH WITHIN AN EMPIRE

Jewish self-government, the distinguishing characteristic of all pre-emancipation Jewish communal organization, was born out of a common desire of the Jews and the Gentile powers that ruled over them to have the Jews conduct their own affairs by their own laws. Since the high priest and his hierarchy had been at the head of the religious community even before the Macedonian conquest, the priesthood was recognized officially and held accountable for the implementation of all imperial policies within the Jewish community. The high priest automatically became an officer of the governing power, and his appointment had to be approved by the ruling government. Moreover, the very law of the Jews, since it was approved by imperial decree, became enforceable by the high priest as the imperial law of Judea. In an imperial charter for Jerusalem issued in 199 B.C.E., Antiochus III officially recognized the Torah as the law of the country and the religious hierarchy of the country as its internal legislative body. By the provisions of this charter, the imperial government undertook to enforce the levitical laws of purity and even the animal tabus of Judaism. Since every subsequent ruling power ratified a similar policy with regard to Jewish internal organization, Judaism became an officially recognized and protected religion. Its religious hierarchy gained the dual status that it held almost until modern times: spokesmen for the Jews to the Gentile world and rulers of the internal affairs of the Jewish community.

The Torah which Ezra had brought was ratified by imperial fiat. In the absence of a Jewish monarchy, the priests often assumed the role of political heads of the Jews as well as that of sacerdotal officers. Put in another way, the political affairs of the Jews were permanently taken over by their religious officials, or, as the Jews expressed it, until God should restore the house of David to its rightful throne. When the Jews gained their independence from the Seleucid empire under the Maccabees, they ratified this communal structure in a popular assembly of 140 B.C.E. as the rightful domain of the Hasmonean dynasty. Simon the Maccabee had merely appropriated for himself and his heirs those rights and duties which had previously been bestowed on the Jewish leaders by the Gentile imperial powers.

When, in 63 B.C.E., the Roman armies of Pompey entered Jerusalem and declared their lordship over the country, the Jewish community returned to the status that had existed under the Persian, Ptolemaic, and Seleucid emperors. Religious autonomy was guaranteed to the Jews under the administration of their high priest, while the political and economic affairs of the country were administered by a Roman official. The latter might be the high priest, a Jewish ruler like Herod, or a Roman procurator. To Rome that made little difference. The crucial point was that the governor of the country was not a sovereign ruler but an agent of Rome. As a religious group, the Jews continued to enjoy full freedom to practice their own way of life without interference. Judaism, in fact, was granted a special status as a "licit religion," that is, one which did not have to incorporate into its pantheon a symbol of the official state religion of Rome.

The Jews, however, refused to distinguish between religious freedom and political sovereignty. For reasons which will be discussed below, the affairs of state were to the Jews as much a subject of their Law as the dietary regulations and the sacrificial ceremonies. Consequently, they revolted again and again until the Temple and with it the hieratic community were utterly destroyed in the wars of 66-73 C.E. and 133-136 C.E.

No Jew questioned the right, indeed, the obligation, of the priesthood to administer the religious ceremonial of the Torah. It could not be otherwise, for Scripture had given them "charge of the Sanctuary, . . . the holy things, and the charge of the altar." During the early stages of Talmudic civilization, however, the Jews split into a number of schools of thought about who should supervise the internal workings of the priesthood and pass on the legitimacy of its personnel and practices. Side by side with the imperial governor and the high priest during the period of Persian and Hellenistic domination, there had functioned a body of "elders of the Jews," or senate, which together with the high priest administered the internal affairs of the country. How this body was chosen we cannot say. Some of its members were perhaps descendants of the Judean aristocracy of Biblical times, while others probably attained the rank of "elder" by virtue of their wealth or political connections. Whatever their origin, this council of elders was accorded official recognition by Persian and Hellenistic rulers. It was from this body, too, that Simon the Maccabee obtained the covenant establishing his dynasty as the legitimate heir to the reins of Jewish government.

In the days of Simon's son, John Hyrcanus, or more probably during the time of Simon's grandson, Alexander Jannaeus, the elders of the country suddenly come into sharper focus. It is in this period that our sources describe a conflict between several factions as to who should constitute the council of state and who should pass on the legitimacy of the way both cult and affairs of state are administered. Specifically, the Sadducees and Pharisees were in open conflict over the question of Alexander Jannaeus' right to the high priesthood. However, the real differences between the two factions lay much deeper. The actual issue had to do with the question of who represented the legitimate successor to the Biblical carriers of religious authority, the prophets. To the Jew of Talmudic civilization, the prophets of earlier days had had quite another function from the one which we attribute to them. Firmly believing that Moses had received the whole Torah from God at Mount Sinai, the Jew necessarily concluded that prophets such as Hosea, Amos, Isaiah, and Jeremiah must have conveyed a message in keeping with the Torah. Reading the prophets the people knew what their function had been. The prophets had come to admonish the people of Israel to observe the Mosaic Torah and to warn them of the consequences of failure to fulfill it. In other words, the prophets had been the early teachers of the Torah, above all, its interpreters in the light of contemporary problems and new situations. Who would continue their role of interpreters of the sacred Book, of critics of the administrators of cult and government in accordance with the Torah's principles?

The Sadducees, adherents of the school of a certain Sadok, argued that the role of interpreter had been entrusted to the officers delegated by the Torah to administer it—the priests and the wealthy aristocracy of the country who had from time immemorial controlled the affairs of Temple and state in their councils. "For the priest's lips preserve knowledge, and one should seek the law at his mouth; for he is the messenger of the Lord of hosts," were the words of the last of the prophets.

The Pharisees argued that the priesthood was merely a hereditary class consecrated to perform the Temple ritual. How the commandments were to be fulfilled was in no wise the private knowledge of the priests. It was the function of the men of the Book, "the disciples of Moses" and the heirs of the prophets, to pass on the propriety even of priestly behavior, and, it goes without saying, on whatever portions of the Torah were not addressed specifically to priests but were germane to the daily life of the people as a whole. "The Torah which the Holy One, blessed be He, gave to Israel," the Pharisees maintained, "was given by the hands of Moses. . . . Joshua took over from Moses; the Elders took over from Joshua; the Judges took over from the Elders; the Prophets took over from the Judges; Haggai, Zechariah, and Malachi took over from the Prophets; the Men of the Great Assembly took over from Haggai, Zechariah, and Malachi." Clearly, the tradition was not a priestly but a *prophetic* one handed over to the Men of the Great Assembly, whom the Pharisees identified with Ezra and other "Men of the Book." Just as the prophets had not been members of one family or tribe, so the bearers of their traditions need not necessarily stem from any particular segment of the people. "The Torah was revealed in the wilderness, publicly and openly, in a land belonging to no one, so that everyone wishing to receive it might come and do so." Accordingly the elders of Israel should consist of expounders of the living Book, be they priests or Israelites, highborn or of obscure origin.

Did the Pharisees, therefore, consider themselves prophets? The question itself would probably have shocked them as rank blasphemy. However, in claiming to hold the key to the meaning of the Mosaic revelation they were continuing an ancient institution, although in a new garb and with a radically different technique.

So long as the Maccabean rulers accepted the Pharisaic view of Jewish law and government, the Pharisees not only approved of their rule but served as propagandists for the men they considered the messengers of God on earth. Some even went so far as to assert that John Hyrcanus had been granted the crown of prophecy along with that of priesthood and kingship. It could well be, one writer asserted, that the Messiah promised by Scripture would stem from the tribe of Levi, to whom the future king of the seed of Judah would have to defer completely.

The break with Alexander Jannaeus and his adherents drove the Pharisees to the very opposite extreme. They rejected him as an illegitimate priest and interloper who had no right to the Jewish government. They insulted him publicly by pelting him with their *ethrogim* (citrons) during the celebration of Tabernacles, while the more fanatical among them joined forces with the Seleucid king and helped him to invade the country. Students of the period have mistakenly supposed that the Pharisees were opposed to all forms of

Jewish temporal rule. That this was not so is shown by their complete about-face during the reign of Alexander Jannaeus' widow and successor, Alexandra Salome. She, realizing that the Pharisees had mass support, replaced her late husband's officials with appointees from the popular party. Led by Simeon ben Shetah, they took over with gusto, reforming legal and ritual procedure in accordance with their own program. To cap their victory, they made the days of their new reforms national holidays, thereby classifying their Saducean opponents with the other enemies of the Jews whose defeats they celebrated annually.

Their victory, however, was short-lived. The internecine strife that erupted in Palestine with Salome's death ended with the incorporation of the country in the Roman imperial machine, and the Pharisees' views on government were relegated to their academies, where they became a dream of the messianic restoration of Israel. Herod, the Idumean usurper, made genuine efforts at humoring and propitiating them. He consulted with them and enforced their views in the administration of cultic matters. But his effort was of no avail. Neither Herod nor the Pharisees would ever willingly accept the domination of the other.

The Pharisees did not attain full control again until after the destruction of the Temple and the collapse of the ancient Jewish machinery for self-government. Their victory then, as they sadly recognized, was a consequence of the victory of Rome over a people and institutions they could now govern almost unchallenged.

In 63 B.C.E., when Pompey arrived in Damascus, three contending Jewish delegations appealed to him to settle the bloody feud then raging between the Hasmonean brothers, Hyrcanus and Aristobulus. Two groups represented the brothers, while a third party claimed to speak on behalf of "the nation." This party openly petitioned to set aside the claims of both aspirants to the throne, "saying," according to Josephus, "that it was the custom of their country to obey the priests of the God who was venerated by them, but these two, who were descended from the priests, were seeking to change their form of government in order that they might become a nation of slaves." Listening with Pompey to the arguments of the three parties was one of his field commanders, Gabinius, who returned to Syria and Palestine as proconsul six years later, and who indicated almost immediately that he had been impressed most by the anti-monarchic representatives of "the nation." Gabinius divided the country into five administrative districts and established over them five councils (*synhedria*) to regulate the Jewish population in its internal affairs. Once again, as under Persian and Hellenistic rule, Jerusalem and its four companion districts were ruled as "aristocracies," as Josephus calls them, the cult being administered by the priests and the society at large by the elders of the country. The ancient Jewish senate had been revived, and under its new name, the Sanhedrin, was to become an enduring institution of the Palestinian Jewish community.

The Sanhedrin was primarily a legislative council which decided upon the interpretation of Jewish law and through its legal interpretations upon the internal affairs of Jewish society. Since Gabinius' reorganization did not last long—it was officially abolished by Julius Caesar in 47 B.C.E.—we are unable to form any substantial conclusions on the powers and procedures of the local councils. However, the name of the institution stuck, and the Jews adopted it as the official name for their higher courts and legislative councils. Local councils consisted of twenty-three elders, appointed apparently by the high court of seventy-one, which held its sessions in the chamber of hewn stone in the Temple in Jerusalem. The supreme Sanhedrin, under the chairmanship of the high priest, restricted its activities to the adjudication of cases of appeal, principally in ritual matters. Affairs of state and civil law were totally in the hands of the representatives of the Roman government, which obviously wished to maintain a close watch on all political, financial, and criminal matters.

Quite apart from the official organs of civil and religious government, the religious associations of Pharisees and Essenes maintained their own courts and councils to govern the conduct of their members. The Essenes and allied ascetic associations renounced as evil all organizations except their own, and consequently they legislated and administered their severe disciplines totally within the confines of their own communities. The numerically larger and more influential movement, the Pharisaic order, also governed autonomously the purely social aspects of its discipline. But although the Pharisees, too, opposed the regulation of Palestinian society by Roman agents, Jewish or Gentile, and utterly renounced the religious principles of Sadduceeism (which, it will be recalled, represented the views principally of the conservative aristocracy), they chose to work within the existing framework of society and to gain control over it. The great majority of the Jewish masses regarded the religious teachings of the Pharisaic leaders as normative, and looked upon these sages as the heirs of the prophets and the authoritative expositors of God's revelation to Israel. Although we cannot be sure, it appears that certain crucial areas of ritual law, notably the regulation of the calendar and the conduct of the high priest in the Temple on the Day of Atonement, were relegated by general consent after the days of Salome to the leadership of the Pharisaic order. Pharisaic prestige and discipline were immeasurably strengthened by the general acquiescence of the people at large in their leadership and program. To the masses the Pharisees doubtless represented one aspect of the long battle against the illegitimate rule of Romanophiles and Sadducean oligarchs.

Although, except for the brief reign of Alexandra Salome, the Pharisees probably never gained absolute control of the Sanhedrin in Jerusalem, they vociferously aired their views on all questions, even at the risk of their lives. No sooner had the traditional institutions of Judaism been suppressed by the Roman war of 67-73 than the Pharisaic survivors refashioned the council of the Jews under its popular name, the Sanhedrin, and declared themselves the legislators and arbiters of Jewish society. The head of the Pharisaic order now became the undisputed patriarch of all Roman Jewry.

The destruction of the First Temple in 586 B.C.E. had, it was generally agreed, vindicated the prophetic school in its battle against the traditional Israelite religion and the policies of its ruling classes. The Second Destruction, in 70 C.E., had a parallel result in the struggle between Pharisaism and other movements within Judaism. Sectarian movements did not die overnight, but Pharisaism rapidly became synonymous with Judaism itself and the Jewish community the subject of Rabbinical control.

Later Jewish tradition, recalling the catastrophic destruction of Jerusalem and its national Jewish institutions, tended to credit Rabban* Johanan ben Zakkai with the rescue of whatever autonomy the Jews succeeded in retaining. Having become convinced that the battle for Jerusalem was lost, he left the city and threw himself at the mercy of the Roman besiegers. Vespasian, the Rabbinic story goes, impressed with the stature—and prophetic gifts—of the man, permitted him to open an academy in the coastal town of Jamnia (Yabneh). Thanks to his resuscitation of the Sanhedrin, the Jewish community of Palestine was in effect able to go on with its way of life.

The fanciful smoothness of uninterrupted Jewish self-government and Rabbinic autonomy is, of course, more of a parable of Jewish survival and faith than a record of historical fact. Rabban Johanan undoubtedly defected to the Romans in despair, and he was in all likelihood immediately thrown into the Roman internment camp at

---

* *Rabban* ("our master"), in contrast to *Rabbi* (actually, *Ribbē*, "my master"), was the title reserved for the Rabbinic patriarch from about 20 C.E.

Jamnia. His "academy," therefore, at first consisted of a group of scholars discussing their tradition quite unofficially, having neither Jewish nor Roman recognition. In fact, when upon his release the Rabbi began to enact certain changes in Jewish ritual practice, he was sharply challenged and bitterly resented. As soon as his former associate Rabban Gamaliel emerged from hiding, Johanan was displaced in favor of the former, who was a lineal descendant of the Davidic house of Hillel. Later legend vindicated Johanan as it did the earlier Jeremiah, for history had "justified" the defections of both. Even his opponents could not help feeling gratitude for the establishment of a communal substructure within which their own control became immeasurably facilitated. Above all, however, the founding of Rabban Johanan's academy at Jamnia summarized to the Jew the fundamental stability of the Jewish community and the *relative* ease with which it recovered its autonomy under the supreme and almost unquestioned control of the Rabbis.

Historically considered, five major factors made for the successful reconstruction of Jewish community under Rabbinic leadership. The first, and unquestionably crucial, circumstance was the fact that the Jewish community, despite the tremendous loss of life and wealth in the war against Rome and despite the almost complete loss of autonomy, remained physically intact. The Jewish population retained control of a sizable portion of the land, and, with the exception of Jerusalem, those areas which had previously been peopled by Jews remained Jewish towns. Slowly but steadily, many of the political exiles returned and resumed business as usual. It was a decimated and impoverished community that survived, but the overwhelming majority of the country was still Jewish. Two principal changes in the Jewish community were to have lasting effects. Jerusalem, the mother city of the Jewish people, was made virtually "Judenrein," and the reins of Jewish government were not to return there until very recent times. In addition, whole blocs of Jewish land had been confiscated by the Roman army and granted to Gentiles or local collaborationists. On the other hand, these displacements resulted in a corresponding increase of Jewish settlement in the northern parts of the country.

Second, if the Jewish population provided the membership for a revitalized community, their religious orientation was responsible for the form it assumed. Two centuries of Pharisaic preaching and instruction in the interpretation of the Torah had won the masses over to Rabbinism. Hillel and Shammai, the outstanding representatives of the two wings of Pharisaism, had already become popular hero types, symbols of saintliness and of the study and fulfillment of the

Torah. Hillel himself was said to be a descendant of the house of David, and the leadership of his family doubtless expressed to many the undying hope for the messianic return and restoration of the Biblical kingdom. Rabban Johanan ben Zakkai, though not a member of the Davidic family, was anachronistically crowned as a personal disciple of the venerated Hillel, thus according additional legitimacy to his assumption of power.

With these sentiments we must couple the active desire of the Pharisees to fill the vacuum that had been created by the Destruction. Although they could not at first have entertained much hope for autonomous rule, they seized whatever opportunity they could to implement their principles and guide the community to a way of life as close as possible to their blueprint of the Law. And finally, over and above their popularity with the masses, their efforts at revitalizing a Jewish community represented Jewish solidarity against the hostile Gentile world. Theirs was the eternal battle of Jacob against Esau, and the people rallied to the symbol of their Biblical Patriarch.

Third, the transition to a Rabbinic community was made infinitely simpler by the half-millennium experience of the Diaspora, of life away from the homeland, removed from Temple and priesthood and predicated largely on voluntary acceptance of religious government. Despite the central position of Palestinian Jewry, the existence of a numerous and widespread Diaspora enabled the Jewish people to become a nonpolitical nation. For land and state, loyal and observant Jews the world over had substituted ethnic and religious institutions designed to bring a measure of the homeland to them. Outstanding among those new foci of Jewish life was the synagogue, with its communal meetings for prayer and for the instruction and discipline of the members of the congregation.

The Jew of Palestine knew full well, observing the thousands of pilgrims who flooded the Temple grounds annually, that a pious Jewish life could be and was maintained by the laity simply out of personal commitment. So strong, indeed, had been the Pharisaic emphasis on individual religious responsibility that Palestine itself already abounded with synagogues. Herod's Temple had contained a synagogue chamber where services were held daily side by side with the altar and sacrificial service. Though no believing Jew would dare to admit it, the priesthood and the sacrifices had become by the time of the Destruction a vestigial relic, necessary only because the Torah prescribed them. With the Temple in abeyance, the Jewish population of the Holy Land itself became a quasi-Diaspora community. Who, therefore, could logically assume the new leadership if not the apprentices and protagonists of lay religion, of synagogal community—the Rabbis!

Fourth, underlying any voluntary community is a faith, a rationale of personal commitment. The Jewish premise was a simple one: God had ordained the Torah as Israel's way of life and had enjoined his children to live by it. The defeat at the hands of the Romans was a profound and palpable calamity. However, it did not spell, as the Christians proclaimed, the bankruptcy of traditional Judaism. Why should it? Had not the Almighty exiled his children and destroyed his sacred house and subsequently restored them once before? Jerusalem might be bare and the Temple a heap of ashes—"and yet for all that," as Scripture clearly asserted, "when they are in the land of their enemies, I will not reject them, neither will I abhor them, to destroy them utterly and to break My covenant with them; for I am the Lord their God." The Jewish people was being chastised severely, but by no means rejected. Their duty was therefore clear: to attempt to make themselves worthy of divine favor by their deeds. Rabbinism was the program of such a fulfillment.

Fifth, the Jewish community owed its survival largely to the Roman policy of toleration. Jewish tradition does not speak kindly of Rome or of most of its emperors. One cannot expect the Rabbis to have been neutral to a Titus who felt that the Temple must be destroyed, "so that the Jewish religion might be utterly eliminated; for with the removal of its source, the trunk [i.e., the Jewish people] would speedily wither." Nor could they take lightly the offensive tax to Jupiter Capitolinus imposed on them as a punitive measure. Yet, in the retrospect of nineteen centuries, Rome must candidly be acknowledged to have dealt with the Jews harshly but not viciously. At no point did it proscribe the Jewish religion, and barring the short period of martial law during the insurrection of Bar Kokhba, it never attempted to prohibit the Jews from congregating and pursuing their religious curriculum. Synagogues arose and were given imperial protection throughout the empire. Rome adhered to its traditional policy of rule by law and of full toleration for ancient religious associations. The very agent of Jewish defeat in Palestine was also the agent of Jewish revitalization as an autonomous Diaspora, a commonwealth within an empire.

THE INSTITUTIONAL PILLARS

The conditions for a Rabbinic community, a society held together not by political power but by religious belief, were in existence. The new Sanhedrin began and remained an academy whose hold over its members lasted only so long as they wished to remain within it. That the Jews were willing to defend their organs of Torah to the death bespeaks a mature and fully crystallized way of life.

At the helm of the Palestinian community stood the Rabbinic patriarchs, who, like the high priests whom they had replaced, became a family dynasty. The house of Hillel, beginning with Gamaliel II (ca. 85 C.E.) held the principate in its hands until the year 425, when Gamaliel VI died without a male heir and the Byzantine court refused to allow the appointment of a successor. Attempts on the part of some of the Rabbis to remove the leadership from the exclusive control of one family were short-lived, because Gamaliel II and his lineal successors had their authority confirmed by the Roman government. The most that a scholarly insurrection could have achieved under the circumstances would be the appointment of a rival as official lecturer in the academy, and this, merely a token move, would have undermined the insurrectionists' own basic drive for a unified and disciplined community. Once again, therefore, the historic Jewish paradox prevailed: the Rabbis, who traced their authority to a Law that transcended human control, submitted to a Jewish leadership which drew much of its power from the mundane office of Rome.

On the other hand, the patriarchs recognized at once that their only chance of success in revitalizing an autonomous community lay in their keeping Rome out of their academies, in other words, in their renunciation of Roman help. Henceforth the machinery of Jewish government would have to be completely internalized and self-imposed. On this point the Rabbis were in entire agreement. The greatest communal offender became the *delator,* or informer, who aided the Roman authorities in keeping a close watch on all Jewish convocations. In Rabbinic theology, individuals defying communal discipline, especially the principles governing relations with the government, were classified with apostates and unregenerate sinners, whose lot would be eternal torture in hell. Jewish solidarity in the face of the Gentiles, though rooted in religious principle, was nurtured and galvanized by the desire for self-preservation.

Jewish organizational unity, however, was more specious than real. Officially the patriarch sat at the head of the academy, which in its executive sessions functioned also as the Sanhedrin. In practice, rabbis with individual followings conducted their own academies and appointed local judges who tried cases in Jewish communities all over the country. At times the authorities of these local academies refused to follow directives of the patriarchal court, and conflict or excommunication ensued, depending upon the seriousness of the issue. After the collapse of the Bar Kokhba revolt, the Rabbis attempted to check the chaos resulting from uncontrolled appointment of judges and agreed to turn over all such administrative matters to the patriarch and his court. But the old practice was resumed as soon as local academies regained their footing. The reason for this lies at the basis of all Jewish autonomy subsequent to the destruction of Jerusalem.

With the dissolution of the high-priesthood and its cultic authority, the Jewish people could be governed only by the Torah. The Jew was obligated to fulfill whatever parts of the Torah could be fulfilled in the absence of monarchy, prophecy, Temple, and priesthood. The only problem that remained for the Rabbis to resolve was the specific ways in which the Torah was to be applied. In other words, they were the repositories or bearers of the Oral Law. Their particular function, however, was not vouchsafed to them by revelation or by dynastic authority. Their claim to recognition stemmed from their knowledge of the Torah and of the traditional interpretation of its word. Consequently, whoever qualified as an initiate of the tradition had as much authority to administer it and to pass it on to his apprentice as anyone else. The Rabbinate from its inception was not a clergy or priesthood. It was a profession to which anyone might gain admittance if he could meet its standards. Thus any three Jews could constitute a court, provided their procedure and decisions were in accordance with Rabbinic tradition. In the absence of a prophetic oracle, early Pharisaism had recognized as legitimate variant interpretations of the Law. "Both views are the words of the living God," they said, and absolute uniformity of teaching and practice would have to await the return of Elijah the prophet. Rabbinic discussion, even the Mishna itself, is replete with differences of opinion and records of divergent practice. Each scholar transmitted the traditions he had received to his disciples, and from among these he appointed "rabbis" (masters) to serve as lecturers and judges.

Difference of opinion and practice was a legacy of Pharisaism which the post-Destruction leadership recognized as a normal phenomenon, though limits were placed on individual freedom. The disturbing thing was the patriarch's inability to control the appointment of judges, the very arm of communal discipline. Old traditions die hard, and the existing situation was rationalized in the criticism that patriarchal appointees did not meet the requirements of scholarship, that they were politicians whose ignorance was commensurate with their wealth and influence. Judah III (275-320 c.e.), the very patriarch who was charged with the appointment of unqualified judges, finally appealed to Rome and obtained a rescript declaring all decisions of unlicensed courts null and void. Patently, this appeal to Rome was an act of desperation symptomatic of the rapid decline of Palestinian Jewry in the third and fourth centuries.

The three centuries of patriarchal rule had an enduring effect on all aspects of subsequent Jewish communal life. In the first place, the prestige of the patriarchs as titular heads of the high court, coupled with the real powers which their position gave them, brought about the dissemination of their own views to the increasing exclusion of others. To be sure, this was a slow process and not without exception, but the decline of one of the two great Pharisaic factions, the school of Shammai, along with its dissenting traditions, was assured by the succession of Hillelite patriarchs beginning with Rabban Johanan ben Zakkai. The Shammaites had not always been in the minority, but Rabbinic tradition has largely obscured the extent of their original influence. It is significant that later tradition paints Hillel as a warm and saintly personality, Shammai as a cold and intemperate scholar. The "Hillelization" of Jewish personal and communal law was further hastened and assured by the redaction of the Mishna (ca. 200 C.E.), which became at once the normative code for the whole community. The great majority of rabbis after the Destruction were of the Hillelite school, and their close alignment with the patriarchal dynasty increased the latter's real sphere of influence.

More important, however, was the lesson of self-discipline that the Rabbis learned in ceding certain issues to the exclusive control of the patriarch. As a group they early realized that in matters requiring general decision, conformity with the views of the majority was essential. No less a man than Rabbi Eliezer ben Hyrcanus— who was, among other things, the patriarch's brother-in-law—was expelled from the Sanhedrin and excommunicated for refusing to accept a vote of the majority on a relatively inconsequential question of impurity. Joshua ben Hanania, second in authority to the patriarch, submitted to Gamaliel II and had to appear with his purse and walking stick on the day which Joshua believed to be the Day of Atonement, simply because the patriarch declared it a normal weekday. As his colleague Rabbi Akiba expressed it to Joshua: "Whatever Rabban Gamaliel decrees [in matters of the calendar], we must obey, as it is written: 'These are the appointed seasons of the Lord, even holy convocations, *which ye shall proclaim in their appointed seasons*' [Leviticus 23:4]"; i.e., whether they are in their proper time or not, these alone are the sacred festivals. Another Rabbi put it more bluntly: the patriarchal court of each generation would have to be accepted as having the same authority as Moses himself. Community required discipline, and it was the patriarch, therefore, who had the right to issue special edicts for communal affairs and to call to account anyone who flouted the respect due to his office. What is remarkable is the relatively infrequent mention in the sources of the use of force. Jewish self-discipline in the medieval world goes back to the period of Talmudic schooling.

The right of the patriarch to command obedience to decisions of a public nature was one aspect of his function as overseer of the general welfare. However willing the masses of the people were to accept the authority of the Rabbis in religious affairs, there were some who felt that the academy was not the sole arbiter of Jewish policy and administration. Two groups stand out in Palestine as having on occasion strongly resisted the policies of the patriarchate: the remnants of the party of independence, and the wealthy families who had formerly controlled municipal affairs.

In 115 C.E. a violent uprising of Jews occurred in Egypt, Cyrenaica, Cyprus, and parts of Asia Minor with the aim of avenging the Jewish defeat of 70 C.E. and the continued harassment of Jewish communities on the part of the Gentile population. Some eighteen years later, Bar Kokhba* led a Jewish uprising which promulgated "the redemption of Israel," minted coins, and even appointed a priest as coleader of the independent community. Though all Jews sympathized with the aims of these revolts, and some rabbis even supported them actively, there can be little doubt that their leaders acted without patriarchal endorsement. The ruthless suppression of these insurrections and the decimation of Jewish populations suspected of disloyalty effectively eliminated aggressive Jewish political activity until modern times.

The wealthy laity, however, never ceased to be a force to contend with in the Rabbinic community. They were the source of revenue and the mainstays of public credit and business. Who could blame them for not always submitting unquestioningly to Rabbinic regulation of taxation, prices, civil litigation, and municipal legislation? Wherever such a class existed—and this holds true for the Jewish community of the medieval world as well—its financial power gave it some measure of control over Rabbinic government. We have already made reference to the appointment of unlearned notables to

---

* Among the recent archeological discoveries in the vicinity of the Dead Sea is a military order from the Jewish general. In it he is named Simeon ben Kosba. "Bar Kokhba" (The Star) is probably a popular pun playing on the messianic hopes that his followers pinned on him.

the Palestinian Jewish judiciary. In Rabbinic times, too, they were necessarily included among the boards of seven councilors governing every Jewish municipality and in the groups charged with regulation of taxation. Two factors served to keep their claims in check. To begin with, the crushing blows which the Palestinian Jewish community suffered after the unsuccessful uprisings battered the economy of the country and the stability of the wealthier classes. With the inflation of prices throughout the Roman Empire in the third century, the economy teetered on the brink of total collapse. Secondly, wealthy malcontents had to acknowledge that they too were subject to the Torah. They too were members of the synagogue, shared in its conscience; so the very Rabbinic morality which openly professed championship of the poor was part of their own morality. In addition to all this, the objective separation of all Jews from Gentile social life prevented the rich from being anything but a strong pressure bloc within the community. They could hardly aspire to control it.

The city council, or notables of the community, governed much in the manner of councils throughout the ancient, medieval, and modern world. They were local groups with a hold only over their own population. The homogeneity of Jewish communal life stemmed from the universal Jewish institutions which, from early Talmudic times, became and remained the pillars of Jewish ethnic-religious association. These institutions were the synagogue and the academy.

Technically, the difference between synagogue and house of study, as the academy was called, is only theoretical. The former, having originated as a surrogate for the Temple service, was endowed with a greater degree of physical sanctity than the academy. Officially it was the communal house of prayer to which the whole community flocked on the Sabbath, and business people on Mondays and Thursdays as well. It also served as a communal assembly hall, local courthouse, charity center, and elementary school. On the other hand, the house of study served as a center of daily services, as the central school of religious studies, and as the communal court for litigation. However, at first the house of study was by no means a popular center. Its frequenters were the Rabbinical scholars and their disciples.

More than any other Jewish institution, the synagogue can be credited with having assured the continuity of Jewish religious life after the second Destruction. Perhaps the most decisive acts of Rabban Johanan ben Zakkai were those which obliged the synagogues to add to their liturgy certain forms which had previously been the exclusive right of the Temple. By a series of ordinances he decisively averted the danger of a static attachment to the memory of a ritual of the Temple mount. The synagogue, the vehicle of local religious expression, was permanently freed to develop in accordance with the needs of the congregations of Jews.

The stabilization and adoption of a uniform order of synagogal service permanently fixed the foundations of communal religious expression. Scripture and personal prayer were the two focal points of Jewish piety. The Torah was read on market days (Monday and Thursday), on the Sabbath, and on festivals and fast days, thus affording each Jew at least one weekly lesson in Scripture. On the Sabbath and festivals, the weekly reading was supplemented by a prophetic passage. The academy at Jamnia also fixed the basic wording of the liturgy but left the door open for free lyrical composition. Since every Jew had to pray, and originally read his own portion when called to the Torah scroll, the role of the priesthood was utterly transcended. Sermons on Sabbaths and before festivals and other occasions for the general population served to instruct the masses in popular ritual behavior and, even more, to inspire them with the importance and relevance of Scripture to their personal lives. The synagogue became the schoolhouse of the Jewish people, and appropriately enough, it was there that the children were sent for their early instruction. On market days, public announcements were promulgated there, and charity collected and distributed. Little wonder then that Jews have generally called their center of worship "synagogue" (*bet ha-knesset*), that is, house of assembly. The house of divine service was the hub of civic and religious life. Hadrian, the Roman emperor at the time of Bar Kokhba's revolt, doubtless knew what he was about when he forbade Jews to congregate even for religious purposes. Though scrupulously tolerant of Jewish religious association, the Romans recognized that the synagogue had replaced the Temple as symbol and center of inspiration and hope for the future.

Synagogal administration usually fell to the wealthy or influential leaders of the local community. They were best equipped to administer and maintain what, as archeological findings have disclosed, were not always inexpensive edifices. These leaders were charged with the hiring and supervision of elementary-school teachers and communal functionaries, and with administering public utilities: a cemetery, a bathhouse, and the public charity chest.

The principles by which the community was governed, since they were the subject of the scholar's study, emanated from the *bet ha-midrash*, the Rabbinic academy. At all times, the most renowned of these academies was the one attached to the office of the patriarch.

To it came not only students, but the heads of other colleges to discuss questions affecting the whole community or matters of law
requiring plenary debate. This academy, as we have indicated, was
the chief center for the appointment of judges and over-all super-
visors of the Jewish community. Besides this center of learning and
legislation, other academies centered about great scholars who held
their lectures in various parts of the country. Often these academies
furnished the judges and teachers for the surrounding villages and
thus maintained their status as an integral part of the community.
Since the academies were the centers for study of the Torah, their
leaders preached that no community was truly complete without its
house of study. And the people, apparently, felt the same way. In
Babylonia, Italy, Spain, France, Germany, and Eastern Europe the
academies (*yeshibot*) and communal houses of study (*bet ha-midrash*)
followed the Jews wherever they went. They served as the Jewish
college and the Jewish forum—and even as communal hostels—where
the people studied their past and adapted it to the present.

It is one of the oddities of Jewish history that Rabbinic Judaism
in its medieval stage was the direct outgrowth, not of Palestinian
legislation and exegesis, but of the reinterpretation to which the
Palestinian tradition was subjected in Babylonia. In one sense, this
was all the more fortunate for later Judaism, since Babylonian
Judaism, as a completely Diaspora civilization, was the logical model
for other Diaspora Jewries to imitate. Perhaps this is a piece of
rationalization. In any case, historical forces certainly assured the
supremacy of the Babylonian schools by the fourth century, so that
in the Middle Ages even Palestinian Jewry adopted the Babylonian
Talmud as its code of law.

Actually, the differences between Babylonian and Palestinian
religion are of major interest only to the Talmudic specialist. For
the most part they derived from the different environments and
varying cultural and economic conditions of the two populations. The
basic pattern was the same in both countries, having been fashioned
by the concept of a separate and protected community formulated
by the Seleucids.

The ethnic and religious centrality of Palestine in the life of the
Diaspora further stimulated imitation of community life in the homeland. Substantial annual contributions were sent to the Temple
treasury, and among the thousands of Jews from all over the world
who made annual pilgrimages to Jerusalem the Babylonians were
among the most conspicuous. So strong was the representation from
this quarter that special consideration was given to traveling condi-

tions in the East when it came to fixing the calendar and the dates of the pilgrimage festivals each year. For its part, Babylonian Jewry actively identified itself with the political causes of the Palestinian community in its wars against Rome. From its midst came some outstanding religious leaders of the homeland, among them Hillel the Elder.

Above all, the synagogue, which was to play a crucial role in Jewish life everywhere, in all likelihood originated in the Babylonian exile, when Biblical monotheism had first had to fashion a center for itself on alien soil. How strong its influence was is illustrated by the active missionary campaign that Babylonian Jews conducted among the Gentile population. One of the most curious events in the first century was the conversion of the queen and prince of the petty kingdom of Adiabene to Judaism. By the middle of the second century Babylonian Jewry was probably the most secure and flourishing of all Jewish communities, and it is no wonder that many Palestinians sought permanent refuge there from the heavy hand of Rome. Parthian toleration had been such as to allow the Jews virtually to fashion their own state within the Babylonian Empire.

At the summit of the community stood the exilarch, who claimed lineal descent from the house of David, but whose real source of power lay in the authority given him by the Parthian and later Persian governments. He conducted his court with royal protocol and had full authority over, as well as responsibility for, the civil affairs of the Jewish community. Jewish judges, tax collectors, and market inspectors were appointed by him, and his authority practically included the power of life and death over the Jews within his domain. Needless to say, he was accountable to the government for the activities of his court and his officers. So established did his office become, and so convenient was the communal arrangement in the sight of the imperial authorities, that the institution endured the changes of imperial dynasty and religion until the twelfth century.

Officially, religious life lay within the purview of the exilarch's powers, since to Jews as well as Gentiles ethnic and religious life were identical. However, in Babylonia, too, the ever-growing number of Rabbinic scholars and the establishment of academies in the second century created a polarity of powers within the community. The arrival of the Mishna and of Palestinian-trained scholars gained for the masters of learning increasing recognition among the masses and power commensurate with that of the exilarch's office. To be sure, we hear of tension and even open conflict between rabbis and exilarchs, but in the last analysis each side had to recognize the authority of the other. Judges were appointed from the academies' rolls, while the yeshibot requested exilarchal approval of their leadership.

The subject matter of the yeshiba curriculum consisted of the elucidation of Jewish law and, beginning with the third century, of the Palestinian Mishna. Like its Palestinian counterpart, the Babylonian academy was primarily concerned with the application of Jewish law, and those aspects of Jewish law relevant only to the Holy Land were largely omitted in the Babylonian curriculum. On the other hand, greater attention was centered on the adjustment of Jewish civil and religious law to the Gentile environment in which the Jews lived. "The civil law of the state is law" (that is, binding upon Jews) was a principle first enunciated in a Babylonian academy of the third century.

Over and above the synagogue, the Babylonian academies developed an interesting medium of communication to the masses of Jewish laity. Two months a year, at the end of the summer and winter, interested laity and scholars convened at the two largest academies, in Sura and Nehardea (later Pumbeditha), for intensive Talmudic discussion. These semiannual retreats served to make the academies living intellectual centers and to keep the population in constant touch with the sources of law and moral teaching.

Many a locality in Babylonia had an exclusively Jewish population. So intense was the pride of Jewish leaders in their autonomous and intellectual community that some rabbis even attributed a special sanctity to Babylonian soil. With the rise of the great academies, some felt that it was forbidden to leave Babylonia even for Palestine. Certainly the historical circumstances which permitted the Babylonian academies to flourish for centuries after those of Palestine had closed or dwindled to inconsequentiality provided a transitional center for the young Jewish communities of Western Europe. Above all, however, it made the Babylonian Talmud, and its recension of the tradition, the normative canon for the whole Jewish world. Thus a Jewish community of the Diaspora mediated the tradition to scores of generations and countries beyond its own.

8

THE RABBINIC HERITAGE

The Jewish communal framework which developed in Talmudic times was only the most tangible product of historical circumstances and of the peculiar ideology of Judaism. Like other societies, the Talmudic rationalized its communal institutions and hallowed them as part of the sacred system of Jewish belief, and this was, in part at least, because these institutions were indispensable for the communication of the religion to the people at large. Without them, or their equivalent, the survival of Judaism as a vital civilization would have been inconceivable.

However, a mere glance at Christian or Muslim history will indicate that practically identical institutions can develop and yet transmit quite different ideologies. To appreciate the practices and aspirations peculiar to Talmudic society and culture, we must focus our attention on the religious outlook which characterized it and which distinguishes it from other stages of Jewish development before and after.

TORAH: SCRIPTURE AND TRADITION

It will perhaps appear strange that a discussion of Judaism should begin with what is at first blush a second step in the religious process, namely, Scripture. Underlying the sanctity of a book there ought presumably to be a conception of God, a theology, and an explanation of the way in which the Deity makes his will known to mortals, that is, a theory of revelation. Nevertheless, our departure from the accepted canons of theological exposition is, we believe, required in fairness to the idiom and mental processes of the culture we are seeking to understand. It cannot be overemphasized that Talmudic Judaism is not to be comprehended as a logical theological system. For what characterizes the Talmudic culture pattern is precisely its Scriptural and, consequently, nonrational framework. Not only are its basic tenets predicated on the text of the revelation, itself above human reason, but far more significantly, its religious and moral ideology is held together by no more than the sequence of the verses of the Bible. In a word, Rabbinic thought with its complex of values and concepts is essentially a running commentary on Scripture. No more than Scripture can the utterances of different schools of thought be fused into a unified theological system. So the varieties of Talmudic thought cannot be reduced to one cohesive structure of ideas and attitudes.

It is idle to ask: What does *Judaism* have to say about the nature of man, about sin, about the world to come, about God himself? The question is as idle when put to the Rabbinic literature as it is unhistorical when put to its Biblical antecedents. The Bible has incorporated within its canon a number of views of God, a number of conceptions of sin, retribution, love, justice, and so forth. The dogmatic theologian and the religiously committed must somehow try to harmonize contradictions and elicit a unitary point of view. The Rabbis could not avoid either the demand of their own minds or the demand of others for basic consistency. However, the structure of the religious community, with its lack of any formalized hierarchy, prevented the definitive resolution of conflicting views on any but the most crucial questions. For the most part, different teachers expounded different solutions, and as in Scripture itself, they were recorded side by side. All later efforts to reduce Judaism to an integrated system of ideas and values—Maimonides is an excellent case in point—were held in no higher respect than the teachings of Rabbi Eliezer ben Hyrcanus, Rabbi Akiba, Rabbi Ishmael, or hundreds of other commentator-teachers. The only question we can in fairness put to the Rabbinic sources is this: What did each of the Rabbis make of one or a number of statements in Scripture? What do their eclectic theologies and commentaries have in common?

It is this common denominator that justifies us in beginning our analysis of Talmudic religion with its conception of Scripture. For not only does the Torah serve as the foundation of Talmudic ritual and values, but whatever conceptions the Rabbis had about God, revelation, human nature, Israel, and even about Scripture, were formally derived from Scripture itself. To be sure, Scripture was not the only source of Talmudic insight and ideology; some of the basic features of Talmudic Judaism are quite new to the Bible. Ultimately the real source and stimulus for a vital orientation to life had to be the environment and the novel challenges which each day produced. However, to achieve a serious hearing and to attain a measure of validity an idea had to be attached to a verse. Occasionally this might involve tearing a phrase out of context, emending the holy text, or, *mirabile dictu,* interpreting a Hebrew word as though it were synonymous with a similar-sounding Greek one! The net effect was the same: the interpretation had been "derived" from Scripture.

Every school of Talmudic thought engaged in reinterpretation of Scriptural verses to suit immediate needs, for all Jews of Talmudic culture agreed on the postulate that the Torah was the first and final revelation of God's will and command. Accordingly, it was eternally relevant and everlastingly binding, and it was the source of all truth and wisdom. "Not only with you do I make this covenant and this oath," Moses proclaimed, "but with him that standeth here with us this day before the Lord our God, and also with him that is not here with us this day." No one should be misled by the ostensible parochialism of Scripture, which often plainly addresses itself to a community with a primitive economy, and so seems totally inadequate to the complexity of the Greco-Roman world. "Scripture speaks in details of its own milieu," the Rabbis explained, but the details merely illustrated principles that were everlasting. Earlier we pointed out that the Talmud is very much alive to Orthodox Jews even in our atomic-technological century. That is because "the Sages [of the Talmud] speak in terms of their own present," while their law and its principles go on forever. The medieval Jew made of the Talmud exactly what his Talmudic ancestor had made of Scripture. Hence Solomon ibn Gabirol, Abraham ibn Daud, Maimonides, or Gersonides could discuss the merits of Platonic and Aristotelian ideas in the light of the words of Moses, Amos and Isaiah, and in the idiom of the Talmud.

The doctrine of an eternally valid Scripture, relevant to the problems of all generations and societies of man, is undoubtedly the most enduring and pervasive legacy of Talmudic civilization to Western society. What the Jewish philosophers and lawyers did to their heritage was amply duplicated by Christian and Muslim, who subjected the New Testament and the Koran to the same legalistic and philosophic tailoring. For centuries, to cite one outstanding example, the Christian Church, which forbade usury among Christians, provided for an uninterrupted source of capital loans by reinterpreting the Deuteronomic law so as to make it apply to Christian creditors, but not to Jews lending money to Christians. Beginning with the Crusades, the Schoolmen argued against this traditional dichotomy and against any form of usury by appealing to other Biblical texts which might prove that Christians and Jews were not "strangers" in the Scriptural sense. When in the sixteenth century Calvin undermined the age-old restrictions against usury and thus smoothed the progress of capitalism, he could do so only by reinterpreting the Biblical verses and "proving" that they were no longer applicable. The history of European economy is thus intimately bound up with the history of the interpretation of two verses in Deuteronomy that were set down in writing in Palestine seven centuries before the Christian era.

In the United States, the Puritan ethic, the American Revolution, and the war over slavery were often grounded in the exegesis of Scripture, for Scripture contained God's revelation and guide for the construction of a just and equitable polity. Throughout the world, in thousands of churches and synagogues, countless sermons are preached on social, political, and economic issues the solution to which is "indicated" by the verses of Scripture. The sermon is the literary form in which the Bible is applied to contemporary issues. Only the sermon, or in Rabbinic parlance, *midrash* (literally, ferreting out, hence, interpretation), has made of the Bible a living book rather than a literary classic read merely for pleasure or edification. The Rabbis made the Bible the cornerstone of Jewish life, and Christianity transmitted their method to every portion of the world that came under its influence.

In Talmudic antiquity, as in the Middle Ages, the legalistic power of the Bible was a fact of daily experience, making itself felt in all those areas of life that were subject to social control and legislation. That Jewish law, like its Christian and Muslim counterparts, was authoritarian, at least in theory, was owing to its Scriptural origin, and Scripture was all-embracing. The contrast with modern canons of behavior and belief is instructive. Even the normally devout and genuinely religious person in democratic society is outraged by prelates who issue religious pronouncements on styles of clothing or who attempt to censor frank and impartial discussion of sex, science, or political legislation. We appeal to our democratic faith and the right to learn the truth and judge according to our *reason*. Modern man regards these things as beyond the purview of religious ritual, and brooks no interference with his privacy.

The Midrashic schools of Talmudic civilization could conceive of relatively few domains which are "private" concerns. One of the most instructive documents for the history of Judeo-Christian civilization is the nineteenth chapter of Leviticus, which is generally known only for part of one verse, that proclaiming the law of brotherly love. Too often the context of this verse is overlooked, and the Hebraic point of view accordingly mutilated. The very chapter that proclaims the lofty ethical ideals of social life insists in the same breath and tone: "Thou shalt not let thy cattle gender with a diverse kind; thou shalt not sow thy field with two kinds of seed; neither shall there come upon thee a garment of two kinds of stuff mingled together." Though Pauline Christianity abrogated much of the Jewish ritual law, in principle it agreed with the Talmudic exegete who stated that "the laws of purity and impurity, of menstruation and of [sacrificial] bird offerings are the essentials of the Torah." The mother and daughter religions differed with regard to which parts of the Bible remained binding and which could be codified, and as to how the details of Scripture were to be interpreted for practical application. But both religions agreed on the postulate of a Scripturally governed life.

The only way that the revelation could be kept relevant to new problems was to interpret the written word so as to make it apply to the activities of the peasant and the businessman, the housewife and the servant, the schoolboy and the scholar. It is this interpretive body of literature that Judaism calls its legal Midrash, or Oral Law. The primary function of Midrash was to make the Torah a living legal document, so that every act of life might be performed in accordance with the divine command. Though the Torah obviously did not spell out the correct behavior for every situation, surely the Revealer must have foreseen every possible contingency and made room for it in His Law. God undoubtedly worded His revelation in such a way as to provide the key to its everlasting application and fulfillment. The Word must, accordingly, be studied and thoroughly examined for hints of the right direction to follow, and a loophole sought where its plain sense has to be relinquished. The kind of Midrash the Jew took most seriously was the Halakhic or legal exegesis, for it gave him the answer to the one question he considered most pertinent to his life: What does God command me to *do*, how would He have me *act* in the face of this or that situation?

From Scripture the Jew inferred, too, that it was not his function to distinguish between important and unimportant commandments. Had not God put the ethical and the ritual together to indicate their equal importance? "Be heedful," his rabbi taught him, "of a light precept as of a weighty one, for thou knowest not the reward of each precept." Another authority put it even more plainly: "If one says 'This law does not seem right,' he has no share in the world to come." Not that the reason for ritual and civil laws was not sought or discussed. As we shall see, a whole body of Midrashic literature deals with the rationale of Jewish life, the whys and wherefores of the Torah. But in the last analysis, the reason was secondary to the performance. Following Rabban Johanan ben Zakkai, who summed up the Biblical laws of purity, the observing Jew felt he must perform the whole Torah: "Neither do the dead impurify, nor do the ashes of the red heifer purify. This is my decree, such is my ordinance; ye may not transgress it!"

The Torah was searched over and over for the detailed ways in which the Jew might fulfill Scripture. The Decalogue forbade work on the Sabbath. What was "work" and what was not? Midrash was the technique by which rest and work were completely defined. From a single command prohibiting cooking a kid in its mother's milk, a whole corpus of dietary laws was derived forbidding the consumption of meat and dairy products together. Scripture, to cite a renowned example of the Midrashic technique, had promulgated the law of retaliation, "eye for eye, tooth for tooth, hand for hand, foot for foot." This, the Pharisees declared, in flat contradiction of the plain sense of Scripture (and of their Sadducean opponents), signifies the requirement that a physical injury inflicted by one man on another must be compensated for in funds. "Why?" the Talmudic authorities asked. "Does the Torah not say *eye for eye?*" The Talmudic reply is a precious specimen of the Scriptural lesson as it was taught in the ancient Jewish schoolhouse. "You might think that where a man put out his fellow's eye, the offender's eye should be put out, or where he cut off his arm, the offender's arm should be cut off, or again where he broke his leg, the offender's leg should be broken. Scripture, therefore, has stated: *He that smiteth any man, and he that smiteth a beast mortally shall make it good.* [Scripture used the word ("smiteth") in both cases to teach us that] just as in the case of smiting a beast compensation is to be paid, so also in the case of smiting a man compensation is to be paid." Verse by verse the teachers proceeded until the hundreds of Biblical commandments had multiplied into thousands.

The first source of law was the text as confronted by the needs and realities of life itself, and mediating between the two was the scrupulous explication of Scripture. At times, the Midrashic method was of itself inadequate, for the scholars could find no means of connecting their own wishes with the provisions of Scripture. At this point they resorted to innovation, provided, of course, they could avoid open contradiction of the Torah. The *takkanah,* or legislated ordinance, if it gained the acceptance of the community of scholars, took on the authority of law and was enforced. In spirit it was intimately bound up with the Midrashic orientation, for its purpose was always to preserve the spirit of the Law as the Rabbis understood it. In the realm of economic life, Hillel the Elder came to the rescue of the small entrepreneur and farmer by the institution of *prosbul,* which enabled creditors to collect their loans even after the seventh year of remission. By guaranteeing repayment, he ensured the uninterrupted flow of credit from the moneyed classes to the poor. Much more significant than the institution itself—which was avowedly borrowed from the Hellenistic courts of his day—is the way in which Hillel rationalized it. To allow the Biblical law of the remission of debts to continue undisturbed, he stated, would risk the violation of the Deuteronomic command, "Thou shalt surely open thy hand unto thy poor and needy brother." In every generation of the Talmudic and post-Talmudic community, new features were added to Jewish life by legislation that plainly had to be fabricated by mortals.

Innovation for the sake of the spirit of the Law brings us face to face with the Rabbinic definition of the spirit of Judaism. No matter how concerned the Rabbis were with ritual performance, the choice of alternatives compelled them to formulate some kind of abstract principle by which the followers of the Torah should be guided. It is here that the Prophetic and Hagiographic books played a crucial role in the definition of Judaism. The spirit of the cult and its ritual was clearly undefinable, except in relative and conjecturable terms. So God had ordained, and so it was to be done. But what had God intended by the injunctions and precepts which He had revealed? To the Rabbinic mind Micah had stated in a nutshell what the prophets had been declaring from the days of Abraham and Moses to the close of the Biblical age: "It hath been told thee, O man, what is good, and what the Lord doth require of thee: only to do justly, and to have mercy, and to walk humbly with thy God." Where Micah and other prophets had protested against Israelite cultism, later Judaism explained, it had only been to deny the automatic efficacy of ritual. Ritual could achieve nothing of itself. The personal *intention* behind it was the crucial factor. The Torah and its rituals were a discipline reminding one at every step of the imperative for justice and humility of behavior, which lead in turn to deeds of mercy and loving-kindness.

Hospitality to wayfarers, visiting the sick, dowering the needy bride, bestowing charity anonymously, attending the dead to the grave and comforting their mourners, and the making of peace between man and his fellow—these became the supreme and symbolic virtues of daily life. Hence social legislation was fashioned along the emotional lines enunciated by the prophetic school. The latter were regarded as the first interpreters of the Torah, and those who claimed their mantle followed in what they regarded as the prophetic footsteps. The cold and impersonal commands of the Pentateuch were charged with the emotional pitch of prophetism, of dedicated worship and loving service. The multiplicity of Talmudic charity laws and institutions, the honor accorded to the communal charity officials, and the incessant concern with the poor and indigent in civil law is one of the glorious chapters in every Jewish code from the Mishna to the *Shulhan Arukh*. Amos' feeling for mankind was codified and incorporated into the sacred ritual.

If law was the heart and body of Judaism, the second type of Midrash, Aggada, or homiletical interpretation, was its lifeblood and marrow. Here, too, the Talmudic doctors clung to the pattern cut out for them by Scripture.

The Torah is not only a law book, it is much more. Considerable portions of the Bible are purely informative; history begins with the first day of creation and ends with the rebuilding of the walls of Jerusalem under Nehemiah. Other portions contain lyrical poetry, liturgical selections, theological reflection, and pure wisdom literature. To what purpose all of this? The conclusion easily imposed itself on the mind of the Jew that the Bible was not only a code of behavior but a guide to the totality of life. In it one would find the clue and the key to every form of authentic wisdom and to every genuine insight. Its historical record of ancient generations—from Adam to Ezra— was not only sacred history but, above all, a parable of all human activity, a model from which all men could profit. The Rabbis declared that prophecies relevant only to their immediate audience were not recorded; only those revelations which were essential for all generations were committed to writing. To the historical portions of the Bible their reaction was the same. God would not have troubled later generations of Israel with a record of mere trivialities. Every detail of Scripture was in reality an archetype, a carefully selected and worded bit of information from which to learn.

Every phrase, verse, and story, every proverb, poem, and prayer—in short, the entire Bible from Genesis to Chronicles—was studied, analyzed, and interpreted. Where the plain sense of Scripture seemed obscure, the exegetes elucidated the text and translated it into their own idiom. Where the Bible had omitted details in a story, they speculated on what probably happened. How did Adam react when he experienced the first nightfall in the Garden of Eden? What did Cain say to his brother Abel just before killing him? What motives lay behind the building of the Tower of Babel? In connection with this kind of speculation we cannot do better than refer the reader to Professor Louis Ginzberg's monumental seven-volume work, *The Legends of the Jews,* where a modern master of Rabbinics has assembled all of the material and transcribed it in the form of a running narrative parallel to the Biblical story. To the Talmudic Jew, ancient history became current events, and the challenges of the day were met under the inspiration of Scriptural antiquity. The feuds between Jacob and Esau, Joseph and his brothers, Moses and Pharaoh, became eternal struggles symbolizing the conflicts of Jews (and for that matter, of all men) throughout history. Thomas Mann's *Joseph and His Brothers* is one of hundreds of literary efforts which drew quite consciously on this genre of Midrashic technique.

Nothing in the homiletical form of interpretation makes the intentions and methods of the Rabbis so plain as does their allegorical treatment of the Song of Songs. A blunt and impassioned compilation of love ditties, the work was incorporated into the Biblical canon only because it was read as a dialogue of love between God and the community of Israel. "Thy two breasts are like two fawns," sings the lover. "Thy two breasts," the Rabbi explained, "are Moses and Aaron." To the ancient, there was nothing strange in this manner of reading, for Greeks and Romans regularly employed the same technique in their own classical poetry and mythology. To the Jew, the text and its Midrash infused a feminine quality of love and warmth into a life of rigor and unending duty. In Aggadic Midrash the imagination ranged freely, releasing the emotion of the devout, and so converting law to love and ritual to caress. The Bible was no longer only the guide and master of the Jew; it was his intimate companion, his alter ego.

Aggada, or the homiletical exposition of Scripture, supplied the Jewish idiom expressive of the phenomena of life and history. Its clichés and catchwords became the vehicles for the communication

of values, ideals, and emotional response. While the Greek philosopher had built a logical structure whereby the universe was systemati-
cally rationalized, the Jew thought and spoke in terms saturated in
value concepts, terms that had moral and emotional overtones, that
conveyed the Hebraic evaluation of every fact as either right or
wrong. The sun, moon, and stars, the elements and animal life—
these were not mere natural phenomena. They were manifestations of
God's love or God's justice depending on how human society experienced them.

Through Aggada the Talmudic Jew engaged in theological speculation. Though open discussion of the essence of God was dis-
couraged officially, the learned Hellenistic milieu, with its mystical
outpourings and theological debates on the nature and essence of the
deity, inevitably penetrated the Rabbinic academy. The visions of
Isaiah, Ezekiel, and Daniel, even the impersonal account of the creation in Genesis, provided fertile ground for Jewish conjecture about
God and His being. But above all, theological expression roamed
freely when it came to the subject of God's relation to man in general and to Israel in particular. To the Jew, naturally enough, the
two most engaging subjects for consideration were the Torah, the
supreme gift of God, and God's selection of the Jews as His chosen
people. The virtues of the Torah, of its precepts, and of its loyal followers were inculcated on every occasion, thus providing the rationale for a militant faith undaunted by subjection, persecution, or
even defeat.

The two forms of Midrash, Halakha and Aggada, grew side by
side. Often a sermon or scholarly discourse was at the same time a
skillfully woven tapestry of legal and homiletical exposition, providing the regimen and its motive together. However, there was a fundamental difference between the Halakha and Aggada in the demand
they made on the individual Jew. Law—civil, ritual, and domestic—
was normative, binding, and absolute. To be sure, there were differences of opinion and practice with regard to questions of the Law,
but the essential point was that a person could be held socially accountable for his behavior, and his peculiarities had better not be
idiosyncrasies. On the other hand, the homily was subjective and hence
essentially without binding force. The only restraints or limits upon
Aggada were the dogmatic presuppositions bound up with the acceptance of the Torah as the revelation. Although Aggadic statements were expressed in terms of traditional value concepts, the latter
were by no means codified forms. The ultimate difference between
the two classes of interpretation appeared in the net result of the
exegesis. A legal statement in Scripture could in theory have only one

possible meaning; in other words, the Law had to be logically derived from the formulation of the precept in Scripture. Legal contradictions had to be harmonized. In contrast, Aggada proceeded, verse by verse, providing no necessary connection between the homily expounded in one verse and the interpretation given to the next. Further still, the very same verse lent itself to any number of Aggadic interpretations and rationalizations even by the same commentator. Homilies varied with their authors or with the same author's moods and insights. What need to harmonize incompatible emotions and reactions, when Scripture itself accorded them an equal hearing?

Rabbinic Judaism, though it has survived to become the oldest organized religion of Western civilization, never could formulate a systematic theology. Individuals like Maimonides, Albo, and Crescas might attempt to formulate creeds, but in the absence of an organized and fully disciplined hierarchy their ideas had no official sanction, and each Jew could accept or reject which of them he pleased. Characteristically the medieval Talmudist regarded the philosopher as an Aggadist, a homiletician whose insights could inspire but not ordain.

Not that Talmudic Judaism had no dogmas, but these, significantly enough, were often stated negatively. So we find in the Mishna: "The following have no share in the world to come. He who denies resurrection, he who denies the divine origin of the Torah, and the Epicurean." Translated into contemporary terms, the statement excludes from the community of Israel whoever denies divine retribution, the sanctity of Scripture and its oral exegesis, and Divine Providence. Actually, these principles of faith all follow from the one assumption that the Torah is God's revelation to Israel. If the Torah and its application in daily life were not ordained by God, the Rabbinic schoolhouse had no meaning. Assume that it makes little difference to God how we act, or that he will not justify the righteous and condemn the wicked, and the perseverance in a Jewish way of life against the current of the whole pagan world is nothing but a masochistic comedy. But how these dogmas were to be translated into a positive creed was left to the individual Jew to decide.

But Rabbinic dogma can also be stated in positive form. From the axiom that the Torah was divine revelation, it followed that the historical accounts it contained were statements of fact. Whatever the significance of these accounts for the future, they were, in the first instance, a record of events which really took place. With one notable exception—the story of Job (which some rabbis considered only a parable)—no fact of Scripture could be questioned or contradicted. Thus the chosenness of Israel was as much a fact of the Bible as the assertion that God rested on the seventh day of creation. Every Jew was certain that God would redeem His people just as the Bible promises. Every believer was as certain of these articles of faith as he was that the Law had to be fulfilled. Beyond these obvious deductions the meaning of faith was the subject of considerable diversity of opinion. Aggadic Midrash never ceased to change so long as the Bible remained the acknowledged source of human guidance.

If the conception of an eternally valid Scripture is the most important of Rabbinic legacies to civilization, there is another Talmudic postulate bound up with it, and hardly less important. God revealed the Torah to *all* of Israel and holds every man and woman individually responsible for its fulfillment. Providence and individual retribution were the logical corollaries of personalized faith. The prophetic assertion that God held each person accountable for his deeds in the moral realm was extended in Talmudic civilization to the cultic-ritual domain as well. For the external, visible Temple cult, Talmudic Judaism increasingly substituted an internalized conscience at least as strong in its grip as that of visible ceremonial. This conscience dictated a ceremonial of its own, often quite colorful and performed in congress with other Jews. But given its internalized character, responsibility rested with the individual, who of course was also subject to social pressure. True, autonomous Jewish society had disciplinary means at its disposal, such as fines, flogging, and excommunication. But its real achievement was the inculcation of a strong sense of guilt in the sinner, and it was this, not physical coercion, in any case poorly developed, that held Jewish society together in a firmly knit unit. Daily prayer and individual proficiency in the Book were but the most obvious elements in the personalization of religious obligation and responsibility. The most far-reaching result of the new conception of faith was an active universalism, directed to converting the pagan to the chosen way of life.

What made the Jew an alien in every community he inhabited was not so much his ethnic attachment—the Jew was not unique in this respect—but his militant insistence on his foreign habits and values. Not only did he behave in Rome as the Jerusalemites do, but he made no bones about concealing his contempt for the misguided, if not downright sinful, civilization of the majority. Whoever takes offense at stubborn and militant sects, like Jehovah's Witnesses, need but read the Book of Esther to appreciate Haman's reaction to Mordecai. It made little difference to the Gentile that the Jewish rejection of Greco-Roman civilization was not intended as a deliberate affront; that it was the only course open to adherents of a jealous monotheism and a levitical code that made a priest of every believer. So much the worse for their superstition, the pagan replied; look at Jewish behavior objectively, and you will find that it bespeaks a deep contempt for the whole human race. The Jew's answer was his actions. The worth of a human being, he declared, depends not on his birth but on what he does. The Torah and its salvation were given to all who would but enter the covenant of Abraham. Thus Talmudic culture broke down forever the ethnic barriers to membership within the Jewish group. Conversion to the faith, submission to the yoke of the Torah—these were the keys to chosenness. For the first time in history a people nullified its ethnic status and reconstituted itself as a church.

It is a widely circulated belief that Judaism does not encourage conversion or missionary activity among the Gentiles. How false this notion is about Talmudic culture may be seen from the early Christian documents, which frankly confess that their easiest access to Gentiles was in the synagogue where the latter came to hear the Jewish sermon. The Talmudic literature records with pride the activities of some of the more distinguished proselytes, a number of whom were of pagan royalty. Simultaneously with its intense ritual separatism, Talmudic civilization proclaimed and fostered a new universalism, without which Christianity and Islam could never have spread as they did. So widespread and recognized did Jewish missionary activity become that Christianity, at the very moment of its break with the Jewish people, proclaimed itself the new and the true *Israel*.

Along with the Talmudic conception of Scripture, the Jewish view of individual religious responsibility altered the course of Western civilization. Jewish-Christian hostility dates back in large measure to the first two centuries, when the two religions openly and heatedly competed for the conquest and salvation of human souls and, in fact, claimed the same name.

Membership in the Torah made of one a fully accepted Jew; indeed, it obligated the convert to *ethnic* Jewish duties and responsibilities. However, so obsessed was the Jewish expounder of the Torah with spreading its message that full conversion was not required of those who wished to observe its law and yet balked at full identification with the Jewish people. "The pious of the nations of the world" and "fearers of the Lord" were two of the religious categories used to designate Gentiles who unofficially accepted more or less of Judaism. All of them had to renounce idolatry—note the negative formulation—blasphemy, murder, theft, and sexual promiscuity, and had to agree to live a strictly moral life in civil transactions. Others adopted one or more of the more commonly known Jewish practices: some renounced pork, others rested on the Sabbath, while women, in particular, were known to light the Sabbath candles in their homes. Though obviously not as deserving as converts, these Gentile fellow travelers were the elect of the nations and were assured of a share in the world to come.

The life of the Torah, besides prescribing rules of conduct and attitudes to the problems of life, made of the Jews a people of the Book in two fundamental senses. The holy Book, or any fragment of it, became a sacred object to the Jews. Before the Torah, Jews are commanded to rise; a scroll that is unusable may not be cast away, but has to be buried or stored. The skins, the ink, the script, and of course the spelling of the scrolls were ritually regulated; the omission of one letter was sufficient to disqualify an entire scroll for synagogal use. Fragments of the Torah, such as those contained in *tefillin* (phylacteries) and *mezuzot* (doorpost mementos) were sacred and must not be desecrated. The language of Scripture became the sacred tongue, and though Talmudic universalism necessarily recognized the validity of study and prayer in any language—Philo most certainly prayed and studied Scripture in Greek—Hebrew occupied a special place in the scale of Jewish values. To be sure, Hebrew was also a vehicle of ethnic identification and preservation. But every ethnic aspect of Jewish life capable of religious association was sanctified.

The physical veneration of the Book was, of course, but the more tangible expression of the awe in which the revelation was held. Profounder worship lay in the study of the contents and meaning of the Torah. Such study became the most honored ritual and profession in Talmudic civilization. It was more than a mere quip when one Palestinian teacher paraphrased a verse in the Bible saying: "Would that the children of Israel leave Me [i.e., God] and pursue my Torah." In the hierarchy of values, Rabbi Akiba and his school argued, study takes precedence over performance, for study is the key to fulfillment. In Rabbinic parlance, wasting time was waste of study time, for every available moment must be dedicated to memorizing and understanding. On this subject the homilists harped without end. The study of the Torah was the Jewish calling, and its followers were assured of the perpetual companionship of the Divine Presence. The renowned little tractate in the Mishna known as The Ethics of the Fathers is really not a treatise on ethics at all, but essentially an exhortation to the acquisition of Torah. "An illiterate does not fear sin," Hillel the Elder said. This statement by one of the fathers of Talmudic Judaism cryptically sums up a whole complex of Jewish values and the Jewish man's vocation on earth. Righteousness, the Talmudic Jew contends, does not consist in spontaneous goodness alone, but in a life disciplined in the heavy harness of the Torah. In one form or another, Talmudic homilists maintained that greater merit accrued to one who fulfilled the Torah out of a sense of duty than to one who did it out of personal choice. Learning in the precept and wisdom of the Torah was the path to performance and consequent acceptance into the kingdom of Heaven.

What we have been describing is, from the historical point of view, the theory expounded by the scribes, elders, and Pharisees in their struggle for authority over Jewish society in the Second Commonwealth. The effect of their teaching was the establishment of a new Jewish aristocracy replacing the traditional priestly and noble classes. Nobility of birth, wealth, or social station was categorically denied as justification of authority. "A learned bastard," the Rabbis said, "takes precedence over an ignorant high priest." This sounds the familiar note of an aggressive class, yes, a subversive one, that is patently advocating the reform, if not the overthrow, of an accepted social framework. To us, the Pharisaic program foreshadows one of the basic features of modern democratic theory.

The new noble was the teacher, together with the man of promise, his disciple. Like all nobility, the Talmudic sages produced their own genealogy, which resembled in some ways the pedigree of the Greek philosopher. Of what import was it whose son you were? What mattered was whose disciple you had been, and how intimate your association with him. Tacitus' complaint that Jewish proselytism broke up stable Roman families was equally applicable to established Jewish homes in Palestine. If what counted was not life, but a life of Torah, one's physical parents were hardly as important as one's spiritual masters. The Mishnaic law is more revelatory here than whole tracts of exhortation. It declares: "[He who seeks] his father's lost property and that of his teacher, his teacher's has first place, for his father did but bring him into this world, but his master that taught him wisdom brings him into the world to come. . . . If his father and his teacher each bore a burden, he must first relieve his teacher and then relieve his father. . . . If his father and his teacher were kidnaped, he must first ransom his teacher, and than ransom his father!" The course of initiation into the Torah, therefore, meant the conscious adoption of a new father, who was heeded and imitated so as to learn the good life. Knowledge of the Book in itself was manifestly useless, for the Law was often applied in a way far different from the ostensible meaning of the injunction. "Exile thyself to a center of Torah" was the Rab-

binic advice to the aspiring student. Only in that way could he become a link in the chain of tradition.

The singular concern of Jews with the education of their children
—the modern, secularized hope for a son who will turn out a lawyer,
a doctor, a professor—dates back to the cultural revolution which
Talmudic civilization produced. In oft-quoted passages, Josephus
proudly boasts of the proverbial learning of Jewish children in the
Torah and, significantly enough, engages in invidious comparison
with the adult populations of the Gentile culture he knew well:
"Above all we pride ourselves on the education of our children, and
regard as the most essential task in life the observance of our laws
and of the pious practices, based thereon, which we have inherited."
Reflecting on the significance of universal education among Jews, he
says:

> Indeed, most men, so far from living in accordance with their own
> laws, hardly know what they are. Only when they have done wrong do
> they learn from others that they have transgressed the law. Even
> those of them who hold the highest and most important offices admit
> their ignorance; for they employ professional legal experts as assessors
> and leave them in charge of the administration of affairs. But, should
> anyone of our nation be questioned about the laws, he would repeat
> them all more readily than his own name. The result, then, of our
> thorough grounding in the laws from the first dawn of intelligence is
> that we have them, as it were, engraven on our souls. A transgressor
> is a rarity; evasion of punishment by excuses an impossibility.

Had he lived in a less hostile atmosphere, or written in his native
tongue, Josephus would no doubt have desisted from such wishful
thinking. Nevertheless, it remains true that in comparison with the
average Gentile, the lay Jew was lawyer, philosopher, and priest all
in one.

Success and achievement have never been an ideal breeding ground
for the human virtues of humility, warmth, and kindliness. Scholars
on occasion all too easily identified the honor of the Torah with its
human bearers, a step that was made all the easier in view of the
oral nature of the Talmudic tradition. To counterbalance this natural
tendency, the sin of pride and the virtue of humility as a *legal* duty
were emphasized constantly. Arrogant Pharisaism was a contradiction in terms. Ideally, the Torah could be fulfilled only in consonance
with the three virtues enunciated by Micah. That not all men lived
up to the ideal is not a reflection on the society or its faith, but simply
proof that men are mortal. We should not indulge in such a truism if
it were not for the one-sided picture of Pharisaism presented by New
Testament writers and exegetes. Tendentiousness, too, is a human

attribute, but regrettably the Gospels have been taken to be objective truth even by historians who should know better.

THE NEW HERO TYPE

A hero, according to the Shorter Oxford English Dictionary, is "a man who exhibits extraordinary bravery, firmness, or greatness of soul, in connection with any pursuit, work or enterprise; a man admired and venerated for his achievements and noble qualities." The hero symbolizes those ideals and values which the members of his society would like to emulate in their own struggles for success and immortality. From the anthropological point of view, the facts of his life—indeed, whether he ever existed at all—hardly matter. The crucial thing is not the real events of his life, but the legends told of him. For these legends are the uncensored transcription of impulses and aspirations that are often repressed in normal converse. A hero, of course, implies a villain, the archetype of all that the society holds mean and contemptible. A seed of low caste, deceitful and arrogant, he represents the eternal foe of the hero (and of his people), whom he constantly seeks to undermine.

And now to the hero and villain types of Talmudic civilization. In the first instance, the most suitable archetypes for Talmudic civilization were the figures of the Biblical narrative from Adam to Esther. Throughout Talmudic times a new genre of pseudepigraphic literature circulated in Jewish society purporting to contain the secrets of heaven and of history, which had been committed to writing by the great figures of antiquity. The very names of these works—generally called apocalyptic because of their form and subject matter—Adam and Eve, Enoch, The Testaments of the Twelve Patriarchs, The Assumption of Moses, Baruch, (Pseudo-) Ezra—reveal the deep awe with which the Talmudic Jew regarded his Biblical ancestor. The heroes here achieved and set down in writing what every Jew in the Greco-Roman world keenly pined for: a direct revelation from the heavenly court on the ultimate justification of the righteous in the end of history. Talmudic legend elaborated on the lives of the Biblical actors and made them participants in the contemporary Jewish struggles with Greco-Roman civilization. Abraham became a saint, Isaac a martyr, Jacob a scholar; needless to say, all three were devout ritualists. Conversely, Esau was none other than Rome the wicked, Balaam was the anti-Jewish propagandist, Jeroboam was the apostate and renegade.

But heroes are forever being born, if we but have the eyes to recognize them. Hillel the Elder came to Palestine at the age of forty, an obscure scion of the house of David—note his pedigree—studied forty years, and ministered to his people for another forty. Like Moses, who did not gain universal recognition until the age of eighty, he lived to the age of a hundred and twenty. So great was his passion for Torah, but so dire his poverty, that when he could not pay the entrance fee to the lecture in the academy, he eavesdropped through a hole in the roof. On this occasion he was so rapt in attention to the lecture that he completely failed to notice that he was caught in a snowstorm and his life imperiled. Later, on a Passover Eve, when the elders of Judea were, to a man, stumped by a ritual problem on which the observance of the festival depended, only Hillel could solve the problem and save the day. For this one feat he was appointed prince of the Sanhedrin. His character and temperament were no less heroic. No one could exhaust his patience, nothing could shake his humility or cool his natural warmth. Even the most negligible of his disciples was worthy of being a prophet, had he but lived in Biblical times.

Like Hillel, Rabban Johanan ben Zakkai—who in defiance of all chronology is called his youngest disciple—lived six score years, the last two of which he spent as president of the Sanhedrin. Like Hillel's, the poverty of Rabbis Joshua, Akiba, Judah, and others was matched by the profundity of their learning. Rabbi Eliezer ben Hyrcanus, the disciple of Rabban Johanan, remained totally illiterate until the age of twenty-two, when he renounced his share in his father's millions and ate dung from the street in order to sit at the feet of the wise. Every schoolboy knew the love story of Rachel, the heiress to a fortune, who married Akiba, an ignorant shepherd, and starved that he might begin to study the alphabet at the age of forty. Not only did he rise to become the dean of Jewish scholars, but he continued to teach until he died a martyr's death with the *Shema* ("Hear O Israel") on his lips.

Nor were the women neglected. The sufferings of Akiba's wife were proverbial even in her own day. Rabbi Joshua's mother, while she bore the future scholar in her womb, visited the academy in order that the atmosphere might seep into her unborn son. Beruria, the wife of Rabbi Meir, distinguished herself by her Rabbinical acumen and profound religiosity. Rabbi Ishmael's mother insisted on the privilege of washing her son's feet, in order to share in the merit of Torah.

The descendants of the very people that first produced mature historical writing—the Books of Joshua to Kings, Chronicles, Ezra, Nehemiah, Esther, and Maccabees—now abandoned historiography as a creative outlet. The historical books that were not canonized—to say nothing of the books of the renegade Josephus—fell by the wayside and became the property of the Christian Church. The fragments of history which have been preserved in the Rabbinic library are only those directly connected with Scripture and the Oral Law. History as a chain of human events ceased to exist, for only Torah was of lasting import, and it had already taken account of whatever history was of significance. Indeed, what use was history to a people whose political existence had been torn to shreds and whose only hope lay in the promises of the Torah?

Torah now took on an added meaning. Not only did it signify the Pentateuch, the Oral Law, and the Prophets. The Midrash of every generation, legal and homiletical; theology, mysticism, liturgy, ethics, and folk tale—all were part of the vast tapestry of Torah, which to the Jew became the mirror of the good life and the reflection of God's will.

THEOLOGICAL IDIOM

It has often been remarked with amazement that a culture so theocratically oriented as the Talmudic should have so *relatively* little to say of its God, and virtually nothing of a dogmatic nature beyond what is explicit in Scripture. God is the creator of heaven and earth, the revealer of the Torah, the judge of mankind, who will one day quicken the dead and restore Israel. How God does these things or why, many a Jew tried to state, but in the end he had to admit that one guess was as good as another.

There was a commonly accepted idiom, however, and it is on this basis that we shall try to formulate a few generalizations about the Talmudic conception of God. Underlying the vocabulary of theological commentary were certain implicit assumptions. We can only formulate these assumptions in a general way, for it is impossible to be precise about a subject concerning which precision and finality were shunned.

Prayers of supplication in Jewish liturgy begin with the rubric, "Our father, our king." There is nothing in these words to convey any distinctly Talmudic conception of God. Indeed, one may comb the Jewish liturgy of Talmudic origin only to find a paraphrase of Biblical verses put together to form a magnificat or a supplication. With the possible exception of the affirmation of resurrection—which the Rabbis "traced" to Scripture—Rabbinic liturgy remained remarkably free of Midrash. The relatively few references to angels are of a later vintage. However, the supplicatory rubric and many like it were on the lips of every Jew, and in unofficial moments Jews spelled out more fully what the words conveyed to them.

If the God of Scripture generally appears to be the stern King and meticulous administrator of justice, the God of Talmudic culture is also the warm and protecting Father, whose chief concern is over the welfare of His children. Present in the writings of prophets and psalmists, the idea is much older than Talmudic culture; yet the frequency with which it is now expressed indicates a distinct shift in emphasis. Wherever we turn in the Talmudic world, we feel that a new intimacy has been achieved between man and God. In keeping with the new religious duties and responsibilities of the individual, God is now near to every man, not only in isolated lyrical moments, but always, everywhere. To Him the Jew may weep about his household problems quite as freely and as fervently as in his supplications for the restoration of His people. God himself, the Rabbis assure the people, is not above weeping at the plight of His children in their exile and their sorrow. God, too, smiles with unconcealed pleasure as He witnesses a debate between two scholars over a technical point of the Law. In other words, God is the head of the heavenly and human families—of the angels and the hosts of heaven, of mankind and the physical world. As the Father, He has all the qualities of a human parent, only infinitely magnified. As Father, He plans, orders, achieves, comforts, chastises, and heeds those who will but call.

God, of course, is no less the King, no less the exacting judge and master. But the God of the Decalogue, the Prophets, Job, and the lyrical psalmist is now felt as a single, if complex, force, present and the same in every variety of circumstance. After the Second Destruction, there arises a new sensitivity in religious and moral matters. It is the outcome of the reforms of Ezra, the wars with Antiochus, and the preaching of Pharisees, Essenes, and visionaries. It takes the form of an unquenchable thirst for God.

The divine-human encounter in its new complexity is signalized in Talmudic idiom by means of two concepts, or moods, if one likes, that conveyed the antipodal manifestations of the Father-King in the universe: God's loving mercy (*rahamim*) and his exacting justice (*din*). As instances of His mercy one might reckon the bounties of nature, His revelations, and His salvation in time of need. His justice, on the other hand, is manifested in such phenomena as war, exile, pestilence, and destruction. Normal and abnormal phenomena, the banal and the miraculous, all reveal God as forever intervening in the order of nature. The universe is an implement in the moral order of things, serving God's purpose to reward the righteous and punish the wicked. Casting a shadow upon these dialectical categories was the eternal question of Job—the problem of the suffering saint and the happy villain. It is the Biblical caveat against any easy solution which would reduce God or his universe to the dimensions of human reason. As we shall see, Talmudic Judaism had an answer to Job's question, but it was an answer that it wisely refrained from applying to the visible world.

How does one approach the omniscient and omnipotent Almighty, the ineffable Holy One blessed be He? His very name (YHWH) was tabu to all but the high priest, who uttered it only on the Day of Atonement. So awesome was his name, so wary was the Jew of taking it in vain, that even "God" (*Elohim*) was not employed in conversation, nor even the euphemistic "Lord" (*Adonai*). How then could one speak to the utterly transcendent creator? By prayer, the Jew replied, by deeds of loving-kindness, by study and fulfillment of the Torah; in short, by bringing oneself fully under the yoke of the kingship of heaven. Obedience to His will moves God to cause His presence to dwell among men. Man can breach the gulf between earth and heaven or widen it. Sin and defection cause God to withdraw, in other words, to leave man at the mercy of the cold and cruel world.

The average Jew of Talmudic times was little concerned over the belief in God. Over and above a perfunctory note of condemnation for a renegade like Elisha ben Abuya, who left the fold despondent and shouting, "There is neither Judge nor justice," one senses in the Talmudic account of him a deep feeling of pity and horror for a man who has lost all hope and has sunk to the last depth of despair. Open denial of God, or atheism, was a rare phenomenon in the ancient world; even the Cynics and Epicureans did not deny the existence of gods. Much more demanding than the philosophic question of belief was the religious question of man's relationship to God, his service to Him, and trust in Him.

The chief source of the Jew's knowledge of God and of the way to serve him was the revelation and its Midrash. To the King, Master, and Father one comes with awe, reverence, fear, loyalty, and love. Here again the Talmudic hero type illustrates in a nutshell what tomes of theory can only adumbrate. The heroine of II Maccabees who urged her seven children to go to their death rather than submit to idolatry became the theme of many an ancient sermon. In the words of the Psalmist, she was "a joyful mother of children." Rabbi Akiba is portrayed as smiling at the moment of his unendurable tortures, virtually thanking his executioners for having enabled him to fulfill the commandment, "Thou shalt love the Lord thy God with all thy heart, and with all thy soul, and with all thy might." The martyr is but the supreme witness to God's call and command.

Martyrdom is an extreme form of the type of experience that a Jew should properly be undergoing at every moment of his conscious life. Every act, no matter how trivial or neutral, must be oriented toward God. Personal cleanliness, eating and sleeping, business, amusement, and marriage are all acts that can be elevated to the service of the Almighty; for each, indeed, there is an appropriate blessing, which rules out the possibility of a purely human area of experience. The Jew was truly a priest forever ministering at the altar of God. Prayer became the surrogate of sacrifice not only in the sense that it was now the vehicle for supplication to God, but in the sense that it made of each Jew a sacerdotal officer, who must ever stand on duty. In one sense, however, Rabbinic prayer was the very opposite of sacrifice; or, to put it in another way, Talmudic prayer followed in the tradition of Hosea rather than of Leviticus. Prayer was supplicatory and emotional, varying from day to day and from one person to another. Such an approach to God bespeaks the personal and individual character of the religious experience enshrined in Rabbinic Judaism. The placing of religious life in the hands of the individual was but a logical consequence of belief in a universal God. The Torah and its God are no longer the property of the Jewish people alone. Whoever accepts the kingship of God and orients his *life* accordingly has entered the fold of the elect.

"Honor thy father and thy mother, that thy days may be long upon the land which the Lord thy God giveth thee." The injunction is hyperbole, for even a fool can see that experience does not bear out the promise. To what avail Torah, to what purpose renunciation, if Rome fiddles while Judea goes up in flames! God's reply to Job failed to satisfy even the most committed Scripturalists, and could not go unamplified. Above all, it contradicted the endlessly repeated assurances of the Torah, Prophets, and Psalmists that God would reward each according to his due. The problem of theodicy could not be left to God alone. History, and in particular Jewish history, made this impossible.

The initial premise of Talmudic as of all subsequent monotheistic thought is that God rewards justly. To deny retribution is to deny divine justice. And to the Rabbis the denial of God's justice is the essence of atheism. The Talmudic solution of this problem served to introduce "other-worldly" religion to Western civilization. "That thy days may be long," God had said, but obviously he could not have meant a span of seventy, or even a hundred twenty years. Length of days could only signify life in a world where ephemerality will reign no longer, where decay, suffering, and death are unknown. Happily, Talmudic culture had inherited the lofty prophetic visions of "the end of the days," when "the wolf shall dwell with the lamb, and the leopard shall lie down with the kid"; when people "shall beat their swords into ploughshares and their spears into pruning-hooks"; when, in short, "they shall sit every man under his vine and under his fig-tree, and none shall make them afraid." What the prophets had fore-seen for mankind corporately, the Talmudic exegete now understood to apply to the individual: not only for men in the future, but for men here and now; all would be reborn new human beings to en-joy "the world to come." The resurrection of the dead, the requital of the righteous and the wicked, each according to his just deserts—this is the sum of the divine assurance.

Israel and the righteous of the Gentiles, all "will have a share in the world to come." This Rabbinic affirmation became a dogma, practically the only one that had no patent foundation in Scripture. Yet so fundamental was it to the individualistic moral orientation of the overwhelming majority of Jews that to deny it, to refuse to affirm it in the daily liturgy, meant automatic exclusion from the religious community. But here, too, no official interpretation or amplification of the dogma was forthcoming. Theories abounded about the world to come, about the state of the human frame and soul in the interval between death and the resurrection, but all of them remained theories. It remained for God to disclose the full truth at His appointed time.

A promise of reward in the future, if it is to be convincing, requires an answer to the obvious question, "Why later? Why not here and now?" What is the explanation of this ephemeral stage of life, with its woes and frustrations? That Talmudic Judaism had no definitive answer to this question perfectly illustrates what we have said con-cerning its undefinitive theology. One preacher might explain that the suffering of the righteous in this world was a test of their devotion to God. Another might with equal plausibility explain that God was settling the small accounts here and now, requiting the sins of the righteous and the virtues of the wicked in this world, so as to be free for categorical rewards in the world to come. Still another might say that the pure of heart were suffering to expiate the sins of their generation. Too many answers are no answer at all; so Job's question remained.

The unwillingness to theologize went along with an unwilling-ness to psychologize in credal terms. Only a system which claims to comprehend God can claim to understand man. Judaism has enter-tained pessimistic psychologies—"Man is basically evil and sinful"—

and optimistic ones—"Man is inherently good." Ultimately no theory could be measured except by one criterion: Did it or did it not imply full acceptance of the law of the Torah and trust in God's command?

THE ELECTION OF ISRAEL

Modern apologists of Judaism often betray an uncomfortable feeling when confronted with the Scriptural and Talmudic statements about God's relation to the children of Israel. Particularly in recent years, traditionalist Jews have sought refuge in the view that the election of Israel, while it implies a special responsibility, does not imply that Israel is superior to other peoples. Yet the fact is that there is only one possible justification for the missionary activity of the Rabbis and for their eagerness to expose new souls to the burden of ritual and Torah. It is the firm conviction that the Jewish people by virtue of its Torah is superior in its faith, morality, and ultimate destiny. There was nothing racial about this belief. Modern theories of racism were as foreign even to the most ethnically oriented of the Rabbis as were modern conceptions of democracy to the most liberal among them. They sought to convert Greeks, Syrians, and Romans into Jews, because they *knew* that they were God's people, that theirs was the only true way of life. To be sure, they felt themselves far more responsible and accountable as Jews for their actions than did Gentiles, but then, as now, *noblesse oblige* meant special rights and privileges. No one, Jew, Christian, or Muslim, could fail to assume that his was the one true religion. Wedded to this conviction, the Talmudic Jew carried all over the world what Scripture had told his ancestors on their own soil.

Reading Scripture, the Jew could see perfectly clearly that the story of creation culminated in Abraham; that the lives of the patriarchs led to the Exodus, and the Exodus to the revelation at Sinai. And bound by the logic of Scripture, he believed that Israel and the Torah were God's chosen possessions. In his relations with God and his fellow men, whether Jew or Gentile, the Jew found himself governed by a regimen of life that at once gave him a key to every situation. His *amixia*, or refusal to break bread or intermarry with Gentiles, was essentially no more invidious in intent than his refusal to copulate with his wife during her menstrual period. All nations had ancestral laws and tabus; those of the Jews were merely more embracing. Not that the Jew of Talmudic culture always acted out of impersonal consideration for the Law. But whatever his motives on occasion, the Jew knew that he was fated to carry out the Law, no matter what the price.

The concern of the Talmudic Jew with Scripture and God's justice inspired the attempt to rationalize God's choice of Israel as the keeper of the Torah. By his own criteria, it was clear that whichever people God had chosen to receive the Torah would as a matter of course have become the elect, the cream of mankind. Why did it have to be Israel? At first blush Scripture proffered no satisfactory answer. "Because the Lord loved you, and because He would keep the oath which He swore unto your fathers"—was not this merely begging the question? No, the exegetes replied; the verse thus cited itself proves that God chose Israel because of the merit of their fathers, because of the piety of Abraham, the devotion of Isaac, and the righteousness of Jacob. By their actions, these men earned the oath and covenant of God for their seed unto all eternity. Were it not for this protecting merit, Israel would long since have been destroyed because of its sins. It is not that the Jews as a people are intrinsically worthy of election; they live by the grace of their fathers. Far more important than this attempt to explain history is the concept of theodicy reflected in the idea of corporate reward and punishment, which so profoundly influenced the Jew's view of the vicissitudes of his people.

The concept of corporate retribution is the one inculcated by Scripture. "I the Lord thy God am a jealous God, visiting the iniquity of the fathers upon the children, and upon the third and upon the fourth generation of them that hate me, and showing mercy unto the thousandth generation of them that love me and keep my commandments." Affirm as he would Ezekiel's doctrine of individual responsibility, the Jew knew that in life the innocent often suffer along with the guilty. The Decalogue passage just cited proclaims a corporate responsibility vertically; in practice, Talmudic Jews applied it horizontally. Allegorically they explained the destruction of the Second Temple as being due to the hatred that existed between two prominent Jews. Let each Jew, then, mind his ways, lest he bring calamity on the whole community. Let no Jew beam with success; his pleasant lot may well be only a reward to his father or righteous neighbor. Can this idea be brought into line with the idea of individual justice? No, but Scripture proclaims both, and God alone knows how and when each principle comes into play.

Yet this rationalization of the election of Israel was not entirely satisfactory. After all, it left the Gentiles out in the cold. At least the Torah might be offered to them! Once again, Aggada stepped into the breach. The nations had been offered the Torah, but they turned it down to a man. Esau (i.e., Rome) would not stand for "Thou shalt not murder"; Ammon for "Thou shalt not commit adultery"; Ishmael (the Beduin) refused to accept "Thou shalt not steal"—and so on. Only Israel willingly proclaimed, "All the words which the Lord hath spoken will we do."

To some extent, this concern with God's motive for the election stemmed from the obsessive concern of the Jew with justice and fair play, in other words, with the translation of the civil law of the Torah to the ethnic sphere. But over and above the religious motive, the realities of life, even the life of Jews themselves, called for an apologetic. Dispersed and under frequent attack from various quarters, the Jews could only stand up to the forces arrayed against them by means of an equally vigorous morale. A fine chosen nation it is, they heard said openly, that was abandoned with its Temple to the Roman legions. The tenacity of the Jew was bizarre enough; but his proselytizing zeal was utterly ridiculous. To offset all this the Jew and his teachers concentrated on the one comfort left them: the promise of the future to God's elect. Their sufferings had a purpose and would be recompensed, if they but continued in the path chosen for them. The solidarity born of their religion gained momentum from each attack from without. So the gulf widened between Jew and Gentile, to be spanned only when the forces of modern democracy broke the ghetto walls and dissolved Jewish ethnic existence.

Nothing is more difficult even for the best-intentioned student than a detached view of Jewish-Gentile relations, not even those of two thousand years ago. We have already seen that present-day accounts of the riots of Alexandria, for example, or the disturbances in Judea, are charged with the suppressed tensions of the twentieth century and have the character of diatribes or apologetics. Here, too, we venture to set forth the hypotheses and assumptions of our ancestors without evaluating them morally.

To the Jew, Scripture made it plain that all Jews were "brothers," all Gentiles "aliens" or "strangers." The dichotomy at once excluded the Gentile from participation in all communal cultic observances and put him beyond the protection of those civil rights in which ethnic or religious elements played a role. In Talmudic society, certainly under the system of Rabbinic authority, a Gentile could not normally give testimony in a Jewish court; a Jew might licitly lend him money on interest and demand repayment of a loan even after the Sabbatical year. On the other hand, Talmudic community leaders ordered that charity be dispensed to Gentiles alongside Jews; that

Gentile dead be buried by Jews and that normal courtesies be accorded them "for the sake of peace." It is thus clear that for all the ritual separation between Jews and the rest of the world, and despite deep-seated antagonism between the peoples of Torah and idolatry, Jews and Gentiles lived side by side harmoniously and peacefully for centuries. Outbreaks of violence were the exception.

It is when we examine the evidence of friction and antagonism that modern sensitivities lead to the temptation to take sides. Essentially the antagonism stemmed from two independent situations, each of which had religious roots. In the Greco-Roman Diaspora Jews demanded—and often received—full protection and equality of rights with the Gentile citizenry. To the Jew a guarantee of rights signified the opportunity to partake in communal activities, yet without having to compromise his own principles. Jews, for example, refused to appear in court on a Sabbath or a festival. In contributing to civic functions, they often stipulated that no Jewish funds be utilized for civic pagan rites. On the other hand, Jews diverted large sums of money annually to the Temple in Jerusalem, a practice to which local Gentile entrepreneurs were extremely sensitive. Add to this the uninhibited remarks which Jews sometimes made about pagan rites and beliefs, and you sense the raw material for a pogrom.

In Palestinian Talmudic society the issue was further complicated by the refusal of the Jews to recognize the legitimacy of alien conquest. Since the Gentile population of Palestine was almost always sympathetic to the foreign conquerors, the Scriptural spark was fanned to a flame. Wherever the Torah had spoken of brother, many an exegete argued, only Jews were meant. Corporate conceptions of justice and responsibility battened on the political-religious realities and reflected solidarity in the face of a common opponent. (Incidentally, the contrast with Babylonian society is most telling. Living in an autonomous community under the protection and good will of the state, the principle that the civil law of the state applies to Jews was upheld as Jewish law.)

Why then the modern misunderstanding of the true significance of Jewish-Gentile relations in Talmudic civilization? In part, the Rabbis of the Talmud were at fault. Interpreting the Torah in the light of the actual situations they encountered, they simply formulated without qualification their response to a problem. (Unfriendly historians have regrettably ignored qualifications even when they were offered.) From the time Talmudic law became canonized, the Jew was left with an undated legacy which later often embarrassed him. That it did not embarrass him too much may be set down to Christian-Jewish relations beginning with the fourth century. However holy the new Roman Empire claimed to be, the Jew felt that it was nothing but Roman through and through. Jews and Christians each contended that the other group was "the stranger" of Scripture, and each group behaved accordingly. The tensions of the Talmudic age were transferred to Europe and preserved for centuries.

One other source for the self-conscious assertion of the election must be mentioned, for here strangely enough the Jews were the cause of their own embarrassment. The effectiveness of Jewish missionary activity, it is well known, immeasurably facilitated Christian preaching of the Gospel to the Gentiles. What is often glossed over is the claim of the Christian preachers to represent the true Israel, their contention that the new sect was the rightful heir to God's revelation to the Patriarchs, Moses and the Prophets. The Talmudic community, beginning with the second century, often found itself forced to defend its claim to the title of Israel. One of the deep sources of tension between Judaism and Christianity—one that never appeared in Jewish-Muslim relations—was the debate of two pretenders to the same title. For reasons of prudence, the Christian Church later chose not to emphasize the question of the Israelite name; but the claim to succession is one which the Church never has given up. The Jew, in turn, all the more aggressively affirmed his lineage and his election against all pretenders. Jacob was again at war with Esau over the primal birthright.

The Jew never suffered a moment's doubt within himself as to who the rightful heir was. He might argue with his neighbor as to why God chose Israel of all nations as keepers of the Torah. But on one point he and his fellow Jews were adamant. God elected Israel for one purpose above all others: to fulfill the Torah and bring its truth to the world. Whatever glorified the Torah was good; whatever discredited it, evil. Israel's mission was to sanctify God's name through the length and breadth of the earth. The most venial of sins was unatonable if it reflected on the Torah: ill manners, shabby dress, legal connivance would undermine a decade of missionary activity. The slightest act of virtue, on the other hand, if it caused a Gentile to say, "Blessed be the God of the Jews who could command such behavior," earned everlasting merit.

The greatest achievement of Talmudic culture on the ethnic level was just this kind of solidarity. The Jews forever kept an eye on the effect of their activity on the world. It is one of the paradoxes of history that few of them could see that if the Jews did not conquer, their Torah did, and thereby brought the civilized peoples under the yoke of the God of Israel.

THE HOLY LAND

Most expositions of Talmudic religion relegate the Holy Land and its place in Talmudic Judaism to a parenthesis in the section on eschatology or retribution, and thence proceed to elaborate on the various theories of the messianic age expounded in ancient Palestine. The chief reason for this misplaced emphasis lies in the effort to treat Rabbinic Judaism as a systematic theology, that is, as a body of abstractions and metaphysical principles. It is argued that a land can only play a contingent role in a religion, that like a ritual or concrete symbol, it is merely the "accidental" embodiment of faith and its imperatives. The theory behind the symbol is infinitely more significant; it is by the theory that the ritual or sacred symbol stands or falls.

However justified such reasoning may be for theology, it is not only totally misleading when it comes to the study of the Talmudic mind, but it also misses the essential factor in nonsystematic religion. Recent anthropological and psychological studies have demonstrated that ancient autochthonous religions were originally a body of rituals and sacred symbols around which the theory (myth or theology) grew later out of a need for rationalization. Religions did not operate as we should like to believe our own religions operate, namely, theology coming first and ritual following as mere symbol. In its treatment of the relative importance of the two types of exegesis, legal and homiletical, Rabbinic Judaism offers an excellent instance of the real order of things. As a general rule, the Halakha came first and the Aggada came afterwards to validate or rationalize it.

In the complex of Jewish rites, symbols, and values, the land of Israel occupies a primary position because of two factors. First and foremost, it is the land of promise designated at the time of the covenant between God and Abraham and is repeatedly reaffirmed throughout Biblical times as the gift of God to Abraham's seed. Nothing is more central in the people's saga. It is always there: in the forty-year sojourn in the desert or in the generations of conquest from Joshua to David. But this factor alone, however important for the early history of Israel, might not have weathered the passage of time, if it were not for the second and more characteristically Penta-teuchal-Talmudic feature of the country. Palestine has ever been one of the pivotal foundations of whole blocs of Jewish law and ritual which cannot be fulfilled beyond the borders of its sacred soil. Because of the cultic sanctity of the land, the Jew of Talmudic civilization, no matter where he happened to live, could no more conceive of Judaism without the land of Israel than he could have conceived of it without the people of Israel.

The central importance of the Holy Land in Jewish religion lies in the fact that Talmudic society took with the utmost literalness those sections of Scriptural law which are introduced with the phrase, "And it shall be, when thou art come in unto the land which the Lord thy God giveth thee." All of the agricultural laws and sacrificial laws, as well as considerable portions of the levitical holiness code and parts of the purely civil law became inextricably connected with Palestine in general and Jerusalem in particular. To fulfill the Torah in its entirety, therefore, required dwelling on the holy soil. In the Rabbinic interpretation of Scripture, even the machinery of the Jewish community structure could function fully only in Palestine: ordination and the powers of the Sanhedrin were the exclusive prerogative of the Holy Land. Consequently, the communal functions that required the vote of ordained scholars could be exercised only in the mother country: civil and capital punishment, regulation of the Jewish calendar, and adoption of universally binding legislation (*takkanot*). The genius of Talmudic Judaism in having transcended the limitations of ethnic group, land, and even priestly intermediacy applied only to the rituals that fell within the jurisdiction of the individual: prayer, the Sabbath and festival rest, dietary laws, and marital relations. The sizable bulk of the Law which Scripture had explicitly associated with the land—fully one third of the Halakha—the Rabbis not only did not attempt to abolish, but actually strengthened and amplified.

Since we have asserted the centrality of Palestine to Talmudic religion, we must deal with a widespread misconception of the Rabbinic attitude to the mother country and the Jewish state. The Talmud, as well as other ancient sources, reveals the existence of considerable conflict between the Pharisees and the Jewish rulers of the Second Commonwealth. Alexander Jannaeus and the house of Herod were often at such odds with the Pharisees and their adherents that not only open hostility but occasional bloodshed resulted. At the time of the great revolt against Rome, Rabban Johanan ben Zakkai, and presumably some of his school, went to the length, it would appear, of utterly rejecting the political campaign, so great was their opposition to the activities of the zealots. Modern scholars conclude that the chief concern of these men was with undisturbed religious practice and the study of Scripture, not with the fight for political independence. In other words, the religious leadership of Talmudic civilization was Torah-centered rather than land-centered.

This antinomy between land and Law is actually nothing but a projection of modern theological universalism onto the Rabbis. But to them the dichotomy would have appeared utterly ridiculous. It is true enough that the Pharisees often went to great lengths in their opposition to the political policies of some Maccabean and Herodian rulers and of political zealots. However, their opposition to particular Jewish governments did not mean opposition to all Jewish government. What they wanted was to control the government themselves; for as keepers of the Torah they regarded their policies as the only ones in consonance with the teachings of Scripture. For example, during the reign of Queen Salome (76-67 B.C.E.), the Pharisaic party ousted the Sadducees from control and took over the administration with a vigorous hand. During the great revolt against Rome, Pharisees and Rabbis fought alongside Essenes and Sadducees, and some of them actually directed military operations. After the collapse of the rebellion, as we have seen, the Rabbis did not in any way shy away from political control. Nor was Rabbinic legislation after the Destruction confined to the cultic sanctity of the country. Since civil law was as much a part of the Torah as sacrificial law, they sought to regulate every aspect of life: labor-employer relationships, prices, real estate equity, market contracts, and so on. As custodians of their people, they even raised purely material enactments on behalf of the general welfare into religious principles. Whatever had to do with Jewish society had to do at the same time with the sacred society and the Holy Land.

Thus, to discourage the mass flight from the country during adverse circumstances, the Pharisaic leaders decreed that anyone leaving the Holy Land automatically incurred ritual defilement. Later Rabbinic law permitted a woman to refuse to follow her husband out of the country, while enabling either spouse to oblige the other to migrate to it from abroad. To prevent ruinous economic competition from foreign markets, they similarly subjected certain imported products to an automatic state of defilement. Sale of Jewish property in Palestine to Gentiles was absolutely forbidden, but it was allowable to purchase land from Gentiles, even if this meant the temporary violation of the more peripheral Sabbath injunctions.

The underlying motif of all Rabbinic discussion of the Holy Land is the intransigent refusal of the Jew to accept the political reality of the world in which he lived. For the greater part of the Talmudic age, Palestine was a vassal territory to one of the Mediterranean empires. For most of the centuries of subjection, Palestine was a servant of Rome, even when its immediate administrators happened to be Jews. But never for a moment did the religious leadership or the Jewish

204 THE TALMUDIC AGE

masses recognize as legitimate the conquest of the country by a foreign power. However passive they were obliged to be in the face of political might, most Jews regarded the Romans as interlopers and their agents as common thieves. Publicans in Rabbinic literature, no less than in the New Testament, are equated with the scum of the earth. Obedience to the ruling powers when necessary was one thing, and the majority of the Rabbis counseled against fanatical and hopeless rebellion, but it was quite another to cooperate actively with the conquerors, even in the interests of law and order. To hand over a Jewish thief to the Romans, as one Rabbi did, was to side with one criminal against another.

The Romans, of course, had come to Palestine on serious business, and their actions said as much. Little remained for the average Jew but to hate his enemy with an intensity that was commensurate only with his impotence. Much of the Talmudic hostility to the Gentile can be understood properly only against the background of Jewish political helplessness. More than on any other subject, the Rabbinic homily on the Holy Land betrays a sense of urgency that stems from a fear of despair. Hoping to keep the people in the land, they pleaded for superhuman patience and infinite trust in God's judgment and promise of restoration. As for the bleak present, God's Presence, they preached, rests only on the land of Israel, and only if the land remains in Jewish hands. Great rewards were in store for those who braved the adverse conditions of Roman rule. The dead of the Holy Land would be resurrected before all others; indeed, the Jew who lies in the consecrated earth can reckon himself buried under the altar of the Lord. God is driven to tears at the sight of His children in exile and at the desolation of the country.

For each of these statements the Talmudist could supply one or more proof-texts from Scripture. But he could not alter the course of history. The Holy Land progressively dwindled in wealth and population and became increasingly a theoretical reality, a symbol of the brilliant past and of a glorious future. That it nevertheless remained a pillar of Jewish life in Palestine and abroad testifies to the deep attachment Scripture and its exegetes had successfully inculcated. The Torah that bound the Jews into a people declared only Zion home and all else exile. Though the Diaspora proved, it could never admit, that the Holy Land and Temple were expendable. Every Jew bore in his heart a sense of guilt at his inability to turn the injunction into a reality.

It was not only by divine decree and Rabbinical exhortation that Zion remained a reality in the life of the Jew. Nothing demonstrates so well the profound emotional grip of the country as the practices of the Jews in the Diaspora. So long as the Temple stood, Jews from all the world sent their annual tax of the half-shekel to the Temple, in addition to voluntary contributions for sacrifices and other Temple needs. The Flavian emperors of Rome knew what they were about when they converted this tax to the coffers of Jupiter Capitolinus; a sacred offering was now being poured into the hated pocket of an idol of the despots of the world. Daily prayer, from early Talmudic times to the present day, has been oriented toward Jerusalem, a practice which has left its mark even on the popular vocabulary: Palestine was spoken of by Babylonian Jews as "the West" or simply as "over there," while European and African Jews designated it as "the East." The pilgrimage—venerated in the Middle Ages by both Christians and Muslims—owes its high religious rank to the honor accorded it by the Jews of Talmudic culture. Even the efforts of Babylonian religious leaders to discourage emigration to Palestine, efforts that stemmed from the fact that Babylonian community life and religious organization had far surpassed that of Palestine by the end of the third century, testify to the normal impulses of the people and the direction of their loyalties.

Even those Jews who frankly preferred to await the return of the Messiah knew that in many ways Palestine governed their lives. The annual calendar was regulated chiefly according to agricultural and husbandry conditions in Palestine. Festal letters and other directives went forth regularly from the mother country along with teachers, preachers, and books. Even children played "Holy Land," as a group of Rabbis learned when they saw youngsters in Rome designating mud pies as "priestly offerings" and "levitical tithes." Judah Halevi, Moses Nachmanides, and Obadiah Bertinoro, like many another pilgrim of a later day, merely carried out in their own lives ideals and dreams on which they had been suckled from earliest infancy. On one level, modern Zionism is a translation of this yearning into a concrete program for reclamation of a land the Jew had always claimed—with Gentile concurrence—to be his own.

We have noted that social and political realities oriented Talmudic culture in two directions: the idealized past of Biblical times and the even more glorious future pictured by the prophets. What the individual hoped would be the divine reward for his present suffering and frustration, the nation awaited as recompense for painful fidelity to its ancestral God and Torah. "Renew our days as of old," the author of Lamentations cried, despite the obvious truth that the garden of man had probably been no greener in pristine times than it was in Exilic or post-Exilic days. In one sense, however, the hope for renewal was justified: the Jew had formerly lived on his own soil, under his own kings, and his own law. All the woes and travails of Talmudic civilization were traced to the curse of subjection and dispersion. Accordingly, all the hopes and dreams for happiness were telescoped into the catchword of "Return." Resurrection, righteousness, peace and plenty for Israel and all mankind—indeed, would not all men be the same?—were forecast for the day of the Return.

"For the vision is yet for the appointed time, and it declareth of the end and doth not lie; though it tarry, wait for it, because it will surely come; it will not delay." These words from Habakkuk expressed the Jewish hope that the end of history had already been decreed and sealed. Practically every prophet from Moses to Daniel had reassured the people on this score. There was nothing to do but to wait and to behave so as to be assured of a share in the final reward. Once again, we must clearly distinguish between dogma and personal speculation. The books of Daniel and of other apocalyptists abound with theories as to the exact date of the messianic End. That people took these religious mathematicians seriously is evident from the Rabbinic excoriation of "calculators of the end." Then as now well-meaning but deluded people managed to convince themselves and others that they were partners to the heavenly secret. No less a man than Rabbi Akiba ben Joseph declared that he could discern the messianic herald in Simeon bar Kokhba. The retort of one of his colleagues has become a classic *bon mot* on the subject: "Grass will have sprouted from your cheeks, Akiba ben Joseph, but the Davidic Messiah will not yet have arrived."

Akiba's hopes and his colleague's retort reflect the two attitudes that pervaded the Jewish community—impatient expectancy and resilient sobriety. So imminent was the sounding of the trumpet of freedom in the minds of the people, that throughout Talmudic times and afterward the Jews were the preeminent prey of messianic pretenders. The faintest rumor of the divine messenger's appearance caused whole communities to pack their belongings and take to the nearest highway on their way to Jerusalem. As each pretender failed to produce the expected sign, that is, met with an inglorious end, the people slowly recovered from their shock and girded themselves for the next chance. How close at hand the event was thought to be may be gleaned from the ritual practices of the Jews of Palestine in Talmudic times. The levitical laws of purity, whose fulfillment was a prerequisite to entering the sacred precincts of the Temple, were accorded careful observance for centuries after the Destruction. The laws of sacrifices and Temple protocol were carefully rehearsed in the Palestinian academy in readiness for the resumption of the normal state of affairs.

More than any other single factor, this preoccupation with the Return kept the Jews an ethnic group with a unified vision of their political role. More than anything else, too, it kept in being the tension born of a universalist and personalized religion that was yet centralized by a land and a Temple site. Even the increased fixity of Jewish liturgy after the Destruction was probably due largely to a profound nostalgia for the Temple service with its rigid protocol and precise regulation. That the Jew failed to resolve this tension until the nineteenth century, when Reform and political Zionism took a hand and separated ethnicism and universalism into separate programs of action, shows how strong were the roots of Talmudic Judaism in all subsequent stages of Jewish history. Judaism continued to profess its hope for the salvation of all society and for the restoration of God's chosen people. It proudly boasted that it was at home everywhere, and proved it, yet never ceased to bemoan its alienation and exile on foreign soil. Modern intellectual Jewish history begins with the renunciation of one or the other half of the messianic ideal. Classical Reform Judaism, secular Jewish democrats, and Jewish socialists adopted the universalist creed and gave up the ethnic aspiration for return to the homeland. The vision of the prophets might well find fulfillment in Vienna, Berlin, or Moscow. What need, therefore, of a Mount Zion? On the other hand, Zionism despaired of a divine salvation or of a Gentile change of attitude, and so took matters into its own hands with the adoption of a humanized program for the traditional restoration.

In Scripture, the Messiah, or anointed one, is a designation used for the high priest and more commonly for a legitimate king. The anonymous prophet popularly called the Second Isaiah refers to Cyrus king of Persia as God's messiah because the exiles of Judea looked to him for the restoration of the Temple. It is clear, therefore, that by the middle of the sixth century B.C.E. the term "messiah" had taken on the added meaning of divine messenger and human savior, a meaning that in ensuing centuries was practically to displace its original sense. Who would be the Messiah and how would his coming be announced? These were questions that aroused the interest of every Jew.

In the usual way, answers were elicited from a combination of relevant verses in Scripture. "Behold," said the prophet Malachi, "I will send you Elijah the prophet before the coming of the great and terrible day of the Lord." The fanatical and implacable prophet of

Gilead was to return from his heavenly home and usher in the new era. Little wonder that in Rabbinic society the personality of Elijah underwent a major metamorphosis. Pastor, counselor and comforter to the Jewish people, he miraculously appears in order to admonish, encourage, and pronounce that the long-awaited day of the Lord will yet arrive. It is he who soothes the faithful and bids them wait patiently for the awful events that God has announced. He will soon make his appearance to all men, proclaiming the new era. Then the great day will have begun.

The day of the Lord, Amos had long since made clear, would be one "of darkness, not of light," and Malachi says much the same thing. It was a simple matter to associate these hints with the fuller treatment of Ezekiel of the battle with Gog and Magog, of that final but most terrible conflict between the human forces of good and evil. The forces of the Lord would, according to God's plan, suffer a temporary setback, but only to tempt the hordes of Gog and Magog still further. Great faith would be required, for the initial setbacks must not deter one from playing his role. The prophets had announced that as a first step in the restoration, God would repair the breach between Judah and Israel and make them again into one people. And to this end God would bring back the remnants of the lost ten tribes of the North and align them in one array with the seed of Judah. Talmudic folklore foresaw that at the head of the rejuvenated people of Israel would stand the king of the lost ten tribes, the Messiah of the seed of Joseph, who would himself perish on the field of battle. But the people would again rally under "the shoot of the stock of Jesse," the Messiah of the seed of David, who would deal the enemy a crushing and final defeat. Then would the visions of all the prophets, of Isaiah, Micah, Jeremiah, Daniel and the others, come to pass: resurrection, peace, prosperity, and universal acknowledgment of the kingship of God.

Is this combination of Biblical fragments the official Rabbinic dogma on the subject of the Messiah? Yes, but only in the sense that no believer would question the words of the prophets, although a Talmudic exegete could declare that these words referred not to the future, but had already been fulfilled. As late as the twelfth century we find a Spanish Jew defending the more common Talmudic opinion that the prophetic promises will yet come to pass. Obviously, the gates of interpretation and speculation, perhaps even of doubt, had not been completely closed. Above all, the theories of apocalyptists and of exegetical computers as to the time of the messianic era, no matter how wide an audience they had gained, could never assume credal finality. "The secret things," the Jews had to admit, "belong unto the Lord our God." Time and again they would hear the clatter of hooves of the Messiah's cavalry, but no bones rose again.

There is a serious objection to this eschatology. The prophetic pronouncements on the Messiah and the Day of the Lord would seem to reduce the role of the individual to insignificance. He is at best but one of the "extras" in a drama, the end of which has long been pre-ordained. If the savior of Israel will come in any case, if the first stage will bring defeat in its wake and will be inevitably followed by victory, what need can there be for personal exertion or sacrifice? Obviously God would make good his promise in His own good time. Did not the Rabbis discourage the people from attempting to hasten the end? The fruit would ripen only in due season; to rush matters would bring on disaster.

The objection is of course a commonplace. If the march of events is ineluctable, if nothing can arrest the arrival of the Davidic Messiah or the classless state—why praise or condemn individuals for their behavior? Judaism had no official answer to the question, nor could it have in an area not covered by the prophets. Yet the preachments against the temptation to leave things to the preordained march of history show that the difficulty was keenly sensed. The various solutions all agreed that the Messiah's date of arrival depended on man. One theory that gained considerable popularity in Rabbinic circles stated that the Messiah had long been due, and that it was only the imperfection of Israel that delayed his coming. Others felt that the time had not yet come, for God would not delay the fulfillment of His promise once the time arrived. But Israel's moral responsibility was undeniable, for God would surely have shortened the ordeal if the people had but given evidence of their worthiness. A third school wisely placed no limits on the period of waiting. The Messiah would not come until a perfect generation appeared. But theory or no theory, the individual was assigned a role of immeasurable importance in this drama of human fulfillment and national restoration. God had created the Messiah; everyone to a man was responsible for making him a reality on earth.

THE LEGACY OF TALMUDIC CIVILIZATION

The complex of institutions and values that were born of Talmudic culture passed on into the Middle Ages virtually intact, unaccompanied by any awareness that an age of eight centuries was drawing to a close. True, the rich community life of Palestine felt the impact of the financial collapse of the Roman Empire and, later, of Persian and Byzantine invasion. The Christianization of the Mediterranean world brought in its wake an incessant harassment of Jewish community activity, a progressive curtailment of its autonomous powers, and outright pogroms and confiscation of property. Many Jews and even whole Jewish communities suffered appallingly. But the culture itself remained intact owing to the strong roots it had struck in the Babylonian community. There Talmudic life continued well into the eleventh century and even beyond it, preserving the ethnic-religious independence of the people at the same time that it acted as a Jewish center to which other communities could look for counsel and instruction, and so bolster their sense of unity and continuity. In the ensuing centuries new Jewish communities spring up throughout Southern and Western Europe, and while their growth is generally veiled in darkness, they all come to maturity with the assumption of a community structure patterned after the Talmudic prototype. The importance of the Babylonian, Palestinian, and Italian communities in this regard is immeasurable. Everywhere the Talmudic law became the constitution of Jewish organization. Above all, the stability of the Babylonian community enabled it to establish the hegemony of its law over Jewish Palestine itself and over the whole of the Jewish world.

Medieval Judaism thus became synonymous with the law of the Babylonian Talmud. The permanent legacy of the Palestinian center was now refracted through the window of an Exilic center that had first grappled with the problem of autonomy under the law of the Palestinian Mishna. What the Bible had meant for Talmudic civilization, the Talmud now meant for medieval Jewish life. The Talmud and the Midrash became the new Scripture by which Jews everywhere were to regulate their daily lives, civil, domestic, and religious, until the beginning of the emancipation in the eighteenth and nineteenth centuries. Whatever the differences between the various Jewish communities during the twelve centuries from the downfall of the Roman Empire and rise of Islam to the emergence of the modern democratic nation-state; whatever the barriers between them, barriers that were geographic, linguistic and even cultural, the law of the Talmud and the vocabulary of its faith were the unitive forces that made all differences seem ephemeral and contingent.

Modern students of Judaism often deplore the relative neglect of Scripture by the traditional Jew of medieval and even of modern society. The neglect is relative, yet it is true that Jewish attention shifted from Scripture to Rabbinic text and commentary. Still, for the traditional Jew, the charge leaves out of account a fundamental consideration. Actually, the Jew continued to read Scripture unremittingly throughout the Middle Ages. But to understand the true meaning of Scripture he had to know the Talmud, which held the clue to its treasures. In the same way the Church of Rome stressed the importance of patristic and canonical literature for the understanding of Scripture. Of what value is a treasure without the keys to the vault in which it is lodged? Jews and Christians alike began to study Scripture afresh, and independently of accepted presuppositions, only after the collapse of the exegetical culture that Talmudic civilization had inaugurated.

Of far more influence on world history than the Talmudic legacy to succeeding generations of Jews was the Talmudic impact on European and Near Eastern civilization. The growth and development of Talmudic culture in Palestine and Babylonia took place within imperial frameworks that tolerated, and in some ways even abetted, the emergence of a Jewish community structure in which the Jew fashioned his own way of life and insulated himself against the Gentile cultural milieu. The Christian and Muslim states of medieval Europe, Asia and Africa followed the Roman precedent with respect to the Jew, even as the Romans and Hellenistic monarchs followed the Persian precedents. Jewish life thus continued to flourish within a self-imposed and tolerated ghetto, which afforded infinitely greater protection against cultural assimilation than a thousand sermons or edicts of toleration.

Over and above the framework of autonomy, and despite the more vocal hostility between Jew and Gentile in the medieval world, Talmudic culture had a far more suitable climate in which to flourish in the medieval world than it ever had in the Hellenistic-Roman world. And this climate was of Talmudic making. Jew, Christian, and Muslim might vilify each other's faith openly and unceasingly, but underneath their condemnations and disputations they moved in a common universe of discourse. All three faiths based their claim to truth and knowledge on a revealed book, which in turn became the subject of exegesis and interpretation and was thus made applicable to changing human experience. All three religions provided their flocks with a regimen of life from cradle to grave which was based on the premise that no differences existed between the secular and the sacred. The new churches, like the mother faith, came with a program of individual salvation that cut across ethnic barriers and created new international alignments. Church, prayer, and the promise of other-worldly retribution—these all stemmed from Talmudic universalism. Debate between the religions, whenever it took place was not about fundamentals but details. Jews and Gentiles, whatever the hatred between them, understood each other extremely well. The Jewish missionaries may have lost to their competitors of the two younger monotheisms the world which they had set about to conquer. But in a profounder sense, they had won: they had called the rules by which the game was to be played. The God of Israel and his moral values became the law of the nations.

Finally, Talmudic culture bequeathed its messianic vision and zeal not only to Christianity and Islam, but to secular modern civilization as well. The cults of nationalism, democracy, socialism, fascism, and communism have all at one time or another appropriated the fervor and soteric claim of the monotheisms against which they revolted. Their byword, each in the name of its own god, reads like an age-old verse originally associated with the advent of the Messiah of the seed of David. "On that day the Lord shall be one and his name one." Each has announced that it alone can bring to pass the prophecy of Zechariah—the prophecy that is the aim and substance of Talmudic civilization.

THE
JUDEO-ISLAMIC
AGE

ABRAHAM S. HALKIN

Born in the Province of Mohilev, Russia, in 1903, Abraham Solomon Halkin came to the United States in 1914. He was educated in the New York public schools and at Columbia University, where he was awarded his doctorate in 1936. He has traveled widely in Europe and Israel and has studied at Oxford University. For a number of years he taught Semitic Languages and Literatures at Columbia University. He now serves both as associate Professor of Hebrew at the City College of New York and on the faculty of the Jewish Theological Seminary. A fellow of numerous learned societies, he is Secretary of the American Academy for Jewish Research. Among his published works are Moslem Schisms and Sects, Ibn 'Aknin's Commentary on the Song of Songs, *and* Maimonides' Epistle to the Jews of Yemen.

9

THE GREAT FUSION

The Muslim conquests of the seventh century were fateful. A stage, as it were, in the migrations of nations, these conquests radically altered the face of Asia and Europe in the earlier and later Middle Ages.

The surge of Arab tribes from the Arabian peninsula northward was the result of economic and social factors, with the added impetus provided by the newly revealed religion preached by Muhammad, the messenger of the Arabs, who eventually came to view his mission as world-wide. Muhammad's message was relatively simple. At first it warned of an impending judgment; but the imminence of this judgment received less and less emphasis in Muhammad's later years. As far as we know, he was not a learned man; his religious beliefs and doctrines were not the fruits of reasoned meditation or logical argument, but the immediate convictions of a deeply religious being, oblivious of scientific or philosophic standards. At the same time he was acquainted with Christian and Jewish tenets, and his own beliefs, teachings, and legislation owe much to them.

During his life as well as afterward, Muhammad's success was phenomenal. In the ten years prior to his death in 632—that is, from the time of his flight from Mecca—the Prophet of Islam succeeded in making himself master of the whole Arabian peninsula, and exacting at least an external confession of faith in the new religion from most of its inhabitants. The following hundred years marked an expansion which made Islam the official religion of southern Asia—except for Asia Minor—from the Mediterranean to India; of Egypt and all of North Africa to the Atlantic Ocean; and of a goodly part of Spain and southern France. This area did not remain fixed, for the history of Islam has been one of constant change. It has continued to spread through the centuries, so that its adherents today are more numerous than ever before.

A NEW HISTORIC PATTERN

Jews, like the other inhabitants of the lands conquered by the Arabs, were deeply affected by the upheaval. The immediate effect did not appear to be great, but the several centuries of Muslim domination wrought changes which were of fundamental importance. One may venture the statement that they involved the creation of a new type of Jew.

Because of the exemption granted to adherents of revealed religions by the founder of the new confession, the Jews, as possessing a revealed Book, were not faced with the alternative of death or conversion to Islam. Muhammad's followers, now the masters of a vast empire, were perfectly satisfied with this arrangement, since the exemption enjoyed by Jews, Christians, Zoroastrians, and others also carried with it the duty of paying a head tax as a ransom. But these favored groups, while they were no doubt happy in their right to remain loyal to their faith, nevertheless resented this tax, as well as the imposts on the produce of farmers and landholders. Indeed, these taxes were such a great burden that they brought many people in the conquered territories over to at least a token profession of Islam. They probably produced conversions from Judaism as well, but to a lesser extent, since relatively few Jews were farmers or landholders. At any rate, we hear of no wholesale apostasies from Judaism to Islam. True, our sources here are scanty, yet if such apostasy occurred echoes of it would surely have survived in the extant records. The probability is that the majority of Jews bore the economic burden and clung to their faith.

Despite the burden, the Jews welcomed the change to Muslim rule, for their lot under the Christians had not been enviable. The restrictions and disabilities they suffered under Byzantine, Visigothic, and African rule were hardly intended to make them well-wishers of the

Christians in the latter's struggle with the Muslims, and their new masters left them pretty much to themselves. We know of only a few persecutions and of some hostile legislation which—save for some social discrimination, anyway—was only sporadically enforced. Until modern times, Islamic administrative policy was generally determined by practical considerations which led to toleration and, on occasion, even privilege. At the same time, however, non-Muslims chafed under the general disdain in which they were held, so that we find Maimonides saying that the yoke of Islam was heavier than that of Christendom—which, however, he had not known at first hand.

Officially the constitutional theory of the Islamic Empire, which was conceived to be a religious community, had no place within it for nonbelievers. But by special arrangement they were given, in return for the head tax (*jizya*), the right of domicile, personal safety, and the opportunity to gain their livelihood. Their cultural and religious institutions and activities were their own concern, with the result that every recognized religious minority set up its own administrative organization and regulated its internal affairs in accordance with its own law. During the early centuries, until about 900, when a semblance of unity still prevailed in the Muslim Empire, the governments of the minorities were also centralized in the head of the community —in the case of the Jews, the exilarch (*rosh-golah*), who lived in Baghdad and was the official Jewish representative, the intermediary between his people and the caliph. As the vast domain of the Abbasid dynasty began seriously to disintegrate in the tenth century, with the dismemberment that went on with few interruptions until the rise of the Ottomans, the minority "governments" likewise split into fragments. But there was no change in principle; the state was still defined in religious terms, and the excluded groups were told to look after their own affairs. The result was the autonomous regulation of civil and religious activities.

The extension of internal autonomy to the Jewish communities under Islam made possible the continuance of a Jewish way of life, or at least the semblance of it, the cultivation of Jewish learning, and patterns of behavior which remained rooted in Talmudic literature, though they underwent an evolution and modification.

From about the ninth to the eleventh centuries, the Jewish communities in the territories conquered by the Muslims were in closer contact with one another than their counterparts in the Christian world. Babylonia and Palestine, the homes and vital founts of the Rabbinic tradition, were within the Muslim empire. Since the seat of the central government was Baghdad in Babylonia, Rabbinic instruction was readily and steadily transmitted to the Jewish communities within the orbit of the capital, just as the problems and inquiries of these communities were easily relayed to the centers of learning. Before the establishment of the Islamic Empire, and for some time after, it was Palestine, rather than Babylonia, that exerted influence in Italy, Byzantium, Egypt, and perhaps France and Germany; but with the ascendancy of Babylonia, Palestine along with the lands of Egypt, North Africa, and Spain became subservient to it.

From about 800 c.e. the Jews of the Muslim world looked to the Talmudic academies of Babylonia for information and guidance. Questions were addressed to these academies on legal matters, on the interpretation of passages in the Talmud, on theological issues, on current affairs, on historical problems, and on proper behavior and tactics. The resulting correspondence created a Responsa literature of which our knowledge has been enormously enhanced by the discovery of the Genizah in Cairo. Important for itself and also for its historical value, this literature marks the beginning of the kind of learned correspondence among individuals and communities which has continued to our own day.

We have already said that the impact of the new society upon the life of the Jews in its midst, if slight at first, gradually became more marked. This was especially true of their intellectual life. As Muslim civilization was assimilated and the Jewish population became Arab-speaking, there arose an atmosphere congenial to new values and new doctrines.

No contact of the Jews with a foreign environment had effects which were comparable in character, or as enduring. Before the rise of the Muslim Empire, Jews who lived in Asia had relatively little acquaintance with the classical culture of Greece. As Greek influence penetrated Asiatic countries during the Hellenistic age, Jews in these countries, notably in Palestine, had become somewhat Hellenized externally but had not, it seems, radically altered their philosophy of life or their religious outlook. Their literary works remained faithful to the content and spirit of earlier post-Exilic Judaism. Even when a new problem of Greek provenance is treated, the solution is in the spirit of Judaism.

Under Islam the Jews had their second encounter with the classical tradition, this time not directly but through the Arabic language. It is to the credit of the Arabs that although they were the victors militarily and politically, they did not regard the civilization of the vanquished lands with contempt. The riches of Syrian, Persian, and Hindu cultures were no sooner discovered than they were adapted into Arabic. Caliphs, governors, and others patronized scholars who did the work of translation, so that a vast body of non-Islamic learning became accessible in Arabic. During the ninth and tenth centuries, a steady flow of works on Greek medicine, physics, astronomy, mathematics, and philosophy, Persian belles-lettres, and Hindu mathematics and astronomy poured into Arabic.

Given this wealth of learning, the gradual shift from Aramaic to Arabic as the vernacular of the Jewish population was a change of radical importance. Not all, but a sizable minority of Jews developed a voracious appetite for the literature in Arabic, not only the imported part of it, but also the Koran and Muslim poetry, philology, biography, and history. Thus they became citizens of the great world. This naturalization in the culture of their environment was of prime importance. The vocabulary of the Islamic faith finds its way into Jewish books; the Koran becomes a proof-text. The Arabs' practice of citing poetry in their works is taken over by Jews. Jewish writings teem with sentences from the works of scientists, philosophers, and theologians. Indeed, Arabic literature, native and imported, becomes the general background of all that the Jews write. And all this goes on for a long time with no hostility toward the foreign learning, no suspicion of its negative or dangerous effects, no awareness that it is the same "Greek wisdom" which Talmudic sources warned Jews to study only when it is neither day nor night.

INTELLECTUAL TRANSFORMATION

It is not surprising, then, that a linguistic transformation took place among the Jews within the Muslim Empire. By the tenth century probably the great majority of them used Arabic as their vernacular. Naturally, the change did not proceed at the same rate among all classes in the various geographic areas, and presumably the previously used Aramaic lingered on in many places. What is surprising is the thoroughness with which the language established itself in the life and culture of the Jewish population. It served not only as their vernacular in conversation but also as their means of expression in writing. Letters, documents, and books were composed in Arabic.

We are face to face here with a phenomenon which has no parallel in Christian lands in the Middle Ages. For although European Jews, like their Oriental coreligionists, spoke the language of the area, their use of it was limited to speech, and hardly occurs at all in their writings. Except for a later parallel in Italy, and except for Yiddish—which is a unique problem—we find no examples until modern times of such a development as occurred in Islam. Even these exceptions are no exceptions, for all they illustrate is the desire of some benevolently inclined individuals to help those who had no access to the body of literature in Hebrew or Aramaic, and this is very different from the universal use of Arabic by people of all classes for all purposes.

How then explain this Muslim phenomenon? Some scholars have suggested that Jewish writers used Arabic in order to reach the masses, who were not conversant with Hebrew, while others have reasoned that these writers found it easier to express their thoughts in Arabic than in Hebrew. Neither explanation will do. There is no reason to suppose that writers in Muslim lands were more conscious of a duty toward the unlearned than their brethren in Christian lands. If anything, the intellectual leaders who wrote in Arabic were rather unsympathetic to the masses. Nor can it be maintained that they found Hebrew a less adequate vehicle for their thoughts than Arabic. For Hebrew could do the work of Arabic, and did, when the necessity later arose for the translation of Arabic works into Hebrew.

The truth probably is that there were no conscious motives behind the widespread use of Arabic. In view of the extensive adjustment of the Jews under Islam, and the degree to which they identified themselves with its culture, nothing is more natural than that they should use in their writings the language which served them in every other need. It simply did not occur to them in their prose works to choose Hebrew as a mark of identification, as do so many in our time who deliberately write in Hebrew in an alien environment. To be sure, some of these writers voice regrets and self-reproach over their use of Arabic. Maimonides is sorry he did not write his works in Hebrew; Ibn Janah, Judah Halevi, and others criticize themselves, and not only themselves, for their neglect of Hebrew, their preference for the "maid," as they called Arabic, over the "mistress," Hebrew. However, nothing came of their compunctions. These men continued to write in Arabic.

The one area in which Hebrew was generally employed was poetry and literary (rhymed) prose. The choice here was probably deliberate, for considering the emotional intimacy of poetry, one would expect Arabic to be the more natural means of expression. It has been argued, probably under the sway of sentiment, that the poets must have felt more at home with Hebrew in expressing their feelings, even though Arabic was their vernacular. This can hardly have been the case. Actually, those poets who turned to Hebrew, and not quite all did, were guided by definite loyalties. To both Muslim and Jewish poets style in poetry and literary prose was as important as content. The creative artist was as proud of the originality of his turns of speech, or of his images, as of the originality of his sentiment or the depth of his emotion. Poetry and literary prose were composed to display the glories of the language, and Jews refused to write to display the beauties of Arabic. Prose was another matter, for there poetic eloquence played no part; and in prose Jews tended to use vulgar rather than classical Arabic.

If it is borne in mind that certain religious considerations attached to the problem of style, the resistance by, and the reluctance of, Jews to write Arabic poetry becomes still more understandable. For Muslims the example of perfect style is the Koran, whose inimitability is one of the principles of their faith. They attempted in all their literary output to emulate their revealed book. Jews, of course, could hardly be expected to take the Koran as their model, even in matters of style. They had their own Bible, in which, it was generally assumed, pure Hebrew was preserved. To them neither post-Biblical nor Rabbinic Hebrew was the same language. As for the basic religious factor, the beginnings of Hebrew poetry are intimately linked to the synagogue and to religion. What little poetry we find in Rabbinic literature consists of the several prayers and odes, all religious in content and almost certainly intended for public worship. The early poets wrote hymns or other forms of religious poetry which the leaders of the synagogue service could introduce into the ritual, to enhance or prolong the prayers. Accordingly, a tradition was soon established whereby—besides the general practice of reciting the prayers in Hebrew—poetic additions were recited in the same medium. In this way the sacred language became fixed as the legitimate tongue of poets and literary men, even when the latter turned from sacred to secular poetry.

The cogency of these reasons becomes even more apparent when we realize that, while the early poets and their successors in the Orient, as well as in Christian lands, took liberties with the language and departed widely from the Biblical mode, their opposite numbers of the Spanish school were much more careful in preserving the Biblical quality of their Hebrew.

Except in this one area, the Islamic influence on Jewish culture is marked and varied. It is manifest in bookmaking; in the marked expansion of thematic material and fields of interest; in the spirit that informs the content of much of the writing; and finally, in the attitudes and philosophies of the men of the age.

Jewish religious lore was studied with great diligence throughout our period. The beginning of the Islamic period coincided roughly with the completion of the Babylonian Talmud, and save for minor alterations or additions, it was accepted as the authoritative source of legal interpretation. It was from Babylonia, appropriately, that the clearest understanding of this voluminous work stemmed, as did the unbroken tradition with regard to its true meaning.

The course of the spread of Babylonian and Palestinian learning and practice to other lands is not clear. Our knowledge of the history of Jewish communities in Europe and other continents during the first millennium of the common era—especially of their cultural level and their religious life—is unfortunately very meager. Still, certain inferences are permissible on the basis of the extant evidence. It may be assumed that some emigration from Palestine to neighboring lands, together with pilgrimages from Diaspora countries to the Holy Land, made for a certain amount of contact between these areas. Similarly, within the Persian Empire, later inherited by Islam, there was probably a parallel communication between Babylonia and the outlying provinces. In any case, it is plausible to assume that prior to the rise of Islam, Palestine within the Byzantine Empire served as the Jewish nerve center of Southern Europe, Egypt, and neighboring North African settlements, whereas Babylonia played the role of guide to the lands within the Persian orbit. How all this worked out in detail we do not know.

With the establishment of the far-flung Islamic Empire, our information becomes more abundant. The change in political suzerainty brought about a reshuffling of allegiances and altered the relations between center and circumference. The Muslim Empire included not only Babylonia and all the lands previously lying within the Persian orbit, but also Palestine, Egypt, North Africa, Spain, and—for a period of about two hundred and fifty years (827-1091)—Sicily and southern Italy. The new alignment, with its consequent linguistic development, resulted in the withdrawal of Palestine from the sphere of Byzantium and probably in the restriction of its communications with both Greek and Latin Christendom.

At the same time another force began to operate which also tended to reduce the importance of Palestine as source and guide of Jewish life and culture. The hegemony of Babylonia became steadily more pronounced, so that the sway of the Babylonian Talmud, Babylonian tradition, and the two old Babylonian Talmudic academies of Sura and Pumbedita extended even to Palestine itself. It seems quite certain that by the time we hear of the propagation of Jewish learning and the reintroduction of a high degree of uniformity in

Jewish life patterns all over the Diaspora, it is Babylonia that is the center of all this. Its spiritual leaders established the Babylonian Talmud as the law of Judaism, and it was they who made the most telling contributions to the character of the many Jewish communities in the Middle Ages.

We cannot trace definitely the methods by which the text of the various Rabbinic works became available throughout the world. A tradition exists according to which an exilarch in Babylonia wrote the Talmud from memory about 750 and dispatched it to the Spanish community. Another story relates that a certain Abu Aaron of Baghdad taught the Talmud in Italy. By whatever means, Rabbinic works became accessible in the course of time to Asiatic and African Jewish groups. Not all Jewish communities came into possession of all the literature at the same time, of course, and no doubt some of it remained unknown to certain communities altogether.

As the Rabbinic texts, particularly the Talmud, could be found in various countries, people turned to their study. These people, with linguistic and cultural heritages very different from those that lay behind the Babylonian and Palestinian Talmuds, naturally encountered obstacles in understanding the works, as well as difficulties in accepting everything in them without reservation. So they turned to the authorities in Babylonia and Palestine for clarification or information. This extensive correspondence served as a means of instruction. A student who did not understand the meaning of an Aramaic phrase, or did not follow the drift of a discussion in the Talmud, or could not decide what the law was, or questioned the implication of certain views or of theological dicta, would address an inquiry to the head (*gaon*) of one of the two academies. In this way men far away from the centers of learning could carry on their education and so become in their turn qualified teachers and guides. Such Responsa, as well as the instruction acquired by students who went to Babylonia, resulted not only in the production of a large body of learning, but in the development of a high standard of study in distant communities, which themselves eventually became foci of Jewish culture and produced eminent scholars, schools, and disciples. According to a variation on a Talmudic saying, after Babylonia declined, Spain and Central Europe took its place.

Along with their activity as teachers of remote students, the Geonim were instructing students in the academies. Their occupation also inspired them to creativeness. Whether a particular work was composed in answer to some question from the outside or was the result of an originally conceived plan, it is impossible to tell.

Of this creative work of the Geonim, and of later writers, it may be said that it shows the effects of the classical approach as transmitted through Islam, both in treatment and in exposition of subject matter. This is particularly true of the scholarship of the tenth and subsequent centuries.

This epoch witnesses numerous compilations of Jewish law as a whole, and of special subjects within it. The compilers were undoubtedly moved by the notion that the ultimate function of Rabbinic lore is to provide guidance for the Jewish people. The volume and variety of this lore prompted them in the preparation of compendia whose object was to state the law more explicitly and make it more accessible. From the tenth century on, they were further prompted by the consideration that a more logical organization, a more methodical presentation, and a more scientific exposition of the law were needed in order clearly to bring out its intrinsic merit. Works with a similar object date from earlier centuries. The *Sheiltot* of Rabbi Ahai, the *Halakhot Pesukot* of Rabbi Yehudai, and the *Halachat Gedolot* of Shimeon Kayyara were all composed during the eighth and ninth centuries and are in Aramaic and Hebrew. In the tenth century and afterward, however, a change took place. It is visible in the works of Babylonian Geonim and of scholars in other lands. First there is the employment of the Arabic language. Nor is this influence the only one. Writers now become much more sensitive than their predecessors to certain requirements of organization and planning. For one thing, they feel the need of attaching an introduction to whatever they write. In a legal compilation, for instance, they explain the purpose of the work, the principles governing the subject, the distinction between general and specific rules, and the method of presentation they are using. In the work of such Babylonian sages as Gaon Saadia (882-942), Hai (939-1038), and Samuel ben Hofni, we find a logic, a continuity, a progression of ideas which one cannot fail to identify as of foreign origin. They provide an impressive example of the influence of environment.

The supreme example is the great Moses ben Maimon—Maimonides—(1135-1204), who more than any of his predecessors, and to the last possible degree, imposed the stringent requirements of logic and the perfection of form on the Halakhic material he undertook to present. Maimonides made three major contributions in the field of Jewish law, and in all of them his love of method and his acceptance of the logic of classical composition are displayed.

The earliest of these is his commentary on the Mishna, an undertaking which took him ten years, some of which he spent traveling from country to country. He completed the work at the age of thirty-three. That he decided to expound the Mishna after working on the Talmud we may assume from the arguments which he offers in his introduction, and also from one of his letters, which implies that he regarded the Mishna as the basic code and the Gemara as commentary, to be utilized as an aid rather than as the core. We may assume further that when he undertook his work on the Mishna he realized it would be preliminary to a code whose preparation he contemplated.

The commentary on the Mishna is a model organization. It opens with a lengthy introduction which summarizes the entire principle of revelation and tradition, distinguishes between acceptable and unacceptable prophets, describes the growth of the Oral Law, elaborates on the significance of the aggadic material in the Talmud, and explains the method of his work. As the need arises he provides similar introductions to other books of the Mishna. Thus he prefaces the last of the six volumes of the Mishna, that dealing with laws of impurity and defilement, with a lucid presentation of the principles underlying the book. Again, the small work Ethics of the Fathers, dealing as it does with ethical behavior rather than with legal rulings, is introduced by a short essay on human psychology. A chapter in the tractate Sanhedrin, listing the kinds of groups and individuals who do not deserve an afterlife, impressed him as sufficiently fundamental to warrant a long introduction in which he analyzes different views of the afterlife, points out what in these views is blameworthy, and proceeds to present his own version, which he contends is the version of the Rabbis themselves. Besides all this, he enumerates what he regards as the thirteen essential beliefs, the very minimum required of anyone who is to be counted a member of the Jewish community. The manner of his commentary also deserves a word. It is a paraphrase of every section that he thinks requires paraphrase, and it is intended to be usable on its own account, without the Mishnaic text.

Maimonides' work in Halakha is his *Code*. He gave it the formal title *Mishneh Torah,* but he generally referred to it as the Composition. It is commonly known as the *Yad Ha-Hazaka* ("The Mighty Hand," from Deuteronomy 34:12, in allusion to the fourteen parts of the volume). The work is intended as a definitive statement of the total Jewish religious prescription. In order to assure its completeness he prepared—this in the third Halakhic book—a list of the 613 positive and negative commandments. The list is prefaced by an introduction in which the laws are grouped into five logical categories, each based on a degree of obligation. The commandments are broken down into fourteen types, so that he divides his work into fourteen books.

Maimonides' idea of preparing a definitive compendium of the totality of Jewish law had important consequences. Although when put to him he denied it, his expectations, as he quite plainly suggests in his short introduction to the *Mishneh Torah,* were that this work, together with the study of the Torah, would provide a Jew with an adequate knowledge of the law. This aim involved attention to the philosophic basis of Jewish law. Accordingly, in the first of the fourteen books, known as the Book of Knowledge, Maimonides presents his views of the Deity, angelology, cosmology, revelation, reward, punishment—in fact of all the principles that he considers cardinal in the Jewish religion. Since his aim is to give a total picture, he includes all of Jewish law in his work, even that which is not observed at the present time or which obtains only in the land of Israel. It is clear why he chose to compile the compendium in Hebrew, while all his major works and minor treatises are in Arabic. Here was a work designed to be as pivotal as the basic works of Judaism. It could only be written in the national language, the language of the Mishna.

The *Mishneh Torah* is a truly amazing monument. Its comprehensiveness, lucid exposition, attention to detail yet simplicity of formulation, its mastery of language and of subject matter—all these things make the work perhaps the most notable of all in its genre. Natural but regrettable is the fact that later works, particularly the *Shulhan Arukh,* replaced it. Yet this masterpiece was never overlooked. In the nineteenth century the students in the Lithuanian academies exercised their wits on the *Yad,* which they called simply "the Rambam" (from the first letters of Maimonides' Hebrew name, Rabbi Moses ben Maimon) and sought to resolve all disagreements between it and other recognized authorities.

THE BIBLE: AGENT OF ENLIGHTENMENT

From the ninth century on, a new kind of interest in the Bible sets in, a desire to expound it directly and immediately, and not to rely for its meaning on the word of the Rabbis. Several reasons may be invoked to account for this phenomenon, reasons which operated with different force among different people. For example, one commentator may have been impelled to undertake his work through a realization of the awkwardness of studying Scripture through

Talmud, and so decided to resort to a direct and simplified interpretation. But even a decision of this kind presupposes a new orientation that involved some sort of departure from the previously forged chain of Bible, Mishna, Talmud.

Right here is the core of the matter. Something happened in the life of the Jewish community under Islam which led to a focusing of attention on Holy Writ for itself, apart from its position as the first link in a process of growth. One factor was the Muslim's adoration of his Prophet Muhammad and of the Koran as the incomparable and inimitable gift conveyed by God through him, which made the Jew feel obliged to display the perfection of his own Scripture and to emphasize its claims. In the environment of a religious movement that sanctified a book from which all of its articles of faith and theological dogmas were derived, the Jews felt impelled to put forward their own claim, to show by a direct study that the Bible possessed an incontrovertible title to recognition as God's sole word, that its subject matter and teachings were all-inclusive. Hence the Bible, especially the Torah, came in for unprecedented attention. Its light had to be made to shine and its unique divine character displayed.

An even more powerful influence toward the direct study of the Bible was the rise of the Karaites, the sect which believed that the traditional Jews had woven a "web of lies," namely, the Talmud, and that true Judaism was contained in the Bible alone. The Karaite battle cry was, "Search the Torah thoroughly." Naturally, the Karaite movement provoked a counteraction among those who remained loyal to the Rabbinic traditions, the Rabbanites. They felt obliged to refute the allegations of the Karaites, and in doing so they adopted the very recommendation of the enemy, that is, the intensive study of the Bible.

Antedating the struggle with the Karaites, the earliest activity in connection with the Bible was the effort to establish one text, so that only one authentic version would circulate among the Jews. A parallel activity was current among the Muslims, who were also engaged in fixing an authentic Koran, a Textus Receptus, that would disqualify all other versions. Among the Jews, it was the school of Masoretes, who developed the Masorah, or the tradition regarding the exact state of the Bible. They took it upon themselves to determine the spelling of words, the right vowels (vowel signs had been developed by Jews in the sixth and seventh centuries), the proper notation for chanting, and the lists of grammatical, orthographic, and lexical peculiarities; and to decide for all time what the text of the Bible was in every detail. All Hebrew Bibles produced since the period of

the Masoretes represent in the main the text established by them.
It is called the Masoretic text, and it is a work of a family of Karaites,
the Asher family.

Emulation of the Muslims and reaction against the Karaites found
expression in the commentaries written by scholars in the Islamic
world. The great Saadia Gaon (882-942), who translated the
Bible into Arabic, also compiled interpretations of most of its books.
Time and again he points out the correctness of the Rabbinic development of the law, or defends the Rabbinic explanation of an
item in Scriptures, with Karaite charges in mind. Further, he emphasizes the rational character of the contents of the Bible, taking as
his postulate that the Bible contains nothing contrary to reason or
human experience, so that anything that appears to be unreasonable
can be explained and made rationally acceptable. Whenever possible,
too, he seeks out statements in Scripture which can be shown to be
the very truths established by reason. And he is concerned to prove
the claim of the Bible to be the revelation of God.

Rationalism is the guiding star of the commentators, but it has
different results in different commentators. They do not all draw the
same inferences from the rational method of approach. So scholars
like Saadia Gaon or Samuel ben Hofni, anxious to display the
teachings of Scriptures in the light of reason, were on occasion more
concerned to read into a text what they liked to see there than to
discover what the text meant. At the same time there developed
a style of commentary known as *peshat,* which, designed to get at
the plain meaning of the Biblical text, kept preconceptions at a
minimum.

It is fair to say that Abraham ibn Ezra (1092-1167), Rashi
(1040-1109), and others generally succeed in this aim. In his introduction to his commentary on the Torah, ibn Ezra, after enumer-
ating four types of interpretations which he blames for going beyond
the text, states his own preference by saying that he "will inquire
painstakingly into the grammar of each word and will explain to
the best of his ability." This was the same method that Rashi and
others cultivated in France. It produced aids to the understanding
of Scripture which are widely used even today. Many editions of
the Bible still include in their apparatus the work of Rashi, who
provided the most popular companion to the text of the Torah, as
they include also the work of Abraham ibn Ezra and others whose
goal was the true understanding of the revealed Word.

But there are differences between Rashi and ibn Ezra. Whereas
the latter represents the type of sober, objective critic, Rashi, coming
from the less intellectualistic environment, accepts much which a

student from the Islamic world would hardly countenance. Often the French commentator offered an explanation or introduced a view he found in the collections of homiletic interpretations of the Torah (*derash*) simply because it seemed to him to be plausible and in accord with the words he was explaining. In typical medieval fashion Rashi illustrated the Bible with examples culled from his own time, without due regard for the anachronisms that were bound to result from such a practice. Nevertheless, his aim, like that of the interpreters in the Muslim milieu, was to help the student of the Bible to grasp it in its literal sense.

Naturally, both the rationalistic style of interpretation, which was essentially enlightened Midrash, and *peshat* underwent a steady evolution. The commentators felt, as the multiplication of their works shows, that they had things to teach that had not been taught before, and changing cultural conditions and attitudes contributed to the development of commentary. In the work of the noted exegete David Kimhi (1160-1235), who lived in Provence, the purpose is still exposition of the literal meaning of the Bible. All his efforts are directed to this end: his attempt to see prophecies in the right historical context; to resolve apparent chronological difficulties; to make the cryptic implications explicit; or to supply the important missing link. At the same time, as an ardent admirer of the philosopher Maimonides, he occasionally indulges in the rationalism so characteristic of the Islamic milieu. But he is much more generous than his Spanish predecessors in his treatment of the Midrash of the Rabbis. Frequently he introduces a Rabbinic exposition of a verse, without however offering it as the correct explanation.

Kimhi's younger contemporary Moses ben Nahman (1193-1270), a native of Spain, a man of noble character and genuine piety, blended *peshat* with a qualified sort of mysticism. Although he tried sincerely to set forth the true sense of the Pentateuch (the only part of the Bible to which he devoted a commentary), his passionate love of Torah and his deep reverence for tradition involved him at times in disagreement with certain more rationalistic scholars who, he felt, misrepresented the correct meaning of God's Word. And while the general tenor of his exposition is toward clarity and simple understanding, there is a steady undercurrent of fervor and of admiration, which occasionally breaks through in edifying comments and wonder at the mystery contained in a verse or a passage.

Over the centuries the exegesis of the Bible attracted hundreds of men in many lands who felt impelled to offer their particular understanding of Scripture to the public. To appreciate properly the wide variety, the many trends, and the peculiar qualities of all these works is a task beyond the scope of this essay. We can only repeat that this brand of exegesis arose in the Islamic world. It was there that the need was felt to reexamine the Bible independently of the great tradition which had grown up around it.

A FLOWERING OF HEBREW LITERATURE

Hebrew poetry and literary prose are among the most interesting and significant examples of "cultures in contact." That the stimulus, at least for nonreligious creation, came from without cannot be questioned. Before the Islamic age, Jewish literature and thought were almost without exception an uninterrupted flow of sacred writings and their poetic interpretation. There was no place in formal writing for the profane or the secular. It is a testimony to the profound influence of environment that beginning with the tenth century Hebrew poetry and literary prose of a nonreligious character undergo an intense development. And it is a further testimony to environment that this new phenomenon caused no surprise or criticism.

Life under Islam, especially in Spain, made new demands on the poets. Many Jews became fond of worldly pleasures; they learned to appreciate the charm of music, the grace of the dance. They participated in drinking bouts, they conversed about women, they joined in literary discussions. They were stimulated by Muslim poets, by their themes and manner of treatment. All of these experiences encouraged the development of a secular poetry. It did not replace religious poetry, but grew alongside it. But the standards and characteristics of secular verse influenced liturgical composition.

Unlike their Palestinian and Babylonian predecessors, the Jewish poets in Spain adopted strict metrical forms. An elaborate scheme of rhythmic patterns was evolved, the basic units of which were either a syllable whose vowel is preceded by one consonant, or one whose vowel is preceded by two consonants. Many poems are a long or short chain of couplets with a uniform rhyme carried by the second line of each couplet. Others are broken into stanzas, with or without refrain, and with a variable number of lines to the stanza. The language undergoes a marked change, which sets it off from the models of the Palestinian school and its successors. Students of grammar in Spain in the tenth and eleventh centuries made remarkable progress, with the result that men of letters became acutely conscious of the exigencies of Hebrew style. Such liberties with the language as the creation of new plurals for nouns, coinage of new words, and variations in the inflection of a verb are all within the framework of the approved principles of Hebrew morphology. Biblical Hebrew became the literary standard in preference to Rabbinic Hebrew. The vocabulary of Mishna and Talmud was used, but adapted to the requirements of Biblical grammar. Deviations from the standard occur under the influence of Arabic or of poetic license, but the output of the period impresses one by its strict adherence to principles, and it is incomparably smoother reading than the work of the Palestininan-Babylonian school, or of its successors in France and Germany.

The poets use conventional themes: praise of a respected person, or a prospective donor, friendship, joyous occasions, sorrow, love, the pleasures of wine, reflections on the world, human aspirations and human frailties. These and similar topics recur regularly. Commonplace in the hands of the poetasters, they take on new life in the works of great poets such as Samuel ha-Nagid (993-1056), Solomon ibn Gabirol (1021-1153), Moses ibn Ezra (1055-1135/40), Judah Halevi (1075-1141), and others. Their compositions are characterized by new ideas, unusual images, exotic metaphors, keen insights, a touching naturalness of feeling. A wine song of Samuel ha-Nagid or Moses ben Ezra, a love song of Halevi, or the elegies of ibn Gabirol on the death of his benefactor—none of these is mere restatement of commonplaces, but fresh, sensitive, and genuine utterance. Originality of theme also marks the work of these poets, and of others like them. There are ha-Nagid's stately odes, full of fervor and piety, on the military victories of the state of which he was vizier; his lyrics on his brother's illness and death, which affect us by their simplicity and directness. Halevi's beautiful lyrics expressing his love of Zion, or celebrating his voyage by sea to the promised land, stand out as major works of art. Ibn Gabirol's lofty poems which voice his unquenchable thirst for knowledge, or his thoughts on life, are distinguished for their depth and universality. Moses ibn Ezra relates his heartrending sorrows as wanderer and exile, and they move us as they must have moved his contemporaries.

Nearly all the poets in Spain wrote religious as well as secular poetry. In both, the effect of the Islamic environment is clearly evident. Whereas the Palestinian and Babylonian poets, with their successors in France and Germany, speak mostly anonymously for their people, their counterparts in Spain speak in their own persons. They first treat of Israel's plight, hopes, sinfulness, and her pleas for God's mercy, with no desire to assert themselves. There is a complete fusion between their own religious and Jewish cravings and emotions and those of the entire people. In the Spanish poets, on the contrary, the personal note is very much in evidence. They compose religious lyrics which are a direct expression of their feelings toward God and so bear the stamp of particular religious experience. Even when their themes are the national ones they share with their brethren in Christian lands, their treatment of them is their own. The way language is employed, the rich imagery, the technical devices distinguish the works of the Spanish writers of hymns, moralistic poems, and admonitions from those of their confreres in other countries. So it is not difficult in the case of an anonymous liturgical verse to determine whether it is a product of the Islamic or the Christian environment.

The art of literary prose was also actively cultivated during this period. Thematically the purpose of this genre was to entertain or to enlighten. Usually employing a narrative framework, the writer either told a story in which plot was the essential, or sought to introduce information or advice of various sorts. In style, all such works were a combination of rhymed prose and metrical poetry. The portions of prose vary in length and end with a rhyming syllable which gives way to a different one after occurring two, three, or more times. Now and then one or more couplets, fashioned in accord with prosodic requirements, break the flow of the prose. The amount of poetry included varies from one work to another, and even in the same work from one chapter to another. In the compositions known as *makamas* the connection between the chapters is often extremely tenuous. In the *Tahkemoni,* by Judah Al-Harizi (ca. 1170-1235), for example, the only connecting links between the chapters are the hero, who appears in all the incidents and adventures that compose the book, and the narrator, who shows up with the same constancy, the two always recognizing each other at the end of each story. Another notable practitioner of this technique is Immanuel ben Solomon dei Rossi of Rome (fifteenth century), whose motive, no doubt, as it was perhaps the motive of others, was the desire to bring all his poems together into one work as parts of a series of tales rather than merely *diwans* of verse.

Often a single complete story is told. Joseph ibn Zabara of Barcelona (twelfth century) in his *Book of Delight* relates his trials as the companion of an ignoble person who persuades him to go on a journey with him. Naturally, the story is packed with fables, tales, information—the whole composing a kind of encyclopedia, which is delightful. Again, Shem Tob ibn Falaquera (thirteenth century) reports the adventures of a man in search of true knowledge. The seeker meets one artisan and specialist after another, each one explaining to him the fundamentals of his craft or pursuit, until he encounters a metaphysician who convinces him that metaphysics is the ultimate science. And Abraham ibn Hasdai (thirteenth century), author of a beautiful tale *The Prince and the Dervish,* adapted from an old Hindu story, preaches flight from mundane interests.

All the many works of this category strive after a distinguished literary style, though not all, of course, are on the same level of achievement. Their popularity made them an effective vehicle for the spread of knowledge among people who would have shied away from more learned works.

The Hebrew poetry and prose fostered under Islam, and destined later to influence Jewish letters in Christian countries, constitute a highly significant chapter in the history of the intellectual growth of the Jewish people.

10

REVOLT AND REVIVAL
IN JUDEO-ISLAMIC CULTURE

The environment of Islam, in which a large proportion of the Jews of the world lived, underwent a steady development, from which of course the Jews were not immune. The various environmental influences did not affect all Jews equally, however. The influence of language was probably the one that penetrated most deeply, since practically every Jew acquired Arabic, but the depth of other influences varied widely. Islamic beliefs and practices, if they attracted the common man at all, did so only in their superstitious aspects. Islamic philosophy and theology could have no appeal except to an intellectual handful. These divergences emphasize the danger of making wholesale generalization concerning the influence of Islam upon Jewry. Any statement made about so complex a subject must be made with caution and hemmed in with qualifications.

In discussing the results of Jewish contact with Islam, it should be kept in mind that the encounter with Islam was at the same time an encounter with elements of Greek origin, and that this fact only intensified Jewish doubts, hesitations, and objections concerning the new environment. In some measure, the Jews under Islam were to go through what the Jews of Alexandria and other Greek cities had been through in their day. True, different conditions somewhat mitigated the clash.

What the Jews under Islam confronted was not the genuine Greek culture of the Periclean age but a version of it adapted to Christian usage, and altered still further by Islam. As such, it was a highly sifted and reconstructed Hellenism, and thus not as radically opposed to Jewish tradition as it was in its pure form. Since the Muslims grappled with it first in order to bring it into line with their own beliefs, they eased the way for the Jews. And the Muslim Jews themselves had a store of authoritative and semi-authoritative literature, some of it a record of the results of earlier reactions to Greek culture, much larger than that at the disposal of Alexandrine Jewry. All in all, therefore, the challenge which the Jew in the Islamic age faced was considerably cushioned. But the truth of this must not blind us to the fact that Greek influence caused a ferment among the Jews of Islam. It was a complicating factor, and its effects could not be avoided.

CULTURAL TENSIONS

What was the cultural atmosphere among the Jews who lived in the Muslim world? Like the bulk of the medieval population, they were children of an age suffused with religion. Not only did this imply faith in Providence, a personal God, it also meant belief in a sacred book, revealed by God through His chosen messenger. On this last dogma the Jews were the most intransigent, since they rejected the claims of both daughter religions, while the Muslims were the most generous, since they recognized the earlier Hebrew and Christian revelations, although claiming at the same time that their keepers had falsified these revelations, and that anyway they had been canceled by Muhammad, who was the last to deliver God's word. However, this quarrel among the three dominant faiths did not seriously impair their agreement in other respects. All subscribed to the dogma of revelation; all believed in reward and punishment and hence in the significance of human actions; all expected an eventual settlement of accounts, individual and cosmic.

No less than their Christian and Muslim contemporaries, the Jewish people found that their cravings and needs were often at variance with their doctrines and traditions; that the pleasures and delights of the world were out of keeping with the austerities and self-denials imposed upon them by Scripture. It was as natural to indulge in the one as it was impossible to forget the other. If there were many who resolved the conflict by subjecting their worldly inclinations to the discipline of religion, there were others who only half resolved it, and suffered, whether consciously or not, from a feeling of guilt.

In this respect the Jewish intellectual did not differ from his compeers of other faiths. But there evolved under Islam a Jewish elite truly unique in behavior, expression, and outlook. The dichotomy that results from two cultures in contest may be taken to account for the peculiar character of this elite. On the one hand, the majority of them appear to have abided fully by the dictates of their religion, which goes some way toward explaining their reflective cast, sobriety, and pessimism. On the other hand, they display characteristics which it would be hard to trace to Jewish origin. Rhapsodic, often Anacreontic in mood, the poets celebrate the pleasures of wine, women, and love, especially in the poetry of their youth, which enlarges without compunction on the physical beauty of women and unashamedly strikes an Epicurean note. Yet one has not the feeling that these are the productions of really happy people. What one senses instead is an underlying melancholy, disappointment, frustration, and disillusionment— the state of mind that modern readers so readily associate with the *Rubaiyat*. And the fact is that besides these poems in praise of pleasure, there are others that speak of the vanity of all things—the deceitfulness of love, the unfaithfulness of friends, the loneliness and sadness which are the human lot.

The conventional idea of the medieval Jew hardly prepares us for the Epicureanism, even libertinism, of poets who, as they advance in years, revert to the more expectable mood of negation. What is more surprising than to find that Samuel ibn Nagrela, the author of works on Jewish law, grammar, and lexicography, the poet who dismisses the world as the "harlot," is also the author of poems which are full of the ferocity of war, the lustfulness of love, and the intoxication of wine? It is another blow to our conventional notions to discover that Judah Halevi enjoyed drinking parties, adored beauty, and rhapsodized over the delights of love, while in his later poems of repentance he reminds himself that time is fleeting and that he has not yet laid up stores for the afterlife.

Of course, such tensions and contradictions were not peculiar to the medieval Jew, though they assume a form in keeping with his special genius. But there were problems peculiar to the Jew because he was a Jew, and these contributed further to the strains and challenges of his existence. Of first importance in this connection was the doctrine of *Galut*—in its plainest sense, the belief, persistently fostered by Jewish literature, that the home of the Jewish people was the land of Israel, and that life elsewhere was life in Exile, or *Galut*. Such a life was a punishment inflicted by God on His people because of their sins. Hope and prayer constantly centered on this tragedy. Sadness about the present was only slightly mitigated by the faith that God in His own good time would bring about a glorious return to the Holy Land and the resumption of a happy life there.

The consciousness of *Galut* did not prevent the Jew from going about the ordinary business of living, even seeking happiness, much in the manner of his neighbors. Yet the Jew never forgot it. When the poet wrote a liturgical composition, or the pietist enlarged upon Israel and her fate, it was foremost in his consciousness. And in times of oppression and persecution *Galut* became a bitter reality. Then the prayers for a return to Zion became anguished cries for help and redemption. If the sense of exile and the hope of return to Zion ordinarily lay dormant in the mind of the Jew, they were nonetheless potent factors in his spiritual makeup.

The hope, whether dormant or quickened, was conceived as being entirely in God's hand. No one thought of taking action on his own initiative or persuading his fellow Jews to do so. Jewish tradition long had it that such action was doomed to failure so long as God was not ready to guarantee its success. This was the universal opinion, no doubt reinforced by the Rabbinic statement that one of the pledges which the people made at God's behest was that they would not force the final redemption. Meanwhile all the people could do was plead and pray and conduct their lives in a way that was pleasing in the eyes of the Lord. More than this was beyond their power. Such an attitude was hardly calculated to focus attention on the favorable opportunity or to encourage interest in political or diplomatic action, let alone military force.

Yet there were times when situations arose that seemed particularly favorable to Jewish hopes, and times when the desire and need of redemption became especially acute. In times of trouble, with the clash of arms resounding through the world like the echoes of the Wars of Gog and Magog, Jewish expectancy rose high; ears became keener, eyes sharper, as the final call of the Messiah was awaited. In times of calamity, when the yoke of subjection became unbearable and patience was strained to the breaking point, Jews in their desperation adopted a peremptory tone toward the Lord, almost a tone of rebuke. And on such occasions it not infrequently happened that someone arose who announced that he was God's messenger come to redeem His people, in a word, that he was the Messiah. This sort of thing would create a stir, but always, at the urging of more "sober" leaders, caution would prevail and the pretender's claims would be exposed.

Now and then individuals or groups decided to change domicile and settle in the land of their fathers, but whether these decisions were the results of messianic stirrings or impulse cannot always be discovered. Judah Halevi, the most celebrated Jewish pilgrim of the Middle Ages, thought that life even in a desolated Palestine was better than life in exile. And centuries before Halevi there was a group, the "Mourners of Zion," who not only lived in Jerusalem, but urged Jews to follow their example. By and large, however, the sense of Exile and hope of Zion left the surface tenor of Jewish life undisturbed.

But there remained the perennial problem which faced all Jews. In all lands they were a minority living amid a population whose religion differed from theirs. And it was a difference of which everyone was conscious. So long as the condition of the Jew was tolerable, his security undisturbed, his economic activity unhampered, and his neighborly relations friendly, the issue of Jew and Gentile remained quiescent, yet with no alteration in the real situation. The Jews were ruled over by Muslims or Christians, so that their status at best was that of a tolerated minority. This social and political inferiority had a theological aspect which the Gentiles exploited to the utmost. To them the position of the Jews was positive proof that they were people rejected of God. And rejected, of course, in the Christian view, because they refused to accept Jesus, or in the Muslim view, because they refused to follow the teaching of Muhammad. The Jews, as convinced of the truth of their religion as the Christians and Muslims of theirs, could not for a moment accept the possibility of rejection by God. They offered explanations of their own. Might it not be that God was still punishing them for sins? For was not Israel always guilty in His eyes? Or perhaps God was testing their loyalty to Him. Or inflicting suffering on them so that their future reward might be richer. God's ways were past understanding. He alone knew the rationale of their fate.

Yet all this defensive reasoning was small comfort in the face of the taunts and derision, the overbearing confidence and disdain, of their critics. How could God put up with this conceit of His enemies? the Jews asked. Why was He not moved to pity at this degradation of His people? This is the constant refrain, even in relatively peaceful times, of liturgical poetry. How can God remain unaffected by the insolence of the Gentiles, by the sight of the heathen lording it over the offspring of Abraham, Isaac, and Jacob, of the children of Hagar enjoying mastery over the children of Sarah? No doubt this anomaly led in some instances to conversion. Certainly, spokesmen of the dominant faiths exerted every effort to "open the eyes" of the recalcitrant Israelites. If there were apostates, the faithful remained all the more loyal to their God and felt themselves all the more deserving of His mercy. Both Judah Halevi and Moses ben Nahman emphasize the special virtue and merit of Jews who fulfill God's commandments in Exile under adverse conditions. For conversion was always open to them—an easy solution of their problem.

Still, the Jew's inner torments and the pain of his sad lot remained, aggravated by his helplessness before the insolence and mockery to which he was exposed. His own common sense as well as that of his leaders always counseled submission and resignation. Anything else would have been futile and foolhardy, for he had nothing more destructive at his disposal than the pen. So the Jews were branded as cowardly and womanish. And the injustice of this charge was felt with a particular poignancy on those occasions when violence broke out against them, a comparative handful. But one must guard against overdrawing the picture. Throughout history the stereotype of the Jew impressed upon the mind of the Gentile melted away at direct personal contact, and in quiet times the self-consciousness and grief of the Jew tended to evaporate.

It is not surprising to find that the Jews who recorded the history of this time exhibited an almost complete lack of interest in politics. They felt themselves to be mere onlookers in that area. With no share in political rule they were often enough its victims, and it was only to this extent that affairs of state concerned them at all. Hence their chronicles are records of persecution and suffering on the one hand, and of cultural, chiefly literary, activity on the other.

If the Jew stood apart from politics, there were many other things in his environment, especially on its religious side, to challenge him. For example, there was astrology, a pursuit which enjoyed a high reputation in the Middle Ages. That celestial bodies were endowed with intelligence and could affect the course of human life was a proposition that seemed perfectly reasonable. Yet for the adherents of monotheism, with its belief that all things come about by God's will, astrology was something of a problem. It was possible to argue that the heavenly bodies of astrology were designed by God to act as His agents, but the prohibition in the Torah against all auguring, necromancy, and astrological aids made the argument questionable. Opinion was divided. The believers could appeal to a considerable number of statements in the Talmud that were predicated on the assumptions of astrology. The disbelievers had the Torah on their side, and even statements in the Talmud, such as the celebrated dictum of Rabbi Johanan that Israel has no constellation, that is, its fate is not ordained by any conjunction of astral bodies. So astrology became a matter largely of personal choice to which the proof-texts could always be adjusted. Maimonides was unreservedly opposed to all manner of divination, while other great men were just as convinced of its truth. Nahmanides (thirteenth century) accepts the religious injunction on the practice yet insists that the truth of astrology cannot be denied. The fact is that the majority of writers in the Middle Ages believed in astrology.

Nor were the Jews impervious to the popular practices based upon the superstitions present in their milieu. The universal respect for tabus and all that goes with them has always proved to be a more powerful force than religious prohibitions or rational arguments. The medieval Jew in both Muslim and Christian lands, no less than his ancestors in antiquity or his heirs in modern times, held fast to his belief in the unseen, and entertained fears and hopes of it. So he was susceptible to the superstitions of his neighbors and borrowed them freely, despite the admonitions of legal authorities or the criticism of sober intellectuals.

On another level is that feature of our period, touched upon before, which consists in the rise of a new interest in the individual. In Biblical literature it is the people of Israel who occupy the center of the stage. Individuals, of course, appear, and not as mere counters either. They are characterized, they speak, they are objects of concern. Yet with all this, the emphasis is always upon the people of Israel. The individual is nothing apart from them or their destiny. And in the indigenous culture of the Jews, with the synagogues as its chief organ, the individual's course in life was set by a ready-made pattern of practices, beliefs, and conventions. The distinction between one man and another was a distinction between piety and sinfulness, between depth and superficiality of religious experience. All distinctions were drawn within a set framework of conduct and attitude.

Now a change occurs among the Jewish writers and thinkers of the Islamic age. They begin to display a marked individualism. They are no longer content to remain anonymous units, unidentifiable voices of an identifiable community. The change shows itself in small things as in great, outwardly and inwardly. For example, according to the normal Jewish view in the past, it was not the author but his work that was important. Examples abound of references not to the writer but to the title of his book. Scholars might be thoroughly familiar with a work without knowing who wrote it. Now neither author nor reader was satisfied with such anonymity. The writer comes forward and identifies himself.

More significant was the change in attitude and outlook, evident not only in the secular and religious poetry of the period but in the work of the philosophers and theologians, who become less concerned with the role and destiny of the people of Israel than with the position and the tasks of the individual.

THE KARAITES

The revolts inside Judaism in the early centuries of Muslim rule were largely brought to a head, if not actually engendered, by influences stemming from the new environment. In some instances they arose from the attempt to incorporate foreign ideas and beliefs into the body of Judaism; in others, outside currents of thought served to release among the Jews dissatisfactions which till now had existed only in an inchoate state.

Of these revolts in the Middle Ages the most significant was that of the Karaites. It arose about 750 under the leadership of Anan ben David, who was of noble family and who, according to tradition, was next in line for the position of exilarch. The story is that he was refused the appointment because of his unorthodox religious views and that in retaliation he organized a faction which seceded from the main body of Judaism. But the causes of the revolt lay much deeper than this story suggests. For under the surface of Jewish life lay a smoldering resentment, always ready to be fanned into flame, against the rulers and authorities. There was a disposition, how widespread we do not know, to look askance at the steady growth of the Oral Law, with its ever widening control over the life of the Jews. People who felt this way were convinced, like the Sadducees of old—some of whose views may have survived among them—that this growth was the result of a conspiracy on the part of intellectuals to impose themselves upon a docile and submissive Jewry. In their view the scholars had invented a method, as artificial as it was baseless, for making the Torah an inexhaustible source of regulations and decisions that had nothing to do with the truth implicit in the revealed words of the Law. They resented the arrogance of these scholars, who set themselves up as the authorized interpreters of the Law, modifying, canceling, widening, or altering the Written Word. This feeling was of long standing, but with the momentous change to Arab rule it became articulate. The change created a climate that was favorable to schism. Preexistent grudges were now ready to burst forth into full-fledged revolt. There is no reason to doubt the story of Anan's disappointment: there is every reason to doubt that it caused his desertion from orthodox Jewry. It merely occasioned it.

Anan's chief tenet was that no Jew need feel himself bound by the reasoning and conclusions of the Rabbis. It was the right, indeed, the duty, of every scholar to study the Written Word for himself, and be guided by its teachings. Anan's slogan "Search the Torah thoroughly" was based upon the belief that such search alone, rather than the fanciful hermeneutic principles of the Rabbis, revealed the true meaning of the Scripture. His *Book of Precepts,* or what remains of it, illustrates this principle, and at the same time illustrates two other things. In the first place, Anan himself, notwithstanding his open revolt against Rabbanism, could not disembarrass himself either of the Talmudic method or of the Talmudic frame of mind. His study of the Bible shows affinities with the system employed by the Rabbis. For example, he employs analogy even to excess; he manipulates words and letters to wring laws out of the Torah; and he employs, besides, other principles familiar from Rabbinic literature. In the second place, again like the Rabbis, he tries to so interpret the Torah as to make it applicable to the whole of Jewish life.

It is clear, therefore, that Anan's objection to Rabbinism is more verbal than real. No more than the Rabbis is he a literalist, and in keeping with the traditional Jewish philosophy he believes that all life necessarily comes within the purview of God's interest, and is directed by His will. If he departs from the old method, it is only in his claim that he "could do it better," and he had found a new key to the understanding of what was inherent in the Holy Writ. Still, unlike the Rabbis, who rely in the main on the Torah and invoke the rest of Scripture as an aid, Anan places all Scripture on an equal footing. The results of his study of the Bible are more stringent and punctilious than those of the Talmudic analysis of the purport of Torah. Thus in order to commemorate Jewish exile he demands that Sabbaths and holidays be occasions of sadness, not of joy. All in all, it is evident that Anan was not moved to revolt by any craving for freedom from the Law. He was a religious man, and there is no reason to doubt that he was anything but sincere in his belief that he was restoring Torah to its pristine sense.

Nor is there any reason to doubt the sincerity of his followers, not all of whom saw eye to eye with him. Indeed, the second half of his slogan was "and do not lean on my opinion," so that disciples appeared who went their own way, offering interpretations that diverged from those of the founder. The result was division and dissension among the followers of Anan. It was only gradually that the several factions consolidated.

The name Karaites, or B'ne Mikra, used to designate those who rejected Talmudic methods in favor of a direct approach to Scripture, came into being after Anan. More a revolt against an existing situation than a doctrine, Karaism attracted every species of rebel. No matter what his hope or grievance, the movement could accommodate him so long as he shared in the common dislike of existing authority. Besides, as has been shrewdly observed, until relatively modern times all uprisings, whatever the grievances behind them, raised a cry for religious reform. Nothing was more natural in a religiously organized society than to ascribe all troubles, material as well as spiritual, to a falling away from the true faith and to look for the cure in a return to the faith, especially as found in the revealed Book. Hence the ranks of the Karaites were swelled with dissenters of every complexion, economic, social, legal, personal, as well as religious. There were those who felt bitter about the division of the community into rich and poor; those who resented the high-handedness of the officials; those who balked at the strictness of the law; and the list could be added to.

Nevertheless, as time went by this diversity of dissent became welded into a single movement, with a tradition peculiar to itself. One impetus toward consolidation was probably the need for a better defense against the devastating onslaughts of Saadia Gaon, whom they came to regard as their arch enemy. At any rate, by the tenth century the sect had acquired an unmistakable identity, with doctrines, laws, leaders, literature, and centers of its own. It won adherents and established communities in many lands. From Iraq and Persia, where the Karaites originated, they spread to Syria and Palestine, Egypt and the Byzantine empire. During the second millennium of the common era they developed centers in the Crimea, in Lithuania, and in western Poland. Each of these centers underwent a period of growth and of decline, and with each change of center there was a change of language; but with the breakup of the Islamic Empire, Hebrew was the language generally employed by the Karaites. There were recurring periods of great cultural activity from the first generation of the movement's career down to about the end of the eleventh century, and another in Constantinople about 1500. After that the Karaite record is not impressive, although individual writers here and there produced works of some merit. The Karaites did not confine themselves to law and theology, which naturally were their chief interests, but produced poetry, commentaries, and a large epistolary literature.

It was not long after achieving unity that the Karaites passed their zenith. They did not follow up their early successes, and their force appeared to be spent. The generations born to Karaism failed to maintain the vigor and zeal of the founders. Instead they settled down into a well-ordered society, with all that implied of stagnation, inequities, vested interests, and apathy. As the years passed, the relation between the Karaites and the Rabbanites varied, the latter remaining always the more numerous, active, and assertive party.

THE NATURE OF RATIONALISM

The majority of Jews throughout the Middle Ages, both in Christian and in Islamic lands, stayed within the fold of Rabbinic Judaism, but this is not to say that they were at one with themselves. Hardly, for the world they lived in was too full of challenges, raised too many questions, to allow at least the thoughtful person to enjoy inner peace. Although some managed in one way or another to remain oblivious to what went on around them, those who were citizens of two worlds, loyal to Jewish traditions on the one hand and admirers of Islamic culture on the other, were shaken by doubts, uncertainties, conflicts. It is these people who left behind a body of writings which provides us with an insight into their problems and also shows us how they went about solving them.

One of these problems was the attack by Karaites and others upon normative Judaism; so that dissensions within the Jewish body were subjected to a searching analysis. The great name here is that of Saadia Gaon. Saadia Gaon is far and away the most vigorous champion of tradition against the Karaites. His arguments are always trenchant and his pen always sharp. But it was not only the critics and maligners from within, but those from without, who inspired much thought and soul-searching. The challenge of the two other faiths had to be met, their claims examined, and their proofs refuted. So in the tenth century David ben Merwan al Mukammas, in the course of his refutation of Christianity—which he had once forsaken Judaism to embrace—goes into an elaborate examination of the Trinity. While the polemical literature appeals largely to Holy Writ, much of it consists also of acute logical reasoning based upon philosophic principles.

Neither the problems posed from within nor those posed from without by the other religions were the only or even the chief concern of the Jews. They were confronted with a much more formidable problem, one that confronted not only them but the dissentient groups as well, and also the Christians and Muslims. It was a problem of accommodation to what may be called the Greek spirit. This spirit, marked by an unbridled rationalism and an insatiable appetite for knowledge, does not appear at first to be compatible with an outlook in which faith is primary; with a revelation which is the standard of all truth; with a divine plan whose mysteries are beyond human probing. The turmoil set up in the religious mind as it caught some of the spirit of free rational inquiry cannot be overemphasized. Nor was the turmoil lessened by the knowledge that no agreement existed among the adepts of rationalism; for such disagreement, it was realized, could hardly be taken as proof they were all wrong.

The issue was not between one set of conclusions and another, but between knowledge arrived at by reasoning, and knowledge imposed through the authority of a Book. To accept on faith or to use one's faculties—this was the problem. The difference between faith and reason viewed purely philosophically need have created no particular anguish of mind, but viewed in its bearings upon specific religious tenets, it was clearly momentous. The conception of God in the Bible and in Rabbinic literature is of a Being who takes a personal interest in each and every one of us, who is capable of pleasure or displeasure, who changes His mind either in response to our actions or to our prayers. Now such a conception of God becomes doubtful when viewed in the light of reason alone, for in this light it appears to violate the requisites of divinity. Or take the belief that God is all-knowing, that to Him things past and future are present, and that He yet endowed man with free will, and so holds him responsible for his actions. But what sort of freedom is this, if God knows in advance what men's actions will be? To the believer it is simple fact that God revealed Himself at a certain time. To the philosopher it raises problems. So the need arises to harmonize faith and reason, revelation and philosophy.

As we have said, Jewish thinkers were not alone in experiencing this need. Christians and Muslims before them had dealt repeatedly with the problems it raised. Thus the Jews had at their disposal a large body of philosophic writings on religion, whether Arabic or translations into Arabic. The originality of the Jewish contribution here lay in their philosophic preferences and the skill with which they harmonized those with their religious beliefs. Without forcing Biblical and Rabbinic texts, or watering down their philosophic prepossessions, they exhibited a singular acuteness in bringing them into line with one another.

It was a cardinal principle of this harmonization that philosophy and Scripture were both true, and since truth is one, the two could not but agree. Not that philosophy and Scripture were on the same footing with regard to either the quality or the kind of validity of the truths they evinced. Scripture as the word of God contained, of course, absolute truth; while philosophy as a human activity could find its truth only in reasoning.

Besides the seeming incompatibility of faith and reason, there was another factor that necessitated a recourse to philosophy. This was the disagreement as to which revelation—Jewish, Muslim or Christian—was the authentic one. And this of course complicated the distinction between revealed truth and human truth. Thus reason had to be employed not only to demonstrate the truths of revelation but the exclusive authenticity of one revelation in particular.

The medieval thinker's great respect for philosophy made him engage all the more willingly in the task of exhibiting the word of God in the light of reason. Believing in the cogency of philosophic method, he felt that its application to Scripture would serve to settle questions, remove doubts, be an antidote to disbelief. The divine word was infallible, but it needed the additional vindication of reason.

Now Biblical writings display none of the conciseness of style, precision of thought, or logical order of presentation characteristic of philosophical writings. So the mere restatement of Biblical propositions in philosophic terms was tantamount to introducing a philosophy into them. Scripture could thus be made the bearer of any philosophic message the interpreter favored, and no matter what philosophy it was harmonized with, its meaning and intent were bound to suffer violence in the process. Not a scientific text, the Bible, once it was decided to wrest scientific truth from it, was elastic enough to yield almost anything desired. So Maimonides writes (*Guide* II, 25):

> Know that if I reject the belief in the eternity of the world it is not because of the text of the Torah which declares that the world was created. For the passages supporting creation are not more numerous than those which indicate that God is a body. Nor are the means of interpreting the texts which favor creation wanting or forbidden. Nay, I could engage in reinterpretation here as I did in the matter of removing corporeality from God.

In order to bring Scripture into line with the teachings of this or that philosophical school, it was necessary to assume that the Bible said one thing and meant another, that in addition to its plain sense there was another, or other senses, besides. This assumption goes by the name of the allegorical method. It is a device applied to a text which, there is every reason to suppose, was not originally intended to serve as an allegory. There is little doubt that everything in the Bible —stories, precepts, everything perhaps except its figures of speech— was meant to be taken in an exclusively literal sense. But now the ancient, sacred Book had to be made to say things suitable to new conditions. For example, Jewish life during the Second Commonwealth was very different from that of the Biblical age, so that the students of Scripture at that time, under the impact of this change, extracted from it by means of the allegorical method what they supposed was in keeping with the requirements of their time. The result was the vast body of literature classified under the headings of Halakha and Aggada. Later the learned Jews of Alexandria, exposed to the influences of a new environment, set about realigning Scripture accordingly, and for the purpose they too resorted to the allegorical method. And now the thinkers of the Middle Ages, once more faced with the problem of reconciling Scripture and philosophy, employed the same method.

Did those who used the allegorical method believe that what it brought to light was in the text itself? So far as the Halakha is concerned, we may say with some assurance that the Rabbis believed that in their elaboration of the Biblical prescriptions they were adhering to the original intent of the Law. It may also be said that in their use of the Bible for Aggadic ends—edification, entertainment, and so on —they were generally aware that they were wresting new meanings from the text but were convinced at the same time that they were in no way displacing its original meaning. It is likely that medieval interpreters, in their zeal to "purify" the faith, made no allowance for a literal interpretation where literalism would be philosophically embarrassing, but these thinkers believed that the writers, whether Biblical or Rabbinic, of the passages in question meant precisely what they themselves supposed them to mean. One thing needs to be emphasized in this connection. Throughout all the elaborations of Jewish law practically no one ever entertained the idea of denying its validity or of suggesting that its fulfillment was less than absolutely obligatory.

There was no consensus among medieval Jewish thinkers about which philosophy was the true one. Since the philosophers differed among themselves, even when they belonged to the same school, the choice of one system rather than another might be due either to a conviction of its truth, or to its popularity, or to its suitableness as a helpmate to a particular brand of Judaism.

During the tenth and eleventh centuries, certain Jewish philosophers in the Orient adopted a version of the system known as Kalam (literally, speech, discussion). Most of them were Karaites, but the most notable was Saadia Gaon, the Karaites' fiercest opponent. The Kalam had a long history, covering a span of several centuries, and its exponents disagreed among themselves on many issues, even major ones. Indeed, the widely respected Orthodox Kalam, known as Ash'arism, differed very radically from the Mu'tazilism, a doctrine with which it broke. However, both systems are called Kalam in distinction to the philosophies that are of non-Islamic origin. For though both Mu'tazilism and Ash'arism set out from premises originally imported from the outside, they were so thoroughly transformed that the system evolved from them was new.

It is only with reservations that Saadia Gaon can be counted a member of the Kalam school. He differs from them with regard to the origin of matter, and in general selects from among their tenets only those that are in keeping with his own original thought. Following the method of Kalam he argues that the world, since it cannot be conceived to have always existed, must have been created. Since it cannot have created itself the world implies the existence of a creator, who is God. In this way, having philosophically established the existence of God, Saadia argues further that God's nature is one and single. Hence he is obliged to interpret all references in the Bible to God's emotions and actions, His limbs and organs as merely ways of speaking, that is, as metaphors. Yet at the same time that he insists upon God's unity and simplicity, he is at pains to emphasize that God is living, omniscient and omnipotent. This was also the position of the non-Jewish Muslim Kalamists.

Saadia argues further that the Law teaches rational truths which, if it were not for the grace of God's revelation to the people of Israel, men would have been long arriving at by their unaided reason and meanwhile they would have strayed blindly from the truth. The same thing is true of the precepts that the Law imposes on us. They are susceptible of rational explanation, whether such explanation has been discovered or not, but we could never have found them out for ourselves. The dietary laws are an example. Saadia attributes free will to men, for only so are reward and punishment justifiable, but he also attributes foreknowledge to God, arguing that this is not incompatible with man's freedom of choice. Again, he undertakes to show that both individual immortality and national redemption are rationally inescapable, that the belief in resurrection does not fly in the face of reason. And so throughout, his loyalty to Judaism and its tradition is unquestionable, yet his standard of judgment is always rational. An especially striking instance is the criteria he lays down for judging a pretender to prophetic inspiration: not a miracle alone, but also the reasonableness of his message.

Another school of philosophy which had Jewish followers, notably Solomon ibn Gabirol, was that known as the neo-Platonic. The school, founded by Plotinus in the third century, consisted of pagan Greeks, and was closed by the Emperor Justinian in the sixth century. Its teachings reached Spain through Muhammad ibn Masarra (tenth century), who gave them out as the teachings of Empedocles (ca. 450 B.C.E.). According to the neo-Platonic view, all reality stems from a spiritual source, called the One or God, by a series of emanations, the last of which is the world of matter. Farthest removed from the One, matter is the cause of evil. Intermediate between the One and matter, and varying in degree of reality according to their distance from the source, are Intellect, the Universal Soul, and Nature. In neo-Platonism God is transcendent and beyond the reach of human intelligence, though mystic union with Him is possible.

An adherent of this system, ibn Gabirol is not on all points in accord with its teachings. In his philosophy, matter, the recipient of form, is universal, in all its forms present to existence. Its origin is directly in God. For Gabirol, therefore, the emanations are universal matter, universal intellect, universal soul, and nature, all of them spiritual beings, each comprehending within itself all its counterparts in the world of matter. Matter itself, a product of nature, is the lowest emanation. The link between God, who is transcendent, and the realities that emanate from Him is to be found in the Divine Will. What Gabirol means here by the Divine Will is not clear; what is clear is his desire to establish a more direct relation than neo-Platonism allowed between God and the world, to involve Him in the process of its coming to be. Gabirol was not satisfied with the neo-Platonic scheme in which God is remote and is eternal order. He conceived of the series of emanations as initiated by an act of volition, a decision on the part of God. Hence his notion of the Divine Will. Such religiously motivated modifications of neo-Platonism are evident in ibn Masarra's version of the doctrine and in the views of the thinkers, Muslim as well as Jewish, who followed him.

Although the philosophy developed by Gabirol played its part in the history of Jewish thought, and was of considerable importance in the evolution of the Kabbalistic system, it was attended by ill fortune. This was due perhaps to the rough treatment his book received in the twelfth century at the hands of Abraham ibn Daud, who upbraided Gabirol for his unsound premises, long-windedness, and failure to quote from Jewish sources, and it was due also to the preeminent role of Aristotelianism in Jewish and Muslim philosophy. Gabirol's book was not translated into Hebrew, though an epitome of it was made by the thirteenth-century Shem Tob ben Falaquera. On the other hand, it enjoyed considerable success among Christian thinkers.

MAIMONIDES AND HIS CRITICS

The most prominent Jewish philosopher of the Middle Ages was Moses Maimonides, who also enjoyed a singular reputation as Talmudist and Halakhist. He was followed by philosophers who were more consistent Aristotelians, who resolved the tension between faith and reason more radically, but it is Maimonides nevertheless who stands out as the master, recognized as such by admirers and critics alike. And his disciples were numerous. Circumstances played a role here, as we shall see, but in the main his reputation is based upon the intrinsic merit of his work. Immensely learned in both Jewish lore and Arabic science, he was the thinker who dealt most comprehensively with Jewish doctrine and practice from a philosophic point of view. His *Guide for the Perplexed* lives up to its title and answers the questions raised by the issue between faith and reason.

His book was not intended for the average man. Indeed, he expresses the hope that it will fall into the hands only of the reader trained in logic and physics. Otherwise, as he realizes, the book is likely to produce confusion rather than clarification. Unlike earlier philosophical proofs of the existence of God, the proof of Maimonides proceeds not from the proposition that the world was created, but that it is eternal. And he proceeds in this way, not because he rejects the idea of creation—in fact, he accepts it—but because the reasoning designed to support it does not strike him as being quite irrefutable. Of God himself nothing can be said except that He is He. To try to characterize Him is to run the risk of impugning His unity. Philosophically we can speak only negatively of God; for example, we may say that He is not weak, or not ignorant. The qualities attributed to God in Scripture have essentially this negative meaning, though as human evaluations of God they take a positive form.

In the Aristotelian view, which Maimonides adopts, the universe consists of a series of concentric spheres, each endowed with a soul and moved by an intelligence. Maimonides identifies the angels of Jewish tradition with these Intelligences, whose number he limits to ten in accordance with the astronomy of the day, and he assumes further that the sublunar world is directly under the influence of the Intellect of the tenth sphere, which is called the Active Intellect. Through the Active Intellect knowledge is bestowed on the human mind. At birth mind is merely a potency, and we may be said to possess only as much mind as has become actualized through learning and achievement. Life after death is not the continued existence of the human body, its appetites, passions, and emotions, but the survival of that portion of the mind which has become actualized. It is this portion that rejoins the Active Intellect and is immortal.

One notices at once how different this theory is from the Jewish beliefs with regard to life after death. To Maimonides resurrection of the body is one of the cardinal dogmas of Judaism, yet he does not discuss it in the *Guide*. This omission was due, as he points out in a special tract, to the fact that the subject is not one that can be argued philosophically, though as a Jew he subscribes to it as a dogma of the faith. Providence, as well as mind, is linked by Maimonides to the Active Intellect. The extent to which we are the objects of divine care depends upon the extent of our moral and intellectual achievements. The further along we are on the road to perfection, the greater God's solicitude. Maimonides rejects the view that animals are similarly under God's care, believing, as Aristotle did, that they are the victims of chance.

In his explanation of prophecy he once more resorts to the Active Intellect. No less than the philosophers, the prophets are beholden to it for their wisdom and learning. In the case of the prophets, however, the Active Intellect impresses itself especially upon their imaginative faculty, which is why they express their teachings in a poetic or literary form rather than in the ratiocinative form of the philosophers. Further, prophetic inspiration does not, as some have held, automatically supervene at a certain level of philosophic insight, but is a gift bestowed by God upon one qualified person rather than another, as He sees fit. To Maimonides, Moses is not to be counted among the prophets, for he towers far above even the greatest of them. In fact, Moses' inspiration flowed not from the Active Intellect, but from a more immediate divine source. The uniqueness of Moses is the assurance of the uniquely divine character of the Law revealed through him. It sets Judaism apart as the only divinely revealed and perfect religion.

The value of the Law is that it fosters soundness of body and soundness of mind. All its precepts and teachings conspire to guide a man to the greatest benefits, moral and intellectual. Everything in the Torah, whether it be a law or a narrative or a genealogy, is significant. Even those laws that appear not to be rational are yet intended to inculcate a moral or intellectual truth, to wean men away from wrong beliefs, harmful excesses, or dangerous indulgences. In its entirety, the Law is the supreme means whereby man realizes himself most fully.

Man's greatest good is to know God, and to know Him is to worship Him and love Him. To Maimonides this is the ultimate knowledge. It surpasses the pious life and knowledge of the Law, which are prerequisites to the highest achievement of all—the philosophic grasp of the physical and metaphysical truths that culminate in a purified conception of the nature of God. It is this kind of understanding that engenders the longing for God and the love of Him. It is the vantage point from which a gifted few from time to time have managed to get a glimpse of the Unknowable, which is beyond the reach of reason.

The phenomenal success of Maimonides' *Guide,* and of his other works, indicates how deeply felt was the need among Jews for a harmonization of their faith with the philosophies of the time. And there is no doubt that works like his had a reassuring effect. They enabled the intellectual to adhere to traditional Judaism and at the same time to abide by the strictest standards of reason. For generations after Maimonides, people in Spain, Southern France, Italy, and the Orient turned to his writings for an answer to their harassing questions.

But the steady stream of books and tracts devoted to reconciling religious faith and philosophic inquiry, both assumed to be unimpeachable sources of truth, was far from meeting with a universal welcome. Not everyone sympathized with the motives or accepted the assumptions of the harmonizers. Many Jews felt with some reason that in this work of harmonization religion was generally at a disadvantage; that in the desire to equate the teachings of Scripture with the conclusions of logic, the mental processes of man enjoyed more respect than the divine guidance of Scripture. Not only was the Holy Book subjected, as they were grieved to see, to the tests of the syllogism, but concessions and reinterpretations occurred in the process. They themselves were not disturbed by the conflicts, whether apparent or not, between reason and faith, and they rejected the primacy that the one seemed to be enjoying over the other. But this attitude represented no abdication of reason. Its spokesmen displayed remarkable acumen and great powers of analysis in their study of the Law. Experts in elaboration and dissection, they were possessed of a fine logical sense. Instead the attitude was rooted rather in their uncompromising adherence to a principle of long standing in Judaism, namely, that there are limits beyond which human reason must not venture—in other words, that there is a vast area which lies beyond the reaches of the human mind. To them it was therefore inadmissible, even sinful, to apply the standard of human reason to divine wisdom, especially as such folly could only result in distortion.

Even before the appearance of Maimonides' great works, Judah Halevi, whom we have already encountered as a poet, raised his voice in protest against the proud presumptions of the philosophers. Under the influence probably of the famous Islamic reformer Abu Hamid al-Ghazali (d. 1112), Halevi composed a philosophic work in which, pointing out the inadequacies of rational construction, he undertakes to show the supremacy of tradition. The *Kuzari,* as Halevi's book is called in Hebrew, consists of dialogues between the Khazar king, in search of the true religion, and a Jewish leader, the Haber, who expounds Judaism to him, after the king has heard representatives of other faiths without being convinced.

Halevi is especially resentful of the philosophic approach to the good life because of its essential indifference to the comparative merits of the several faiths. In this approach the ultimate objective is the knowledge of God. Religion is recommended because it inculcates the proper moral qualities in man, but no attention is paid to the question of which system of religious morality one ought to follow. Yet the question, says Halevi, is of the greatest importance, so it is anything but an indifferent matter whether a man professes Judaism, Christianity or Islam. He tries to show that the cardinal beliefs and prescriptions of religion, of the true religion, of course, flow from sources which reason cannot tap, from experiences that are incomparably more valid than conclusions of reason. Not that Halevi has any desire to blacken reason or even philosophy in religion, provided it recognizes that the questions which affect the heart and soul of the religious man are beyond its scope. His object is not to deny philosophy but to put philosophy in its place, to show that in the final analysis it starts with assumptions and ends with more theories. How then can philosophy, if this is its nature, be placed on the same footing with, let alone challenge or disprove, the physical experience of the Jewish people who witnessed the theophany on Mount Sinai, the historic truth of prophecy, and the crucial character of the land of Israel in its fulfillment? Philosophy of its very nature cannot provide the satisfaction, the emotional experiences, which the Jew derives from the observance of his religion, nor the conviction that they alone are capable of inspiring in him the sense that he is in the good graces of the Lord and will benefit from His promises. So it is not reason but experience that assures us that Judaism is the only true path.

The philosophic approach was also uncongenial to those who, without disparaging the intellect, were more attracted to the contemplative than to the intellectual life. Bachya ben Pakuda (eleventh century) is an example. His ethical treatise *The Duties of the Heart* remains to this day a popular work. In his introduction Bachya states plainly that he is not interested in argument or sophistry, but this disavowal does not prevent him from recognizing that a correct knowledge of certain fundamental premises about the nature of God is essential to a proper conception of the religious way. For this reason his first chapter is devoted to an examination of the problems of creation, God's unity, His attributes, and so on, in which he leans heavily on Saadia Gaon. But his major interest is the life of piety and meditation, as his whole book testifies. He treats of such themes as worship, trust, sincerity, repentance, and love of God, which is to say that his concern is with the inwardness of religious experience, with "the duties of the heart." This concern is more in keeping with the neo-Platonic than with the Aristotelian view of life and religion.

Although Bachya's war against externalism in religion is fully in the spirit of Judaism, the influences that affected him were at least as much Islamic as Jewish. One such influence especially was the Sufi trend in Islam, with its emphasis upon the inner, contemplative side of religion. The mystical bent displayed by Bachya and others, as for example Abraham, the son of Maimonides, is evidently one that can be shared by adherents of different faiths.

The onslaught by orthodoxy on the philosophers and their teachings broke out at the time of Maimonides and increased in intensity after his death. Several things brought the tension to a head. For one thing, the work of Maimonides, more than that of any of his predecessors, brought the Talmudic scholar face to face with philosophy. Hitherto philosophical discussions of theology had been confined to books that only the initiated were likely to read. But Maimonides, for whom philosophic explanations of God and His attributes, of the heavenly bodies, and of the elements were essential to religion, accordingly included them in his commentary on the Mishna and his voluminous compendium of Jewish law. The result was that the innocent student of Talmud, when he turned to Maimonides' commentary or the *Code*, found not what he expected to find, but philosophic theories presented as the substance of Judaism. It may be assumed that many a learned man reacted unsympathetically to what he thus found, even if he was not as articulate on the subject as Abraham ben David of Posquières (1125-1198), who made more than one criticism of the *Code*. For example, he takes exception to Maimonides' statement that it is heretical to think of God as corporeal, pointing out that "many greater and better people than he think so on the basis of Scriptural passages and of Aggadic statements."

The fact of Maimonides' fame only outraged readers the more when they came to realize the full implications of his philosophical versions of Scripture. To the traditionalists the spread of his teachings was a threat to Judaism. God purified of all human traits and feelings was not the personal, kind, confidence-inspiring divine Presence with which the Jews had long been familiar. The feeling of discomfort aroused by Maimonides' philosophical conception of God was still further aggravated by his views on Providence. To make the divine care of man dependent upon his intellectual development, practically an automatic result of it, is a far cry from the Jewish view of a solicitous, merciful God, concerned with all men alike and the immediate master of the fate of each and every one. In the same way Maimonides' doctrine of the afterlife appeared to be alien to the Jewish belief with its rich variegated lore. The abstract notion according to which immortality was nothing else than the merging of the human mind with the Active Intellect was psychologically unsatisfying and traditionally unfounded. It seemed to have nothing to do with the concrete doctrine of future reward and punishments. There was much else in Maimonides to irritate the traditionalist: his views of prophecy, of the revelation on Mount Sinai, of the studies that go to make the perfect man, above all his view that if Scripture was to attain the clarity and rationality of philosophy, it needed to be subjected to philosophical canons and reinterpreted in their light.

One thing, however, needs to be emphasized about this conflict between the traditionalist and the philosopher. It was not, as has been all too often supposed, a conflict between obscurantism on the one side and enlightenment on the other. Apart from the vagueness of both these terms, it is simply not true that those who were opposed to the attempt to philosophize the faith, rejecting its method as well as its results, were all untutored in the culture of the day. On the contrary, some of them were well versed in the sciences and no strangers to philosophy. The stand they adopted was not the result of narrow-mindedness, but of resentment at what they thought was the attempt to make tradition subservient to an alien mistress. On the other hand, it is equally necessary to bear in mind that the philosophic harmonizers were, almost all of them, sincerely devoted to Judaism and its traditions and sincerely and utterly convinced that what they were doing needed doing.

Even during Maimonides' lifetime the opposition made itself heard, and the sage felt compelled to refute the charges of heresy brought against him and defend his orthodoxy and pious intentions. After his death the controversy grew fiercer. Letters and epigrams were exchanged between Maimonists and anti-Maimonists, and the debate often became acrimonious, marked by personal slander and insult. Exacerbated by bans and counterbans, the debate was climaxed by a public burning (in 1232) of the *Guide to the Perplexed* and the first book of the *Code*. This, of course, did not solve the problem, but it did appear to act as a safety valve, for thereafter the tide of passion receded, though the number of Maimonides' disciples continued to increase and his opponents witnessed the phenomenon with anxiety and pain. The quarrel broke out again at the beginning of the fourteenth century, just as the Jews were about to be expelled from France, and resulted in a ban, issued by the greatest Talmudic authorities of the time, prohibiting the study of philosophy before the age of twenty-five. By that time, it was hoped, the student would have so fortified himself with a knowledge of Jewish tradition and become so steeped in the Jewish way of life that he could confront the reasonings and conclusions of philosophy without danger to his faith.

From the thirteenth century onward there is a reaction against freedom of inquiry, the right to probe accepted beliefs. The reaction was brought about not only by those in the Jewish community who were opposed to the attitudes and principles of the philosophers but also by economic, political, and social factors. The less liberal climate that came to prevail within the Jewish group was paralleled, even anticipated, by a similar current within Christendom and Islam. Toward the end of the twelfth century, partly owing to the successful struggles against the Crusaders, a dynasty came to power in Egypt which was committed to the defense of orthodoxy in Islam against enemies from within as well as without. As may be imagined, the situation made for a restriction of thought and in one instance at least for violence by government order. Similarly, Christian authorities in Europe undertook a vigorous campaign to stamp out heresy, and passing from a battle of words to military action, they took to the massacre of heretics, as in Provence. It was not solely by peaceful means that the supremacy of the Catholic Church was established in the early years of the thirteenth century. Together with the reconquest of Spain from the Muslims in the same century, this brought a zeal and fanaticism that made an end of tolerance. In order to secure its hold, the Church established schools of theology, engaged in public debate, introduced the Inquisition—indeed, did everything possible to cope with schism and error—and it is likely that this new mood encouraged the aggressiveness of the antirationalists.

Whether as cause or effect it is hard to determine, but the closer contact between Spain and the Franco-German center in the thirteenth century also probably strengthened the position of traditional Jewish learning and the attitudes associated with it.

Still, the two or three open clashes in the Jewish world between the protagonists of philosophic inquiry and its opponents did not result in the unqualified victory of the latter. Individuals arose in Spain, France, and Italy who continued with greater or less distinction to indulge in rational examination of God and the world. Yet the fact remains that the cultural climate was no longer as propitious to such activity as it had been before. For one thing, the lot of the Jews as a whole became more precarious than ever. In France the Jewish communities were destroyed by the expulsions that followed each other in the fourteenth century. In Spain they were faced with martyrdom or conversion in 1391 and the following two or three decades, and thereafter lived in tragic circumstances till they were banished altogether in 1492. In Germany the Black Plague of 1348-49 marked the beginning of a series of expulsions which continued for some three centuries. For another thing these unhappy events occurred at the same time that a wave of intensified pietism swept over both the Christian and Muslim worlds. And this in turn had the effect upon Jews of enhancing the prestige and appeal of traditional Judaism as it was practiced in northern France and Germany. In fourteenth- and fifteenth-century Spain the spokesmen for the traditions and loyalties of Judaism were German scholars and rabbis, and those who came under their influence.

Thus a change in circumstances brought about a change in outlook and philosophy, and it was not a change that was favorable to free inquiry. The whole-hearted and undivided dedication to the values which were accepted as genuinely Jewish—Talmud as a way of life and a constant subject of study; pietism which had no need of reason to bolster its premises and conclusions; a morality which allowed no scope to the individual—such dedication became the order of the day.

The result was hostility not only to any challenge to traditional religion, whether it came from philosophy or theology, but even to the orthodox use of reason. Outside Spain and Italy, Jews lost almost all interest in secular poetry and literary prose, in the physical and mathematical sciences, and even in medical studies, for which they had long been famed.

THE MYSTICISM OF THE KABBALA

Philosophy, with its reliance upon reason, came finally to be replaced by Kabbala, a system of mystic, esoteric wisdom. Kabbala has a long history, and represents in fact not one but several systems. In the later Middle Ages, as cultivated in southern France and in Spain, and eventually in other lands as well, Kabbala concerned itself with many of the problems that had exercised the minds of the philosophers, such problems as the Godhead, creation, good and evil, and so forth. But it differed from philosophy in several fundamental respects. Although its chief tenets are of neo-Platonic origin, they are presented not as reasoned conclusions, but as matters of fact requiring no proof other than Scripture or Rabbinic writings. The Kabbalist took over innumerable terms from Scripture, assimilating them to the language and concepts of his system, which, as a result, appears in an essentially Jewish garb. Throughout, the postulate is that, besides the plain sense of all ancient Jewish texts, they have also an inner sense, which is their true meaning. In all the vast literature of Kabbala there is no trace of a non-Jewish source or influence. In so far as persons appear at all, they are always Jewish sages, some of them anonymous and of hoary antiquity. Indeed, the very name Kabbala, which dates from about the eleventh century, means Tradition. It implies that the doctrine is not the product of human minds but was handed down the centuries through the mediation of initiated luminaries, like Rabbinic lore (which is also known as Kabbala).

Kabbala developed its own peculiar style of discussion and exposition. To the Kabbalist, Scripture is a repository of names and symbols standing for the emanations whose source is the Infinite; so that the language he employs is extremely figurative. It was often forgotten in the heat of discussion that this language was not a literal transcription of tangible realities, that its symbols were symbols and not things.

The authority of the teachings of Kabbala grew with the passing centuries. Its prestige was especially great during the sixteenth and seventeenth centuries, when, as the result of the teachings of Isaac Luria (1534-1572) and his disciple Hayyim Vital, it was able to offer in terms of cosmic events an explanation of both exile and the future redemption, and so provided a means as well of realizing the hope of Israel and the world. In this period Christians, too, were attracted to Kabbala, and they studied it assiduously.

In Kabbala, which eschewed all alien contributions, traditional Judaism undoubtedly scored a victory. The traditional version seems thereby to have established itself as the only genuine version, reasserting, so to speak, its indigenous character. But it would be a mistake to overemphasize this matter of what is and what is not indigenous. There has always been some degree of intercommunication between peoples and cultures, so that some measure of give-and-take has always occurred. No matter at what stage or at what period, every culture has yielded to influences from without. Yet when the fusion of elements, native and foreign, has become so complete that members of the group themselves do not know which is which, it is only the historian who has any interest in distinguishing them. For all practical purposes the two are one. The Muslims, for example, if they were aware that philosophy and science were foreign imports, had no doubt that their philology and history were indigenous growths. Yet the historian knows that these, too, underwent influences from the outside. Similarly, among the Jews, all memory of non-Jewish influence in Rabbinic literature was obliterated by the veneration in which Mishna, Talmud, and Midrash were held. They enjoyed an authority which made it inconceivable that foreign influence should have infiltrated any part of them. Indeed, any discovery of an affinity between Rabbinic and Greek views was hailed with pleasure, for it confirmed the belief that the Greeks got what wisdom they possessed from the Jews. It was only their sins and consequent tribulations that deprived the Jews of their rightful possessions, with the result that the sciences and philosophy passed as the creations of the Greeks, or Persians, or Christians. For those who repudiated it, philosophy was in this sense something foreign and incompatible with the resolve to abide loyally by what from time immemorial had been recognized as genuinely Jewish.

During the late Middle Ages and early modern times, intellectual activity in Jewish centers of learning was concentrated on Talmud, Kabbala, and pietistic works. Yet though the influence of Islamic culture declined, it did not disappear altogether. In Spain there were Jews who kept the Islamic influence alive, and even produced a literature of Islamic coloring. Nor did this influence end with the expulsion of the Jews from Spain, for a cultural activity of much the same nature and scope was in progress in Italy. This activity dates from the twelfth or thirteenth century, and was itself ushered in by the Italian Renaissance, when the theater and music and the arts began to attract the attention of Jews, and gained recruits among them. In some measure, even the exiles from Spain, scattered as they were over many lands, managed to keep up the cultural interests that their fathers and forefathers had promoted in an ungrateful country. Thus here and there were little islands in which the wider culture was kept alive long enough to be handed on, though in vastly different conditions, to the fathers of modern Hebrew literature in the late eighteenth century. A good example of this somewhat tenuous continuity is the work of the Italian scholar and artist, Moses Hayim Luzzatto (1707-1747). To some historians he belongs in spirit to the late medieval world, while to others he is the father of the intense literary activity which is going on in the state of Israel today.

THE LEGACY

Did the Jews under Islam leave a permanent legacy? And what is its import for the contemporary Jewish world?

The answer to our first question is yes. Jewish productivity, literary and philosophical, was great under Islam, and much of it can still stir us. Among the poets and writers of literary prose, there are a fair number who are as lively and fresh as ever. If they have few readers today, that is because of the cultural upheaval of our time, which has alienated us from our heritage. But the fact remains that if we are looking for distinction of thought, for sentiment and diction, to say nothing of techniques or the crystallization of ancient lore, we shall find them in a large part of the poetic output of Islamic Jewry; just as we shall find depth, clear thinking, and honest scholarship in its prose.

There is also much to be learned from the cultural activity itself, for underlying that activity was a state of mind that we might well emulate today. It may be called a sense of intellectual responsibility. The encounter with Greek thought was a profoundly disturbing event in the life of the Jews under Islam. The modern world offers a parallel. Then, as now, the exposure to new winds of doctrine produced confusion and perplexity at the same time that it stimulated a rethinking of old problems.

What evokes admiration is the way in which the Jews of Islam addressed themselves to the task that faced them. It was not only that they were steeped in Judaism, but they were otherwise thoroughly informed, as for example in Greek philosophy. They could thus speak with authority. Their knowledge acted as both an aid and a restraint. Grounded in the essentials of the Jewish faith on the one hand and in the tenets of the philosophers on the other, they were in a position to measure the possibilities and impossibilities or reconciliation between them. There was no vagueness here, no muddled, ill-informed attempts at compromise. Immense subtlety, skill, and learning went into their harmonizations, but they knew what they were about and their loyalty to Judaism—not a diluted Judaism, either—never wavered.

We have spoken of intellectual responsibility. The learned men who were engaged in working out the rationale of a way of life which would violate neither Torah nor the particular philosophy they adopted were earnest seekers of the truth. To them as to their medieval confreres generally, truth was no merely relative matter, dependent upon time and circumstance. Absolute truth was their aim, and no other truth existed. Conventions they knew, man-made regulations and laws, but these had nothing to do with the truth they were after. Since truth for them was not one thing today and another tomorrow, they approached their task with the greatest seriousness and sense of responsibility, and set forth their conclusions not as more or less plausible hypotheses, but as unqualifiedly true. In their view, if they were not thus true, they were not true at all.

Contrast this whole intellectual ambiance with that prevailing among Jews in the twentieth century. In so far as the task of harmonizing their faith with the intellectual currents of the time is recognized at all, it is commonly undertaken by people who, versed as they may be in the ideas and moods of the day, are deficient in Jewish learning. The results are not of the happiest; indeed, they may be said to be superficial and shoddy. It must be added, however, that the task has been considerably complicated by the changes that have taken place in Jewish thought since the Islamic period. Moreover, those changes occurred in a milieu that was no mere continuation of that in which philosophic inquiry flourished, but rather a break with it.

It was the milieu of German-Polish Jewry which broke decisively with the postulates and conclusions of their predecessors in Islam, and the dominance for centuries of German-Polish Jewry stamped Judaism with a character which by force of circumstance became its normal character. What happened was a reversion—with modification, of course—to Talmud and Midrash, to the outlook of the medieval Franco-German world. And so the Judeo-Islamic factor was reduced to a minimum. Accordingly the harmonizer of today is confronted, apart from all else, with a set of problems that are incomparably more difficult than those that confronted his medieval counterpart.

Besides all this, we have lost confidence in the possibility of finding truths at all. Relativism has come to pervade every branch of intellectual inquiry. Absolutes only raise a smile. What is profoundly important is that this change has robbed us of the earnestness that was so marked a characteristic of our ancestors. We are no longer committed to the truth of Judaism as they were committed to it. To them it was a truth so unquestionable that no other truth could possibly be incompatible with it. Hence the imperative necessity to demonstrate that the two truths, one philosophical, the other religious, were one truth. With us that commitment and conviction have been replaced by a sentimental attachment to the "legacy" of Judaism, or by a belief in the social benefits of religion, or by a need for the peace of mind it bestows. Since our religious convictions are vague and accommodating, they are compatible with almost any other belief we may happen to hold. If we are concerned with harmonization at all, it is only in the sense of finding room for a cherished but somewhat antiquated bequest.

In contrast to our own time, the notion that every religion is true after its own fashion would have been inconceivable in the Middle Ages. To the medieval Jewish believer the only true religion was the one he professed; all the others were necessarily false. He might admit that Christianity and Islam were superior to paganism, but he could not admit that they were on a par with Judaism. Accordingly, what he emphasized was not the general preamble of faith that the three religions shared in common, but those teachings in which Judaism differed from them. It did not matter that their proofs of God's existence were the same, that they ascribed the same attributes to Him; what did matter was the uniqueness of Moses, the eternity of the Law, the indispensability of its prescriptions. To the modern man, on the contrary, it is the common core rather than the differences that matters. No doubt social and cultural factors are involved in this change of attitude. But this apart, the change itself has been momentous in dictating the goals as well as the methods of present-day approaches to Judaism. The goal of these approaches is mainly to save Judaism—a rather vague Judaism, it should be added—to find a place for it in the modern world, in the hope that once this is achieved Jews will remain within the fold. Obviously this is a far cry from the aims and motives of our medieval "defenders of the faith."

This change of attitude toward religion helps also to account for the great disparity between Jewish achievements in medieval Islam and Jewish achievements in modern Europe and America. Notwithstanding the affinities between our world and theirs, the Jews under Islam created a rich and varied Hebrew literature, one so noteworthy that the period has been called "the Golden Age," while the modern Western world has nothing comparable to its credit. It is true that in Russia and Poland—the centers of Jewry in the nineteenth century—Hebrew literature underwent a remarkable development, but under conditions unique to those two countries. This phenomenon can hardly be credited to the West, any more than the burst of literary activity in Israel today can be so credited.

It would appear, then, that where Judaism was a vital force, as in Islam or Eastern Europe, Hebrew poetry and prose flourished, and when it ceased to be such, as in the West, these arts tended to die away. We have already seen that in Islamic society there was what might be called a neutral area in which men of different faiths could work together without hurt to their identity. This was the case in medicine, mathematics, science, and philosophy. Yet if Jews, Muslims, and Christians could work together in these fields, each faith carried on in an environment of its own; each was conscious of its affiliations. And this consciousness revealed itself even in their secular writings. A work by a Jew usually opened with praise to God or some reference to the Lawgiver. Even the sort of proof-text as quoted from Scripture served to identify him, and even his handwriting, for he wrote in Hebrew script. Anonymity might cloak his name but not his religion. Of course, such a climate fostered a recognizable Jewish literature, even when written in Arabic. And one special way for the Jew in Islam to assert his identity, his solidarity with his group, was through the production of poetry and prose in Hebrew.

Today a very different picture confronts us. The Jew is participating in the culture of his time, but in an atmosphere in which religion is a strictly private concern. So the work of Jews, no matter in what field, bears no specific stamp. And since art has become a purely personal expression, it is not surprising that the Jew, especially as his religion has become a somewhat tepid affair, feels no need of a Jewish approach or of the Hebrew medium. Thus the literary and philosophical achievements of the Jews under Islam find no parallel among the Jews of the modern Western world, despite affinities between cultural conditions then and now.

Still, the Golden Age of Hebrew literature remains and much may be learned from it. Conjectures concerning "what would have happened if . . ." are out of place in a historical survey, yet one cannot help regretting certain unfortunate historical circumstances which forced the Islamic age in Jewish life and letters to give way to a spirit that was so largely alien to it. One can only hope that the impetus which came from Eastern Europe in the last century and which has gathered force so remarkably in Israel will yet have the result of reclaiming for modern times the glory that was Spanish Jewry.

THE
EUROPEAN
AGE

CECIL ROTH

Cecil Roth was born in London in 1899. He served in the British Army during World War I and then returned to Oxford, where he studied history, specializing in Italian and Jewish history. He has been Reader in Jewish Studies at Oxford since 1939, and he has become familiar to Americans through his books and lectures, as well as to thousands of American troops who heard him in Europe during World War II. He is the author of hundreds of scholarly articles and more than thirty books, including A Short History of the Jewish People, The Jews of Medieval Oxford, *and* The Last Florentine Republic, *which have been translated into six languages. He considers his greatest honor the fact that the Nazis included him, with Anthony Eden and Winston Churchill, in a list of the first five hundred persons to be arrested when they landed in Britain.*

11

A MILLENNIUM IN EUROPE

For at least twenty-one centuries before the rebirth of the Jewish state in 1948, Jews had been living in Europe, and for a period nearly that long organized Jewish congregations were to be found there. Culturally, the European period may be said to date from at least the tenth century, since we have documents from that time which attest an intensive Jewish literary and spiritual productivity. After the middle of the eleventh century, with the decay of the great academies of the East, came the poets and philosophers of Spain and the Talmudists of Germany and France. From then on, Jewish genius flourished almost exclusively on European soil. Indeed, from the completion of the Babylonian Talmud down to the publication of the Jewish Encyclopedia in America in 1906, hardly a single major cultural product originated outside Europe.

Today the great majority of the Jews of the world are of immediate European descent, and time was when nearly ninety percent of them actually lived in Europe. The European age of Jewish culture, representing as it does a span of some thousand years, thus lasted as long as the periods of the First and Second Temples combined, from the accession of Solomon to the destruction of Jerusalem by the Romans; it lasted twice as long as the Talmudic age in Babylonia; five times as long as the Hellenistic age in Alexandria; and fifteen times as long as the Jewish experience in America thus far. In no other part of the world did the Jews suffer as much, yet their history in Europe is not merely a history of agony and abasement, but of creative achievements so great that they have affected, even molded, Jews and Judaism down to the present time.

It will be my task here to try to distinguish some of the major European contributions, extending over a millennium, to Jewish life rather than to Jewish letters.

The American reader of this volume hardly needs to be reminded that, notwithstanding the fact that Judaism is rooted in a remoter past and in yet more ancient lands, the European experience is implicit in American Jewish life, perhaps even more than that experience on its Christian side is implicit in American life as a whole. The United States, at the end of the eighteenth century, evolved something which was in certain respects novel in human history, and however much European models and influences and echoes may be traced in it, we can say that here is something essentially American. At that time Jews had already been resident on the North American continent for well over a century, and it was not long before American Jewish life began to attain significance. Yet even today American Jewry is still living off the cultural and religious heritage which it brought from the other side of the Atlantic. The ancestors of the overwhelming mass of American Jews came from Europe; American Jewish ideals are European in origin; American Jewish literature is still in the main European. It is impossible to understand American Jewry, or to appreciate its problems, or for that matter its achievements, except in a European context.

THE EUROPEAN EXPERIENCE

Jews first settled in Europe perhaps as early as the close of the Biblical age, certainly at the beginning of the second century before the Christian era, and they were to be found in Rome well before its fall. Their number increased as the result of the Romans' large-scale deportations of Palestinian prisoners of war, as well as by peaceful migration to the capital of the Empire, and even by conversions—for at one time Judaism was an active proselytizing faith. From the third century of the Christian era at the latest, there were communities and synagogues all over the European continent, from the Bosporus to the Atlantic seaboard. The Roman emperors treated the Jews (as they did all other subject races) with mild tolerance, tempered however with resentment at the fact that they persisted—as no other group did—in adhering to their stubborn monotheistic religion and their paradoxical hope of national regeneration.

When the Roman Empire adopted Christianity in the fourth century, a novel and intolerant spirit began to establish itself and to increase in strength in the new Europe as the Middle Ages advanced. In due course the Christian Church evolved an elaborate anti-Jewish code, which one may say reached its final form in the Fourth Lateran Council of 1215, and which was reinforced by the popular prejudice that it had itself half reluctantly stimulated. Jews and Christians were not to dwell together, to trade together, to work together. The unbelievers were not allowed to engage in honorable professions such as medicine, lest they should attain improper influence over their patients. They were excluded from handicrafts, and so reduced in many lands to pawnbroking and old-clothes dealing. They were not to own land or even to live outside towns, though they were hypocritically blamed sometimes for being divorced from the countryside. In the places where they were suffered to exist, they were crowded into separate, fetid streets, later called ghettos, and marked off from other men by a special garb or badge of shame. At intervals they were compelled to listen to conversionist sermons, and as late as the nineteenth century their children were sometimes seized and baptized by force.

Meanwhile, as the result of their isolation and of the unremitting propaganda against them, their physical security continuously deteriorated. From the period of the First Crusade (1096), outbreaks of violence against them became appallingly frequent throughout Europe. Preposterous charges, such as the accusation of ritual murder at Passover time, were increasingly common. The resentment thus stimulated finally resulted in a series of expulsions from one country after the other—from England in 1290, from France in 1306 and 1394, from Spain in 1492, from Portugal in 1497, from most of the cities of Germany during the period of stark tragedy which succeeded the massacres (on the absurd charge of poisoning the wells) at the time of the Black Death in 1348-49. By the end of the fifteenth century the Jews had been excluded from the whole of Western Europe except some parts of Germany and of Italy, where political disunity fortunately prevented the pursuit of any single policy. Henceforth they were concentrated overwhelmingly in the two great eastern empires of that age: the Ashkenazim or Northern (literally "German") Jews in Poland, the Sephardim or Southern (literally "Spanish") Jews in Turkey.

At the close of the sixteenth and during the course of the seventeenth century, a more tolerant atmosphere began to spread in some lands of Western Europe, especially England and Holland. This was the result partly of the new tendencies in religion, partly of the modern spirit of mercantile enterprise, which paid more attention to a man's economic utility than to his race or faith. Semiemancipated communities of a new sort now slowly established themselves in these countries and in their overseas dependencies, where the American Revolution achieved for the first time complete equality for all regardless of religious belief—an equality that was temporarily imitated in Western Europe at the time of the French Revolution, and in a more deliberate fashion when liberalism triumphed (as was then thought, for good) in the second half of the nineteenth century.

This progress, however, affected a relatively small minority of the Jews. The great masses in Eastern Europe, formerly in Poland but now mostly in the Russian Empire, were wholly unaffected. From 1648 onward, outbreaks of massacre in this area resulted in herds of refugees, who created or reinforced the various communities of Western Europe. In the nineteenth century, when elsewhere a new era seemed to have dawned, successive waves of "pogroms" (as they were henceforth termed), coupled with new anti-Jewish legislation, brought about the emigration from Russia of hundreds of thousands more— the ancestors of most of the Jews in the United States, the British Empire, and many other lands today. This new persecution ended only with the Russian Revolution of 1917, which on the other hand resulted in the severance from the Jewish people (and as it seems from Judaism) of the three million Jews left in Russia proper.

Meanwhile, the relics of the old anti-Jewish feeling, given a "new look" on a pseudo-scientific basis under the name of antisemitism, were being fostered, especially in Germany, through jealousy of the rapid progress made by emancipated Jews in that country. As the result of many factors—political, psychological, economic—this became the fundamental principle of the Nazi government which took power in 1933, and which later deliberately set about the extermination of European Jewry. From 1939 to 1945, between 5,000,000 and 6,000,000 Jews perished out of the 9,000,000 who had formerly lived in the lands through which the German fury swept. Today there are left in Europe fewer than 3,500,000 Jews, or approximately thirty percent of the total number in the world, as against at least eighty-five percent a hundred years ago. Of these European survivors one-half or more live in Russia, and one-quarter in the satellite countries behind the Iron Curtain, their future share in the great adventure of Jewish life being doubtful.

Much that is of first importance in Jewish life may yet proceed from Europe. There are still in that continent reserves of strength, based on the traditions of a thousand years, which should not be underestimated. There is no inherent reason why the European survivors, notwithstanding their losses, should not develop once again a spiritual productivity comparable to that attained in the past, for in things of the mind God is not on the side of the big battalions; in fact, the great ages of creativity in Jewish history were the achievement of relatively small groups. After all, there are still in Western Europe as many Jews as there were at any time in the Middle Ages, and theoretically at least, their potentialities are equally great. But the age of European predominance in Jewish life, which lasted for a thousand years, has without question come to a sudden and unspeakably tragic end.

CONTEMPORARY SIGNIFICANCE

What is the greatest contribution of the European Jewish groups to the common store, and to mankind, in the course of these twenty centuries? What fundamental lesson does their experience hold for posterity? I have spent much time pondering the problem since I was invited to collaborate in this book, and I have come to a firm conclusion. It is that they continued to exist, above all that they continued to exist *as Jews*. That this fact profoundly influenced the world is something to which we will revert: the point I wish to emphasize here is that this continued existence is itself a tremendous achievement. No other group in history has ever withstood such constant, unremitting pressure, century after century. But the Jews experienced it, defied it, survived it, and emerged at the end unbroken and unbowed, to achieve in our own day their greatest and most unbelievable triumph.

They never questioned for one moment the validity of their faith. They never doubted that they or their children or their children's children would one day witness God's consolation. They were filled with unbounded certainty that in due course they would be restored, a free people again, to their own land—and by this unbounded certainty of theirs they made it not only possible, but certain. Scoffing strangers considered them timid. Yet they showed a courage unexampled in all human experience in braving the contempt and hatred of their neighbors, in maintaining their faith when they knew that apostasy would automatically bring them security and largesse, in continuing to live in isolation among their enemies even after the horrors of bloodthirsty, frenzied attacks.

Let us take one very familiar episode. Everyone has heard the terrible tale of the ritual murder accusation in England in 1255, associated with the name of Young Hugh of Lincoln, and recalled by Chaucer in his *Canterbury Tales*. Without going into the details, I should like to call attention to a facet of the story—of all such stories —which we generally tend to overlook. In the tiny Jewish community of not more than two hundred souls at the most, over ninety persons were arrested and nineteen were put to death. Nevertheless, the communal life continued, the survivors came back to their former homes and built up their lives anew, turning once again to the solace of their studies. Every face they saw in the street was that of a potential murderer, every footstep at night might be that of an assailant, every sound of voices that penetrated the closed shutters might be the precursor of a pogrom. If they made a journey, they might never return; if they smiled at a child in the street, they ran the risk of being accused of a foul crime. Still, with indomitable courage, they maintained themselves, a proudly separate people. A word to a priest, a ceremony at the baptismal font, and they would have been free forever from this constant, gnawing fear. Yet hardly one of them succumbed to the pressure. And this was the case, not in Lincoln alone in the middle years of the thirteenth century, but in every city of Europe, from the North Sea to the Vistula and from the Baltic to the Mediterranean, for a dozen centuries.

The psychology of the Jewish people has greatly altered during the past generation. We have changed from a passive to an active attitude, and there is a tendency in some circles to regard the long generations of Jewish pacifism almost with contempt. There is no need to argue for or against the merits of this attitude, and the historian may recall that there were in the past some significant exceptions to the pacifist tradition. But this is not the point. We have to remember that *in historic fact* this resistance preserved the Jews and Judaism. The secret of a nation's endurance is the inability to accept defeat. This was the supreme characteristic—and for us the supreme service—of the European age in Jewish history.

What was it ultimately that prevented the Jews from giving in during these centuries of almost intolerable suffering? There was obviously something in addition to, though implicit in, their conviction that their beliefs were true. It was the unswerving certainty that in due course their sufferings—as a people, not merely as individuals—would end, and that they would be restored to their former land. This certainty was bound up with the doctrine of the Messiah, and in the course of time was given far-reaching mystical and theological extensions, but the fundamental conception remained very simple: that in

God's good time, and in the not-too-distant future, conditions would change drastically for the better and a happy state of affairs would be established on earth for Israel—and for the rest of believing mankind, if they gave up their evil ways.

Judaism did not dwell, in the exclusive way of Christianity, on bliss in the afterworld, nor did it consider that the Messianic manifestation at the end of days would be a "day of wrath and destruction." Steadfastness would ultimately receive its reward—*in this world;* a state of perfection would ultimately be attained—*in this world.* Thus there was in the Jewish outlook an inherent optimism. It believed in the perfectibility of humanity. It considered that to despair of redemption was one of the sins that would not be forgiven at Judgment Day. It thought of the Golden Age as being in the future, not in the past. The worse external conditions grew, the more profound and deep-rooted was the certainty of deliverance—and if we examine Jewish history in detail, we see that those few Jewish people who succumbed to the pressure of the environment did so not because they suffered more than the others, but because they gave up the optimistic conviction of ultimate deliverance. It was a conviction that in later times made it natural for Jews to take a prominent part in movements for the abolition of war and the establishment of universal peace, indeed, in many movements aimed at improving the lot of mankind. This optimistic outlook is of the greatest significance too for the present age, when scientific developments have given a grim actuality to Christian conceptions of the Last Day and the destruction of the world. As against this, Judaism teaches that to despair of the future is one of the gravest of all sins, because the perfect age, for which every man must work, still lies before us.

Their ages-long resistance endowed the Jews with many of the qualities which now seem to be characteristic of them: a physical courage which expressed itself in the power to endure rather than to inflict; an adaptability to new circumstances and to new lands and callings; a remarkable resilience, of which we have had the outstanding instance in our own day; and a physical wiriness and tenacity often more effective than sheer strength. On the other hand, adversity also inevitably endowed them with some unpleasing characteristics. They became timorous in small matters, notwithstanding their unbelievable gallantry in great ones. They lost to a great extent their appreciation for, as well as their physical contact with, the fields and the countryside. They tended in all circumstances—and not unnaturally—to become suspicious of their Gentile neighbors. To circumvent the unending tangle of restrictions placed on all their economic and personal activities, some of them learned to practice petty deceit. There were other characteristics of ghetto Jews in their greatest abasement which were by no means admirable. What was surprising, however, was not that this came about, but that it proved so superficial and so evanescent. Petty deceit never degenerated, as it might so easily have done, into widespread and serious criminality; and generally speaking, the offenses associated with the Jews were relatively trivial. Moreover, a generation of freedom usually sufficed for ghetto characteristics to be discarded and for the Jew to become indistinguishable in most respects from other members of the social group to which he belonged. The tragedy is that in the process he sloughed off, not only the superficially acquired characteristics, but also in many cases the fundamental Jewish virtues and way of life.

What is the lesson of Jewish survival, not only to the Jews themselves, but to the world at large?

The question is in a way preposterous for a Jew. For Jews must know that the great achievement of our ancestors was that, by their persistence, they preserved Judaism. But from a nonsectarian or even a rationalistic point of view, the persistence of the Jewish tradition has also had far-reaching importance. Throughout the ages, the Jew has influenced mankind by remaining always what may be called an Eternal Protestant. Confident of the validity of his own faith, he has consistently refused to believe as other men believed, however much opinion was against him. Led by the Maccabees, the Jews refused to succumb to the attempt at Hellenization in the second century B.C.E., and thus made possible not only the survival of Judaism, but also the emergence of Christianity and Islam. Their implacable stubbornness secured them exemption from the general compulsion to conform to the state religion of the Roman Empire. And in the Middle Ages, in Europe, they and they alone stood out against the attempt of church and state to impose uniformity of belief everywhere.

This nonconformity served to keep alive some degree of freedom of thought in the world. It made people of intelligence realize the possibility that there might be another point of view, and so prevented their own thought from becoming wholly canalized. The mere existence of Judaism kept Christianity continually on the *qui vive;* the constant Christian polemic directed against Judaism, and aimed at converting its adherents, stimulated the argumentative faculty of Christians and made it necessary for them to find a philosophical justification of their faith. But above all, the presence of the Jew compelled people of every faith to think for themselves. It may be said that during the Middle Ages, Judaism was in a way the conscience of Europe: an uncomfortable companion, always questioning, always

doubting, always compelling thinkers to reexamine and to justify the bases of belief, always reminding the majority that its conclusions might not be beyond question or argument.

The theory that the Jews directly and consciously stimulated the
various movements for Church reform, down to and after the birth of
Protestantism, cannot be substantiated; yet the presence of the Jew in
the background certainly had something to do with them, as is evident
from the fact that in many cases the reformers went to the Jewish
quarters to study Hebrew and to learn the Jewish interpretation of
this or that disputed point of Scripture. The fact that Judaism itself
avoided a multiplication of dogma and that argument was the lifeblood of the Talmudic system of education must necessarily to some
extent have influenced the Jews' neighbors.

Jewish contributions to Occidental civilization in every sphere—
political, social, scientific—have been owing largely to the exercise
of those critical faculties which the Jew, because his background,
thought, and beliefs have not been those of the majority of the population, has possessed to an eminent degree. By finding the weak spots
in older systems, he has helped to build up the new. Even today, we
can see how in Central and Eastern Europe this Jewish solvent seems
to be at work exposing the weak spots in the new Communist totali-
tarianisms, as it was at work a generation ago exposing those in the
capitalist society of the time.

What in the Middle Ages was to some extent the passive achievement of the Jewish group, simply by virtue of its existence, came to
be from the French Revolution onward the conscious work of individuals. Apart from religion, the Jew's greatest significance to mankind
in the period we are considering perhaps lay in the fact that he was
—as he should remain—the Eternal Protestant.

THE VITAL INSTITUTIONS

Something more than a body of belief was necessary to secure the survival of the Jewish group, and what it stood for, throughout this period of isolation and tribulation. This something more was provided
during the previous epoch of their history. It was the way of life
that had been evolved in the East during and after the period of the
Second Temple, which now became part of the texture of their being.

It is not far from the truth to say that, while Babylonia created
Judaism, Europe created the Jew. By the time the Babylonian Talmud
was completed, the whole structure of traditional Jewish observance as
we know it had been fully elaborated. How far—or rather, how

widely—it was actually applied is another matter. To some extent, it was even then (as it had apparently been in Palestine in an earlier generation) the religion of the scholars and their votaries. The mass of the people adhered to it in its broad outlines, but did not necessarily do more than this. In a certain sense Jewish history in the following five or six hundred years is the history of the establishment of the universal hold of Talmudic Judaism, in its last and least detail, on the Jew. In our generation we hear searching, though frequently ill-informed, criticisms of this great code of life. But let there be no mistake about it: but for that code, the Jew and Judaism would not have survived in the period of stress, agony, and division through which they were to pass.

The agency through which this pattern of life entered into the bloodstream of the Jewish people was a remarkable system of education which extended from the cradle to the grave, and which evolved partly because of the peculiar economic circumstances of the European Jewish community. The older system of religious training in Palestine had been based on the relatively restricted subject matter of the Bible. Now there was added to this the vast body of the Talmud, which between, say, the tenth century and the eighteenth century was the universal instrument of Jewish education in every land—an education not confined to the children, but extending to adults and continuing throughout life. This above all gave European Jewry its characteristics and powers of endurance. It is not my task here to describe how this came into existence, or by what means it was carried into effect. What I wish to emphasize is its result, which was of incalculable importance.

In the first place, this system of continuous education conferred on the Jews everywhere a fundamental unity. No matter where they lived or what languages they spoke, the pattern of their lives was in essentials the same. A Jew from the most distant part of the world arriving in a strange city would find in the Jewish quarter a way of life which was essentially identical with his own: not merely the same beliefs but the same ceremonies, the same religious services, the same intellectual interests, the same outlook. This reinforced Jewish unity; one might almost say, re-created the Jewish unity which had been shattered with the destruction of the Jewish center in Palestine. The oneness of the Jewish people was not merely religious or merely racial, but was based on an identical historic experience and pattern of life.

Second, the triumph of Talmudic study as an all-embracing ideal, filling every moment of leisure, created conditions in which small, physically isolated Jewish communities could exist. Hitherto Jews had lived in the main in self-sufficient, concentrated groups, sometimes (as in Alexandria) in great urban agglomerations, sometimes (as in Mesopotamia) in fairly cohesive rural colonies, closely interconnected. In Europe they found themselves for the first time scattered about, tiny minorities in the midst of a vast, alien, and usually hostile sea. The average Jewish community of the Middle Ages did not number more than a hundred or two hundred people; one of five hundred was large, one of two thousand was vast. Moreover, there was seldom any other community within a day's journey, and if there chanced to be one, it was in all likelihood similarly diminutive.

Indeed, one of the significant changes in Jewish life in recent generations has been the great increase in the size of what might be termed the viable Jewish community. It is not until a group has reached perhaps a thousand or two thousand in number that it now considers itself able to maintain adequately the fundamental communal institutions and services and preserve its cultural identity. The tiny communities of the Middle Ages, however, not only did this, but made positive contributions to Jewish life, and the reason lay in their self-sufficient, all-embracing, leisure-consuming intellectual life, in their passionate devotion to study. The little villages of northern France in the Middle Ages were the places of residence of the Tosaphists, who wrote the famous glosses on the Talmud. Rashi lived and worked in Troyes, where there were probably not more than a score or two of Jewish families, all imbued with a zeal for scholarship. Even in an age of relative decadence, an eighteenth-century Italian ghetto with a population of a couple of hundred managed to maintain a self-sufficient cultural life and a public able to appreciate and write Hebrew poetry. In the last century some of the small centers in Russia and Poland produced a scholarship that has become proverbial.

This universality and intensity of intellectual interest underwent full development first among European Jewry in the Middle Ages, and although its subject matter changed it left its mark for good on the Jewish people everywhere. It is part of the heritage that has passed back again to Palestine in our own time. The intellectuality of the Kibbutz, the book-awareness of Tel-Aviv and Haifa, the hunger for learning in the young Israeli, are an inheritance from his European forebears.

Inevitably, in speaking of the Middle Ages, we are compelled to use the term "the Jewish community." Thereby perhaps we run the risk of conveying the impression of a body such as is familiar to us in the Jewish world today—a preponderantly religious organization, having as its main function the maintenance of the synagogue together with certain subsidiary charities and organizations. But the historic European Jewish community was perforce far wider than this.

The Jews were a corporate body, bound together by ties of which religion was only part, and responsibilities of which the synagogue was only one. Over against the outside world, it was an entity distinguishable by its religion, whose main function was the exaction from its members of its allotted—and overwhelming—quota of taxation. Whether the synagogue was maintained or not was a matter of indifference to the government. From an organizational point of view the place of worship was secondary, and indeed was not infrequently left to the liberality of some communal Maecenas. What concerned the community as such was something far wider: it was, one may say, the social organization of the Jews as a body. Religious leaders might —and generally did—take the lead, but this was because they, as scholars, were expected to discern the principles implicit in the Rabbinical regulations and to guide social legislation accordingly. Illustrating this fact are the famous "Takkanoth" of Rabbenu Gershom ("The Light of the Exile," ca. 1,000), which contained regulations for the social guidance of the Jewish collectivity in the new circumstances of European life: that unfair competition should be avoided; that judicial machinery should be available to secure redress of injustice; that private correspondence should not be opened by a stranger, and so on. Even Gershom's famous prohibition of polygamy, which the Jewish religious code indubitably permitted, was essentially a social regulation.

It became generally agreed that only a rabbinical synod could abrogate this legislation or any part of it. And indeed throughout the Middle Ages there were from time to time gatherings of rabbis who concerned themselves to a great extent with similar regulations for the communities or groups of communities which they represented. These conventions took place with such frequency and to such effect that a work on the subject, by Louis Finkelstein, is entitled *Jewish Self-Government in the Middle Ages*.

In due course, organized semilegislative gatherings of the representatives of Jewish communities of entire provinces or countries, with lay as well as rabbinical participation (not that in Jewish life there was any hard-and-fast distinction between the two elements), took place in England, France, Germany, Spain, Italy, and especially in Poland, the seat for upward of two and a half centuries of the famous Council of the Four Lands. For the most part, to be sure, these bodies had to address themselves to the hard and ungrateful task of raising money to satisfy their merciless taskmasters, yet at the same time they were inevitably concerned with all the problems relating to the internal regulation of their communities. An old record tells how in England's North American colonies in the seventeenth century, colonial legislative assemblies "broke out," as it were spontaneously. Such legislative synods "broke out" too in medieval Jewish life, with results that were sometimes remarkable. Perhaps one outcome of this was the fiery devotion which Jews were later on to manifest for the institutions of representative and parliamentary government.

INTELLECTUAL STANDARDS

Let us try to distinguish some of the features of the European Jewish cultural atmosphere of the past. First and foremost, as we have said, was its universality. Judaism has always been a religion of instruction —which explains why the suppression of Jewish schools in Soviet Russia has been singularly successful in undermining the Jewish religion. Before the destruction of the Second Temple, the pagan philosopher Seneca had admitted that the Jews alone, of all peoples, knew the reasons for their religious rites and ceremonies, while Josephus records with pride that "our principal care of all is this, to educate our children well." Nevertheless, it was in Europe that this passion for education was developed to its fullest extent.

Until the nineteenth century—perhaps until our own day—there has never been at any time so literate a society as European Jewry in the medieval and post-medieval periods, not even ancient Greece— where achievement, it should be recalled, was made possible only through the existence of a vast substratum of slaves. Every boy, at least, was taught to read, but most went far beyond the rudimentary stage into advanced scholarship. It must be admitted that our knowledge here is imperfect and that there may have been an unrecorded proletariat whose existence would belie the picture. But so far as our records go, it is arguable, at least, that in England, France, and Germany in the thirteenth century, and in Poland in the sixteenth and seventeenth, every Jewish male child capable of such study was introduced to advanced Rabbinic and Talmudic learning. We have a picture of Jewish life in Poland before the tragedy of 1648 in which the whole country is depicted as a hive of Hebraic studies. In every house either the householder was a scholar, or his son, or a son-in-law, or some student whom he was privileged to support. Sometimes all of these were together under one roof, and there was no house in the entire country, we are told, from which the voice of study did not rise each day, an acceptable offering to the Lord. In this way the Jewish intellect was sharpened, generation after generation, by continuous exercise, from earliest youth, upon the acute Talmudic dialectic. Indeed, Moses Maimonides himself foresaw the great good of messianic times as lying in the fact that there would then be an abundance of leisure which could be for the study of Torah.

To the medieval Jew the Talmud meant much more than intellectual enjoyment. It brought him into relation with another world—vivid, calm and peaceful—after the constant humiliation of his ordinary activities. It provided him with a second existence, wholly different from the sordid round of every day. After each successive outbreak was stilled, and the shouting of the mob had died down, he crept back to the ruins of his home, put away his Jewish badge of shame, and set himself to pore again over the yellowed parchments. He was transported back into the Babylonian academies of a thousand years before, and there his anguished soul found rest.

Yet the Talmud was by no means an antiquarian study. It was a guide to life, and the basis upon which European Jewry erected a remarkable superstructure of discussion and elaboration whereby the fundamental Rabbinic principles were applied to changing scenes and conditions, somewhat as English and American jurisprudence was expanded by the vast mass of case law. It was discussed theoretically by the descendants and pupils of Rashi in closely argued glosses which henceforth accompanied the Talmudic text; it was applied to practical cases which came up in daily life in the Responsa which European Jewish scholars produced ceaselessly from the eleventh century onward. It was made more accessible in a series of codifications which scholars of the Spanish school in particular compiled in order to help the uninitiated or the hurried businessmen to arrive at practical decisions. The important point is that the study was alive. The text on which it concentrated was of immemorial antiquity, the problems to which it was applied were those of the day, with the result that the law which the rabbis administered in the medieval Jewish quarter did not suffer by comparison with that practiced by the justices in the royal courts outside.

This absorption in matters of the intellect prepared the Jew for the scholarly pursuits he so whole-heartedly took up in the age of emancipation, as it prepared the way for his contributions to civilization in all its branches at a later date. It also had an incidental result of supreme importance. If the greatest good was to study, then a man's excellence was to be measured in terms of his intellect, not of his wealth. The wealthy man was envied, but not so much for his wealth as for the opportunity it afforded him to indulge in study and other *mitzvot*. Hence the spirit of the Jewish community has always been, except in some decadent interludes, democratic; and hence too, in every country of Europe, Jews were foremost in the nineteenth- and twentieth-century fights for parliamentary institutions.

It must not be imagined that this absorption in the Talmud at any time excluded wider intellectual interests. The Talmud itself touched on such a wide variety of subjects that its proper study was a liberal education. Moreover, in order to understand Rabbinic law fully it was sometimes necessary to stray beyond the bounds of strictly Talmudic literature—to know something of astronomy, for example, so as to comprehend the regulations relating to the calendar, or of anatomy in connection with the ritual slaughter of animals for food. And in addition, the traditional intellectual disciplines always included many elements which were outside the Talmud, as the work of the famous Rashi testifies. Rashi was the embodiment, as it were, of devotion to Talmudic study, but he also wrote the classic commentary on the Pentateuch—still used and respected by non-Jewish scholars even today.

The same breadth existed in various other subjects of literary interest. In every country the liturgy continued to be enriched by a constant output of Hebrew hymns, which shows, by the way, that Hebrew continued to be a living language. The beauty of the works of the Spanish school of Hebrew poets of the Middle Ages is universally known, but it should not make us overlook the more somber productions of Northern Europe, less mellifluous but of a tremendous spiritual force and profundity of anguished feeling. The horizons of the crabbed rabbinic student were enlarged by the mystic currents which enriched ritual observances with a deeper meaning and added to Judaism an entire literature, the most important example of which is the Zohar.

Medieval Jewish intellectual life was to a great extent self-contained, but this is not to say that it was immune to outside influences, or was without influence itself. Inevitably there was some contact between Jewish and Christian scholars, if only in the course of business; and such contacts could not fail to leave their mark on both sides. Nor was this the case in the Muslim world alone, where the Jews were involved in Arabic culture. As is now becoming plain, it was the case also in Christian Europe, where, for example, certain influences of secular literature and even of the writings of the Church fathers are discernible in some Rabbinic compositions. On the other hand, the medieval Jewish Biblical commentaries were known to contemporary Christian scholars, such as Nicholas de Lyra, and affected Christian Bible exegesis. Moses Maimonides' *Guide for the Perplexed* became in its Latin version a medieval classic, and influenced the thought of the Schoolmen, from St. Thomas Aquinas onwards.

Thus there grew a large body of religious and Rabbinical literature which constituted the basis of much of European Jewish life. But Jewish literature was of much wider scope than this, and it was constantly being enriched by the opening up of fresh perspectives generation after generation, not infrequently under external influences. The religious poetry of the early Middle Ages was succeeded by secular poetry. After Dante's *Divine Comedy* became known to the world, its earliest imitation was an account in Hebrew of a visit to the afterworld by Immanuel of Rome. Drama began to be written in Hebrew in the sixteenth century, and literary criticism began at about the same period. After the expulsion from Spain the Jews in the Balkans and Italy preserved the literary and poetical standards of the Andalusian school associated with the names of Judah Halevi and Solomon ibn Gabirol. In due course, these were transplanted to Holland, thereby making possible the eighteenth-century revival associated with the German Meassefim, and this in turn was the prelude (by way of the Russian Haskalah movement of the early nineteenth century) to the remarkable literary renaissance of our own generation.

The Jews of Italy in the sixteenth century and the Sephardim of Amsterdam in the seventeenth may be said to have begun seriously the tradition of a vigorous Jewish literature in the vernacular. Out of the latter there arose in the nineteenth century the work of the *Jüdische Wissenschaft,* or "Science of Judaism." This application of modern Occidental standards to Hebraic studies resulted in a tremendous literature on every aspect of Jewish intellectual life—first in German, then in French, Italian, and other languages, latterly in Hebrew again, and (thanks to the devotion in particular of American Jewry) in English. It is to this that we owe almost the whole of our modern Jewish historiography, our literary criticism, and our coordination of the Rabbinical disciplines in the modern sense. There is as it were an unbroken genealogical connection between the first whisperings of Jewish literature in Europe a thousand years ago and the latest Israeli novel or Anglo-American work of Jewish historical research.

THE INFLUENCE OF JUDAISM

European Jews combined their tremendous Jewish devotion with a certain realization of their position as Europeans. They were to a great extent extruded from European life, but they persisted in contributing to it nonetheless. Apart from their activity as intermediaries they played a far from negligible part in the general intellectual life. The medical writings of Moses Maimonides and of Isaac Israeli were stud-- ied in the European universities down to the period of the Renaissance, and for some time afterward. Abraham ibn Hiyya of Barcelona was perhaps the outstanding figure of twelfth-century European science. It has been said that he stands at the beginning of an age of creativity which ends with another Jew, the globe-trotting polymath Abraham ibn Ezra. Jewish poets writing in the vernacular are encountered in medieval France, Spain, Italy, and Germany. Jewish astronomers and physicians served many European courts, and were responsible for important improvements in observational instruments. The scientific equipment of the expeditions of Columbus and Vasco da Gama was in good part Jewish in origin. A school of Jewish mapmakers, who were considered preeminent in their day, flourished in Majorca. In the sixteenth century Jews collaborated to some extent in the Italian Renaissance, in particular in the renewal of music and the drama, besides contributing in the *Dialogues of Love* of Leone Ebreo (son of the famous statesman-exegete Don Isaac Abrabanel) one of the philosophical classics of that fecund age. At this period, and for some time after, the Marrano element provided many of the important figures of European medicine and science, as well as of Spanish and Portuguese literature.

All this led up to the amazing outburst of the nineteenth century. With the fall of the walls of the ghetto the pent-up Jewish genius rushed forth and immensely enriched many diversified fields. There was no branch of European life in which Jews did not now participate, and which they did not enhance. In politics and literature, in art and poetry, in science and medicine, in drama and music, Jews figured with singular preeminence. Heine in literature, Einstein in physics, Pissarro in art, Mendelssohn in music, Disraeli in politics, Ehrlich in medicine.

One thing, however, cannot fail to impress itself on us. The Jews of the Middle Ages, though they made outstanding contributions to the general cultural life, were profoundly rooted in the Jewish tradition. Their wide secular culture was not developed at the cost of, or in spite of, but one may say as a natural sequel of, their profound Jewish knowledge. They served the world at large: they led their own community. Moses Maimonides was the most eminent of medieval Jewish physicians, the most brilliant of medieval Jewish philosophers; at the same time he was perhaps the greatest Talmudist of the Middle Ages. His Halakhic writings began a new era in Rabbinic studies and are still regarded as fundamental. No other medieval Jewish scholar achieved the same stature, but every one followed the same pattern of achievement: distinction in the non-Jewish sphere being combined with distinction in Jewish life, and secular learning invariably intertwined with Hebraic study.

The unity created throughout the Jewish world by the triumph of Rabbinic Judaism and the spread of Talmudic learning was to have an effect of vast importance. Not allowed to be a citizen in any land, the Jews became perforce a citizen of the world, and as a citizen of the world he performed an irreplaceable service. For one of his greatest and most characteristic functions throughout history has been his part as an intermediary—not only intellectual, but economic, social, and political as well. In addition to his role as the Eternal Protestant, he was also the "International Jew"—a title properly of pride, not of obloquy. He always had the advantage of standing astride more than one civilization. He had personal connections and interests not hemmed in by political borders. He had a realization of lands and cultures lying far distant from those of his own environment. He had access to foreign languages. His kinsfolk were scattered in many lands, so that in every country there was some coreligionist who could act as his correspondent or his agent, or give him hospitality, or extend him credit. Hebrew could carry him, at a pinch, from one end of the world to another, and lay open to him the intellectual treasures of every age and every land.

Thus he was admirably qualified to interpret people to people. He traveled for business, introducing the amenities of civilization from one country to the other. The function of the Jews in the Dark Ages in France and Germany, and in the later Middle Ages in Poland, was in this respect very similar to that of the German Jewish itinerant merchants who played a significant part in opening up the American Middle West in the nineteenth century. But the Jew carried with him (and the parallel still applies) not only commodities but ideas: tales of distant lands, inklings of new developments, rumors of events in the great world beyond. His coming was eagerly anticipated in remote villages and homesteads, for he brought with him a whiff of fresh, invigorating air from the outside world; and if in due course he opened a store to sell his wares it became the veritable cultural focus for the entire area. This explains in part the policy of the medieval papacy toward the Jews, for the Church was not unnaturally nervous of this rival center of enlightenment, which even if it was not anti-Christian (as zealots alleged) was certainly non-Christian.

There was another way in which the Jews left a profound mark on Occidental civilization. It consisted in their work as translators and intellectual intermediaries between country and country. The medieval world was made up, it may be said—though with reservations—of two self-contained sections: the world of Christianity, with its culture largely expressed in Latin and its derivatives; and the world of Islam, based on the Arabic language and literature. Of the two, the latter was for a long while the more advanced in many respects. In the course of their migrations the Arabs had encountered the ancient Hellenic culture which evolved in Greece and then (after the conquests of Alexander the Great) flourished especially in Egypt and Syria, had absorbed it, assimilated it, and vastly developed it, above all in the world-famous schools and academies of Muslim Spain. Thus the writings of Aristotle and his contemporaries were preserved only in Arabic versions. Western Christendom had entirely lost this tradition, but was aware of it, and looked wistfully and hungrily southward to the Muslims, who were its present custodians, but whose language they could not speak or read.

It was fortunate for the development of medieval civilization that in the Jews there was an "international" element which could act as an intermediary. Sometimes, perhaps, a Spanish rabbi would translate for his own edification some classic of Greek philosophic or scientific literature from Arabic to Hebrew; his version would be carried north of the Pyrenees and there rendered into Latin. Sometimes a patron of learning would commission direct translations from the Arabic of works which interested him. Sometimes an eager Christian would approach a Jewish scholar and obtain from him the gist of some scientific treatise, which he would jot down perhaps in the vernacular, subsequently rendering it into a more erudite tongue. But in each case the part of the Jew was of great significance. From this process there emerged what is known as the Latin Renaissance—the revival of thought and science in medieval Europe which had its finest flower in the work of Dante Alighieri and which anticipated in many respects the great fifteenth-century Renaissance which succeeded it.

This was a characteristic service of European Jewry, dependent on the Jewish experience and mentality, which has made Jews in all ages so valuable as intermediaries. It was because they were Jews—because they had international connections, because they had an inkling of intellectual conditions beyond the frontiers of the lands in which they lived, because they had in the Hebrew language a unique medium of international intercourse and understanding—that they were able to perform this service.

As the cultural unity of Europe, based to a large extent on the use of Latin, began to disintegrate, and national cultures emerged, the Jew again was in a position to fulfill a similar important function, this time on a smaller scale. The task was not one of interpreting continent to continent, but of interpreting country to country.

It is no coincidence that in the nineteenth and twentieth centuries some of the foremost exponents of the literature and thought of one country to another, and some of the most active workers for international understanding, were Jews. Indeed, their characteristic economic function as well, that of introducing new processes, making capital mobile, and so on, was to a great extent made possible by their past experience. Similarly, after the great wars of the nineteenth and twentieth centuries the Jews—through their personal connections, their economic interests, their intellectual contacts, and also their humanitarian activities—played a major role in reestablishing normal relations between formerly hostile states—a function particularly marked after World War I.

It is to be feared that the annihilation of the Jewish element in so many parts of Europe is going to make the reconstitution of a balanced world again in our day far more difficult. Future generations may decide that, when all things are taken into account, this was the greatest crime of the Nazis against humanity at large.

12

THE SUCCESS OF
THE MEDIEVAL JEWISH IDEAL

Let us try to picture to ourselves a day in the life of an ordinary Jewish household, in some normal European community, of England or France or Germany, in the Middle Ages. The same picture would apply, of course, to Italy or Spain or Greece, with certain differences, but I specify one of the Northern European communities for two reasons: one, that their conditions of life were rather harder, and their triumph over them therefore all the more memorable; and the other, that the medieval communities of these countries are more specifically the direct ancestors of Ashkenazi Jewry, and thus of the greatest body of Jews in the world today, including almost the totality of those in the United States. With certain reservations, however, the characterization is true in essentials of any Jewish community of the old type at all periods after the fall of the Roman Empire and (in Eastern Europe) down almost to our own times.

THE HOME

Let us call our typical Jewish householder Master Benedict; this would be the vernacular equivalent by which a man known in Hebrew as Rabbi Baruch, or Berachiah, would normally be called. His wife is Mistress Rachel (I think she would have been known in France or England as Bellaset, or Belle Assez, in recollection of her Biblical homonym who was "of beautiful form and fair to look upon"). Certainly they would have married early in life—perhaps when he was in his early twenties, she no more than sixteen or seventeen—and the probabilities are that they would have had a large family. Not all would survive childhood, but, for reasons that will appear later, a larger proportion would survive than was usual among non-Jews at the time.

The day began early, when the *shamash,* or beadle, of the community (the *Schulklopfer,* as he was called in Germany) went around from door to door arousing the faithful and summoning them to service. How this worthy himself was aroused betimes I do not know, but there were primitive alarm clocks even then. In the half-light, the family dressed. The first thing done by Master Benedict on getting out of bed was to wash his hands and face (at least), reciting the prayer of thanks to the God who had fashioned man so marvelously and revived him to face a new day. Doubtless, this formality was sometimes carried out perfunctorily, and it was certainly not as adequate as the daily bath, but it is important to note that such ablutions were prescribed by religious discipline. To put it plainly, the Jew washed regularly; and this could not be said of every element in the population. Add to this that the hands always were rinsed before prayer, before eating, and after exercising the bodily functions; that the women totally immersed themselves once a month; and that pietists, at least, indulged in ceremonial ablutions each week—and it will be realized how far elementary hygiene had become part of daily life among the Jews. Nor do we find among Jews the principle of abstaining from ablution for the glory of God, as was the case in certain Christian circles.

There were many other Jewish ritual prescriptions which, while doubtless part of the religious discipline, had obvious hygienic facets: the washing of the meat, the ban on the flesh of a dead or dying animal, the covering of the blood of a slaughtered bird or animal, the prohibition to utter a prayer even at home in the presence of ordure, the women's period of abstention, the ritual spring cleaning to remove leaven on the approach of Passover, and so on. It thus becomes possible to understand why the Jewish quarter was sometimes free from diseases which ravaged the rest of the town; and why in that credulous age Jews were sometimes accused of responsibility for the deliberate spreading of contagions to which they appeared immune.

By and large, Master Benedict must have lived in a far more salubrious fashion than his neighbors.

We left the household getting dressed in preparation for the activities of the day. This was not a distinctive process, since, generally speaking, there was no great difference in outward appearance between Jew and Christian. Representations of medieval Jews show them dressed in the normal fashions of the environment. On the other hand, the men were usually (though by no means invariably) bearded, and they sometimes tended to retain the costumes of the lands from which they derived (for example, to wear Moorish costume in Spain well after the Christian reconquest), or to preserve antiquated fashions—especially for synagogal wear, as is the case in our own day with the Hasidim, who deck themselves out on Holy Days in the picturesque costume of Polish burghers of the sixteenth century.

It was this similarity of outward appearance that led the Church from the thirteenth century on to insist that Jews should wear at all times a badge to distinguish them from other men. It was generally in the form of a red or yellow circle sewn over the heart—later sewn on a hat of the same colors for men or a veil for women. There was a specious justification for this: to insure that there should not be unwitting intercourse between members of the two opposing faiths. But the inevitable result was that when Master Benedict went outside he could be recognized and insulted even from afar.

THE SYNAGOGUE

Every member of the family had recited a prayer on rising, but normally only the men went to synagogue each morning, leaving the women to see to their household duties. The synagogue was not likely to be far away, for it was by their own desire as well as external compulsion that the Jews tended to live together in the same quarter or street. Sometimes a difference in the architecture of this part of the city could be discerned immediately. Both for reasons of security and because of their widespread awareness of foreign fashions, the Jews seem to have been the pioneers of domestic architecture in stone in Northern Europe, their well-built houses sometimes contrasting sharply with the lathe-and-plaster cottages by which they were surrounded: even to the present time, some of the oldest dwelling houses in England, for example, are associated with the names of the Jews who built them or inhabited them many centuries ago. On the other hand, in the Middle Ages the Jewish quarter was not necessarily apart from the rest of the town, but was sometimes on a main street. The ghetto, barred off from the rest of the town and restricted to Jews, was a relatively late phenomenon.

As Master Benedict hurried to synagogue, perhaps already wrapped in his *tallit* and *tefillin,* he overheard muttered curses and imprecations from his neighbors who were setting up their stalls or the peasants who came in from the countryside to sell their produce, and recognized the Badge of Shame which he wore. In the synagogue he was safe. The building was generally modest, sometimes no more than an upper room set aside in the house of a communal magnate, seldom what may be termed "monumental." There were many reasons for this. One was Gentile jealousy; another was the smallness of the Jewish community. But there were other factors of more basic significance. We must not forget the intimate nature of the Jewish conception of divine worship. The Jew did not go to synagogue to be prayed for or prayed at, or to witness and participate in a "mystery" performed by a priest, but to pray and to study. Hence a monumental synagogue in the modern sense, where the congregant is reduced to the status of auditor in a service conducted for him, was out of place, and its evolution in recent times has implied a completely new attitude (a change not altogether for the better) toward the function of the place of worship. Moreover, to the Jew the highest service of God was charity. Hence to lavish money on the synagogue, when there were hungry to feed and naked to clothe and orphans to support, was considered a perversion of religion.

Attention has recently been called to the fact that so few really old artistic synagogue appurtenances have survived to our day. One reason for this was that in case of need they were sold unhesitatingly so that the proceeds could be used for the relief of suffering. This is not to say, however, that loving care was not lavished on the synagogue appurtenances, which were fashioned of precious metals and fine brocades; while such things as the Ark and the Reading Desk were executed perhaps by master wood carvers or metal workers. Even in the poverty-stricken Polish communities of the seventeenth and eighteenth centuries the same standards prevailed; it was only in the course of the nineteenth century that Jewish ritual art became standardized and cheapened.

Besides the synagogue appurtenances, there were those which Master Benedict used at home: the silver beaker for the *Kiddush* on Friday evening, the spice container for *Habdalah* after the Sabbath, and the dish for the *Seder* service on Passover Eve. (It was not until the seventeenth century, however, that the latter fashion reached its climax.)

Illuminated manuscripts also enhanced the attraction of the service, especially the Passover *Haggadah,* the most charming of Jewish rituals, and later on the Scroll of Esther read on Purim. Not infrequently, in Northern Europe especially, scenes from life and representations of the human figure were introduced without qualm into such codices. But perhaps the essential Jewish art was calligraphy, and it is a joy even to gaze at the lettering of some codices of the period, every stroke of which seems to reflect the piety and devotion of the scribe. Contrary to what is so often believed and stated, the prevailing esthetic sense of the age was by no means suppressed among medieval European Jews.

The *bet ha-knesset,* or house of assembly, in which Master Benedict prayed was a good deal more than a place of prayer. It was the place for study and discussion, the place where communal assemblies were held and communal business transacted. If there were no other provision for the purpose, the wayfarer or the needy would be allowed to pass the night there. Adjacent to it, in a wealthier community, would be the house of study, the *hekdesh,* which served as hospital and hospice, as a "dance hall" where communal weddings were celebrated, and as the *mikvah* for ritual ablutions. The synagogue was thus the "communal center" as well. One of the disasters of European Jewry in the nineteenth century was that this ideal was abandoned and the synagogue assimilated to the church; it became a place of worship and nothing more. Conversely, one may say that one of the great achievements of American Jewry—which has now begun to react on the Old World as well—has been the revitalization of the conception of the communal center, one more lavishly equipped than anything that the European Middle Ages could have envisaged, though not necessarily so effective or perhaps so comprehensive.

Another point is worth emphasizing. In the church, the service centered on the priest. In the synagogue, there was no equivalent to this. The services could be rendered by anyone—they did not require special training or spiritual qualification: perhaps today Master Benedict has assumed the honor of acting as the *sheliah zibbur,* the "emissary of the congregation." In larger communities a sweet-voiced *hazan* was appointed (though it was considered necessary that he be properly qualified morally and intellectually as well). Similarly, in the medieval synagogue there would as likely as not be no "rabbi" in the modern sense, though there might be a scholar, "first among equals," whose intellectual preeminence was recognized and who enjoyed for that reason rather more authority than the others. When later on the salaried rabbi emerged in Jewish life, it was regarded as something of a lowering of standards, justified only because it was economically impossible for a man to engage gratuitously in what had become a full-time occupation. Even so, other scholars probably existed in the community who had the rabbinical qualifications and, though they were not dependent on this for their livelihood, were intellectually on the same level as the rabbi and discussed points of law and interpretation with him as equals. It was not that the rabbinate was on a lower level than today, but that the lay membership of the community was on a far higher one.

We have assumed that in normal circumstances our Master Benedict would attend service every morning (and every evening too, for that matter). There was no question of the synagogue being a place of Sabbath resort only, much less of its being open only on that day. Indeed, there was probably little difference in the attendance on an ordinary weekday and on the most solemn occurrences of the Jewish religious year, so far as the men were concerned. Children attended regularly too, so the synagogue (or rather the synagogues, including the private prayer rooms) provided sufficient accommodation for the whole community.

The worship was vocal, hearty, and unrestrained, with universal participation: no question of decorous spectatorship of functions performed by another—though in the Middle Ages rigid church decorum in the modern sense was unknown in any religious group. It is to be noted that an integral part of every Jewish religious service, even in that age of universal scholarship, was a modicum of study. Readings from the Bible or from Talmudic literature were always interspersed in the prayer book, and the services were never services of prayer only. Not only on the Sabbath morning, but in the afternoon as well and on at least two weekdays, a reading from the Pentateuchal scroll was included in the service, a practice which went back to the very beginning of organized Jewish religious life. The traditional term *shul* for the synagogue among Ashkenazi Jews (paralleled by *escuela* among the Sephardim, *scuola* in Italy, and so on), though it applied originally to the Jewish group, reminds us perpetually of the educational function of the true Jewish place of worship. An American scholar, the late Professor Nathan Isaacs of Harvard, once hit on the suggestive phrase "study as a mode of worship" to describe this all-important facet of the traditional Jewish life. The phrase hardly needs elaboration, and it is not far from the truth to say that the strength of Judaism in the past depended largely on this principle.

It is a truism to observe that the services which Master Benedict recited were in Hebrew. But what must be emphasized is that they were universally understood by the congregation. There was no question of reciting propitiatory formulas in a dead language. Everyone knew enough Hebrew to understand at least the daily prayers, and most could even presumably follow the extraordinarily difficult language of the abstruse hymns recited on special occasions. From this ensues an important corollary: that a concomitant of the system of worship was the highly developed system of education. There was no question of accommodating worship to the standard of culture. The standard of culture had as its minimum level the requirement of worship.

During the service (if it was one of the days when the Torah was read) a boy who had just completed his thirteenth year might be "called up," without fuss or preparation, to the Reading of the Law, thus performing a *mitzvah* or religious precept for the first time in public. It is to be noted that this did not necessarily take place on the Sabbath, nor was it an occasion for the resplendent celebrations that have developed in recent generations. Far more importance was of course attached to another ceremony which also might take place on this day, in the synagogue itself, during the service: the initiation of a newborn male child into the Covenant of Abraham, to the accompaniment of special hymns and general rejoicing.

Not long after this, there will be the ceremony of his "cradling," when a scholar holding a Bible blesses him as he lies in his crib and prays that the infant will study and fulfill all that is written in the Book. The linen used during the circumcision ceremony will be made by the mother into a binder for the Scroll of the Law, embroidered with the infant's name and appropriate benedictions, and he will present this to the Torah on the first occasion when he is taken to synagogue. He will be formally introduced to study on the appropriate occasion, Pentecost, the feast of the Giving of the Law, when he will be carried to the synagogue wrapped in his father's cloak, taken to the *Almemor* to assist in wrapping the Scroll after it has been read, and given honey to lick from a slate on which the letters of the Hebrew alphabet are written for him to learn, so that the words of the Torah will be indeed sweet in his mouth. By losing these things, Jewish life has lost a great deal of its color and intensity. They were part of the very pattern of the existence of Master Benedict and his contemporaries.

The synagogue service would doubtless be succeeded by an hour of Talmudical study, perhaps under Benedict's guidance, for those whose work made it impossible for them to devote a great part of the day to the subject. The congregation would then break up and Benedict would return home, where meanwhile Rachel his wife and the other womenfolk of the household had been preparing the very simple first repast. Had they lost, spiritually, by not being present at the service in the synagogue, and did this fact emphasize their inferiority in the scheme of life? Hardly; not at least when we take into account the status of women in the medieval world generally. For in the Jewish scheme of things man and woman were relegated to two different spheres. The one was supreme in the synagogue and the house of study, the other was supreme in the home, and it is wrong to think of the latter as being inferior to the former. The reverse, in one respect, for when a family lived in isolation Judaism could be perpetuated without the one, whereas it could not exist even in the most populous community without the other. In the home woman was paramount, and every detail of the domestic routine had its religious aspect. From the separation of the dough on Friday to the ritual preparation of the meat, from the distinction of dishes to the kindling of the Sabbath Light, from the Passover cleansing to her period of purification— every action was imbued with a religious significance, so that the home became a veritable sanctuary over which she presided as priest- ess. If it is true that with the men we have "study as a mode of worship," in the case of the women the conduct of the home was a perpetual act of service.

It may be added that the economic emancipation of women was relatively far advanced among the Jews. In the Middle Ages we very often find women engaging in business on their own account, not only as widows continuing the transactions of their late husbands while their children are minors, but very frequently in their husbands' lifetimes. Later on it became usual for some women to engage in trade so their husbands could have leisure for their studies. Whatever the details of the situation in law, this inevitably implied a great de- gree of emancipation in fact. In the sixteenth century, a number of Jewish women emerged (Gracia Mendes and Bienvenida Abravanel are two outstanding examples) who were numbered among the out- standing communal leaders of their day.

Perhaps one of the indictments that may be made against the tradi- tional Jewish scheme of life was that female education was over- looked. Yet the fact remains that women scribes are on record who copied with understanding highly intricate Talmudic treatises, that women were even known on occasion to answer difficult Rabbinic problems or to conduct public lessons, and that one of the grand- daughters of Rashi is said to have acted as his amanuensis. Leaving such exceptional cases aside, we often find girls having lessons with their brothers from private tutors or from their parents, and a Talmud Torah for girls is said to have existed in Rome in the fifteenth century; indeed, in Italy women often acted as the primary teachers.

Hence average women such as our Mistress Rachel could read, if not write. Moreover, they knew large numbers of Hebrew words and phrases which had entered into daily speech, they learned by rote some of the standard Hebrew prayers and their meaning, they joined in singing the table hymns, they listened to the discourses in synagogue, they heard their fathers and husbands discussing points of Rabbinic law, they were familiar with a vast store of legendary lore, and they were supposed to have mastered those domestic regulations prescribed by tradition which were their special care. Hence the least educated or even illiterate Jewish woman of the Middle Ages enjoyed a relatively higher degree of Hebraic culture than her more sophisticated and better-trained contemporary descendant of either sex. It has been pointed out that in the memoirs of the garrulous seventeenth-century autobiographer Glückel of Hamelin—who has been styled the German-Jewish Pepys—in which a vast amount of Rabbinic legend and ethical teaching is embodied, one third of the total vocabulary is Hebrew. It is certain that the women's devotion to Judaism was in no way feebler than that of the menfolk; this was proved in a thousand instances of martyrdom. A Spanish moralist points out sadly that in that country, weakened by the neglect of learning and the pursuit of worldly comfort, relatively few of the Marrano element adhered to Judaism when the final disaster broke, "and those few were mostly women."

The match between our Benedict and Rachel had no doubt been arranged by their parents. The young couple had not necessarily been consulted, though obviously their preferences had been considered, and Jewish law gave the bride the opportunity to break off the match if she had an aversion to the partner intended for her. Master Benedict had not known, and had no desire to know, another woman. It would be wrong to think that monogamy was a new institution in Jewish life when Rabbenu Gershom of Mainz established it about the year 1000. His ruling only crystallized a tendency that had already been prevalent long before, for the society reflected in the Talmudic literature, which set the standard for later Judaism, is essentially a monogamous one, although one or two exceptions may with difficulty be traced.

In the European world, the conjunction of this tradition with the prevailing European ethic, however tenuously observed, made the tendency into a principle. Among the Jews of the Muslim world, where another example prevailed, it remained no more than a tendency, but monogamy was accepted by European Jews whole-heartedly and without reservation. There can be no doubt as to the higher level of family life and of sexual morality among the Jews than among their neighbors, if only because the restricted society made it unavoidable. Moreover, the Jewish outlook, as expressed in Rabbinic teaching, emphasized the dignity and importance of the functions of wife and mother, as contrasted with the Catholic idealization of celibacy. It was a natural corollary that woman's physical treatment was more humane. Even in England, down to the seventeenth century, wife beating was recognized by law as being an ineluctable privilege of the husband, but the Rabbis condemned it as an un-Jewish practice: "It is not the way of our people to beat their wives as the Gentiles do," naïvely declared one eminent authority.

Before sitting down to table, Master Benedict saw to it that one of his children fed the domestic animals, in fulfillment of the Rabbinic interpretation of Deuteronomy XI:15: "And I shall give grass in thy field to thine animal: and [then only] shalt thou eat and be satisfied." Some people even insisted that it was a religious duty to keep a domestic pet for the purpose of fulfilling this precept (as we find, incidentally, in the scenes depicted in various illuminated Haggadahs). The meticulous Rabbinic code could broaden and humanize the Jew's life even in such details.

The meal over, Mistress Rachel would prepare her children for school, and perhaps take them there herself, for although she was absolved from the obligation of study, her husband had told her that she acquired merit vicariously from the performance of this duty. Then she would return to continue her household duties, passing through the marketplace on the way home to replenish her stores. One may imagine what an ordeal it was sometimes, especially just before Easter, when the recollection of inflammatory sermons in the local churches was still fresh, or after some murderous outbreak which had only recently subsided. Yet relations between Jew and Gentile were not always strained. Left to themselves they got on well enough together—much to the distress of ecclesiastical fanatics, who inveighed and fulminated against such intimacies on every possible occasion. We have emphasized the harshness and unfriendliness of the environment, but we should not overlook the interludes of gruff cordiality.

While Mistress Rachel was engaged in her duties about the house, duties that were much the same among every class and in every land, her husband would have set about the main occupation of the day. We have seen that the medieval Jew in Northern Europe was forced by circumstances and indeed by law to embrace the profession of moneylending. It would be misleading, however, to leave the reader with the impression that, even in the most restricted medieval community, the whole body of the Jews depended for its livelihood on this unloved occupation. This was true of the communal magnates during a relatively short space of time and in a relatively small geographical area of Western and Northern Europe. But even where the principal householders relied on it, there were inevitably servants and teachers and scribes and other dependents who were associated with it only indirectly. Everywhere we find other favorite vocations represented.

So long as it was possible for them to do so, many Jews clung to agriculture, even in Germany and Central Europe. Rashi is believed to have been a winegrower, as many French Jews of his generation were. It would be possible to interpret medieval Jewish economic history as a record of how the Jews endeavored to maintain some sort of foothold in the various branches of the textile industry in which they were traditionally interested, and how down to the late eighteenth century the Gentile guilds persistently opposed and fought them and secured governmental intervention for their exclusion.

It is likely that the moneylenders themselves, through whose hands articles of personal adornment passed continuously, often worked as jewelers and silversmiths, or that they sold the fine embroidery for which the Jewish womenfolk were famous. Certainly they sometimes imported articles for sale; since the characteristic Jewish occupation in the early Middle Ages was that of international merchant, Jews thus performed an invaluable function in bringing the products of other countries (that is, many of the amenities of life) from one area to another. Over a great part of Southern and Eastern Europe, however—and to some extent in Northern Europe as well—the bulk of the Jews were artisans and manual laborers, notwithstanding all attempts to exclude them. They were weavers, dyers, tanners, silk manufacturers, and metal workers; the Jewish quarter in Sicily or Sardinia, for example, was discernible from afar by the constant hammering. Here, too, a number of the Jewish proletariat engaged in the basest manual work, as porters or as stevedores and port workers, callings which their descendants later took with them to Salonica and the Balkans, and which were thereafter transferred to Israel. There was of course a similar situation in Russia and Poland, where down to our own days vast numbers of Jews followed the humblest and most laborious callings.

THE JEWISH QUARTER

Inevitably, it was always the wealthy Jew—the medieval financier, the seventeenth-century merchant—who was in the forefront of the picture and who engaged the attention of the chroniclers. This occurred partly, at least, because it was such wealth which stimulated persecution and was the ultimate reason for the ludicrous accusations raised against all Jews. But at all times the vast majority of Jews were poor, and in many cases miserably so. Even in the communities which were grouped about wealthy financiers, in Northern Europe and in Italy in the Middle Ages, there was a large proportion of penniless dependents; indeed, owing to the frequent murderous outbreaks against them, and the great toll especially among those who had to travel, it is to be imagined that the number of resourceless widows and orphans in the medieval groups was at all times disproportionately high. Paupers and pedlars not far removed from pauperdom were very numerous indeed in the communities of a later period. It is computed that in the eighteenth century, even in Western Europe, one-third of the Jews were actually paupers, one-third lived close to the subsistence level, and only one-third were in settled circumstances, however modest. One of the reasons for the mass emigration from Eastern Europe to the Anglo-Saxon countries at the end of the nineteenth century was, in addition to the intensification of persecution there, the appalling increase of poverty among the Jews which resulted from it.

In spite of all these reservations, moneylending became perforce the characteristic Jewish occupation during the later Middle Ages, in the same way as international trade was during the Dark Ages. We must therefore assume that our typical householder, Master Benedict, was dependent on it for his livelihood.

Moneylending is not a full-time occupation. The capitalist usually sits and awaits his client, and meanwhile has nothing to occupy his time. This enforced idleness could in ordinary circumstances have had very serious results on the entire fiber of life, but the Jew, with amazing success, turned it to his advantage. He had come into Europe with a vast textbook of Jewish lore, the Talmud, which required leisure to study it; now he was providentially provided with leisure. He took advantage of the opportunity to the full. Whether he lived alone in a remote village, or in a diminutive community of France or England or the Rhineland, he devoted all his ample spare time to the elucidation and the elaboration of the beloved code. This fact explains why Jewish scholars and scholarship of this age are so often associated with minute places which hardly figure in the normal works of reference, and why the knowledge of the Talmud now became so amazingly universal. As had so often happened in the course of his history, the Jew snatched triumph out of the jaws of disaster.

A standard was thus set which one may say continued to prevail over most of the Jewish world until our own day. Even those whose occupation was different and more exacting—the craftsmen and the day laborers—accepted the same intellectual criterion, although they might be unable to achieve it; and in areas where these elements were strong, circles for the study of Talmudic laws or legend were established to beguile the simple man's leisure. There was probably not very much to distinguish the Jewish from the non-Jewish home at this time except one thing. In the average Jewish home, such as Master Benedict's, there were books, each containing an entire library of minuscularly written works—for parchment was scarce and valuable. In the average non-Jewish home, books were unknown.

Study could be of three types. The householder might sit conning the beloved folios by himself; or he might assemble a band of like-minded students around him, in synagogue or *bet ha-midrash,* and discuss with them the problems arising out of the text; or if his competence was sufficient he might engage in the hallowed duty of instructing his colleagues or the youth—perhaps the greatest of all *mitzvot.* Let us assume that this last was Master Benedict's main occupation. For this he neither expected nor received any payment, though as the Middle Ages advanced, instruction tended to be taken over—at least in major communities—by the professional and salaried rabbi.

The course of study is interrupted, for word is brought from home that a knight, Sir Front-de-Boeuf, has ridden into town and urgently wishes to see our Master Benedict. He leaves his books and colleagues and hurries back to his house where the visitor is awaiting him. The two men are face to face: the one a gentle-spoken scholar, the other an illiterate fighting man, living in relative luxury off the unremitting labors of his half-starved peasantry, and with little thought beyond the tourney and the chase. There was no compulsion on the knight to borrow; in most cases, probably, he needed the loan for some extravagance—building a castle, buying jewelry for his own adornment or his wife's, foreign travel under the guise of "pilgrimage" or "crusade." Now he would perhaps be wheedling and conciliatory. But Master Benedict knew full well that this attitude would change when the time came for repayment, and he might remember perhaps that the knight was one of those needy debtors who had been among the ringleaders of a massacre in this very street not long before. Moreover, he had to remember that most of the profit he received would be paid over to the royal treasury, the silent partner in all his transactions, so that it was almost impossible for him to be moderate in his terms. Nevertheless, it is pleasant to realize that conditions would tend to become more favorable after initial transactions had established some degree of mutual confidence.

It might be, indeed, that Sir Boeuf did not want a loan, but had come to Master Benedict for advice of a different sort. For in every land the Jews had a reputation as physicians, based in part on the fact that they could read medical literature (of which there was a more than adequate supply in Hebrew) and in part on the fact that, in Christian Europe, they kept alive something of the great traditions of Arab medicine, in which some Jews had themselves solidly collaborated. Often the same person was an affluent businessman, a learned rabbi, and an eminent physician. This was the case not only in the southern countries but also—though to a lesser extent—in the lands of restricted opportunity in the north, with which we are here principally concerned.

A few outstanding names emerge, but it may be said that on the whole the Jewish physicians probably stood on much the same level as their neighbors, except that they would tend to be rather less prone to superstitious practice. What was perhaps more important was that this proclivity to medicine, coupled with the long habituation through many generations to study and with the Rabbinic insistence that the service of suffering humanity is the service of God, prepared the way for the great tradition of Jewish eminence in modern medicine, which, beginning as a trickle in the seventeenth century, was to become a mighty flood in Germany in the nineteenth and now in America in the twentieth.

While Master Benedict was poring over his books, Mistress Rachel and the other women had been busy with the housework. They were generally unassisted, unless they had some Jewish damsel about the house, for it was sternly prohibited by the Church for a Jew to have a Christian in his employment, especially for domestic work. (As late as the nineteenth century, in Italy, it was even forbidden for Christian washerwomen to enter Jewish houses, or for kindly neighbors to look after the fires in Jewish homes on the Sabbath—and how the Nazis revived such regulations is still fresh in our recollections.)

The women sang as they worked, for the most part, the same songs in the vernacular—French or German or Spanish or Italian—which they heard from their neighbors. It is memorable that the exiles from Spain took away with them into their new homes many such ballads which they preserved many centuries after they had been forgotten in the Peninsula, and which Hispanic scholars are now avidly collecting. To these, however, were added semireligious ballads in the same languages and style on the themes of Jewish experience and life, perhaps interspersed with Hebrew words and phrases. We must bear in mind the fact that even in the Middle Ages the Jews of the various countries, however close they were in spirit to other Jews, and however much condemned by their Gentile neighbors, were at the same time children of the countries in which they lived, to which after all they could not fail to be passionately attached. There is an old and suggestive story that many generations after the expulsion of the Jews their descendants were in the habit of procuring citrons from Spain for use on the Feast of Tabernacles, in nostalgic recollection of their former beloved home.

The popular culture of the Jews was inevitably that of the environment. They spoke the same languages, sang the same songs, shared the same tastes, cooked the same dishes, adopted the same folklore. If Jewish communities in different countries were much the same, it is also true that the Jews of France were in many ways very French, while those of medieval Italy shared the outlook of their fellow Italians. The vernacular permeated the social and even the intellectual lives of the Jews, except perhaps in places (such as Poland and Turkey, at a later date) where they lived in large and almost impenetrable masses with a self-sufficient and unquestionably superior cultural life. That Rashi and his contemporaries interpreted difficult words and passages in Old French—among the earliest specimens of that language now extant—is generally known. It is less familiar knowledge that in almost every country there were translations of the Bible, and even of the prayer book, and that there was a store of light-hearted table and wedding hymns in the vernacular, in the composition of which the most pious rabbis participated.

The hour of the midday meal has arrived, and Master Benedict's family sits down to table. Notwithstanding some specific details, perhaps brought over from a former land of residence or bound up with Jewish symbolism, the cuisine was, like the daily speech, normally characteristic of the land of residence. The well-to-do Jew doubtless ate luxuriously, though the traditional dietary restrictions imposed some limitations on his indulgence. But the meal differed from that of a non-Jewish household of similar standing in that there was relatively little drinking. For sobriety was even then a mark of the Jewish home, and the fact besides that the Jew would not touch wine prepared by non-Jews severely restricted (especially in northern countries) the amount of alcoholic liquor available. Another difference was in the nature of the conversation around the table, for at that time men took seriously the aphorism that a meal in which no word of Torah was spoken was like the sacrifice of the dead.

I suspect that on summer afternoons there was somewhat less busyness than in the mornings, and that the younger element at least had a stronger capacity for physical enjoyment than the sources might lead one to imagine. On one or two occasions (such as the thirty-third day of the Omer, the scholar's festival) lessons were suspended, and country excursions, and sports for the young men, were usual. The synagogal hymns, especially for Passover, the springtide feast, show a keen appreciation of the beauties of nature. On Pentecost, when green rushes were strewn on the synagogue floor and flowers placed before the Ark, the countryside invaded the Jewish quarter; and on Tabernacles, when the ritual palm branch and citron were arduously and expensively acquired in accordance with Biblical precept, there was a visual reminder of the natural products of the Holy Land.

It was not a question of only these special occasions, however, but of day-to-day life. On the Sabbath, certainly, the women sauntered abroad to take the air, and the rabbis discussed the problems of what jewelry and adornments might be worn without constituting a "burden." There is extant a curious record of how when a doe found its way into Colchester, one day in the thirteenth century, the beadle of the local synagogue joined his neighbors in giving chase. We know of Jewish champions in wrestling and fencing in medieval Germany, and that in the sixteenth century the Jews of Mantua maintained their own tennis court. The Rabbinical Responsa, solemnly discussing what sports were or were not permitted on the Sabbath, incidentally indicate what was not objected to on other days—and it is obvious from these documents that there were some who did not scan the Sabbatical prohibitions too closely.

All this indicates, I think, that the intellectualization of the Jew was not exclusive of other interests, and that as Master Benedict paced the street of the Jewish quarter in the afternoon sun, pondering on his scholastic problems, the sound of laughter and games and perhaps even of flirtation assailed his ears.

This would be so especially at Purim, when the Jews, like their neighbors at about the same season of the year, threw themselves into merrymaking. In a large community, later on, there would even be a Purim fair in the Jewish quarter. But the spirit was the same everywhere, and among all classes. Perhaps this year our Master Benedict has been elected the Purim King, with absolute power over his neighbors in all matters of merrymaking and authority to impose fines in terms of wine and strong drink. Or if he was regarded as the Rabbi, or head of the Yeshiba, he would have his functions that day usurped by his pupils, who would appoint their own mock rabbi (like the "boy bishop" of the Christian world at Carnival) to mock the teachers, usurp the synagogal functions, recite daring parodies of the most solemn prayers, hold a mock Seder service complete with imitative Haggadah, and invade for once the women's section of the synagogue, and exact a forfeit from said Mistress Rachel herself.

THE VISITOR

Toward evening there is an unwonted stir in the Jewish quarter, centering on Master Benedict's house. A stranger has arrived! It must have been a rare and tremendous event in the small Jewish groups of the Middle Ages, unless they lay on an important trade route. It was probable that the isolated community might pass months without seeing a single strange face; all the more noteworthy, therefore, is the intellectual vitality it was able to maintain.

Communications then were dangerous and difficult. It is not easy to imagine the great risks run at this time by the merchant or anyone else who traveled from place to place—but especially by the Jew, marked off for insult and obloquy. Benjamin of Tudela, who traversed the whole civilized world at the close of the twelfth century and is described as the first medieval traveler who generally told the truth, has left a record of some thousand places he visited and some hundreds of scholars he met; but he has left to our imagination the many risks he ran and the escapes he was vouchsafed in the course of his long years of travel. Greatly daring, let us imagine that the visitor whose arrival in Master Benedict's home has caused such a commotion is none other than Benjamin of Tudela himself.

As soon as he had entered the town, he would have inquired for the Jewish quarter (the *Juiverie* it would be termed in French, *Jewry* in English). Once there, he would find himself among his own people, safe at last after the perils of the journey. No matter from what country the stranger came, his hosts would treat him as one of their own flesh and blood, a part of their Talmudic way of life. There was competition for the privilege of entertaining Benjamin. It was not only that this was considered a primary *mitzvah*, but there was also avidity for news of the great world outside, of new books that had been written in faroff lands, or reports of ingenious interpretations or decisions of some world-renowned rabbi in a distant community.

The question inevitably arises, what language was the medium of communication in such cases? Over much of the Mediterranean world it was of course Arabic. In a good part of Northern Europe, down to the fourteenth century, it was apparently French—the "international" Jewish language of this area before the concentration of Jews in Germany and the rise of Judeo-German and Yiddish. But what happened when, say, a Jew from England came to Italy, or a Jew from Cologne visited Toledo? The inevitable medium of communication among them was Hebrew, the language of which every Jew had at least a smattering by reason of his religious education; and it is on record that in the twelfth and thirteenth centuries this was usually employed in Northern Europe in intercourse with "foreign" Jews. To imagine that Hebrew was a wholly "dead" tongue before its nineteenth-century revival is thus incorrect.

Perhaps the globe-trotter has brought with him, together with other letters from Jews elsewhere, a special communication for our Master Benedict: an inquiry, of course in Hebrew, on a point of Rabbinic law (*Sheelah*) from an eminent authority abroad, who was canvassing opinions from other scholars on some perplexing legal problem which had been submitted to him. We may imagine the voluble discussions which would ensue in the synagogue or the *bet ha-midrash*. In due course, after proper deliberation, Master Benedict would prepare his quill and find a piece of parchment (perhaps, if the matter was urgent and supplies were scarce, he had to cut it off the margin of a book) and pen his learned reply (*teshubah*), in readiness for the next wayfarer in the reverse direction.

It is worth while to bear in mind the fact that these learned communications themselves were a bond of even closer personal union between scholarly Jews in different parts of the world. Men who corresponded in this manner obviously had some degree of trust in one another. That the Jews of the Middle Ages invented "credit" in the modern financial sense, as has been too readily asserted by some economic historians, is probably untrue, but they possessed it as a social reality.

The stranger would be particularly welcome if like Benjamin of Tudela he came from or had been to Erez Israel—to go there was the ambition of every Jew, and no small number were able to carry it out, notwithstanding the hourly dangers of the way. At intervals Jews from every country went to the Holy Land on pilgrimage or to settle there; and from time to time—in England and France at the beginning of the thirteenth century, in Sicily in the fifteenth, as in Poland in the eighteenth—there were organized proto-Zionist movements. Except for that brief interval after the Crusades when the Palestinian Jewish settlement was reduced almost to nothing, collections for the maintenance of the Palestinian academies and the support of the Palestinian poor continued throughout the Middle Ages, and it was inconceivable that any Jew should withhold his support.

If the stranger brought news from Palestine—as Benjamin of Tudela did when he returned to Europe in 1173—how joyously he would be greeted, what eagerness there would be to entertain him, how anxiously his hearers would hang on his words, with what pathetic inquiries he would be bombarded. And what fantastic stories, perhaps, he would report. It would be a day to be remembered and recalled for many years.

Like all Jews—at that time, at least—the visitor from Spain is interested in books, and Master Benedict eagerly displays his library of nearly twoscore bound volumes. It was in fact a far greater collection than was to be found in any local monastery. There were, of course, in addition to the Bible, the standard Jewish classics, the most important being the Talmud, comprised by a marvelous feat of calligraphy in a single weighty volume (for this was before the days when that great product of the human intellect had been condemned by the Popes and burned by the cartload in Paris and elsewhere). There were the usual subsidiary handbooks of Jewish law, and Rashi's already classical Bible commentary, and a great folio decorated in the Gothic style containing the festival prayers, and Mistress Rachel's richly illuminated copy of the Haggadah for Passover Eve, and a rare collection of the Responsa of the Geonim. Of course, the medieval Jew did not know the original Josephus (or any of the other classics of Hellenistic Judaism), but Master Benedict possessed and cherished the Hebrew chronicle of Jossipon, which was based upon Josephus, though it contained in addition many legendary elements. This was the only historical work he owned, other than some accounts of recent persecutions, written to commemorate the heroism of the martyrs.

By the side of such works, which were to be found in Jewish homes all over the world, the visitor found several which were less familiar to one who like himself came from Southern Europe. There was, for example, that remarkable collection of godly anecdotes delineating the proper action of the virtuous man at every juncture, the *Sefer Hasidim* or Book of the Pious, recently compiled under the auspices of Master Benedict's kinsman, Rabbi Judah, "the Saint," of Regensburg. Benjamin of Tudela opened the volume at random and read a couple of passages, noting with some amusement the difference between this pragmatic approach and the philosophical detachment of the Spanish ethical classics (such as Bahya's *Duties of the Heart*) with which he was familiar:

> If a woman is on a journey and she hears that the Gentiles are attacking the Jews and fears that she will be violated, . . . she may disguise herself as a nun, so that they will think that she is a nun and not lie with her.

> A man once told another: "I have gone about dressed as a Christian priest among the Christian women, so that they should think that I

am a priest and not assault me." Another man recounted: "I have studied the books of the Christians, and when I am among them I sing hymns in their language." The wise man said: "Of such as these the Bible says: 'These are ordinances in which a man should not live' " (Ezekiel 20:25).

It once happened that they wanted an old man to marry a young virgin, but the old man did not wish to take her lest he should cause her to sin. They said to him, "Nevertheless, she wants you." The old man went to her and took off his hat and said to her: "Look, my head is streaked with gray and so on because of old age, so you cannot say that you did not know." She replied: "It is enough for me if I am allowed to wash your feet, only that I may be called by your name and bear children who will be wise."

If you see men whispering together and you want to know what they are saying do not ask them, because by so doing you will cause them to lie: if they wanted you to know they would have told you, and since they do not want you to know they will not tell you the truth.

If a man is holding a book in his hand he should not show his anger with his hand, by hitting the book or by hitting others with the book. The teacher who is angry with his pupil should not hit him with a book, and the pupil should not protect himself with a book from blows, unless he is in mortal danger.

There were two pious men in a town who had books which needed binding, and there was in this town a Christian priest who was an expert bookbinder, more skillful than the Jews. One of the two pious men used to give his books for binding to a Jew who was not so expert as the priest, for he said: "I do not wish such a one to touch my books." . . . The other pious man held that there was no objection, but stood over the priest to make sure that he did not use the pieces of parchment which were cut off for binding his Christian literature.

The next work that Benjamin picked up gave him cause for surprise, familiar though it was to him. It was Maimonides' *Guide for the Perplexed,* in the Hebrew translation so skillfully executed by the physician Samuel ibn Tibbon. The book was already well known among the Jews of South Europe, with their philosophic bent, but among the Ashkenazim it was generally frowned upon; for its rationalistic outlook had scandalized many scholars and it had been committed to the flames by some zealots. It seemed incongruous that a profound Talmudist such as Master Benedict should have in his library so questionable a work; and the visitor even caught a glimpse of a Biblical commentary by a Karaite, obviously well thumbed. Yet when he told his host in the course of conversation that in Cyprus he had come across some heretical Jews who observed the Sabbath from daybreak instead of from nightfall, the other burst into a violent tirade against these perverters of the honor of God's covenant with His people. Were he able, Master Benedict averred, he would suppress them by force—aye, even by the sword. But there was no innate contradiction between Master Benedict's ingrained tolerance in the matter of ideas and literature and his intolerant indignation in the other. Self-discipline was necessary in order to maintain the Jewish people as an entity; freedom of discussion was its lifeblood.

If the community were a large one, and there were many visitors, private hospitality was incapable of coping with them. In these cases there was not infrequently some sort of private ghetto hostelry for strangers who could afford to pay, though even so, personal hospitality for meals was very usual, especially on the Sabbath. The poor, on the other hand, were looked after in such circumstances by some charitable organization.

In the small medieval community (or the small modern community in Russia or Poland, for that matter, so long as it retained its former simplicity and integrity) the Jews constituted as it were one large family. Every man's mourning was general mourning, every man's joy was a general joy. All participated in celebrations, all participated in grief, all helped the needy, all comforted the mourners, all visited the sick, just as though the nearest of kin were concerned. But as the community grew in size, this became more difficult. Hence special associations ("Holy Brotherhood," or *Hebra Kadisha,* was the normal term applied to them, though this is now restricted generally to the burial society) were organized to perform—not by way of charity, but rather as a social duty—such kindly services as could not now be left to spontaneous neighborliness: visiting the sick, burying the dead, dowering the bride, supporting the needy, educating the young, redeeming the captives, and so on. At the end of the ghetto period, a well-organized community of a couple of thousand souls might have several scores of such associations, covering the entire gamut of life. As a result the charity organization of the Jewish quarter became more comprehensive than that outside it. When in the nineteenth century the Jews emerged from the ghetto into the modern world, they brought this same spirit, though somewhat bereft of the former personal warmth, into the great communities of Europe and America. Here the Jewish charitable system became famous, affecting to a considerable extent the charitable and relief organizations of many modern countries before the rise of the welfare state. This has brought us a good way from the simple, spontaneous system by which the stranger or the needy would be succored by his coreligionists in the tiny medieval Jewry, but the two are closely connected.

The exercise of this spirit of charity was never confined to fellow Jews. Some people taught that this was advisable for reasons of policy ("because of the ways of peace"). But the great ethical classics repeated the Talmudic prescription that it is a man's duty to relieve the poor of the Gentiles and to visit their sick and to bury their poor, just as though a coreligionist were in question; for as the Psalmist said (Psalms 145:9), the tender mercies of God are over *all* his works. I suppose that this was not always acted on—one must try not to overidealize—but a Christian beggar can seldom have been turned away from Master Benedict's door without a crust, if only for reasons of tact. Did Jewish beggars, one wonders, ever have the temerity to go to a monastery?

On the Sabbath, the pattern of the day was different. It was not, as in later generations, simply an interlude set apart from the rest of the week by special clothes and food and synagogue attendance. It was marked off from other days by its entire texture.

As he returned from synagogue in the half-light on Friday evening after greeting the Princess Sabbath, Master Benedict would find his house prepared, Mistress Rachel bedecked in her best to greet him, the table spread with special food and covered with a white cloth over which the Sabbath lamp shed its soft radiance. (It must be remembered that on most occasions people ate off the bare boards, and contented themselves after nightfall with a minimum of the sparse and expensive illumination.) The repose prescribed by Jewish law on the Sabbath was complete, many later stringencies having been added to the thirty-nine major labors listed in the Talmudic literature. But—and this is important—they were not regarded as stringencies. They were definitions, the observance of which kept a man from creative labor.

The Sabbath rest was strict, but far from making the day lugubrious, it insured an all-pervasive atmosphere of cheerfulness and joy. And it is worth while to bear in mind the fact that, because of the high standard of education, the observance was never mechanical or unintelligent. The scholar knew, as the ignoramus did not, at what point the restrictions might be disregarded, in accordance with the basic Rabbinic principle that a man was to live through the precepts, not die through them. Thus the all-pervading joy of the Sabbath made itself felt as a proper prelude to the ecstasies of connubial union. For it is impossible to understand the Judaism of our fathers unless we realize that asceticism was as remote from its spirit as was excess.

Conscious that (as legend told) the two angels who accompanied him home had blessed him with the hope that the same good fortune would be his next Sabbath, Master Benedict blessed his children in the pattern set by the Patriarch Jacob, and chanted in Mistress Rachel's honor the glorious panegyric of the "woman of worth" which concludes the Book of Proverbs, before "sanctifying the day" over a brimming goblet of wine.

The meal that she had prepared was ampler than on other days. After this came the leisurely recital of the grace, accompanied by the chanting of table hymns, half sacred and half secular, often to tunes popular among the general population at the time, and set to the same meters. These, for which the use of the vernacular was not disdained, have well been called the "medieval Hebrew minstrelsy," and it was in their composition that the Jewish troubadours and minstrels who were familiar in every country doubtless received their training. The stranger at the table, if he had remained over the Sabbath, would call down long and elaborate blessings on his host's head in the course of the benedictory formula. On the next morning the services might be somewhat later and more leisurely, with a greater accompaniment of song; and the discipline of study would be somewhat less rigid, concentrating on ethics and legend rather than on strictly legal matters, and better adapted perhaps for the less learned who were free from other occupations on this day.

HERITAGE TO POSTERITY

During the week, on the other hand, the day would end for Master Benedict and his household in much the same sober manner as it had begun. Toward nightfall, there was evening service in the little synagogue, again filled almost to overflowing, and this was inevitably followed by the hour of study and discussion in the failing light. Home, then, to the warmth of the faggots, the sparse evening meal, and the bookish conversation at table. Afterward, in the dim flickering of the rush light, the men elaborated their learned preoccupations, and the youths sang, and the women spun or tried their eyes on fine needlework—a mantle or binder perhaps for the Torah Scroll, if not some object of personal wear. For there was little to do, in those days, during the hours of darkness, and in wintertime all would go betimes to bed.

When the rest of his household had retired, one thing more remained for Master Benedict. After the fashion of his day and his people, he had determined to leave behind him in writing moral and practical advice for his family, to guide them in their daily actions when he should be dead. And with the anti-Jewish outbreaks that were now becoming so common, what man knew whether he would live out even half of his allotted span? Drawing his chair up to the table, and cutting a new point to his quill pen, Benedict first noted down the amount of the profit that he expected to make from the transaction that he had completed with the needy knight, Sir Front-de-Boeuf, earlier in the day. Fifteen marks, if all went well. One-tenth of fifteen marks would be one mark and a half, or twenty shillings. It was important for him to reckon this out and to have it in writing; for it was his practice, as that of most of his pious neighbors, to devote to charity the tithe of all his profits, just as their ancestors had brought to the Temple a tithe of the produce of their fields.

This finished, he began to write in his minute, angular, almost Gothic Hebrew hand the Ethical Will that he had in mind. He had decided to base it on that of his kinsman, Rabbi Eliezer of Worms (whom men called "the Great"), who had died a hundred years or more ago, before the tragic pilgrimages which the Christians called Crusades had begun to make European Jewish life a nightmare. Practical advice, and spiritual guidance, and injunctions on the observance of the ritual precepts, figured almost in confusion, for they all combined to make up the Jewish way of life:*

My son! Give glory to God and show him your thanks, for he made you and brought you into the world. Be careful therefore to keep your body clean and free from pollution, for it is the resting place of your soul.

My son! Always keep a jar of water at your bedside. When you get up in the morning, wash your hands before you begin to dress, and on no account touch your eyes until you have washed.

My son! Always be among the first ten in synagogue each day, for thus you have merit and reward for all those who take part in the service.

* These passages with their characteristic mixture of practical and ethical precepts are taken almost literally from the Testament of Rabbi Eliezer the Great—which was extremely popular among the Jews of Northern Europe—so as to convey a completely faithful picture of the Jewish outlook of the time. It would have been easy enough to idealize, by inventing or anthologizing, but this is not the intention here. The advice regarding the care of books, etc., is, however, adapted from the twelfth-century Testament of Judah ibn Tibbon.

My son! When you go to synagogue, enter into the presence of your Maker with fear and trembling, and when you pray know before Whom you stand.

My son! Make a point of visiting a sick man, for thus his suffering is eased. But do not fatigue him by staying too long, for his illness is enough for him to bear.

My son! Help in the burial of the dead, and after the funeral comfort the mourners so far as is in your power.

My son! Be considerate of the feelings of a poor man, by giving him alms in secret, and on no account before others. For this reason also give him food and drink in your own house—but do not watch him while he is eating. And do not overwhelm a poor man with words, for God will fight his cause.

My son! Take heed for the joy of the Sabbath, honoring it with food and drink so far as lies in your power.

My son! Eat grass rather than beg from others. If you have to ask for help, take only what you need desperately, and die rather than be a burden on your neighbors.

My son! Pay attention to your books, inspecting them at every New Moon, and the bound volumes at least once every quarter, for I left you well provided, so that unlike others you need not borrow.

My son! Never refuse to lend a book to one who needs it for his studies, so long as you can rely on him to return it; but make a note of the title before it leaves your house. And my son! take particular care of your library, covering the bookcases with carpet so as to preserve the books.

My son! You must have children, to train in the study of the Torah, for through them you will have merit to enjoy eternal life.

My son! Avoid grossness with your wife when you awake at night and seek her; and do not walk behind a woman in the street, or between two women, lest you should be led astray.

My son! I command you to love your wife, and if you value my precept show her honor with all your might. Devote your mind too to your children, be gentle with them as I was gentle with you, and strive to teach them as I taught you: and if they should seem a little unwell do not neglect them, but seek medical advice at once.

Master Benedict ended his writing. He put down his pen. He locked away his Ethical Will in the iron-bound chest that contained his most precious belongings. He recited the final night prayer and lay down by his wife's side. Another day had passed for this imaginary ancestor of ours, uneventfully (thank God) but not unfruitfully. In such a series of identical days the Jewish people was kept alive, Judaism was maintained, Jewish ideals developed. They are the tiny, unbreakable links in the chain that unites each one of us with our remote past—and thereby with one another.

THE
MODERN
AGE

SALO W. BARON

Salo Wittmayer Baron was born in Tarnow, Austria, in 1895.
He received higher degrees in history, law, and political sci-
ence from the University of Vienna and a rabbinical degree
from the Jewish Theological Seminary in Vienna. After teach-
ing for a number of years at the Jüdisches Pädagogium there,
he was appointed Professor of History and Librarian at the
Jewish Institute of Religion in New York where he served
from 1926 to 1930. Since then he has occupied the chair of
Jewish History, Literature, and Institutions on the Miller
Foundation at Columbia University. He has been a member
of numerous national and international learned societies and
educational and welfare organizations, and has lectured widely
in the United States, Europe, and Israel. His books and studies
number more than two hundred and some have appeared in
German, French and Hebrew. Among his many standard
works are The Jewish Community: Its History and Structure
to the American Revolution *and* A Social and Religious History of the Jews, *which originally appeared in three volumes*
and is now being expanded into fifteen. He is also participating
in the creation of UNESCO's Scientific and Cultural History
of Mankind. In the preparation of the manuscript, he was
assisted by his wife, Jeannette Meisel Baron.

13

THE DYNAMICS OF EMANCIPATION

The last two centuries in Jewish history have often been called the era of emancipation. Despite certain similarities with conditions in the Greco-Roman world, this was, indeed, the first time in the whole history of the Dispersion that Jews were formally declared citizens of their respective countries with the same rights and duties as their non-Jewish compatriots. At the same time they were expected to become fully integrated into the political, socio-economic, and cultural structure of the surrounding civilizations without completely giving up their identity. Precisely because of the unprecedented nature of this great experiment in both general and Jewish history, a great many novel problems arose for both the Jews and their neighbors, on the solution of which mankind at large is still laboring today. The mere fact that most of us live in countries where Jewish equality is not only formally guaranteed but also largely achieved in practice must not create the illusion that these age-old problems are approaching their ultimate solution.

Before describing the individual stages of the struggle for Jewish emancipation we must first rectify some serious misconceptions which, in the course of the last several generations, have obscured the nature of these great historic processes. Adopted during the protracted struggle for Jewish equality, in which progressive Jews fighting side by side with progressive Christians greatly molded public opinion, these misunderstandings have gained wide currency among the general public, as well as among scholars. Now that the struggle for the formal acceptance of equality is largely over—although the time still seems remote for the champions of genuine equality to rest on their laurels—these fallacies offer real stumbling blocks to the full understanding of the present historic situation.

Jewish champions of egalitarianism have often been permeated with such messianic fervor that they were prone to paint the emancipation era all white against an abysmally dark background of "medieval" sufferings. The medieval civilization came to be accepted in Jewish historiography and by the Jewish public at large as a period of complete Jewish rightlessness, in which the wandering *Ahasver* was hunted from place to place, frequently expelled, if not massacred, always treated with disdain by his rapacious overlords, and tolerated on the lowest possible plane only because his economic and fiscal functions as tradesman, moneylender, and taxpayer were urgent necessities for the countries of his settlement. It was from this state of bondage and serfdom that he was "emancipated," that is, achieved liberty and human dignity.

So deeply had this misconception sunk into the minds of the Jewish people and their liberal non-Jewish friends, that when Hitler came to power in 1933 the Nazis and their opponents alike often spoke of the revival of the "medieval" status of Jewry. The Nuremberg Laws of 1935 did contain a number of provisions borrowed directly from medieval legislation, such as the "badge," the exclusion of Jews from certain occupations, and their strict segregation from "Aryans." However, even in the 1930s and still more in the 1940s, it became manifest that through this comparison we were maligning the Middle Ages. After all, the medieval civilization was a long era of human history which, despite its manifold shortcomings, was essentially an era of law and order. One need not be a romantic of the neo-Thomist schools of philosophy to realize the genuine values of that hierarchic civilization, which at least formally was based upon the acceptance of a moral order and the quest for justice.

To understand properly, therefore, the distinction between the pre-emancipation and the emancipation eras we must remember that European society during the Middle Ages was a corporate society divided into "estates," each endowed with a specific status in public law as well as in practical life. Within that corporate structure Jews formed a separate corporate body. Under these circumstances to speak of lack of equality makes no sense. Equality with whom? There certainly was no single legal status into which Jews might fit. Compared with the other groups in the population, the Jewish community certainly did not enjoy all the rights of either the nobility or the clergy. Its status could generally be compared with that of the burghers, although in time, with the growth of cities, the bourgeoisie became the leading component of the Third Estate, as a rule much superior to Jews. However, one must never forget the essential fact that wherever Jews were tolerated at all, they enjoyed incomparably more rights and suffered fewer burdens than the villeins—that unfree, downtrodden mass of humanity which constituted the majority of every Christian population in late medieval Europe.

For this reason emancipation did not mean a sudden elevation of Jews to a superior status, without their having to pay a very substantial price for it. The greatest loss they sustained in return for equality consisted in the sharp curtailment of their ethnic-religious autonomy. We shall see that only after a protracted uphill struggle did the modern Jewish communities salvage some of the prerogatives they had enjoyed in the pre-emancipation era—a struggle which must be renewed in every generation under changing environmental pressures.

In fact, emancipation was an even greater necessity for the modern state than it was for the Jews. The modern state, particularly the democratic state, could be established only after the abolition of the corporate distinctions and by the substitution of the egalitarian for the corporate structure of society. To leave the Jewish group as a corporate body apart, endowed with a specific system of rights and duties, had become an outright anachronism. Even antisemites came to feel that revocation of Jewish emancipation would offer only a temporary solution. Sooner or later the Jews would have to be eliminated from the body politic. Many friends of Jews merely argued in favor of total absorption as the more humane alternative.

Another fallacy connected with this peculiar relationship between the Jews and the state is the widespread assumption that all Jews were in favor of emancipation. This is simply not true. Not only many communal leaders and officials, whose vested interests in the old type of community were suddenly undermined by the new evolution, but also a great many of the rank and file cherished their accustomed ways of life, and found the price of equality too high. Of course, under the pressure of a constantly growing population Jews found it absolutely necessary to enter new occupations. They found, therefore, that the removal of certain civil disabilities was an inescapable necessity. All agreed that civil equality, or what the Germans called the *privatbürgerliche Gleichberechtigung,* would be a great blessing. But many had compunctions about accepting full political equality, which included the electoral franchise and military service, but which also presupposed their giving up their segregated mode of living and long-practiced communal controls. While these conservative circles were never quite so vocal as were the progressive spokesmen of emancipation, their opposition made itself felt clearly during the French Revolution, especially in Amsterdam in 1796. It came to the fore again in Southwest Germany in the 1840s, in Galicia in 1867, and elsewhere. Finally, a compromise was sought by modern Jewish nationalists in a combination of political emancipation with national minority rights. Under this new system, they hoped to restore much of their old communal self-determination under a new, secular guise.

The very fact, however, that even these modern nationalists never budged from the principle of Jewish equality of rights as a basic prerequisite for minority rights showed how far the Western world had traveled on the road toward an egalitarian society. Liberals of all faiths came to recognize what a Jewish publicist had proclaimed from the columns of the Leipzig *Orient* in 1848: "He who believes that a country can be free while legally withholding human rights from a single resident knows nothing of the essence of liberty."

In the twentieth century Jews abandoned all opposition to the principle of equality. No longer were there learned and eloquent spokesmen of Orthodoxy like Akiba Eiger and Moses Schreiber to preach vigorously against emancipation as such. At the most, Orthodox leaders denounced the fundamental values of Western civilization and, like their Christian or Muslim counterparts, contrasted the anarchy and libertarianism of modern civilization with the orderliness and the supremacy of moral law in their religious tradition. But even they did not doubt that, under the existing conditions of modern society, mankind required the system of equal treatment for all. This late conversion to egalitarianism must not blind us, however, to that initial lack of unanimity which still characterizes certain more fundamentalist wings in other religious movements.

A third widely held misconception has long been the high, indeed, excessive appreciation of constitutional and legal declarations of equality. Jewish scholars and public alike, largely recruited from Continental countries inured to written constitutions and protracted struggles for constitutional changes, viewed the progress of emancipation entirely in the light of legalistic reforms. This tradition, which saw in the French Revolution and its official pronouncements the first real harbingers of equality, is still very much alive. Only under the impact of both the Anglo-Saxon tradition of unwritten laws and the realization of how quickly even ironclad constitutional guarantees could be evaded in practice, have we come to evaluate more adequately the relative force of legal enactments and their ultimate dependence on underlying socio-economic, cultural, and political factors.

Jewish experience in Anglo-Saxon countries may serve as an excellent illustration of that supremacy of life over law. Legally Jews were not formally readmitted to England by Cromwell and his early successors. For a long time the Jewish community in the British Isles lived precariously under a law which never implied that the expulsion decree of 1290 was abrogated by Parliament. In a famous case of one Elias de Paz, whose will had provided £1,200 for a yeshiba, a leading British tribunal argued in 1744 that "such a bequest for the propagation of the Jewish religion" could not be granted, since that religion "is not taken notice of by any law, but is barely connived at by the Legislature." Hence the Court decided to turn over £1,000 to the Foundling Hospital in London for Christian religious instruction. Nonetheless, many Jews prospered under this system, economically and culturally. An Englishman, John Toland, was the first to advocate full emancipation in his *Reasons for Naturalizing the Jews in Great Britain and Ireland, on the Same Foot with All Other Nations,* published in 1714. Seven years later another Englishman, James Finch, could with equal vigor espouse the restoration of the Jews to the Holy Land. It was also possible for the British Parliament in 1740 to pass a Naturalization Act for the North American colonies in which Jews and Quakers were specifically exempted from certain general regulations so that they might become naturalized citizens without offending their religious sensibilities. As early as 1697 the London Stock Exchange, soon to become the world's leading bourse, reserved permanently for Jews twelve of its 124 seats. On the other hand, when statesmen tried to rush matters and extend the Naturalization Act to the homeland before the public was ready for it, the effort failed. Prime Minister Pelham, though successful in steering his "Jew Bill" through Parliament in 1753, had to yield to the anti-Jewish clamor and propose the bill's revocation within less than a year.

In the American colonies, in the meantime, Jews were given many rights by inadvertence, while they were refused others without any animus. Laws enacted against Catholics, who for religious as well as international reasons constituted a problem, were sometimes couched in terms excluding Jews, too, from the enjoyment of certain rights. In other instances, the legal phraseology was so narrow that only Catholics were excluded. In more than one colony the status of Jews was superior to that of their Catholic compatriots. Similarly, in the absence of specific regulations Jewish residents of the colony of New York were allowed to vote even before the Naturalization Act of 1740. Only when in 1737 a defeated candidate challenged the election on the score of illegal Jewish voting did the Colonial Assembly recognize the validity of that objection, because Jews had no right to vote for Parliament in the mother country. Life proceeded apace, however, and despite this Assembly resolution Jews were again recorded as voters in New York in 1761.

In contrast thereto, the apparent victory of the Jewish delegations at the Paris Peace Conference of 1918-19 and the inclusion of provisions for Jewish equality—in some countries also of national minority rights—in the peace treaties under international guarantees proved a dismal failure. Interwar Poland may serve as an excellent illustration. The Polish delegation, headed by Paderewski, formally signed these treaties and accepted without demur further instructions on implementing them from Clemenceau, chairman of the Peace Conference. More, in order to safeguard Polish national pride the National Assembly in Warsaw inserted the same provisions in its newly adopted constitution, making it appear that, of its own volition, Poland was extending just and equal treatment to her minorities. Yet we all know the tragic experiences of Polish Jewry between 1918 and 1939, when the Polish government found one excuse after another to evade its constitutional responsibilities. Protection by the country's own constitution, reinforced by international guarantees, thus proved to be but a broken reed.

Not that legal equality is to be slighted. Law, in the ultimate sense a derivative factor and largely a reflection of existing socio-political realities, nevertheless, when once adopted, becomes a social force in turn. Ringing proclamations of equality, like those of the French Revolution, became a new driving force, greatly accelerating the realization of the egalitarian ideals. Failure to define a status clearly and unequivocally can also become a source of serious complications in the case of sudden shifts in public opinion or under temporary power constellations. Soon after the enactment of the Nuremberg Laws a prominent American jurist subjected them to careful juridical analysis. It was a shock to his listeners, and may still be a shock to many readers, to discover that, if a political machine like that of Huey Long in Louisiana had succeeded in pushing through a legislature a set of similar enactments, some of them could not be invalidated by the United States Supreme Court, because they would not run counter to clear-cut provisions in the United States Constitution. We must bear in mind at the same time that such a tragic eventuality would presuppose a revolutionary change in the sentiments of the American people or at least of its active majority. Once such a radical transformation were to take place, no constitutional provisions, however outspoken, could stem the tide. We need but recall the Weimar Constitution with its vigorous, beautifully defined safeguards for democratic equality. Yet it was swept away by the first severe storms of a revolutionary upheaval.

EMANCIPATION IN WESTERN DEMOCRACIES

Despite this failure to spell out Jewish rights in detail, the progress of emancipation in the Anglo-Saxon countries was fairly rapid. In the United States, particularly, where the presence of many diverse denominations, all of them minorities, made the continued existence of established churches impossible, a system of mutual toleration and full liberty of conscience became an absolute prerequisite for survival. Jews were treated as but one of these numerous denominational groups to whom freedom of conscience and worship was guaranteed by the Constitution.

It was all done so inadvertently that in his well-known letters to the Jewish and other denominational groups George Washington could glibly speak in terms suggesting that full equality had already become the governing principle of public life. He readily forgot that the states had yet to pass their own constitutional provisions which, as it turned out, sometimes seriously impinged upon that general principle. North Carolina, for example, retained religious tests for public office even beyond the Civil War (to 1868).

Wherever public opinion favored a particular Jew, exceptions were devised by competent lawyers. When in 1808 Jacob Henry was elected to the North Carolina legislature no one raised any question. But after his reelection a year later, a fellow legislator demanded that his seat be vacated because Henry "denied the divine authority of the New Testament and refused to take the oath prescribed by law for his qualification." After a lengthy debate in which Henry delivered one of the classic addresses on the subject of equality, he was allowed to retain the seat under the subterfuge that the constitutional restrictions affected only appointive, not elective, offices. Even better known is the protracted struggle for Jewish equality in Maryland, which after several setbacks by the electorate ended in the victory of the progressives and the removal of Jewish disabilities in 1828. Yet even today Maryland's legal structure includes provisions which an anti-Jewish administration or judiciary could well apply against Jews. The same holds true of some other states in the Union.

More significantly, the pros and cons of the Jewish question have always been decided, especially in democratic countries, by public opinion. Thomas Jefferson saw it very clearly when in a letter to Mordecai M. Noah he complained that public opinion often "erects itself into an Inquisition and exercises its office with as much fanaticism as fans the flames of an Auto-da-fé." In defiance of all egalitarian laws, or in their circumvention, American Jew-baiting found many avenues of expression in social and economic discrimination. In periods of high tension, such as the 1930s, antisemitic propaganda could endanger the very continuity of that egalitarian tradition. The experience of the Nazi era has taught most Americans, however, the lesson that liberty is indeed indivisible and that one could not set in motion new discriminatory processes without undermining the very foundations of democracy.

In England, too, emancipation was gaining ground by gradual enactments and precedents set by life, rather than by any sweeping declarations. In fact, the famous struggle for emancipation in England, extending over a quarter of a century and culminating in the legislation of 1857, was really concerned only with the form of oath to be taken by members of Parliament. Being couched in Christian terms, this oath could not be taken by a conscientious Jew. To force Parliament's hand the City of London (the main business section) five times elected Lionel de Rothschild as its member, and five times Parliament refused to seat him. But all through that period Jews could not only hold municipal offices, to which they were specifically admitted by a law of 1845, but as Lord George Bentinck, leader of the Conservative party, observed, they could occupy the posts of Privy Councillor, Secretary of State, Keeper of the Great Seal, and even that of Prime Minister, were it not for the "incidental necessity" for a Prime Minister to have a seat in Parliament. It is small wonder, therefore, that, despite millions of words spoken and written for or against the removal of the Parliamentary disability from English Jewry, and despite that debate's vast international repercussions, the correspondent of the New York *Asmonean* reported from London on January 10, 1850:

> I must not omit to mention that the Jews, as a body, are quite indifferent in England to Jewish emancipation. It appears to me that it is but the ambition of a few individuals in the Jewish community in England who care at all about it, whether Jews may sit in Parliament or not.

Before very long Jews were admitted to the highest offices in England. William Gladstone was the first to select the Jew, Sir George Jessel, to serve as a solicitor general (1871). Later on a loyal Jew, Sir Rufus Isaacs, could successively occupy such important offices as Lord Chief Justice, British Ambassador to the United States during Britain's crucial efforts to draw America into World War I, and finally as Viceroy of India. Jewish equality had become so deeply rooted in England that it easily stood the strain of the grave emergency of the 1940s. Even when Ernest Bevin delivered his antisemitic speeches, when Palestinian "terrorists" executed British sergeants and Israeli fliers shot down members of the RAF, no one in a position of responsibility suggested the curtailment of the rights of British Jewish citizens. The "lunatic fringe" of Mosleyites and other fascists made less headway in England than almost anywhere else.

In contrast with this Anglo-Saxon evolution, Continental emancipation proceeded in the full light of history and by way of solemn declarations. The French National Assembly debated the Jewish question for nearly two years, before it finally decided to grant Jewish equality in two stages: the Sephardic Jews, chiefly concentrated in Bordeaux and elsewhere in the South, were emancipated in January, 1790, or about six months after Bastille Day. But it took more than a year and a half longer—until September, 1791 —before Ashkenazic Jewry living in close settlements in Alsace-Lorraine was granted the same status. In between, all the pros and cons were aired not only in the Assembly but also in the press and the various revolutionary clubs in Paris and the provinces. In many ways all the arguments heard in later years in favor of, or against, Jewish equality had essentially been voiced already in that grand debate.

Although starting from the same basic assumptions as did the American Revolution, the French Assembly, facing a Jewish population about twenty times the size of the American, for the most part segregated from the rest of the population culturally as well as economically, proceeded at a much slower pace. The very fountainhead of both revolutions, the French Enlightenment, maintained a rather ambivalent attitude toward the Jews. Because many spokesmen of Enlightenment saw their major task in attacking Catholic institutions, in fact all established religions, Judaism, too, came under sharp assault. It was easy to blame Judaism for all the misdeeds of Christianity as well, since both of them were rooted in the same

Hebrew Bible. Searching to replace the divisiveness of sectarian religions by an all-embracing cosmopolitan humanitarianism, most
leaders of the Enlightenment had even less patience with Jews, with
whom they maintained but few personal contacts, and Judaism, of
which they knew very little. Typical of a great many others is
Voltaire's tirade in his much-debated article, "Juifs" in the *Diction-
naire philosophique:* "In short, we find in them only an ignorant
and barbarous people, who have long united the most sordid avarice
with the most detestable superstition and the most invincible hatred
for every people by whom they are tolerated and enriched. Still we
ought not to burn them." This attitude was prevalent in revolutionary
circles and on one occasion the Jacobins of the Champagne passed a
resolution demanding the expulsion of Jews from their province.

The majority, however, especially in Paris, felt that the shortcomings of the Jewish people were but the effect of oppression and
persecution. Once the disabilities were removed and the Jewish
people subjected to the educational processes of the new humanitarian environment, the Jews would divest themselves of their unwelcome characteristics and become members of the *grande nation.*
Amalgamation with the majority was considered an integral part of
that egalitarian process by both the French liberals and the relatively
few Jewish spokesmen. In its extreme form the Revolution preached
a new religion of reason to replace all existing religious traditions in a
vast humanitarian embrace, and seized by revolutionary enthusiasm,
some young Jews became devotees of the new religion, cast off their
old religious "shackles," and at times offered such religious implements as scrolls of law for the public bonfires.

The opposition was no less vocal. Its chief spokesmen were worlds
apart. On the one hand, Abbé (later Cardinal) Maury argued with
the self-assurance and dignity of a Catholic prelate that Jews would
never become incorporated into the French nation, that they would
always constitute a "state within the state," and only utilize their
new freedoms to strengthen their separatist institutions. No matter
how many rights they might secure and how joyously they might be
welcomed into French society, they would never cease to be a distinct, unassimilable minority. On the other extreme, the radical deputy Reubell, representative of the Alsatian peasantry—which in the
prerevolutionary *cahiers* had sharply assailed Jewish business practices—now violently argued against Jewish equality on economic
grounds. The removal of existing disabilities, he contended, would
only play into the hands of Jewish usurers and exploiters and enable
them the more effectively to buy up all available land and further
ruin the suffering farmers. Reubell's arguments were backed up by

small but widely scattered pogroms, in which portions of the Alsatian peasantry gave vent to their new feelings of freedom.

In the end the progressive groups won and the principle of equality was generally adopted. With the growth of the revolutionary Terror opponents of egalitarianism were threatened as outright counter-revolutionaries. But revolutionary spokesmen, whether moderate Girondists like Count Clermont-Tonnère or radicals like Robespierre, made it perfectly clear that they expected the Jews speedily to divest themselves of their ethnic separatism and become part and parcel of the French nation. Most Jews, or at least their vocal representatives, accepted that condition and the process of amalgamation proceeded apace.

But its tempo did not appear sufficiently rapid to impatient observers, of whom Napoleon was one, and that autocrat sought to accelerate it through the resources of the Jewish community itself. By convoking with great pomp an Assembly of Jewish Notables, followed by the still more solemn revival of the ancient Sanhedrin, he hoped to obtain from the Jewish leaders satisfactory answers to twelve questions prepared in advance, so as to expedite that process of integration. These governmentally selected Jewish leaders were perfectly willing to follow the emperor's lead, but balked on one point. They refused solemnly to encourage intermarriage between Jews and Christians as the most eminent means of assimilation. Napoleon proceeded to buttress these resolutions by a number of typical dictatorial police measures, as well as by the establishment of a new "consistorial" system which reorganized the existing Jewish communities under close state supervision.

Only the consistorial system survived the Napoleonic regime. It lasted fully until the separation of state and church in France in 1906, and still freely operates on a voluntary basis today. Abetted by the vast internal migrations and profound economic changes, the integration of French Jewry into the national body politic proceeded more successfully than in most other countries. Before very long French Jews and many of their coreligionists abroad extolled the French Revolution in almost messianic terms. Representative of their feelings is the declaration of Colonel Max Cerfberr, President of the Central Consistory, at the beginning of the Revolution of 1848:

> The two principles which the Republic had inscribed on its flag, equality and fraternity of all men, have emerged from our holy Scriptures. It was the voice of our prophets which proclaimed them for the first time. Transferred by our immortal Revolution from the religious to the political sphere, they have lent strength to liberty. . . . For

this reason our faith combines with our patriotism in making us cherish this new era of our history.

SPRINGTIME OF NATIONS

The impact of the French Revolution was immediately felt all over the Continent. Even the remote Tsarist Empire took fright lest the Russian Jewish masses listen to the clarion call of the Sanhedrin and swing over to the French side during the forthcoming conflict. For this reason Tsar Alexander I suspended the evacuation of his Jewish subjects from the villages. More permanently, the French legislation was adopted, sometimes under the pressure of the French armies, in the Netherlands, the western parts of Germany, and in Italy. The Netherlands unwaveringly continued the Jewish emancipation after Napoleon's defeat, and also after their separation in 1830 into the two states of Holland and Belgium. In a few small states of both Italy and Germany, Jewish equality likewise survived the shock of the restoration of 1816.

In most Central European countries, however, a sharp reaction set in. Here Jewish communities of considerable numerical strength looked back upon centuries of their own cultural and communal development, but also faced an unbroken tradition of hostility from the medieval era. One of the major differences between Germany and Western Europe consisted, indeed, in this unbroken continuity of the antisemitic heritage. While England, the Netherlands, and France were able to make a fresh start in the Jewish question during the era of resettlement, Jews had never been completely expelled from Germany in the earlier centuries and hence carried with them irrefragable memories of Jew-baiting ever since the tragic age of the Crusades. These traditions were not completely broken by German Enlightenment, in which such representative figures as Gotthold Lessing and Johann Herder were much more friendly to Jews and Judaism than their French predecessors had been.

In view of the economic importance of the German Jewish communities and many of their leaders, who as "court Jews" went hand in hand with the princes in building up the modern German state (to quote Werner Sombart), the conflict between pro-Jewish and antisemitic sentiments dominated the public mind to an extent unparalleled in the West. For this reason the debate on the Jewish question assumed in Germany unprecedented dimensions. In many ways the German-speaking countries, during the last two centuries, served as the main laboratory for the Jewish question, with vast experimentation in both directions.

Even emancipatory ideas found their first clear formulation in the Germany of Lessing and Moses Mendelssohn. Under the influence of Enlightenment, Christian Wilhelm Dohm published the first comprehensive work advocating the "amelioration" of the civil status of the Jews. Although not yet propagating full emancipation, this work, which was also translated into French, marshaled most of the arguments later presented by champions of Jewish equality. Count Mirabeau was so impressed by the ideas expounded in the Mendelssohn-Dohm circle that upon his return from a visit to Berlin he published a booklet on Mendelssohn in which he advocated fundamental reforms in the position of Jews in the modern world. These words of the most influential leader of the French Revolution in its early stages fell upon receptive ears in France and exerted an influence far beyond its borders. At the same time anti-Jewish voices of no less force and persuasiveness were heard from one end of Germany to the other.

In reaction to the French Revolution, the attitude to Jews on the part of the German ruling classes underwent a great change. At first the Austrian heirs of Josephinism grew frightened by the radicalism of the movement. Without revoking Joseph II's Tolerance Edict of 1781, which had laid the groundwork for a rapprochement between Jews and Christians, they discontinued further reformatory steps. In time, however, many German states came under direct or indirect French domination and adopted constitutions modeled after French patterns. Ultimately even defeated Prussia underwent a great reformatory upsurge in the so-called Stein-Hardenberg era, and promulgated a sweeping decree of Jewish equality in March, 1812. Only the admission of Jews to public office was still reserved for future legislation. More, the Prussian statesmen, Hardenberg and Wilhelm von Humboldt, became the chief spokesmen of Jewish emancipation at the international Congress of Vienna which, in 1814-15, tried to settle the complex European problems arising from the dissolution of the Napoleonic Empire. Characteristically supported by Austria's Metternich, later the leading European reactionary, these Prussian statesmen secured the inclusion of a pro-Jewish article (16) in the newly adopted constitution of the federated states of the new Germany.

Although weakened by a powerful opposition, led especially by the petty bourgeois leaders of the free German cities, that new Confederate Act of 1815 promised future legislation to establish full equality of Jewish rights throughout the Confederation. It also pledged all member states to maintain the existing legal status of the revolutionary era. This constitutional provision was not only in itself a major international commitment, inasmuch as the Germanic Confederation now consisted of wholly sovereign states bound together in a miniature league of nations, but also enjoyed the specific international guarantees of all signatories of the Treaty of Vienna. As a result, the European world was startled to see in the years 1816-24 a series of formal pro-Jewish interventions by Austria, Prussia, Great Britain, and even Russia against anti-Jewish measures in Frankfort and the Hanseatic towns.

By one of the frequent reversals in German-Jewish relations, these promising beginnings were submerged in a sudden wave of reaction. In 1819 German Jewry awakened with a start at the sight of the sudden outbreak of the Hep-Hep movement. Although involving few casualties, the revival of this battle cry against Jews and its rapid spread through the German states opened up abysmal possibilities before a generation which had lulled itself into a sense of security and the belief that the attainment of complete Jewish equality was only a matter of a relatively short time. In the vast antisemitic literature which appeared before and after 1819, most of the arguments of later German antisemitism, including even its racial features, were eloquently advanced. They were invested with the high academic dignity—so appealing to Germans—of professorial pronouncements.

This avalanche of antisemitism generated a new Jewish reaction, however. More and more Jews now decided to take matters into their own hands. Until that time Jewish spokesmen such as Mendelssohn, Friedländer and the Frankfort Jewish representatives at the Congress of Vienna had operated behind the scenes. Most of what they hoped to achieve could be attained only by "lobbying" and the strategic use of douceurs. Now Jewish leaders began to stand up and fight for their own rights and those of all downtrodden humanity. In Gabriel Riesser, German Jewry produced a dignified, eloquent, and persuasive champion for Jewish emancipation. In a series of pamphlets and in a special periodical which he defiantly called *Der Jude* (rather than *Der Israelit,* or some other less "objectionable" designation), he argued for Jewish rights as an integral part of human rights owed all German nationals.

More significantly, Jews also entered the general political arena. Before long they assumed positions of leadership in liberal and radical movements. Even before the Revolution of 1848, publicists such as Ludwig Börne and revolutionary leaders such as Karl Marx and the "socialist rabbi" Moses Hess were among the most effective spokesmen for long-overdue changes in the political structure. During the Revolution, Jewish leadership came to the fore in a most dramatic fashion. In Vienna, where the Metternich system was suddenly overthrown, two young Jewish physicians, Adolf Fischhof and Joseph Goldmark, became the chief architects of the revolutionary movement. As head of the Committee on Security, Fischhof appeared as the uncrowned emperor of Austria. Antisemitic rumor had it that he had taken over the emperor's prerogative, and, though a Jew, marched at the head of the church procession on Corpus Christi Day. The German National Assembly included a number of influential Jewish deputies. Among them was Gabriel Riesser, who, in recognition of his struggle for Jewish rights, was elected one of the vice-presidents of that great constitutional parliament.

In Italy, too, the Revolution was often led by Jews, both converted and professing. The head of the new Venetian Republic was a converted Jew, Daniel Manin, but his cabinet included two loyal Jews. It is less surprising that France, where Jewish emancipation had been in effect for half a century, also included two prominent Jews in its new cabinet. One of them, Michel Goudchaux, became Minister of Finance, allegedly in order to reassure the Paris bankers and industrialists that the Revolution would not go too far. The equally crucial Ministry of Justice was handed over to the staunch champion of Jewish rights Adolphe Cremieux, although his appointment necessitated the transfer of the Bureau of Cults to the Ministry of Public Instruction. It would indeed have been ironical for a Jew to appoint the bishops of Catholic France.

True, the Revolution soon gave way to a more or less pronounced reaction everywhere. However, many states, including Prussia, did not dare abrogate the principle of equality. More, Jews never thereafter retired to their own corner. Under the reactionary regimes they joined the ranks of the opposition and furnished talented leadership to all liberal wings from left of center to the extreme Socialists and Communists. Curiously, even the conservative movements now had Jewish leaders, although largely recruited from baptized circles. In England it was Benjamin Disraeli, the "Hebrew conjurer" as Carlyle chose to call him, who became not only one of Britain's great empire builders, but also the regenerator of the Conservative Party. Many observers viewed with amazement the tragicomic spectacle of Prussia's conservative Junker Party being led by another Jewish convert, Friedrich Julius Stahl. The articulateness of Jewish leadership was so great that the *Deutsche Eisenbahn-Zeitung* went to the trouble of computing the following statistics of the parliamentary speeches delivered by Eduard Lasker, the Jewish leader of the most influential National-Liberal Party in Germany. In the eleven years from 1865 to 1876, Lasker is said to have spoken 927,745,328 words and introduced 7,344 resolutions, of which fully 7,211 were adopted. During these same years Ferdinand Lassalle organized the German Labor Party, which soon became the ideological and practical pace-setter of world socialism. While Hohenzollern Germany and Hapsburg Austria-Hungary still discriminated against Jews in public administration and military service, the Jewish role in domestic and international policies of both countries continued to expand until, after World War I, the Weimar Republic established a full-fledged democracy with intensive Jewish participation.

Italy, too, witnessed the spectacle of a Jewish Prime Minister, Luigi Luzzatti, and two other cabinet ministers representing a Jewish population of less than 40,000. Simultaneously a Jew served as Mayor of Rome. There were also eleven Jewish generals in the Italian army, as well as a host of professors, bankers, and leading professionals in almost all departments.

This political progress generated much ill will and contributed to the rise of a new, post-emancipatory brand of antisemitism. But instead of quietly accepting such hostility as inherent in Jewish Exilic life, Jews now vigorously fought back. Jewish communal leadership began broadening its struggle for Jewish rights in each particular country, and evinced deep concern for the treatment of Jews everywhere. Under Jewish prompting a relatively small local persecution, the Blood Accusation in Damascus in 1840, and even the conversion against his parents' will of a single Jewish boy, Edgar Mortara, in 1858, became matters of international concern. In 1860, French Jewry organized the Alliance Israelite Universelle, which undertook to coordinate the struggle for Jewish equality all over the world. National jealousies prevented Jews of other countries from associating themselves directly with the Alliance, but the Board of Delegates of American Jews, organized in 1859, the Anglo-Jewish Association, formed in 1871, and similar groupings elsewhere actively collaborated in this struggle. Finally, the world-wide Zionist movement took over the leadership in the quest for an international solution of the Jewish question.

THE PRICE OF LIBERTY

As time went on the original messianic expectations of emancipation had to be toned down. Keen observers began to realize that emancipation, while indubitably benefiting the individual Jew and improving the socio-economic position of the whole people, also set in motion forces menacing their very survival. The wave of conversions to Christianity which occurred in the early nineteenth century in Prussia may not have been as extensive as it appeared to contemporaries and later historians alike, but it did hoist a danger signal. So did the continuing arguments from Christians that in order to achieve true emancipation Jews had better give up their "segregated" forms of living, abandon their Talmudic traditions, and preferably inter-marry. Such a policy, if consistently pursued, would have spelled disaster to the Jewish people.

Apart from the menace of total assimilation, the new materialism and religious skepticism were undermining the internal strength of the people. As early as the 1840s, the noted novelist Berthold Auerbach was shocked by the exclusive pursuit of life's external pleasures on the part of Vienna's gilded Jews. He heard many young Jews repeat a current *bon mot,* "Why should I do anything for posterity, what has posterity done for me?" From another angle the Orthodox leader Israel Hildesheimer wrote in 1867 that in his earlier years nine-tenths of the Jewish youth were either "deprecators of religion, religious traitors or, at best, wholly indifferent." It is small wonder, then, that patriotic Jewish thinkers such as Samuel David Luzzatto began viewing emancipation as such with consider-able suspicion. Disillusioned by the failure of the Revolution of 1848, this great master of Italian Jewish scholarship began em-phasizing the differences rather than the similarities between Judaism and the Christian civilization, particularly the latter's Hellenic matrix.

By the time emancipation reached the masses of Jews in Eastern Europe, therefore, it began to be considered a practical necessity, rather than a vehicle of ultimate humanitarian redemption. In Tsarist Russia especially, which in the latter part of the nineteenth century harbored nearly half of the world Jewish population, some earlier emancipatory measures had been discredited by the government's outright conversionist aims.

Curiously, the Russia of Catherine II was one of the first countries to admit Jews to the enjoyment of political rights by allowing them to participate in municipal elections. That very regime, however, also laid the foundations for the Pale of Settlement (beginning in 1791), which bottled up the ever growing Jewish masses in a few western provinces. The overtly progressive agricultural colonization of Jews sponsored by the governments of Alexander I and Nicholas I was quickly turned into an instrument of governmental coercion and denationalization. It was completely discredited by the simultaneous eviction of Jews from villages, purportedly for the protection of the exploited peasantry. Military service, which in Austria and elsewhere was often the harbinger of Jewish equality, lost whatever patriotic glamor it might have had for Russian Jewish youth by its overtly discriminatory and Christianizing functions. The *Rekrutchina,* in particular, that forcible enlistment of Jewish children for service extending over decades, was clearly an effort to wrest these children from parental and communal control. The total number of such draftees during the twenty-eight years of that system's operation (1827-55) may have been relatively small. According to the best estimates, in the years 1833-54 only 21,043 Jewish "cantonists" had become its victims. Yet the impression it made upon the entire community when children were seized on the streets by governmental "catchers," or, worse yet, had to be selected by the Jewish leaders themselves for ultimate estrangement from Jewish ways of life, was profound and enduring.

For this reason the realization increasingly dawned upon the growing Jewish intelligentsia that the Jewish question could not be solved without the total overthrow of Russia's established order. Especially when the era of Alexander II had passed and the liberation of the Russian peasantry in 1861 was not followed up by Jewish emancipation, more and more younger Jews joined the various radical movements. Reciprocally, the greater the share of Jews in the revolutionary movements, the more repressive became the governmental attitude under the last two tsars, Alexander III and Nicholas II. No sooner did Alexander III ascend the throne than a wave of governmentally inspired pogroms swept over Russia in 1881, and was followed by the sharply restrictive May Laws of 1882. Jews in Russia and elsewhere—in fact, the whole outside world—were shocked by the reappearance of this violent method of settling Judeo-Gentile controversies. These pogroms, moreover, were repeated, again with the foreknowledge of government, on a still larger scale in 1903 and 1905.

Some leading Russian statesmen did not even bother to conceal their ultimate intentions to eliminate all the Jews in the country. A famous saying attributed to Constantin Pobedonostsev, Procurator of the Holy Synod and Russia's evil genius for a quarter-century (1881-1905), defined as the objective of imperial policy that one-third of Russian Jewry emigrate, another third become Christian and the final third perish. Using the excuse that in southern Russia Jews allegedly constituted ninety percent, and in the interior of Russia forty percent, of all revolutionaries, a leading minister, Wenzel von Plehve, candidly informed a Jewish delegation from Odessa in 1903: "We shall make your situation in Russia so untenable that Jews will be forced to leave it to the very last man." That is why von Plehve lent a receptive ear to Theodor Herzl's scheme of opening Palestine for large-scale Jewish immigration.

While some Jews sought the remedy in a revolutionary dictatorship of the proletariat, others, bearing in mind particularly the overwhelmingly middle-class and petty bourgeois status of the Jewish population, demanded the establishment of a liberal democracy along Western patterns. Many of the leaders came to the conclusion, however, that equality of rights was not enough. For reasons which will be explained in another context this was also the period of the rise of Jewish nationalism. Voices were more and more frequently heard claiming that emancipation as such was, to quote Ahad Haam's famous essay, nothing but "bondage within freedom." To secure liberty alongside of equality the Russian Jewish leaders began demanding the supplementation of equality of rights by a system of national minority rights. The short-lived but for a time quite influential League for the Attainment of Equal Rights for the Jewish People in Russia, organized in March, 1905, postulated "national rights, and a comprehensive system of communal self-government, the freedom of language and school education." A combination, therefore, of equality and national self-determination was to replace the previous association of equality with national integration in the majority peoples.

The Russian Revolution of 1905 provided a preliminary answer. It gave the Jews a modicum of equality, although it left much room for discrimination and continued governmental oppression. National minority rights were still merely in the debating stage when World War I broke out, followed by the successive democratic and Communist revolutions of 1917. Their effect upon Jews will be considered in a later chapter.

Resistance to Jewish equality was not limited to Tsarist Russia. Rumanians, Poles, and other East European nations fought bitterly every effort of their own progressives, as well as of foreign powers, to secure equal treatment for their substantial Jewish minorities. Rumania, which was just emerging into complete independence in 1878, had to sign on the dotted line that she would grant equality of rights to all citizens. Nevertheless, she succeeded in evading the provisions of Article 44 of the Berlin Treaty by one subterfuge or another. She defied the formidable interventions of Bismarck and Disraeli, of Austria and the United States, and when World War I came thirty-six years later, only about one percent of the Jewish population had become individually naturalized by special acts of parliament. Rumania signed even more specific provisions for equality in the Bucharest Treaty with the Central Powers in 1918, and the treaties of Saint Germain and Trianon with the Allied and Associated Powers in 1919. Nonetheless, she again successfully evaded her responsibilities in the interwar period.

In Poland there actually was a reversal of early pro-emancipatory trends. Just before the final partitions of Poland in the 1790s, the memorable Quadrennial Diet had enacted a reform legislation which, though not going the whole length of the French National Assembly, opened up new vistas of freedom and cooperation between Jews and Poles. Polish Jews, indeed, fought for Poland's national independence under Kosciuszko, and again during the uprisings of 1831 and 1863. After 1831 many Jews also joined the Polish emigration which kept all liberal forces in Europe aware of the Polish struggle for liberty. Yet partly stimulated by the Tsarist policy of "divide and rule," the relations between the two oppressed minorities constantly deteriorated, until the Polish nationalists proclaimed a universal boycott on their Jewish neighbors shortly before World War I. The Paris Peace Conference could legitimately point out to the Polish delegates that "in view of the historic development of the Jewish question and the great animosity aroused by it, special protection is necessary for the Jews in Poland" (Clemenceau's letter to Paderewski of June 24, 1919). But the history of the next two decades of Polish sovereignty is filled with tragic pages of constant governmental and social pressures. More refined and better concealed than the measures taken by the Tsarist regime, these measures no less effectively undermined the very basis of Jewish subsistence. Polish Jewry in the 1920s and 1930s was just as much in a state of permanent flight as Russian Jewry had been before 1914, except that now practically all frontiers, including those of the United States, were closed to mass immigration.

THE CLIMAX OF EMANCIPATION

The story of emancipation, as it has unfolded itself before our eyes, shows how recent an achievement Jewish emancipation really is. One could make a good case for the contention that emancipation has not yet had a chance to prove itself, in either its favorable or unfavorable features.

We need but think back half a century to realize that at that time the large majority of world Jewry, living in Tsarist Russia, Rumania, the Ottoman Empire, and several other countries, had not even been granted equality on paper. The Young Turk Revolution of 1908-09 might have opened a new era for the Jews in the Balkans, western Asia including Palestine, and parts of North Africa. But the decaying Ottoman Empire could not implement these revolutionary slogans because of the Italo-Turkish and Balkan wars, soon followed by World War I and the empire's disintegration.

Moreover, fifty years ago even the minority of Jews which happened to live in democratic countries was little emancipated in reality. In the United States, for instance, Jews may have enjoyed substantially equal rights ever since the American Revolution, or for more than four generations. Yet most Jews living in the United States in 1906 had themselves been born and bred in Russia or Poland, Rumania or Turkey. They did not change overnight by the mere transfer from an area of nonemancipation to one of equality. Whatever use they made of the new economic and even cultural opportunities granted them by democratic countries, their outlook on life, their mores and ideologies, altered but slowly and imperceptibly.

After World War I the proclamation of egalitarian constitutions by the Soviet Union, Poland, Rumania, and the other successor states of the Tsarist, Hapsburg, and Ottoman empires created the temporary illusion that world-wide emancipation was finally to become a reality. The few peripheral areas, such as Yemen and Morocco, could be disregarded. Hopes ran high, indeed, that they too would soon fall in line with an utterly irresistible historic process.

These hopes were quickly dashed. Not only did Poland, Rumania, and other states immediately sabotage their own constitutional provisions, but there arose in Weimar Germany the powerful countermovement of Nazism. We shall see that this new movement, which soon gained acceptance in many circles outside Germany, demanded in the first place complete disfranchisement of Jews. One of the antisemitic arguments of that period was that Jews themselves had forfeited emancipation by not living up to their part of the bargain. A myth was now actively propagated that the former liberal regimes had granted Jews equality of rights on the *condition* that their assimilation would speedily follow. Since the Jews had failed to become assimilated and insisted upon the retention of their ethnic-religious identity, they had allegedly broken the contract. Its annulment, therefore, was perfectly in order. One need not expatiate on the spuriousness of this argument; the less so as the Nazis and their allies desired assimilation even less than emancipation. With even greater fervor than disfranchisement, they preached dissimilation and total segregation of Jews—all that merely as a step toward the "final solution of the Jewish question," which was total elimination of Jews from Europe, if not from the rest of the world as well. Under this counterattack, which was gathering strength in the late 1920s and the 1930s, Jewish equality actually retrogressed even in countries which did not alter their constitutional systems.

It was, therefore, only after World War II that world-wide Jewish equality received a new lease on life. I happened to be present in Paris in 1946 when the peace treaties with Italy, Hungary, Bulgaria, Rumania, and Finland were being negotiated. Unlike the first Paris Peace Conference of 1919, the assembly of statesmen in 1946 offered a rather somber spectacle. The Jewish delegations played an even more subdued role, particularly since the Hitler persecutions had revealed the political impotence of the Jewish people. Nonetheless, they did not have to struggle for equality. No delegation on either side proposed any kind of constitutional regulations which would controvert the principle of equality of all citizens. Even outside these five countries no voices were heard overtly demanding discrimination against minorities. Despite the tensions generated by the Zionist movement, the Arab countries, including the newly arisen states of Syria, Lebanon, and Jordan, professed adherence to basic equality of rights. Few of them have lived up to these constitutional requirements with respect to Jews. Under one subterfuge or another Iraq and Syria were able to make life much more unbearable for their Jewish citizens than it had ever been under the nonegalitarian Ottoman regime. Nevertheless, here were official constitutional safeguards of a universality never achieved before.

Even more importantly, the majority of the Jewish people now lived in democratic countries, particularly the United States and the British Commonwealth. Nor were they for the most part newcomers. By far their largest number were born and bred under conditions of emancipation, went through American, British, or French schools, fought in two world wars, and became integral parts of the majority peoples. This time it seemed, indeed, that the great human experiment of Jewish emancipation could undergo its final test in the crucible of history. One should not be surprised, indeed, if historians of the future would date the beginnings of real Jewish emancipation not with 1787 or 1790 or even 1848, but rather with the first postwar year of 1946.

Together with this great achievement, the negative aspects of emancipation have also manifested themselves in their full force. Long before 1946, publicists and historians had often spoken of the "crisis of emancipation." I have, myself, often compared the internal crisis in Jewish life generated by the new equality with the crisis of the First Exile. In 586 B.C.E. the question had arisen as to whether Jews could survive the loss of national independence and maintain their identity as a minority on foreign soil. Owing to the peculiar evolution of pre-Exilic Jewish religion and society, it was possible for Exilic leaders like Ezekiel to furnish the first affirmative answers to this query. In patient elaboration by generations of prophets, priests, and sages from Ezekiel to Hillel, these answers were finally evolved through what we call Pharisaic-Rabbinic Judaism, and found their classical expression in the two Talmuds. Armed with these solutions, the Jewish community, living its own autonomous life, could face different, often hostile, majorities. It could adapt itself to a variety of civilizations while maintaining its own unbroken historic continuity. This unprecedented solution remained substantially valid after the Second Fall of Jerusalem and all the way down to the emancipation era. What emancipation now demanded from the Jews, however, was that they give up their status as a minority facing the majority, and become part and parcel of that majority itself. From now on Jews were to be Americans *and* Jews, Englishmen *and* Jews, Swiss *and* Jews, and so forth, sharing the political, economic, and even cultural concerns of their countries, and retaining only in relatively small areas their religio-cultural identity.

Could Jews—and Judaism—survive such a total reshaping of their status and way of life? The answers furnished by a century and a half of emancipatory progression were inadequate in so far as the interdependence of the Jewish people the world over caused developments in nondemocratic countries to have a direct bearing on Jewish destinies in democratic countries as well. During the last decade the apparent universalization of equality removed that obstacle. But was emancipation, itself, quite genuine? Have not certain socio-economic and cultural forms of discrimination been able to survive even under the most outspoken egalitarian provisions? Is a modicum of discrimination really necessary to keep at least some Jews within the fold?

Answers to these questions can only emerge after a fuller consideration of the other factors which have shaped the destinies of the Jewish people in the modern era. One of them was the worldwide movement of modern nationalism.

14

THE IMPACT OF NATIONALISM

Behind the tragic failures of emancipation, as well as behind some of its celebrated victories, lay a deep-rooted dichotomy. In its origins, emancipation was essentially the child of the Enlightenment, which in its cosmopolitan fervor minimized all national, linguistic, and religious differences. Even those who were not prepared to go the whole length of replacing all established religions by a new, truly universal religion of reason believed that all differences separating men from men had largely been the result of ill will and human mismanagement. Once permeated with the rays of true reason, these differences would melt away, and the essential Man would emerge as the master of creation. In practical application, however, it quickly turned out that Man was an abstraction, and that in historic reality he always appeared in groups, social, religious, and national. So it came about that the same French Revolution which proclaimed the Rights of Man also became the protagonist of the new nationalism which has dominated men's minds ever since.

From the Jewish point of view that dichotomy likewise led to a serious misunderstanding. The main exponents of Jewish emancipation during the great struggle in Central Europe before and after 1848 were at the same time children of the Enlightenment and of its opposing movement, Romanticism. As enlightened rationalists they demanded recognition of Jews as men endowed with the natural qualities and privileges of all humanity. As Romantics, however, they felt the great power of historic heritages, of those man-made and history-made divisions that were particularly evident in the rival nationalisms. It dawned upon these champions of emancipation that the assimilation demanded from Jews could in practice not be accomplished by assimilation to some abstract mankind but had to be carried out in conjunction with one or another historic nationality. In other words, Jews were not merely to become "men," but specifically Frenchmen, Englishmen, Germans, and so forth. Many Jewish leaders were prepared to accept even that formulation. But there was a stubborn kernel of resistance in the rank and file, especially in those countries whose cultural level was low. It seemed to make sense when Jews were asked to become Frenchmen, Americans, or Germans. But to become Latvians, Lithuanians, or Ukrainians, nationalities which themselves were just awakening to the significance of their national cultures and destinies, seemed utterly unrealistic. Yet nationalism as it developed became ever more exacting and ruthless. Ultimately it threatened to destroy not only the Jewish people but all of Western civilization.

CHARACTER OF MODERN NATIONALISM

In the decisive debate on Jewish equality in the French National Assembly, Count Clermont-Tonnère concluded his appeal in its behalf by exclaiming that, if the Jews should refuse to become Frenchmen, "let them be banished." Here was the basic intolerance of the new nationalism. In the past, nationalism was always intertwined with religion—a combination which injected into every national consciousness a certain supranational ingredient. But now nationalism itself became a religion with the same exclusiveness as the old monotheisms. "Thou shalt have no other gods before Me" became as much a nationalist as it had once been a religious slogan.

Accordingly, a deep-rooted, fine, human loyalty to one's own people became distorted into an all-devouring passion. The nation became completely secularized, a law unto itself. The supremacy of a moral order, at least postulated by all ancient and medieval religions, now gave way to the untrammeled doctrine of national sovereignty, which by definition means that the state is not subject to any outside will. And along with sovereignty there developed an ever increasing emphasis on the principle of noninterference in the internal affairs of other sovereign states. Humanitarian intervention by one power in the affairs of another, as, for example, in behalf of the persecuted Jews of Damascus or Rumania, became less and less frequent. Finally, nationalism degenerated into the ruthless totalitarianism of our own day.

At first Western nationalism seemed to bring the Jews equality and so liberation from the ghetto. National unity presupposed the dissolution of the medieval corporate societies and the integration of all citizens into the body politic. Many Jews could, therefore, easily delude themselves into believing that the new nationalism would bring them salvation. They often tried to outdo their neighbors, becoming the most ardent and vociferous German, Hungarian, or French nationalists.

Now religion was declared to be "a private affair of the individual," and hence Jews, too, could continue worshiping their God in the privacy of their homes and synagogues, but in all other respects be members of the dominant nationality and partake of its political and cultural life. Progressive Jews were perfectly willing to accept that arrangement. Such a loyal Jew as Gabriel Riesser solemnly declared that German Jews are but "a group of people who do not wish to have national existence of their own, such as had formerly been imposed upon them by their enemies, but who think and feel as Germans." In the United States, too, Isaac Mayer Wise spoke of America as being his Promised Land.

Yet Jews found themselves faced with difficult alternatives. It was easy enough to declare themselves Englishmen, or Americans, or Italians, but in areas inhabited by mixed nationalities the choice was always fraught with danger. In the eastern provinces of Prussia, Jews faced a local Polish majority which the Germans tried to denationalize. Because of their age-old differences with the Poles, as well as the attraction of the superior German *Kultur,* most Posen Jews sided with the Germans. They paid for this choice with the deepened hostility of their Polish neighbors during the insurrectionary movements of 1846-48. Throughout the nineteenth and early twentieth centuries Jews found themselves in the awkward situation of siding with the German minority against the Czechs in Bohemia and Moravia, and with the Magyars against the local Slavonic and Rumanian majorities in Hungary. In Galicia they had to support the Poles against the Ruthenians, while across the border they were accused, not without some justification, of fostering Russification of Polish and Ukrainian areas, despite their own sufferings under the Russian knout. These difficulties repeated themselves in all multinational areas after the rise of the new states in the interwar period.

Even today Jews find themselves in many unhappy situations because of the conflict between the Catholic French and the Protestant English in Canada, or the struggle between the Afrikaaners and the English-speaking white population of the Union of South Africa.

In all such cases the unreality of Jews joining one national group as against another was easily demonstrated in periods of crisis. After the rise of Czechoslovakia, for example, many Jews who had formerly professed to be German nationals were almost overnight counted as members of the Czech nationality, culturally as well as politically. The only alternative, of course, was to stand up and declare themselves to belong to neither of the two opposing ethnic groups, but to be members of an independent Jewish nationality.

Western nationalism's appeal to the Jews was heightened, at least in its heroic stage, by its messianic fervor. Modern nationalism inherited from the old monotheistic religions not only their exclusiveness, but also their profound belief in a forthcoming end of days, an era of ultimate fulfillment. There were many variations on that theme, but all of them ultimately stemmed from the Judeo-Christian messianic tradition. Many Americans who were not believers in the fundamentalist sense nevertheless spoke of America's "manifest destiny" with a truly religious devotion. In the same vein Fichte declared the German nation to be a *Menschheitsnation,* a nation dedicated to the service of humanity. The Polish mystic Andrew Towianski and Poland's greatest poet, Adam Mickiewicz, saw in the Polish people another personification of Isaiah's suffering Messiah; they expected that Israel and Poland, working hand in hand, would ultimately redeem mankind. Stimulated by Mickiewicz, Guiseppe Mazzini proclaimed the Italian nation the true messiah, able to overcome even the dualism between heaven and earth, thought and action, spirit and matter.

Such messianic credos elicited in Jewish hearts many a responsive echo. Since the realization of the messianic dream had always presupposed an era of sufferings and self-sacrificing devotion, many Jews were ready to offer the sacrifice of their own ethnic loyalties on the altar of that humanitarian redemption. Others, however, saw the realization of the messianic ideal through their own, genuinely messianic Jewish nationality.

ANTISEMITISM, OLD AND NEW

Under the impact of both emancipation and nationalism the age-old forms of Jew-baiting underwent profound changes. Not that the old arguments had been silenced. There still was—and is—much talk about the original Jewish sin in repudiating Christ, about the Jews' share in the crucifixion and their alleged self-condemnation before Golgotha, "His blood be on us, and on our children" (Matthew 27:25). Especially during Easter Week, Christian pulpits all over the world resounded with the old accusations. The New Testament stories were told over and over again in Sunday schools. Children and adults alike were usually made to believe that the story of the Gospels had a direct bearing on contemporary Jews.

The manifold efforts in modern times to promote mutual understanding between the leaders of the various denominations usually produced much oratory but had little impact upon the rank and file. During the "Springtime of Nations" an effort was also made to transcend the bounds of the denominational divisions. An "Ecclesiastical Association for All Denominations" was organized in Leipzig in 1848 with the participation of such representative Jewish scholars as Zacharias Frankel, Adolf Jellinek, Samuel Holdheim, and Julius Fürst. Fraternization went so far as to make possible occasional use of synagogues for church services. But all these efforts, constantly repeated by associations foreshadowing our own societies of Christians and Jews, exerted little influence on public opinion.

Many of the "Christian" political parties were hostile to the Jews. Christian socialism, in particular, often combined the anti-Jewish tradition of the old Christian apologias with the new socialist attacks on Jewish capitalism which so deeply muddied the waters of European socialism in the nineteenth century. True, the early English Christian socialists had little to say about the Jewish question. In Germany, Catholicism was often on the defensive, particularly during the *Kulturkampf* of the Bismarckian era. Hence the Christian-Socialist Party of Bishop Ketteler in the mid-nineteenth century and the Center Party in the German Empire after 1871 were often defenders of Jewish rights. These leaders realized that as an embattled minority they could not quite countenance discrimination against another minority. It was the Protestant pastor Adolf Stöcker who in the 1880s assumed leadership of the antisemitic movement. He even organized international antisemitic congresses.

In Catholic Austria, on the other hand, the Catholic Christian-Socialist Party, led by Karl Lueger, formed the first organized anti-semitic party. It became so popular among the masses of the German-speaking parts of Austria that Lueger was elected burgomaster of Vienna. Ultimately Emperor Francis Joseph I, who had vetoed Lueger's election, had to yield to the popular clamor. Lueger's party also became the largest party in the Austrian parliament, and remained so after the dissolution of the Austrian Empire, within the newly created Austrian Republic. Only after the bitter experiences of the Nazi occupation and the elimination of the overwhelming majority of Austrian Jewry during World War II did the present heirs of that political party, still in control of the Austrian Republic, tone down their antisemitic policies. Starting with less of a Jew-baiting heritage, the new Catholic parties of De Gasperi, Adenauer, and Bidault, which became so influential in postwar Italy, Western Germany, and France, respectively could dispense altogether with any anti-Jewish program. In the United States, Father Coughlin's Catholic brand of antisemitism was short-lived. When it became manifest that his agitation was against America's national interest, the Catholic hierarchy itself silenced its most eloquent radio priest.

In all this agitation the religious issue played an ever decreasing role. The idea of religious intolerance had become obnoxious and deeply at variance with the self-interest of other religious minorities, varying from country to country. The new propaganda, whether carried on by religious or secular spokesmen, now concentrated on national and social problems. Since many Jews had risen to economic affluence and political power, it was easy for Jew-baiters to clamor against the alleged Jewish domination of their national economies or political structures. This issue was to envenom the relations between Jews and the early socialists, and became paramount in the attacks on Jews and Judaism by ultranationalists of all countries and denominations.

The classical exponent of this brand of antisemitism was Edouard Drumont. Before him Wilhelm Marr, who may have been responsible for coining the term "antisemitism," proclaimed in 1879 in mock despair, "the great historical triumph of Judaism, the record of a lost battle, without any extenuation for the beaten army." Marr and his confreres, writing after the crisis of 1873, claimed that Germany had become wholly dominated by Jews. In his *La France Juive,* Drumont discussed with more learning and eloquence the alleged Jewish domination of France. First ignored by the French public and press, this volume speedily caught the attention of readers and became a best-seller. In its very first year (1886) it appeared in a hundred editions in French, and was soon translated into German, English, Spanish, and Polish. Together with Drumont's journal, *La Libre Parole,* it began molding French public opinion to such an extent that a decade later the charges against a Jewish captain, Alfred Dreyfus, could be seized upon by the reactionary forces as a pretext for undermining the Third Republic. Among the anti-Dreyfusards of the years of 1895-1903 was also a young lieutenant,

Philippe Pétain, who toward the end of his life finally succeeded, with the aid of the German occupation forces, in destroying that republic. For liberals the world over, however, the Dreyfus Affair became a warning of what antisemitism meant for their own future. Zola's *J'accuse* and Clemenceau's vitriolic attacks on that miscarriage of justice demonstrated that even these abysmal forces of prejudice and bigotry could be overcome by a nation's progressive forces, once they realized that their own future was at stake.

In most other antisemitic movements the attack on democracy and liberalism was not quite so apparent. True, in Russia the Black Hundreds who attacked Jews were also the protagonists of general reaction and the suppression of all liberal opinion. However, not all progressives in, and outside, Russia realized that intrinsic nexus. Some were even persuaded that there was a grain of truth in the antisemitic contention of the Jewish quest for domination, nationally and internationally. In Russia, finally, the idea of a Jewish world conspiracy received its classical formulation. Advisers of Tsar Nicholas II, who had not hesitated to finance antisemitic propaganda literature from his private purse (archive materials published after World War I showed that he had disbursed more than 13,000,000 rubles for this purpose), also encouraged a monk, Nilus, to prepare in 1903 a forgery which later came to be known as the *Protocols of the Elders of Zion*. Here an old French romance of non-Jewish content was converted into the alleged record of a meeting of Jewish elders planning world conquest. For some fifteen years Nilus' fabrication remained limited to a Russian audience, but immediately after World War I it had a strange career and was translated into many languages. Republished by Henry Ford under the title *The International Jew,* and expounded at great length by Alfred Rosenberg and other leading antisemites, it became the most influential forgery of the twentieth century.

The idea of a Jewish world conspiracy found ready acceptance not only among the masses of uncritical believers, but even among statesmen and politicians. Count Lamsdorf, who as Russia's Foreign Minister must have known of the origin of the Nilus book, in all seriousness suggested in 1905-06 to Emperor William II a Russo-German alliance for combating both the international Jew and the equally international Freemason. Incidentally, this alleged alliance between Judaism and Freemasonry became another shibboleth of modern antisemites, including the French Royalist Party gathered around the *Action Française*. Here, however, nationalist opposition to Germany and Catholic enmity to Protestantism could be combined with anti-Judaism. To quote Charles Maurras, the *Action Fran-*

çaise's most eloquent spokesman, "There exists a great maritime power: it is Anglo-Saxon and Protestant, and hence twice barbarian. There exists a great military power: it is German, Protestant, twice barbarian. There exists a great financial power: it is cosmopolite and Jewish, that is both barbarian and anarchist." For Catholic France, according to these extremists, there was no other way but to revert to the ideals of the period before the French Revolution.

AMBIGUITIES OF RACIALISM

In these socio-political denunciations of Jews we find a secularized antisemitism fully corresponding to the secularized nationalism of the period. Once the argument was raised that Jews dominated the nation, they were necessarily identified as an independent entity. Rather than preaching integration, secular antisemitism thus demanded segregation and legal, as well as social, preventives against Jewish control over national life. From here it was only a step to racial antisemitism, but it was not till the nineteenth century that race was gradually elevated into a supreme principle affecting all walks of life. True, the terms Aryan, Semite, and the like were introduced primarily by students of languages and cultures to classify and distinguish certain groups of languages akin to one another. In time, however, the idea of race began to be employed in a naturalist vein, and from there transferred to the realm of history and contemporary affairs. Count Gobineau, often considered the father of modern racial theory, was neither the first thinker to expound it, nor did he propose its application to the Jewish question. Curiously, the first writer to make use of racial arguments in connection with Judaism was Disraeli, who considered himself a proud and loyal Jew, although, as he used to say, a Jew of Calvary as well as of Sinai. "All is race, there is no other truth," declared one of his heroes, Tancred. Even more proudly he explained the fact of Jewish survival by the natural superiority of Jews. "All which proves that it is in vain for man to attempt to baffle the inexorable law of nature, which has decreed that a superior race shall never be destroyed or absorbed by an inferior." While Disraeli's rhetoric was never taken too seriously even by his devotees, Gobineau's theories were immediately put to use by the antiabolitionists in distant America.

In time racial antisemitism gained more and more fanatical adherents. Here antagonism to Jews could be justified on immutable natural grounds. If Richard Wagner had an axe to grind against the Jews in music, he could blame their alleged lack of creativity on their racial insufficiency. Moreover, racialism could be utilized in combating Christianity as well, by blaming the shortcomings of the Christian faith on its Jewish founders. Some racial antisemites like Houston Steward Chamberlain tried to salvage at least the personality of Jesus for the Aryan race by claiming, against the overt Gospel tradition, that he was of non-Jewish Galilean origin. But the majority was perfectly willing to forego Jesus along with the Apostles because of their Judeo-Christian ethics. Racialism of this kind can be understood only against the background of unbridled nationalism, particularly in Germany. Fichte still tried to glorify Lutheranism by means of a nationalist reinterpretation of Protestant Christianity. But Friedrich Nietzsche preached an anti-Christian "reevaluation of all values" that greatly appealed to a generation which had lost all its moorings in the traditional system of ethics. A prominent Bible scholar, Paul de Lagarde, argued in favor of the creation of a new national German religion:

> Catholicism, Protestantism, Judaism, naturalism must give way to a new conception of life so that they be remembered no more than are the lamps used at night after the sun shines over the mountains. Or else the unity of Germany will become ever more questionable from day to day.

As the imperialist clashes grew in intensity, such opposition grew into a vociferous chorus. "Woe unto the people," exclaimed Ernst Wachler in the leading anti-Jewish organ *Der Hammer,* "which will behave in a Christian fashion, in an era when the struggle has begun for the possession of the earth." To such imperialists and nationalists it mattered little that even their hero, Nietzsche, had admired the perseverance of the Jewish race. ("The Jews are without any doubt the strongest, most tenacious and purest race now living in Europe.") In their haste to get rid of the stumbling block of Judeo-Christian ethics, and what they considered its main exponent, the international Jewish spirit, German nationalists of all brands, including those led in Austria by the half-demented parliamentarian Georg von Schönerer, wished to eliminate the Jewish factor from German public life.

These exponents of racialism found ready listeners in many other countries as well. In the United States, then in the midst of a great industrial revolution and mass immigration of Southern and Eastern Europeans including Jews, racial antagonism—heretofore directed only against Negroes and Indians and later against Orientals, especially Chinese and Japanese—ultimately turned against Jews, too. In the growing agitation for closing the doors to certain types of immigration the Jews became one of the main targets. Here the racial element was played up, although with less pseudo-scientific rigor than in Germany or France; some historians, such as Henry Adams, injected it even into their interpretation of American history.

All these trends were overshadowed in the interwar era. Germany, defeated and humiliated, sought to salve its pride by blaming someone else. The Jews appeared as the ideal scapegoat, since so many of them had become leaders of leftist parties whose pacifist agitation during the years of World War I could now be denounced as a "stab in the back" at the "victorious" German armies, still fighting on foreign soil when the war ended. Aggravated by a serious economic crisis, caused by the prevailing anarchy and inflation but readily attributed in the popular mind to Jewish profiteering, the unrest among the masses was easily diverted from the social revolution into anti-Jewish channels. Out of this turmoil was born the National Socialist movement which was soon to grow into a monster.

Theoretically the National Socialist program was a hodgepodge of ideas previously expounded and of methods previously employed. With utter disregard of the intrinsic truthfulness of these ideas, or even of their consistency with one another, Hitler and his cohorts went about remaking Germany and, before long, also shaping a New Order in Europe in their own image. Without explicitly committing themselves to displacing Christianity, since they feared religious martyrdom as an element of religious regeneration, they nevertheless preached a basic new "religion of blood and honor." The Reich Minister for Church Affairs, Kerrl, declared succinctly in 1937: "There has now arisen a new authority as to what Christ and Christianity really is. This new authority is Adolf Hitler." Nationalism, too, underwent a complete reinterpretation; above the older vital ingredients of territory, state, and language, there now began to loom the supreme criterion of race. Consciously using this pseudo-scientific test, and knowing well enough that few members of the German nation could live up to the alleged Teutonic characteristics in physical appearance or mental behavior, they recklessly employed it for propagandist purposes not only in Germany but the world over.

We need not go over the thrice-told tale of the Nazis' meteoric rise to power in Germany, and their subsequent ruinous drive for world domination. Long before they proceeded with their ruthless extermination of millions of Jews as a "final solution of the Jewish question," they used the Jewish issue to divide nations against themselves. By propagating racial antisemitism, and hence lending it the permanent unchangeability of a natural law, and by playing up the dangers of world communism—with which in 1939 they were prepared to strike a mutually favorable bargain—they succeeded in undermining the internal cohesion of the nations they planned to invade.

Within a year after their rise to power, Hitler and his associates organized in Hamburg and Erfurt centers for world-wide propaganda among both the *Auslandsdeutsche* and the native Jew-baiters. In May, 1934, there already existed more than 350 national and local units which, directed from the Hamburg headquarters, effectively propagated Nazi ideas in a multitude of local adaptations. So effective was this foreign propaganda that the French Right welcomed even the Munich surrender as a lesser evil. As one of its leaders, Thierry-Maulnier, explained in 1938, "A French defeat would really have been a defeat of France, and a French victory would have been less a victory of France than a victory of the principles rightly considered as leading straight to her ruin and to that of civilization itself." It is small wonder, then, that at the hour of decision the French national will was found wanting and all of France was easily overrun by the Nazi hordes.

Even in America the impact of Nazi propaganda in the mid-thirties was enormous. When, in 1935, *Fortune* Magazine polled the people on the question, "Do you believe that in the long run Germany will be better, or worse off, if it drives out the Jews?" it received remarkable answers. Only 54.6 percent of those asked replied that Germany would fare worse; 14 percent felt that she would be better off; and fully 31.4 percent answered that they did not know. Regionally the pattern was even more discouraging. For example, in the western states other than the Pacific coast, the answers that Germany would be worse off dropped to 41 percent, and almost half (49.2 percent) of those asked claimed not to know. With the continued successes of German diplomacy in the following four years, and the intensification of Nazi propaganda, the number of convinced antisemites in America, too, grew by leaps and bounds. Only when Germany overreached herself and started World War II did reason, buttressed by the national self-interest of the Allied Powers, begin to reassert itself.

Even then, however, the previous propaganda bore tragic fruits. Because all opponents of German expansion had effectively been denounced as Jewish "warmongers," any effective action by the Allied leaders in behalf of European Jewry was considered diplomatically "unwise." In contrast to World War I, moreover, when influential Jewish communities were found on both sides of the front, the whole Jewish people now supported the Allied cause unquestioningly. Nothing had to be done to capture Jewish good will. In the arena of power politics no greater misfortune can befall a group than being taken for granted.

For these reasons even the Western world stood by passively in the face of one of the starkest tragedies in the history of mankind. Before the outbreak of the war the gullible Western public wishfully believed that the Nazi bark was worse than its bite, and at worst expected the German government to go through the motions of deporting a few Jews to some distant territory like Madagascar. According to Count Galeazzo Ciano, William Phillips, the American Ambassador, approached the Duce on January 3, 1939, on order of President Roosevelt, suggesting the transplantation of German and Austrian Jews to Ethiopia and surrounding colonies.

The Duce [we are told] rejected this proposal, and said that only Russia, the United States and Brazil have the material possibilities for solving the Jewish question, allotting to the Jews a part of their territories. He declared himself favorable to the creation of an independent Jewish state, and in general he promised to support it.

That Mussolini spoke with his tongue in his cheek was doubly evident to one familiar with the story of the various attempts to secure freer admission of Jewish immigrants to the United States during this period. Congress not only refused to relax the rigid immigration laws, but even Senator Robert Wagner's reiterated attempts to secure admission for a specified number of children, particularly orphans, remained without avail. During World War II the administration went through the motions of establishing a War Refugee Board and of sending agents to Turkey and other countries adjacent to Nazi-occupied Europe, in order to salvage prospective victims of Nazi barbarism, but the results of these half-hearted efforts were extremely meager. Only in Italy, Bulgaria, and Denmark, where the local population refused to collaborate with the Nazi *Gauleiters,* did a substantial proportion of the Jewish population survive the Nazi onslaught. In other lands, especially Poland and the Ukraine, the Nazis succeeded in fanning age-old local hatreds, and substantial segments of the population, themselves trodden under the Nazi heel, gladly cooperated with the Nazi extermination squads.

Nor was the reaction of the world's religious bodies to the Nazi attack more direct and consistent. True, both Catholic and Protestant churchmen, even within Germany, early sensed the incompatibility of the new Nazi religion with their traditional faiths. But there were relatively few religious martyrs. Foreign churches were slow in recognizing the peril. At the beginning of the Nazi regime the

Vatican actually concluded with it a Concordat, the first treaty of its kind embracing all of Germany. Only in 1937 did the Papacy realize that Nazism might actually be a more dangerous enemy than communism. It was then that Pope Pius XI, in cooperation with his Secretary of State, Cardinal Pacelli (now Pope Pius XII), composed his famous encyclical, *Mit brennender Sorge*. Here the Papacy protested vigorously against the doctrine of race and "the heresy of speaking of a national God, of a national religion." To convey its ideas to the German Catholics the Papal chancery actually used a subterfuge to smuggle thousands of copies of that circular in diplomatic pouches and to have them distributed to every German parish by young Catholic bicycle-riding priests. On Palm Sunday the Catholic pulpits in the Third Reich resounded with this sharp denunciation of racism. In 1938, the Pope coined his famous epigram that "spiritually we are all Semites." However, the churches did little beyond verbal protestations. Only during the war did individual priests and pastors at great risk to themselves save a number of prospective victims.

Nazism has been defeated; Hitler is dead. But how permanently has that specter been banished from the public life of nations? Historic experience has shown that a career like Hitler's invites emulation. Napoleon Bonaparte was also defeated in the end. Nonetheless, his startling rise to power created in its wake a lot of little Napoleons, including Mussolini and Hitler himself. There always exists the danger that some ambitious young man endowed with a magic appeal to the masses may again utilize the instrumentality of racial antisemitism in his quest for power. The fact that the racial doctrines have been convincingly exploded by all impartial scientists offers little reassurance. Here again, Hitler has taught the effectiveness of the Big Lie. No country can say to itself, "It can't happen here." On the other hand, one would be unjustifiably rash in asserting that "it must happen here." But it would certainly be extremely naïve to look forward to a speedy disappearance of antisemitism from the world scene after it has demonstrably accompanied all Jewish life in the Dispersion for more than two thousand years.

VARIETIES OF JEWISH NATIONALISM

In the early discussions on Jewish nationalism one often heard the heated assertion that the new Jewish national movement was but a reaction to antisemitism. Jewish nationalists often considered such a statement outright slander. They would have been less agitated had they realized that such reactions are historically quite legitimate. After all, antisemitism and its opposite, philosemitism, are to the Jewish people what foreign relations are in the life of nations.

Until the era of emancipation no one doubted the existence of a Jewish nationality. In an era when religious disparity overshadowed all ethnic-cultural differences, Jews were generally considered a separate cultural entity. Under secular modern nationalism, on the other hand, the fiction arose that Jews were nothing but a religious group. The protagonists of this idea forgot that such divorcement of nationality from religion in the Christian world had been the result of a protracted evolution from the Reformation through the American and French Revolutions, the decisive factor being the deadlock of the Wars of Religion. Judaism, which had not gone through that process, would have had to undergo an even greater transformation, since the doctrine of the chosen people and the Jews' physical descent from Abraham, Isaac, and Jacob had always been an integral part of their faith.

Orthodox Jews persisted, therefore, in adhering to their traditional type of nationalism even under the new conditions. For the most part neither the Orthodox masses nor their religious leaders were much interested in philosophic speculations. They rarely devoted much time to analyzing their traditional doctrines in the light of modern conditions and concepts. Only the Western Orthodox and the numerous sympathizers with Orthodoxy among the romantic secularists tried to reformulate the old beliefs in modern terms. Samson Raphael Hirsch had no difficulty in explaining to himself and to his Neo-Orthodox followers the continued existence of a Jewish national feeling based upon the doctrines of the Torah. To men of the type of Isaac Breuer of Frankfort, the Jewish people had always been and would always remain a nationality of its own kind, a *Religionsnation*. Even as a nationality it was dedicated, in his opinion, principally to the cultivation of its religious heritage. The other categories of nationalism such as language, territory, and statehood were decidedly secondary, if not wholly unimportant.

Except for the radical reinterpreters of Judaism in the Reform movement and its allied wings, the doctrine of the chosen people remained a complex problem among Jews themselves as well as in their relations with the Gentile world. Many apologists tried to blunt its edge by numerous variations on essentially the same theme. Perhaps the most eloquent reformulation was offered by Heymann Steinthal, who, together with another loyal Jew, Moritz Lazarus, was the recognized founder of the new discipline of ethnopsychology. Steinthal explained:

We call ourselves the chosen people not in order to indicate the height on which we stand or ever stood, not in order to appear superior to our fellow men, but in order constantly to visualize the chasm separating our reality from the ideal tasks of our morality, the chasm between our shortcomings and the model life sketched for us by the prophets. The ugliness of each act of vulgarity and coarseness shall seem to us more repulsive when we have to admit to its being found in a "kingdom of priests," and even in the virtues which he might feel entitled to claim shall fall short of the demands of a "holy nation."

Such an explanation hardly satisfied even Christian liberals. Nor did it appeal to those Jewish nationalists who were looking for absolute "normalcy," that is, the complete similarity of the Jewish national sentiment with that of other peoples. Yet so overpowering has been that religious heritage going back to the ancient prophets and sages that few secular nationalists could completely divorce themselves from the idea of a Jewish mission. Nor could the ancient messianic idea be completely disposed of. Even a Marxian socialist like Moses Hess could only endeavor to give it a completely secular interpretation when he claimed that "the messianic era is the present age, which began to germinate with the teachings of Spinoza, and finally came into historical existence with the great French Revolution."

Much more significant were the newer brands of Jewish nationalism, which caught the spirit of the modern national movements. Like most contemporary non-Jewish nationalists, the exponents of Jewish ethnic aspirations considered them realizable only through some territorial concentration of Jews which would enable them to pursue their own cultural aims without interference from non-Jewish majorities. Ultimately, as we shall see, these yearnings gave birth to the Lovers of Zion, and finally to the Zionist movement. For a long time, however, these expectations were by no means limited to the Holy Land. Perhaps the earliest dramatic espousal of them was Major Noah's Ararat project in the vicinity of Buffalo. While not devoid of features usually associated with a publicity stunt, that project made an impression even on leading European Jews. Noah made it clear, however, that he did not envisage Ararat as a permanent replacement for the Holy Land. In his "Discourse on the Restoration of the Jews," delivered in New York in 1845, he admitted that all attempts to colonize Jews in other countries had failed and would fail in the future. He merely believed that the United States, which had given Jews equal rights and had never persecuted them, "has been selected and pointedly distinguished in prophecy as *the* nation which, at a proper time, shall present to the Lord his chosen and trodden-down people and pave the way for their restoration to Zion." A European Jew of that very period, on the other hand, advocated large-scale Jewish colonization in North America. In a memorandum submitted in 1832 to the Rothschilds, one Issachar ben Isaac of Hesse suggested such colonization also as a means of relieving the pressures at home. This entire problem of territorialism versus Zionism was to remain a burning issue in the modern Jewish nationalist struggles.

Other voices began to be heard, however, which advocated one or another form of Jewish nationalism without any territorial solution. These ideas germinated in those fateful 1840s when a newly arisen Jewish intelligentsia, culturally if not yet politically emancipated, tried to clarify to itself and to the outside world the puzzling position of the Jews in a modern environment. The Damascus Affair of 1840 had deeply moved even such "assimilated" young Jews as Moses Hess and Ferdinand Lassalle. In his youthful fervor the latter dreamed of organizing a military campaign to take revenge on the persecutors of Jews in the Near East. Soon thereafter the Revolution of 1848 stirred many European nationalities to seek liberation from both absolutism and national oppression. Once again, a characteristic voice was heard in America. An Orthodox rabbi, Isaac Leeser of Philadelphia, keenly awake to the changes in the world affecting the destiny of his people, saw in the new revolutionary trends a great opportunity for the resurrection of the Jewish nation. He wrote in his *Occident:*

> And if ancient Germany again becomes a nation—if Poland throws off successfully the chains of mighty oppressors—if fair Italy takes a rank as one people . . . why should not the patriotic Hebrew also look forward to the time . . . when he may again proudly boast of his own country. . . . Where is the heart that would not swell with a mighty sensation, could he once more see our fair land restored to its former beauty, when . . . the waste cities be built up again, and the son of David rule in righteousness among his equals?

It was not in the United States, however, but in the Hapsburg Empire that these Jewish national aspirations began taking on real flesh and blood. Austria, later Austria-Hungary, was the ideal breeding place for European national ideologies. Like the United States, which had to pioneer in religious liberty because of the presence of many denominations with none in decisive majority, that Central European Empire, especially after its separation from the Germanic Confederation in 1866, could hope to establish peace among its warring nationalities only by a new libertarian approach. Progressive thinkers had already tried to meet that challenge in the new draft constitution submitted in 1848 by the Committee on Constitutional Affairs to the Austrian Parliament in Kremsier, in which Article XXI provided that "every ethnic group has the inviolable right to cultivate its nationality and particularly its language."

Among the most ardent exponents of what we may perhaps call liberty of national conscience was the Jew, Adolf Fischhof. Had the empire listened to his counsel, which was proffered over several decades, it might not only have been a pioneer in the area of national minority rights, but probably also have averted its own ultimate dissolution after World War I.

Fischhof himself did not apply that lesson to the position of the Jewish people. He probably would not have gone the whole length, as did his colleague Goldmark, who in an open session of Austria's Constitutional Assembly exclaimed, "If it be true that we [Jews] are awaiting the coming of a messiah, he must be coming in 1849. If we are no longer oppressed, we need no messiah." Fischhof nonetheless would have subsumed the Jews under the respective nationalities amid which they lived. There were others, however, much closer to the Jewish heritage, who drew their own conclusions. Moses Ehrenreich, a Galician-born rabbi and disciple of Luzzatto, warned that "in our quest for proving ourselves as citizens of the country which we call our Fatherland . . . we must not forget the interests of our nationality." He therefore urged the readers of the leading Viennese Jewish weekly to cultivate Hebrew as their national language. Another member of the same circle, Simon Szanto, suggested the adoption of Jewish national colors, advocating even then the selection of blue and white.

Austria missed this opportunity of establishing national freedom. Hence the remaining decades of its imperial existence were filled with nationalist strife. In the clamor of nationalist claims and counterclaims the Jewish voice, too, was heard, but it was not the single voice of a people, but a true Babel of voices. Some Jews were nationalists, even extreme nationalists, but they professed allegiance to the German, Magyar, Polish, Czech, or other nationality. Yet when the first Austrian parliament, elected by popular franchise, convened in 1907, it included a Jewish "national" club of four members, in addition to many other influential Jewish parliamentarians in the other national or political parties. Ultimately one province, the Bukovina, introduced elections to its provincial diet by national *curiae,* with each nationality guaranteed a certain number of seats. The Jewish nationality was fully recognized by law.

Curiously, in the nearby province of Galicia the dominant Polish majority succeeded in sabotaging such a formal recognition. In order to prevent even indirect acknowledgment of the presence of a Jewish national minority, the administration prohibited the listing of Yiddish as a person's customary language (*Umgangssprache*) in the regular population census of 1910. This struggle had some humorous features, too. Not wishing publicly to advocate a breach of the law, the nationalist leaders called on the Jewish masses to file returns in accordance with *emes* (truth). In one public assembly, the story has it, the district governor, thinking that *emes* meant the Yiddish language, got up and declared, "Several speakers have urged the audience to enter *emes* in the returns. Since *emes* is not recognized in Austria, I adjourn the meeting."

Out of this welter of argument and counterargument emerged that great intellectual élan which endowed the Zionist movement with such outstanding leaders as Theodor Herzl, Max Nordau, Nathan Birnbaum (Matthias Acher), and many others. Equally significant was the redefinition of nationalism advocated by the Austrian socialists, Karl Renner and Otto Bauer, the latter a Jew. Austrian realities defied any objective definition of nationality, since the usual criteria of language, territory, and statehood had to be subjected to numerous qualifications. So a purely subjective definition of nationality was suggested. Nationality was called simply a *Schicksals- und Kulturgemeinschaft*, a community of destiny and culture. The decision whether a particular individual shared past experiences, future destinies, and common cultural interests with a particular group was in the ultimate sense up to him.

Even in monolithic France, advanced students of problems of nationality and race realized that the usual objective definitions could not cover the entire range of historic reality. In his essay on *Qu'est-ce qu'une nation?* (1882), Ernest Renan declared that nationality is but a plebiscite repeated daily. Jews could, of course, participate in such a plebiscite and declare themselves members of a Jewish community of destiny and culture. Their contentions were further reinforced by many doctrines of such leading Western nationalists as Fichte or Fustel de Coulanges. The latter's declaration that "true patriotism is not love of the soil, but love of the past, reverence for the generations which have preceded us," found doubly receptive ears among Jews who could not point to a common territory, state, or even language as their distinguishing characteristic.

At the turn of the century Russian Jews ever more insistently demanded recognition as a national minority. Unlike Austrian Jewry, which had been emancipated since 1867 and faced daily political struggles in and out of Parliament, Russian Jewry was still engaged in hopeless combat for equality of rights against the background of pogroms and the May Laws. In drawing up programs for the future era of equality, therefore, it did not have to impose upon itself the shackles of political realism. Jewish leadership could indulge in maximalist programs, since even minimal demands appeared impossible of attainment.

Emphasizing the failure of Western emancipation to solve the Jewish question definitely, Chaim Zhitlowsky in 1892, and soon thereafter Simon W. Dubnow, formulated their demand for Jewish minority rights supplementing Jewish equality of rights. Being a historian of note, Dubnow buttressed his ideas of Diaspora nationalism by proofs from, and his own reinterpretation of, Jewish history. He believed that the core of Jewish survival through the ages was Jewish communal autonomy, which enabled the Jewish people to determine the course of its evolution under different circumstances and varying environmental pressures. Jewish autonomism became the keynote of his historical outlook as well as of his political demands. Using Hegelian terminology, he argued that before the French Revolution Jews had enjoyed extensive autonomy but no equality. This medieval "thesis" was reversed by the "antithesis" of the emancipation era, namely equality without autonomy. But the time had come, he insisted, for a historic "synthesis" of equal rights plus communal self-government.

A similar program with a proletarian background, first advocated by Zhitlowsky, was gradually adopted by the newly formed and growingly influential Jewish socialist party, the Bund. At first its Marxist international ideology militated against any postulate of Jewish national rights. For a number of years the Bund leaders tried to justify the existence of a separate Jewish party on the purely strategic ground that they could reach the Jewish workers only through the medium of Yiddish. In time, however, more and more Bundists agreed with Juli Martov (Zederbaum) that "a working class which is content with the lot of an inferior nationality will not rise up against the lot of an inferior class. . . . The growth of national and class consciousness must go hand in hand." Against the opposition of the dominant groups in Russian socialism, the Bund insisted more and more vigorously on the separate existence of a Jewish nationality and its right of self-determination in all matters pertaining to culture and education. Ultimately there also emerged a Populist party, led by Noah Prilutski, which went to the extreme of demanding that the new Russian Parliament consist of represent- atives of nationalities. While such joint concerns as foreign policy and defense would transcend nationality lines, these national rep- resentations should play the preeminent role in shaping all other domestic policies. Consistently, they also expected an international extension of that principle. When during World War I the idea of a League of Nations began rapidly gaining world-wide adherents, many Jewish Diaspora nationalists demanded that the League be an association not of sovereign states, but of ethnic cultural nationalities.

The wartime slogans of national self-determination, so prom- inently incorporated in President Wilson's Fourteen Points, seemed to bring these dreams close to realization. In the great semimessianic fervor with which the "war to end wars" was finally concluded, it was readily overlooked that national self-determination was promised only for those areas of Central and Eastern Europe which would lead to the dissolution of the Austro-Hungarian and Ottoman empires, and that it would only affect one formerly Allied country, Russia, which had deserted the Allied camp after the Communist Revolution of 1917. No one seemed seriously to suggest the extension of that principle to the victorious countries as well. At best, one could hope that the clauses providing for minority rights in the newly created, or newly enlarged, countries, from the Baltic to the Aegean Sea, would at some future time be broadened under the sponsorship of the League of Nations to embrace the entire world.

Jewish leaders happened to be in a particularly favorable strategic position to bring about the incorporation of safeguards for national minority rights in the peace treaties of 1919. When the frontiers were redrawn to suit the appetites of the Allied and Associated Powers, hardly any Poles or Czechs were left under foreign domina- tion. They had no interest, therefore, in demanding national minority rights, but on the contrary viewed them as a limitation of their countries' sovereignty. Germans, Austrians, Magyars, and Turks, on the other hand, who saw many of their nationals transferred to alien, even hostile, regimes were members of the defeated alliance of Central Powers and had little influence during the peace negotia- tions. They strained their few remaining resources to wrest from the vindictive Allied statesmen some territorial concessions, in order that fewer of their nationals be surrendered to their enemies. Only Jews were to remain a permanent minority behind all new frontiers. They also possessed in the Western Jewish leaders sufficiently influential spokesmen to persuade the Peace Conference of the desirability of minority rights as a means to pacify the ever disturbed areas of mixed ethnic groups.

It was one of the paradoxes of history that Western Jewish leaders, who would never have dreamed of demanding minority rights within their own countries, became most instrumental in securing the adoption of this revolutionary principle in international law by the world's leading statesmen. Louis Marshall, American Jewry's influential representative in Paris, would have fought tooth and nail any suggestion that American Jewry be treated as a national minority. Yet, he felt that if East European Jews demanded minority rights for themselves, it was his duty to fight for the realization of the principle.

Thus began a long tale of woe, called the system of minority rights during the interwar period. Apart from the Soviet Union, which had voluntarily enacted comprehensive minority legislation, only two countries, Czechoslovakia and Estonia, tried to respect the minority safeguards. Others, especially Poland and Rumania, shirked their responsibilities under one excuse or another. Kemalist Turkey went further. By appointing notables of the Jewish, Greek, and Armenian minorities and calling them to special meetings in which these governmentally appointed leaders solemnly renounced their minority rights, Mustafa Kemal Pasha secured nullification of them. Theoretically, to be sure, even legitimately elected representatives could not have foresworn their rights without the approval of the League of Nations as the guardian of the peace treaties. However, since none of the minorities in the new Republic of Turkey dared to petition the League against infractions of their rights, these remained a dead letter. The League itself, moreover, suffered from a case of bad conscience, for its protracted debates had unmistakably revealed the majority's unwillingness to fulfill the original promise of the universalization of minority rights.

Outside the League membership, too, the idea of national minority rights made little headway. In the United States, Louis Adamic eloquently espoused the idea of this country's being a "nation of nations"—a term first coined by Walt Whitman—but neither his nor any other ethnic group advocated formal, constitutional safeguards for minorities. If I may mention a personal experience, the dichotomy between American and European Jewry never appeared to me more clearly than when the late Professor Dubnow honored me in 1937 by a review of my *Social and Religious History of the Jews*. In his generally sympathetic review, the revered dean of Jewish historians took issue in particular with my failure to demand minority rights for

American Jews. As if there were any shred of feasibility in such a program, or as if American Jews themselves would have supported it!

Experience has shown, moreover, that even in Europe the formal minority safeguards have proved a dismal failure. Perhaps the most dramatic reversal took place in Czechoslovakia after 1945. Its President, Benes, who for some forty years had struggled for minority rights in the old Austro-Hungarian Empire and then in the interwar period had tried loyally to apply that principle in the new republic, now made a complete turnabout. Realizing that minority rights had fostered Sudeten German and Magyar irredentas which had helped plunge his country into utter misery, he and his associates now decided to transform the resurrected Czechoslovakia into a national state. Most Germans and Magyars were expelled, while the Jews were advised by their friend returning from the London Exile that they would either have to choose emigration to Palestine, or else become Czechs by nationality as well. In the Jewish case, for reasons to be discussed in another context, the minority provisions of the Soviet Union had likewise proved ineffective.

Today this problem has become largely academic. The areas of Jewish settlement where the Jews had lived a fairly full national life have been destroyed by Hitler. The struggling groups which have remained alive have either sought to emigrate to Israel or the United States, or else made peace with their Communist rulers and meekly accepted a large measure of denationalization. In the Western countries, Jewish nationalism of that type has gained few adherents even among nationally minded Jews.

Are minority rights, then, to be entirely relegated to the limbo of history? Have the Jews who, early in this century, belonged to the most outspoken, influential theorists of ethnic cultural nationalism now suddenly ceased being a nationality outside Israel? What is the position of Jews behind the Iron Curtain? Or are there forming before our own eyes three distinct types of Jews: the nationals of the State of Israel; the nonreligious national minorities in the Soviet Union and her satellites; and the purely religious nonnational minorities in the Western Hemisphere, the British Empire countries, and elsewhere in the free world? Answers to these perplexing problems can only be given by a fuller understanding of the cultural, religious, socio-economic, and political realities of Jewish life under varying political systems in the world, and particularly of the evolution of Jewish life in both Israel and the United States.

15

THE ENDURING HERITAGE

In common with all other peoples, contemporary Jews are the products of their history. Even those Jews who are unfamiliar with their heritage, or resent it to the extent of wishing to escape it, are the end links of specific chains of historic evolution. Jewish history in its various stages from the Biblical through the Talmudic and medieval periods has created certain problems which required fundamental decisions and these decisions were unaffected even by the breakdown of the ghetto civilization.

A CLASSIC MINORITY

Except for the relatively short period from Judges through the fall of Samaria, and the far briefer span of half a century under the last Maccabeans, the majority of the Jewish people have always lived outside their own country as a struggling minority. This minority status has persisted in modern times. We shall see that as a result of the emancipation crisis the precariousness of minority existence showed itself more plainly, and the establishment of a homeland where at least a segment of the people could live the normal life of a majority became an imperative necessity. Most Jews, however, continued living among the different majorities of the respective countries of their settlement.

It would be nice if Jews could feel that they were just one among many religious minorities. In the United States, religious diversity is fully recognized by law, and by and large accepted by public opinion. We now have in this country some three hundred religious denominations, each claiming, and as far as the law goes enjoying, complete independence. The differences within some major denominations, moreover, often go so far as to approximate sectarian divergences. Certainly, from the legal point of view, Judaism is but such a major denomination with many internal differences among its adherents.

Not in theory, however, and still less in practice, can the Jewish religion be simply equated with any Christian denomination. After all, whether one is a Methodist or a Baptist, an Episcopalian or a Lutheran, even a Catholic or a Greek Orthodox, one still belongs to the great body of the Christian faith and civilization, which has come down the ages in forms often unfriendly to Judaism. One need but consider the observance of Sunday laws to see how meaningful the Lord's Day is to the overwhelming majority of the population, even those nominal Christians who never go to church. As a religious group, the Jewish community does not recognize Sunday as a holy day. And yet, yielding to environmental pressures, most Jews do observe Sunday as a holiday in some fashion or other. At times Jewish religious institutions themselves have been forced to organize special Sunday services which are more than mere weekday services, to provide Sunday schools for children, or to celebrate most religious weddings on Sundays, and so on. The all-embracing character of the Sunday day of rest, with or without the support of governmental blue laws, has resulted in the irony that some Orthodox Jews go to work on Saturdays and rest on Sundays. From the Orthodox point of view, such behavior is a major transgression, one of the capital crimes of Biblical and Talmudic law. In fact, the Jewish Sabbath, with its essential idea of *total* rest, cannot even be compared with the Saturday of the Seventh Day Adventists, or the Friday of the Muslims. The Sabbath idea, which ancient Judaism developed, as far as we can tell, independently of any other religion or civilization—indeed, in defiance of antagonistic governments from Babylonia to Rome—is substantially different from the weekly day of rest celebrated by its daughter religions, and from the various secular days of rest.

True, the Jewish Sabbath has often been honored in the breach in recent years. In its radical departures from the established Jewish law, Reform Judaism has altered the character of the Sabbath, either eliminating or tempering some of its stringent legal prohibitions. Even so the Reform Sabbath is fundamentally different from the Lord's Day. It is no denial of the Judeo-Christian foundations of our civilization to point out that there are certain fundamental differences between Judaism and Christianity, differences which far transcend those between the Christian denominations.

Of course, there are also Muslims, Buddhists, and adherents of other non-Christian religions, whose divergences from the Christian tradition are as great as, or greater than, the Jewish. In modern times, moreover, both agnosticism and militant atheism have become such formidable powers that an alliance of all religious groups against them has become imperative. Facing a common enemy, the different religions have rightly toned down their divisions and emphasized their similarities. But it would be rash to overlook these divisions, which are especially likely to make themselves felt at critical moments.

For example, there is the Passion of Christ as told in the Gospels. These accounts have deeply envenomed Judeo-Christian relations for the last nineteen centuries. Liberal churchmen and teachers may try to play them down, yet the fact remains that the Gospels are Sacred Scripture to untold millions, and their simple meaning cannot easily be interpreted away. No one can tell how important a role the story of ancient Jewry's part in the Passion of Christ still plays in antisemitism today. Psychological studies of the effects of Sunday school teachings on adult life have been inconclusive. But it stands to reason that a story heard or read time and again in childhood and after cannot but leave a permanent mark. And the prejudices thereby created always stand ready to be mobilized.

Gone is the time when educators and publicists believed that there were easy correctives for such heritages of ancient bigotry. We have all come to learn the overwhelming force of irrational motives in individuals, and still more in groups. This is not to say that antisemitism cannot be combated, in some measure at least, through long-range education. But education, however prolonged or effective, is not likely to stamp out completely hostilities that have so protracted a history. The other factors in antisemitism, economic, social, and cultural, only tend to reinforce the religious animosities. Of course, the right of each man to adhere to his own convictions is fundamental to democratic coexistence. It is easy for a nonbeliever to be religiously tolerant, and today many Jews as well as non-Jews are not real believers even though they may attend religious services. Yet there remains the majority for whom their religious tradition means a great deal and who are neither saintly enough nor historically minded enough to appreciate a faith other than their own. In practice what tolerance usually comes to is a sort of enforced forbearance toward differences which one cannot help, but which one heartily dislikes. Even in those persons who are essentially indifferent in matters of religion, old atavisms well up in periods of great emotional stress or social crisis.

In short, as a result of a long historic evolution, the Jews constitute, even in the period of emancipation, a distinct and distinguishable group within the non-Jewish societies. Our easygoing age is not marked by the tragic sense of life, or a feeling for those fateful heritages that are consciously or unconsciously carried down the ages by groups of human beings. It is both the strength and weakness of religions that they are at once the most enduring as they are the most divisive factors in human civilization. Whenever group conflicts are fired by sectarian fanaticism, they are likely to break out into an all-consuming conflagration. In quieter periods they may be held under control, even thrust underground. But they cannot simply be conjured out of existence by any amount of reasoned argument.

VARIETIES OF RELIGIOUS ADJUSTMENT

Nevertheless, the emancipation era has brought about many adjustments in the field of Jewish religion. Students have dealt dramatically with the effect upon traditional concepts of Biblical criticism, of the philosophic teachings of Spinoza, and of the school of Mendelssohn. But of equal, perhaps even greater, significance were the social developments that affected the masses. The very force of the Enlightenment stemmed from the widespread rejection of the traditional modes of living by certain classes of the population. Even if these classes at first formed only a minority in their respective communities, they had an economic and intellectual influence often out of proportion to their numbers. As the traditional patterns of Judaism disintegrated, new rationales emerged, and those in turn stimulated still further changes.

In Italy and Holland as far back as the seventeenth century, voices demanding change were heard with ever greater insistence. By 1770 an anonymous writer (Mordecai van Aron de Pinto) demanded the abolition of the Sabbath and holidays for economic reasons. He argued that the observance of these Jewish days of rest entailed the loss of too many working days in business and greatly increased household expenses. Others demanded the relaxation of the ritual food commandments, as being particularly objectionable during extensive business trips and as a stumbling block in the growing social intercourse with non-Jews. Of greater significance than these occasional outbursts were the changes in life, such as the growing disregard of the Sabbath rest and ritual food commandments, that were taking place in certain circles of upper Jewish society and even among simple workingmen. The enhanced position of women in the upper bourgeoisie and nobility of France and Germany had repercussions in the Jewish community as well, where women often enjoyed educational opportunities that were not always open to men. It was considered perfectly legitimate to give daughters instruction in foreign languages and general sciences, whereas men's education was limited to the Talmudic fields. At times a highly educated or even half-educated woman looked down upon her Talmudically learned but unworldly and linguistically limited husband. Many of these women brought up on Enlightenment literature despised the traditional Jewish mores and helped undermine the allegiance of their children to the Jewish heritage.

Even within the synagogue reformatory trends appeared among the worshipers before they appeared among their leaders. The growing dissolution of communal controls and the lessening prestige of the rabbi and scholar, in a society increasingly dominated by prosperous but unlearned businessmen, robbed Hebrew learning of its predominance. Even in the traditional community there had been a revolt of the unlearned against the rabbinic hegemony which took the form of the Hasidic movement. In the West the revolt stemmed from the upper classes, who were no longer Rabbinically learned, nor admirers of such learning.

Accordingly the demand for synagogue services and sermons in the vernacular became more and more frequent. Although scholars might point to Talmudic precedents for preaching and reciting prayers in any familiar tongue, the use of German, for example, in Central and Eastern Europe—except Italy—was considered a radical innovation. Again, the great informality of Orthodox congregations was compared with services in Christian churches and condemned for being indecorous. Still more radical was the demand for the artistic enhancement of Jewish services through use of the organ. To conservatives such an innovation on Sabbaths and holidays was a desecration. Ultimately men and women began praying together, although the family pew became a major issue only in the middle of the nineteenth century.

All these socially potent factors were reinforced by the newer trends in Jewish philosophy and theology. Many young intellectuals who had gained access to secular learning began to view Judaism through the eyes of their non-Jewish neighbors. Plagued by a feeling of inferiority, they either abandoned their faith or sought out apologias for it. Disturbing, too, was the charge of excessive Jewish "legalism." In Central Europe, especially, many thoughtful young Jews were impressed by the attacks on religious tradition stemming from Voltaire and the Enlightenment generally. Still others came under the sway of Hegelian philosophy. In either case, they reached the conclusion that the Jewish religion demanded excessive subjection to the yoke of traditional law, so that that yoke ought to be lightened and the individual given greater freedom and discretion in his religious observances.

Rigid communal controls also evoked sharp opposition. Zalkind Hurwitz, an influential publicist of the early period of the French Revolution, was particularly vehement in denouncing the supremacy of the rabbis in the Jewish community. Even before July 14, 1789, he considered the reduction of rabbinical powers a prime requisite for the moral and political regeneration of the Jewish people. The Revolution, at least in its more moderate period, before the proclamation of the Religion of Reason, gave him the opportunity to propagate this idea throughout France and wherever French was read. And the repressive measures employed by the existing communal organs added fuel to the accusations. When, in 1824, twelve members of the congregation Beth Elohim in Charleston, South Carolina, submitted a memorial to the vestry demanding reforms in the existing ritual, they were rebuked by the elders without further discussion. Thereupon they organized the Reformed Society of Israelites, the first Reform group in the United States. Although short-lived, this organization was portentous of things to come. In England, too, the organization of a West End Synagogue in London in 1840 with a moderate Reform program evoked sharply repressive measures, even actual excommunication, on the part of the Chief Rabbinate and the United Synagogue. On the other hand, in Germany the activities of reformers often met with the encouragement of the communal elders and governments. In the newly created kingdom of Westphalia, under Napoleon Bonaparte's brother Jerome, an influential leader, Israel Jacobson, became a lay pracher, and a protagonist in revamping the synagogue liturgy. He was followed by the elders of the leading community of Hamburg, many of whom accepted without demur Gotthold Salomon's revised prayer book of 1819.

The Hamburg ritual evoked widespread controversy throughout Central Europe and also attracted the attention of Jews in other countries.

From these early beginnings grew a powerful Reform movement which reached its acme in Germany in the middle of the nineteenth century, and in the United States several decades later. It was easy for opponents to equate emancipation and reformation. The distinguished Moravian Talmudist, Mordecai Banet, not only condemned the Reform prayers as sinful, but declared that the sole purpose of Reform was "to curry favor with Christians." This was an overstatement certainly. Of course, the quest for equality of rights strengthened the forces making for the integration of Jews into Western society. By removing many of the "segregationist" laws, Reform facilitated closer social and cultural relations with the Gentile world, and promoted political as well as cultural emancipation. Yet there is no reason to doubt the reiterated disclaimers of Abraham Geiger and other leading reformers that they were moved by any but religious considerations. As we have seen, demands for religious Reform preceded political emancipation. Indeed behind these demands were the same social forces that shaped cultural and economic emancipation during the seventeenth and eighteenth centuries. At the same time one need not deny the impact of the struggle for emancipation upon the thought of ordinary Westernized Jews whose outlook was uncomplicated by theological nuances.

The extent of Reform varied. Extreme reformers like the members of the Frankfort Reform Society in the 1840s, and later Felix Adler in New York, rejected even circumcision. To Adler, at that time a professor of philosophy at Columbia University and soon thereafter founder of the Ethical Culture movement, this ritual appeared as "simply barbarous in itself and utterly barbarous and contemptible in its origin." Coming from a former rabbinical student and son of the leading Reform rabbi, Samuel Adler, this declaration called forth sharp condemnation even from Isaac Mayer Wise, one of the recognized leaders of the Reform movement, who dismissed Adler as an "unknown little Professor of Semitic languages." The issue was debated time and again in both Germany and America. Yet circumcision has remained the accepted form of admission to the Covenant of Abraham among the overwhelming majority of Reform Jews.

On the other hand, few reformers entertained the same scruples about other provisions of Talmudic law, especially those relating to the Sabbath commandment or to ritually permissible food. In their excessive zeal, opponents of Reform made the frequent mistake of equating Reform with Karaism, because of the reverence of both for the Bible. But while Karaites repudiated Talmudic law, they adhered all the more rigidly to Biblical law, which they reinterpreted in terms of their own growing body of Oral Law. Reform, on the other hand, was perfectly prepared to disregard Biblical command-ments as well, in so far as these no longer suited modern conditions or needs. It was felt that so long as a Jew adhered to the main religious and ethical postulates of the ancient prophets, he was free to subject the Bible itself to searching scholarly criticism and to dis-regard all those legal requirements set down in Scripture because of special historical reasons. Once again opponents saw in this effort but a method of reducing Judaism to a shadow of itself, so that it would no longer be an obstacle to complete assimilation. Yet there is no reason to believe that such were the motives of the leading Reform theologians. Emil G. Hirsch, the son of another prominent Reform rabbi, Samuel Hirsch, and himself a leading American preacher, succinctly stated:

> My Radicalism—and it is that which I imbibed at the feet of my own father and teacher, and found in the instruction of my master Geiger, both of blessed memory, the Radicalism of Einhorn and Samuel Adler —intends to be more Jewish than ever was official orthodoxy. We hunger for more Judaism, not for less of it. If we lay little stress upon ceremony, it is because we do not regard with Paul, Judaism to be a dead Law. The law we believe in accordance with the results of modern criticism to be of non-Jewish origin. Judaism stands for ideas. . . . Into the non-Jewish symbol or custom the Jewish spirit poured its golden wine and thus made even the symbol speak of the nobler view.

The fact is that the life of a pious Reform Jew is as demanding as that of an Orthodox Jew.

Because of its underlying individualism and its preachment of individual conscience, reminiscent somewhat of Protestantism, Re-form was in danger of splitting up into a variety of mutually ex-clusive sects. That danger existed even in Germany, where a measure of communal unity was guaranteed by public law. In order to meet the danger, the leaders of Reform tried to unite the various factions in special rabbinical conferences or mixed lay and rabbinical synods. The early conferences of Brunswick, Frankfort, and Breslau in the 1840s, and the two great synods of Leipzig and Augsburg in 1869 and 1871, made history far beyond the confines of the Germanic Confederation. There the major issues were thrashed out with such thoroughness that in the following six decades, until the rise of

Nazism, little of fundamental importance was added to the theory and practice of Reform.

In America, on the other hand, the danger of anarchy was doubly great because of the newness of most communities, their lack of traditional roots, and the total noninterference of the government under a system of separation of state and church. For a while it looked as if every Reform congregation would represent a different wing of the movement. Certainly almost every Reform rabbi of the latter part of the nineteenth century considered it incumbent upon himself to produce a prayer book of his own. It was owing to a large extent to the great organizing ability of Isaac Mayer Wise, together with the distinguished theological thinking of David Einhorn, that the American Reform movement achieved a certain singleness of purpose and organizational solidarity. For the past eight decades the Union of American Hebrew Congregations, the Central Conference of American Rabbis, and Hebrew Union College (more recently joined by the Jewish Institute of Religion) have given the movement a definitive sense of direction. Through the democratic processes of debate, majority and minority votes, congregational autonomy, and respect for centralized leadership, the movement was able to absorb a variety of approaches and adjust itself to speedily changing needs. In the twentieth century the American branch has exerted a powerful influence on Reform movements all over the world. With the aid of German leadership, it helped organize also a World Union for Progressive Judaism, which has served as an important sounding board for Reform ideas in various countries.

Curiously, despite the fervor of theological debate the difference between Reform and traditionalism goes much less deep in the realm of religious fundamentals than in that of ritualistic practice. One obvious explanation is the fact that Judaism has always placed far less emphasis upon the dogmatic elements than upon the way of life. Until Maimonides no one had even attempted to formulate clearly the beliefs which were to be considered binding on every Jew. Even the so-called 613 commandments of Judaism were never enumerated in any uniform fashion; in medieval times rabbis were still debating which regulations were to be subsumed under the total of 365 prohibitions and 248 positive commandments. The dogmatic teachings formulated in Maimonides' famous thirteen principles, although recited daily by many an Orthodox Jew in his prayer, *Ani Maamin,* have not been universally accepted. Two centuries later Hisdai Crescas reduced them to a total of six or seven principles, while Joseph Albo, Crescas' pupil, reduced them to three altogether. Taking Albo's classification as a basis, Professor Samuel S. Cohon has rightly emphasized that Reform Judaism believes in all these three principles, including the "stems" derived from them, and only repudiates a number of further subdivisions, which Albo calls "branches." The principles and "stems" accepted by Reform consist of the following: (1) God's existence including His unity, incorporeality, timelessness, and perfection; (2) revelation, including prophecy and the prophet's perfection; and (3) retribution, including God's omniscience and providence. Among the "branches" which appear questionable are: creation *ex nihilo,* Moses' rank above other prophets, eternity of Torah, human perfectibility through the fulfillment of commandments, resurrection, and the doctrine of the Messiah.

Perhaps the sharpest controversy arose over the messianic doctrine. Here the early Reformer's antinationalism came clearly to the fore. Apart from spiritual objections to the idea of a physical redeemer, Reformers objected to the restoration of the Jews to Zion as a necessary prerequisite for ultimate redemption. Many of them believed that the messianic future was to be brought about gradually by the realization of Israel's prophetic ideals through the persistent efforts of believers in ethical monotheism. Because of these efforts the Jewish community, happily and permanently living in the various countries of its dispersion, was to be the true Messiah. Likewise the Hebrew language was to play but a secondary role. For these reasons the early Reform prayer books almost invariably eliminated references to a personal Messiah or restoration to Zion, and reduced the Hebrew prayers and Scriptural recitations to a minimum.

Under the impact of the growing Zionist movement, however, there has been a steady decline in the antirestoration sentiments of the Reform laity, and even more of the Reform rabbinate. We shall see that in the political struggles of the day the anti-Zionist stand of most Reform bodies was maintained through the period of the Balfour Declaration and the establishment of a Mandate in 1922, but underwent abatement in the later 1920s. In the 1930s most Reform rabbis and laymen became firm pro-Zionists. Spiritually, too, there has been a growing recognition of the yearning for the restoration to Zion as a significant ingredient of the Jewish faith. Beginning with the inclusion of the national anthem, *Hatikvah,* in the Union hymnal, which was adopted by the Central Conference of American Rabbis in 1930, this reevaluation has made steady progress. More recently, this change in point of view became embroiled in the political controversy which gave birth to the American Council for Judaism. But majority Reform opinion has resumed much of the traditional coloring.

In general, Reform has become less and less militant in recent decades. Its greatest strength always lay in countries with a powerful Protestant tradition. Next to Germany and the United States, it flourished especially in the Scandinavian countries, and to a lesser extent in Hungary, with its strong Protestant minority. Wherever Catholicism was dominant Reform made little headway. France, Belgium, Italy, and Austria had few, if any, Reform congregations. In Poland, the Catholicism of the majority combined with the strong nationalist sentiments of the Jewish minority to reduce Reform trends to a minor public role. The same is true of the Greek Orthodox countries and in some measure even of England, where the established Church retained much of its Catholic tradition. Under Islam, finally, there were neither the spiritual nor social preconditions for the growth of the Reform movement.

There has been little demand for religious reform in Israel, which is not surprising. The population has been mostly recruited from Eastern Europe or the Muslim lands, so that what Reform congregations exist were established by the relatively few German and American settlers. Their recognition has become a major public issue, for since the Turkish period many areas of civil law, including marriage, divorce, and inheritance, have been determined by the religious laws, and administered by the religious authorities of the respective denominations. The chief rabbinates of the Ashkenazic and Sephardic communities have been recognized by the law of the land (Ottoman, British-Mandatory, or Israeli) as supreme in these spheres. They have consistently denied recognition to non-Orthodox rabbis as organs of such religious administration. Vigorously as the American Reform rabbinate has protested against this discriminatory policy, and much as the socialist majority has resented such encroachments of the synagogue on the state, this legal tradition of many decades has been successfully upheld by the strong and unwavering support of the Orthodox minority.

Publicists and historians have often spoken of the "petrification" of modern Orthodoxy. Viewing all Jewish history in terms of intellectual development, they claim that rabbinic scholarship reached its zenith in the sixteenth or seventeenth centuries, and that what followed was merely derivative. In their opinion this decline in intellectual vigor testifies to the drying up of the creative mainsprings of Rabbinic Judaism. While Orthodoxy may still carry on for some years, they say, it is bound ultimately to lose out in the struggle with the new creative forces in religion and society.

Such an analysis is evidently one-sided. To begin with, there is no way of measuring human creativity, nor the energy that goes into producing monuments of scholarship. If there were a machine that gauged the brain power of individuals, it might have shown that one or another nineteenth-century rabbi had greater mental energy than many a medieval *gaon* or modern philosopher or scientist. If Immanuel Kant in Koenigsberg, Karl Marx in London, and Sigmund Freud in Vienna left a permanent imprint on human civilization, this by itself is no evidence of superior mental capacity. Their greater influence may have been due mainly to the different subject matter with which they dealt and the range of interest of the public to whom they appealed. Nor is there any objective criterion of "originality." In modern times originality has come to be measured by the extent to which the scholar, writer, or artist departs from accepted views. In medieval civilizations generally that type of originality was frowned upon: it was considered heretical, subversive of the established order. Certainly such great men as Avicenna, Maimonides, and Thomas Aquinas would have repudiated any suggestion that they were introducing "innovations" into the established system of doctrine, ethics or law. The most creative and most widely honored contributions of that time consisted precisely in reformulating established systems in such a fashion as to meet new intellectual and social needs. The same thing holds true for rabbinic learning throughout the ages. Bound by tradition, it developed through a process of interpretation and reinterpretation that constantly brought learning up to date and whetted the speculative appetites of students and masters.

Nor was there any "petrification" with respect to the learned man's emotional attachment to his studies. Using as a criterion only the student's deep concern for learning, one may readily assert that an old-type yeshiba *bahur* considered his Talmudic *pilpul* (dialectic) —what he called "living waters"—with greater zeal than is displayed by the vast majority of American university students even in such "exciting" departments as physics. It would hardly make sense to declare on that account that physics, medicine, law, or sociology is a "petrified" subject. One wonders how many modern university students would, unless faced with examinations, spend the entire night from Thursday to Friday in going over the week's lessons. Yet just this was the habit in the *bet ha-midrash,* which existed in many Jewish communities till recent times, not to mention the enormous financial sacrifices attendance at yeshibot entailed, the sleeping on hard synagogue benches and getting along on a starvation diet—all for the sake of the acquisition of that "petrified" learning.

The productivity of rabbinic scholars remained extremely high down to the end of East European Jewry during the Hitler era. In the years 1938 and 1939, on the eve of its great tragedy, Polish Jewry produced a formidable number of books in such traditional rabbinic fields as Law, Aggada, Kabbala, and Hasidism, together with traditional commentaries on the Bible. The impressive thing is that Polish Jewry, harassed politically and economically, and linguistically divided into Hebrew, Yiddish, and Polish reading groups, was yet able to produce in those two years more works of the kind just mentioned than were produced in any two decades of the seventeenth century, when rabbinic learning was in its heyday all over the world. Apart from quantity, moreover, many of these works were distinguished for their quality. If they had been written a thousand years earlier they would now be counted among the revered classics of Jewish literature. And the same thing may be said of some of the numerous rabbinic works which have appeared in the United States during the last decade.

Rabbinic learning has been the matrix of all Jewish intellectual pursuits even during the last few generations. A Polish Jewish labor leader once voted in favor of a large appropriation for a local yeshiba, explaining to an amazed inquirer that out of that yeshiba would come the future leaders of the Socialist Bund. It is a matter of record that most of the Hebrew and Yiddish writers and scholars, as well as a great many Zionist and socialist leaders, received their early training in one or another field of rabbinics. Not that this influence of rabbinics on all Jewish life was accepted without question. Hasidism, that great revolt against rabbinic hegemony, proclaimed the primacy of good deeds and pious living over the intellectual attainments of rabbinism. Israel Baal Shemtob, "the Besht," himself not a learned man according to customary definitions, in many respects led this revolt of the half-learned or illiterate masses. His type of learning was emotional rather than intellectual. His leading disciple, Baer of Meserich, claimed that Israel "taught me the language of the birds and of the trees. He revealed to me the secrets of the saints and the magic spells. He led me into the book *Mayene ha-hokhmah* [Source of Wisdom] and explained every letter to me." Nevertheless, rabbinism itself soon conquered the Hasidic leadership. Baer, the great Maggid, was a distinguished rabbinic scholar. In his homilies, which attracted pupils from all over Poland, he combined much traditional learning with old and new ethical teachings. Rabbinically trained also was the great mystic Solomon Zalman of Ladi, founder of the important Hasidic movement of Habad. He finally produced a new *Shulhan Arukh* of his own in order to bring rabbinic learning up to date, and insisted that Jews continue studying the Talmud as intensely as ever. He ordered every congregation to organize adult study groups which, by assigning different Talmudic tractates to individual members, would collectively complete the study of the entire Talmud in the course of each year.

At the same time Hasidism injected new elements, or at least a new intensity, into the concern with spiritual matters among the masses of Orthodox Jewry. Many, indeed, were the Hasidim who took literally such advice as that given by the Besht in his alleged testament:

> Every man must devote all his capabilities to the service of God, for all things are intended to serve God. Under no circumstances of life must this service be intermitted. For instance, a man may be walking and talking with other men, and he cannot then be studying the Torah. None the less must he on those occasions cleave close to God, in full consciousness of His uniqueness. Or the man may be on a journey, and thus unable to pray in his usual fashion. At such times he must find a mode of service other than prayer.

Even today, living in the materialistic environment of New York City, there are numerous Hasidim to whom deep spiritual preoccupations are not just a matter of fine words or a theatrical pose.

Of course, like every other human institution, Hasidism as it came into contact with the hurly-burly of life degenerated from its original purity. The idea of the zaddik, especially, of a charismatic mediator between the Deity and the masses of his followers, lent itself to innumerable abuses. Zaddikism itself could become a mere worldly career. Once established, the movement became as reactionary as it had once been revolutionary, and opposed all further changes in the Jewish outlook. The quarrels among the Hasidim themselves injected another divisive force into the Jewish community. Geographically the movement was limited to Poland and its appeal elsewhere was only to immigrant groups from Eastern Europe. If today it plays a considerable role in Israel or the United States—and has nuclei in the ghettos of London and Paris—it is only among first-generation immigrants.

The spiritual impact of Hasidism has been enormous. Even the opposition of old Rabbinic Judaism did not save it from coming under the influence of certain Hasidic approaches, which led to the re-emphasis upon long-accepted mystical and ethical teachings. For example, the Musar (Ethical Behavior) movement, associated especially with the name of Israel Salant of Lithuania, went back to the ethical teachings of such classical writers as Bahya ibn Pakuda or Israel ibn al-Naqawa, which were given new meaning and intensity under the stimulus of the spiritual message of Hasidism. Musar classes came to be a common feature of the Lithuanian and other yeshibot. Even secular writers in both Hebrew and Yiddish developed a romantic leaning toward Hasidic teachings. In the works of Micah Joseph Berdichevsky, particularly, despite their Nietzschean tendency, Hasidism assumed a Western garb. Yitzhok Leib Peretz retold Hasidic tales with such artistic effect that they appealed even to the most secularized readers. Through the works of Martin Buber, Hasidism, at least in its so-called neo-Hasidic garb, has entered the realm of Western theology. Combined with Buber's own philosophy of religion, Hasidism has elicited considerable interest among non-Jews. Nevertheless, in its original form Hasidism was, and remains, a variant of Jewish Orthodoxy. Whether Hasidic or Mitnagdic (anti-Hasidic) Orthodox Judaism has continued to pursue its millennial career along traditional lines.

The emancipation era was another major influence on the Orthodox camp. Apart from its great losses to other Jewish movements, both religious and secular, Orthodoxy was confronted with the challenge to its own ways of thought and life. Not surprisingly, German Orthodoxy, in the overheated atmosphere of the struggle for emancipation, was the first to look for spiritual answers to the new conditions that arose from Jewish equality. In contrast to the Reform leadership, which advocated the abandonment of many traditional forms in favor of integration, Samson Raphael Hirsch and his successors, especially among the Breuer family, preached unflinching adherence to all traditional commandments. At the same time they were prepared to make concessions in the theoretical realm, so long as these left religious fundamentals unaffected. In his apologia for the traditional faith Hirsch made use of the teachings of the then universally revered German critical philosophy. This approach figures in his influential *Nineteen Letters of Ben Uzziel,* as in his other writings, and also in the journal, *Der Israelit,* which he founded in Frankfort.

This brand of Orthodoxy differed greatly from that prevailing in Eastern Europe. There the very study of the German language, or of modern philosophy, was shunned by Orthodox rabbis and their followers. Entrenched in their traditional mode of living and little affected by the struggle for emancipation, which in the Tsarist realm was not to become a reality until 1917, Eastern Orthodoxy was prepared to repudiate all secular studies. Yet Neo-Orthodoxy, with all its secular orientation, resembled the old in its unwavering adherence to all the commandments. Indeed, precisely because the continuance of the traditional Jewish mode of living was so much more difficult in the assimilatory German environment, Neo-Orthodoxy often developed a certain rigidity and artificiality, which appeared incongruous to Eastern Orthodoxy.

In spite of their differences, both wings of Orthodoxy were prepared to collaborate on all issues affecting world Jewry, especially in the area of politics. In 1911, the Agudas Israel was organized under the leadership of German Orthodoxy, but with the cooperation of many Eastern rabbis and laymen. True, even this organization was too radical a departure for extremists of the kind represented by the Hasidic chieftains of Belz in Poland. But a substantial number of the Orthodox now saw the merits of organization for the pursuit of their domestic as well as international aims. In Palestine, Orthodoxy entered fully into partisan politics and, highly intransigent, often succeeded in imposing its will upon the majority parties.

The influence of modern secularism and emancipation was felt even in communities which nominally retained the character of the old ghetto life. In interwar Poland the Orthodox group succeeded in persuading the Pilsudski regime to include in the communal statute a provision that any person failing to observe Jewish law could be eliminated from communal membership. These artificial supports failed to impress the public, however. The opposition saw in them nothing but political moves to get rid of unwelcome antagonists. In the long run such antics lost Orthodoxy adherents in its own group, and helped pave the way for the victory of the radical labor parties in the Jewish communal elections in 1936.

In the United States the great problem is the general superficiality of Orthodox allegiance. Many so-called Orthodox Jews are outright sinners before the Law, breaking the Sabbath rest commandment, taking lightly the dietary provisions, neglecting their stated prayers, and generally living in a way which would have appeared as an abomination to their East European ancestors. When rumors of the prevailing religious laxity in America reached the Eastern European rabbinate in the nineteenth century, some of them—as for example, Israel Meir ha-Kohen, author of the famous ethical treatise *Hafes Hayyim*—took a stand against the immigration of Jews to the United States. Israel Meir, it is reported, long refused to take leave of friends and relatives prior to their "treasonable" departure overseas. Because of pogroms which made emigration imperative in the 1880s, the rabbi changed his mind and unbent sufficiently to suggest certain minor alleviations in the religious observance of American immigrants, without for a moment allowing the same tolerance at home. Once in this country, however, most immigrants showed little respect for religious scruples. Even if they did not belong to the substantial socialist or anarchist groups, they either threw overboard the entire burden of the Law or made all sorts of compromises to suit their own convenience.

It is extremely difficult to assess the numerical strength of Orthodoxy in America, as in other countries of the Dispersion. The preponderant majority of Jewish congregations in the United States are no doubt at least nominally Orthodox, but not even their number is known exactly, much less the size of their membership or the extent of their religious conformity in and outside the synagogue. Yet we may say that Orthodoxy is stronger today in the United States and Western Europe than it has been for several decades past.

Like Neo-Orthodoxy, the Conservative movement began as a response to the challenge of Reform, and even more to those fundamental social and cultural factors underlying Reform itself. Limited largely to Germany and the United States, Conservatism must not be mixed up with, for example, the so-called *status quo* communities in Hungary. The latter merely succeeded in avoiding the split between Reform and Orthodoxy, and in maintaining the old unitarian community. Neither the beginnings of the Conservative movement, or as it was called in Germany, the positive-historical school, nor its philosophy have ever been clearly delineated. Zacharias Frankel lost sympathy with the increasingly radical Reform movement, and in a dramatic move seceded from the Rabbinic Conference of Frankfort in 1845. But he had no sooner published his famous treatise on the methodology of the Mishna than he was sharply attacked by Samson Raphael Hirsch for his critical approach to that matrix of Talmudic law. Trying to steer a middle course, Frankel and his associates founded the Jewish Theological Seminary of Breslau and issued a scholarly periodical, the *Monatsschrift*. For nearly ninety years the Breslau seminary was a major center of Jewish scholarship, and under the leadership of Frankel and Graetz became the fountainhead of the Conservative rabbinate in Central Europe. In the United States the transition from modern Orthodoxy to Conservatism and from Conservatism to moderate Reform was often so blurred that it is not easy to classify such leading nineteenth-century rabbis as Isaac Leeser, Marcus Jastrow, and Benjamin Szold. As the founder of the Jewish Theological Seminary in 1888, Sabbato Morais may, if only on that account, be definitely considered an early leader of the Conservative movement. With the assumption by Solomon Schechter of the presidency of the seminary in 1901, the movement underwent a still further development.

It is the strength as well as weakness of Conservatism that it tries to mediate between extremes. If one fancied Hegelian categories, one might interpret the modern evolution of Jewish religion in terms of thesis, antithesis, and synthesis. The thesis, old Orthodoxy, generated the antithesis, Reform, while Conservatism represents the synthesis of the two. But this middle position often meant wavering between one extreme and the other, and imposed restraints on any attempt to define principles. Such reluctance, to be sure, is characteristic of all Judaism. Orthodoxy itself never agreed upon a system of dogmas and beliefs, although its general outlook appears unmistakably in the classical literature from the Talmudic age down. Reform in both Germany and the United States tried on several occasions to formulate its credo, but even the so-called Pittsburgh Program of 1885 never enjoyed more than limited acceptance in the Reform camp, and has since largely been discarded in the progress of Reform ideology. Nevertheless, even compared with Orthodox and Reform theology, Conservative thought is much less definitive.

Conservatism shares with Reform the belief in freedom of thought and in the importance of critical investigation of the historic documents of Judaism, while it shares with Orthodoxy the belief in the substantial validity of the traditional law and ritual. More than either Orthodoxy or Reform, it professes genuine reverence for history, not only for traditions, but institutions. Characteristic of Conservative utterances are the "views on the synod" expressed by Schechter at a time when the convocation of a synod of rabbis and laymen was one of the most heatedly debated issues in the American rabbinate. Schechter declared:

> If the synod should become a blessing, it must first recognize a standard of authority, and this can be no other than the Bible, the Talmud and the lessons of Jewish history as to the vital and the essential in Judaism. When, for instance, history testifies that Judaism was prepared to suffer martyrdom rather than give up the Sabbath and the Abrahamitic rite, we know that their abolition would mean death to Israel.

Perhaps because of this attachment to history, the Conservative movement waxed in strength with the rise of Jewish nationalism and Zionism. Even in Germany, the anti-Herzlian *Protestrabbiner* were recruited largely from the Orthodox and Reform groups, whereas the Conservatives were more sympathetic to Herzlian ideas. For example, Heinrich Graetz, after a trip to Palestine, became quite friendly to the Lovers of Zion movement long before the Basel Congress. With numerous theological reservations, Schechter, too, was essentially pro-Zionist. As the movement gathered momentum in the twentieth century, Conservatism became ever more staunchly Zionist. With few exceptions the Rabbinical Assembly of the Jewish

Theological Seminary fought valiantly for Zionist principles and policies. And many thoughtful nationalists joined the Conservative camp, especially its Reconstructionist wing.

Theologically, the Reconstructionist Mordecai M. Kaplan went further than most of his Conservative colleagues in postulating, much in the manner of Reform, considerable freedom to modify the existing rituals. But bred on the national doctrines and revering historical institutions, he and his associates have stood for adherence to the commandments as time-honored Jewish "folkways." At the same time Reconstructionism has been awake to American realities. It has advocated the adaptation of these "folkways" and of Conservative thought generally to American ways of thinking. Shunning the use of the phrase Jewish nation, as misleading within the framework of the American idiom and national outlook, the Reconstructionists called for the recognition of Judaism as a religious civilization which embraces much more than religious beliefs or rituals. On the international level, they have evinced considerable attachment to Ahad Haam's idea of a Jewish cultural center in the Palestinian homeland.

Notwithstanding all this, Reconstructionism has refrained from laying down formal principles for its adherents. Like the rest of the Conservative movement, it has allowed great leeway, both practical and theoretical, to each congregation. The difficulty has been not its intellectual, but its emotional emphasis. It has been more like a theological school, appealing to a select number of thoughtful students, than a sectarian trend enlisting mass support. Nevertheless, it has introduced new elements into the Conservative movement as a whole and has also influenced the thought of not a few Orthodox and Reform leaders.

With the progressive rapprochement of the various religious wings of American Jewry, Conservatism has made more progress in recent years than either Orthodoxy or Reform. It has often managed to unify whole communities on a middle-of-the-road religious basis. The responsiveness of Conservatism to the differing demands of its constituencies has been facilitated by that very indefiniteness of doctrine which appears to some critics as its major theological drawback. Some Conservatives look forward to the day when American Jewry will transcend the differences between Orthodoxy and Reform and enroll under the banner of Conservative doctrine and practice. This might indeed happen if, as Kaplan has frequently demanded, the American communities should transform themselves into all-embracing "organic" communities. Cognizant of the existence of powerful secular groups and institutions, the leaders of Reconstructionism yet expect that ultimately these "organic" communities would be primarily religious in character. In this way the American Jewish community, representing a comprehensive religious civilization, would inherit the ethnic-cultural tradition of European Jewry.

NEW CULTURAL MOLDS

The roots of Haskalah lie in the Jewish Enlightenment, which itself was deeply influenced by the European Enlightenment. Like its antecedents in Italy and Holland, the Berlin Haskalah of the eighteenth century tried to reform Jewish life on the basis of rational criteria. The great admiration shown for Moses Mendelssohn by his disciples has obscured the fact that they departed radically from his philosophical and religious ideals. Mendelssohn himself clearly recognized the supremacy of the activist element in Judaism. "Among the provisions of Mosaic law," reads a typical Mendelssohnian injunction, "not one states: Thou shalt believe or not believe. They all emphasize: Thou shalt do or not do! One cannot issue orders to faith, for it does not accept any other orders than those to which it reaches through conviction." Mendelssohn's disciples were far more radical, especially Lazarus ben David, who developed a theory irreconcilable with Judaism in any of its traditional forms.

Furthermore, in the *Meassef,* the Berlin and Koenigsberg Maskilim traveled far on the road toward secularization. To them Hebrew literature no longer meant religious writings primarily, but works of critical scholarship of the type produced earlier by Azariah dei Rossi. The latter's main historical work was now reprinted as a model of independent research, and such exponents of a more rational approach to Jewish problems as Leone da Modena were enshrined as examples to be followed. In addition to scholarship, these reformers were concerned with belles-lettres, practical educational reforms, problems of grammar and style, and hence with improvement of the "barbaric" Hebrew then in vogue. Poetry and drama now became the chief vehicles of expression. The Jewish public was now introduced to Western scholarship and letters through translations into Hebrew or Judeo-German, the latter soon to become full-fledged Yiddish. Much of this literary output was of an inferior quality, certainly as measured by the prevailing standards of German literature. For the most part the translations were of second- and third-rate German stories and poems. The great works of art then being produced by Lessing, Goethe, and Schiller were overlooked.

Nevertheless, this ferment resulted in new approaches to both Hebrew and Yiddish letters. Avenues were also opened up for the entry of Jews into literature and the general sciences. Significant of things to come was the work of a member of the Mendelssohnian circle, Solomon Maimon, a native of a Polish ghetto, who became one of Immanuel Kant's leading disciples. He was highly appreciated for his dialectical keenness of mind by the great Koenigsberg philosopher, and his work had considerable influence on the subsequent evolution of German idealism. Incidentally, it may be noted that Kant was interested in Hebrew studies and espoused the idea of establishing a Hebrew chair at the University of Koenigsberg. He wished to see it entrusted to Isaac Euchel, author of Yiddish as well as Hebrew works.

On the whole, the influence of Mendelssohn and his school on German Jewry was short-lived. At first the Jews were greatly impressed by the high standing accorded to Mendelssohn by German thinkers and by society at large. Leading Jewish circles in eighteenth-century Germany were delighted to read in the press a memorial couplet for the sage of Dessau:

> There is a God, so Moses taught;
> But Mendelssohn the proof has brought.

To be sure, some non-Jewish writers resented this exaggerated praise. A wag wrote a parody on that verse:

> The wise believe 'cause Moses taught it;
> From Mendelssohn but fools have caught it.

But men like Friederich Schleiermacher resented such parody. To them Mendelssohn was the thinker who had raised himself by his boot straps from the Dessau ghetto to a leading position in contemporary German philosophy. Nevertheless, his philosophy became antiquated so quickly that even his most devoted disciples could not follow in his footsteps. Within half a century after his death, German Jewish thought had left the whole approach of the Mendelssohnian age far behind.

In Eastern Europe, however, these Haskalah influences had more enduring repercussions. Beginning with Menahem Mendel Lefin Satanower, a member of the Mendelssohnian circle, who wrote both in Hebrew and in Yiddish, the Haskalah established itself firmly among the East European intellectuals. In the so-called Galician Haskalah, Jewish scholarship celebrated memorable victories and was superior to much of the scholarship that preceded it in the German Haskalah and to that which was to follow it in the Russian. Nahman Krochmal has rightly been considered the most original nineteenth-century Jewish philosopher. In his *Guide for the Per-*

plexed of Our Time this quiet and retiring scholar of the Zolkiew ghetto employed Kantian and Hegelian approaches for the purpose of an original, truly Jewish reinterpretation of Jewish history against the background of world history. His friend, Solomon Judah Leb Rapoport, became one of the founders of the new Science of Judaism, which, as we shall presently see, endeavored to find still another intellectual bridge between Judaism and the outside world. Satirists like Isaac Erter, educators of the stamp of Joseph Perl, modern reinterpretors of Talmudic learning like Zevi Chajes and a host of lesser writers, publicists, and scholars testify to the vigor of the intellectual ferment in that border country between Polish and German culture in the decades before emancipation.

From Galicia the Haskalah movement spread to Russia, partly through the agency of émigrés from Galicia, especially those who went to Odessa, which soon developed into a major center of Russian Jewry. For example, Simhah Pinsker helped establish modern Jewish learning in Odessa by his famous publications in the field of Karaite lore and in the history of Hebrew vocalization. In Russia, however, the Haskalah turned more definitely to the field of belles-lettres, as the names of Abraham Mapu, the Lebensons, Judah Leb Gordon, and others show.

All these forms of Haskalah were decidedly intermediate. They sufficiently caught the spirit of the modern age to introduce Western secular approaches into Jewish intellectual life. As such they were offshoots of the European Enlightenment, although in their later stages they received many impulses from German romanticism and the idealistic philosophy. Yet in essence, they did not address themselves to emancipated Jews. As soon as emancipation became a reality, as in France and Holland after the Revolution, or an immediate prospect, as in most parts of Germany after the Napoleonic era, Haskalah was largely discarded as an outworn separatist form. Certainly, Heinrich Heine and Ludwig Börne, and even Zunz and Geiger were anything but Maskilim. The Haskalah performed a major function in the immediate preemancipatory period in Germany, Galicia, and Russia. Its basic preachment, "Be a Jew at home, and a man on the street," withered away under the dictates of full emancipation, which demanded that the Jew be a Western man even at home. On the other hand, Haskalah's revival of both Hebrew and Yiddish letters bequeathed a significant heritage to the subsequent period of Jewish nationalism. Accepting the premise of emancipation, nationalism went beyond Haskalah, demanding that the Jew be a Jew on the street also. However, what was now anticipated was a Western, emancipated Jew—one cognizant of his Western nationalism and employing his national languages of Hebrew or Yiddish for literary expression.

A different attempt to reconcile Judaism with Western civilization was made by the founders of the *Wissenschaft des Judentums,* the Science of Judaism. Here too there was no uniformity of approach. Among these early luminaries were such different scholars as the Galicians Krochmal and Rapoport, the Italians Joseph Samuel Reggio and Samuel David Luzzatto, and the Germans Zunz, Jost, and Geiger. Reggio was essentially a spokesman of the Italian Haskalah. Luzzatto denounced any form of assimilation to Western ways of life even at the price of emancipation. A few years after the Revolution of 1848, which had both impressed and disappointed him, he addressed himself to the public in Italian:

> In short, Judaism must be liberated from external oppression, as well as free itself from everything that has intruded itself into it through external influence. Be that through the imitation of Chaldean civilization . . . of the American, or any other kind of civilization, in fact of all of them which, not having (as does Judaism) as a basis the two principles of mercy and heavenly reward, have not, and will not, be able to preserve themselves, as Judaism has preserved and will preserve itself.

At the other extreme, Isaak Markus Jost went so far in accepting non-Jewish judgments of Jewish history, wherever his conscience as a scholar permitted, that he often antagonized his readers by an excess of objectivity. For example, he was ready to admit that the expulsion of Jews from France in 1306 had some justification—a stark heresy to other Jewish historians and to the public at large. Abraham Geiger was a leading reformer who utilized his historic researches to buttress the Reform outlook. Leopold Zunz, like his younger friend Moritz Steinschneider, tried to steer clear of political and religious controversies and devoted himself to gathering data on the Jewish past. Not that either Zunz or Steinschneider refrained from interesting asides which revealed their private biases no less clearly than the lengthy tirades of outspoken propagandists. Yet in the main their work was dominated by a scholarly objectivity.

Critics have considered this objectivity a major weakness, showing that the new Science was too factual and disengaged. Except in Germany, where unbiased scholarship was generally valued, the Science aroused little interest. On the other hand, the brilliant scholar Graetz, with his eloquence about Jewish sufferings and glorification of the achievements of Jewish men of learning, became extremely popular. It mattered little that he was severely criticized by such learned contemporaries as Geiger and Steinschneider. His history completely superseded the work of Jost, not only because of the intervening advances in Jewish scholarship, but also because of Jost's noncommittal attitude. Zunz alone among these early masters enjoyed universal reverence, if not popularity.

Zunz, Ludwig Philippson, and others agitated for the establishment of chairs of Jewish studies in the universities. Apart from the prestige factor, which was a matter of great moment to a generation beset with feelings of inferiority on its emergence from the ghetto, the protagonists of the idea looked for a more objective treatment of Jewish subjects before detached university audiences than was possible in rabbinical seminaries. They felt, too, that collaboration with professors in other university departments would broaden the outlook of Jewish researchers and reduce the dangers of extreme parochialism. But the Prussian authorities especially had little sympathy for the idea. Aside from the general disparagement of Jewish studies in uninformed academic circles and the antipathy for Judaism among Prussia's bureaucracy, there was hardly any understanding of the peculiarities of Jewish culture, nor of the difference in methodological approach necessary to its comprehension. In the early years of his membership in the Berlin Society for the Science of Judaism, Heine had warned that "one must not treat Judaism in the manner of modern Protestantism." But at the same time a committee of leading Berlin scholars, including August Boeckh and Leopold von Ranke, came to the conclusion that most of the pertinent philosophical, philological, and historical subjects were already being taught at German universities. This betrayed a misunderstanding that has not yet disappeared. Many university administrators, even in America, view Judaism as nothing but a religion, and so regard a chair of Jewish studies as on a par with a chair of church history or any other purely religious discipline. It requires a familiarity with the complexities and unique character of the Jewish past and present which not even all Jewish intellectuals possess to realize that the subject is one that calls for a special, highly refined method of study.

One area of Jewish history, however, has always been of major concern to general scholarship: the Old Testament period and the centuries immediately preceding or following the rise of Christianity. Curiously, for many decades Higher Criticism of the Bible attracted relatively few Jewish devotees. After Geiger, no distinguished Biblical critic appeared until the twentieth century, owing probably to a fear of manhandling Scripture, which was considered perfect and unerring. Besides, a great deal of Biblical scholarship from De Wette to the school of Wellhausen displayed decided antisemitic overtones. Thus Friedrich Delitzsch tried to prove that the Bible was completely unoriginal and owed everything to Babylonian prototypes. Other scholars, including James Breasted, postulated the Bible's total dependence on Egyptian culture. Jewish Biblical scholarship, therefore, in so far as it went beyond the philological and theological interpretation of texts, was concerned with an apologetic defense of Scripture, rather than with an objective analysis of its Oriental background.

But the very progress of Biblical scholarship has removed the necessity for such apology. The better known the ancient Near East has become through archeological excavations and the unparalleled growth of detailed information, the brighter the Biblical traditions have shone with respect to both their authenticity and their originality. Accordingly, many Jews, inspired by a genuine desire to discover the truth, have recently found their way into the realm of Biblical scholarship. Moreover, the rise of Israel has reawakened a deep interest in Biblical history, which after all is the best known and most important part of the history of the country itself. Today Biblical archeology has become a national pastime in Israel, with many an Israeli layman turning amateur archeologist.

While in Israel Jewish scholarship has been an integral part of the intellectual growth of the nation, in the countries of the Dispersion mere lip-service is often paid to the ideals of Jewish learning, and there is little communal action to promote it. Still, despite all difficulties, American Jewish scholarship has made very great strides in the last two generations. It already has to its credit a number of outstanding works comparable in quality to the best produced in Germany or Israel. In one area, however, where American scholarship might have been expected to lead the way, the field of collaborative scholarship, little has been accomplished. though the beginnings were auspicious. Having marshaled the resources of world scholarship for the production of the first Jewish Encyclopedia in the early years of this century, American students have since carried on largely in splendid isolation. Which is a real pity, for the genius of American scholarship has often consisted in mobilizing financial and organizational resources for the production of major works which individual scholars have neither the time nor the capacity to compose.

REBIRTH OF LITERATURE AND THE ARTS

Yiddish literature, too, emancipated itself early from the shackles of Haskalah. From its inception in the Middle Ages, Yiddish writing catered to the masses, and the early romances which circulated in the Germanic folk-tongue were often frowned upon by the Hebrew-writing intellectuals. Yet those works, as well as the Yiddish para-phrases of the Bible, met a real need among the illiterate classes, including most women. It was a folk literature and remained so in the nineteenth century and after.

Artistically inferior, but socially very significant, romances such as those produced by Shomer (N. M. Schaikevitch) had a tremendous circulation, as did the popular poems of Hillel Klibanoff. In the latter part of the nineteenth century there appeared a stellar triad of great novelists, Mendele Mokher Sforim (Sholem Jacob Abramovitch), Sholem Aleichem (Sholem Rabinovitch), and Yizthok Leibush Peretz. The first two depicted in unforgettable colors the life of the old *shtetel*. In Mendele's realistic descriptions there runs a deep vein of satire, while Sholem Aleichem's are shot through with a more dispassionate humor. Unfortunately, owing to their very realism, the works of these two men have begun to date. The old *shtetel* is hardly more than a memory today. But Peretz, who dealt with such peren-nial topics as Hasidic ideals and behavior, has stood up much better.

Besides these three giants, Yiddish literature has had a great many distinguished novelists, playwrights, poets, and publicists. In Amer-ica, especially, the immigrant masses created a peculiar brand of literature, which was a contribution not only to Jewish culture but to the whole realm of American letters. Certainly the sweatshop con-ditions at the turn of the century found no better reflection in any language than in the Yiddish poems of Morris Rosenfeld. Abraham Reisen, David Pinsky, H. (Halpern) Leivick, and others have left their mark on Yiddish as well as American writing.

Of great influence too was the Yiddish theater. Starting with popu-lar melodramas whose lineage went back to the medieval Purim plays, the theatrical arts gained a firm hold on the East European and later the American Jewish public. The Yiddish stage was en-riched by such prolific playwrights as Abraham Goldfaden and Jacob Gordin, the latter the author of no less than eighty plays. Numerous translations were made from foreign languages, and often adapted to the tastes of the Yiddish-speaking public. At the turn of the century, the artistic level of the theater reached great heights, accentuated by the deep devotion of stage people and public alike. A famous German visitor to New York in 1904, the historian Karl Lamprecht, was so impressed with Yiddish theatrical performances that he wrote: "In ancient Hellas, too, they must have played theater with such religious consecration." Perhaps the greatest triumph of the theater was celebrated in the Yiddish, as well as Hebrew, per-

formances of S. Ansky's (Solomon Zangwill Rapoport) *Dybbuk.*
Unfortunately, in recent years the Yiddish theater has steadily
declined in both attendance and artistic quality. With the destruction
of Polish Jewry the great Vilna Art Theater and other Polish theatrical groups went out of existence. For a time the Soviet Union encouraged the Yiddish theater, as it did other phases of Yiddish
culture. In the 1920s the Moscow Art Theater, though ideologically
restricted to plays with a more or less outspoken revolutionary message, still kept up a creditable level of achievement. Together with
the rest of Yiddish creativity, however, theatrical production began
withering away in the inhospitable clime of the totalitarian regime of
the 1930s. The decline was accelerated during World War II until
the Jewish theater ceased functioning altogether. Nor has it revived
in the postwar era, although according to newspaper reports sporadic
performances took place in 1955. Most of these seem to be limited
to a few stars and the audiences are largely recruited from the older
groups in the population—an ominous augury for the future.

Of special importance was the development of Yiddish journalism.
From the time of the biweekly *Kurant,* which appeared on Fridays
and Tuesdays in Amsterdam in 1686-1687, the Yiddish press made
great progress in many countries. In 1912 there were a hundred
periodicals, including twenty daily papers. Less than two decades
later this number increased to four hundred periodicals and fifty
dailies. At the same time there was also a considerable increase in
the publication of books. In 1928 more than a thousand Yiddish
books appeared (622 in Poland, 224 in the Soviet Union, and
102 in the United States). Some American dailies, such as the *Forward,* counted their circulation in six figures.

Yet in the 1920s pessimists were shaking their heads. They contended that even in Poland a large segment of the youth had stopped
speaking Yiddish and preferred to use Polish or, for Jewish literary
purposes, Hebrew. Russification and Americanization proceeded
with great rapidity. In the United States the Yiddish press itself
served as an Americanizing agency, furnishing the immigrants with
news about their environment and helping them in their economic
and social adjustment. Ever fewer of the younger generation spoke
Yiddish. The Yiddish press had to compete with a powerful American press designed for a heterogeneous public and having at its
disposal a vast network of correspondents. Thirty years ago, in the
midst of the great flowering of Yiddish culture, one already heard
predictions of its speedy disappearance.

Although the prophets of gloom were for a time vindicated by
the unprecedented historical catastrophe which destroyed the main

centers of Yiddish-speaking Jewry, their predictions have not been borne out. The American Yiddish press still carries on valiantly, though on a diminished basis. Since many Americans are habitual readers of several papers, many people now read their Yiddish paper as well as their English daily. They find it worthwhile because no paper in English, not even one so comprehensive as the *New York Times,* is able to supply all the worthwhile Jewish news items, and even general news is often presented from a Jewish angle in the Yiddish papers. Further, the Yiddish press has always been the chief refuge of Yiddish litterati, especially because of the shrinkage of other publishing media. A number of important Yiddish weeklies, monthlies, and quarterlies in the United States have maintained or even improved upon their high literary and scholarly level of three or four decades ago. But the Russian Jewish press has suffered total eclipse, not even the Moscow *Emes* or the Biro-Bidjan *Shtern* have appeared regularly in recent years. Israel, despite the aversion of many Hebraists to Yiddish, now boasts of a fairly substantial Yiddish press.

More than Yiddish letters, modern Hebrew literature owes its revival to the national movement, which led to the rebirth of Hebrew as a spoken language. Gone was the pessimistic outlook on the future of Hebrew that was characteristic of the last writers of the Haskalah period, especially Judah Leb Gordon. The feeling of permanence now enhanced both the literary value of the new literature and its appeal to an ever more discriminating audience. In the wake of the new optimism some of the best minds of East European and Palestinian Jewry were inspired to create distinguished works of poetry, fiction, and scholarship in the now secularized Hebrew language.

With this secularization went new literary approaches. In previous generations Hebrew authors had produced mainly legal compendia, Kabbalistic and Hasidic homilies, and ethical works. Now the majority turned to the novel and short story. Similarly, even in the Golden Age of Spain, Hebrew poetry was predominantly sacred and liturgical in character, although Gabirol, Halevi and especially Immanuel of Rome produced a great many memorable secular poems as well. Now poetry followed the usual Western genres of epic, lyric, or dramatic poems. In structure and content these were largely European poems in Hebrew garb, although their style and spirit often owed a great deal to the Hebraic heritage of former ages. Ahad Haam, one of the leaders of this Hebrew renaissance, pointed out that traditionally Jews valued particularly their scholarly rather than their belletristic literature. Yet in his very influential periodical,

Ha-Shiloah, he had to assign considerable space to poets and novelists. But it does violence to both Jewish literary tradition and the facts to apply, as some historians have done, Western standards to modern Hebrew literature and treat it from the point of view of belles-lettres only.

At the turn of the century, the Hebrew essay was still greatly in vogue. It was not by his novels but his essays, together with his periodical, *Ha-Shahar,* issued in Vienna, that Peretz Smolenskin led a whole generation of Hebrew readers to turn their backs on the Haskalah ideals. Moshe Leb Lilienblum effectively propagated the new brand of Hebrew nationalism. And Ahad Haam, himself one of the grand masters of modern Hebrew prose, acted as a guide and a mentor to a generation of students and readers who, even if they violently disagreed with his "cultural" brand of Zionism, deeply admired his lucid presentation of the Zionist rationale.

At the same time modern Hebrew poetry and fiction suddenly flowered. Poets like Hayyim Nahman Bialik and Saul Tchernikhowsky restored Hebrew poetry to the heights formerly attained only by the great Spaniards of the eleventh and twelfth centuries. Bialik used such traditional themes as the massacres of Jews (*Massa Niemirov*) or the virtues of the old-type Talmudic education (*Ha-Matmid*), while Tchernikhowsky was a "Hellene" who injected into Hebrew literature the appreciation of beauty and the zest for life of the ancient Greeks. Both lent the Hebrew tongue a new suppleness and inspired untold thousands of readers with a deep appreciation for the new Jewish national values. The same thing holds true for such distinguished prose writers as Berditchevsky, the alleged Hebrew "Nietzschean." It is a curious fact that while the battle between Hebraists and Yiddishists was raging on the political and educational fronts the great writers, including Bialik, Mendele, and Peretz, wrote in both languages with equal distinction.

The new secular approaches found expression, too, in a great diversity of topics and points of view. For the first time it became possible for even a convert to the Greek Orthodox Church, Constantin Asher Shapira, to become a celebrated Hebrew poet who gave memorable expression to his deep yearnings for the beauty of the old ghetto. Other romantic writers, like Berditchevsky, Judah Steinberg, Asher Barash, and S. J. Agnon, glorified the Hasidic ideals, though not necessarily as members of the Hasidic movement. As a Nietzschean Hasid, Berditchevsky was a truly paradoxical illustration of the vast range of the new literature in Hebrew. A host of realistic narrators described life in its ugliest as well as its seemliest aspects. There were naturalists and propagandists for one or another socialist ideology, such as A. D. Gordon, G. H. Brenner, Gershom Schofman, Uri Zevi Greenberg, and Abraham Shlonsky. Some of these writers figure in the new Israeli literature which, though maintaining unbroken continuity with its earlier Diaspora prototypes, has developed certain peculiar features of its own.

Israeli preponderance is especially evident in the Hebrew press and theater. While a book may appeal to a small élite, the press especially requires a considerable number of regular subscribers and advertisers. A theater is altogether dependent on local audiences sufficiently numerous and devoted to maintain it beyond a few performances. In all these respects the Hebrew public in the Dispersion cannot measure up to its Yiddish counterparts numerically. Only in Israel has there been a sufficiently large number of Hebrew newspaper readers and theater-goers to justify the publication of morning and afternoon papers, weeklies and monthlies, and to maintain regular theaters, especially the famed Habimah and Ohel. In the Dispersion, it was only occasionally that there appeared such magnificent theatrical troupes as the original Moscow Habimah, whose meteoric career in western Europe and America illuminated the Hebrew cultural horizon. Historically, these noteworthy achievements of the Hebrew drama, which goes back to the sixteenth century, are doubly remarkable, for the works were written largely without reference to any theatrical performance. But in Mandatory Palestine, and now in Israel, the drama exists on a secure footing.

More remarkable still is the fact that many publishers, in the face of every difficulty, persevered in issuing Hebrew dailies in Russia and Poland in the latter part of the nineteenth century, indeed, down to the eve of World War II. Like the Yiddish press, the Hebrew papers and magazines provided the training ground and literary outlets for many gifted writers, including David Frischman, the leading Hebrew feuilletonist. Perhaps the most significant journalistic venture of all was the Warsaw *Ha-Sefirah,* founded by a self-taught East European astronomer, Hayyim Selig Slominsky. The paper reached its peak under the editorship of Nahum Sokolow. Hebrew periodicals also appeared in many other countries. The first socialist Jewish periodical, published by the professed atheist Aron Lieberman, was the London *Ha-Emet.* The United States, too, was the scene of manifold journalistic enterprises in Hebrew, so manifold as to make up an extensive bibliography which was published as far back as a quarter-century ago. Most of the nineteenth-century publications, however, were short-lived, as was the attempt to publish a Hebrew daily after World War I. But the weekly *Ha-Doar* has enjoyed a long and fruitful career of more than three decades. The fact that it

managed to survive the death of its founder and moving spirit, Menahem Ribalow, is a sign of its enduring vitality.

An author writing in Hebrew or Yiddish, or for that matter in
Ladino, Judeo-Persian, or any other Jewish dialect, if he is of any
consequence, automatically makes a contribution to Jewish culture.
On the other hand, when anyone writes in a non-Jewish language, if
he contributes to the Jewish heritage at all, it is only because of his
Jewish subject matter or some peculiarly Jewish approach. So it is
often difficult to distinguish a Jewish writer in English, French, German, Russian, or any other language from his non-Jewish counterpart.
This is true not only in such religiously or nationally neutral areas as
the physical sciences, but in the humanities and social sciences. The
case is even clearer with regard to artists using other than linguistic
media. After endless debates about the nature of Jewish art and
music, it is still impossible to put one's finger on a particularly Jewish
style in architecture, sculpture, or painting, or a Jewish spirit in music.
Of course, the old liturgical music has certain peculiarly Jewish
features. But most modern Jewish productions, whether in music or
the other arts, might be the work of non-Jews. Only here and there a
connoisseur will detect, or thinks he detects, a certain undefinable
ingredient which stamps this or that art as Jewish.

Such indistinctness must remain a feature of much of Jewish
creativity in the Dispersion, since most Jewish scholars, artists, and
writers will undoubtedly use the media fashioned by their environment. Unless the subject matter itself is of direct Jewish concern,
their contribution is to the general culture, and only indirectly to
Jewish culture. Nevertheless, in so highly nuanced a realm as the
cultural, even indirect contributions have a profound bearing on the
cultural physiognomy of a group. Unlike politics and economics,
where different interests are usually intolerant of each other and
mutually exclusive, cultural life embraces differences and grows by
cross-fertilization. It is the aggregate of both direct and indirect contributions which will ultimately account for the richness and genuine
survival value of Jewish culture in the Dispersion.

16

THE CHALLENGE OF
MATERIAL CIVILIZATION

The size and structure of Jewish as well as world population have undergone a tremendous change in the last two or three centuries. True, our knowledge of the variations in Jewry's numerical strength throughout history, even in modern times, is very inadequate. We do not even know how many Jews there really are today in the United States or the Soviet Union, the two countries of largest contemporary Jewish settlement. What their numbers were a century or two ago is equally debatable. Nor are we very well informed about the birth or mortality rates, the ratio of Jewish marriages (including mixed marriages) and divorces, and the effect of these things on Jewish communal life. On the factual side generally, we have yet to amass sufficient data not only for the correct interpretation of the Jewish past, but also for the formulation of enlightened public policies today. Worse still is the indifference of the Jewish public toward this kind of knowledge. Communal leaders, who in their private business would never dare to make important decisions without first securing the basic statistical information, nevertheless glibly pass judgment on vital courses of action affecting the future of the Jewish communities without the slightest attempt to obtain even what information is available.

Suffice it to state here that we have reasons for assuming that the total Jewish population in 1800 did not much exceed two million. In one of the most startling expansion movements in history, the Jewish people grew during the nineteenth century to well over twelve million before the outbreak of World War I. Despite various retarding factors and incipient signs of biological decline in many areas, the global number increased by another four million in the quarter-century between 1914 and 1939. Soon thereafter some six million lives were suddenly swallowed up. Notwithstanding the fairly rapid postwar recovery, the world Jewish population now probably stands at the level it had attained more than forty years ago.

CHANGING POPULATION TRENDS

The reasons for both growth and contraction can be given here only briefly, and hence in a somewhat oversimplified form. So long as the Jewish people lived its old ghetto life, very early marriages combined with a minimum of birth control to produce an extraordinarily high birth rate. Orthodoxy, in particular, has always claimed that the Biblical blessing to Adam and Eve "Be fruitful and multiply" (Genesis 1:22) was the first *commandment* recorded in Scripture. Until recently, many Jews took that commandment so seriously that, after ten years of barren marriage, they availed themselves of their right to a divorce. As late as the beginning of this century, Russian Jewry had the high birth rate of more than forty per thousand population. However, in this respect Jews did not materially differ from the Slavonic and Arab masses among whom the majority of them lived. The major difference consisted in the fact that Jewish mortality was much lower. While we cannot give any definite figures for the older periods, it may well be that instead of a general mortality in the first year of perhaps 250 or 300 infants among every 1,000 born and an additional 200 during the subsequent four years, the Jewish rate was only half of this. After the age of fifteen, too, Jewish mortality was less than that of the general population.

Various factors account for this phenomenon. We need merely mention the deep appreciation of life characteristic of the Jewish people throughout the ages; the intensity of Jewish family life, which made all parents strain their resources to the utmost to nurture their children to maturity; the greater availability of medical care even in small Jewish settlements; and the great measure of communal responsibility which included the care of the sick, orphaned, and aged. In times of peace few, if any, Jews starved to death, while recurrent famines in Tsarist Russia alone devastated millions of their neglected neighbors. As late as 1932, it is said, five million Soviet citizens died from starvation as a result of the failure of crops or transportation.

Negative factors, especially conversion from Judaism and inter-marriage, caused only a minor retardation of the upward trend. To be sure, there was a wave of conversion in Prussia at the beginning of the nineteenth century. And less conspicuously, but steadily, there was a slow erosion of Jewish numbers by Christian missionary efforts which, often being governmentally financed, exacted a toll among Jews all over the world. It has been estimated that the London Society for the Promotion of Christianity Amongst the Jews spent on the average $5,000 to convert a single Jew in England, Palestine, and other countries. As a matter of fact even in the staunchly Orthodox *halukkah* settlement of Jerusalem, Ludwig August Frankl found in 1856 a sizable group of converts to Christianity. Similarly, among the Orthodox Jews of Russia more than 100,000 are said to have found their way to the baptismal font in the course of the nineteenth century. Nevertheless, compared with the total number of Jews living at that time these defections had a greater moral than biological significance.

Nor was intermarriage a threat to Jewish survival at that time, although upper-class Jews often married outside the fold. The Men-delssohn family was often mentioned by opponents of Haskalah as an illustration of the latter's destructive influence, and later one could frequently see a scion of one of the noble but impoverished families restoring his family's fortunes by marrying off a daughter to a wealthy Jewish banker or industrialist. Bismarck often encouraged such un-ions. But not until the twentieth century did mixed marriages in Germany and other Western countries make a real dent in the Jewish population. They did so in Russia after the Revolution of 1917, so that within nine years the first census of the Soviet Union showed a ratio of twenty-five percent of mixed marriages in the Russian interior. In Trieste in 1927, the ratio of mixed marriages went up to fifty-two percent.

One must bear in mind, however, that statistically each Jewish marriage involves two Jewish partners, while a mixed marriage affects only one Jew. That is why a ratio of twenty-five percent really means only one marriage out of seven. Moreover, mixed marriages did not necessarily mean the permanent loss of the Jewish mate to Judaism. Even on the European Continent some Christian wives joined the Jewish faith. In America, it seems, losses are almost fully balanced by gains. Perhaps the most serious result of mixed marriages was that so many of them, especially on the Continent, were childless or limited to one offspring. In any case, mixed marriages have thus far affected the Jewish people only in a subsidiary fashion.

Late in the nineteenth century Western Jewry began showing pronounced symptoms of biological decline. Natality now declined much more rapidly than mortality. Ultimately the average age of the population went up to such an extent that the death rate, affecting especially the older age groups, actually began increasing. Observing these facts in Germany, Dr. Felix A. Theilhaber, who combined experience as a gynecologist with studies in sociology, published before World War I a book called *The Decline of German Jewry*. Here he figured out that German Jewry as such no longer reproduced itself and that without the aid of East European immigration it would sooner or later vanish from the earth. The book caused a furor in its day, but its author's predictions turned out truer than he himself had anticipated. The Prussian census of 1925 showed that while during the preceding five years the general population had increased by more than 3,000,000, Prussian Jewry had lost 18,000 members. Conditions went from bad to worse, and by 1931 another sociologist calculated that if that generation of German Jews were merely to maintain its biological strength, it would have to average seven children per married couple. In other words, German Jewry seemed to be leaving the scene of its millennial history even before it came under the heel of the ruthless tyrant.

To a lesser extent these factors operated also in other Western lands. Local surveys made in American communities in the mid-1930s showed a constant decline of the Jewish birth rate. In Buffalo, for example, it was shown rather conclusively that the Jewish population no longer reproduced itself, and what was true of Buffalo undoubtedly held true for other American communities, especially New York, by far the largest of them. The outcome was that the natural increase of the Jewish people the world over declined from some 150,000 in 1930 to some 80,000 only eight years later. It is small wonder that many students of Jewish population were predicting that within another dozen years the Jewish people would become stationary and even begin declining, and this without the help of massacres or wars. The prediction proved to be true, despite the rather rapid increase of North African Jewry and the high birth rate among Palestinian Jews.

Once again, however, this time quite unexpectedly, the negative trends reversed themselves. The American Jewish community participated in the reversal which took place in the United States generally during World War II. Our knowledge of the Jewish birth rate and all other population factors since 1940 is extremely limited, and even the few population surveys of recent years, for instance in Los Angeles and in Essex County (Newark), New Jersey, have furnished little conclusive evidence on this score. Yet it appears that, though slightly lagging behind the general increase in American natality, that of the American Jews has brought about a rejuvenation of the whole Jewish community. Israel, now the third-largest country of Jewish settlement, has consistently maintained its high birth rate. Since it has a generally low death rate everywhere, the Jewish people has undergone a biological renaissance.

MIGRATION: FACT AND FICTION

Population increase is usually a powerful stimulus to economic and cultural expansion, while periods of decline are for the most part concomitant with economic stagnation and general psychological lassitude. We need but recall our own depression years of the 1930s and the declining birth rate that accompanied them.

Without the stimulus provided by the increase of the Jewish population in the nineteenth century, the remarkable achievements of Jewry during the emancipation era would have been impossible. At the same time, growing population pressure created much misery. Down to the middle of the nineteenth century the growing masses of Polish Jewry had vast opportunities for expansion within the three partitioning powers of Russia, Austria, and Prussia. The partitions coincided with the southward expansion of Russia toward the Black Sea and the occupation of the vast underpopulated regions which came to be called the New Russia. Even when, beginning in 1791, the Pale of Settlement started to exclude Jews from the great expanses of the old Russian interior, these long neglected neo-Russian, now largely Ukrainian, lands were able to absorb a considerable surplus of the Jewish population. Here the Tsarist regime, anxious to colonize the newly acquired provinces, welcomed Jewish settlers. For example, Odessa was founded as a city by the Duc de Richelieu in 1803, and only a century later it was one of the largest Jewish communities in the Tsarist realm; indeed, it was the leading center of the Russian Haskalah and later Zionism. Again, Polish Jewry spoke of the "discovery of Volhynia" during the 1830s and 1840s, for that province, which had long belonged to independent Poland, now underwent a minor industrial revolution, so that it could absorb not only a great many new workers but also traders and professionals.

Similarly, the segment of Poland which went to Austria in 1772, soon known as Galicia, found unexpected possibilities for geographic expansion. Neighboring Bukovina, incorporated into Austria in 1775, had practically no Jews at that time, but by 1900 so many Galician Jews had immigrated into that province that it actually exceeded Galicia's Jewish ratio of ten percent. Slovakia, across the Carpathian Mountains, had a relatively small Jewish population before 1772, but soon thereafter, largely owing to Galician immigration, its Jewish communities began increasing by leaps and bounds. These in turn expanded internally within Hungary, and soon raised the old but rather tiny Jewish settlements in Buda and Pest into a leading community. Galician and Hungarian Jewry also had considerable leeway for westward movement within the Hapsburg Empire. Vienna, which at the beginning of the nineteenth century admitted but a limited number of precariously "tolerated" Jewish families and saw its first modern synagogue only in 1821, was to become a century later the second-largest Jewish community in the Old World. Joining hands with the Ukrainian Jews, Galicians also penetrated in increasing numbers into the so-called Danubian Principalities (Rumania), then under Turkish suzerainty. Moldavia, it appears, had only 12,000 Jews in 1800, but a century later, despite severe governmental restrictions, this number rose to almost 200,000, largely owing to the immigration from Galicia and the Ukraine.

Posen Jewry, in the third segment of partitioned Poland, at first encountered much greater difficulties. After the Napoleonic Wars the Jews of Prussia's eastern provinces constituted the large majority of the country's Jewish population. However, because Prussia, which was to play such an enormous role in the history of German unification, had come out of her defeats and victories of the Napoleonic era with a checkered territorial pattern, its government prohibited the movement of Jews from one district to another without special permit. Of course, this legislation did not completely check Posen Jewry's transplantation to other parts of Prussia or even to other German states. Polish Jewish immigration into the old Germanic Empire had been under way ever since 1648, and could not be completely stopped by these artificial barriers. But only when these restrictions were removed in 1848 did Posen Jewry set out on its memorable march. Despite its continued natural increase, it constantly lost in absolute numbers and still more so in its ratio to the population at large. The two administrative districts of Posen and Bromberg, for example, showed a decline from 76,757 Jews in 1849 to 35,327 in 1900. The Jewish ratio in the city of Posen dropped from 20.5 percent in 1832 to 4 percent in 1905. Many of these Posen Jews found their way into Berlin, which soon held one of the large European Jewish communities. Many others joined their coreligionists from Bavaria, Hesse, and other German lands on their trek to Western Europe or overseas. At first the Bavarian Jews looked down on these "Polaks." Yet to outsiders in America or England they always appeared as part and parcel of the "German" immigration. Before long these distinctions disappeared altogether before the onrushing waves of later immigrants from farther east.

From all this it is plain how little historical validity there is to the internal dissensions between the so-called Russian, Lithuanian, Polish, Galician, Hungarian, Rumanian, and German Jews. Few families can really trace their descent to Jews who lived in Germany or Hungary before 1772. Subsequently the overwhelming ratio of growth of former Polish Jewry, and its constant internal and external migrations and frequent intermarriage with other groups, have so thoroughly blended them all that their previous national origins have become completely meaningless. To all intents and purposes the vast majority of the Hungarian, Rumanian, and even German Jews now living in America had their preponderant ancestry in prepartition Poland.

Needless to say, however, the absence of historic justification did not prevent these "national" groupings from asserting their superiority over one another. Half a century ago, even in America, German Jews refused to fraternize with their coreligionists from any East European country. "Litvaks" had little use for Poles or Galicians, and vice versa. For a Russian Jew to marry a Hungarian Jew amounted to intermarriage. Communal positions, in particular, were often reserved for persons of a particular "national" origin. Today these prejudices, what is left of them, often merely evoke a smile on the part of observers. But half a century ago the distinctions were very serious indeed.

Much more extensive were the international Jewish migrations in the latter part of the nineteenth century. Scholars and public alike, looking for some dramatic initiation of new historic periods, have often connected the large-scale German Jewish emigration with the Revolution of 1848, and attributed the East-European mass migration to the Russian pogroms of 1881 and the May Laws of 1882. Even today one often hears of families glorying in their descent from Forty-Eighters, or connecting the exodus of their ancestors with one or another era of Russian persecution.

This mythology quickly withers away in the more dispassionate climate of historical facts. True, there was a great upsurge in the quest for freedom in 1848. In Austria, especially, there arose a regular "On to America" movement, and many societies were organized to promote emigration to the United States. In a prophetic mood the Austrian writer, Leopold Kompert, hailed not so much the prospective émigrés themselves as their offspring as "the sons of the free." Yet so far as the records go—and they are admittedly incomplete—a few Jews left for the United States or England as a result of the Revolution, and some of those who did ultimately returned. There is no reason to assume that the Jewish ratio in the general German emigration varied much from year to year. It is likely, therefore, that as in the case of non-Jews, more Jews left Germany for America in 1847 than in 1848 or 1849. The upward trend, however, which had begun soon after 1816 but assumed significant proportions in the 1830s, continued despite some temporary setbacks. It reached its peak in the 1850s, but fell off during the American Civil War and again in 1871, after the rise of the Second Reich, whose industrial expansion soon created a shortage of manpower in Germany itself.

For similar reasons we must not view 1881 as the turning point in East European Jewish migrations, which had been fully under way in the 1860s, and rapidly increased after 1869. Owing to the attraction of the American industrial revolution after the Civil War, the greater ease and speed of steamship travel, the fact that steamship companies sent out their own agents to solicit immigrants, and the greater facilities extended to émigrés by Jewish welfare organizations—the growth in the numbers of new arrivals would undoubtedly have occurred even without the sharp change in policy after Alexander III's accession to the throne. As a matter of record this was the period of the staggering increase of the "New Immigration," coming from Austria-Hungary, Italy, and Russia in that order. Most remarkably, while the figures for Jewish emigration from Russia increase sharply from decade to decade after 1870, the Jewish ratio in the general Russian immigration to the United States was constantly declining. Further still, Galician Jewry, though not affected by pogroms or May Laws, nor locked up behind the Pale of Settlement, nonetheless had an even higher percentage of immigrants to America. Pogroms and May Laws undoubtedly aggravated Russian Jewry's bad economic and social situation and induced a substantial number of more well-to-do and educated Jews to leave the country. But these factors were not the chief ones.

In any case, this migratory movement assumed mass proportions almost reminiscent of the barbarian migrations at the end of antiquity. In the twenty-four years before World War I, or within less than a generation, fully thirty percent of all European Jews changed their residence from one continent to another. To the overseas migrants one must add untold multitudes who moved from one country to another within Europe (during those years London and Paris, too, became major centers of Jewish life) or settled in some other part of the same country. A Galician Jew moving to Vienna did not figure in the statistics of international migration any more than there was a statistical record of an American Jew who changed his residence from Chicago to Miami. Yet the former actually required greater psychological adjustments to his new environment than if he had moved to the Lower East Side in New York. This was indeed an entire generation on the move.

Not surprisingly, ideological adjustments and controversies accompanied this great commotion. Internally, it generated the rival movements of Am-Olam (Eternal People) and Hoveve Zion (Lovers of Zion). The former, borrowing the title from a then much-debated essay by Perez Smolenskin, wished to combine the mass emigration with economic restratification of the Jewish people, which loomed very large in the minds of progressive Jewish leaders of all camps. It demanded, therefore, a more regulated migration and the establishment of Jewish agricultural colonies in America, where Jews were undisturbedly to cultivate their heritage while developing new patterns of productive living. These same ideals were espoused also by the Lovers of Zion, except that this group believed that only Palestine offered the proper soil for complete Jewish cultural and economic regeneration.

Many other Jews shared some of these aspirations. Just as Baron Edmond de Rothschild became the greatest promoter of the early Jewish agricultural colonies in Palestine, without necessarily professing the whole range of Zionist ideals, so did another great Jewish philanthropist seek similar solutions elsewhere. Baron Maurice de Hirsch, who refused help to Theodor Herzl in the establishment of a Jewish homeland in Palestine, was nevertheless prepared to stake his entire fortune on Jewish agricultural colonization in the New World. After tentative explorations by a mission he had sent to Argentina he established the Jewish Colonization Association (ICA) in 1891, endowing it first with £2,000,000. He bequeathed to it an additional £6,000,000 a few years later. This amounted to some $40,000,000, which at that time had many times the purchasing power of a similar sum today and probably exceeded the resources of any other philanthropic organization. Baron de Hirsch envisaged the transplantation in twenty-five years of some 3,000,000 Jews from Tsarist oppression to the freedom and productive farming or small-scale industry in the New World. True, the pace of Jewish colonization in Argentina never reached the projected 125,000 annually. Even when the ICA expanded its operations to Brazil, established a Baron de Hirsch Fund in the United States and other countries, and finally participated also in the settlement of Jews in Palestine—as late as the 1930s, its subsidiary the Palestine Jewish Colonization Association (PICA) controlled fully one-third of all Jewish owned land in the country—its impact upon both migrations and restratification of Jews was not decisive.

Nor was opposition to Jewish immigration absent in Western countries. At the end of the nineteenth century the United States and Great Britain witnessed the rise of anti-immigration societies and extensive public debates in the press and legislative bodies. Many arguments were employed, among them the racialist, according to which the physical and mental makeup of the American population was constantly deteriorating through the absorption of millions of Austro-Hungarians, Italians, and Russians. Some of these arguments were heard by congressional committees as well as by a British Royal Commission and, at least indirectly, contributed to the rise of a quasi-racialist antisemitism.

Curiously enough, even in Jewish circles immigrants were not altogether welcome. A Circular Letter issued in 1849 by Anglo-Jewish leaders asked the German Jews to restrict their immigration to England. On the other hand, British philanthropic agencies sought to steer as many clients as possible toward America. The American Jewish leaders were under greater constraint, since they could not send arrivals to any other country. But even they counseled Europeans to exercise great moderation in transplanting Jews to the New World. Representatives of the Board of Delegates of the American Jews at the Paris Conference of 1878 publicly sounded a warning against indiscriminate Jewish migrations. Some twenty years later, however, when the debate took an anti-Jewish turn, Jews largely closed their ranks and together fought for the maintenance of the existing liberal immigration laws.

Nonetheless, Britain adopted her Anti-Alien Act of 1903, and after some years of hesitation the United States followed suit. In 1924 the United States enacted its first quota system, allocating special percentages to various countries. With modifications in 1928, further sharpened by presidential executive orders, the distinction was drawn between the welcome "old" immigration from the British Isles, Germany, and the Scandinavian countries and the far less desirable "new" immigration from Southern and Eastern Europe.

Having already passed a law excluding Orientals, America thus embarked upon discrimination among ethnic groups. All protests of Jews and progressives remained without avail, especially since on this issue labor favored a restrictive policy and therefore often joined hands with its reactionary archenemies. The result was that after 1928 immigration sharply declined. During the economic depression of the early 1930s the United States actually lost more emigrants than it gained from those who were still permitted to find refuge on its shores.

Britain and the United States, the world's leading democracies, thus set the pace for the anti-immigration policies of most countries in the Western Hemisphere and elsewhere. In the late 1920s and early 1930s Jews of Poland, Hungary, and Rumania were looking in vain for avenues of escape. Even such clearly underpopulated countries as Argentina, Brazil, South Africa, and Australia shut their gates to Jewish migrants. Australia came to regret bitterly its anti-immigration policies when during World War II it found vast stretches of its continent exposed to potential Japanese conquest because there was no settled population to resist the invader.

France alone welcomed immigration during the 1920s, but became much more selective in the more crucial 1930s. In the first decade after World War I she tried to make up for some of her war losses by admitting about 1,500,000 immigrants from such friendly countries as Poland. But from the beginning the French government sought to replenish its manpower in mining, heavy industry, and agriculture—all occupations for which few Polish Jews had had preliminary training. That is why, despite their great desire to leave Poland, proportionately fewer Jews than Poles immigrated to France.

With the rise of Hitler, the quest for new outlets became doubly urgent. It testifies to the usual human short-sightedness that German Jews did not fully avail themselves of the existing opportunities for emigration. Without changing the existing immigration laws, which Congress in any case stubbornly upheld, President Roosevelt ordered his consuls abroad to interpret them as liberally as possible, and long before the Anschluss in 1938, he merged the small Austrian with the very much larger German quota. Remarkably, that combined quota was never utilized to the full until the last prewar year, 1938-39, after the sharp rise in Nazi persecutions that began with the assassination of Von Rath in November, 1938. Now only the blindest of the blind resisted immigration to free countries.

Jewish communities the world over now became seriously concerned with finding havens of refuge for the condemned European Jewries, but the major international agencies did not get much beyond talk. A special High Commissioner for Refugees appointed by the League of Nations, James MacDonald, speedily submitted his resignation in a letter which is a moving testimony to the futility of intergovernmental action when none of the governments is ready to set an example of self-sacrificing hospitality. Special international conferences like those convoked at Evian in 1939 and in Bermuda in 1941 degenerated into debating societies. The prevailing mood of the free countries was perhaps best expressed by the Australian delegate at the Evian Conference. Australia had not had, he claimed, any racial problem of its own and did not wish to create one by admitting a large number of Jews.

Most astonishingly, even the horrors of concentration camps and the extermination of millions of Jews were not sufficient to arouse the conscience of mankind and to force nations to suspend their restrictions on immigration. Apart from the protracted closing of Palestine's frontiers to large-scale Jewish immigration by the White Paper of 1939 until the creation of the new state in 1948, all nations persevered in their basically restrictive policies. In the United States the post–World War II McCarran and McCarran-Walter Acts reached a new height of illiberality, even overt racialism. To be sure, after the destruction of so many Jewish lives and the opening of Israel's frontiers to the survivors the Jewish people were no longer so vitally interested in freedom of migrations. Thousands of Jewish refugees still availed themselves of the existing opportunities to settle in the United States and other free countries, but the large majority of would-be émigrés now found their way to Israel.

Does this mean that the Jews can now relax and consider international migrations as a matter of individual rather than collective concern? Or shall we rather assume that the wandering Jew has not yet come to rest and that perhaps ever new avenues of Jewish migration will have to be sought, especially if the countries behind the Iron Curtain should open up? Answers to these perplexing problems can only be given in the context of the other socio-economic factors which have always operated as the main driving forces of human migration.

ECONOMIC CHANGE AND SOCIAL ATTITUDES

Besides broadening its geographic base, the Jewish people greatly intensified its economic endeavors during the last century and a half. These two movements were, of course, interrelated. Before 1772 practically the entire Jewish people were concentrated in Poland, the Ottoman Empire, Germany, and Italy. Outside these four regions only small segments carried on their old life in Iran, India, Morocco, or struggled for new footholds in Western Europe and its American colonies. Most Jews, therefore, lived in small hamlets (the old *shtetel*), even rural districts, and largely derived a livelihood from crafts, trades, innkeeping, and agencies of all kinds. Today, half of world Jewry lives in the Western Hemisphere. The other half is concentrated in the Soviet Union, Israel, the British Empire countries, and the French Union. Great Britain alone has more Jews today than Poland, Turkey, Germany, and Italy combined. In all these newer lands most Jews live in metropolitan areas from Los Angeles to Moscow and Tel-Aviv. Together with the removal of disabilities through the progress of emancipation, this transfer of Jewish population from backward to the most advanced countries and from small towns and villages to world metropolises naturally led to a total revamping of the Jewish economic structure as well.

Yet at first glance the change may not appear so great. Two hundred years ago half the Jewish people earned a living from one or another branch of commerce, more than a third from industry and handicrafts, and the rest from communal service and such professions as the rabbinate, teaching, and the like. There was a sprinkling of Jewish landowners and tillers of the soil, but their total number hardly exceeded two or three percent of the Jewish population. It was this occupational maldistribution, as well as the large number of Jews without permanent employment, the so-called *Luftmenschen,* which caused so many adverse observations on the Jew's "parasitic" existence and inspired the numerous calls for reform. Today, after mankind's greatest industrial revolution, the occupational statistics of world Jewry—if such were to be compiled— would probably still show that nearly half lives from some form of merchandising, perhaps a third is engaged in industrial endeavor, no more than two to three percent cultivate the soil, and the rest are professionals or civil servants.

Shall we say, then, that nothing has changed? Such a conclusion would be wide of the mark. Great qualitative changes have taken place, but apart from these, it makes a difference whether one is an Old World petty shopkeeper, moneylender, or communal scribe, or as today, is a leading businessman, banker, civil servant, or scientist. Environmental conditions have changed even more radically. At the end of the eighteenth century the few Jews engaged in agriculture confronted civilizations like the Polish, Turkish, etc., where eighty to ninety percent of the population consisted of peasants. Today the world's leading agricultural country, the United States, succeeds in producing tremendous surpluses with a farming population which, according to the latest census figures, has declined to 13½ percent and continues to decline. American Jewry's ratio of two percent is, therefore, no longer specially disproportionate. An industrial country like Britain has long been able to survive with an agricultural population of no more than seven percent. At the same time there has also been a vast increase of non-Jewish merchants, chain-store employees, and other white-collar workers. In short, during the last two centuries the gap has constantly diminished, not so much because the Jews have adjusted themselves to the economies of the Western world as because the Western world's occupational distribution has become, if one likes, more and more "Jewish."

No one could have predicted that development in the eighteenth century. The generation of Mendelssohn and its early successors were influenced by the "Physiocratic" outlook on life, which viewed agriculture as the only truly productive occupation with all other human activities merely derivative, if not altogether parasitic. Even when Adam Smith and the other liberal economists displaced the Physiocratic school of economics, Jewish leaders still thought largely in Physiocratic terms. From this standpoint, the Jewish economic structure appeared entirely askew. That is why almost every reform proposal connected with emancipation also envisaged restratification of the Jews. Governments and voluntary societies of all kinds propagated such "amelioration" of Jewish status through retraining Jewish youth for "productive" occupations, particularly on the soil. Already Joseph II in Austria had tried to place some of the newly acquired Jewish subjects of Galicia on land. More firmly Tsars Alexander I and Nicholas I undertook large-scale Jewish agricultural colonization in the neo-Russian provinces, especially in the vicinity of the Black Sea. That this Tsarist action was accompanied by overtly anti-Jewish measures, such as the expulsion of Jews from villages within the Pale of Settlement, could hardly endear this ambitious enterprise to the Jews themselves. Nevertheless, this was a significant experiment in introducing Jews to agricultural settlements of their own.

In Russia itself this movement received a new impetus after the Revolution of 1917 when the majority of Jews found themselves suddenly "declassed" under the new Communist order. Jewish shopkeepers and even many petty artisans and professionals were ousted from their economic positions and had to look for new occupations. Agriculture beckoned as a major hope. The government, at that time still very friendly to the Jewish minority, claimed merely to be righting an ancient wrong when it allowed Jews to share in the distribution of land confiscated from churches and landlords. A law of 1924 specifically provided that, while only farmers were entitled to such a share, Jews, even if not previously engaged in farming, might receive an allocation of land. The Revolution thus wished to remedy the effects of Tsarist hostility which had kept Jews out of agriculture. Governmental propaganda, abetted by local Jewish leaders and significantly supported by large funds, agricultural machinery, and other facilities supplied to these Jewish farmers by the Agro-Joint—a subsidiary of the American Joint Distribution Committee —persuaded large numbers of Jews to start a new life in Jewish agricultural colonies, which were to be developed into autonomous regions. According to official governmental statistics by 1929, no less than 350,000 Jews or some twelve percent of the total Jewish population derived their livelihood from agriculture.

Unfortunately, this honeymoon did not last. Even before the ruinous World War II and the Nazi extermination of untold numbers of Jewish farmers, the Jewish colonies began deteriorating and ceased to attract new settlers. The successive Five-Year Plans created such a shortage of industrial labor that many Jewish and non-Jewish farmers heeded the call of rapidly expanding urban opportunities. Before long, as we shall see, some Jews also listened to rival appeals to settle in far-eastern Biro-Bidjan. While this enterprise proved to be nearly a total failure, it prevented Russian Jewry from continuing with its agricultural experiment.

Meanwhile, the Am-Olam movement had undertaken to transplant thousands of Russian Jews to the United States and settle them there in agricultural colonies. American Jewish leaders, too, wished to see their coreligionists join the westward trek in the rapidly expanding American frontier of the nineteenth century. Influential publicists such as Michael Heilperin enlisted the support of Jewish philanthropists with the object of helping these newcomers overcome the staggering initial difficulties. Unfortunately, neither the human nor technical material nor the necessary technical implements were sufficiently prepared for this gigantic enterprise. A number of colonies were indeed founded as far south and west as Louisiana and the Dakotas, but most of them died aborning. The sites were poorly selected, the settlers untrained and completely inexperienced, the climate strange. No wonder that so many succumbed to the first major flood, drought, or blizzard. Yet some colonies survived, especially those close enough to the major eastern population centers to become dairy and truck farms, for which the old *shtetel* had somewhat better prepared their inhabitants. The colony in Woodbine, New Jersey, for example, developed into what was in some respects a model farm.

Conditions improved rapidly in 1900 when the newly formed

Jewish Agricultural Society embarked upon a more rational, less emotionally fraught, program. Making slow progress during the first years of this century, Jewish farming underwent a great spurt during World War I's agricultural boom. The same effect on a lesser scale was produced by the Great Depression. In the early 1930s some Jews, like their non-Jewish fellow Americans, often returned to the soil which offered them at least a minimum of subsistence. Later on the Society found a fairly large group of interested settlers among German and other refugees. Since 1939 the Jewish agricultural population in the United States has been stabilized at approximately 100,000, or some two percent of American Jewry. Despite many differences in detail, there has also been a similar agricultural development among Canadian Jews.

Jewish agricultural colonies at the other end of the hemisphere, however, suffered from what might be called an excess of prosperity. From the beginning, working under the patronage of the ICA, the Argentinian Jewish colonists did not have to rely on themselves alone, for the ICA with its vast resources could always bail them out. In the first twenty years 30,000 Jews were established in such new villages as Moiseville, named after Baron de Hirsch. Here World War I proved a curse in disguise. Because Argentinian agricultural output, much sought for by the Allied nations, had risen to unprecedented heights, many Jewish farmers were able to pay off their long-term debts to the ICA and to acquire full title to their land. These acquisitions were often followed by a wave of land speculation, with some of the Jewish property sold to Gentiles. While the original colonies still retained their Jewish identity, they were no longer permeated with the great fervor of the early doughty pioneers. The children of the pioneers often found their way into Buenos Aires, and today the colonies form but a relatively small segment of Argentina's Jewish population, estimated at some 350,000.

In short, economic idealism, even if supported by such large funds as were invested by the ICA, American philanthropists, and the Agro-Joint, was not sufficient to overcome stubborn economic realities. After all, the general trend of the age was toward transplantation of millions of farmers to urban occupations. Whether because of adversity or of excessive prosperity, therefore, many of these ventures withered on the vine. Only in Palestine, where it was reinforced by deep national yearnings, did the restratification of the Jewish people and its return to the soil make genuine headway.

Jews encountered less difficulty in entering modern industry on both the managerial and the labor sides. Long before emancipation a substantial proportion of the Jewish people lived from crafts, especially tailoring, which, because of the Biblical prohibition of mixing wool and linen, assumed a special religious coloring. Wherever Jews lived in large numbers, as in medieval Spain or modern Poland, they formed artisan guilds among themselves. These associations frequently maintained synagogues and social services of their own, forming subcommunities within the general Jewish community.

It was not too difficult, therefore, for Jews to enter upon modern industrial endeavor. Although labor conditions in factories, especially those of Eastern Europe, differed greatly from those in small private establishments, Jewish workers could continue living in cities. Those who immigrated to Western Europe or the New World found that factory work was their most direct means to a livelihood and adjustment to the new environment. Fully one-sixth of the East European Jewish immigrants into the United States listed their occupation as tailors; though doubtless exaggerated, this figure indicates that most of them expected to join the needle trades after their settlement in this country. In Paris many Jews became capmakers, almost monopolizing that profession.

Of course, there were also many Jewish entrepreneurs, in both the Old and New Worlds. When German exports to Russia ran up against an insuperable tariff barrier, German industrialists developed the great textile center in Lodz from where they freely exported their wares to the rest of the Tsarist Empire. Polish Jews joined the German factory owners not only in Lodz but also in Bialystok and other centers. Even earlier Jews had entered the sugar-refining industry in the Ukraine in a prominent way. Other Jews helped exploit the oil fields in Baku, Galicia, and Rumania. Railroads all over Europe and America owed a great deal to Jewish initiative and finance capital.

Most significantly, Jewish workers coming from Eastern Europe to the New World or England were pioneers in developing labor unions. Class struggle had existed even in the old Jewish community. In Tsarist Russia, especially, the policies of the administration often created much dissension within the community itself. For example, the enforced cooperation of communal leaders in recruiting Jewish youths for the Tsarist armies led not only to the victimization of the poorer classes, but also to much resentment of the discriminatory policies pursued by these leaders. Perhaps much of the repudiation of traditional ways of living by the Russian Jewish Communists after 1917 was the result of that deep-rooted disaffection of the masses.

In any case, the Jewish working class in Russia, and to a lesser extent in Galicia and Rumania, was fully prepared to listen to the socialist message. All through history Jewish communal life was permeated with the ideal of social justice. This, even more than immediate wage benefits or improved conditions of labor, became therefore an integral part of Jewish unionism. It has been observed that in the United States, as elsewhere, many Jewish labor leaders remained working for their unions even when they had economically more attractive alternatives. In this way Jewish unions injected a peculiar ingredient into the Western labor movements.

For example, when the Amalgamated Clothing Workers of America and the International Ladies Garment Workers Union called their famous strikes of 1909, they made significant labor history. During the strikes public opinion led to demonstrations against police suppression and court injunctions in an unprecedented fashion. Even "socialites" like Anne Morgan and Mrs. August Belmont actively sided with the strikers. Jews were even more directly affected. Quite early the Boston philanthropist Lincoln Filene and, under his prompting, Louis Brandeis, looked for a compromise settlement. Ultimately the leaders of the American Jewish Committee, Jacob Schiff and Louis Marshall, were drawn in. Generally the Committee, then the only Jewish defense agency in the country, was not directly concerned with problems of hours and wages. But this strike, bitterly fought on both sides by Jews, became a major Jewish issue, with repercussions in all Jewish community life. Falling back on the old communal tradition of settling disputes by mutual agreement, they secured a final contract (the "protocol") which, at least indirectly, established a vital precedent for American industry as a whole. Before long the needle trades acquired a permanent "impartial" chairman to regulate conditions of labor to the mutual satisfaction of management and labor, and to forestall protracted labor conflicts. The system has proved itself marvelously; there have been no major strikes since 1933. No other unions have pioneered social welfare plans for their members that are as humane and farsighted. Ben and Sylvia Selekman were not guilty of gross overstatement when a quarter-century ago they spoke of the Jewish tailors who "have immeasurably enriched America. For while their fellow workers— diggers of coal, forgers of steel, weavers of cloth—are still [in 1930] widely denied a collective voice, the masses in the needle trades have been revealing what free, responsible citizens can contribute toward the development of life and industry."

When these words were written they were already recording past history. With the sharp decline in Jewish immigration after 1914, the needle trades recruited more and more non-Jewish workers. In 1937 a study undertaken by the Conference on Jewish Relations showed that of 5,720 workers reporting, some 607 had been initiated in the decade of 1908-1917. Of these no less than 526 were Jewish. During the next decade of 1918-1927, the 329 Jews were but a minority of the 665 initiates. The percentage dropped still further in the following decade (1928-1937): of a total of 3,880, only 962 were Jews. Despite its initial advantage the Jewish share thus fell to but 38.6 percent, while that of Italians already exeeded 56 percent in 1937. Since that time still newer groups of immigrants, including Puerto Ricans and Negroes coming up from the South, have further displaced the Jewish membership in the rank and file, if not in the leadership of these unions.

This transition has already created important economic and social problems within the Jewish community, which has increasingly tended to become a middle-class group, with an ever diminishing proletariat, if American workers can still be called by that name. If these trends continue American Jewry's social stratification may soon resemble that of the Jews of Germany rather than of the East European masses at the beginning of the century.

Mercantile endeavors have thus resumed their traditional place in the American community. Whether because of force of circumstance, or because of the normal predilections of a predominantly urbanized community, or because of the lure of greater profits, European Jewry had made the transition from an economically well diversified group to a preeminently mercantile people during the Middle Ages. Even in Eastern Europe and the Ottoman Empire, where Jews had to look for employment in all branches of industry —pre–World War I Salonica actually had a Jewish longshoremen's union—commerce remained the most rewarding occupation for many Jews.

Unhampered by the Physiocratic tradition, we can now view merchandising in all its forms with much less bias. Through their commercial undertakings, international and local, Jews have made tremendous contributions to human progress, and are still doing so today. Let us mention merely the humblest of all Jewish tradesmen, the peddler. Neither American nor Jewish historiography has done justice to this inconspicuous, but vitally important, builder of Jewish communal life in our own as well as many other countries. A characteristic endorsement (dated Februrary 5, 5610/1850) was entered by Rabbi Isaac M. Wise, then still in Albany, into the record book of a Palestinian messenger, Rabbi Aaron Selig Ashkenazi. While urging his readers to contribute to the aid of the poor of the Holy Land, Wise added "since many of our members are absent from the City, nothing could be done in his favor until Pesah next." Evidently the absence till Passover of numerous congregants peddling in upstate New York doomed to failure any major communal action.

What the peddler achieved was more than merely making a living for himself. By bringing ever new merchandise to the attention of villagers, he created ever new wants and thus helped lay the foundations for the American mass market, and indirectly for American mass production. In many ways he was performing the functions divided now between advertising men, salesmen, mail-order catalogues, and radio announcers. In a period when even newspapers were scarce, he served as a major agency of communication between city and countryside, between one county and another, one state and another. By keeping alive these vital channels of communication, he also served as an important link in cementing the unity of the American nation.

If the peddler happened to be a Jew, he performed still another vital function. Thomas Huxley, the great biologist, himself rather an agnostic, once extolled the impact of the Bible on Western civilization. Among its other virtues, he declared, "it forbids the veriest hind who never left his village to be ignorant of the existence of other countries and other civilizations, and of a great past stretching back to the furthest limits of the oldest civilizations of the world." In many an American, Canadian, or British village, too, most people might never have heard of a town or river fifty miles away, but they all knew of Jerusalem, Bethlehem, and Nazareth. They all had heard of the river Jordan. What the Bible did as literature, the Jewish peddler often accomplished as the living embodiment of that Biblical tradition. To many villagers the appearance of a Jew in their midst served as a living reminder of a civilization spanning continents and centuries.

The peddler soon gave way to the traveling salesman or shopkeeper. There followed the large department stores, chain stores, and mail-order houses, in all of which undertakings Jews have left a permanent mark not only in the United States, but also in England and all over the Continent. And they have been equally active in such related occupations as that of accountants, efficiency experts, and public-relations men. The whole area of mass production so dependent on mass distribution has had many Jewish protagonists. The dissemination of news, previously indirectly performed by peddlers, has since been replaced by an enormous network of newspapers, magazines, and radio and television stations. In all these mass media Jews have played a great role. In fact, from 1848 on German and Austrian antisemites never ceased complaining of Jewish domination of the press. While these accusations were exaggerated, there was no denying that such leading papers as the *Berliner Tageblatt, Vossische Zeitung, Frankfurter Zeitung,* and *Neue Freie Presse* were owned and to a large extent run by Jews. To a lesser extent the same phenomenon occurred in other countries, including the United States and the British Commonwealth, particularly in the newer communication industries, like radio and television.

However, one traditional Jewish occupation, banking, has been declining in recent years. Ever since medieval feudalism forced Jews off the soil and into moneylending, they have played a preponderant role in Europe's credit system. With the rise of modern capitalism, money and credit became the very lifeblood of the new economy. And Jewish bankers were in a position to influence the flow of production and international exchanges among advanced nations. As "court Jews" of German emperors or princes, as contractors for British and Dutch armies, as cofinanciers of such major undertakings as Columbus' voyage of discovery, or William and Mary's expedition to England, they transcended the field of economics and exerted a powerful influence on the political and cultural evolution of the Western world. They reached their climactic achievement in the first half of the nineteenth century, through the House of Rothschild. The Austrian Ambassador to Paris, Count Apponyi, was not exaggerating when he reported home that the influence of the Paris Rothschilds far exceeded that of any great European power. Although the Revolution of 1848 seemed to undermine the foundations of that great financial power, young Disraeli was able to enlist the aid of the London Rothschilds in Britain's dramatic acquisition of control over the Suez Canal, that vital link in her lifeline to India. Rothschild capital, directly or indirectly, also fructified much of the American railroad system and industry. Connections with other Jewish bankers enabled Joseph Seligman to raise substantial American loans in Frankfort and elsewhere during the Civil War. According to Abraham Lincoln, this financial support was a decisive factor in the outcome of the Civil War.

In the last several decades, however, the Jewish banker has become much less prominent. To begin with, his greatest functions were taken over by corporate banks. In countries where Jews had lived for a long time and taken deep roots in the banking system, many of them successfully negotiated the transition from private to corporate banking. In Germany, Austria, Italy, and to a lesser extent France and Russia, Jews exerted powerful, at times controlling, influence on many corporate banks. In Germany, in fact, the Jewish directors of the three big D-banks (Deutsche Bank, Dresdener Bank, Diskonto Gesellschaft) served as a major target for Nazi attacks. On the other hand, in the English-speaking countries Jews have always played but a minor role in the gigantic banking corporations. The Bank of America, the Chase Manhattan, and the National City Bank have occasionally had a Jew in a more or less important executive capacity, but at no time have Jews exerted a controlling influence. The fact is that for many years they justly complained of discriminatory personnel policies employed against them by many corporate banks. The same minor role was played by one or another Jewish director of the Big Five London banks, which until the recent rise of Wall Street to world leadership, deeply influenced the whole world economy.

Even these corporate banks began losing their preeminent position in business and industry. During the two world wars even the largest banks were unable to provide the enormous amounts needed by governments; they could at best serve as subsidiary agencies. Today banks borrow more from governments than governments from banks (including the Federal Reserve System and the Bank of England). The Senate hearings of 1939 revealed the growing independence of big industry from finance capital. It may be said, therefore, that at this stage of American and world capitalism the Jews contribute more significantly through other channels than through the credit system. In this way another great economic element of segregation, or at least differentiation, of Jews from the rest of the population has gone into the discard.

Perhaps the greatest transformation that has taken place in Jewish economy in the last one hundred and fifty years has been the large-scale entry of Jews into professions. With emancipation and the removal of disabilities Jews staged a regular run on Western professional careers. Not only did they find law, medicine, and other professions relatively lucrative, but they also seemed thus to satisfy their ancient craving for learning. In time, the legal and medical professions, especially, attracted a disproportionately large number of Jews. With their typical self-irony Jews in New England used to joke about every Jewish family having a lawyer, except for those which had two or three lawyers. Less a matter for joking was the antisemitism this phenomenon inspired, especially in Germany. But for a variety of reasons, among them the attraction of other professions such as science and engineering, the proportion of Jews in law and medicine has declined in recent years. In the United States, for example, it appears that Jewish enrollment in medical schools fell off from an average of some eighteen percent in the 1920s to some twelve percent in 1939. If this downtrend was somewhat reversed in recent years, this change was owing to other social factors.

It is especially worthy of remark that a change seems to have occurred in the Jewish attitude to learning. In the old ghetto community and in the early immigrant communities of Western Europe and the New World as well, the traditional Jewish love for learning lay behind the preference for certain professions. Today American Jewish youth show signs of sharing with their non-Jewish compatriots a certain contempt for "intellectualism." This is not the anti-intellectualism of the Hasidic movement which stressed piety, good deeds, and mystic communion with the Deity. It is rather of a purely materialistic brand. Perhaps the threats of war and atomic annihilation have helped revive that old reckless attitude of *carpe diem,* characteristic of other human periods of crisis and uncertainty. The new attitude has spread to many parts of the Old and New Worlds, even to Israel, where the generation of sabras, and still more their children, evince definitely less intellectual devotion than the first settlers.

In any case, the gap between Jews and non-Jews has greatly narrowed. The number of Jewish students at colleges and universities has been steadily increasing, but the number of non-Jewish students has grown even more rapidly. Within less than a decade American colleges will apparently have to graduate about five million students every four years. In other words, here, too, the Jewish occupational distribution is becoming more "normal," not because of any major changes in Jewish occupational preference, but because the outside world receives an ever more "Jewish" occupational coloring.

IMPACT ON VARIOUS ISMS

The socio-economic evolution here sketched is naturally interrelated with the various social movements in recent generations. Jews have evidently prospered most under a liberal system of economics and government. Democracy, which had genuinely appealed to Jews because of its mainsprings in the prophetic insistence on the dignity of man, and its affinity to the egalitarian mode of life of the old Jewish community, now had a redoubled attraction for Jews because of the greater economic opportunities it offered to the ever growing Jewish population. It had removed most traditional disabilities, and because of its connections with economic liberalism it had opened broad new avenues for Jewish enterprise and imagination. Certainly the marvelous economic expansion of modern Jewry would have been impossible without the liberties enshrined by the American and French Revolutions, which guaranteed equal treatment for Jews as individuals, rather than as members of a segregated, inferior group.

Right here, however, we find a serious catch. Even during the French Revolution farsighted observers had detected a basic contradiction in the revolutionary triad of Liberty, Equality, and Fraternity. Full liberty, they contended, means "war of all against all," and the rule of the strong. In the economic sphere it means that the rich get richer, while the poor become poorer. If one wishes to counteract the power of the strong in favor of equality, one must necessarily curtail liberty. In advanced capitalism there has indeed been a growing concentration of power in corporate enterprises. Radicals, and even moderate liberals, have often vigorously denounced these corporate "monopolies." Not only outright socialists, but also New Dealers and other progressives, have sponsored antitrust, fiscal, and labor legislation.

On the whole, the majority of Jews favored such restrictions, having learned from bitter experience that for the most part economic concentration operated against them. Moreover, by age-old tradition Jews felt most comfortable when they were their own bosses. Wherever economic liberty was furthest advanced, the Jews found the road easier. Yet they could not get along with liberty without equality; their long communal experience had trained them for a certain balance between the two, as well as between authority and freedom. Accordingly they desired some such equilibrium for modern society at large. In mankind's great struggle to achieve this balance—the present division of the world is that between libertarian democracy and egalitarian communism—the Jewish people may yet be given the opportunity of finding new solutions to that perennial riddle.

Judaism and fascism are intrinsically incompatible. Not that fascism is necessarily antisemitic. In the first fifteen years of Italy's Fascist regime there were no overt anti-Jewish policies. Mussolini even indulged in such gestures as inviting students persecuted in their homelands to study at Italian universities with full tuition scholarships. Nonetheless, fascism as such—its glorification of the state and its corporate regimentation—ran counter to the deep-rooted traditions of Judaism, as well as to the long-range interests of the Jewish people. Well before 1938 many Jewish scholars in Italy lost their university positions because they refused to swear the required loyalty oath, and there was a constant diminution of Jews in leading positions in government, arts and sciences, and even in business. Even without joining the Axis, therefore, Fascist Italy would doubtless have gradually reduced the Jewish share in the country's public life to a minimum.

Where Fascist seeds fell upon an antisemitic soil, as in interwar Poland, their impact on Jewish life was felt immediately. With the government's increasing controls over industry and commerce, and its consciously discriminatory policies, Jews were speedily eliminated from one occupation after another. For example, the tobacco industry, and especially the tobacco outlets, had long been predominantly in Jewish hands. No sooner did the industry become a government monopoly than the number of Jewish workers and tobacconists declined catastrophically. Ultimately, only such Jews could sell tobacco as were able to make arrangements with non-Jewish figureheads in possession of government licenses. On the other hand, if neither Franco, Salazar, nor Peron pursued consistently anti-Jewish policies— for a time during Hitler's ascendancy both Spain and Argentina did reveal strong leanings toward anti-Jewish discrimination—this was owing to peculiar local circumstances. The Jewish communities of Spain and Portugal were numerically insignificant, and these governments' attitudes were largely measured by their reception of Jewish refugees. Here, of course, international considerations greatly modified the dictators' preferences. In Argentina the threat to the substantial Jewish community appeared greater, as some protagonists of the Peronista movement preached a return to the medieval Spanish traditions of intolerance. Harking back to inquisitorial ideologies, some spokesmen of the new regime even extolled the "penitential" value of violence. Fortunately for the Jews, the general libertarian traditions of the country were reinforced by the growing dissensions between the Catholic Church, extremely powerful in that predominently Catholic country, and the Peronista party.

Much more significant for the past and also, it appears, for the future of world Jewry is the relationship between the various socialist movements and the Jews. At first socialism seemed to assume a definitely hostile attitude, not only to Judaism as a religion—most socialists preached agnosticism—but also to the Jews as such. Arising in Western Europe, where Jews were largely concentrated in mercantile occupations, the early socialist parties evinced a strong anti-Jewish bias. Even where, as in Amsterdam, a large segment of the Jewish population belonged to the proletariat—indeed, lived on communal charity—it failed to provide the proper human material for socialism. To Fourier most Jews appeared as outright social parasites. In a typical antisemitic vein he preached forcible restratification of Jews and their resettlement on the land. The rise to power of Jewish banking firms led some socialist writers to join in the antisemitic outcry against so-called Jewish financial domination. One of Fourier's pupils, Toussenel, sounded the battle cry of contemporary antisemites in a book with the telltale title of *Juifs, Rois de l'Époche* (Jews, Kings of Our Period). Most significantly, Karl Marx himself, though a descendant of rabbis going as far back as Rabbi Meir Katzenellenbogen of Padua, went on record with two rather Jew-baiting essays. Marx argued that Judaism was nothing but the spirit of civil society (*bürgerliche Gesellschaft*) and that, with the passing of that society as a result of the forthcoming revolution, it was bound to go out of existence. He was prepared to minimize even the heatedly debated problem of Jewish emancipation. In the words, "The social emancipation of the Jew is the emancipation of society from Judaism," Marx epitomized his view of the Jewish question. Even Moses Hess, though loyal to Jewish tradition, subordinated Jewish equality to the social problem. Reminiscing later on the Damascus Affair, he admitted that he had mastered his impulse to do something for the persecuted Jews by giving higher priority to his socialist efforts.

In time, however, socialist opinion changed. The more Western socialism veered toward an alliance with democracy, the more it recognized the egalitarian claims of the Jews. Furthermore, the old equation of Jews with capitalists had to be abandoned in the light of East European realities. There the vast masses of Jews were known to live in dismal poverty. A large segment made a living through hard physical labor, and fitted very well into the picture of a proletariat, if not necessarily of an industrial proletariat after the Western pattern. Before long the German Socialist Party, leading the world's socialist movements in numbers and ideological insight, repudiated in its official platform any kind of antisemitism. Finally, August Bebel, leader of that Party at the turn of the century, ridiculed all antisemitism as the "socialism of fools." In London, not only Friedrich Engels but also Marx's own daughter personally agitated among the newly immigrated Jewish workers in Whitechapel. Miss Marx allegedly studied Yiddish in order to become a more effective propagandist among these promising recruits to the cause.

This opposition to antisemitism was deepened by the increasing utilization of antisemitic slogans for the combating of socialism and with the appearance of prominent Jewish members in the socialist parties in all countries. When, in the Dreyfus affair, the conservative circles of France tried to use Dreyfus as a means of undermining the Third Republic, Jean Jaurès, the recognized socialist leader, became an outspoken Dreyfusard. Similarly, Russian socialism in all its forms sharply combated Tsarist antisemitism as being an integral part of Tsarist tyranny.

While objecting for a time to the formation of a special Jewish socialist party, Lenin sharply opposed any form of antisemitism. When he came to power, he not only continued the egalitarian provisions inserted into the constitution by the previous Lvov-Kerensky regime, but also tackled the antisemitic problem directly. In July, 1918, he outlawed antisemitism as a counterrevolutionary crime. He also delivered a radio address in which he declared that anyone acting in an antisemitic fashion thereby aided and abetted the restoration of Tsarist traditions, and hence undermined the Revolution. This address, frequently rebroadcast over the entire network of the Soviet Union, even after Lenin's death, understandably made a great impression. Russia was frequently cited abroad as the only country which had formally outlawed antisemitism. Of course, foreign apologists often overlooked the difference between the Soviet Union, where freedom of speech was in general sharply curtailed, and the Western democracies, where even many Jews had come to feel that formal outlawry of antisemitism might endanger rather than enhance civil liberties.

In any case, outlawry was not enough. Not only was Jew-baiting too deeply ingrained in the Russian population through several generations of antisemitic propaganda from press and pulpit, but the Communist regime itself gradually changed its attitude. The law was never revoked. The constitution of 1936 fully retained all egalitarian principles. But many other paragraphs in that constitution were evidently formulated as goals toward which public life was to be steered, rather than as binding laws for the present. The more deeply totalitarian and nationalistic the Soviet Union became, the more manifest was the chasm separating it from traditional Jewish values. Ultimately it not only reduced the Jews' long-cherished national minority rights to a shambles, but, especially in the period of the recent cold war, it began suspecting Jews of "cosmopolitanism." With their interterritorial connections and traditionally international outlook, Jews, even if avowed Communists, appeared as unreliable partisans in the approaching conflict with the Western democracies. Toward the end of Stalin's life a lurid story about a Jewish doctors' conspiracy seemed to open the road toward untrammeled persecution of Jews and their speedy elimination from all positions of trust and confidence. Since Stalin's death and with the attempts at rapprochement with the Western powers, this governmentally sponsored anti-Jewish orientation has been greatly toned down. However, the situation is still far from reassuring. Apart from antisemitism, moreover, the totalitarian system of education and the overpowering pressures of its one-track ideology have already sapped the vitality of Russian Jewry to such an extent that many keen observers have expressed doubts as to the possibility of its survival for many more generations.

Within the European socialist movements there emerged, beginning in the 1870s, specifically Jewish parties. At first they were very restrained about their Jewish character. When Aaron Lieberman began publishing the first Jewish socialist paper in Hebrew, he made it clear that he was not propagating any kind of Judaism, but was using this medium the better to acquaint Jewish workers with socialist principles. When asked by a Vienna court, as was usual, to state his religion, he answered succinctly, "I am a socialist." Essentially the same line was adopted by the later publishers of Yiddish socialist papers and, especially, by the leaders of the Jewish Socialist Party, the Bund. For many years after its formation in 1897, the Bund disclaimed all national aspirations and avowed that a special Jewish party was needed only for the more effective propagation of socialism among the Jewish masses. When the Bund changed its mind and, beginning in 1903, advocated national minority rights for Jews, it had a hard time defending this new position before its comrades in the Russian Socialist Party. The latter, totaling no more than some 50,000 members, looked askance at the presence of a large "separatist" Jewish party consisting of about 30,000 members. At that time Lenin was the most vigorous opponent of such Jewish separatism. In two remarkable essays, republished as late as 1913, he declared,

> The Jews in the civilized world are not a nation, they have become most of all assimilated. . . . The Jews in Galicia and Russia are not a nation, they unfortunately (and not through their fault, but owing to the Purishkeviches) are still a *caste*. . . . These facts indicate that "assimilation" can be denounced only by the Jewish reactionary petty bourgeois, who wish to turn back the wheel of history, and to force it to move, not from the conditions of Russia and Galicia to the conditions of Paris and New York, but in the opposite direction. . . .
>
> Whoever directly or otherwise puts forward the slogan of Jewish national culture (however well intentioned he may be) is the enemy of the proletariat, the defender of the *old* and *caste* element in Jewry, the tool of the rabbis and of the bourgeoisie.

By a major historic irony, four years later Lenin himself expressly recognized the Jews as a national minority in the Soviet Union. He had evidently yielded to the all but unanimous desire of Russian Jewry, which had shortly before found expression in the election of nationalist Jewish deputies to the Constituent Assembly.

Within the Jewish socialist movement itself divisions arose. The Bund consistently adhered to its Diaspora nationalism. It saw the salvation of the Jewish people in the progress of socialism, combined with Jewish communal autonomy and the cultivation of Yiddish culture. Other groups, however, synthesized their socialism with Zionism. Ber Borochov, especially, tried to harmonize his internationalist, Marxist outlook with the idea of the national restoration of Jews to Palestine. We shall see how great a role Labor Zionism played in the upbuilding of the Jewish homeland and, more recently, in the creation and administration of the new state of Israel. Nor was Labor Zionism a monolithic group. After the Revolution of 1917, especially, there developed a deep cleavage between the left and the right Poale Zion, between pro- and anti-Russian orientation. The cleavage still persists, especially between the adherents of Mapai and Mapam.

Looking at the world scene today one cannot fail to notice the difference in the political and economic structures of the Jews living under the Western democracies, those residing within the Soviet orbit, and finally the new citizens of Israel. In the Western world Jews have become an essentially middle-class group. Correspondingly, they are dominated by middle-class ideologies. Even their labor leaders tend to approve the capitalist order of society and the basic principles of political and economic liberalism which, after all, have been so beneficial to their people. In the Soviet Union and her satellites, on the other hand, the Jews have increasingly become integrated into the Communist economy—in whatever stage of realization of its Communist ideal the latter may be. In so far as they can still guide their own destinies, they are exponents of strong social controls. Israel, a nation in the making, is oscillating between economic liberalism and socialist controls. Of course, Israel does not live in a vacuum and the pressures of a divided world on the one hand, and of world Jewry on the other, tend to color deeply its domestic policies as well. On the whole, however, the preponderance of democratic labor parties in Israel, and their relative weakness within the Jewries of the Dispersion, are but a reflection of the varying socio-economic structures of these segments of the Jewish people.

17

THE EMERGENCE OF ISRAEL

Contrary to appearances, modern Zionism together with the rise of the new state of Israel have been part and parcel of the emancipation movement. The very comprehensiveness of the Zionist ideal—its appeal to many wings of Jewry from the ultra-Orthodox to agnostics, from reactionaries to socialists—is in itself not only the effect of the millennial traditions of the Jewish past, but of the perplexities of the emancipation era, and the quest for integral solutions.

The fact is that the rise of the state of Israel would have been impossible without emancipated Jewries. For it required the trained manpower, the modern scientific and technical knowledge acquired by Jews in general schools and universities, and the tremendous financial resources which became available to the Jewish people only as a result of its full participation in the economic development of Western countries. Nor would Israel have been possible without the armed forces, which in part had been prepared by service in the Western armies during World War I and II, or above all without the political influence exerted by the masses of American and other Jews taking an active part in the political life of their respective countries. Every major step in securing international recognition for the Jewish postulates from the days of Montefiore to Herzl, and still more from the Balfour

Declaration to the United Nations resolution of 1947, came about only through the political activism of the emancipated Jewish communities. Finally, even the continued existence of Israel would have been impossible without the economic, fiscal, military, and administrative machinery developed by Jews under the opportunities of emancipated living.

On the other hand, Zionism achieved a new sense of urgency as a result of emancipation. In the preemancipatory period Jews, pursuing their accustomed way of life, had developed many effective substitutes for the missing state and territory. They had in their autonomous community a surrogate, however imperfect, for independent statehood, while their ghetto, whether or not formally established by law, gave them the illusion of possessing a territory of their own. Moreover, their sense of kinship with Jews of other lands was little disturbed by their geographic dispersion. *Kelal Yisrael,* the totality of the Jewish people, was not merely an ideal, but in many respects a living reality. As late as the seventeenth century, Jews living in cities as far apart as Cracow and Safed knew more about each other than about their Christian or Muslim neighbors two or three streets away. The *Shulhan Arukh* compiled by Joseph Karo, a son of Spanish refugees in the Ottoman Empire, could immediately be subjected to criticisms and supplementation by Mordecai Yafeh of Venice and Posen, and Moses Isserles of Cracow. The joint work of Karo and Isserles soon became the standard code of Judaism. At the same time most Jews, even the more educated, knew little and cared less about the controversies between Lutherans, Calvinists, and Catholics, and for a time even between a Galileo or a Newton and their old-time opponents.

Now under conditions of emancipation the old system began to break up, as did the unity of the Jewish people. Not only did Jews lose their traditional substitutes for state and territory, but they were expected to become integrated into the national majorities among whom they lived. For example, there was real danger that American Jews, now often considering themselves first Americans and then Jews, would lose their sense of identity with French, Argentinian, and other Jews who might feel the same way about their countries. In recent years the cleavage between Western Jews and those living behind the Iron Curtain has underscored these dangers of separation. In the early years of the Communist Revolution, when Russian Jews, enjoying their national minority rights, built an imposing structure of Jewish education with some 350,000 pupils attending schools (from grammar schools to sectors of universities) in which Yiddish was the language of instruction, some of their spokesmen considered most Western Jews "bad," assimilated Jews, since they sent their children to general schools. Reciprocally, Western Jews looked down upon Russian Jews because they were prepared to throw overboard the traditional values of the Jewish religion and Zionism.

Under these circumstances the building of a Jewish homeland in Palestine which would focalize all Jewish life appeared as an imperative necessity to thinking Jews. Here, even before achieving sovereignty, the Jewish community was not subject to the pressures of assimilation. The Yishub could hardly have become either Turkish or Arab or British. Moreover, here was a modern community, not merely a survival of the old ghetto community. Romantics of all kinds might cherish, even exaggerate, the memory of ghetto life, but hardly anyone could deny that that life had been doomed by emancipation and that it could no longer serve as the animating force in the preservation of Judaism in the modern world. By developing purely Jewish, and yet modern, values a Jewish homeland would provide the standard by which the Jewishness of the respective national groups could be measured. In short, Zionism presupposed emancipation, while emancipation made Zionism an inescapable necessity.

RELIGIOUS MOTIVATIONS

Behind the Zionist movement were, of course, the Jews' ancient yearnings for restoration to the land of their forefathers. In the home, school, and synagogue every growing child received a deep indoctrination in that messianic ideal, in the darkest moments of history even more than in the brightest. At times Jews were ready to follow false messiahs. The latest and in some respects the most influential of these, Shabbetai Zevi (1626-1676), demonstrated anew the overpowering appeal of the Holy Land. It is difficult to imagine today a group of bankers and big businessmen, all level-headed realists, prepared suddenly to pick up all their belongings and follow the call of the King Messiah. Yet this is what actually happened to the communal elders of the Sephardic community of Hamburg, as is shown by a number of remarkable entries in their congregational minute book. Even Shabbetai's ultimate conversion to Islam did not completely undermine his disciples' faith in his message. Before long one of them, Abraham Cardozo, of Marrano origin, developed the theory of *Misvah ha-baah ba-averah* (a commandment achieved through the commission of a sin). Vastly expanding this Talmudic doctrine, and undoubtedly influenced by rationalizations current among the secret Jews of the Iberian Peninsula, Cardozo now taught that release from the ceremonial law may indeed be the prelude to ultimate redemption.

Whether sharing these revolutionary views or repudiating them, Shabbetians filled the Jewish world with their heated public controversies, and still more with their underground agitation. In many ways they were indeed the harbingers of the new age of Enlightenment and emancipation through which ran the persistent expectation of return to Zion.

Out of this spiritual élan came the first mass migration of Jews to Palestine in modern times. Pilgrimages had, of course, never ceased. Back in 1211, for example, partly under the stimulus of the Crusades, three hundred West European rabbis journeyed to Palestine. Now under the leadership of Yehudah he-Hasid fully a thousand Jews, recruited from Poland, Germany, and other countries, settled in Palestine in 1700. They were followed by many other rabbis, mystics, and ordinary Jews. Indeed, many of them believed that they would thus be spared the underground migration which awaited all bodies buried elsewhere before they could arise from the dead in the messianic age. To most Jews even such exalted descriptions of the Holy Land as were uttered by the great Hasidic rabbi, Nahman of Bratslav, were utterly convincing. He wrote:

> And even now that we are exiled from our land for the vast number of our transgressions, Erez Israel still persists in holiness because of the strength of the hidden Torah and the love that seeks no returns, the love that was hidden in the land even when it was still in the hands of the Canaanites. That is why we are always waiting to return to our land, for we know that in secret it is ours.

That Nahman took his teachings seriously was evidenced by his own departure for Palestine at the age of twenty-six. To achieve this goal he and his family had to sacrifice a great deal. "You will proceed to your future father-in-law," he wrote in 1799 to his eldest daughter, "your older sister will become a servant, your little sister will probably be taken into some home out of pity, your mother will become a cook, and I shall dispose of all my household for traveling expenses." Of another Hasidic leader the story is told that he was so convinced of the imminence of the advent of the Redeemer that he always kept two saddled horses in his stable, lest he lose a moment in heeding the call of the messianic *Shofar*.

Such intensity of feeling was, of course, not characteristic of the common man. Under the influence of early capitalism and the growing enjoyment of the amenities of life, voices began to be heard even in the eighteenth century, proclaiming that the Messiah had better not come and disturb the existing satisfactory state of affairs. But the majority repeated with great devotion the numerous prayers for return to the land of Israel. Meanwhile, welcome was extended to the recurrent arrival of messengers from the Holy Land, who collected funds for Palestine relief. This was not ordinary charity, for almost everyone believed that by dedicating their lives to study and good deeds on the holy soil, the Palestinian communities were redeeming the soul of all Israel. Financial support for the remnant that was in Zion was therefore considered by many donors an eminent means to the forgiveness of sin.

Nor was the belief in the ultimate Jewish restoration to the Holy Land limited to Jews. Pious Christians of all denominations included genuine believers in such restoration as a necessary prerequisite for the second coming of Christ. So convinced were even the medieval churchmen of the necessity of keeping Jews until the end of days that Duns Scotus, for example, living in the hostile environment of pre-Expulsion England, suggested that the Christian world maintain some Jews at its expense on a distant island. From among the British missionaries in particular, there arose champions of both Jewish equality and the restoration of Jews to Palestine—another illustration of the intrinsic nexus between emancipation and Zionism. Typical of their approach is the memorandum submitted to Lord Palmerston, then Foreign Secretary, by 320 Christian petitioners:

> Your Memorialists beg leave further to remind Your Lordship that the Land of Palestine was bestowed by the Sovereign of the Universe upon the descendants of Abraham as a permanent and inalienable possession nearly 4000 Years ago, and that neither conquests nor treaties among men can possibly effect their Title to it. He has also decreed that they shall again return to their Country and that the Gentiles shall be employed as the means of their restoration.

While explaining the religious fervor behind Zionism, these ancient doctrines and emotions could also be directed into anti-Zionist channels. Many rabbinic and Hasidic leaders believed that redemption had to be accomplished in a supernatural way by direct divine intervention, so that any merely human effort to bring the Jews to their country was not only futile but impious, for it endeavored to "push the end" ahead of the predestined time. Although gradually an increasing number of Orthodox joined the Zionist wing, the Mizrachi, and even many members of the ultra-Orthodox Agudas Israel viewed the rise of the new state with growing sympathy, there remained a core of intransigent objectors to any purely human solutions. To the present time, a remnant in Jerusalem calling itself *Neture Karta* (Watchman of the City) so far repudiates the reality of the state as to refuse to accept ration cards. In the earlier years of utter austerity, it preferred starvation to the surrender of its principles. In the Dispersion, too, the Belzer rabbi is reported to have issued a manifesto in the summer of 1955 urging his Israeli followers to boycott the national elections.

Another group of religious objectors came from the Reform camp. Zionists have frequently attributed Reform's antagonism to its utter preoccupation with the quest for equality. But this is an oversimplification of extremely complex phenomena. Not only did some leading Reform rabbis in all sincerity deny the connection, but in its early enthusiasm the Reform movement envisioned a thorough reorientation of the Jewish faith in the direction of universalism. In many ways Reform was as genuine a child of European Enlightenment as were Haskalah and many of the agnostic trends in Judaism. Its early protagonists were convinced that the Jewish religion must cast off all its "particularist" shackles and become the religion of humanity. In this respect the Jewish people—not nationality—still had a function to perform by missionizing for its ideals of ethical monotheism. Such a program could only be hampered by the restoration of Jews to a small Near Eastern country. Time and again Reform leaders cited the old Rabbinic saying that "God has bestowed a benefit upon the Jews by dispersing them among the nations," and that this would facilitate the Jewish mission.

Not all Reform leaders were of one mind, however. From the outset there were some influential spokesmen preaching reconciliation between Reform and Zionism. In America, where the Reform movement reached its greatest intensity, Herzlian Zionism found an immediate response among such influential Reform rabbis as Bernard Felsenthal, Gustav Gottheil, and the youthful Stephen S. Wise. As late as 1918, it is true, the Central Conference of American Rabbis by a substantial majority went on record against the Balfour Declaration and its implementation at the forthcoming Peace Conference. Yet the progress of Mandatory Palestine on the one hand, and the entry into the Reform ministry of many younger men with an East European pro-Zionist background on the other, brought about an increasing rapprochement. By the 1930s the actual majority of Reform leaders, both in this country and abroad, adopted a pro-Zionist stand. After first including the *Hatikvah* in the Reform hymnal, the Central Conference voted with increasing majorities in favor of pro-Zionist solutions. The diehards did not completely disappear, however. Finding themselves in a minority, some of them finally organized, with the aid of sharply anti-Zionist laymen—not necessarily of the Reform persuasion—the American Council on Judaism. But on this plane the political issues far overshadowed the original religious objections to Zionism. In fact, the course of recent history has reduced such religious objectors, whether Orthodox or Reform, to an insignificant minority.

THE HUMANITARIAN ELEMENT

Palestine carried great appeal to Jews, and even to Christians, on purely humanitarian grounds. Diaspora Jewry took all the more pride in its support of the Palestinian remnant and in personal pilgrimages, as the Christian world, too, generation after generation, sent to the Holy Land thousands of pilgrims and settlers and helped maintain there numerous monasteries and religious schools. The more ruinous were the fiscal exactions of the Turkish administration in Palestine, the more unbridled the tyranny and arbitrariness of local officials, the more readily did world Jewry extend a helping hand to its downtrodden coreligionists. In the introduction to his famous prayer book, Jacob Emden, a prominent German scholar of the eighteenth century, voiced the keynote of that Diaspora attitude:

> Everyone in Israel must in his heart steadfastly resolve to go to Erez Israel and to remain there. But if he cannot go himself, he should, if his circumstances permit—whether he be a craftsman or a merchant—support some person in that country, and so do his part in restoring the Holy Land, which has been laid waste, by maintaining one of its rightful inhabitants. He must feel the desire to pray there before the King's palace, to which the Divine Presence still clings, even in its destruction. Therefore he who does not live in that country cannot give perfect service to God.

In this way there arose the philanthropic system of *Halukkah* which dominated Jewish life in Palestine from the beginnings of the Zionist colonization. In the nineteenth century the increase in immigration gave rise to curious "national" divisions. The few Jews from Germany and Holland organized a Kolel Hod which claimed to be the rightful recipient of all the relatively large contributions from these countries. It wished to distribute all such receipts only among former compatriots. Other Jews naturally objected, and began organizing independent national committees of their own, until everyone realized that such anarchical distribution seriously interfered with fund-raising abroad. Ultimately the various Ashkenazic Kolelim got together and formed a general committee headed by the distinguished rabbi, Samuel Salant. Ironically, American Jews, whose compatriots were substantial contributors to the *Halukkah,* but who had no Kolel of their own, received no support whatever.

Additional difficulties arose in connection with the methods of fund-raising. Devoted as the Jewish communities abroad may have been to the Palestine ideal, they often required the additional stimulus of personal visits by a Palestinian messenger. Such messengers were usually fêted by the local leaders, and allowed to address congregations and to engage in fund-raising on a large scale. As far back as the seventeenth century, however, it was realized that the cost of dispatching messengers for a period of months or even years ate up most of the revenue. That is why many communities adopted resolutions discouraging the dispatch of messengers and pledging themselves to raise the necessary funds without such outside aid. But the results were disappointing. Communities often faced too embarrassingly complex local problems to enable them to concentrate on the relief of distant coreligionists. On the Palestinian side, some messengers developed a vested interest in fund-raising and, defying resolutions of the kind just mentioned, reappeared in increasing numbers. These experiences of European Jewry were duplicated in the nineteenth century in America. Much as the local leaders tried to organize Palestine Relief on a permanent basis—Tarumat ha-Kodesh was organized in New York in 1833 and functioned there for many decades—and much as the leading rabbis including Isaac Lesser publicly appealed to the Jerusalem elders not to dispatch messengers, these visitors kept on arriving and attaining considerable financial success.

The *Halukkah* system survived even more serious attacks from both Palestinian members and occasional Western visitors. Perhaps the most devastating critique was contained in a report submitted in 1876 to the Board of Jewish Deputies in England by two of its most respected members, Samuel Montague (later Lord Swaythling) and Asher Asher. This report was circulated privately and received considerable attention from the Jewish press in both England and America. Among other matters it criticized the system under which every newborn child automatically became a charge on the charitable chest "and hence procreation is regarded as a legitimate means of livelihood"! Some recipients used their money to lend it at usurious interest to Arabs. The funds arriving from Eastern Europe were distributed by rabbis "who insist before dispersing a dollar to others, on apportioning the larger part to themselves." Finally, in their use of funds for education the local leaders confined teachers to instruction in Hebrew and Talmud, while parents who allowed their children to be taught Arabic or some European language were excommunicated. These objections to the *Halukkah* system swelled into a powerful chorus after the rise

of the Zionist movement. Zionists objected vehemently to the demor-
alization that resulted from an entire community living on charity,
and sought to substitute productive work in its stead.

Nonetheless, messengers kept on arriving and *Halukkah* kept on
being distributed to an ever increasing number of recipients. In retrospect, one must pay homage to the numerous distinguished messengers
whose influence on the world community cannot easily be exaggerated. When Hayyim Joseph David Azulai, the famous eighteenth-
century polyhistor, arrived in a Western country, whether it was
Tunisia, Italy, France, or England, his great learning, combined with
his charm and worldly wisdom, left a permanent imprint upon these
communities and sometimes even upon non-Jews. An acute observer,
Azulai was able to leave behind also a travel diary which is one of the
most informative documents on Jewish life in the period before the
French Revolution. Another Palestinian messenger of that time, Hayyim Isaac Carigal, traveled extensively in the New World. We possess a charming description of his impressive personality from the pen
of Ezra Stiles, then Congregational minister in Newport and later
president of Yale University.

On many occasions such messengers were asked to arbitrate local
disputes. In all cases they kept alive, not only the connections between
Palestine and Diaspora Jewry, but between the various communities
of the Dispersion themselves. Had not even Shabbetai Zevi begun his
career as a messenger? Perhaps his great early successes as a preacher
during his fund-raising journey inspired him, as well as many of his
followers, with the idea that he was to be the chosen redeemer.

This tradition of humanitarian aid for Palestine Jewry remained
alive even after *Halukkah* came into considerable disrepute. Philanthropy always had great appeal for Jews. The designation *rahmanim
bne rahmanim* (merciful sons of merciful sires) applied to themselves by generations of Jews was for them an endless source of pride
and gratification. That is why the humanitarian appeal of helping
downtrodden Jews in Palestine, or those seeking refuge there, had
great potency even with anti-Zionists. During World War I, when
the Turkish administration suspected Palestine Jewry of pro-Allied
sympathies, so that Governor Djemal Pasha imprisoned thousands of
the Zionist settlers, the whole Jewish world, regardless of its ideology,
tried to help them. This phenomenon repeated itself during the interwar period. When persecuted Polish or Rumanian Jews of the
1920s were knocking at the gates of Palestine, they found a sympathetic hearing and even financial support from quarters which sharply
rejected the Zionist political demands. Such non-Zionist Americans as
Louis Marshall and Felix Warburg joined hands with the Zionists in

the formation of a Jewish Agency for Palestine in 1928. Ultimately, under the blows of Nazi persecution, the idea of Palestine as a haven of refuge for endangered European Jewry began to dominate even Zionist thinking.

Although essentially running counter to the idea of a reborn nation, self-reliant in its economic and cultural endeavor, this program of salvaging as many Jews as possible from the horrors of the Nazi concentration camps loomed large in all Zionist and world opinion. The public of the Western world, horrified at the Nazi atrocities and conscience-stricken at its own inactivity, found some comfort in the idea of bringing the surviving remnant back to the land of its forefathers. In the name of that human salvage President Truman effectively proposed the admission of 100,000 Jews to Palestine in 1946, a suggestion which was to open the floodgates for the subsequent diplomatic and military storms which led to the proclamation of the new state. It is also in the name of this basic idea of salvage, rather than productive selectivity, that one of the first measures taken by the new state was the adoption of the "Law of Return." Thenceforth all Jews, regardless of age, sex, country of origin, and even of their ultimate usefulness to Israel society, were to be admitted to the country as of right.

CULTURAL ASPIRATIONS

Superimposed upon these religious and humanitarian sentiments was the quest, in recent generations, for the cultural rebirth of the Jewish people, for which the soil of Palestine was considered preeminently suitable. This notion, an offshoot of modern nationalism, general as well as Jewish, was nurtured from the mainsprings of European romanticism. Phrases like "national spirit springing up from the national soil" were now freely bandied about. True, the heritage of Enlightenment was still strong enough for these younger nationalists to believe in their ability to remake the world in the name of a preconceived program. But they no longer believed that such a program could be designed by reason alone; it had above all to be based on history-rooted emotions and traditions.

Such a spiritual rebuilding of the Jewish people's life became an increasing preoccupation of those thoughtful Jews who had moved away from the traditional Orthodox rationales for Jewish existence, yet did not wish to see Judaism submerged in the surrounding cultures. The first to formulate clearly this hope for a cultural regeneration of the Jewish people was Moses Hess, who wrote in 1862, that he believed in the continued progress of mankind and saw the messianic end of days only in the development and education of humanity to its highest point. "We are on the eve," he exclaimed, "of the Sabbath of history and should prepare for our last mission through a thorough understanding of our historical religion." Not that Hess really wanted a revival of the traditional Jewish religion, whether in its Orthodox or Reform interpretation; rather, he viewed the historic heritage of the Jews as a set of humanitarian ideas to be realized by purely cultural efforts.

Western Europeans like Hess still spoke largely in religious terms, since this was the only basis of Jewish communal coexistence. In Eastern Europe, where the masses of Jews lived their Jewish way of life, spoke their Jewish language, and were subject to fewer assimilatory pressures, these cultural aspirations could take on an outright secular coloring. We recall the rise of the national movement among the East European Jews, its penetration into labor circles, and its revival of Yiddish as an instrument of the national renascence. Other leading intellectuals felt that Hebrew, rather than Yiddish, should become the instrumentality of national rebirth. In a remarkable essay on "The Renascence of the Spirit," written in 1902, Ahad Haam (Asher Ginzberg) insisted that "there exists no people among those now living, or those which have long disappeared, of which we may contend that it is older than its national language. There has existed none which has lived for long periods of time in the light of history before learning its national language." This shaft was, of course, aimed at Yiddish, which had made its appearance in history not earlier than the twelfth or thirteenth century, whereas the Jewish nationality had already been in existence for some thirty centuries before. At the same time, Ahad Haam realized that for the full development of Hebrew culture, one required a national home. Hence his espousal of "cultural Zionism," namely, the restoration of a segment of the people to Palestine, where it could undisturbedly dedicate itself to the development of a modern, secular Hebraic culture for the benefit of all Jewry, indeed, of all mankind.

Not that Ahad Haam wished to leave the revival of Hebrew to the Yishub alone. He knew that although it had always been the language of the Jewish intelligentsia, Hebrew had long been in disuse as a daily language. However, many Jews had used it in their regular correspondence, business records, legal documents, and a variety of other "secular" undertakings. At times, especially when Jews from different countries met, they got along best by conversing in Hebrew, however haltingly. When in the nineteenth century East European Jewry had become ready for a press of its own, the first journals launched, especially those which lasted at all, were in Hebrew. Even socialist Aron Liberman, professedly agnostic and international-minded, published the first Jewish socialist paper in Hebrew under the characteristic Hebrew title, *Ha-Emet* (The Truth).

A concerted effort was made to convert the ancient "holy tongue" into a language of the home and the street. Outstanding among the protagonists of the revival of Hebrew was a young fanatic, Eliezer ben Yehuda, who insisted on speaking Hebrew to all his friends, even to non-Jews. A powerful Hebrew movement in press, letters, and practical education was making headway in the Dispersion almost as quickly as in Palestine. But only extremists believed that the whole people would speak Hebrew in its daily exchanges outside the cultural center in Palestine. Even there, it required almost superhuman efforts to turn a national imperative into a practical actuality. The protagonists realized that they had to conduct a two-front war. On the one hand, they had to overcome the resistance of those who believed that Jews should learn only the languages of the majority nations. Even in Palestine it required a protracted struggle, not only against inertia, especially that of older settlers, who continued speaking Yiddish and other languages of their home countries, but also against a conscious Germanizing effort in the schools established in the Holy Land by the German Jewish *Hilfsverein*. In a dramatic strike of the teachers of that school system in 1913, the Hebraists won. Even more difficult was the other front, the struggle against the other national language, Yiddish. Many nationalists, especially among the socialists and populists, sharply repudiated Hebrew as the language of religion and reaction. In the heated controversy between Hebraists and Yiddishists, the leading Zionist Nathan Birnbaum joined the populist camp. The Tchernowitz Conference of 1908 and such organs as Birnbaum's *Dos Volk* declared war on the protagonists of Hebrew. The Hebraists fell back on Judah the Patriarch, the compiler of the Mishna, who, confronted with a Jewish people speaking Aramaic-Syriac in the midst of the great Greco-Roman civilization, exclaimed: "Either Hebrew or Greek—why Syriac!" This battle cry was echoed three generations later by a Babylonian sage living under Persian domination, who likewise insisted that Jews should speak either Hebrew or Persian, but not Aramaic. Now many Zionist leaders sang in a chorus: "Either Hebrew or Russian" (or Polish, or any other majority language) "—why Yiddish!"

Such a program was not easy to fulfill. The Hebrew vocabulary was still limited to the religious, scholarly, and business areas where it had been customarily applied. Objects in daily use, new technological discoveries, a variety of technical terms in sciences, law, and even education—all required a new terminology. Undismayed, Ben Yehuda and a host of Hebrew teachers and writers proceeded to coin new terms. Some of these were readily accepted, others repudiated. Single-handedly Ben Yehuda undertook to prepare a gigantic dictionary, of the kind usually compiled as a collective project under the auspices of a major academy of learning. One lifetime was not enough for such a project and it has been completed only in recent years by several workers under the editorship of N. H. Tur Sinai. But it was the volumes which appeared in Ben Yehuda's lifetime, or immediately after his death, that pointed the way. In a more organized fashion Palestinian Jewry, at the beginning of this century, organized a linguistic committee, recently replaced by the Language Academy, which was in charge of expanding the language by placing its stamp of approval on terms already in use or by inventing new ones. In recent decades dictionaries of technical terms have appeared, supplying the necessary terminology for use in agriculture and industry, as well as in schools of higher learning.

No less gigantic was the educational effort. Here, too, it was a two- or perhaps even a three-front battle. Most parents of the older generation sent their children to the usual heder or Talmud Torah, followed by a yeshiba. There traditional Hebrew subjects were taught exclusively, but the language of instruction was usually Yiddish. On the one hand progressive parents preferred to send their children to Russian, Polish, English, or other secular schools, governmental or private, while on the other, within the nationalist camp, there was the old division of Yiddish versus Hebrew education.

It is a remarkable testimony to the great vitality of the Eastern and Central European Jewries in the interwar period that they succeeded in erecting a tremendous educational structure along all these lines. While a substantial proportion of Jewish youth attended the traditional hadarim and yeshibot, and while another ever increasing number went to Polish public and private schools, there sprang up a vast network of both Tarbut (Hebrew) and Cisho (Yiddish) schools offering a comprehensive primary and secondary education in general and Jewish subjects. Scores of thousands of graduates of these schools not only did very well in their subsequent university studies in Poland and elsewhere, but furnished many of the leaders for Jewish communal work in Palestine and other countries. Americans, who have witnessed the recent growth of the Jewish day school from about two percent of all Jewish school children a decade ago to some seven percent today, can realize what such a vast school system must have meant to the East European Jewish communities. Many American schools, too, have adopted the Hebrew language of instruction, just as the

Sholem Aleichem school system here and in Canada has for several decades past cultivated the Yiddish language. In Palestine the school has all along been almost exclusively Hebraic, and has served as the major vehicle of unification of the various groups of Jewish immigrants making up the population of Israel.

Hand in hand with this revival of the Hebrew language and Hebrew education went a marvelous efflorescence of modern Hebrew letters. A secular form of Hebrew literature had been growing up even before the national movement. The Haskalah, whether of the older Italian, Dutch, or German kind, or of the newer Galician or Russian variety, invariably made use of Hebrew for its literary creations. But in these cases Hebrew was a means rather than a goal in itself. In fact, by propagating Westernization, Hebrew literature could actually become a vehicle of assimilation and denationalization. So great, however, was the power of the language itself and the spiritual heritage with which it was imbued, that even the protagonists of Haskalah could not escape its great positive impact. In moments of great despondency Yehudah Leb Gordon may have written a bitter poem, "We are a Herd, not a People." But even he and his confreres unwittingly became the forerunners of the great Hebrew renaissance.

More recently Palestine has understandably taken over leadership in the field of Hebrew letters, but Diaspora Jewry, including that of the United States, has contributed its share.

After the rise of political Zionism, Zionist cultural aspirations received a new, powerful stimulus from the political agitation. True, Ahad Haam never joined the new Herzlian movement. In the first years after the Basel Congress of 1897, the great Hebrew publicist heaped ridicule on the Basel program, but his constructive criticisms proved helpful in rectifying certain ill-conceived or ill-executed measures in Palestine. Most of his disciples joined the organization and worked within it. Without opposing political Zionism they merely doubted its feasibility at that time. Among the early exponents of cultural Zionism was Chaim Weizmann, who was destined more than any other single individual to contribute to the realization of political Zionism. Among the other leaders from 1902 on was Martin Buber, who was increasingly drawn back to the religious mainsprings of the Jewish tradition, particularly Hasidic mysticism. His brand of cultural nationalism had mystical and philosophic undertones which lent his national preachment an all-embracing humanitarian tinge.

Outside the circle of cultural Zionists, the old idea of Israel's mission, often ridiculed by secularists, gained ever new adherents under one guise or another. Just as Hess always insisted that his nationalism went hand in hand with humanitarianism, the cultural Zionists preached the erection of a cultural center in Zion as a great service to humanity at large. That is why, long before there was any prospect of political autonomy in the homeland, the Zionist World Congress, under the prompting of Zwi Hermann Schapira and Weizmann, went on record as sponsoring a Hebrew University in Jerusalem. This was not to be merely a school of higher learning, but a center where the entire people would be regenerated in the service of humanity. Almost the first thing the Zionist leaders did after the liberation of Jerusalem by Marshal Allenby in 1918, was to lay the foundation stone for the university. Six years later it was opened with neither faculty nor student body, but with the unshakable conviction that here would soon arise the cultural center of the Jewish people.

Since that time, the Hebrew University has grown into a major institution of learning. It has been joined by other schools like the Technion and Weizmann Institute of Science, and several others are now abuilding. At the same time the university gave refuge to some old East European centers of Rabbinic learning which were transferred to Israel before or after the Nazi occupation. Jerusalem alone now harbors more than a hundred yeshibot. The output of books and magazines has reached phenomenal proportions for a country the size of Israel. More than a thousand volumes, many of them quite weighty, saw the light of day in 1955 alone. The constant increase of subscription lists of the various encyclopedias has no parallel abroad. For example, the Encyclopedia Hebraica, something akin to the Britannica in Hebrew, is now being distributed among some forty-five thousand subscribers. Considering the size of the Israeli population, this is tantamount to six or seven million subscribers in the English-speaking world. Theatrical performances, Philharmonic concerts, and art exhibits usually compare in quantity and quality with those in the larger countries. In short, Israel has become a major cultural center of world Jewry. The extent to which it will exert direct influence on Jewish culture in the Dispersion is, of course, too early to tell. But there is no question that already Israelis have quickened many domains of Jewish cultural life in other countries, just as Israel has greatly benefited from the influx of Jewish scholars, writers, artists, and technicians from other lands.

POLITICAL DRIVES

All these centuries-old religious, philanthropic, and cultural impulses were brought into focus by the rise of political Zionism. The latter sprang from the new political self-assertion of European and American Jewry, dating from before 1848 and now channeled into the newly awakened national consciousness. Progressive Western or Westernized Jews in particular, despondent over the failure of emancipation to solve the Jewish problem, became keenly aware of the great power of post-emancipatory antisemitism and felt the need of a political shelter for the Jewish people. Political Zionism was looking for a haven for individual Jews, one that would "provide a remedy, complete tranquility and national glory for them," while the Lovers of Zion sought to provide only a "secure refuge" for Judaism and a cultural bond of unity for the nation as such. Ahad Haam was aware of the difference. He wrote:

> In the West it is the problem of the Jews, in the East the problem of Judaism. The one weighs on the individual, the other on the nation. The one is felt by Jews who have had a European education, the other by Jews whose education has been Jewish. The one is a product of antisemitism, and is dependent on antisemitism for its existence; the other is a natural product of a real link with a culture of thousands of years.

Allowing for some exaggeration, natural with the leading exponent of cultural Zionism, we may readily admit that the Zionist thinking of the intellectually "emancipated" Russian physician Leo Pinsker and of the fully Western, in fact, almost completely assimilated, journalist and writer Theodor Herzl owed its character to the seeming hopelessness of the struggle against an ever recurring antisemitism. In his famous *Auto-Emancipation,* Pinsker, under the great shock of the Russian pogroms of 1881, argued that antisemitism was a permanent psychopathological phenomenon against which the Jew's only recourse was self-emancipation and the creation of an independent state for himself. Herzl's national consciousness was awakened by what he witnessed at the Dreyfus trial. Here in the very European country which had led the world in the liberation "of the Jew, after a century of full-fledged Jewish participation in French culture, the alleged disloyalty of a single Jewish army officer could set ablaze the ancient hatreds." To Herzl this world-shaking event proved that sooner or later a powerful antisemitic movement was bound to arise in every country, quite independently of what the Jews do or fail to do.

A man of great vision, Herzl was also impatient. For him the slow process of Palestinian colonization by the Lovers of Zion, with the assistance of Edmond de Rothschild, appeared intolerable. In his opening speech at the first Basel Congress, he remarked that at that pace it would take nine hundred years before all Jews could be brought back to the Holy Land. In fact, this was an underestimate, for in 1897, and for many years thereafter, the natural increase of world Jewry far exceeded the number of those absorbed by colonization. Only international action on a grand scale, Herzl insisted, could definitely settle the Jewish question.

The immediate response of large groups to this appeal cannot be explained by the sheer power of Herzl's personality and charm. The idea of Jewish colonization in a separate territory had been debated for decades by Jewish and non-Jewish thinkers in many lands. Because of deep-rooted religious traditions and the ever present complications of the so-called "Eastern question," Palestine loomed uppermost in the minds of both Jews and Christians. The Ottoman Empire had long been in a state of dissolution, saved from utter collapse only by the rival interests of the European powers. These conflicts came to the fore especially during the war between the Sultan and his powerful vassal, Mehemet Ali of Egypt, in 1838-40. When Turkish suzerainty over Palestine was reestablished with the aid of the Western powers, many Englishmen realized their country's peculiar weakness in the Near East. For centuries past France had enjoyed the formal right to intervene in the affairs of the Latin Christians throughout the Ottoman Empire. Austria, too, claimed that right. Russia, the Ottoman Empire's hereditary enemy, was in an even more favorable position to "protect" the Porte's numerous Greek Orthodox subjects. Great Britain and Prussia alone among the leading powers had no one to protect, because few Protestants lived permanently in the Near East. Many a British diplomat, including Colonel Churchill and the several British consuls in Jerusalem, suggested, therefore, that Britain might take under her wing the populous and influential Jewish communities throughout the Near East, particularly in Palestine.

It was this combination of imperial interests and genuine humanitarianism—which carried far greater weight in the diplomacy of the mid-nineteenth century than it does today—together with the old religious appeal of Jewish restoration to the Holy Land, that induced Lord Palmerston in 1840 to make a daring suggestion to the Porte. Thenceforth, he proposed, all Turkish subjects of the Jewish faith who felt wronged by any local administrator or judge should be allowed to appeal directly to the Sultan through the mediation of the British consular authorities. This suggestion was, of course, repudiated as an infringement on Ottoman sovereignty, but in practice British consuls, especially in Palestine, often interfered in behalf of non-British Jews, although the existing agreements restricted "consular" protection to subjects of each particular power. For example, a consular dispatch from Jerusalem in 1849 contained a petition by Isaiah

Burdaki, leader of the Russian Jews in the Holy Land, requesting British "protection" for his coreligionists, most of whom had become "stateless." While this cooperation between Britain and Palestine Jewry was often clouded by controversies arising from the activities of English missionaries, British interest in Palestine Jewry appeared as one of the "constants" in the checkered diplomatic negotiations concerning Jewish rights throughout the nineteenth century.

At the same time, some English Jews began taking more positive action. Sir Moses Montefiore evinced a deep interest in Jewish colonization, envisaging it, of course, more as a philanthropic than a national venture. During Mehemet Ali's control over Palestine, Sir Moses negotiated with him for a charter for such colonization in return for his aid in floating an Egyptian loan on the London market. Although the negotiations came to nothing because of Mehemet Ali's defeat, they did point up possibilities for the future. In 1842, Montefiore was also instrumental, together with the British consul in Jerusalem, in transmitting to the British government an elaborate plan for colonization prepared by Abraham Benisch, later a well-known editor of the London *Jewish Chronicle*. Once again the suggestion that a company be organized to finance large-scale settlement of Near Eastern Jews in the Holy Land, with the full diplomatic assistance of the British government, was not lost on subsequent generations. In fact, this problem never disappeared from the "agenda" of thoughtful Jewish leaders until a group of Lovers of Zion going under the name BILU (an abbreviation of *Bne Yaakov lekhu ve-Nelkha,* Sons of Jacob, Let Us Go) succeeded in establishing some of the first important Jewish colonies in Palestine such as Rishon le-Zion (founded in 1882).

Under Herzl's leadership the new Zionist organization undertook large-scale political negotiations with the object of establishing, under some sort of international guarantee, a "national home" for the Jewish people. The use of this somewhat equivocal term was well advised, for though its adherents knew well enough that what they had in mind was a Jewish state, the bluntness of a demand for political sovereignty would certainly have alienated the Sultan and probably many European statesmen also, while a "national home" could be achieved with the direct cooperation of the Ottoman government. It was indeed with the Porte that Herzl began his early negotiations. He hoped to obtain from the Sultan a formal charter admitting persecuted Jews to the Ottoman Empire provided they became Ottoman subjects. In return the Sultan expected Herzl to organize a Jewish banking syndicate to consolidate the shaky Turkish debt structure. The Sultan probably hoped to put over his scheme of financial assistance on the diplomatically inexperienced interlocutor and give as little as possible in return. Ultimately Izzet Pasha reported to Herzl that "the Sultan was willing to open his Empire to all Jews willing to become Ottoman subjects, but the Government would in every instance decide the area of settlement, with Palestine ruled out altogether." The Ottoman Jewish company could colonize Mesopotamia, Syria, Anatolia—in a word, anywhere except Palestine. Some of Herzl's advisers were so anxious to secure international recognition of their movement that they were prepared to accept even so much. Herzl, however, feared that such a charter might prove a serious impediment to the attainment of his ultimate goal.

Herzl proceeded to enlist the support of other powers. In a dramatic, widely publicized interview with the Kaiser in the Holy Land, he sought the assistance of Germany, at that time at the height of its imperial expansion. The Hohenzollern regime, planning the penetration of the Near East by means of the Berlin-Bagdad railway, was at first inclined to favor the settlement in Palestine of Yiddish-speaking Jews, who would help spread the German language and culture. However, on second thought the imperial administration realized the inherent dangers. Some German statesmen feared that any governmental sponsorship of Palestine colonization might be misconstrued as a desire to get rid of German Jewry via emigration, and hence as a nod of approval for the rampant German antisemitic parties.

The Tsarist regime felt no such compunctions. Its Minister of Interior, von Plehve, discussed with Herzl the problem of directing the Russo-Jewish emigration to Palestine. But the Tsarist government soon realized that the Russian Zionists, rather than merely concentrating on the task of transplanting Jews to the Holy Land, preached the cultural awakening of the Jewish people, tried to reorganize the Jewish educational system, and even demanded national rights for the Jewish minority. He wrote to Herzl on August 12, 1903:

> So long as Zionism consisted of the desire to create an independent State in Palestine and promised to organize the emigration from Russia of a certain number of its Jewish subjects, the Russian Government could very well be favorable to it. But from the moment that this principal object of Zionism is abandoned in order to be replaced by a simple propaganda for the national concentration of the Jews in Russia, it is natural that the Government cannot in any case tolerate this new departure of Zionism.

Similarly unsuccessful was Herzl's effort to persuade the Vatican to endorse the Zionist idea. After some preparation through a converted Jewish intermediary, Herzl had an interview with both Pope Pius X and his famous Secretary of State, Merry del Val. The Cardinal was diplomatic but firm. He would go along with the scheme provided the Jews were first converted to Catholicism, and he added:

> Certainly to me the Jew who is baptised from conviction is the ideal. In such a Jew who acknowledges the Divinity of Christ I find the physical descendant of Christ's people united with the spirit; so St. Peter and St. Paul. The history of Israel is our own. It is our foundation. But before, as you request, we declare ourselves for the Jewish people, it must first be converted.

The Pope was even more outspoken. "We cannot favor this movement," he declared.

Herzl obtained his only real diplomatic success in his negotiations with the British government, whose able Colonial Minister, Joseph Chamberlain, caught something of Herzl's vision. With his help and that of British Jewish leaders, among them Lord Nathaniel Rothschild, who had previously avoided Herzl, but now noticed that Her Majesty's Government was taking him seriously, the Zionist leader negotiated with the Foreign Secretary, Lord Landsdowne, about assigning to the Jews a territory in the vicinity of El-Arish on the Sinai peninsula. Although disputed by Turkey, Egypt's suzerainty was sufficiently established for the British Protectorate to allow colonization in this vicinity, but the trouble was the aridity of the land.

The British government was soon induced to make another grand offer. It suggested that the Zionist movement undertake to colonize Jews in the British Crown Colony of Uganda in East Africa. This underpopulated country, with a moderate climate because of its high elevation, could accommodate many Jewish colonists. Some British settlers there objected to Jewish mass immigration, but the government was prepared to overrule them. Herzl rightly considered this British offer a major victory. It represented the first public recognition by a major power of both the Jewish people's claim to separate territory and the World Zionist Organization as its authorized spokesman. Meanwhile, a revolt broke out among the Russian Zionists led by Menahem Ussishkin. At a Kharkov meeting the Russian leaders protested against any idea of colonizing Jews outside Palestine, and even rejected Herzl's argument that Uganda could at least serve as a preparation for the ultimate immigration to Palestine.

After Herzl's death, the Uganda project was completely abandoned, but it left its traces in an important splinter group, led by Israel Zangwill, which had favored acceptance of the British proposal and now formed a new Jewish Territorial Organization (ITO) to continue the search for an appropriate territory in which to colonize Jews. The Zionist Organization itself, which even before Herzl's death had included an articulate group of "practical Zionists," now tempered its expectations of an internationally guaranteed charter in favor of less dramatic, but more enduring, practical colonization. Retaining much of the cultural program, the practical Zionists concentrated on the economic and educational expansion of the Yishub. They were convinced that, whatever the cost in money and effort, the creation of such strategic positions in the Holy Land would, in the long run, prove more fruitful than diplomatic negotiations.

Apart from the "practical Zionists," who differed from the Herzlian group in method rather than goals, there emerged two other important factions which, though they were to add to the richness of Zionist ideology, at the same time complicated the organizational tasks. The first formally recognized faction was the Mizrachi, which insisted upon building Zionism on the basis of the Orthodox religious tradition. The second faction, the Jewish socialists, had reconciled in their minds Jewish nationalism with their basic international ideals, and among them were devoted Zionists who felt that the ultimate solution of the Jewish question, even in the social sense, required the foundation of a Jewish homeland. These Zionist-socialists soon split up into many subdivisions, the most influential of which were the Poale Zion under the leadership of Ber Borochov, and the Ha-Poel ha-Zair under A. D. Gordon. The latter movement was altogether ready to forego Marxism and the class struggle, and to achieve the realization of its national, as well as socialist, programs through "love" and cooperation, and particularly through preaching its "religion of labor."

Whatever their party affiliations, all these Zionist groups cooperated down to the outbreak of World War I in enlarging and strengthening the Yishub, particularly its agricultural segment, with the aid of such national institutions as the Anglo-Palestine Bank and the Jewish National Fund. The Russian pogroms of 1903 and 1905 created a much greater demand for immigration to Palestine, and the "second" Aliyah beginning in 1905 made more rapid headway than the first Aliyah of the BILU. The number of Jewish colonies, which by 1893 had reached twenty-one, increased to forty-seven in 1914. Despite the great repression by Djemal Pasha during World War I they continued growing, so that at the beginning of the Mandate in 1923 there were seventy-four.

At the same time industrial endeavor received an even greater impetus. A regular urban proletariat organized in strong labor unions made its first appearance, as did the nucleus for a Jewish police and army in the form of the Ha-Shomer, a volunteer national guard which stood watch over the Jewish colonies against Arab raiders and marauders. In 1909, a few Jewish settlers built a new township on the sand dunes on the outskirts of Jaffa and named it Tel-Aviv. In short, slowly but surely there was emerging a small but self-contained, economically and culturally vigorous community which could well form the nucleus for a future commonwealth.

THE PALESTINE MANDATE

The Yishub and behind it the world Zionist movement were in a strategic position to make use of the great crisis of World War I. Ber Borochov urged his followers to "face reality" in the midst of the war, and wrote:

> The practical colonization work in Palestine, with its experiences, its sacrifices, its inevitable mistakes, has created those political *facts* which have paved the way for our present status. No matter how small and weak the Jewish colonies might be, no matter how great the shortcomings in their system of colonization—they did more towards enlightening the Jewish nation than a thousand beautifully-worded programs and diplomatic negotiations. A fallen *Shomer* plays a greater role in the realization of Zionism than all declarations. *The best guarantee of Zionism lies not in a charter but in the Zionist Movement.*

Ironically, within half a year after these words were written, the foundations for the charter were laid: the Balfour Declaration of November 2, 1917. To understand this first Allied commitment, we must realize that for a long time World War I hung in the balance. Before the United States' entry into the war, the European Entente and the Central Powers in particular were on the lookout for partisans. The sympathies of Jews, especially in the United States, might, so it was thought, prove decisive for the outcome of the war. Jews were reputed to have control over vast capital, and it was Lloyd George who, at the inception of the war, had predicted that it would be the last silver bullet which would determine the victor. Not only the man in the street but statesmen and financiers were prone to exaggerate the size, power, and solidarity of Jewish finance capital. It was still the day, we must not forget, of great and influential private bankers, such as J. P. Morgan. So the effort to capture the good will of the Jews, especially those in neutral nations, appeared worthwhile.

But there was a complicating factor here owing to the West's alliance with Tsarist Russia, the arch-foe of the Jewish people. It mattered little that at the outbreak of the war the Russian generalissimo, Nicolai Nicolaevich, addressed an appeal to "my beloved Jews." However, with Turkey's entry into the war on the side of the Central Powers, the Allies could bid for Jewish support with the promise of a

Jewish national home in Palestine; when victorious they would proceed to dismember the Ottoman Empire. True, the Allied statesmen had also been secretly negotiating with the Arabs, whom they incited to rebel against their Turkish overlords. In these secret negotiations, above all with Hussein, the Sherif of Mecca, such British representatives as Hogarth and McMahon made promises, rather vague and far from binding, concerning the extent of the Arab state which was to arise from the Ottoman ruins. The responsible British ministers knew of these negotiations, yet went ahead with their public commitment in behalf of a Jewish national home.

It was an idealistically tinged realism which prompted Lloyd George and Arthur James Balfour, his foreign secretary, to go on record as favoring the Zionist idea. In 1936, Lloyd George himself testified publicly in Parliament that the Declaration had been issued in full realization of Britain's own interest. Another member of the War Cabinet, Winston Churchill, likewise stressed its adoption as the result of "the dire need of the war" and "with the object of promoting the general victory of the Allies, for which they expected and received valuable and important assistance." The Declaration, moreover, soon secured the approval of the other Allied powers, especially France, Italy, and, somewhat more guardedly, the United States.

The text betrayed the protracted negotiations which preceded its promulgation. To pacify non-Zionist Jewish circles, which included the addressee of the Declaration, Lord Lionel Walter Rothschild, the British government made it clear that by establishing the Jewish national home "nothing shall be done which may prejudice . . . the rights and political status enjoyed by Jews in any other country." Then, as later, much ink was spilled about the "dual allegiances" of Jews. Only Gentiles already predisposed to believe the worst of Jews evinced real concern about such divided loyalties, purportedly characteristic of all ethnic minorities, but this phantom has not been laid until today. Noteworthy too is the fact that the original formula suggested by the Zionist group was a pledge by the British government of support for "Palestine as a Jewish national home." This was changed to read, "The establishment in Palestine of a national home for the Jewish people," and the way was thus left open for diverse interpretations. In fact, in a subsequent White Paper in 1922, Winston Churchill argued that Britain had never expected Palestine to be as Jewish as England was English. Still, the Declaration marked the first definite recognition by a great power of the Jewish claim to Palestine.

Jews all over the world hailed the Declaration and its subsequent endorsements by other governments and leaders of public opinion as ushering in the ultimate realization of their ideal. They knew that the road ahead would be difficult, but looking back at the distance they had already traveled against tremendous odds, they felt convinced that final success must be theirs by dint of hard work and sacrifice.

As soon as the war was over much of the Allied enthusiasm for the rebirth of the Jewish people cooled off. At the Peace Conference, all ideals of national self-determination and of making the world safe for democracy withered away in the icy climate of power politics and insatiable greed for territorial expansion. Involved in daily tasks of administration, and observing from narrow range the hostility of the Arab population, many officers of the Allenby staff and, later, civil administrators considered a Jewish national home utterly impracticable. Even those who were not from the outset pro-Arab, or otherwise prejudiced against Jews, often believed that their leaders in London had lost sight of the Palestinian realities. When the Crane Commission arrived in Palestine for an eight-day visit in the summer of 1919, its members were informed by the local officials that the plan was not working.

Nevertheless, the statesmen reassembled in San Remo in 1920 and decided to establish a League of Nations Mandate over Palestine and entrust its administration to Great Britain, which was to be obliged to implement the Balfour Declaration. As soon as the League was formed in 1922, Palestine was formally proclaimed a territory under an A mandate, that is, substantially a sovereign state in being, whose actual exercise of sovereignty was but temporarily suspended. When its population became ready for self-government, the mandatory power was to hand over the reins of government to the native population.

The provisions of the Mandate contained in themselves the seeds of their destruction. On the one hand, like the other mandates, the Palestinian provided for the early establishment of self-governing institutions, while on the other its main import was the establishment of a Jewish national home and the encouragement of large-scale Jewish immigration. Under the conditions then existing in the country, these two propositions proved irreconcilable. Any democratically elected legislature would close the country to Jewish immigration and land purchases. It was of little help that Britain from the outset eliminated Trans-Jordan from the area of Jewish colonization, separating it for the first time in history from western Palestine. Britain's subsequent efforts to organize some sort of advisory legislative council with no Arab minority foundered on the rock of Arab refusal.

Here lay the crucial difficulty. It is not true, as is frequently alleged, that Herzl and the other Zionist leaders did not know of the existence of Arabs in the country. But they could not anticipate that after

World War I European nationalism would spread to the Arab world with such fury and intensity. The national movement, to be sure, had been under way since the days of Mehemet Ali and his son, Ibrahim Pasha, but it had not really penetrated beyond intellectual circles. Nor were Zionists or Western statesmen fully cognizant of the atavistic Muslim view that a country conquered by the sword of Islam could only be taken away from her by the sword. With the glibness of European colonizers, Britons and Jews often underestimated the Orient's resistance to Western ways of life. While Arab nationalism meant ultimate Westernization, the masses of fellaheen and their spiritual leaders resented the importation of Western ideas by Jewish colonists, who constituted not merely a thin layer of foreign bureaucrats, as in other colonial countries, but an important segment of the population. Further, the new ways invited emulation, and hence were doubly resented by the influential landlord class, which feared the introduction of revolutionary ideas among the country's oppressed peasantry. Thus arose a strange coalition of various Arab groups, united only in their resentment at the new immigration and their opposition to the Jewish homeland. The result was the increasingly sanguinary clashes with the Jews in 1920, 1921, 1929, and especially 1936-38.

Here Zionist ideals clashed with bitter reality. All through the period before and after the establishment of the Mandate, Zionism preached social justice as much as national rebirth. Opposing "realists" had often raised the question whether any country was ever colonized without the aid of a mother country, which alone could furnish the necessary military and naval support against a hostile population, small as it might be. But one might point to two precedents in Jewish history. Did not the exiles from Egypt build the First Commonwealth? Similarly, did not the manpower, financial resources, and diplomatic skill of the Jews of Babylonia pave the way for the establishment of the Second Commonwealth? Neither group of ancient settlers had a motherland behind it. Zionism flattered itself that it could create a third precedent of successful colonization without a mother country, and with the ultimate consent, moreover, of the natives themselves. But the latter calculation proved to be mistaken. In the days of Herzl such consent might still have been forthcoming. After the Hussein-McMahon correspondence and the rise of several Arab states around Palestine it became decidedly too late.

Meanwhile, the Zionist movement proceeded with its program of colonization, helped by the League of Nations Charter, while the Mandatory Power became ever more reluctant. The statesmen in London were still fairly favorable. Their broad vision of human affairs enabled them to see the local difficulties in perspective. Not so the administrators on the spot, who were beset with a variety of unprecedented procedural problems. The Arabs still fell within the comprehensible pattern of a colonial people governed according to the usual colonial methods. Jews, however, were Europeans, with European aspirations and demands, and were disrespectfully oblivious of the obstacles placed in their way by the colonial administration. The first High Commissioner, Sir (later Viscount) Herbert Samuel, whose appointment was hailed by some British statesmen as that of a new Nehemiah, often had to lean backwards because he was a Jew. Only under the strong hand of Marshal Plummer was peace and order fully maintained. But under his weaker successors, disturbances only confused an already puzzled British Civil Service.

With less and less assistance from the Mandatory Power, the Zionist World Organization, originally recognized by the Mandate as the Jewish Agency for Palestine, serving the Mandatory Power in an advisory capacity, continued to build national institutions with ever increasing effectiveness. It opened up the country to Jewish immigration, and from the outset accommodated the "Third" Aliyah. Owing to the great Jewish crisis in newly independent Poland, immigration reached a total of over 33,000 in the single year 1925. Seven years earlier only twice as many Jews had lived in all of Palestine under Djemal Pasha's hostile regime. True, after 1925 economic conditions deteriorated to such an extent that two years later the number of emigrants from Palestine exceeded that of new arrivals. But after this setback the figures climbed again and reached unprecedented proportions after the rise of Hitler to power. In 1935 alone, Jewish immigration exceeded 63,000. Although the tempo was again retarded in subsequent years, owing to the Arab uprising, by 1939 the National Home already embraced a community of some 600,000 Jews, or about thirty percent of the population. Hand in hand with this numerical growth went economic expansion in both city and countryside. However difficult and costly its purchase became, land under Jewish control increased slowly but decisively. The intensive cultivation of citrus fruit created an important export article, while the social experimentation of the collectivist Kibbutzim and of the urban workers organized in the Histadrut proceeded apace, to the amazement of the outside world.

To some impatient leaders the pace was not fast enough. The old cleavage between practical and political Zionism, though on a new plane, reappeared in Vladimir Jabotinsky. Profoundly dissatisfied with the tempo of practical achievement, he organized a Revisionist Party in 1925 and demanded the return to ambitious Herzlian methods, methods now more military than diplomatic. Jabotinsky, bent upon promoting the exodus of Polish Jewry, did not hesitate to negotiate even with the notoriously antisemitic Polish government. This action evoked a storm of indignation, despite the precedent set by Herzl's negotiations with von Plevhe, and the later arrangement made by the Zionist Organization itself with the Hitler regime. This so-called *Haavarah* made it possible for thousands of German Jews to leave for Palestine and take with them as much as 15,000 marks' ($6,000) worth of German goods each, the aggregate amount of which greatly enlarged the absorptive capacity of the country and enabled it to admit many other immigrants. Here *Realpolitik* overruled the obvious sentimental objections to such negotiations. One merely wishes that German Jewry had read the signs of the age earlier and remembered the scolding of their ancestors by Rabban Johanan ben Zakkai, "You were unwilling to pay the head tax to God, 'a beqa a head'; now you are paying a head tax of fifteen shekels to the government of your enemies." German Jewry paid, in 1938, the enormous penalty of 800,000,000 marks. If it had had the foresight and spent the same amount on Palestine ten years earlier, before it was financially weakened by the economic depression and Nazi hostility, it might indeed have created for itself a haven of refuge, able to absorb most exiles from the Hitler regime.

Under the impact of the Arab uprising in 1936, the Zionists closed their ranks. The policy of *Havlagah* (self-restraint) revealed the remarkable discipline of a people following a determined leadership. Despite Arab provocations and the assassination of many Jews, the Jewish population did not react by violent retribution, but left it to the Mandatory Power to preserve public order. On the other hand, eight hundred Arabs, a total exceeding that of British and Jewish victims combined, fell during that uprising, many at the hands of fellow Arabs. This Jewish self-discipline was both a sign of political maturity and of inner certainty that the National Home could no longer be uprooted.

In those turbulent years of Nazi expansion and the Arab uprising, the creation of a Jewish state was first formally suggested, not by a Jewish body, but by the Royal Commission, headed by Lord Peel, which investigated the causes of the uprising. Opinion among the Palestinian Jews, as later at the Zionist Congress, was sharply divided over the proposal. It is regrettable that nothing came of the Peel recommendation, for, if carried into effect, it would have obviated many a World War II tragedy. After its fairly universal repudiation, the British government reversed its strong policy and increasingly yielded to Arab pressures. After a futile London Conference, with Arabs and Jews meeting separately, the government issued its notorious White

Paper of 1939, which restricted Jewish immigration to 15,000 a year for the next five years, after which no Jews were to be admitted at all without Arab consent. Britain, then on the defensive against the Axis Powers, pursued her futile policy of appeasement not only in Munich, but also in the Near East.

As on the international scene, so in Palestine, this policy backfired. During World War II, Britain found little support in the Arab world. The defense of Egypt was left almost entirely in the hands of British troops, which included a contingent of Jewish volunteers from Palestine. In fact, the latter would have been much more numerous had Palestine's British administration freely accepted them rather than waiting for an equal number of Palestinian Arabs to enlist. All through the early war period the Zionist leaders pressed for the creation of a Jewish army to be recruited in the United States and other neutral countries. Ultimately a compromise was struck and a Palestinian Jewish Brigade fought valiantly on the Allied side in Italy and Germany. Not only did it cover itself with glory on the battlefield, but it exerted heroic efforts to save the surviving remnants of Eastern and Central European Jewry. At the same time the Palestine hinterland helped supply the British armies with food, medical supplies, and even weapons during their strenuous North African campaigns. Other war supplies had to be transported through the infested Mediterranean or all the way around the Cape of Good Hope, so that Palestine's growing industrial output proved of great assistance to the Allies.

In the war emergency the Arab uprising subsided and the country enjoyed a sort of internal truce. Independently of the British forces, the Yishub formed its own army, the Haganah, which was tacitly recognized by the British as a reserve force in case the Germans broke through the defenses of El-Alamein and reached the Suez Canal. The training received during the war was to stand the Haganah in good stead in the hour of decision.

In the meantime, living up to the restrictions of the White Paper, the British administration tried to shut the gates to immigration after the admission of the first 75,000 Jews. All appeals having failed in the face of Nazi extermination, the Jews organized a large-scale illicit immigration. In chartered ships, often far from seaworthy, thousands of immigrants eluded the British patrols and landed under the cover of night on some Palestinian beach, where they were rapidly distributed among the Jewish settlements. Sometimes, however, a boat was caught and its human cargo sent back to almost certain death. On her enforced return journey, the *Struma* sank in Turkish territorial waters, with but few survivors among its eight hundred passengers.

World indignation was aroused and in Palestine itself passions were fanned to a white heat. When the European phase of the war ended in May, 1945, the Yishub rebelled against the continuation of British "atrocities." From among Revisionist circles, especially, there emerged the Irgun Zvai Leumi, and the Stern group, which retaliated in kind. The blowing up of the King David Hotel, the breach of the Acco prison walls and liberation of its political prisoners, and the hanging of two British sergeants were some of the highlights of this much-publicized "terroristic" campaign. But the majority of the Yishub quietly continued building up its military and economic resources, bringing in as many illicit immigrants as possible, and preparing itself for the unavoidable day of reckoning.

THE STATE OF ISRAEL

Out of this turmoil of 1946-47, the state of Israel was born. The events are too recent to require extensive recital here. Most contemporaries will remember the formation of the Anglo-American Commission of Inquiry, its extensive and noteworthy hearings, its final recommendations, and ultimately the debates at the United Nations. Finally came that crowning achievement, the United Nations resolution of November, 1947, to partition Palestine between a Jewish and an Arab state, with an international enclave in Jerusalem. Weary of her Mandate, Britain announced that come what may, her troops would evacuate Palestine on May 15, 1948. Obviously, Ernest Bevin, Britain's implacably anti-Zionist Foreign Minister, hoped that in the free-for-all that would follow this withdrawal, the armies of the seven Arab states would easily overcome the Yishub.

The six months which elapsed from the time of the United Nations decision to the British evacuation were a period of feverish activity for Jews in Palestine and abroad. Despite the frequent vagaries of American foreign policy, which during the war produced the Roosevelt-Ibn Saud understanding, and in the spring of 1948 seemed to lead to the abandonment of the United Nations resolution, this country remained the Yishub's staunchest supporter. The Soviet Union, which in November, 1947, voted for the Palestine resolution, was still bent primarily on getting Britain out of the country. But when in May, 1948, the hour of decision struck, the Yishub found itself alone in confronting the array of Arab armies. Undaunted, it immediately proclaimed its independence, and on its very first day was formally recognized by President Truman. The intervention of the Security Council led to the first cease-fire, which helped alleviate the position of beseiged Jewish Jerusalem. The second cease-fire, however, imposed by the Council under severe sanctions, was entirely to the advantage of the Arab armies, which were thus saved from almost total annihilation. Even today, many Israelis, especially of the Herut faction, believe that the cease-fire order should have been rejected and all Arab troops expelled from Palestine on both sides of the Jordan. Strategically feasible, such an overt defiance of the Security Council would undoubtedly have led to severe reprisals.

Eight years of Israeli independence are hardly enough to provide a historical perspective. The formative years of any new state are always years of flux. And there is the complication in Israel of the unfinished business of a peace treaty. The state enjoys *de jure* recognition by most of the world's nations, though by none of its immediate neighbors. It required great ingenuity and effort on the part of the United Nations representative, Ralph Bunche, to secure by separate negotiations with the Arab states and Israel even the present uneasy truce. Iraq is not even a signatory to the armistice pact. Egypt is still blockading Israel and refuses transit through the Suez Canal to any cargo destined for Israel. Interventions by the great powers and censures by the Security Council have thus far remained without avail. The Arab countries also maintain an economic boycott of Israel, even to their own disadvantage, since they would normally export more goods to the new country than they would buy from it.

Besides all this is the festering wound of the Arab refugee problem. The mass psychosis was generated by the Arab leaders, who advised their compatriots to leave, promising them a speedy victorious return. The promise never materialized. The number of actual refugees is controversial. The official lists of the United Nations Refugee Organization now count more than 900,000. But this number includes many local residents who succeeded in insinuating themselves into the relief rolls. While all births are speedily recorded, deaths are often unreported for months, even years, because the families benefit from the increased dole.

Were logic alone to determine the course of human affairs the Arab refugee problem could be settled very quickly. Iraq and Syria are crying out for additional settlers. Iraq's cultivable area is even now used only to the extent of one-fifth or one-quarter. With irrigation of the long neglected lands, this country, it has been estimated, could readily accommodate more than 3,000,000 immigrants. Such a mass immigration of Palestinian Arabs, akin in language, culture and religion, would greatly benefit both the newcomers and the country at large.

Readmission of any substantial number of refugees by Israel would be suicidal. These refugees do not conceal their deep hostility and hope that a "second round" would end in Israel's complete defeat. What it would mean if Israel agreed to the suggestion that it should admit two hundred thousand refugees for the sake of good will and peace may be appreciated through a comparison. It would be like suggesting to the American government that for the sake of good will and peace it open the gates to the influx of twenty million Chinese Communists. Even then the United States, separated from China by the Pacific Ocean, would be far less endangered than Israel, which is surrounded on all sides, except the sea, by Arab nations. On the other hand, the state of mind among the Arabs is such that, to quote an informed British observer, any Arab statesman who recommended the resettlement of refugees away from their present concentration would be immediately assassinated.

Many persons also express concern about the present frontiers of Israel. From a strategic as well as an economic point of view these frontiers obviously leave much to be desired. A mere glance at the map will show that the Tulkaram triangle juts out into Israel's territory to a distance of some twenty miles from the sea. Here Israel's area could be quickly cut in half, separating Galilee and the northern coast from Jerusalem and Tel-Aviv. Yet one must bear in mind that, with the exception of the brief periods under David, Solomon, and Alexander Jannaeus, neither the First nor the Second Commonwealth ever had clearly defined or strategically easily defensible boundaries. Still, both managed to stave off all invasions by neighbors and surrendered only to the overwhelming power of such distant empires as Assyria, Babylonia, and Rome. No other boundaries would have proved more defensible against these imperial overlords. A genuine international guarantee of the existing frontiers would, therefore, help to remove one of the gravest sources of apprehension, and even domestic party strife.

There is still the unfinished business of a written constitution. A very eloquent draft was prepared by the international jurist Leo Kohn and his associates soon after the proclamation of independence. From the point of view of style and high ethical standards, it is a pity that it did not become the law of the land. From the outset, however, objections were raised in principle and also with regard to individual provisions. The Religious Bloc parties in particular insisted that Israel needed no other constitution than its God-given Torah. Israel is managing, therefore, with a series of fundamental laws adopted *ad hoc*.

Of course, countries can live with unwritten constitutions, as has Great Britain for many centuries past. Israel's main task now is to fuse its underlying, historically diverse, legal systems. Its legal structure is still dominated in part by modified traditions of Turkish law, and consists also of important innovations introduced by the British Mandatory legislation, largely in consonance with Anglo-American legal principles. At the same time the people are trying to revert to the teachings of Bible, Talmud, and the rest of Jewish law as it operated through centuries of Jewish communal autonomy. To merge these diffuse elements into a single legal structure would be difficult enough even if Israel's population had not come from so many countries with so many diverse legal traditions and mores. Most of the Israeli lawyers are graduates of Central or Eastern European law schools and so place great emphasis on Roman and Teuton law, which differs radically from the earlier Turkish and Anglo-American elements. Yet, the country's legal profession, especially its judiciary, has admirably handled a difficult situation, and a new legal structure, workable if not always self-consistent, is gradually emerging from this juristic Babel.

Similarly, the complex party system which has aroused concern among sympathetic observers has thus far operated in a fairly satisfactory fashion. Predictions were often heard that Israel would follow the checkered career of the French parliament and its short-lived cabinets. What even a world power like France could ill afford might prove disastrous to a struggling new country of Israel's size. In practice, however, the government of Israel has shown a remarkable stability. Throughout the eight years of its national existence, indeed, during the preceding two decades of its fairly effective self-government, the Jewish National Home has been ruled by the same party, Mapai, and even by the same statesmen. Whether in combination with the General Zionists or with the Religious Bloc, such labor leaders as Ben Gurion and Ben Zvi were in charge of the main branches of the administration and the old National Council, just as they have held the main cabinet posts since 1948. To be sure, the recent elections, showing a gradual erosion of Mapai's voting power, may be ominous for the future development of the party system. One may only hope that a way will be found to secure some balance between authority and freedom, between firm governmental controls and liberty of political expression and association, which, as a new country beset with difficult problems, Israel needs even more than the rest of the world.

Another major problem arises from the country's peculiar population structure. Given the fundamental character of the Law of Return, it has strained all its resources to admit Jewish immigrants. Israel's Jewish population more than doubled in the first five years of its national existence. This influx has slackened in the last two or three years, partly because the country's absorptive capacity had reached its limit, and partly because of the emptying of the main reservoirs of Jewish manpower in Europe and the Near East, such as the D.P. camps, Bulgaria, and Yemen. More recently only precarious North African Jewry has furnished large contingents of migrants.

The great question is whether the countries behind the Iron Curtain will open their doors for Jewish emigration. Many Rumanian, Hungarian, Polish, and possibly even Soviet Jews are apparently anxious to leave for Israel as soon as they are allowed to do so. In the case of Jewish citizens of democratic countries, there is no legal obstacle to their emigration to Israel, but so far only a relatively small number of idealists and skilled technicians have chosen the road to Jerusalem. Such immigration, if it became great enough, would have the effect of slowing down the progressive Orientalization (carping critics say "Levantinization") of the population. The government of Israel is anxious to promote this emigration publicly, despite the explosive reactions among Jews in Western lands who are fearful that the specter of "double allegiance" will thus be evoked. Like the whole accusation of divided allegiance, this may be only a figment of the imagination. Yet, because it is widely believed in, it constitutes a considerable problem.

Israel's melting pot has thus far proved even more effective than similar assimilatory processes elsewhere. Although the country is suffering from a great shortage of Hebrew teachers—some time ago there were three thousand vacancies—Hebrew education, particularly of children, has made tremendous progress. Army service and the *Hakhsharah*—pioneer agricultural training—have likewise brought together young people of diverse origin and converted them into full-fledged Israeli citizens. Nonetheless, the task ahead is still staggering. Complaints are heard about economic and social discrimination by the entrenched older segments of European origin against the more recent Near Eastern and North African arrivals. Marriage between Ashkenazic and Sephardic Jews is sometimes spoken of as "intermarriage." Although no one envisages the emergence of a full-fledged racial problem in Israel, the strains and stresses incident to amalgamation of diverse groups into a united nation are causing much individual hardship. The presence of some 170,000 Arabs, both Muslim and Christian, has only made the problems of the melting pot still more complex. In principle the fundamental laws call for the complete equality of all citizens. The Arabs have full franchise and send their own elected representatives to the Knesset. Yet their loyalties are not above suspicion, so that the government has had to adopt certain emergency police measures curtailing some of their freedoms, at least until peace is restored. Government and public alike are fully aware that their treatment of the Arab minority cannot but affect the position of their correligionists in other lands.

Finally, there are tremendous economic problems. Thus far the country has been greatly aided by foreign funds. UJA campaigns and Israel Bond drives in the United States and other countries; investments by private capital; loans extended to Israel by the United States government and foreign financial institutions; and in the last three years the goods imported from Germany under the heading of restitution for Jewish "Material Claims," have all greatly helped Israel's economy. In this Israel is not unique, for many of the older and most powerful nations, including Britain, France, and Italy, have likewise depended for several years on Marshall Plan funds for their reconstruction. Even today American foreign aid is still an indispensable budgetary resource of many lands.

In eight years Israel has made tremendous strides toward self-sufficiency. Despite centuries of neglect and shortage of water, Israel's agriculture is nearly supplying all of the country's needs in foodstuffs and farming raw materials. Industrial progress is even more startling. The country is, of course, short of such basic raw materials as coal and iron. It has spent some $40,000,000 annually in importing oil from distant countries, being unable to get it from neighboring Iraq or Saudi Arabia. However, the newly drilled oil wells are already supplying liquid fuel and gas for Israeli industry. Intensive research aimed at the direct utilization of sun rays for power is under way. This is a promising undertaking, indeed, in a country blessed with cloudless skies for months on end. Before long atomic energy may displace the need for traditional fuels, and Israeli scientists may well be able to convert simple sea water into all the energy the country needs. In short, Israel no longer requires the proverbial "miracle" to achieve a self-supporting economy, even one with a relatively high standard of life.

What will all this mean to world Jewry? It is difficult for us to envisage a time when there will be no Bond, UJA or JDC campaigns. Perhaps the cessation of "emergency" situations abroad would create an "emergency" in American Jewish community life, such that the loss would be greater to American Jewry than to the foreign recipients. But for the near future Jewry in the Dispersion will still have to marshal vast resources in money, manpower, and diplomatic and technical skills to help Israel weather the recurrent crises which it is bound to face.

Israel has already repaid much of its debt to Diaspora Jewry, however, and it is going to do so in an ever increasing measure. During the few years of its existence it has already instilled in a great many older and younger Jews a new sense of pride and belonging. No matter what complications may arise for many Jewish groups because of Israel's international conflicts; no matter how many sacrifices in money and energy Israel's upbuilding will require also from Jews of other lands; and no matter how many heartaches will be occasioned by certain acts of the Israel government or its people of which individual Jews elsewhere may not approve—all these will be episodes, quickly forgotten in the perennial historic procession of the Jewish people, in whose vanguard Israel, together with the best of the other Jewish communities, will be marching. This may best be exemplified by the impact it has already made, and will increasingly make in the future, upon the destinies of American Jewry.

18

THE AMERICAN EXPERIENCE

The fund-raising efforts of American Jewry have not been the only extraordinary feature of a community life which from the beginning lacked the usual attributes of Exilic life. Legally, American Jewry suffered from some discrimination, not so much from specific anti-Jewish bias as from certain general regulations. At no time did Jews receive special "privileges" which would have spelled out their rights and duties within the country and would also have regulated to some extent the limits of their communal self-determination. Except for the dramatic settlement of the twenty-three refugees in New Amsterdam in 1654, which caused a great stir, and a subsequent controversy with Governor Peter Stuyvesant, their arrival was hardly noticed by contemporaries, so that it is extremely difficult to find out their names and the time and place of their settlement.

It accrued to their benefit to be thus ignored by law. Long before emancipation, they were often treated on a par with other citizens simply because no laws had been enacted against them. Yet it was also the case that their self-government lacked the usual guarantees of public law which it enjoyed in most European countries. At times, as in New Amsterdam or New York, the ruling groups withheld from religious minorities the right of public worship. Here the Jewish community had to struggle inch by inch for permission to establish a cemetery or to acquire land for a synagogue—all matters taken for granted in almost any Old World community. Perhaps because it had thus to rely upon itself, American Jewry pioneered along novel ways of communal coexistence, ultimately to serve as a model for most countries of the Dispersion.

Looking back at the three centuries of American Jewish group life, one is struck by the well-nigh universal Jewish feeling of being at home in America. From the outset the overwhelming majority of Jews came with the intent to remain here permanently and to build new homes for themselves and their children.

We are not well informed about Jewish migratory movements in the earlier period. But as soon as immigration statistics became more ample and reliable, particularly during the period from 1899 to 1943, when Jewish immigrants and visitors were supposed to list themselves as "Hebrew" by race, they showed an unusually high ratio of immigrants to reemigrants. The figures for the twenty years of 1908-27 are especially significant, for the period can be subdivided into (1) six years of continued mass immigration (1908-14), (2) the practical cessation of the flow of new arrivals during World War I, (3) the resumption of the influx (1918-24) with a new relative peak reached in 1921, and (4) the final three years (1924-27) under the newly restricted immigration. Year after year, the Jewish group was the least prone to leave these shores. Some 1,040,000 Jews in all entered the country, but only 53,000 departed, representing a ratio of but 5.11 per cent. Even during the six prewar years of relatively free migration, a percentage of 7.14 departures for 100 Jewish entries was indeed extraordinarily small. During the following decade, 1915-24, the ratio dropped to 1.55 percent, to rise but slightly to 2.67 in the subsequent three years. Compared with the Jews, the Irish showed a ratio of 8.58 percent for the whole period, and of 10.84 percent during the decade of 1915-24, undoubtedly owing to the attraction of the new Irish Free State. Next came the Scotch and the Germans, with a ratio ranging from 10.5 to 14.5 percent during the twenty-year period. Most significantly, the peoples from whose midst the large majority of Jewish immigrants had come had a much higher ratio of returnees. For every 100 Poles who had entered the country more than 40 departed. In 1915-24, owing to the rise of independent Poland, there was an actual excess of Polish emigration, 135 departures for every 100 entries. In the case of Russians, Rumanians, and the Balkan peoples total departures in the twenty-year period ranged from 78.5 to 124 percent. In the case of Rumanian and Balkan Slavs the ratio rose steadily until, from 1925 to 1927, for every 100 entering the country, 340 Rumanians and 367 Balkan Slavs departed.

Perhaps even more remarkable is the story of the Great Depression, whose dark and tragic years are still the living memory of the present generation. While many Americans looked for a way of rebuilding their shattered fortunes by returning to the soil, others chose the road of emigration. At the same time the harsh restrictions of the immigration laws were made doubly stringent by presidential orders. As a result, in 1932 and 1933 more than three times as many American residents left the country as there were foreigners coming into it. In 1934 there still was a surplus of some 35 percent of émigrés. In 1935 there was a slight surplus of immigrants, but this was entirely owing to the large excess of Jewish immigration which had persisted during the preceding years as well. While the number of Jews who succeeded in scaling the barriers of immigration remained very small, the figure of those who sought their fortune elsewhere never exceeded one-sixth in any year. In fact, Jews were the only ethnic group among those listed in the government statistics whose immigration exceeded emigration year after year.

Remarkably, too, more Jewish émigrés left for Canada or Mandatory Palestine than for their countries of origin. According to Palestinian statistics more than 1,800 American Jews settled in that country during the first seven years of the Mandate, 1923-29.

In all these respects the American experience was altogether unique. Not even Great Britain or Canada revealed the same unwavering line. Unquestionably many East European Jews had entered England and Canada only to use these countries as midway stations in order either to accumulate enough funds or else to secure the necessary visas for entry into the United States. Many of them found acceptable positions and established human relations which caused them to stay on in British Empire countries, even after they were able to proceed to America. These and other Jewish communities thus benefited permanently from the tremendous American pull. Many more immigrants, however, adhered to their original intention. In 1923-24, for example, some 4,300 Jews entered Canada but 7,920 departed, 7,421 of them for the United States. During two years of the 1930s (1936-38) Jewish departures from Canada to the United States exceeded by some fifty percent all Jewish entries.

These figures reflect the prevailing state of mind among the American Jews. Without underestimating the force of antisemitism even in this country, we can say that the American Jewish community nevertheless has had very little of the traditional feeling of *Galut*. It matters little whether we consider this attitude as mere wishful thinking, or lulling one's self into a false sense of security, nor does it matter that German Jews in the nineteenth century, and perhaps even Spanish Jews in the thirteenth century, also had little foreboding of an imminent disaster. Even Israeli thinkers have conceded that it would be wholly unrealistic to speak of American Jewry as part of a *Galut* and substituted for that term the more neutral word, *Tefutsot,* or Dispersion. There is indeed, a deep moral and psychological chasm between the two terms.

WELFARE PIONEERING

Because of that conviction of permanence, American Jewry gradually but solidly built up its communal life along novel lines. With generation after generation of immigrants knocking at its gates, it had to allot to philanthropy a much greater role than was usual in the traditional Jewish community.

All through the ages, to be sure, communal as well as private charities had played a tremendous role in the Jewish communal structure. The leaders of the London community correctly stated in 1678 that "it is a general virtue of all the congregations of Israel, in all the places where they dwell, to establish and form a Hebrà, which shall practice the meritorious and urgent charity which is due to the sick and dead." Medieval rabbis actually permitted the diversion of gifts and legacies for the building of a synagogue to the erection of a hospital and the care of the sick. In modern times hospitals sprang up in all major Jewish communities in the Old and New Worlds.

Amercian Jewry went further, not only in establishing magnificent institutions for the healing of the sick, but in turning them into great training centers for physicians and other medical personnel. More than in any other Jewish community, Jewish hospitals in America glory in their interdenominational character. Although almost wholly supported by Jewish funds, and under wholly Jewish management, they now regularly take care of more non-Jewish than Jewish patients. Further, like other American benefactors, for instance the Rockefellers, American Jewish philanthropy has in recent decades done a great deal in promoting health centers abroad. The magnificent achievement of the American Hadassah in building a comprehensive system of medical care in Mandatory Palestine, and more recently in Israel, has been crowned by the creation, in conjunction with the Hebrew University, of a full-fledged medical school whose graduates have already begun to serve the manifold needs of the new country. Incidentally, these opportunities for higher training have also helped in some measure to counteract the existing discrimination in admission of Jews to medical schools, internships, and residencies. Quite recently Yeshiva Medical School has opened its doors in the city of New York.

On the other hand, the care of the dead has been greatly neglected. Traditionally this was a major communal responsibility, although like most other charities it was often delegated to a special association, called *Hebrah Kadishah,* the Holy Association. While all the other associations bore specific names, such as *Hebrah Kadishah Bikkur Holim* (the Holy Society for the Visitation of the Sick), that for the care of the dead required no further qualification. In the Old World it often enlisted the active participation of the most learned and highly respected citizens. In this country, too, New York and Newport had Jewish cemeteries long before they had synagogues, since Jews could also worship in private homes. In the mid-nineteenth century many benevolent societies began providing, among other services, funeral accommodations for their members. Many a western and southern community, too, started with the organization of a benevolent society, rather than a congregation. In more recent decades the Landsman-shaften and workmen's lodges have often provided for the burial needs of their members. But the community at large has often been derelict in supervising existing funeral parlors and private cemeteries.

No wonder, then, that commercialization of funeral services has reached positively disgraceful dimensions. There has always been a conflict between the financial motivations of cemetery administration and those of the families in mourning. Even the old communities used to withhold decent religious burial or refuse permission to erect a tombstone in order to force the hand of recalcitrant members and miserly contributors to communal charities. However ugly these proceedings were, they resulted in strengthening the communal controls. In this country, the benefits of the system accrue entirely to private entrepreneurs, while its shortcomings deeply reflect on the honor and dignity of the entire community. Nor is there any prospect of remedial action in sight.

More directly beneficial to an immigrant community has been the assistance given to new arrivals or prospective immigrants. Naturally enough, the primary responsibility rested on relatives. The dramatic story of Aaron Lopez of colonial Newport, who sent one of his ships to Lisbon to pick up his brother with a wife and three children, demonstrates to what lengths some early American Jews went in bringing close relations to this country. Lopez's brother apparently was in danger of prosecution by the Portuguese Inquisition. Such a danger confronted all Marranos, but doubly so a man whose brother had publicly reverted to Judaism in the New World. Apart from relatives, however, the community was always ready to help. At times, when the influx of immigrants was relatively small, some prosperous communities had no members on their relief rolls, as happened in both Cincinnati and Boston in 1849. The correspondent of the New York *Hasmonean* contrasted the idyllic situation in Boston with that of the Old World Jewish community of Amsterdam, which had long earned the designation of New Jerusalem. There, of a population of 22,000 Jews, 4,000 contributors to charity supported fully or partially 16,000 coreligionists.

With the sudden influx of new settlers the pressure on the American communities increased greatly, and newly organized charities took over the task of seeing the immigrants off their ships, finding them shelter and employment, retraining and "Americanizing" them. At the turn of the century the United Hebrew Charities did yeoman work, as the HIAS (in the 1920s temporarily cooperating with the ICA under the name of HICEM) did later and as the National Refugee Service, more recently renamed the United Service for New Americans, is doing now. From the 1880s, American Jewry no longer waited for the new arrivals, but often sought them out in their old lands. Representatives of American groups were stationed at strategic points in Europe to give prospective immigrants legal and financial assistance. On a much larger scale, the Joint Distribution Committee, while concentrating on the reconstruction of Jewish communities devastated during the two world wars, also performed major services in planning and directing the flow of Jewish migration to this country.

The number and variety of charitable societies, each trying to fill a certain lacuna in the welfare structure, became so great and the distinction between genuinely helpful and mistaken efforts so difficult to draw, that by the end of the nineteenth century some sort of over-all control had become an urgent necessity. So long as each city had only one congregation (even the largest Jewish communities, New York and Charleston, had only one Jewish congregation each at the beginning of the nineteenth century) the congregational board had exercised a measure of control over these semiprivate undertakings. With the proliferation of congregations, as well as of benevolent societies, such control disappeared. Individual donors, too, exposed to a barrage of appeals for a multitude of causes, often lost their bearings. Not having a *kehillah* (community) of the old type, as it still existed in most European countries, American Jewry had to develop new methods of fund-raising and allocation. Beginning with Boston in 1895, the Federation movement made rapid progress. While the much more ambitious project of organizing a New York *kehillah,* begun in 1909, proved unsuccessful, its welfare committee, established in 1912, prepared the ground for the Federation of Jewish Philanthropies, which was organized in 1917. At first the pessimists seemed right: the increase in revenue owing to such consolidation was very slight. But their fears that endowments for specific causes, dear to a particular donor's heart, would no longer be forthcoming, proved groundless. After a few hesitant years, every one of the established federations grew by leaps and bounds, to reach fantastic proportions in the years after World War II. In 1932 these local groups were further united under a Council of Federations. While leaving complete autonomy to each federation, the Council has helped them think through certain common problems and initiate certain joint plans. Independently there arose the gigantic machinery of the United Jewish Appeal, the Israel Bond drives, and other vast national fund-raising campaigns.

Many sneer at such "pocketbook" Judaism. But one must bear in mind that financial sacrifices belong to the oldest and most widespread rituals in religious worship. Animal sacrifices by a nomadic tribe meant essentially the parting with some of man's most cherished possessions in order to propitiate the deity. Perhaps American Jews do not part company with too many of their cherished possessions; perhaps the sacrifices are not large or hurtful enough. But they represent the same basic approach. One could push that parallel even further and claim that we are witnessing the evolution of a new ritual reminiscent of the ancient ceremonial repasts. Fund-raising dinners with a sequence of exhortatory after-dinner speeches deeply tinged with emotion and a ritualistic offering of names could well become a new liturgical form. The payment of a regular contribution, if done in the name of an ideal, or even because of the impact of public opinion and the force of imitation, may indeed become the dominant new form of communal allegiance.

However, psychologically the vast majority of contributors evince little of that sense of ritualistic devotion. Some limit themselves to sending checks annually to their selected charities and feel that they have thereby fulfilled their duty toward the Jewish community. If they happen to be large contributors, they frequently delegate the responsibility of writing such checks to their secretaries. Certainly the amount of time and energy it takes to comply with such obligations in no way compares even with the minimum attendance at religious services during one day a year.

More significantly, fund-raising has necessarily injected a quantitative standard into communal service. At all times major contributors or taxpayers have played a more or less preponderant role in communal affairs. Even in the so-called democratic communities of medieval and early modern Europe wealth carried great weight. In many cases rabbinic decisions emphasized that in communal action a balance must be struck between the will of the majority of constituents and that of the largest financial contributors. This has indeed been an ancient bone of contention between the protagonists of established churches, like the Church of England, and the champions of separation of state and church. While admitting some dependence on the state and changing constellations in party politics, the former claimed that, in the long run, the established churches were better off because they did not have to cater to the rich. In the United States even congregational life has become dependent on the good will of wealthy groups; in fact, too many congregations resemble clubs of the rich, rather than places of worship for the masses of humble and downtrodden. But in the field of charities this quantitative aspect, naturally enough, assumes even greater significance.

Another adverse feature, indeed, a source of weakness as well as of strength, is the great emphasis on efficiency. From the point of view of pure fund-raising, of course, the more efficient the machinery, the better it is. I recall a discussion I had nearly thirty years ago with a distinguished leader of one of the great federations. This was in the Roaring Twenties. At that time the Board had figured out that, since the federation had a total expenditure of $5,000,000 a year, it would suffice to find a hundred donors obligating themselves to contribute $50,000 each for the budget to be fully covered without the fanfare and expense of a campaign. Young and brash as I was at the time, I asked two questions: First, how certain were we of continued prosperity and the ability of a hundred contributors to donate $5,000,000 annually? Secondly and more importantly, was it wise to build a federation structure on so narrow a base? Because of peculiar American conditions, the federations had developed into the closest substitutes for over-all Jewish communities. The larger the number of contributors, therefore, the more intensive was the collaboration of the Jewish public at large in this concerted Jewish effort. Even if the cost of raising small contributions exceeded the revenue therefrom, in the long run it paid to draw in as many contributors as possible.

Efficiency requires other sacrifices as well. According to Maimonides, a man who gives a thousand dollars to a thousand poor people performs the commandment of charity in a much higher degree than one who devotes a thousand dollars to a single cause. Ethically, undoubtedly, there is great value in the act of charity as such, regardless of its ultimate effectiveness. The very idea of federation, on the other hand, and of all other fund-raising efforts in the United States is to eliminate duplication of effort, to value efficiency above psychology. With it also goes the greater professionalization of social work. For more than a thousand years the Rabbis had tried to stem the professionalization of learning. According to the Talmud, teaching of the law, administering it, and all other Rabbinic functions were to be performed free of charge. In time, these high expectations proved unrealizable, and there emerged a regular communal bureaucracy headed by salaried rabbis. However, nonprofessional learning remained in very high esteem and the word of a learned layman carried as much weight as that of the official rabbi. In our own complex society, the increasing division of labor has brought about the rise of a communal bureaucracy of professional social workers including communal executives and fund raisers. Well-trained technicians have become almost a necessity, not only for major fund-raising but also for the proper distribution and the ultimate use of these funds. But we have had to pay for this efficiency the high price of relegating to a secondary role the host of lay officials who used to be the leaders in the ancient *hebrah*. The great strength of the old communal service was its deep and self-sacrificing devotion to Judaism. Today, much communal work is performed by well-trained technicians, whether or not they have any emotional stake in their work.

RELIGIOUS CURRENTS

Some of these approaches have been carried over into the domain of religion. Quantitative measurements have been applied where they least belong. Time and again the main emphasis is laid upon the rise in membership of individual congregations or of their central bodies, as if that were the core of religious progress.

Such was not always the case. For more than half the period of organized Jewish life in this country, all communal life was concentrated around the synagogue. Even here there was a noteworthy difference between the New and the Old World. Generally, early American congregational life was controlled by Sephardim who developed it along the patterns of Sephardic congregations in Amsterdam and London—with one essential difference. In Amsterdam, three Sephardic congregations had been founded in the first quarter-century after the settlement of Jews in the city in 1593. But no sooner did large groups of German immigrants come than the three congregations closed their ranks and forced the Ashkenazim to organize their own congregation. In London, too, in addition to the Spanish-Portuguese Congregation established in 1656, there grew up an independent Ashkenazic Great Synagogue. A great chasm separated the two groups. Nothing of the kind occurred in America. Apparently more Ashkenazim than Sephardim lived in New York even in 1730, when Shearith Israel consecrated its first building. Yet for nearly a century this growing Ashkenazic majority was willing to submit to the control of a predominantly Sephardic board, to pray according to the Sephardic ritual, and to live within the synagogue precincts, if not at home, as if the entire population were Sephardic. Nor was marriage between members of the two groups seriously frowned upon, as it was in London and Amsterdam.

In time, however, the population growth gave rise to new congregations, and even minor internal conflicts led to the separation of dissident groups. The first city to boast two permanent Jewish congregations was Philadelphia. Rodeph Shalom, founded in 1802, was the first independent Ashkenazic congregation in this country. New York followed suit, and in 1825 a dissident group departing from Shearith Israel formed an independent Ashkenazic congregation, B'nai Jeshurun. Once unity was breached there was no end to subdivisions. Discussing the Oneness of God, Maimonides and other philosophers made it perfectly clear that there is a basic difference between one and any other figure. Having given up their traditional unity, more and more splinter groups formed congregations of their own. It is estimated that by 1860 New York possessed twenty-seven congregations.

Of course, the majority of newer communities had but one congregation each. The Censuses of Religious Bodies conducted by the United States since 1850, though not necessarily accurate, give a fair picture of that congregational growth. In 1850, of thirty-seven synagogues in the country, fourteen were located in the state of New York and eight in Pennsylvania. Only two other states, Ohio and South Carolina, had three congregations each. Curiously, Georgia, whose community dates back to 1733, the very year of the founding of that colony, had no synagogue recorded in that census. In the following ten years the situation changed rapidly, the total number of synagogues rising to seventy-seven. Ohio now had eight synagogues; Louisiana added four to the original one; California, which had none in 1850, had five ten years later. Despite the retardation of immigration during the Civil War this growth continued at an accelerated pace. By 1870 no less than a hundred and eighty-nine congregations were counted. Astonishingly, the state of Maine had twenty-three congregations, almost half the number of those of New York.

A most remarkable census took place in 1890, when for the first and only time the government inquiries differentiated between Orthodox and Reformed congregations. The figures are incomplete. Maine, for instance, listed in this census neither Reform nor Orthodox congregations, and hence disappeared from the list entirely. While the 316 Orthodox congregations were largely concentrated on the eastern seaboard (152 in New York State alone), the 217 Reform congregations were distributed all over the country. Only 27 were in the state of New York, but are listed as having a seating capacity of 19,000 as against 21,000 of all the Orthodox synagogues. By 1906 the total increased to 1,769, to reach twenty years later the substantial figure of 3,118. The last official census of 1936 showed an increase of but 600 congregations (to 3,728) in the intervening decade. There are well over 4,000 now, but we shall know better after the forthcoming census. Regrettably, owing to a sudden outburst of congressional economy, no 1946 census was taken, and the missing link will never be completely restored.

The census of 1916 is unique in furnishing data about the languages used by these congregations, although only 1,537 of 1,901 congregations listed reported pertinent facts. Naturally, the largest group (818) listed Hebrew only. Both Hebrew and Yiddish were listed by 691, while 9 listed Yiddish only. On the other hand, 15 used German and Hebrew; 3 mentioned Arabic and Hebrew; and one, named Volunteers of America, claimed to have 520 members and listed Hebrew, Italian, and English. Still another mentioned German, Italian, and Yiddish but evidently by oversight failed to mention Hebrew. It may be assumed that many answers to these and other questions were somewhat arbitrary. But successive listings in decennial censuses would have shed considerable light, not so much through their absolute figures as through the changes and trends they would have revealed from decade to decade. One could wish that all these censuses had been more comprehensive and had offered more comparative data.

With respect to recent developments we must rely upon statistics published by the Union of American Hebrew Congregations for the Reform group, the United Synagogue for Conservative Judaism, and the partial data supplied by the least well-organized Orthodox Unions. The religious upsurge during and after World War II has helped increase tremendously both the number of congregations and their total membership. All three groups claim to have more than doubled their membership since 1940. Major contributory causes of this phenomenon have been the wave of prosperity which placed more and more Jews in the position of paying the relatively high membership dues; the growth of suburban communities, which, without entirely depleting the membership of old congregations, created many new ones; the vast internal migration, especially to the West, Southwest, and South, which brought about the formation of many new communities and the multiplication of congregations in such vastly expanded communities as Los Angeles and Miami; and last but not least, the decline of agnosticism and militant atheism among Jews.

Obviously congregations are not identical with synagogue buildings. People have often wondered why Jews in colonial New York did not put up a much stauncher fight for the right of public worship. One must bear in mind, however, that public worship in Judaism means nothing more than an assembly of ten adult male Jews in any locality. The very word synagogue, like the Hebrew word *knesset,* means assembly, not the house of assembly, the *bet ha-knesset.* Such an assembly of ten men meeting in a cave, in an open field, or a private home performs the same congregational worship as that instituted in the most elaborate structure. Hence New York Jews could well wait three-quarters of a century before they erected a synagogue building of their own. Curiously, unlike most communities in the Old World, the colonial and early American Jews were unable to raise the necessary funds from their own resources. Shearith Israel sent out a moving appeal in 1728 not only to Jewish communities and individuals in the New World but also to some benefactors in London. Much the largest single contribution, £150, came, in fact, from Abraham Mocatta of London. A similar appeal was issued a century later by B'nai Jeshurun (1825), the newly formed congregations in Cincinnati (1825), New Orleans (1828), and others. As late as 1863, the Jews of Washington were able to build their first synagogue only with the aid of other communities. On the one hand such appeals betrayed a certain unwillingness of members to suffer hardships comparable with those of most European communities, which ever since the Middle Ages had somehow managed to build synagogues with their smaller resources. On the other hand they offered testimony to both American inventiveness and democratic cooperation. From the beginning, whatever local patriotism animated the individual, communities did not militate against their feeling of solidarity with the other Jewries of the New World. Interterritorial giving had indeed become a major feature of the American Jewish community, until in the last two generations it has been able to repay many times over the financial benefactions it formerly received from its European coreligionists.

It is small wonder, then, that these communities felt quite early the urge to cooperate on a national basis. After the American Revolution there existed only six regular communities. But no sooner did their number increase with the influx of German Jews in the 1830s and the 1840s than a national federation began to be advocated by such outstanding leaders as Isaac Mayer Wise and Isaac Leeser. Wise, especially, dedicated most of his long and fruitful career to the task of unifying American Jewry under one representative body. A preliminary step was taken in 1859 with the organization of a Board of Delegates of American Jews devoted to the defense of Jewish rights in other countries. In the twenty years of its existence it placed American Jewry so to say on the map of Jewish world affairs. While mostly following the lead of the somewhat younger Alliance Israelite Universelle (organized in 1860) and the Anglo-Jewish Association (established in 1871), it asserted its independence during the important international conferences of the 1870s. Wise was not satisfied, however, with its limited scope and finally succeeded in establishing in 1873 the Union of American Hebrew Congregations to provide domestic communal guidance as well. The Board of Delegates was soon absorbed by the union.

By a curious historical twist, this effort at unity turned out to be a major divisive element. At the time of its organization the Union undoubtedly enjoyed the backing, active or passive, of both communal leaders and the rank and file, mostly recruited from among the German immigrants. But the 1870s witnessed the first major upsurge of East European Jewish immigration. The latter consisted primarily of Orthodox Jews, with a sprinkling of socialists and other agnostics. Neither group was prepared to recognize the supremacy of the Union. Before long the Orthodox groups tried to establish at least for New York City a chief rabbinate of their own along European lines. After preliminary negotiations, including approaches to several European rabbis of distinction, one of them, Jacob Joseph, accepted the call and became the first Orthodox Chief Rabbi of New York (1888). From the beginning he had to combat the opposition not only of Reform and socialist groups, but also of many autonomy-loving Orthodox congregations. Gradually his spiritual authority was reduced to that of his own congregation. Somewhat more successful were the attempts to establish a Union of American Orthodox Congregations which embraced at least a segment of the Orthodox congregations of the country. The foundation of the Isaac Elchanan Yeshiva or Theological Seminary in 1897 (reorganized in 1908) gave orthodoxy a major training and spiritual center which, though not quite so all-embracing and authoritative for the Orthodox movement as Hebrew Union College was for Reform, did lay the foundation for more united efforts.

In between there crystallized a mediating movement soon called Conservative Judaism. First represented by such rabbis as Morris Jastrow and Benjamin Szold, who were not quite clear about their theological position, the new movement led to the establishment, in 1887, of the Jewish Theological Seminary under the leadership of Sabato Morais. Subsequently reorganized in 1902 under the presidency of Solomon Schechter, who was especially invited for this purpose from his readership in Rabbinics at Cambridge University, the Seminary became a central institution of both learning and spiritual guidance for the growing group of Conservative congregations. These were soon organized under the United Synagogue of America.

Within these three groups there was not only room for major differences in theology and ritual, but also considerable organizational latitude. American synagogues soon embraced many activities not usually associated with religion. More than the Christian churches, which had likewise expanded in all directions (according to Eduard C. Lindeman, a metropolitan church which he observed carried on thirty-nine different activities between 7:30 A.M. and 10:00 P.M. of a single day), the synagogue could claim venerable precedents. It always was a "house of the people," although this designation borrowed from Jeremiah had for some reason a sectarian connotation to Talmudic sages. But it was always a center of all communal life, secular as well as religious. Now this functional expansion proceeded so rapidly that, at times, such secular and social activities as athletics seemed to overshadow the synagogues' original spiritual functions. Even theologically, each congregation retained a great deal of autonomy. True, Orthodox congregations felt bound by the law of the *Shulhan Arukh,* and Reform congregations, on the other hand, largely submitted to sets of principles formulated from time to time by the Central Conference of American Rabbis. Nevertheless, much leeway was left for the wishes of congregational members and the theological predilections of their rabbinical leaders.

Many observers have deplored this lack of unity and centralized controls. Such criticisms, it should be borne in mind, stemmed less from protagonists of religion than from exponents of Jewish ethnicism. Having for the most part grown up in the effectively organized European communities, the champions of Jewish nationalism had always viewed the Jewish community as the most eminent vehicle for Jewish survival; to some it appeared as the nearest substitute for the missing Jewish state. They gloried, therefore, in the power of the medieval Jewish community and especially in such central organizations as the Council of Four Lands in early modern Poland. While realizing that under conditions of emancipation no community could possibly exercise similar authority, the nationalistic-minded spokesmen yet wished to approximate that older model as far as possible. A most comprehensive effort in this direction was made by the protagonists of the New York *kehillah.*

Those interested in purely religious affairs, however, had the feeling, not always clearly articulated, that religion as such might benefit from less organization. After all, in its ultimate sense, religion rests upon the individual conscience and each man's direct communion with his Deity. Kierkegaard actually claimed that a truly religious man often joins a congregation only out of cowardice, because he does not dare to stand up alone before his Creator. This is a patent exaggeration. Organized religion helps satisfy purely spiritual cravings in a different but equally legitimate way. In any case, from the standpoint of religious creativity, full religious autonomy, the right of any group of like-minded worshipers to express their spiritual yearnings in their own way, seems to be a desirable goal. The ridicule frequently heaped upon those nineteenth-century reformers who felt obliged to produce a new prayer book for each congregation was less justified in principle than because of the frequent spiritual and esthetic inadequacies of these liturgical creations.

Today the three religious movements have settled into more or less standardized forms. The transitions from one to another are so gradual, however, and are represented by so many local variants that the differences between them constantly diminish. If such drawing together opens new vistas for the reunification of American Jewry on a religious basis, we must not forget that it has become possible largely because of the decline in the intensity of religious feeling. Mutual toleration is often the function of religious indifference, rather than of a growing belief in the legitimacy of one's neighbor's religious principles. In this respect Thomas Jefferson was far from wrong when, in thanking the Jewish preacher Jacob de la Motta for a copy of the discourse delivered at the consecration of a synagogue in Savannah, he observed:

> It excites in him the gratifying reflection that his country has been the first to prove to the world two truths, the most salutary to human society, that man can govern himself, and that religious freedom is the most effectual anodyne of religious dissension; the maxim of civil government being reversed in that of religion, where its true form is, "divided we stand, united, we fall."

One may indeed hope that the religious differences will not be replaced by some standardized minimal type of Judaism, which will raise few objections only because no one will really care to raise them.

CULTURAL AND EDUCATIONAL EXPERIMENTS

If the American congregation has not lived up to the ideals set by the old religious leaders, American Jewry's cultural and educational achievements have left even more to be desired. In fact, promotion of Jewish education has only recently become a matter of community-wide concern. In the colonial and early American periods, the congregations were far too small to provide adequate instruction, so that the teaching of Jewish as well as general subjects had to be left to the discretion of parents and of whatever individual teachers the latter were able to secure. The first Jewish school established in this country was the Polonies Talmud Torah at Shearith Israel in New York. Founded in 1803 through a bequest by Myer Polonies, a native of Poland, this school offered instruction in a varying number of subjects and with varying success over a period of forty years. The Jewish education of the early American Jewish leaders was very limited. When writing a Yiddish letter to his mother, Haym Solomon had to use the assistance of a slightly better informed coreligionist. Often the knowledge of Hebrew among the spiritual leaders did not exceed the level usually attained by a young boy in an East European yeshiba. However inadequate, most instruction given to Jewish children was denominational in character, as was practically the entire educational system.

From the middle of the nineteenth century public education competed with both congregational and private Jewish schools. For a number of years New York Jewry debated the desirability of maintaining full-fledged Jewish schools, without, however, subscribing to the Catholic and fundamentalist denial of the state's right to regulate the education of their children. It was largely a question of expediency as to whether some form of Jewish education could be combined with the public school, which was prohibited by law from giving religious instruction. Wherever that law was circumvented and children were taught the Bible, the temptation to teach it from the Christian point of view was very great. In other words, the proponents of special Jewish schools were principally guided by their fear of the assimilatory effects of the public school.

Inescapably the public school won out. The Jewish community simply could not afford a ramified day-school system. Even today it cannot compete with the Catholic Church, which can draw on its nuns and monks for its teaching staffs with relatively little expense. Moreover, many Jews objected to day schools because they segregated Jewish children from the rest of the school population. With Americanization of the immigrant and the melting-pot ideology looming paramount in the minds of Jewish leaders at the turn of the century, the very idea of a communal day school appeared as a heresy. All that was considered feasible or desirable, therefore, was supplemental Jewish education of varying degrees of intensity. Most Reform congregations were satisfied with Sunday schools, which gave two or three hours of instruction in such Jewish subjects as Bible, Jewish history, and religious customs. Orthodox and Conservative congregations usually insisted upon weekday attendance as well; for the most part, two additional afternoons a week completed the curriculum. Needless to say, relatively little could be learned in a school year with long summer vacations and many holiday intermissions, by attendance of less than ten hours a week. Many children, moreover, attended only for two or three years. Very few continued their schooling after their bar mitzvah or confirmation ceremonies. A substantial number, at times the majority, received not even that minimum of Jewish training.

Much as enlightened parents deplored this situation, they found the competition of the public school further intensified, as American education became more and more comprehensive and catered to more and more of the pupils' interests. Not only were the hours of instruction lengthened now, but grammar and high schools added to their curricula a good deal of informal, semivoluntary education, both social and athletic. With the great emphasis on athletics in and out of school, moreover, many boys wished to spend their free hours outside in athletic games, and objected to attending a Hebrew school two or three additional hours in the afternoon. Some resented being different from their schoolmates of other faiths, whom they watched enjoying their leisure after school hours. Most parents were not genuinely interested in the education their children received in the Jewish schools, but simply complied with a social obligation. At best they wanted their children to acquire the facility of reading Hebrew prayers by rote so that they might participate in synagogue worship. Nor were the teachers altogether of the highest caliber. Before 1940 the salaries of Hebrew teachers were exceedingly poor, their prestige rather low. Hence the profession attracted, for the most part, either recent arrivals from abroad, who had considerable difficulty in communicating with their pupils in English, or teachers who considered Hebrew teaching a stopgap until they secured more remunerative and satisfying employment, or else people who were unsuccessful in other jobs.

Much of the anarchy in Hebrew education came from lack of interest among communal leaders. Until recently it was left to individual congregations, special associations maintaining Talmud Torahs, or to parents and private teachers to cope with the situation as best they could. Only a few ideologically directed enterprises showed what could be achieved through intelligent, directed effort. Early in the century the Yiddish-speaking proletarian groups embarked upon an ambitious program of maintaining Yiddish schools. As a result, a network of Sholem Aleichem schools arose in this country and Canada which, though confronted with the additional difficulty of teaching Yiddish in a less and less Yiddish-speaking environment, can boast of some remarkable educational attainments. Dedicated teachers and parents succeeded also in establishing fine Orthodox yeshibot and modern Hebrew schools with a Zionist program. But these stand out against a background of ineffectual Jewish education.

Conditions have greatly improved in the past two decades, during which the community as such has awakened to its responsibility toward Jewish education. Historically, communal responsibility for education is one of the oldest and most universal aspects of Jewish communal effort. The Jews have rightly prided themselves on having pioneered in the field of universal elementary education for boys from the age of six even before the Second Fall of Jerusalem. Everywhere even the poorest of communities sought to supplement individual efforts by parents and teachers. America lagged behind. But in recent decades boards of Jewish education have been founded and subsidized, or even maintained outright, by federations. The Jewish Education Committee in New York, begun with a large grant from a private foundation, is carried on the budget of the Federation of Jewish Philanthropies. These boards set up new standards which raised considerably the level of Jewish education. Simultaneously, the improvement in the economic status of teachers, the increasingly improved programs at the various teachers colleges, and the even more stringent requirements for certification of qualified teachers gave the Jewish schools a more competent body of instructors. Parents, too, had become aware of their own lack of Jewish education, and desired to give their children what they had missed. Community agreement on requirements, such as nonadmission to a bar mitzvah ceremony without previous school attendance for a prescribed number of years, has likewise served as a strong stimulus.

All these factors have led to increased attendance at Jewish schools on all levels. The nation-wide enrollment has often reached fifty percent of children in particular age brackets; more than half of those now attend schools more than once a week. Perhaps the most startling development has taken place in the Jewish day schools. As late as 1940 only two percent of Jewish school children attended such schools; now the ratio exceeds seven percent. Non-Orthodox parents will often send their children to such schools because of the high quality of instruction they offer, even in general subjects, or because they like the integration of the Jewish into the general curriculum, or because they see in such a school the only opportunity of giving children a more intimate knowledge of the Jewish heritage. Graduates of these schools will undoubtedly furnish a substantial proportion of the professional communal manpower (rabbis, teachers, and social workers), and also provide the community with a lay elite much better informed about Jewish life and letters. To protagonists of the day school, such a Jewish elite far outweighs the disadvantages of "segregation." Some sort of segregation, they claim, exists in many public schools with a preponderant Jewish student body, and from another angle in all private schools which promote segregation along class lines.

With all these substantial improvements, however, American Jewry still has a long and arduous road to travel before the majority of its youth will receive adequate training in Jewish subjects and acquire genuine familiarity with their Jewish heritage.

Progress in the higher echelons of Jewish education has been even more marked. Even Talmudic learning of the old type has received a new impetus through the transplantation of several yeshibot from Europe to America. Hundreds of Jewish young men now receive advanced Talmudic training which favorably compares with that previously obtained only in Eastern Europe or Israel. The seminaries, too, have increased their enrollment and extended their curricula to a variety of allied fields. For example, it is now possible to receive professional training for cantorial work. Since the suspension of the Graduate School for Jewish Social Work in 1939, no specialized training in this field is offered, which is doubly regrettable, since, as we have mentioned, Jewish social work in all its ramifications occupies a focal position in Jewish communal life. The short-lived Training Bureau for Jewish Communal Service which functioned in the first postwar years only partially filled the gap. Some work along these lines is being done, however, at Yeshiva University's School for Community Service, and similar projects at other schools are being discussed. But this is still a major item of unfinished business in Jewish higher education. On the other hand, the various Jewish teachers colleges, Hebrew and Yiddish, have made good strides in the last two decades, as have purely academic forms of instruction by the growing number of Jewish chairs at universities and colleges, including Brandeis University and Dropsie College. In this process the B'nai B'rith's Hillel Foundation has contributed directly, through its efforts to establish such chairs as well as by more informal instruction in Jewish subjects to students on various campuses throughout the country. Since its establishment in 1923 the foundation has extended its range of activity to some 120 campuses in the United States and Canada (a Hillel Foundation was even established at the Hebrew University in Jerusalem), where Jewish students are given an opportunity to satisfy a variety of social, religious, and cultural needs. On the other hand, youth organizations of all kinds—the Menorah movement, Young Israel, Zionist youth groups, and others—have for many decades stimulated concern for, and action in, Jewish fields on the part of young people acting on their own initiative.

Many social groups have combined Jewish activity with more informal social and educational enterprises. From its inception the synagogue has served as a social center as well, but in America men often wished to get together on a purely social basis. The earliest Jewish social club on record is one that was organized in Newport in 1761. Since that time clubs of all kinds have been started by Jews in various parts of the country. But with rare exceptions their Jewishness has consisted almost exclusively in their Jewish membership, rather than in any particular activity.

Quite a few clubs were essentially reactions to the extensive discrimination practiced by non-Jewish clubs against Jewish applicants for admission. Such discrimination also allegedly underlay the formation of the first Jewish fraternal orders. Curiously, Freemasonry was permeated with humanitarian ideals transcending the bounds of religion, race, or nationality. For this reason as well as because of its mysterious rituals, it always appeared suspect to extreme nationalists. In recent decades antisemites in Germany, France, and other countries sharply attacked the supposed alliance between Freemasonry and international Jewry. It is doubly ironic, therefore, that in America various masonic lodges have themselves practiced discrimination against Jews. This was not always the case. In fact, one of the early Boston Jews, Moses Michael Hays, served for four years (1788-92) as Master of the Masonic Grand Lodge with Paul Revere as his deputy. But later, with the increase in the number of Jews, it appears, some lodges began practicing discrimination or at least some Jews felt discriminated against and proceeded to organize their own fraternal orders.

In founding the Independent Order B'nai B'rith in Essex Street, New York, in 1843, Henry Jones and his eleven German Jewish associates went far beyond the usual objectives of a lodge. Without being too specific about their program, they adopted a constitution the preamble of which reads:

B'nai B'rith has taken upon itself the mission of uniting Israelites in the work of promoting their highest interests and those of humanity; of developing and elevating the mental and moral character of the people of our faith; of inculcating the purest principles of philanthropy, honor, and patriotism; of supporting science and art; alleviating the wants of the poor and needy; visiting and attending the sick; coming to the rescue of the victims of persecution; providing for,

protecting, and assisting the widow and orphan on the broadest principles of humanity.

This program was so broad and sweeping that there was apprehension
lest the members' attention be diverted from religious work to purely
secular activity. Although the order tried to steer clear of the controversy between Orthodoxy and Reform, it failed to unite American
Jewry. Further, it was not long before it faced competition from new
orders. One of the original founders, Hirsch Heineman, proceeded
within six years to organize a new Independent Order Free Sons of
Israel. Afterward an Independent Order Sons of Abraham and several
others were formed.

The B'nai B'rith has reached into Germany, Austria, and other
countries. Today its United States membership alone consists of some
350,000. Together with numerical growth went a growing diversifi-
cation of programs and activities, such as the above-mentioned
Hillel Foundation. Equally significant have been the order's social
services, including vocational guidance. More recently B'nai B'rith
entered the political arena and became the driving force behind
the formation of the American Jewish Conference during World
War II. It has retained its interest in the struggle for Jewish rights
abroad. Domestically, its Anti-Defamation League has for the last
thirty years carried on a persistent struggle against antisemitism. It
was particularly vigorous during the heyday of antisemitism in the
1930s. For many years B'nai B'rith has also had a strong youth organization and more recently it has adopted an expanding program of
adult education.

In some respects related to the orders were the Landsmanshaften.
Organizations of this type are almost as old as the Jewish Dispersion.
Even in ancient Rome several synagogues were founded by persons
hailing from the same original community or province. After the
expulsion from Spain and Portugal, Iberian exiles formed Sevillian,
Lisbon, and other congregations in Constantinople and Salonica. Similarly, in the period of the great American immigration, arrivals from
certain East European communities were drawn into larger "family"
groups bent upon assisting newcomers in finding jobs, securing medical care, and providing for them in emergencies. Relief activities were
but a part of the program, however. Usually the Landsmanshaften
satisfied the craving of new settlers for social intercourse, and at times
formed congregations of their own. The membership increased by
leaps and bounds, since in many instances before 1939 more Jews
from East European townships had settled in the United States, or
even in New York alone, than had remained behind. Some of these
Landsmanshaften joined larger groupings, if indeed they had not

themselves originated from provincial Landsmanshaften which then split into local subdivisions. In time federations of Ukrainian Jews, Rumanian Jews, Galician Jews, and so forth focused in themselves many social and educational efforts of large segments of the Jewish population. Although their heyday is long past, enough of them are still functioning today to represent a significant variant of the Jewish social clubs. One wishes that more information were available about the historic evolution and sociological function of these survivals of Old World loyalties. A variant of the Landsmanshaft has been the family society, which may be said to revert to still older, preterritorial groupings of clan societies.

Most of these organizations, except perhaps the independent orders and family societies, have decidedly Old World antecedents. American Jewry has made another significant contribution, however, by developing "Jewish Centers." With the nineteenth-century influx of German Jews, who had brought with them strong cultural interests, outlets were sought beyond the confines of the existing synagogues. After 1848, at a time when America witnessed the rise of numerous political and cultural societies, Jews, too, wished to get together for nonsynagogal activities. In 1850 a group of Philadelphians organized a literary group which adopted the characteristic name of Young Men's Hebrew Literary Association, while the first American Young Men's Christian Association was founded more than a year later, in December, 1851. The American Jewish organization took the same name as an English movement established a few years earlier, but there is no evidence that the Philadelphia group knew anything about its existence. Similar literary associations began springing up in other American cities including Baltimore, New York, and Boston. Before long, however, they gave way to the more comprehensive, philanthropic as well as educational Young Men's Hebrew Associations like the one founded in New York in 1874.

A new impetus to these Ys and Jewish Centers, as many of them came to be called in the twentieth century, came from the formation of the Jewish Welfare Board during World War I. A federation of Jewish Centers, under way for several years, was founded in 1911, but it was still very weak when the war created a new need. With the large enlistment of American Jews in the armed forces, the government had to provide chaplains and other religious and social services for Jewish servicemen. Because of this immediate need and its appeal to the patriotic sentiments of American Jews, the newly created Welfare Board enlisted widespread support. It was recognized by the government as representative of all Jewish communal groups. Only incidentally did the Welfare Board become connected with the Jewish Center movement.

As soon as the war was over, however, this secondary function became primary. Without arrogating to itself any controlling powers, the board tried to focalize the disparate efforts of the individual centers, to offer them guidance in programming, planning for buildings, and budgeting. More recently it has also undertaken to help train personnel for the centers' specialized functions. To be sure, World War II and the Korean War diverted much of these energies toward new war efforts, the Welfare Board also maintaining a Bureau of War Records to keep track of the number of Jewish servicemen, casualties, recipients of decorations, and so forth—a much-needed activity in view of the numerous antisemitic aspersions concerning alleged Jewish "shirking." Nevertheless, its planning and advisory services for the Jewish Centers have remained the mainstay of the organization.

The problem of "Jewish content" in the Jewish Center programs has been a heatedly debated issue for many years. Practically all centers pay lip service to the importance of Jewish content. In practice some of the activities of all centers, and most of the activities in some, are entirely devoid of any denominational or specifically Jewish cultural ingredients. Many centers pride themselves on attracting large numbers of non-Jewish youth. The debate has calmed down recently, but the progress of Jewish education on this informal level has been spotty. Nevertheless, the center movement has been a major American contribution to Jewish educational efforts in the emancipation era. The 350 centers now functioning in the United States and Canada and spreading out to Latin America, South Africa, and even Israel have significantly influenced a large section of Jewish youth now grown into adulthood, and the movement holds out even greater promise for the future.

In recent decades the summer camp has spread along with the center movement. Most camps are social and athletic and pursue few educational aims. However, there has been a growing realization among educators that summer months can be used to great advantage for educating young people for better citizenship, and also for a richer Jewish cultural life. Such camps as Massad try to cultivate Hebrew as a spoken language and to give children a taste of Israeli life. The various Ramah camps and those run by teachers colleges and Jewish Centers have incorporated many educational features into their normal camping programs. So have the Yiddish-speaking camps run by the Arbeiter Ring (Workmen's Circle), which are designed for education and indoctrination as much as for healthful social living. The Brandeis Youth Organization centered on the West Coast has adopted a very ambitious program of cultural creativity on a more adult level. All these undertakings are still in their early stages of evolution. But they already constitute a major American pioneering contribution which has been serving as a model for other Jewries.

A CREATIVE CULTURE IN THE MAKING

In spite of all this varied activity, many critics have asked whether American Jewry is capable of any genuinely creative achievement in the field of Jewish culture. Looking back on three centuries of organized Jewish life in this country, one can fully understand these criticisms. It is a matter of record that in the first two centuries American Jewry was unable to produce even a single Hebrew book of its own. Some Jews studied Hebrew, and one of the first known American Jewish intellectuals, Judah Monis, achieved a certain fame because he produced the first Hebrew grammar in this country. For this achievement he was given a master's degree at Harvard University. Soon thereafter, when duly converted to Christianity, he was allowed to teach Hebrew to Harvard students, who at that time were mostly students of divinity. But none of the prominent Jews of the Revolutionary era seems to have had any real knowledge of Hebrew. Haym Solomon required as much assistance in writing a Hebrew letter as he did for his Yiddish correspondence. We have an official authorization issued by Bernard Gratz to Solomon Etting in Lancaster, Pennsylvania, which is written in an absolutely barbaric Hebrew. Not even Gershom Mendes Seixas, the minister of the Spanish-Portuguese synagogue in New York, was a student of Hebrew, as may be judged from a Hebrew address which he helped Sampson Simpson prepare for his graduation from Columbia College. Conditions were so bad that when Isaac Hart of Newport received a Hebrew letter from Hebron in Palestine he went to Ezra Stiles, the Protestant divine, to translate it for him. As late as 1848 a permit for kosher wine in New York was obtained after the text was formally translated into English by another non-Jew, Professor William L. Roy. To be sure, shortly before this, a Jewish scholar, Isaac Nordheimer, published in New York a Hebrew grammar and the first part of a Hebrew concordance. But he died in 1842, leaving no Jewish successor. On the whole, the criticism voiced by I. W. Carpeles in 1785 that "the majority of inhabitants of the lands beyond the sea

[America] are not scholars and do not understand our sacred language" was still true even in the middle of the nineteenth century.

It was not until 1860 that the first Hebrew book, *Abne Yehoshua,* a homiletical commentary on the "Sayings of the Fathers," was published by a recent immigrant from Poland, Joshua Falk ben Mordecai ha-Kohen. Although the author announced on the title page that "if my book will find favor in your eyes and you will buy it from me for its full price . . . I shall print a second book about which I know for sure that everyone will be delighted with it," apparently not enough readers accepted this invitation. The loss to Hebrew letters was not great.

In the meantime, however, Jewish learning made some progress in English-language publications. The first English translation of the Hebrew prayer book was published by Isaac Pinto in 1776, because he had found that Hebrew, "being imperfectly understood by many, by some not at all; it has been necessary to translate our Prayers in the language of the Country." The real upsurge of Jewish learning began only with the activities of such rabbis as Isaac Leeser, Isaac Mayer Wise, Samuel Hirsch, and David Einhorn. Whether writing in English or in German, these men, especially Einhorn, made significant contributions to Jewish theology before 1860.

After the Civil War there was a sudden flowering of both Hebrew and Yiddish letters. Yiddish, in particular, achieved a high literary quality in the fields of drama, poetry, and journalism. The Hebrew litterateurs had a harder time. A Hebrew daily failed after a few months. But Hebrew magazines like the *Hadoar* have appeared regularly, and Hebrew poets of distinction have also emerged in the American environment. Even greater strides have been made in scholarship. Just as old Rabbinic learning has found a new home in this country, so has, even earlier, the modern *Wissenschaft des Judentums.* Early in this century American scholarship organized and largely produced the Jewish Encyclopedia, the first work of its kind in any language. Since that time American Jewish learning has produced many monumental works of scholarship. In fact, in recent years the United States has ranked next to Israel as the main center of Jewish learning. At the same time, even more energies have been devoted to the cultivation of general arts and sciences. In the twentieth century, especially, the roster of American Jewish writers, artists, musicians, jurists, and scientists has been truly formidable.

In the face of these ever growing achievements, the critics have emphasized the fact that most of the manpower, certainly in the Jewish fields but also in the general sciences and arts, has been recruited from abroad. Certainly such men as Sholem Aleichem and Morris Rosenfeld, Schechter, Ginzberg, Neumark, and Einstein came to this country as fully formed personalities. In the last two or three decades native-born Jewish scholars and writers have begun to emerge, but only a few have achieved the eminence of their predecessors who came from Europe. More significantly, the critics rightly point out that nearly all basic approaches, almost all fundamental philosophies of Jewish life, have been formulated abroad, while American thinkers have only given them an occasional twist or modification to fit the American conditions. This criticism becomes quite significant now, since European Jewry can no longer supply America with the necessary ideologies, methods, or even intellectual manpower. Many anxious souls are asking, therefore, whether there is any future for a creative Jewish culture in America.

No one, of course, can predict the future. However, judging by past achievements elsewhere, these queries reveal undue impatience with the tempo of history. American Jewry has not yet achieved the stature of any of the great centers of Jewish learning such as ancient or medieval Babylonia, medieval Spain, early modern Poland, or medieval or nineteenth-century Germany, but we are apt to forget that even now American Jewry is still a young community by historic standards. Not only did the vast majority of American Jews settle in this country within a century or less, but even if one takes the entire three centuries of their residence here, it is still a relatively short span of time for an original culture to develop.

Every one of the chief ancient centers required half a millennium or longer of silent growth before Jewish culture became deeply rooted and developed new and original forms of its own. True, in modern times the progress has been speedier. Jews transplanted into the Netherlands, whether from Spain, Germany, or Poland, immediately proceeded to build cultural institutions and create literary monuments. But this was not a genuine Dutch Jewish culture. Here, as in the Ottoman Empire, the Spanish exiles, and to a lesser extent their German and Polish counterparts, simply continued living their old cultural life with little reference to their immediate environment. In the Balkans until the twentieth century, most descendants of the exiles spoke Ladino and rarely, if ever, participated in the cultural life of their Turkish, Greek, or Slavonic neighbors. In America, too, as soon as cultural leaders arrived from Europe during the last hundred years, they succeeded in transplanting Yiddish and Hebrew letters and learning along the lines fully developed in the older countries. But for a native American Jewish culture, the community has simply been too young and not yet deeply enough rooted in the soil of this land. Perhaps now, with the large majority of American Jews having been born and educated in this country, we may look forward to some genuine cultural achievements bearing a preeminently American coloring.

PATTERNS OF SURVIVAL

Problems of Jewish cultural creativity are but part of the larger problem as to whether, and for how long, Jews can survive in America. The negative argument is often presented in a twofold way. On the one hand, believers in the permanence of antisemitism predict that sooner or later the Jews of every country *must* be overwhelmed by some major cataclysm. They argue that all through history every Jewish community, however flourishing, was destroyed by such an elemental outbreak and American Jewry cannot hope to escape that fate. On the other hand, those observers who believe in the permanence of American democracy and its egalitarian institutions are convinced that Jews will disappear precisely because they are too well off.

Both these arguments can be supported with plenty of evidence from history. Certainly in the thirteenth century no one could have predicted that a few generations later Spanish and Portuguese Jewry would be eliminated from Iberian soil. So certain of their position in the country were the Aragonese Jews in 1219 that, facing the threat of a discriminatory badge because of the resolution adopted two years earlier by the Fourth Lateran Council, they threatened to leave the country if the king resorted to force. King and Church yielded. Yet within less than two centuries the descendants of these Jews faced a large-scale "holy war" preached against them by antisemitic rabble-rousers. By the end of the fifteenth century they were told to leave.

More recently, as late as thirty years ago no one would have predicted that Germany would fall back into barbarism and attempt its savage "final solution of the Jewish question" so soon thereafter. In fact, Jews under the Weimar Republic had suffered so little from social discrimination that when the catastrophe finally struck, it found them totally unprepared mentally. Our Cassandras here say, "Wait for the next depression and you will see in America, too, an outbreak of antisemitism of unprecedented ferocity." No student of social sciences will be careless enough to predict that such an upheaval is impossible here. Neither will he predict that it *must* happen here. There are no unbreakable historical laws.

That there is a causal relation between economic depressions and antisemitic outbreaks is historically far from proved. There certainly is no evidence that in the past American depressions (1873, 1907, 1921) we had any significant upsurge of anti-Jewish feeling. If during the Great Depression after 1929 antisemitism made headway on the American scene, the main cause may have been the world-wide Nazi propaganda. As a matter of record, the antisemitic movements reached their height in the United States, not during the low points of the Depression in 1930-32, but rather in the late 1930s, when many ravages of the Depression had already been healed and the American economy was again forging ahead. Of course, despair generated by unemployment and the shattering of family fortunes creates a more receptive audience for agitators of all kinds, including those who preach bigotry and hatred toward any chosen scapegoat. But in general, depressions, like other social revolutions, merely accelerate trends already existing in the body politic.

In short, while it is *possible* that some cataclysmic anti-Jewish upheaval might some day put an end to American Jewry, it does not appear likely. Its occurrence would presuppose such a total revamping of the American social and political system, such a total abandonment of the national heritage and radical deviation from the course of American history, that for the time being at least one can relegate the possibility to the realm of pessimistic nightmares.

American Jewry's disappearance as a result of total assimilation is a more tangible danger. Has not the emancipation era as a whole created a deep crisis in Jewish living? This crisis is, naturally enough, most direct where emancipation is at its fullest. One might even quote the historic precedent of China. Because that country so rarely discriminated against foreigners, including Jews, it proved to be in the long run the most assimilatory power in history. The Jews in China, too, of whom we have definite historic traces since the ninth century and who probably settled there several centuries earlier, on and off formed communities of their own. Yet sooner or later these communities were swallowed up in the mainstream of Chinese culture, leaving behind only the debris of architectural monuments, inscriptions, and books. Even in the twentieth century there was a Chinese Jewish community in Kai-Feng, consisting largely of racial Chinese probably with some admixture of original Jewish blood, but this was only a remnant of a much more flourishing community in that and other localities. Would not the same thing happen to Jews in America?

Here the answer, based upon Western history, is definitely in the negative. One might even paradoxically assert that American Jews—indeed, all Western Jews—could not disappear even if they all wished to do so. Historic experience shows that whenever large masses of

Jews were suddenly converted to Christianity or Islam, as was the case of the Marranos, the Italian *Neofiti,* the survivors of the Almohade persecutions in North Africa and Spain, or the Turkish *Dönmeh,* they were not absorbed by society at large, but overtly or clandestinely formed a distinct group for generations thereafter. As late as 1904 the Prime Minister of Spain, Miguel Mauras, was chided in open session of Parliament as a *Chueta,* that is, a member of the Marrano group living on the Balearic Islands as Christians since 1492. In the 1920s a Galician engineer, Samuel Schwartz, discovered in Oporto, Portugal, a group of several thousand people who still had distinct knowledge of Jewish customs and festivals. After the publication of Schwartz's book, *Os Cristãos-Novos em Portugal,* in 1925, the world became keenly aware of the existence of a sizable crypto-Jewish community in Portugal four and a quarter centuries after the so-called Expulsion of 1496. The chances are, therefore, that even if the whole American Jewish community were suddenly to adopt Christianity, the result would only be the emergence of a new group of American Judeo-Christians still presenting all the complexities of the Jewish question but devoid of the feature that makes Jewish life worthwhile, namely, its magnificent heritage. Actually, the majority of American Jews do not wish to be converted and have no thought of disappearing. On the contrary, it is manifest from all that has been said here that the forces of survival in religion, education, and culture are more strongly operative now than they were three or four decades ago. The impact of the state of Israel is also becoming more noticeable as time goes on.

Since neither forcible elimination nor voluntary disappearance seems to be a realistic possibility, the only genuine question is what kind of Jews there will be in America and elsewhere a century hence. No one in his senses will have the temerity to predict the type of Judaism and Jewish community which is likely to emerge from the great turmoil of our present world. Yet one thing may confidently be asserted: If American Jewry turns from quantity to quality, if it builds its communal coexistence less upon the quantitative criteria of financial success, statistically measurable memberships or school attendance, and costly and outwardly impressive buildings and institutions, and devotes more attention to the cultivation of the genuinely creative personality and of the substantive and enduring values in religion and culture, the new type of American Jewry will be a cause of pride and satisfaction. To put it bluntly, if someone were to guarantee that in the next generation American Jews will harbor one hundred truly first-rate scholars; one hundred first-rate writers and artists; one hundred first-rate rabbis; one hundred first-rate communal executives; and one hundred first-rate lay leaders—the total number would not exceed five hundred persons, a negligible and statistically hardly recognizable segment of the Jewish population—one could look forward confidently to American Judaism's reaching new heights of achievement.

Jewish historical-ethical monotheism, expressive of the unity of God, of the universe and mankind, is needed more than ever in our divided world. Perhaps the greatest task now confronting humanity is how to establish the supremacy of the moral order above all other sovereignties, including that of the state. A history-oriented and messianically driven religion alone can counteract the destructive forces of nature, nowadays magnified by the new man-made means of destruction.

In the service of that religion and with this ideal in mind, the Jewish people still has a tremendous mission to perform. Its destiny has made it not only a world people in the course of its history, but has also placed it in a strategic position for service—service to be sure combined with suffering—in this critical epoch of human history. Destiny willed it that the two largest agglomerations of Jews should be found today in the United States and the Soviet Union, the two world powers whose rivalry or cooperation will fatefully determine the whole course of human evolution. The third-largest group of Jews, which before long may outstrip the second, is located in Israel, at the edge of the turbulent Asiatic-African populations, and has an irresistible drive toward reshaping existing international relations. Before the Jewish people a great book of human and Jewish destiny stands open; in it is mirrored its millennial experience in its progression through many civilizations. If only our present generation and its successors can become fully cognizant of their heritage, if only they will delve ever deeper into the mysteries of their people's past and present, they will not only make certain of that people's creative survival, but also significantly help in charting mankind's path toward its ultimate, let us hope messianic, goals.

SUGGESTIONS FOR FURTHER READING

This book is an interpretation of Jewish culture and experience and it should not be used as a substitute for the historical record of thirty-five or more centuries. But if, as the introduction contends, the importance of history is in the light that it throws on our present situation and the guidance it affords for intelligent action, then this story and interpretation of some of the major ages and ideas of Jewish history should give the reader a firm sense of continuity with his forebears as well as a new awareness of his ideals, loyalties, and responsibilities.

The book may be most profitably used as a guide. Like any guidebook, it directs the traveler to the points that the writers consider of primary interest. But even the most experienced guide will acknowledge that there remain uncharted terrain and—especially in the region of history—embarrassing riches. Moreover, the descriptions of the points of major interest are limited, not only by the pages of the guidebook, but also by the exactness of the guide's descriptive powers and the range and quality of his vision. The traveler may find some of the descriptions inexact from his own vantage point and he will surely discover his impression of certain objects and subjects at odds with those of the guide. He may even wish to depart from the prescribed routes and wander off into byways. He will probably give intense interest to those parts of the terrain that have personal and special meaning for him.

This supplementary section is not intended to be a bibliography, for any respectable list of the sources of Jewish history would require a solid volume. The aim here is only to direct the reader to some of the best accessible literature which will allow him to retrace the paths of the writers and to gain for himself the sense of the past that grows out of direct association with those who have made history and have shaped our thought. In short, this section is simply a commentary on original and interpretive sources.

While a number of primary works or anthologies of texts in Hebrew are mentioned for certain readers who are at home in that tongue, it is assumed that the larger body of general readers and students will turn to works written in or translated into English. The most direct and thus the most satisfying experience can be gained from reading accounts by contemporary writers of each age and entire works of representative thinkers and writers, in spite of the observation of the poet Bialik that reading a translation is like kissing through a veil. Another way of sampling the materials of Jewish history and thought and at the same time of covering large areas of experience is to read anthologies or selections prepared by experts. This method has obvious advantages, but it provides only glimpses which the editor regards as representative but which in fact reflect his own standards and scale of values. Both methods of reading are useful and informative, though wide reading in fuller sources in either Hebrew or English is recommended.

Because many of the books mentioned may not be easily accessible in local libraries, full information is given about each reference. Wherever a work is available in an inexpensive paper-bound edition, the reference to the original trade edition has been omitted. For those interested in building a reference library, specific information about books mentioned either in the body of this volume or in the following pages may be obtained by writing directly to individual publishers or to the Jewish Book Council of America, 145 East Thirty-second Street, New York 16, New York. An asterisk (*) denotes books with authoritative, extensive bibliographies.

INTRODUCTION

The reader will probably want to move quickly on from the introduction to the story itself, and it is probable that like many introductions this one can be read with fuller appreciation as a concluding chapter. But some readers to whom the theme of "living" history and the methods of historiography are challenging may want to examine more adequately this basic concept and some of its assumptions. The little volume *History as the Story of Liberty,* by Benedetto Croce (#17 in the Meridian Books Series, Meridian Books, N.Y., 1955, $1.35), gives a classic statement of the thesis that history "exists for the purpose of maintaining and developing the active and civilized life of human society." Though Arnold J. Toynbee's *A Study of History* may be criticized, a historical work of such widespread influence cannot be ignored. The best approach to it is the one-volume abridgment by D. C. Somerville (Oxford, N.Y., 1947). A necessary antidote to Toynbee's treatment of Jews and Judaism will be found in Maurice Samuel, *The Professor and the Fossil: Some Observations on Arnold J. Toynbee's A Study of History* (Knopf, N.Y., 1956). An equally influential interpretation of history, in both the Communist and non-Communist worlds, is based upon Marxist doctrine and is generally known as "historical materialism." V. Gordon Childs, an eminent authority on prehistory, gives a brief, clear, and sympathetic exposition of this approach in his essay *What Is History?* (College Paperbacks, Abelard-Schuman, 404 Fourth Ave., N.Y. 21, N.Y., 1953, $1.00). The knife of criticism is incisively applied to all the above-mentioned viewpoints by Isaiah Berlin in *Historical Inevitability* (Oxford, N.Y., 1954); although somewhat overconcentrated, this essay is nevertheless a magnificent assertion of free choice in history. There is an exciting inquiry into the lessons of history in Herbert J. Muller, *The Uses of the Past* (Mentor, 501 Madison Ave., N.Y. 22, N.Y., 50 cents).

Although Ernest Renan remarked almost one hundred years ago that "the philosophy of history is the achievement of Judaism," there is not yet a substantial work in English on that theme. Helpful to any reader who wishes to pursue this topic are a suggestive essay by Morris R. Cohen, "Philosophies of Jewish History," in *Reflections of a Wondering Jew* (Marboro Books, 222 Fourth Ave., N.Y., N.Y., $1.00), and a number of extremely readable historical essays in the first part of *Personalities and Events in Jewish History,* by Cecil Roth (Jewish Pub. Society, Phila., 1953). Some illuminating essays on phases of the Jewish intellectual tradition are included in E. R. Bevan and Charles Singer (eds.), *The Legacy of Israel* (Oxford, N.Y., 1927).

The importance and meaning of the issues raised in this introduction, even if considered after the whole book has been digested, depend largely upon the depth and range of the reader's knowledge. For a rapid survey of the thousands of years of Jewish history, there are numerous one-volume works. The solid Max L. Margolis and Alexander Marx *A History of the Jewish People** (Jewish Pub. Society, Phila., 1927) is recommended. But any such survey is merely *hors d'œuvres:* one can find the banquet only in the classic many-volume works. The condensation of Heinrich Graetz's original eleven-volume German work into the six-volume English version, *History of the Jews* (Jewish Pub. Society, Phila., 1891-95), despite reservations expressed here, may be still read with pleasure and profit. Those familiar with German or Hebrew should read Simon R. Dubnow's ten-volume *World History of the Jewish People.* The major contemporary work is Salo W. Baron's *A Social and Religious History of the Jews* (Columbia University Press, N.Y., 1952), in three volumes, but now being expanded into at least ten, of which the first two are in print. Volume Three of the first edition, which contains notes, bibliography, and index, is indispensable for the student. For the evolution of communal institutions, the standard work is Salo W. Baron, *The Jewish Community: Its History and Structure to the American Revolution* (3 vols., Jewish Pub. Society, Phila., 1942). For general reference the epoch-making *Jewish Encyclopaedia* (10 vols., Funk and Wagnalls, 1901-06) is a mine of information, and the more recent *Universal Jewish Encyclopedia* (10 vols., Universal Jewish Encyclopedia, N.Y., 1939-43), although not of the same high quality, is useful for material on the last half-century. Two compendia of essays can be recommended: Louis Finkelstein (ed.), *The Jews: Their History, Culture, and Religion** (4 vols., Jewish Pub. Society, Phila., rev. ed., 1956) and *The Jewish People: Past and Present* (4 vols., Central Yiddish Culture Organization, N.Y., 1946-54).

1, 2, 3, 4   THE BIBLICAL AGE

The open sesame to the Biblical age is the Hebrew Bible. There is a handy Hebrew-English edition, with the Masoretic Hebrew text in parallel columns, *The Holy Scriptures* (2 vols., Jewish Pub. Society, Phila., 1955). The Jewish Publication Society's *The Holy Scriptures According to the Masoretic Text* (1 vol., Phila., newly reset, 1955) is the "authorized version" of English-speaking Jewry. Prepared some forty years ago by a group of eminent scholars and now undergoing revision, it is widely acknowledged to be one of the best translations of the received Hebrew. Of the innumerable English translations, the King James Version of 1611, while archaic, is of unsurpassed beauty. The Revised Standard Version (Thomas Nelson, N.Y., 1952) is much more up to date, but still basically a Christian version. While the various attempts to translate the Hebrew Bible into a modern American idiom are inferior as literature, the use of one of them as a companion text—for instance, James Moffat, *The Old Testament: A New Translation* (Harper, N.Y., 1922)—can help to clarify much that is obscure in the standard versions.

For the archeological, historical, and literary backgrounds, the following up-to-date, authoritative accounts are recommended: W. F. Albright, *The Archaeology of Palestine* (Penguin Books, Baltimore, rev. ed., 1954, 85 cents); R. H. Pfeiffer, *Introduction to the Old Testament** (Harper, N.Y., 1941); and Harry M. Orlinsky, *Ancient Israel** (Cornell University Press, Ithaca, N.Y., 1954). Hebrew readers have the advantage of the best comprehensive Biblical encyclopedia, *Encyclopedia Mikraith* (Jerusalem, 1950—), of which the first two volumes have appeared, and for a commentary on Biblical literature they may turn to M. H. Segal, *The Law, the Prophets and the Hagiographa* (Tel Aviv, 1947—). The Second Commonwealth is covered admirably in Joseph Klausner, *A History of the Second Commonwealth* (5 vols., Ahiasaf, Jerusalem, 1949-51), which is now being translated into English.

The reader will find a stimulating exposition of general ancient Near Eastern thought in Frankfort, Wilson, Jacobsen, and Irwin, *The Intellectual Adventure of Ancient Man* (University of Chicago Press, 1946). The study of the thought of this age should be supplemented by a reading of Yehezkel Kaufmann, *The Biblical Account of the Conquest of Palestine* (Magnes Press, Jerusalem, 1953) as an example of this writer's critical interpretation of a Biblical text, and especially his monumental Hebrew work, *A History of the Religion of Israel* (8 vols., Tel Aviv, 1937-56). There is illuminating material in G. E. Wright's excellent monograph, *The Old Testament Against Its Environment* (Alec R. Allenson, Chicago, 1954). For further material on the Apocalyptic as a link between Judaism and Christianity, see H. H. Rowley, *The Relevance of Apocalyptic* (Redhill, London, 1944). Among the numerous works on the interpretation of Biblical ideas and their role in Western civilization, the following are recommended: H. H. Rowley, *The Biblical Doctrine of Election* (Lutterworth, London, 1950); D. B. Macdonald, *The Hebrew Literary Genius* and *The Hebrew Philosophical Genius* (Princeton University Press, N.J., 1933-36) and Robert Gordis, *Koheleth—The Man and His World* (Bloch, N.Y., 2nd ed., 1956).

5, 6 THE HELLENISTIC AGE

The reader will find an over-all sketch of this intriguing epoch in W. W. Tarn, *Hellenistic Civilization* (Arnold, London, 3rd ed., 1952), and an equally good account of the Jewish experience in Max Radin, *The Jews Among the Greeks and Romans* (Jewish Pub. Society, Phila., 1915). There is an excellent essay on the adaptation of Judaism to Hellenism by Elias Bickerman, *The Maccabees* (Schocken, N.Y., 1947). Anyone interested in examining more closely the analogy of the Hellenistic age with our own will discover illuminating discussion in Eric Fischer, *The Passing of the European Age* (Harvard University Press, Cambridge, 1943). The following should enable the reader to pin down the major cultural elements of the age and their cross-fertilization: Saul Lieberman, *Hellenism in Jewish Palestine* (Jewish Theological Seminary, N.Y., 1950); Robert Pfeiffer, *A History of New Testament Times* (Harper, N.Y., 1949); H. H. Rowley, *The Zadokite Fragments and the Dead Sea Scrolls* (Blackwell, Oxford, 1952); and for those who read Hebrew, Avigdor Tcherikover, *The Jews in Egypt in the Hellenistic-Roman Age in the Light of the Papyri* (Hebrew University Press, Jerusalem, 1945).

For studies of two preeminent Jewish figures in the Greco-Roman world, consult Henry St. John Thackeray, *Josephus, the Man and the Historian* (Jewish Institute of Religion, N.Y., 1924) and the monumental work of Harry Austryn Wolfson, *Philo: Foundations of Religious Philosophy in Judaism, Christianity, and Islam* (2 vols., Harvard University Press, Cambridge, 1947).

To glimpse the mind and spirit of this age, there is no substitute for reading the works of contemporary authors. A comprehensive corpus of Jewish-Greek writings that were excluded from the canon of the Bible are available in R. H. Charles (ed.), *The Apocrypha and Pseudepigrapha of the Old Testament* (2 vols., Oxford, England, 1913). Freshly edited and translated individual books include: Moses Hadas, *Aristeas to Philocrates* (Harper, N.Y., 1951) and *The Third and Fourth Books of Maccabees* (Harper, N.Y., 1953); and Sidney Tedesche and Solomon Zeitlin,

The First Book of Maccabees and *The Second Book of Maccabees* (Harper, N.Y., 1950-54).

The flavor of Philo of Alexandria comes through in the anthology selected and edited by Claude G. Montefiore, "Florilegium Philonis" in the *Jewish Quarterly Review* (VII, London, 1894-95). The complete works of Philo are presented with the original text and English translation by F. H. Colson and G. H. Whitaker, in the Loeb Classical Library, *Philo* (10 vols., Harvard University Press, Cambridge, 1932-41). The writings of Josephus, to be completed in 1958, are also in the Loeb Classics (9 vols., translated by H. St. John Thackeray and Ralph Marcus, Harvard University Press, Cambridge, 1926—).

7, 8   THE TALMUDIC AGE

Despite a century of critical investigation of Talmudic sources, few qualitative advances have been made over the original synoptic works produced by the nineteenth-century German school of Jüdische Wissenschaft. Scholarship in this field has tended recently to restrict itself to the study of texts and the investigation of individual topics. A new synthesis of the culture of this age is a desideratum.

For a brief historical survey of the epoch, see Judah Goldin, "The Period of the Talmud" in Louis Finkelstein (ed.), *The Jews* (Jewish Pub. Society, Phila., rev. ed., 1956), Vol. 1, pp. 115-215. The best one-volume exposition of the contents and methodology of Talmudic and Midrashic sources is H. L. Strack, *Introduction to Talmud and Midrash** (Jewish Pub. Society, Phila., 1945). Some of the major social and religious ideas of the epoch can be followed in Louis Finkelstein, *The Pharisees: The Sociological Background of Their Faith* (2 vols., Jewish Pub. Society, Phila., 1938); George F. Moore, *Judaism in the First Centuries of the Christian Era* (3 vols., Harvard University Press, Cambridge, 1927-30); Solomon Schechter, *Some Aspects of Rabbinic Theology* (Macmillan, N.Y., 1909); Joseph Klausner, *The Messianic Idea in Israel* (Macmillan, N.Y., 1955); Louis Ginzberg, *Students, Saints and Scholars* (Jewish Pub. Society, Phila., 1928) and his *Of Jewish Laws and Lore* (Jewish Pub. Society, Phila., 1955); and Max Kadushin, *The Rabbinic Mind** (Jewish Theological Seminary, N.Y., 1952).

The best exposition of Rabbinic dogma is the Hebrew Prayer Book. A useful edition is Philip Birnbaum, *Daily Prayer Book* (Hebrew Publishing Co., N.Y., 1949). A classic example of early Midrash is the exegetical portion of the Passover Haggadah, and the edition edited by Nahum Glatzer (Farrar, Straus & Cudahy, N.Y., 1953) is recommended. A superb compilation of a cross-section of the Tannaitic mind and method is Judah Goldin's translation of *The Fathers According to Rabbi Nathan* (Yale University Press, New Haven, 1954). For a characteristic "legal" Midrash, see a Tannaitic commentary, *Mekilta de-Rabbi Ishmael*, edited by Jacob Z. Lauterbach (3 vols., Jewish Pub. Society, Phila., 1933-35). For Hebrew readers there is a standard anthology, Jacob Ravnitsky and Hayyim Nachman Bialik, *Sefer Ha-Aggadah* (3 vols., Dvir, Tel Aviv, 1940).

Some phases of the tensions of the age and the attempts at adjustment are treated in the following works: Solomon Zucrow, *Adjustments of Law to Life in Rabbinic Literature* (Stratford, Boston, 1928); Louis Finkelstein, *Akiba: Scholar, Saint and Martyr* (Covici-Friede, N.Y., 1936); Joseph Klausner, *Jesus of Nazareth* (Macmillan, N.Y., 1929).

For detailed information on events, ideas, schools, personalities, law, and so on, the standard encyclopedias should be consulted. Most of the collections and anthologies of Midrashic and Talmudic literature in English are poor. A useful popular book is Abraham Cohen, *Everyman's Talmud* (J. M. Dent, London, 1932). The one standard work of Aggadic literature is Louis Ginzberg, *Legends of the Jews* (8 vols., Jewish Pub. Society, Phila., 1919-25). For Hebrew readers there is an important volume of essays by a learned, original scholar: Gedalia Alon, *A History of the Jews in Palestine During the Mishnaic and Talmudic Epochs* (Hakibbutz Hameuchad, Tel Aviv, 1954).

While the twentieth-century reader cannot easily digest the turgid literature of this epoch, some knowledge of the sources is indispensable for an understanding of Talmudic civilization. Fortunately the reader can turn for the first time to some fairly adequate translations. The entire Mishna is available in a handy one-volume edition: Herbert Danby, *The Mishnah* (Oxford, London, 1933). Of the numerous Aggadic collections, the reader may explore one Tannaitic Midrash that is characteristic: *Midrash Rabbah* (10 vols., Soncino Press, London, 1939). The complete Talmud has been rendered into English by a group of scholars in Britain: *The Babylonian Talmud* (35 vols., index, Soncino Press, London, 1935-52). The thousands of Responsa remain an uncharted sea; but the reader will find an illuminating introduction to this literature in Solomon Freehof, *The Responsa* (Jewish Pub. Society, Phila., 1955).

9, 10   THE JUDEO-ISLAMIC AGE

In view of the recent establishment of the state of Israel in the belt of Arab and Islamic states and their growing interdependence in future decades, this age has taken on new meaning. Consequently the reader may well be interested in one or two books that portray the epoch and discuss mutual cultural influences. A stimulating presentation of the relations between Arabs and Jews is given in S. D. Goitein, *Jews and Arabs: Their Contacts Through the Ages* (Schocken, N.Y., 1955). The culture of this epoch and its relation to Hellenic civilization is carefully studied in G. E. von Gruenbaum, *Medieval Islam* (University of Chicago Press, 1947). There is an excellent portrait of Islam's administrative, economic, social, and cultural life, with a good chapter on Christians and Jews, in Adam Mez, *The Renaissance of Islam*, translated by Bukhsh and Margoliouth (Luzac, London, 1937). A lively treatment of Jewish participation in Islamic states may be found in Walter J. Fischel, *The Jews in the Political and Economic Life of Medieval Islam* (Royal Asiatic Society, London, 1937).

Much of the Genizah material has been made available in English in the works of Professor Mann; see especially, Jacob Mann, *The Jews in Egypt and Palestine Under the Fatimid Caliphs* (2 vols., Oxford, 1920-22). In Hebrew there is a particularly well documented portrait of medieval Jewish communities under Islam: Eli Strauss, *The Jews of Egypt and Syria under the Mamluks* (2 vols., Mosad Kuk, Jerusalem, 1944).

The following should enable the reader to get a fuller view of the two important movements discussed here: Leon Nemoy, *Karaite Anthology* (Yale University Press, New Haven, 1952), and an admirable study of Kabbala in Gershom G. Scholem: *Major Trends in Jewish Mysticism** (Schocken, N.Y., 3rd rev. ed., 1954).

Before exploring the great books of this period, it may be helpful to understand the spirit of some of its men of genius. Of those who are referred to in these chapters, there are two worth-while studies in English: Henry Malter, *The Life and Works of Saadia Gaon* (Jewish Pub. Society, Phila., 1921) and Abrahams and Yellin, *Maimonides* (Jewish Pub. Society, Phila., 1908). A meaty summary of the chief thinkers of this age will serve those interested in the development of philosophic and religious thought: Isaac Husik, *A History of Medieval Jewish Philosophy* (Jewish Pub. Society, Phila., 1916). A more recent work in German and Hebrew, and now being translated into English, is Julius Guttmann, *The Philosophy of Judaism* (Mosad Bialik, Jerusalem, 1941). Hebrew readers will find many admirable essays on medieval personalities in the learned journals such as *Tarbiz, Siyyon,* and *Hatekufah.*

Probably the best introduction to the imaginative literature of this age is a reading of its magnificent poetic output. Among the books in the Schiff Library of Jewish Classics the following translations, printed with the original Hebrew text, are excellent: Nina Salaman, *Selected Poems of Jehudah Halevi* (Jewish Pub. Society, Phila., 1924); Israel Zangwill, *Selected Religious Poems of Solomon ibn Gabirol* (Jewish Pub. Society, Phila., 1923); Solomon Solis-Cohen, *Selected Poems of Moses ibn Ezra* (Jewish Pub. Society, Phila., 1934).

Although the philosophic books of this era cannot be read lightly by the layman, a study of several influential works alluded to in the text will be rewarding. See the translation of the *Kusari* by Hartwig Hirschfeld, *Judah Hallevi's Kitab Al Khazari* (Cailingold, London, rev. ed., 1931); Moses Maimonides, *The Guide for the Perplexed,* translated from the Arabic by M. Friedlander (Dutton, N.Y., 2nd ed., rev., 1925); Saadia Gaon, *The Book of Beliefs and Opinions* (Yale University Press, New Haven, 1948); Abraham Maimonides, *Highways to Perfection,* translated by Samuel Rosenblatt (2 vols., Johns Hopkins University Press, 1938).

An insight into the ideas and values of Jewish life during this epoch as well as their roots in earlier times can be gained by a study of Maimonides' monumental *Code.* Moreover, this formulation of Jewish theory and practice is a mirror of the legal, social, and religious basis of classical

Judaism. A complete translation has been undertaken by a group of scholars under the aegis of the Yale Judaica Series, and the following volumes are now available: Jacob J. Rabinowitz, *The Book of Civil Laws;* A. M. Hershman, *The Book of Judges;* Herbert Danby, *The Book of Acquisition;* Herbert Danby, *The Book of Cleanness;* Hyman Klein, *The Book of Torts;* Solomon Gandz, *Sanctification of the New Moon.*

11, 12   THE EUROPEAN AGE

A perceptive portrait of medieval Jewish communities is given in two works of Cecil Roth, *The Jews of Medieval Oxford* (Oxford Historical Society, London, 1951), and, especially for Gentile-Jewish relations, *The History of the Jews in Italy* (Jewish Pub. Society, Phila., 1946). There is a charming, somewhat overidealized picture of the personal social life of the ordinary Jew of the period in Israel Abrahams, *Jewish Life in the Middle Ages* (Jewish Pub. Society, Phila., 2nd ed., 1932). Covering in a scholarly fashion every aspect of Jewish social life in medieval Spain on the basis of original sources, and the best work of its type in English, is Abraham Neuman, *The Jews in Spain: Their Social, Political and Cultural Life in the Middle Ages* (2 vols., Jewish Pub. Society, Phila., 1942). Also see the admirably written chapters dealing with this period in Marvin Lowenthal, *The Jews of Germany* (Harper, N.Y., 1936). Communal development in terms of administration and sanctions is treated, with copious documentation in Hebrew and English, in Louis Finkelstein, *Jewish Self-Government in the Middle Ages* (Jewish Theological Seminary, N.Y., 1924). The reader looking for documentation will find useful a collection of sources illustrating every aspect of medieval life in Jacob R. Marcus, *The Jews in the Medieval World: A Source-Book, 315-1791* (Sinai Press, Cincinnati, 1938); the Hebrew reader can turn to Abraham Kahana, *Sifruth Ha-Historia Ha-Yisraelith* (Warsaw, 1922).

Personal values and social ideals are vividly illustrated in contemporary autobiographies, letters, memoirs, travel books, and the like. The following can be read with enjoyment and profit: Leo W. Schwarz, *Memoirs of My People: Through a Thousand Years* (Rinehart, N.Y., 1943), E. N. Adler (ed.), *Jewish Travellers* (Bloch, N.Y., 1931). A remarkable collection of testamentary documents, characteristically Jewish, on which excerpts in these chapters are based, is Israel Abrahams, *Ethical Wills* (2 vols., Jewish Pub. Society, Phila., 1926); the most charming, graphic, and informative Jewish autobiography, vividly illustrating Jewish life in Germany in the seventeenth century as seen through the eyes of an intelligent, active, and far from repressed woman is *The Memoirs of Glückel of Hameln,* translated by Marvin Lowenthal (Harper, N.Y., 1932). There is an interesting selection of contemporary letters in Franz Kobler, *A Treasury of Jewish Letters* (2 vols., Farrar, Straus & Cudahy, N.Y., 1954).

While the role of the Hebrew Bible as guide, reader, and textbook is apparent in the above literature, the best approach to its actual impact and meaning is through the classic commentary of Rashi. The most serviceable translation, printed together with the Hebrew text of the Bible, covers the complete Pentateuch: M. Rosenbaum and A. M. Silberman, *Pentateuch with Rashi's Commentary* (5 vols., Shapiro, Valentine, London, 1929-33). The moral outlook of the Jew of the ghetto period is splendidly expressed in a relatively late ethical classic, Moses Hayyim Luzzatto, *Mesillat Yesharim* ("The Path of the Upright"), translated by Mordecai M. Kaplan (Jewish Pub. Society, Phila., 1936). One can turn with pleasure to a few of the representative imaginative writings that have been rendered into English: Joseph ben Meir Zabara, *The Book of Delight*,* translated by Moses Hadas (Columbia University Press, N.Y., 1932), and Dante's contemporary, Immanuel ben Solomon of Rome, *Tophet and Eden* ("Hell and Paradise"), (University of London Press, 18 Warwick Sq., E.C. 4, London, 1921).

13, 14, 15, 16, 17, 18   THE MODERN AGE

The nineteenth and twentieth centuries are too near to us to apply the broad perspective that is possible in the preceding ages. It is difficult, if not impossible, to determine which forces in society are running their course and which ones are approaching full tide. Moreover, the cumulative information at our disposal is not easily controlled and some of it has not yet been carefully studied. Nevertheless, if we do not wish to be swallowed up by history it is possible—and necessary—to develop a sense of direction.

The general background to the modern and contemporary epoch is presented, with different emphases, in the one-volume and many-volume Jewish histories mentioned on page 487. They can be supplemented with two useful surveys: Ismar Elbogen, *A Century of Jewish Life* (Jewish Pub. Society, Phila., 1944), and Israel Cohen, *Contemporary Jewry: A Survey* (Methuen, London, 1950). For individual events, persons, and movements the student should consult one of the standard encyclopedias.

Emancipation in practice has shown many variations. The scope of participation by Jews in general culture is developed in Cecil Roth, *Jewish Contributions to Civilization* (Macmillan, London, 1938), and A. A. Roback, *Jewish Influence in Modern Thought* (Sci-Art Publishers, Cambridge, 1929). The halting of this historical process in Germany and its implications for the present generation can be studied in Marvin Lowenthal, *The Jews of Germany* (Jewish Pub. Society, Phila., 1936); Hannah Arendt, *The Origins of Totalitarianism** (Harcourt, Brace, N.Y., 1951); and Gerald Reitlinger, *The Final Solution* (Beechhurst, N.Y., 1953).

For the bases of modern antisemitism—racial, economic, social, psychological, and religious—the reader should consult the following: Koppel S. Pinson (ed.), *Essays on Antisemitism* (Conference on Jewish Relations, N.Y., rev. ed., 1946); N. W. Ackerman and M. Jahoda, *Antisemitism and Emotional Disorder* (Harper, N.Y., 1950); Maurice Samuel, *The Great Hatred* (Knopf, N.Y., 1940).

Nationalism has been and remains one of the most potent factors in the complex of modern culture. The reader who wishes to grasp the general background of this historical force can turn to C. J. H. Hayes, *The Historical Evolution of Modern Nationalism** (Macmillan, N.Y., 1926), or Hans Kohn, *The Idea of Nationalism** (Macmillan, N.Y., 1948), and particularly Salo W. Baron, *Modern Nationalism and Religion* (Harper, N.Y., 1947). The powerful impact of nationalism on modern Jewish life and thought has been recorded in an immense literature, but much of it is unavailable in English. The reader will find a succinct sketch of Dubnow's theory in Israel Friedlaender, *Dubnow's Theory of Diaspora Nationalism* (The Maccabean, N.Y., 1905), and the concept and its implications for the Jewish minority in Oscar I. Janowsky, *Jews and Minority Rights,* 1898-1919 (Columbia University Press, N.Y., 1933). The varieties of Zionist nationalism can be approached, for want of any comprehensive account in English, through the following: Leon Simon, *Studies in Jewish Nationalism* (Longmans, Green, N.Y., 1920); Moses Hess, *Rome and Jerusalem,* translated by Meyer Waxman (Bloch, N.Y., 1918); Achad Haam, *Essays on Zionism and Judaism,* translated by Leon Simon (George Routledge, London, 1922); Frances Burnce (ed.), A. D. Gordon, *Selected Essays* (League for Labor Palestine, N.Y., 1938). Motivations for adherence to these viewpoints can be discovered in personal documents, e.g., Marvin Lowenthal (ed.), *Theodor Herzl's Diaries* (Dial, N.Y., 1956); Jacob de Haas, *Louis D. Brandeis,* a biography with a solid section of Brandeis' Zionist writings (Bloch, N.Y., 1929); Chaim Weizmann, *Trial and Error* (Harper, N.Y., 1949); and an excellent biography of Jabotinsky by Joseph B. Schechtman, *Rebel and Statesman* (Yoseloff, N.Y., 1956).

Phases of the cultural and religious developments in modern times are touched upon in the standard histories and compendia referred to on pages 487-488, but there is no comprehensive treatment of the immense literature in any one-volume work. For the liberal and reformist phase the standard book is David Philipson, *The Reform Movement in Judaism* (Macmillan, N.Y., rev. ed., 1931); but one should check some later divergences in the Yearbooks of the Central Conference of American Rabbis. See also Leo Baeck, *The Essence of Judaism* (Schocken, N.Y., 1948). An informative account of the Conservative movement is given in Marshall Sklare, *Conservative Judaism* (Free Press, Glencoe, Ill., 1955), and the philosophy of the Reconstructionist movement is expounded in Mordecai M. Kaplan, *Judaism As a Civilization* (Macmillan, N.Y., 1934) and *Judaism in Transition* (Behrman, N.Y., 1941). For an exposition of the neo-mystical trend within this group, see Abraham J. Heschel, *God in Search of Man* (Farrar, Straus & Cudahy, N.Y., 1955). Of the sparse literature in English interpreting the Orthodox-traditionalist view, see Leo Jung (ed.), *Israel of Tomorrow* (2 vols., Herald Square Press, N.Y., 1946), and Jacob Agus, *Banner of Jerusalem: Life, Times and Thought of Abraham Isaac Kuk* (Bloch, N.Y., 1946). Stimulating modernist views are presented in Hayim Greenberg, *The Inner Eye* (Jewish Frontier Assn., N.Y., 1953), and Horace M. Kallen, *Secularism*

Is the Will of God (Twayne, N.Y., 1955). Of the numerous excellent Jewish periodicals which contain many splendid studies, the most extensive and richest in English is *The Menorah Journal* (N.Y., Vols. I-XLIII, 1915-56, indexed).

To understand the Enlightenment to which the Haskalah was a reaction, the reader should turn to Volume II of Preserved Smith's standard *History of Modern Culture* (Holt, N.Y., 1930-34) or the admirable little paperbound book, Isaiah Berlin, *The Age of Enlightenment* (Mentor, 501 Madison Ave., N.Y., 1956, 50 cents). There are no corresponding volumes on the Jewish Enlightenment and most of the basic literature is unavailable in English. The stirrings of Enlightenment in eighteenth-century Berlin come through in a famous autobiography of a philosopher, *Solomon Maimon: An Autobiography* (J. C. Murray, Boston, 1888) and some fundamental principles are elucidated in Moses Mendelssohn, *Jerusalem: A Treatise on Religious Power and Judaism* (Phila., 1851). Useful, though dated, is Jacob S. Raisin, *The Haskalah Movement in Russia* (Jewish Pub. Society, Phila., 1913). For developments in art, music, and literature, there are a number of helpful volumes. An introduction to the major Hebrew writers and their works may be found in Shalom Spiegel, *Hebrew Reborn* (Macmillan, N.Y., 1930), and Simon Halkin, *Modern Hebrew Literature* (Schocken, N.Y., 1950). For individual authors and books, consult the comprehensive bibliographical index, Sylvia Landress (ed.), *Palestine and Zionism* (cumulative vols., Zionist Archives and Library, 250 West 57th St., N.Y.). A survey of the rebirth of Yiddish letters is given in A. A. Roback, *The Story of Yiddish Literature* (Yiddish Scientific Institute, N.Y., 1940). A clue to developments in the fine arts is given in the following: A. Z. Idelsohn, *Jewish Music in Its Historical Development* (Holt, N.Y., 1929); Franz Landsberger, *A History of Jewish Art* (Union of American Hebrew Congregations, Cincinnati, 1956); Rachel Wishnitzer, *Synagogue Architecture in the United States* (Jewish Pub. Society, Phila., 1955).

The mental structure of society is closely meshed with its physical structure; the intellectual climate of the modern age can be fully grasped only in the light of the economic and social forces that have shaped it. Unfortunately, solid literature on this subject is meager in English. For statistics and trends in Jewish migration, except for recent decades, the reader will find a general account in Arthur Ruppin, *Jews in the Modern World* (Macmillan, N.Y., 1934) and *Jewish Fate and Future* (Macmillan, London, 1940). Much can be learned about the character of this movement from a study of the great waves to the United States, which may be followed in Samuel Joseph, *Jewish Immigration to the United States from 1881 to 1910* (Columbia University Press, N.Y., 1914). Recent developments are summarized and occasionally evaluated in the annual volumes of the *American Jewish Year Book* (57 vols., AJC–Jewish Pub. Society, Phila.). For the relation of Jews and Judaism to modern capitalism, a good introduction is the volumes of Count Egon Corti, *The Rise of the House of Rothschild* and *The Reign of the House of Rothschild*

(Cosmopolitan, N.Y., 1928); and the classic but controversial Werner Sombart, *The Jews and Modern Capitalism* (Dutton, N.Y., 1913); the latter should be read in the light of the critique of Nathan Reich, "Capitalism and the Jews" in *The Menorah Journal*, Vol. XVIII, pp. 5-19. There is no single work dealing with the reciprocal relations of Jews and the various "isms," and existing studies are scattered in periodicals and the press. It may be helpful to consult the encyclopedias under separate headings.

The emergence of the state of Israel should be studied in the perspective of the historical factors and traditional concepts that shaped its substance. In addition to the references given on page 495, the reader may consult the standard historical work by a Zionist leader and scholar, Nahum Sokolow, *History of Zionism, 1600-1918* (2 vols., Longmans, Green, London, 1919). For up-to-date accounts of the origin and promulgation of the Balfour Declaration and its consequences, see the second part of Christopher Sykes, *Two Studies in Virtue* (Collins, London, 1953), and Barbara W. Tuchman, *Bible and Sword: England and Palestine From the Bronze Age to Balfour* (New York University Press, N.Y., 1956). The best theoretical study of the Mandate is J. Stoyanovsky, *The Mandate for Palestine: A Contribution to the Theory and Practice of International Mandates* (Longmans, Green, N.Y., 1928). A good description of the Yishub in the interregnum period may be found in Abraham Revusky, *Jews in Palestine* (Bloch, N.Y., rev. ed., 1935), and the broader issues are solidly analyzed in a publication of the Esco Foundation, *Palestine: A Study of Jewish, Arab and British Policies* (2 vols., Yale University Press, New Haven, 1947). An eyewitness story by a diplomat gives a dramatic account of the events leading to the UN decision to create the state of Israel: Jorge García-Granades, *The Birth of Israel* (Knopf, N.Y., 1948). For the role of the Jewish survivors of Nazi rule in the making of Israel, two complementary accounts may be read: Leo W. Schwarz, *The Redeemers* (Farrar, Straus & Cudahy, N.Y., 1953), and Jon and David Kimhe, *The Secret Roads* (Farrar, Straus & Cudahy, N.Y., 1955). A brief account of subsequent developments is given in J. D. Hurewitz, *The Struggle for Palestine* (Norton, N.Y., 1950). There is a compact study of the constitutional issues in Emanuel Rackman, *Israel's Emerging Constitution 1948-1951* (Columbia University Press, N.Y., 1955). Several books dealing with the Israel-Diaspora (or Galut) concept can be recommended: Yitzhak F. Baer, *Galut* (Schocken, N.Y., 1947); James Parkes, *End of an Exile* (Library Publishers, N.Y., 1954); Ben Halpern, *The American Jew: A Zionist Analysis* (Theodor Herzl Foundation, N.Y., 1956); Maurice Samuel, *Level Sunlight* (Knopf, N.Y., 1954). For the mentality and ideas of a living architect of the state, see David Ben-Gurion, *Rebirth and Destiny of Israel* (Philosophical Library, N.Y., 1954).

Broadly speaking, contemporary American historians are at their best in dealing with economic, military, and political aspects of the United States and rarely penetrate the diverse interacting strains in our cultural and intellectual growth. A welcome change in view, though hardly adequate, is Merle Curti, *The Growth of American Thought* (Harper, N.Y., 1943), in which diverse cultures and group distinctions are recognized. On the other hand, much of the writing on Jewish life in America by Jewish authors and scholars has been, until very recently, apologetic or polemical. Serious readers will want to examine Salo W. Baron, "American Jewish History: Problems and Methods" in *Proceedings of the American Jewish Historical Society* (N.Y., Vol. XXXIX, 1950, pp. 207-266), and a bibliographical essay, Moses Rischin, *An Inventory of American Jewish History* (Harvard University Press, Cambridge, 1955). Of the more recent literature, a number of volumes will provide helpful glimpses into Jewish historical and cultural growth. For the early period, see Jacob R. Marcus, *Early American Jewry* (2 vols., Jewish Pub. Society, Phila., 1951-52) and *Memoirs of American Jews* (3 vols., Jewish Pub. Society, Phila., 1955-56); Abram V. Goodman, *American Overture: Jewish Rights in Colonial America;* Lee M. Friedman, *Jewish Pioneers and Patriots* (Jewish Pub. Society, Phila., 1942). There is a useful compilation of documentary material, marred by a tendency to overemphasize negative factors: Morris U. Schappes, *Documentary History of the Jews in the United States* (Citadel Press, N.Y., 1950). The role of the Jews in the Civil War is treated in B. W. Korn, *American Jewry and the Civil War* (Jewish Pub. Society, Phila., 1951). A popular account of Jewish experience in America can be found in Rufus Learsi, *The Jews in America: A History* (World, Cleveland, 1954). For the story of our neighbors in Canada, see Louis Rosenberg, *Canada's Jews: A Social and Economic Study of the Jews in Canada* (Canadian Jewish Congress, Montreal, 1939).

The emerging patterns of contemporary American Jewish life can be vividly glimpsed in the growing autobiographical literature in the United States. Though engaging as personal documents, the following can be recommended for the light they throw on cultural issues as well as their literary distinction: Maurice Samuel, *I, the Jew* (Harcourt, Brace, N.Y., 1927); Ludwig Lewisohn, *Mid-Channel: An American Chronicle* (Harper, N.Y., 1929); Marvin Lowenthal (ed.), *Henrietta Szold: Life and Letters* (Viking Press, N.Y., 1942); Stephen S. Wise, *Challenging Years* (Putnam's, N.Y., 1949); and Meyer Levin, *In Search* (Horizon Press, N.Y., 1950).

The following should interest the reader who is concerned with communal and institutional history: Hyman B. Grinstein, *The Rise of the Jewish Community in New York, 1654-1860* (Jewish Publication Society, Phila., 1945); Stuart E. Rosenberg, *The Jewish Community in Rochester, 1843-1925* (Columbia University Press, N.Y., 1954); David and Tamar de Sola Pool, *An Old Faith in the New World; Portrait of Shearith Israel 1654-1954* (Columbia University Press, N.Y., 1955); and Charles Reznikoff and U. Z. Engelman, *The Jews of Charleston* (Jewish Pub. Society, Phila., 1950).

INDEX

References to names are chiefly limited to those persons who are discussed at length. Subject matter dealing with cultural growth is stressed. Chapter headings, subheadings and bibliographical references are not included.

Abraham ibn Daud, 142, 249
Abraham ibn Ezra, 228
Abraham ibn Hasdai, 233
Abraham, patriarch, 4, 189
Abu Aaron of Baghdad, 223
Academies, Talmudic—in Jamnia, 160f.; etymology of, 168f.; in Babylonia, 171; semi-annual retreats at, 172; discussion of God in, 182; Responsa literature of, 218; at Sura and Pumbedita, 222; role in psychology of medieval Jews, 280
Activism, 272, 328, 330, 379, 420
Against Apion, 123
Aggada—the lifeblood of Judaism, 180; imagination ranges freely in, 181; discussion of God in, 181
Agriculture and agricultural colonization, 120, 331, 399ff., 404, 405, 435, 437, 438, 452
Ahad Haam (Asher Ginsberg), 333, 378, 387, 430, 433, 435
Akiba ben Joseph, Rabbi, 166, 174, 186, 190, 193, 206

Alexander the Great, 97, 103, 145
Alexandria, ancient, 115, 116, 125
Allegorical method of Scriptural interpretation—124, applied to Song of Songs, 181; the Second Temple, 197; use by Maimonides, 246
Allegory. *See* Allegorical method
Am-Olam movement, 405
American Jewish Committee, 408
American Jewry—European experience implicit in, 268; origins in Ashkenazi Jewry, 287; revitalization of concept of communal center in, 291; status in colonies, 319f.; progress of emancipation of, 321f.; antisemitism and equality, 322; participation in defense abroad, 330; European psychology of, 335; new center of gravity, 336; impact of Nazi propaganda on, 348; restrictive immigration laws, 349; rejects concept of Jews as American national minority, 358; Reform Judaism in, 366–370; Rabbinic scholarship in, 372;

American Jewry (*cont.*)
Hasidic groups in, 373f.; superficiality of Orthodox allegiance in, 375; development of Conservative Judaism in, 376ff.; rise of Jewish scholarship in, 384; Yiddish activity in, 385, 387; Hebrew journalism in, 389; changing birth rate in, 394f.; migration to, 398; farming population of, 404, 405f.; social stratification of, 409; role of peddler in, 410; youth contempt for "intellectualism," 413; non-Zionists' participation in Jewish Agency for Palestine, 429; Jewish schools in, 432; feeling of being at home of, 456, 457f.; immigration statistics, 456–457; development of welfare concepts and institutions in, 458–463; concepts and organization of religious groups in, 463–469; educational and cultural progress in, 470–478; future of creative Jewish culture in, 478–481; survival and future of, 480–484
American Joint Distribution Committee, 405, 406, 460
American Revolution, 323, 414
Amos, 57, 58, 59, 60, 62, 63, 65
Amos, Book of, cited, 58, 59, 60, 63, 65
Anan ben David, 241
Antiochus Epiphanes, 84, 105, 106
Antisemitism—inaccuracy of term, 115; letter of Claudius warning antisemites of Alexandria, 116; of Roman minister Sejanos, 118; agitation in Rome, 119; false charge of usury, 120; forms of in Hellenistic age, 131ff.; hostility to Talmud, 144; in Christian Church, 269; ritual murder accusation in England, 272; of Voltaire, 324; unbroken heritage in Germany, 326; in Tsarist Russia, 331–333; in Nazi Germany, 335f.; sources in Christianity, 342; adoption of racialism, 345f.; longevity of, 350; no easy correctives for, 362; a stimulus to emigration, 397f.; charge of Jewish domination of the press, 410; fascist variety of, 414–415; opposed by Lenin, 417; Pinsker regards as permanent psychopathological phenomenon, 435; struggle of

Anti-Defamation League against, 475; the future in America of, 481–482
Apocalyptic literature and thought, 86, 111, 189, 206
Apologetics, 123, 198, 342, 384
Apostasy, Jewish, 123, 127, 130, 132, 164, 189, 216, 238, 245, 269, 271, 331, 332, 388, 393, 422, 478
Arabic language, 218, 219, 245, 427
Arabs, 215, 216, 443, 444, 445, 446, 447, 449–450, 452
Aramaic—absorption of Greek and Latin words, 107f.; shift to Arabic under Islam, 219
Archeology, 103, 108, 110, 112, 113n., 136, 167n., 169, 384
Architecture, 103, 108, 121, 289, 390
Aristotle and Aristotelianism—his alleged description of a Jew, 114; Philo's knowledge of, 133; ideas interpreted in idiom of Talmud, 175; role in medieval philosophy, 249ff.; translated by medieval Jews, 285
Ark, in Bible, 27, 35, 47, 53; in post-Biblical Judaism, 290, 302
Art, Jewish, 390, 434. *See* Archeology
Ashkenazim, 269, 287, 306, 323, 426, 452, 463–464
Assimilation—in Israelite religion, 77, 78; of proselytes, 80; of alien influences during Second Temple, 89; in Palestinian Jewish community, 111; cultural assimilation under Islam, 224ff.; in France, 325f.; rejection by Nazis of, 335; Hebrew as a vehicle of, 433; the question in America of, 482–483
Assyria—Habiru in, 3; world empire of, 65, 66; cultural contact with Jews, 95
Astrology—in Hellenistic culture, 101; in Middle Ages, 239
Astronomy, 100, 219, 281
Auto-Emancipation of Pinsker, 435
Autonomy—in province of Judah, 83; in Ptolemaic empire, 104; in Hellenistic cities, 115; as a source of communal strength, 149; practiced by Pharisees and Essenes, 159; recovered by Rabbis, 160; disciplinary instruments of, 184; in Muslim empire,

217; curtailment resulting from emancipation of, 317; as core of Jewish survival, 356; as surrogate for statehood, 421

Babylonia—Habiru in, 3, 5; community of exiles in, 72, 73, 81; cultural contact with Jews, 95; adjustment of Jewish life to Parthian culture, 147; Jews loyal to Palestinian community, 170; role of Exilarch, 171f.; completion of Talmud, 222
Babylonian Talmud. *See* Talmud
Badge of shame, 269, 280, 289, 316
Banking, 119, 403, 411, 416
Bar Kokhba, 163, 165, 167, 206
Ben Gurion, David, 451
Ben Yehuda, Eliezer, 431, 432
Ben Zvi, Isaac, 451
Benjamin of Tudela, 303–307
Bet ha-Knesset, 169. *See also* Academies, Education, Synogogue, Talmudic Judaism
Bet ha-midrash, 169, 170, 371
Bialik, Hayyim Nahman, 388
Bible, view of paganism in, 11ff.; canonization of, 82f.; Greek translation of, 125; adopted by Christianity, 138; made a living book by midrashic interpretation, 176; a guide to totality of life, 180; new interest created by Muslims and Karaites, 227–230; translation into Arabic, 228; Karaite exegesis, 242ff.; allegorical interpretation by Maimonides, 246; opposition to rationalistic interpretation of, 252; Christian study of, 275; Rashi's commentary on, 281; influence of Jewish commentaries on Christian exegetes, 281; source of principles of French Revolution, 325f.; Biblical criticism in Reform movement, 367; modern interest in Biblical scholarship, 384
Biological decline and growth, Jewish, 394, 395, 396
B'nai B'rith, 473, 474–475
Book of the Wars of YHWH, 41
Book of Yashar, the, 34, 41
Brandeis, Louis, 408
British Jewry. *See* England
Buber, Martin, 374, 433

Caesar, Julius, 115, 118, 159
Calendar, Jewish, 151, 159, 205, 281
Calvin, John, 176
Canaan and Canaanite society, 3, 4, 5, 6, 19, 21, 31ff., 95
Canadian Jewry. *See* American Jewry
Capitalism, 342, 411, 412, 414, 423
Catastrophe of European Jewry, 402, 405, 429, 447, 448
Catholic Church and Catholicism. *See* Christianity
Charity, 169, 290, 307, 310–311, 424, 426–428, 458–464, 462
Chosen People. *See* Election of Israel
Christianity—trinitarian monotheism of, 101; role of Septuagint in birth of, 125; inroads made on Diaspora Jews, 127f.; roots of martyrology in Judaism, 138; birth in Talmudic age, 144; Deuteronomic law of usury reinterpreted, 176; abrogation of Jewish ritual law, 177; proclaimed the "true Israel," 185; Rabbinic messianism in, 212; dogmas shared with Judaism and Islam, 235; Karaite refutation of, 244; influence of Gabirol in, 249; anti-Jewish code of, 269; relation of Jews to reform movements in, 275; medieval Jewish commentaries' influence on Christian exegesis of Bible, 281; difference from Judaism of, 331; sources of modern antisemitism in, 342; assault of antisemitism on, 346–347; attitude of Papacy to Nazis, 349f.; Christian denominations cannot be equated with Judaism, 361–362; Christian belief in restoration of Palestine to Jews, 424; anti-Zionism of Papacy, 438–439
Churchill, Winston, 266, 442
Circumcision, 130, 293, 366
Citizenship—in Hellenistic cities, 115; provision in emancipation for, 315; in the state of Israel, 452
City-state—Canaanite, 38, 48; Hellenistic, 98, 115
Claudius, Roman emperor—letter on Jewish privileges, 116
Cleopatra, 99, 117
Clermont-Tonnère, Count, 325, 339

Codes of law—Mishna promulgated, 152; Babylonian Talmud adopted, 170; Maimonides' *Mishneh Torah*, 225

Colonization, Jewish. *See* Agricultural colonization

Commerce, 297, 316, 403, 409f.

Common law—in force alongside Torah, 50; influence of Hellenistic, 126

Communal organization. *See* Jewish community

Communism—98, 329, 347, 357, 404, 417, 419

Concentration camps, 402, 429

Conservative Judaism—origin and development of, 376–379; founding of Jewish Theological Seminary, 467

Conversion of Gentiles. *See* Proselytes and Proselytism

Cosmopolitanism, 25, 42, 51, 323f., 417

Covenant of Israel—at Sinai, 19ff.; morality of, 60

Crafts, 119, 290, 297, 403

Crises in Jewish history. *See* Cultural tensions

Cultural tensions—between prophetic and popular religion, 59; in Judea under Persian empire, 102; in Hellenistic age, 131ff.; in Talmudic age, 149f.; transferred to Europe, 200; in Judeo-Islamic age, 235ff., 244ff.

Cyrus, King of Persia, 81, 207

Daniel, Book of, 81, 85, 86, 206

David Kimhi. *See* Kimhi

David, King, 47, 48, 49, 50–53, 67

Day of Atonement, 160, 166, 193

"Day of YHWH," 64f., 67, 209

Dead Sea Scrolls—relation to Biblical criticism, xxiv, use of text of Isaiah, 67n., discovery and evaluation of, 111–112; creates interest in Jewish sects, 146; letter of Bar Kokhba, 167n.

Democracy—primitive, 39; in Israel's monarchy, 46; foreshadowed in Pharisaism, 187; messianic vision in, 212; in medieval Jewish community, 280f.; attack of antisemitic movements on, 344; appeal to Jews, 413

Deuteronomy, Book of, cited, 40, 46, 52, 63, 69, 71

Diaspora—rejection of pagan civilization in, 77f.; a religious-national body, 82; envoys aid morale of, 106; etymology of, 113; economic and social conditions in, 119f.; loyalty of Jews in, 123f.; concept of Zion in, 135f.; "double loyalty" in, 137; hegemony of Palestinian community in, 151; transition to Rabbinic community in, 162; role of Babylonian Talmud in, 172; relation to Holy Land, 204, 236f.; relation of antisemitism to, 350; survival value of Jewish culture in, 390; relation to state of Israel, 419, 453f.; doctrine of *Tefutsot*, 458; contemporary discussion of, 498

Dietary laws, 73, 125, 151, 178, 248, 301, 364

Diplomacy—envoys to Rome, 106; Herzlian, 435–439

Dogma, Jewish—stated in negative and positive form, 183; of the world to come, 195; of the Messiah, 208; in the Muslim world, 235; of resurrection, 250f.; conduct more important than, 368

"Double loyalty," 137, 442

Dreyfus affair, 416, 435

Dubnow, Simon M., xviii, xxiii, 356, 358

Ecclesiastes, Book of, 51, 87

Economic conditions and relations— in Hellenistic age, 98f.; in Diaspora, 119; institution of *prosbul,* 179; in medieval Jewry, 269, 294, 296–298, 299; Jews on London Stock Exchange, 319; economic importance of German Jewry, 326; demand for abolition of Sabbath for economic reasons, 363ff.; modern occupational distribution, 403ff.; restratification in Soviet Russia, 404; participation in industry, 406f.

Ecumenical, etymology and meaning, 97

Education, Jewish—universal in Judea, 102; in Hellenistic age, 124; role of Talmudic synagogue in, 169;

training of teachers, 170; curriculum of Babylonian yeshiboth, 172; semi-annual retreats at Babylonian academies, 172; Josephus on, 188; argument the lifeblood of, 275; an all-embracing system, 276, 279–280; status of medieval female in, 294–295; role of Talmudic study in, 298–299; vitality of rabbinic educational system, 371f.; Hasidic adult education, 372f.; Yiddish school system in Soviet Russia, 421; school systems of Eastern and Central European Jewries, 432f.; higher education in Israel, 434; elementary education in Israel, 452; development in the U.S., 470–474; the Jewish Center movement, 476

Egypt—Habiru in, 3, contact with Israel, 95; antisemitism and taxation in, 119–120, 436

Einstein, Albert, 283, 479

Election of Israel—rooted in monotheism, 43; consciousness, in Diaspora, 79; in Aggadic literature, 182; dogmatic nature of, 184; Talmudic view of, 196ff.; integral part of Judaism, 351; problem for modern Jews, 351f.

Elephantine (Yeb), Egypt, temple at, 81; military colony at, 113n.

Eliezer ben Hyrcanus, Rabbi, 166, 190

Elijah—struggle against Jezebel, 54, 64; instrument of peace, 86; symbol of messianic society, 165, 207f.

Elisha ben Abuya, 193

Emancipation—modern era of, 315; misconceptions of, 315ff.; Jewish opposition to, 317f.; progress in Anglo-Saxon countries, 321ff.; at Congress of Vienna, 327; Jewish survival menaced by, 330–331, 336–337; integration linked to nationality by champions of, 339; religious adjustments in age of, 363ff.; population increase a stimulus to, 395; Shabbetians as harbingers of, 423

End of Days, 12, 66, 69, 70, 195, 341, 430

England, ritual murder accusation in, 272; legal status of Jews in, 319; progress of emancipation in, 322ff.; quota system in, 400

Enlightenment (European), 323f., 326, 327, 338, 363, 364, 365, 379, 381, 423

Equality—extended to all in Talmudic Judaism, 143; in the Diaspora, 199; curtailment resulting from emancipation of, 317; provisions in Paris Peace Conference for, 320; New lease of life after World War II, 336

Eschatology—prophetic view of, 64; vision of Isaiah, 66–67; transformation of, 86; Rabbinic ideas of, 209

Essenes—relation to Hasidim, 106; origin and beliefs, 111–112; monasticism adopted by Christianity, 138

Esther, Book of, 184

Europe—early contact with peoples of Asia Minor, 96; religious tensions of Talmudic period transferred to, 200; longevity of Jews in, 267; Judaism the conscience of, 274f.

Excommunication, 164f., 166, 184

Exilarch, head of Babylonian Jewry, 171, 217

Exile and exiles—Babylonian exiles, 57; by Assyrians, 65; letter to, 74; return of, 77; law of, 78; cult without sacrifice in, 81; doctrine of *Galut*, 236; sense of exile, 238; Karaite concept of, 242; doctrine of *Tefutsot*, 458; contemporary interpretation of, 498

Exodus, Book of, cited, 11, 15, 16, 19, 21, 22, 24, 26, 29

Exodus, the, 15, 19, 25, 26

Expulsions of Jews, 118, 269, 319, 324, 404

Ezekiel, 78, 150, 197

Ezekiel, Book of, cited, 6, 78

Ezra, 81ff.

Faith—and reason, 245, 245f., 250

Family—life in Middle Ages of a, 287–311; attendance in synagogue, 364; indoctrination in messianic ideal in, 422

Fascism, 414, 415

Freedom—in Israelite religion, 12; in Second Commonwealth, 155; limits on individual, 165; served in Middle Ages by nonconformity, 274

French Jewry, after the Revolution, 324–325; opposition to communal control of the rabbis, 365; immigration to, 401; Dreyfus affair, 416

French Revolution, 318, 325, 326, 327, 338, 345, 352, 414

Freud, Sigmund, 371

Fund-raising, Jewish, 453, 455, 461–462, 466

Future, doctrine of—in prophetic eschatology, 66–69; promise to God's elect, 198; Talmudic orientation toward, 205; rejection of despair for, 273

Gabirol, Solomon ibn, 231, 248f.

Gaius Caligula, Roman emperor, 117

Galut, 237, 238, 457–458, 498. *See also* Diaspora, Exile and exiles

Games and sports, 205, 301–302

Gamaliel, Rabban, 161, 166

Genesis, Book of, first philosophy of history, 42, 50

Gentile Jewish relations—condemnation of Gentiles' paganism, 89; hostility in Alexandria, 116; antisemitism in Hellenistic age, 131–132; source of hostility in Talmudic age, 149f., 185, 198; quiescent in peaceful conditions, 238; ghetto qualities in, 273–274; in medieval times, 296, 301, 305–306; effect of emancipation in France on, 324–325; wave of reaction in Germany, 328; New Testament as a source of hostility in, 362

German Jewry—unbroken heritage of antisemitism, 326; economic importance of, 326; emancipation in, 327; antisemitic reaction to equality, 328; Jewish socialist leadership in, 328–330; Nazis' "final solution," 335f.; Reform movement in, 366; Haskalah movement in, 379f.; biological decline in, 394; penalty paid to Nazis by, 446

Ghetto, 269, 274, 277, 283, 307, 340, 360, 380, 392, 413, 421

Ginzberg, Louis, 110, 181, 479

Gnosticism—influence on Essenes, 112; later influence on Judaism, 113; influence on Jewish mysticism, 138

God—in Israelite religion, 10ff.; Kingdom of, 42; monotheistic idea of, 59f., in Israelite religion, 69; loyalty in Diaspora to, 80; Jewish gospel of redeeming God, 91; in Aggadic literature, 182; Talmudic conception of, 192; in the light of reason, 245; proof of existence, 248; Gabirol's conception of, 248ff.; Maimonides' conception of, 250–251; dogma regarding existence of, 369; Hasidic conception of, 373

Gog and Magog, 208, 237

Graetz, Heinrich, xviif., 2f., 376, 377

Greco-Roman. *See* Hellenistic culture and society

Greco-Roman culture and society—extent of, 97; influences on Jews and Judaism, 107ff.

Greece. *See* Greek culture and society

Greek culture and society—conflict with Judaism, 91–92; impact upon Jews, 97ff.; accommodation to in medieval Judaism, 244ff.; Luzzatto's opposition to, 331; influence on modern Hebrew poetry, 388

Greek terms in Hebrew language, 100, 106–108

Guide to the Perplexed—philosophy of, 250–252; public burning of, 255; influence on Schoolmen, 281; translation of, 306

Guide for the Perplexed of Our Time, 380–381

Habakkuk, 72, 79, 206

Habiru, 3ff.

Hadassah, Women's Zionist Organization of America, 458

Haggadah, 291, 296, 302, 305

Hai ben Sherira, Gaon, 224

Halakha—as a way of life, 109; as legal exegesis, 177f.; binding on individual Jew, 182; associated with land, 202; Maimonides contribution to, 225f.

Halevi, Judah—description of Israel, 95; pilgrim to Holy land, 205, 238; attitude toward Hebrew and Arabic, 220; range of his poetry, 231; epicureanism of, 237; merit of *mitzvoth* in exile, 238f., philosophy of, 252–253

Halukkah, 393, 426–428

Hanukka, antiquity of, xxi; festival of, 151

Hasidim—in Maccabean times, 106; relation to Essenes, 111; dress of, 289

Hasidism—origin and development of, 372–374; ideals expressed in writings of Peretz, 385; in writings of Agnon, 388; Nahman of Bratslav's attitude to Holy Land, 423; Belzer rabbi's anti-Zionism, 425; Buber's mystical interpretation of, 433

Haskalah, Jewish enlightenment, 379–382, 388, 395

Hasmoneans. *See* Maccabees

Hebrew language—absorption of Greek and Latin words, 107f.; role in Judeo-Islamic culture, 219–221; use by Karaites of, 243; medieval use of, 284, 292f.; advocated by nationalists as national language, 354; struggle for supremacy with Yiddish, 431; development in Palestine of, 431–432; in U.S. census of 1916, 465; development in America, 478–479

Hebrew literature—in period of the Judges, 41ff.; in period of First Temple, 56; flowering under Islam of, 230–231; Karaite contribution to, 243f.; Haskalah contribution to, 379ff.; modern development of, 387–390, 433; development in America, 478–479. *See also* Bible, Hebrew language

Hebrew University in Jerusalem, 434, 458, 473

Hebrews, 4, 6

Heine, Heinrich, xxiv, 283, 381, 383

Hellenism. *See* Greek culture and society

Hellenistic culture and society—extent of, 96; resemblance to modern world, 97ff.; polity in, 97–98; philosophies in, 101; influence on Jewish ruling classes, 105, 110; Jewish literature in, 122–123; achievement of Judaism in, 137ff.; difference of modern citizenship from, 315

Hellenization. *See* Hellenistic culture and society

Hero-types in Jewish history—Talmud as a source of, 144; the teacher, 187; in Talmudic culture, 189ff.

Herod. *See* Herodians

Herodians—recognition of Herod as king of Judea, 107; reconstruction of Temple in Jerusalem, 108; wealth of, 120; acceptance of Pharisaic doctrine, 158

Herzl, Theodor, 333, 355, 399, 420, 435–439

Hess, Moses, 329, 352, 353, 416, 429, 430, 433f.

Hillel—methods of interpretation, 110; origin of, 132; Pharisaic school of, 161f.; personality of, 166; institution of *prosbul*, 179; on Jewish values, 186f.; as hero-type, 190

Hirsch, Baron Maurice de, 399, 406

Histadrut, 445

History—role of, xivf.; premonarchic view of, 33; philosophy of, 42, 96; prophetic view of, 62ff.; Talmudic view of, 191; medieval conception of, 239; racialist interpretation of, 346–347; Krochmal's philosophy of, 381; neglect of role of peddler in, 409

Hitler, Adolph. *See* Nazis

Hittites, 30, 95

Holy Land, the. *See* Land of Israel

Horace, cited, 129

Hosea, 57, 61

House of study. *See* Academies

Idolatry—appearance in ancient Israel, 29; nonexistence in early monarchy, 48; view of classical prophecy, 68; of the nations, 70, 75; disappearance after Fall, 79; versus monotheism, 123

Immigration. *See* Migration

Immortality, 87, 225, 248, 250f.

Impurity—Biblical concept of, 27f.; apocalyptic concept of, 87; laws essential to, 177

Individualism, and society—in Hellenistic age, 98; in Pharisaic doctrine, 162; law binding on individual, 182; impact of concept on Western civilization, 185; responsibility for reali-

Individualism (*cont.*)
    zation of messianic society, 209; new
    interest under Islam, 240f.; in Re-
    form Judaism, 367
Industrialism, 406–407, 415
Ingathering of Israel's dispersed—
    proselytes included, 80; concern of
    eschatology with, 86, 88
Integration—assumption of emancipa-
    tion, 315; attempt of Napoleon, 325;
    in Tsarist Russia, 333; opposed by
    antisemites, 345; imperative of as-
    similation, 421
Interfaith, 262, 342
Internationalism—of medieval Jew,
    284–285; in ideology of Bund, 356
Isaiah, 60f., 65, 66, 67, 68, 70, 71, 79.
    See Second Isaiah, Prophecy.
Isaiah, Book of, cited, 61, 66, 67, 68,
    70, 80, 81
Islam—origins of, 215f.; status of Jews
    in, 216–217; flowering of Hebrew
    literature under, 230ff.; elements of
    Greek origin in, 235; cultural atmos-
    phere of Jews under, 235f., influence
    on Karaism, 241ff.; conversion of
    Shabbetai Zevi to, 422; theory of re-
    ligious war in, 444
Israel—relation to Habiru, 4; struc-
    ture of, 5; elements of ancient cul-
    tures in, 6ff.; cult in, 11f.; election of,
    14; in Egypt, 15f.; culture of, 25ff.;
    conquest of Canaan, 31ff.; new role
    of, 68; among the nations, 95; record
    of growth in Hebrew Bible, 143;
    messianic restoration of, 158
Israel, Kingdom of—Baal cult in, 54f.;
    prophecy of Fall of, 57
Israel, Land of—in Israelite religion,
    76; relation to Diaspora, 203ff.; in
    doctrine of *Galut;* 236f.; relation to
    rationalism, 253; in Nahman of
    Bratslav, 423
Israel, State of—opposition to religious
    reform in, 370; archeology a national
    pastime in, 384; new literature of,
    388f.; high birth rate in, 394–395;
    opened to survivors of Catastrophe,
    402; labor parties in, 419; role of
    emancipated Jewries in emergence
    of, 420f.; anti-Zionists in and out-
    side, 424f.; adoption of "Law of Re-

turn," 429; higher institutions of
    learning in, 434; birth of, 448–449;
    recognition and nonrecognition by
    Arab states, 449; Arab refugee prob-
    lem, 449–450; constitution of, 450–
    451; political parties in, 451; immi-
    gration in, 451–453; melting pot in,
    452f.; Arabs in, 452; economic prob-
    lems and progress in, 453
Israeli. *See* Israel, State of
Italian Jewry—participation of Jews in
    Revolution, 329; in public life of,
    329; fascist antisemitism in, 414–415

Jamnia, academy at, 160f., 169
Jeremiah, Book of, cited, 59, 73, 74, 75
Jeremiah, prophet—element of divina-
    tion, 58; ideal of justice, 61; cham-
    pions Josianic reform, 72; doctrine
    of, 73; polemic against idolatry, 79
Jerusalem—symbol of Davidic dy-
    nasty, 52; siege of, 73f.; prayer di-
    rected toward, 81; eschatology
    bound up with, 81; Zadokite priest-
    hood of, 102; followers of Jesus in,
    127; preeminence of, 136; Roman
    devastation of, 160f.; center of Rab-
    binic learning, 434; UN resolution
    regarding, 448
Jesus of Nazareth—followers of in
    Jerusalem, 127; cited on proselytes,
    128; activity in Talmudic period, 144
Jewish Community, the—communal
    organization of Essenes, 111; civic
    rights of, 113; organization in Hel-
    lenistic cities, 115; organization in
    Rome, 117; preservation of records
    by, 122f.; in Palestine and Babylo-
    nia during Talmudic age, 147;
    emergence of Talmudic community,
    148ff.; ethnic-religious function of,
    150; self-government in, 152; transi-
    tion to Rabbinic community, 162;
    close contact in Muslim world, 217;
    spread in Europe of, 268; the viable
    Jewish Community, 276–277; demo-
    cratic character of, 280; modern
    struggle for prerogatives, 317; en-
    hanced position of women in, 364;
    the "organic" Jewish community,
    378; subcommunities of artisan
    guilds, 407; ideal of social justice in,

408; Halukkah system of charity, 426–428; pioneering of American Jewry in communal coexistence, 456ff.; idea of *kehillah* in America, 460f.; vehicle of Jewish survival in America, 468

Jewish Encyclopedia, 267, 384, 479

Jewish people, the—adaptability of, 95; synagogue the schoolhouse of, 169; a people of the Book, 184; emphasis on, 240; change from passive to activist attitude, 272; unity in medieval times of, 276; corporate structure of, 316f.; shortcomings of, 324; a distinctive group in non-Jewish societies, 363; increase of population a stimulus to, 395; population shift to Western Hemisphere, 403

Jewish Question, 322, 326, 330, 332, 336, 356, 436

Jewish Welfare Board, 476–477

Jews. *See* Jewish people

Job, Book of, cited, 56, 88

Johanan ben Zakkai, Rabban, 160, 162, 166, 168, 190, 446

Jonah, Book of, date of composition, 56

Jordan, state of, 112

Joseph and His Brothers, 181

Josephus—as historian, xvii; cited, 103, 104; his description of Essene community, 112; description of Diaspora, 114; regarding citizenship in Hellenistic cities, 115; decree of Dolabella cited, 115f.; his apologetic treatise, 123; cited, 158; the Josippon chronicle, 305

Joshua, 29, 36

Joshua, Book of, cited, 42, 43

Josiah, King of Judah—struggle against paganism, 56; reform of, 71f.

Journalism, Jewish, 386, 387, 389, 410f., 430f.

Judah Al-Harizi, 232

Judah ha-Nasi, Rabbi, 136, 152

Judah, Kingdom of—Baal cult in, 54, 55; prophecy of Fall of, 57, 73; exile, 74; a Persian province, 81

Judaism—beginning of, 76; contrast with Hellenism, 91f.; essence unaffected by Hellenization, 107; influence of Gnosticism on, 113; culture and religion synonomous in, 122; a protected religion, 154; Rabbinic definition of spirit of, 179f.; medieval interpretations of, 239ff.; preservation of, 274; attacked by Enlightenment, 323f.; Luzzatto's defense of, 331; election of Israel an integral part of, 351; cannot be equated with American Christian denomination, 360f.; adjustments in emancipation era, 363ff.; small emphasis on dogma, 368–369; incompatibility with facism, 414

Judges, Book of, cited, 33, 34, 36, 38, 39, 41, 42, 44

Judeo-Christian culture — idea of world brotherhood in, 97, 98; legacy of Hellenistic Judaism to, 137f.; role of Leviticus 19 in, 177; differences between Jewish and Christian civilization, 331, 362; messianic element in modern nationalism, 341; interfaith associations, 342

Judeo-German. *See* Yiddish

Judeo-Islamic culture—role of Talmud in, 217; linguistic transformation in, 219f.; new interest in Bible during, 226f.; flowering of Hebrew literature in, 230–233; cultural atmosphere of Jews in, 235f.; concept of exile in, 236f.; role of Karaites, 241ff.; role of philosophy in, 238ff.; role of Kabbala in, 257ff.; legacy of, 259ff.

Jüdische Wissenschaft. See Science of Judaism

Justice, 60f., 109, 408

Kabbala—influence of Gabirol on, 249; origin and outlook of, 257ff.; the Zohar, 281

Kalam. *See* Philosophy, Saadia

Kant, Immanuel, 380, 381

Kaplan, Mordecai Menahem, 142, 378

Karaites and Karaism—influence on study of Bible, 227f.; role in medieval Judaism, 241ff.; decline of, 243f.; Biblical commentary by, 306; Reform movement equated with, 367; studies in lore of, 381

Kibbutz, 277, 445

Kimhi, David ben Joseph, 229

Kings, Book of, cited, 46, 48, 53, 55, 56, 63
Koran, 219, 221, 227
Krochmal, Nahman, 380–381, 382
Kuzari, cited, 95; philosophy of, 252–253

Labor unions, 407–408, 409, 445
Landsmanshaften, 459ff., 475, 476
Law. *See* Laws of nature; Mosaic Law; Oral law; Natural law, Torah
"Law of the Monarchy," 46, 50
Law of nations—secular counterpart of world brotherhood, 98; Jewish religio-cultural sources of, 212
Leeser, Isaac, 353, 427, 466, 479
Legends of the Jews, The, 181
Lenin, Nikolay, 417, 418
Leviticus, Book of, cited, 25, 63, 166
Liberalism, 344, 352, 413, 419
Liturgy—prayer formulated into, 85; adopted by Christianity, 138; cited, 145; Temple forms added to, 168f.; increased fixity of, 207; influence of secular verse on, 230; theme of suffering in, 238; enriched in Middle Ages, 281
Logos, 135, 138
Luzzatto, Samuel David, 331, 382

Maccabees, 106, 107, 109, 155, 157, 274
Maccabees, Books of, cited, 104, 105
Maimonides—attitude toward Christianity and Islam, 217; regarding his use of Arabic, 220; content and variety of his works, 224f.; opposed to divination, 239f.; allegorical interpretation of Scripture, 246; philosophy of, 249–252; opposition to, 254ff.; on study of Torah in Messianic age, 280; influence on Schoolmen, 281; medical writings of, 283; translation of the *Guide,* 306; formulation of dogmas, 368f.
Malachi, 57, 85, 86, 207
Man—nature of, 87, 88, 185, 209, 240, 251, 339
Mann, Thomas, 181
Mapai, 419, 451
Mapam, 419
Marranos, 283, 295, 422, 483

Marriage, 124, 196, 291, 295, 391, 393, 452
Martyrs and Martyrology—roots of Christian martyrology in Judaism, 138; Akiba as, 190; as witness to divine call, 194
Marx, Karl, 328, 356, 371, 416
Marxism. *See* Communism, Socialism, Soviet Jewry
Master Benedict, composite medieval Jew, 287–311
Materialism—in conversion of ancient Israel, 78; Hellenistic contempt for, 101; threat to Jewish survival, 331; in anti-intellectualism of Jewish youth, 413
Mattathias, 106, 107
Matzoth, bread of haste, 20
Medicine, 121, 219, 257, 283, 299f., 412, 458
Mendelssohn, Moses, 327, 363, 379, 380, 404
Messiah—Davidic symbol of, 52; as redeemer, 86; from tribe of Levi, 157; Rabbinic doctrine of, 208ff., 236f.; role in Jewish survival, 272–273; role in Polish nationalism, 341; rejection of, 423
Messianic pretenders, 167, 206, 237, 422
Messianism and Messianic society—role in the background of Restoration, 82; ultimate conversion of mankind, 109; the "Return," 205; apocalyptic belief in, 206; Rabbinic doctrine of Messiah, 208, 236f.; role in Jewish survival, 272–273; study of Torah in Messianic age, 280; in French Revolution, 325f.; in modern nationalism, 341; realization through Jewish nationality, 341; secular interpretation of, 352; opposition of Reform Judaism to, 369; indoctrination in home, school and synagogue in 422; movement of Shabbetai Zevi, 422
Micah, 61, 179
Middle Ages, the—Talmudic civilization the basis of communal life in, 144, 209, 223; historical writing in, 239; influence of Maimonides in, 249ff.; freedom of thought in, 274;

the Jewish community in, 276–277; Jewish self-government in, 278–279; role of Talmud in, 280; Jews as intellectual intermediaries in, 284–285; a typical Jewish household in, 287–311; popular culture shared by Christians and Jews, 301; misconception in Jewish historiography of, 315–316; role of Yiddish in, 384

Midrash—as written Torah, 83; etymology and influence, 176; Oral Law in, 177; technique of, 178f.; becomes a new Scripture, 210

Migration, 332f., 334, 346, 349, 375, 397, 400f., 408f., 423, 445, 452, 456f.

Military service, 332, 447, 476–477

Minorities, 216f., 340f., 409

Minority, Jewish, 217, 238, 337, 340f., 356, 358, 359, 360

Minority Rights, 320, 333, 354, 417

Misconceptions of Jews and Judaism—of relation to paganism, 8f.; exclusiveness of post-Exilic Judaism, 84; role in "eastern" and "western" cultures, 96; Roman defeat proclaimed bankruptcy of traditional Judaism, 163; that Judaism does not encourage conversion, 185; Gentile Jewish relations in Talmudic culture, 199; Talmudic attitude toward land and religion, 201; conflict between faith and reason, 255; Hebrew a dead language, 303–304; accepted fallacies regarding modern emancipation, 315ff.; idea of a Jewish world conspiracy, 344–345; fiction that Jews are only a religious group, 351; charge that Rabbinic Judaism is petrified, 370–372; alleged superiority of Jewish national groupings, 397

Mishna—promulgated, 152; difference of opinion in, 165; in Babylonia, 171; negative statement of dogma in, 183; concept of teacher in, 187; problem of autonomy in, 210; Maimonides' commentary on, 224f.; Frankel's methodology of, 376

Mishneh Torah of Maimonides, 225ff.

Mission, 70, 352

Mistress Rachel, composite medieval Jewess, 287–311

Mitzvah—Biblical concept, 28; Talmudic concept, 178ff.

Monarchy—law of, 36; and prophecy, 45ff.; democratic element in, 46. *See* Polity

Moneylending, 119, 151, 176, 296–298, 316, 403

Monotheism—relation to paganism, 11f.; role of Moses, 14ff.; in institution of Judges, 39; rooted in popular religion, 59; extended everywhere, 150; modern secular cults appropriate soteric claim of, 212; modern nationalism and, 339; need for survival of mankind of, 484

Montefiore, Sir Moses, 437

Morality—foundation of Torah, 23f.; in Biblical wisdom, 51; primacy of, 60f.; Jeremiah's doctrine of, 73; role in winning converts to Judaism, 129; contribution of Talmud to, 144; poor and rich in concept of, 168; Bachya's treatise on, 253; medieval literature of, 305f., 310f.

Moses, formulation of monotheism, 14ff.; first prophet, 16f.; parallel to Muhammad, 18; as hero-type, 190; uniqueness of, 251; ranked above other prophets, 369

Moses ibn Ezra, 231

Muhammad—parallel to Moses, 19; prophet of Islam, 215; adoration of, 227; as a trustee of revelation, 235; Jews reject teaching of, 238

Music, 283, 300, 309, 345, 390, 434

Muslim. *See* Islam

Mystery-cults, 101, 129

Mysticism—in Philo, 134f.; in Nahmanides, 229; in Ibn Gabirol, 248f.; in The Zohar, 281; in Land of Israel, 243; Buber's Hasidic, 433. *See also* Gnosticism, Hasidism, Kabbala,

Nahman of Bratslav, 423

Nahmanides, Moses, 205, 229, 238, 240

Nahum, prophet, 72

Nation and nation-state. *See* Nationality, Nationalism, and Zionism

National self-determination. *See* Self-determination

Nationalism—takes on character of exclusive religion, 339; secularization

Nationalism (*cont.*)
   of the nation, 339f.; rejection of
   Jewish nationality, 340; messianic
   element in, 341; use of antisemitism,
   343f.; Nazi reinterpretation of, 347;
   fiction of Jews as a religious group
   of, 351; the issue of territorialism in,
   352–353; Hebrew as national language, 354; Dubnow's theory of Diaspora nationalism, 356; Arab nationalism, 444f.
Nationalism, Jewish—a reaction to antisemitism, 350; Orthodox Jews per-
   sist in traditional type of, 351; issue
   of territorialism in, 352–353; theory
   of Diaspora nationalism, 356; demand that League of Nations be an
   association of ethnic cultural nationalities, 357; Haskalah contribution
   to, 381; contribution to Hebrew revival of, 387; and socialism, 418f.
Nationality, Jewish, 339, 340, 341, 351,
   353, 354, 355, 356f.
Nazis, 286, 300, 316, 335, 347–350,
   368, 401, 405, 412, 415
Nehardea, 172
Nehemiah, 82ff.
Nehemiah, Book of, cited, 84
New Testament. *See* Christianity
New York Times, 387
Numbers, Book of, cited, 26, 29, 41, 50

Occupations, Jewish. *See* Agriculture,
   Banking, Commerce, Crafts, Economic Conditions, Industry, Money
   lending, Professions
Optimism, 65, 196, 273
Oral Law, 165, 177, 241. *See also* Aggada, Midrash, Torah
Orthodox Judaism—leaders denounce
   values of western civilization, 318;
   persists in traditional type of nationalism, 351; analysis of criticism and
   program of, 370–376; Hasidic influence upon, 373; censuses of American congregations of, 464f.; organization in U.S. of, 467

Paganism—mistaken for fetishism, 8;
   morality of, 24; and prophecy, 37;
   in monarchic period, 53ff.; deification of man, 62; idolatrous deification

of reason, 92; in Hellenistic-Roman
   period, 101; use of pagan symbols by
   Roman Jews, 126
Palestine—as holy land, 76; in Persian
   empire, 101; decline of Jewry in,
   166; a foundation of Jewish law and
   ritual, 201; agricultural colonies in,
   399f., 406; the Yishub in, 422; pilgrimages of rabbis and mystics to,
   423; Christian belief in restoration to
   Jews of, 424; Halukkah system in,
   426–428; messengers to Diaspora
   Jewries from, 428; persecution of
   Zionists for pro-Allied sympathy in
   World War I, 428; revival of Hebrew
   in, 430–432; Herzl's diplomacy for,
   436–439; British interest in, *idem.;*
   Bilu's colonies in, 437; Ha-Shomer,
   the national guard in, 440; the
   League of Nations' Mandate for,
   443–447; immigration to, 445; policy of *Havlagah,* 446; Jewish Brigade
   and Haganah, 447; birth of state of
   Israel, 448–449; American Jews in,
   457
Passover—antiquity of, xxi; first festival of, 20; character of, 26; pilgrim
   festival, 136; ritual spring cleaning
   on approach of, 288; medieval cus-
   toms of, 290–291; synagogal hymns
   for, 302
Patriarchs, Biblical, 4, 5, 42, 50, 189;
   Rabbinic, 160, 164, 165, 166, 167
Paul (Saul) of Tarsus—"apostle to the
   Gentiles," 128; activity in Talmudic
   age, 144
Peace, 67, 206, 272, 273
Peddler, 409–410
Pentateuch—history in, 25; accepted as
   revealed Law, 151; Rashi's com-
   mentary on, 281. *See also* Torah
Pentecost, 293, 302
Peretz, Yitzok Leibosh, 385
Pessimism—among Essenes, 112; in
   Talmudic religion, 195; in Judeo-
   Islamic culture, 236
Pharisaism and Pharisees—the Macca-
   bees and, 107; political and religious
   beliefs of, 109f.; acknowledge possi-
   bility of prophecy, 156f.; interpreters
   of Mosaic revelation, 157; schools
   of, 161; recognition of variant inter-

pretations of the Law, 165; interpretation of *lex talionis,* 178; foreshadows modern democratic theory, 187; distortion of in New Testament, 188
Philanthropy. *See* Charity, Social Work
Philistines, 30, 31, 37
Philo of Alexandria—description of Essene community, 111; description of Diaspora, 114; enjoyment of full citizenship by Jews, 115; writings of, 123; considers Septuagint divinely inspired, 125; opponent of idolatry and polytheism, 126; Wolfson's interpretation of, 127; attitude toward proselytes, 130; portrait of, 132; debt of Christianity to, 138; universalism of, 139
Philosemitism—of Poppaea, wife of Nero, 119; in modern society, 351
Philosophy, Jewish—Philo of Alexandria, 132ff.; medieval concern with, 245f.; system of Kalam, 247ff.; neoplatonic influence in medieval Jewish thinkers, 248ff.; Maimonides' contribution to, 249–252; Halevi's view of, 253; opposition to study of, 255–256; replaced by Kabbala, 257; newer trends in, 365f.
Pilgrims and Pilgrimages, 136, 151, 162, 170, 205, 222, 238, 424, 425
Pirke Abot, Mishnaic treatise, 107, 186, 225, 479
Plato and Platonism, 133, 175, 248ff.
Polish Jewry—evasion of minority rights of, 320; governmental reform and oppression, 334; intellectual productivity of, 372; Yiddish theater in, 386; expansion of, 395
Politics and political power—entry of Jews into arena of, 328f., 420, 446, 450–451
Polity—political institution of Judges, 38; tribe as political unit, 38; primitive democracy, 39; monarchy and prophecy, 45; law of monarchy, 46; included in Talmudic culture, 148; priests as political heads, 154; tie between religious freedom and political sovereignty, 155f.; primacy of civil law of the land, 172; Scripture as guide for just polity, 176; preoccupation with "Return" in, 207; autono-

mous community a surrogate for statehood, 421. *See also* Messianism, Monarchy, Self-government, Zionism
Polytheism—early, 7ff.; in Hellenistic age, 123; combated by Philo, 126. *See also* Idolatry, Monotheism, Paganism
Pompey the Great, 107, 146
Population, Jewish, 114, 331, 336, 391ff., 395f., 451–453, 460
Prayer—as cult in exile, 80; creation of the synagogue, 81; monotheistic form of, 151; in the Temple, 162; in the synagogue, 169; element in personalization of religious responsibility, 184; study as, 186; oriented toward Jerusalem, 204; recitation in morning, 288; character public worship, 292; study and, 292
Prayerbooks, 292, 301, 365, 368, 369, 426, 479
Priesthood and priests, Jewish—cult in Jerusalem, 102; preservation of geneologies, 124; relegated to cultic jurisdiction, 152; dissolution of cultic authority, 165
Professions, 120, 412
Prophecy—apostolic, 20; cultic, 36; monotheistic character, 37; prophetic theocracy, 40; and monarchy, 45; struggle against Baal worship, 54ff.; classical prophecy, 57ff.; eschatology of, 65ff.; preservation by the Pharisees, 109; Rabbinic social legislation based upon, 79; Maimonides' conception of, 251; source of principles of French Revolution, 325f.; ethical and religious postulates of prophets in Reform movement, 367
Proselytes and Proselytism—appearance in Babylonian Exile, 80; a product of Jewish universalism, 89; Judaizing of Idumea and Galilee, 106; conversion in Diaspora, 106; appeal of Paul among semiproselytes, 127; Philo's attitude toward, 130; pattern adopted by Christianity, 138; missionary campaign of Babylonian Jews, 171; semiproselytes required to renounce idolatry, 185; in Islam, 216. *See also* Antisemitism, Mission

Protestant Church and Protestantism. *See* Christianity

Proverbs, Book of, 51, 56

Psalms, Book of, 44, 51, 56, 85, 87, 308

Purim, 291, 302

Rabbenu Gershom, 278

Rabbi, etymology, 160n., medieval role of, 291–292; declining prestige of, 364

Rabbinic Judaism. *See* Talmudic Judaism

Rabbinical seminaries, 368, 376, 378, 467, 473

Rabbis, the. *See* Talmudic Judaism

Racialism—absent in Talmudic outlook, 196; adopted by antisemitism, 345; immigration policies actuated by, 400f. *See also* Antisemitism, Nationalism

Rashi (Rabbi Solomon ben Isaac), 228, 277, 281, 297, 301, 305

Rationalism—the guiding star of Biblical commentators, 228; problem in medieval Judaism of, 244ff.; role of Maimonides in adoption of, 252; antirationalism of Kabbala, 257f.; effects of Enlightenment, 324, 338

Reconstructionism, wing of conservative Judaism, 378–379

Reform Judaism—problem of chosen people in, 351; alters character of Sabbath idea, 362; demand for reform of ritual, 365; movement in Germany, 366; in the United States, 366–370; changed attitude to Messianic doctrine, 369; considers mission of Jewish people to spread ethical monotheism, 425; censuses of American congregations, 464f.

Refugees, 349, 402, 429, 446, 449–450

Relativism, 260, 261

Religion and comparative religion. *See* Christianity, Islam, Judaism, God, Monotheism, Mysticism, Rationalism, Values and value concepts

Responsa—origin and character of, 145; in Babylonian academies, 218f.; in medieval Europe, 280; discussion of sports on Sabbath, 302; writing of, 304

Revelation—in Philo, 135; in Pharisaic doctrine, 64; Talmudic postulate, 157; Maimonides' discussion of, 225; Saadia's concern with, 228; need to harmonize with reason, 245; dogma of, 369

Reward and Punishment, 193, 194, 196, 235, 273

Ritual, 60f., 147, 161, 178, 365, 366, 377, 461, 468

Rome—Jewish envoys to, 106; organization of Jewish community in, 117

Roosevelt, Franklin Delano, 401

Rosh Ha-shanah, 83

Rothschild, Baron Edmond de, 399, 436

Russian Jewry—effect of French Revolution on, 326; comprises half of world Jewish population, 331; governmental policy for, 332; demand recognition as national minority, 356; high birth rate of, 392. *See* Soviet Jewry

Ruth, Book of, cited, 49

Saadia ben Joseph, Gaon, 224; translation of Bible into Arabic, 228; struggle against Karaites, 243–244; use of Kalam by, 248

Sabbath—importance in Babylonian exile, 81; observance of in Hellenistic age, 116; discussion of sports on, 302; heretical view of, 307; medieval pattern of, 308–309; joy of, 311; differs from day of rest of other civilizations and religions, 361; demand for abolition of, 363

Sacrifices—sacral meal, 22; exemption from military service to make, 116; in Temple at Jerusalem, 151

Sadducees, 107, 109, 156, 241

Samaritans, 85, 149

Samuel, Books of, cited, 33, 37, 42, 45, 46, 48, 49, 56, 61

Samuel ha-Nagid, 231

Sanhedrin, 109, 159, 160, 164, 166, 225, 325, 326

Satan, 86, 89

Schechter, Solomon, 376, 377, 479

Schoolmen, medieval—attitude toward Deuteronomic law of usury, 176; in-

fluenced by Maimonides, 281; neo-Thomism, 316
Schools. *See* Academies, Education
Science of Judaism, 282, 381, 382, 383
Scriptures. *See* Bible, Torah
Second Commonwealth, The—importance for understanding of Talmudic culture, 146; Pharisaic struggle for authority in, 187, 202
Second Isaiah, 61, 70, 79, 207
Secularization. *See* Assimilation, Emancipation, Nationalism, Zionism
Self-determination, 333, 357, 443, 455
Self-government—origin and purpose of, 150f.; in the Middle Ages, 278–279; in Russia, 333, 356; in United States, 455
Sephardim, 269, 323, 452, 463
Septuagint, Greek translation of Hebrew Bible—occurrence of word "diaspora" in, 113; considered divinely inspired, 125; use by Philo, 134; made possible preaching of Gospel in Diaspora, 138
Sexual morality, 185, 196, 278, 288, 295, 305–306, 311
Shabbetai Zevi, 422, 428
Shammai, 161, 166
Sheelah. See Responsa
Shekinah, Divine Presence, 76, 186, 204, 426
Shema ("Hear, O Israel"), 190
Sholem Aleichem (Sholem Rabinovitch), 385, 433, 479
Shulhan Arukh, 180, 226, 372
Simeon ben Shetah, 158
Slavery and Slaves—legal protection in Hellenistic society, 99; ransoming of, 120; laws of, 151
Social Justice. *See* Justice
Social Work, 473, 474
Socialism—in Hellenistic age, 98; Jewish leadership in, 328–330; attack on Jewish capitalism by, 342; secular interpretation of messianic idea by, 352; Jewish socialist party (Bund), 356, 418; Jewish workers and, 407f.; hostile attitude toward Judaism, 415
Solomon, King, 47, 48, 51, 52, 53, 54
Solomon ibn Gabirol. *See* Gabirol
Song of Deborah, the, 33, 42

Song of Songs, 51, 181
Sovereignty, 339, 422
Soviet Jewry (USSR)—undermining of Judaism in, 279; minority rights ineffective in, 359; Yiddish theater in, 386; decline of Yiddish press in, 387; growth of mixed marriages in, 393; declassing of Jews in, 404; anti-semitism in, 417; declining vitality of, 417; Jews recognized as national minority in, 418; Yiddish school system, 421; desire to emigrate to Israel in, 452
Spinoza, 134, 352, 363
Study. *See* Academies, Bible, Education, Synagogue, Talmud
Sukkoth, 124, 136, 157, 301, 302
Sura, 172, 222
Survival of Jews and Judaism—role of communal institutions, 173; contemporary significance of, 271; role of Messianic doctrine in, 272; role of Talmud in, 275ff.; threatened by emancipation, 330–331, 336–337; racialist theory of, 345; Gentile contribution during Nazi occupation to, 349; communal autonomy as core of, 356; value of culture in, 390; threat in Soviet Union to, 418; Jewish community in America a vehicle of, 468; role of American Jewry in, 480–484
Symbolism, 17, 83, 126, 134
Synagogue—a new creation, 84; architecture of, 108; in Rome, 117; focus of Talmudic community, 162; Roman protection of, 163; functions in Talmudic society, 169f.; role in medieval Judaism, 278, description of, 289f.; use for church services of, 342; changes in, 364; of artisan guilds, 407; source of indoctrination in messianic ideal, 422

Talmud—character of, 144; adoption of Babylonian Talmud as code of law, 170; role of Babylonian Talmud in Diaspora, 70; application of principles to present, 172; becomes a new Scripture, 210; patterns of behavior in Muslim empire rooted in, 217; completion of Babylonian Talmud, 222; attitude toward astrology,

Talmud (*cont.*)
239f.; hold on the Jew, 276; glosses of Tosaphists on, 277; role in life of medieval Jews, 280; studied in synagogue, 293

Talmudic (Rabbinic) Jewry. *See* Talmudic Judaism

Talmudic Judaism—the Rabbis acquainted with Greco-Roman culture, 110; a universalist religion, 143; role of Talmud in, 144; time and place of, 145ff.; centrality of Jewish community in Palestine, 147; authority shifted to scholar in, 164f.; role of Patriarch in, 164; role of synagogue in, 169f.; lack of a theological system in, 174; a running commentary on Scripture, 174; role of Biblical interpretation in, 176; role of Torah in, 180; role of dogma in, 183; new hero-types in, 188ff.; concept of Holy Land in, 201ff.; pilgrimage in, 205; doctrine of Messiah in, 207; eschatology in, 209; legacy of, 210f.; prominence in Muslim world of, 217; Karaite revolt against, 241ff.; universal hold on Jews, 276; Jewish unity created by, 284

Taxation, 120, 163, 167, 217, 278, 316

Tcherikover, V., 119, 126

Tchernikhowsky, Saul, 388

Tefutsot, 458

Tel-Aviv, 277, 403, 441, 450

Ten Commandments, the—origin and significance, 22; application of Midrash to, 178; corporate responsibility in, 197

Teshubot. See Responsa

Theater, 385–386, 389, 434

Theodicy, 194ff., 197

Torah—cult laws of, 47; crystallization of, 50; moral and religious guide, 50; equality of prophecy with, 57; in Josianic reform, 71; redaction of, 82; creative exegesis of, 83; universal essence of, 85; as civic-religious constitution, 101; doctrine of in Hellenistic Judaism, 134; its meaning expressed in liturgy, 145; becomes public domain, 151; recognized as law of the land, 151; prophets the early teachers of, 156; Jewish people governed by, 165; reading of in Talmudic age, 169; a revelation of God's will and eternally relevant, 176; whys and wherefores in Midrash of, 178; a guide to the totality of life, 181; mirror of good life, 191; conquest of West by, 200; heightened interest under Islam, 227; Rashi's commentary on, 228; Karaite view of, 241ff.; instrument of self-realization, 251; role in Messianic society, 280; reading in synagogue of, 293; spoken at meals, 301; as constitution of state of Israel, 450

Totalitarianism, 275, 339, 417

Toynbee, Arnold J., xvi, xx, xxiii

Tribes of Israel. *See* Israel

Truman, Harry S., 429, 448

United Nations, 421, 448, 449

Universalism, 32f., 75, 139, 143, 150, 184, 194, 484

Usury. *See* Moneylending

Values and value concepts—Aggada as traditional value concepts, 182; Hebrew and study in scale of, 186; linked to lifeways, 188; Land of Israel in complex of, 201; in medieval Jewish thought, 239ff.; relativism and, 260; values of western civilization denounced by Jews, 318; Jewish homeland as a laboratory for, 422

Voltaire, 324, 365

Weizmann, Chaim, 433, 434

Wellhausen, Julius, 7, 384

Western civilization—legacy of Hellenistic Judaism to, 137ff.; Talmudic concept of eternally valid Scripture in, 176; Talmudic religion the oldest organized religion of, 183; impact of concept of individual religious responsibility on, 184; introduction of "other-worldly" religion to, 194f.; legacy of Judeo-Islamic culture to, 259ff.; influence of Jews as intellectual intermediaries on, 284–285; Jewish denunciation of values of, 318

Wise, Isaac Mayer, 340, 366, 368, 409, 466, 479
Wolfson, Harry Austryn, 127, 134, 135, 138
Woman—emancipation in Hellenistic society, 99; behavior in pogrom, 124; status of *aguna*, 145; Alexandra Salome, 157; as hero-type, 190; in relation to Land of Israel, 203; beauty celebrated by poets, 236; role in medieval home and community, 293–295; steadfastness among Marranos, 295; humane treatment of, 296, 311; enhanced position of, 364; conversion of Gentile women to Judaism, 394
World Jewry. *See* Jewish people
World War I, 333, 335, 348, 357, 392, 406, 416, 420, 428, 441
World War II, 336, 349, 405, 420, 447, 461, 477
Worship. *See* Liturgy, Prayer

Yabneh. *See* Jamnia
Yahweh. See YHWH
YHWH, name of God, 16; at Exodus, 20; relation to Baal, 36f.; as King, 42; Israel the "Servant" of, 79
Yiddish, language and literature, 303, 356, 379f., 381, 384–387, 416, 418, 421, 430, 465, 477
Yishub. *See* Palestine, State of Israel, Zionism

Zangwill, Israel, 439
Zechariah, 61, 212
Zechariah, Book of, cited, 81
Zerubbabel, 81, 82
Zion, 68, 70, 135f., 204, 237, 423
Zionism — proto-Zionist movements, 304; leads quest for an international solution of Jewish question, 330; origins in nationalism of, 352; influence on Reform Judaism, 369; synthesis of socialism and, 419; part of emancipation movement, 420; religious motivations in, 422ff.; religious anti-Zionism, 424–425; reconciliation of Reform Judaism and, 425f.; opposition to Halukkah system, 428; creation of Jewish Agency for Palestine, 428f.; cultural Zionism of Ahad Haam, 430; struggle of Hebrew vs. Yiddish in, 431; rise of Herzlian (political) Zionism, 435ff.; British interest in Herzl's plans, 436–439; anti-Zionism of Papacy, 438–439; Zionist-Socialists, 440; evolution of Balfour Declaration, 441–442; Revisionism in, 445f.; Jewish state proposed by Peel Commission, 446; organization of illicit immigration (Aliyah Beth), 447–448; birth and development of state of Israel, 448–453
Zionist Movement. *See* Zionism
Zionist Organizations. *See* Zionism
Zunz, Leopold, xvii, 381, 382, 383

ABOUT THE EDITOR

LEO W. SCHWARZ, the editor of this volume, was educated at Harvard University and at the Jewish Institute of Religion, specializing in classical and Semitic philology and the history of religion. During World War II, Mr. Schwarz served in General Patton's Third Army and won a field commission in the Normandy campaign. In the postwar years he served as director of the American Joint Distribution Committee in Germany and was the American representative of the Hebrew University of Jerusalem.

Mr. Schwarz is the editor of the Rinehart Judaica series, which includes the anthologies *The Jewish Caravan, A Golden Treasury of Jewish Literature, Memoirs of My People* and *Feast of Leviathan;* and *The Root and the Bough,* a collection of eyewitness accounts of the Jewish experience in Europe during World War II. He is the author of *Where Hope Lies, The Redeemers* and *Refugees in Germany Today.*

Mr. Schwarz and his wife live in New York City, where he was born.

CULTURAL

EXTERNAL INFLUENCES

Near Eastern Cultures:
Amorite, Canaanite, Babylonian,
Egyptian, Assyrian, Hittite, Persian

> • • •

ca. 2500 B.C.E.
to
ca. 300 B.C.E.

• •

Hindu and Persian Cultures
Greco-Roman Civilization
Apostolic Christianity

> • • •

ca. 300 B.C.E.
to
ca. 300 C.E.

• •

Greco-Roman Civilization
Parthian-Sassanian Culture
Patristic Christianity

> • • •

ca. 330 B.C.E.
to
ca. 500 C.E.

• •

Byzantine Culture
Islam (Muslim Culture)

> • • •

7th Century
to
13th Century

• •

Medieval Christianity
European Renaissance
Protestant Christianity
Early Enlightenment and Emancipation

> • • •

10th Century
to
18th Century

• •

Science and Technology   *EMANCIPATION*
Industrial Society   *NATIONALISM*
Political Isms   *DEMOCRACY*
Religious Freedom   *ZIONISM*

> • • •

19th
and
20th Centuries

• •